GERMANY'S COLD WAR

THE NEW COLD WAR HISTORY

John Lewis Gaddis, editor

GERMANY'S COLD WAR

The Global Campaign to Isolate

East Germany, 1949–1969

WILLIAM GLENN GRAY

The University of North Carolina Press Chapel Hill & London

© 2003
The University of North Carolina Press
All rights reserved
Set in Charter and Meta types
by Keystone Typesetting, Inc.
Manufactured in the United States of America

Library of Congress Cataloging-in-Publication Data
Gray, William Glenn.
Germany's cold war : the global campaign to isolate
East Germany, 1949–1969 / by William Glenn Gray.
    p. cm.
Includes bibliographical references and index.
ISBN 0-8078-2758-4 (alk. paper)
1. Germany (West)—Foreign relations. 2. Germany
(West)—Economic policy. 3. Germany (West)—Foreign
relations—Germany (East) 4. Germany (East)—Foreign
relations—Germany (West) 5. Hallstein, Walter, 1901–
6. Recognition (International law) 7. World politics—
1945– I. Title.
DD259.5 .G46 2003
327.430431′09′045—dc21   2002006444

07   06   05   04   03   5   4   3   2   1

Contents

Acknowledgments ix

Abbreviations xiii

Introduction 1

Chapter 1. Containing East Germany in the Early 1950s 10

    Constructing the Diplomatic Blockade 13

    East German "Sovereignty" and the Western Response 21

Chapter 2. Staving Off Collapse 30

    A Shifting Landscape: Geneva and Moscow 31

    The Blockade Slips 39

    The Bonn Ambassadors' Conference 44

    "Managed Relationships" and the Isolation Campaign 49

Chapter 3. Yugoslavia Crosses the Line 58

    Grasping for Openings 59

    Damascus, but Not Warsaw 65

    A Failure of Deterrence 74

    The Hallstein Doctrine 81

Chapter 4. Scrambling for Africa 87

    Otto Grotewohl's Journey 88

    Doubts and Hesitations: The Berlin Crisis 95

    Bonn's Counteroffensive 102

    Guinea: The Exception That Proved the Rule 107

Chapter 5. Development Aid and the Hallstein Doctrine:
A Trajectory of Disillusionment 116

    Bonn's Billion-Dollar Aid Program 117

    The Shock of the Belgrade Conference 123

    Experiments in Economic Leverage 131

Chapter 6. The Perils of Détente 140

    De Gaulle, Détente, and the "Policy of Movement" 141

    Planning the Breakthrough 147

    "New Measures" in Ceylon and Zanzibar 155

    The Apex of West German Vigilance 162

Chapter 7. The Peculiar Longevity of a Discredited Doctrine 174

    The Debacle: West Germany's Expulsion from the Arab World 174

    The Contest Goes On 182

    Unification Hysteria and Erhard's Political Demise 191

Chapter 8. Of Two Minds:

  The Grand Coalition and the Problem of Recognition 196

    The Ulbricht Doctrine 197

    The Coalition "Cambodes" 205

    A Qualified Breakthrough 212

Conclusion 220

    The Halting Progress of a German Sisyphus 221

    A War within a War 226

    The Hallstein Doctrine and German Unity 229

Notes 235

Bibliography 323

Index 343

Maps

1   West Germany's Diplomatic Network, December 1955 *56*

2   East Germany's Trade, Consular, and Diplomatic Network, December 1955 *57*

3   West Germany's Diplomatic Network, December 1963 *150*

4   East Germany's Trade, Consular, and Diplomatic Network, December 1963 *151*

5   East Germany's Trade, Consular, and Diplomatic Network, December 1969 *216*

Acknowledgments

Specialists in German history will have already flipped to the back; the list of archival sources there will tell them all they need to know about the making of this book. Such readers can probably anticipate many of the names I am about to mention. For all other interested readers—and for the pleasure of my own personal recollection—I shall make an effort to identify here the many individuals who have assisted me in the course of this six-year endeavor.

My first debt is to the professors and students of Yale University. Seminars led by Henry Ashby Turner Jr. and Paul M. Kennedy, my two principal mentors, yielded the immediate inspiration for the book at hand. To them I owe an abiding interest in relating German topics to the broader currents of international history. Students who passed through Yale in the 1990s had the pleasure of seeing Paul Kennedy's research group, International Security Studies, blossom into one of the country's premier venues for the promotion of multiarchival, truly cosmopolitan history. Thanks go out to Ann Carter-Drier and Rose Pawlikowski for running a tight ship, and to the institute's associated faculty—among them Bruce Russett, John Gaddis, Will Hitchcock, and Ted Bromund—for bringing to Yale a constant stream of guests from the worlds of academia, diplomacy, and beyond. For me personally, ISS was a welcoming environment on many levels: intellectual, social, material. Not least, I am thankful to the institute and to the Smith Richardson Foundation for funding my original research in 1996–97. There is, of course, much more to Yale than ISS: Professors John Merriman, Jay Winter, and Diane Kunz were outstanding teachers; Suzanne Roberts at Sterling Memorial Library was most helpful in collecting papers of relevance to my project; and Florence Thomas guided me and many a graduate student through the mysterious institutional corridors.

At work in the field, I found no exceptions to the general rule that German archivists are extraordinarily knowledgeable and professional. Knud Piening at Germany's Foreign Office was friendly as well; he and his colleagues helped to make my months there enjoyable and productive. Much the same can be said for Hans-Otto Kleinmann at the Archive for Christian-

Democratic Politics in St. Augustin and Christoph Stamm at the Archive of Social Democracy in Bonn. My stay at the Archive of German Liberalism in Gummersbach was brief, and my visits to the Konrad Adenauer House and the Ludwig Erhard Foundation even briefer; but that is all the more reason to thank Monika Fassbender, Engelbert Hommel, and Andreas Schirmer, respectively, for helping me find the essentials quickly. Happily, I was able to spend many weeks at the Federal Archives in Koblenz, where the Herren Hoffmann and Braband provided excellent advice about the files of the Ministries for Development Aid and All-German Affairs. That I had access to two important collections there, the papers of Heinrich von Brentano and Baron von und zu Guttenberg, was due solely to the kindness of Michael von Brentano and Baroness Guttenberg. One final stop of special import during that trip was the Press and Information Office in Bonn, where Frau Klimmer supplied me with great stacks of newspaper clippings.

To my delight, I learned that Germany does not have a monopoly on top-notch archivists. At the Quai d'Orsay in Paris, Grégoire Elden was kind enough to communicate with me in German, sparing me from having to explain my project in broken French or—worse still—American English. He placed at my disposal temporary finding aids for the years 1960–70, material which he was only then cataloging. If there was any period of my research that was more fruitful than those weeks in Paris, it can only be the month spent at the National Archives in College Park, Maryland. (No doubt the liberal photocopying policies at both sites are part of the explanation.) The NARA is typically an anonymous environment, but on several occasions Ken Heger proved himself a competent guide through the tangle of finding aids. I have no one in particular to thank at the Public Record Office in London, but the smooth functioning of the vast operations there is surely testimony to British administrative prowess.

From the beginning, audiences and individual readers supplied me with helpful comments. Among the first was Klaus Hildebrand, who graciously allowed me to air provisional conclusions to his *Oberseminar* in Bonn in April 1997. Upon my return to New Haven, readers included Jeremi Suri, Tom Maulucci, and a very special dissertation group consisting of Fernande Scheid, Michael Shurkin, and Richard Lofthouse. Pertti Ahonen, now at Sheffield, shared all of his own chapters on West German expellees with me while providing thoughtful observations about my work. More recently, Paul Steege at Villanova and Brian Vick at Stanford have demonstrated collegiality and friendship with their comments on portions of the revised manuscript. Those revisions are, in turn, a reflection of upbeat and insightful reader's reports by Marc Trachtenberg and Thomas Alan Schwartz; I thank them for their suggestions and hope that they find the changes to their liking. Of all readers, Henry Turner has been the most attentive: in matters of both style and substance, the guidance provided by this master historian is exemplary.

For a dissertation to become a book, scholars typically require a period of contemplation and an injection of fresh archival sources. During the academic year 1999–2000, New York University's Remarque Institute proved instrumental in both regards. Tony Judt and Jair Kessler have fashioned a marvelous center for European studies at the southern end of Washington Square Park. Their biweekly seminars at the Remarque are noteworthy for creative catering and, more importantly, the informality and intensity of discussion. I am also thankful to Volker Berghahn for introducing me to his doctoral group at Columbia University. Understandably, then, I did not gladly take leave of New York in the fall of 2000; but I have been delighted to discover just how stimulating intellectual life can be on the South Plains when one's colleagues are as engaged as those at Texas Tech University. Thanks to the leadership of Allan Kuethe and now Bruce Daniels, Lubbock has become a congenial place to do European history. I must resist the temptation to list all the members of my new department, but two have shown special interest in my career as a historian: David Troyansky and Patricia Pelley. Generous assistance by the Remarque Institute and the Texas Tech history department funded summers in Germany in the years 2000 and 2001, allowing me to expand the original scope of research to consider East German perspectives. Sylvia Gräfe at the Federal Archives in Berlin-Lichterfelde and Ulrich Geyer at the Politisches Archiv des Auswärtigen Amts in Berlin provided invaluable orientations to the vast mountains of East German material.

I feel tremendously honored to be included in a series edited by John Gaddis, and I thank him for encouraging me to submit the manuscript promptly. At the University of North Carolina Press, Chuck Grench expedited the acquisitions process miraculously; perhaps he owes much of this efficiency to such able assistants as Ruth Homrighaus and Amanda McMillan. Equally impressive are the feats of the editorial staff: Ron Maner, Kathy Malin, and Stephanie Wenzel succeeded in smoothing out many of the excesses of my effusive prose. As a first-time author, I am especially grateful that the press has cooperated in producing just the sort of history book I have always wanted to publish, replete with a dense scholarly apparatus and a lengthy bibliography. Thanks to their meticulous grasp of detail, the editors saved me from a number of minor slips; those errors that remain originated with me, and I gladly bear responsibility for them.

Traditionally, scholars reserve their families for last; for it must be true that the contribution of loved ones, though intangible, has had the greatest weight. In my case, the role of my parents has not been abstract at all. Many years ago, just as I was starting graduate school, my mother became Dr. Janet Glenn Gray. Her example as a scholar of European history shaped me from an early age—though I must add that my father, Rev. James Gray, was every bit as instrumental in suggesting that I pursue a career in academia. In closing, I would most like to honor two individuals from an earlier generation, Dr. Gerald Glenn (1911–98) and Mrs. Margaret Gray (1908–2000). Neither will have the opportunity to hear me lecture or to read these words; but their sacrifices for my education made all the difference. It is to these two grandparents that I dedicate this manuscript.

Abbreviations

ADN	Allgemeiner Deutscher Nachrichtendienst (East German news service)
CDU	Christian Democratic Union
CSU	Christian Social Union
DM	German mark (the West German currency)
ECE	Economic Council of Europe
ECOSOC	United Nations Economic and Social Council
EEC	European Economic Community
FDP	Free Democratic Party
FRG	Federal Republic of Germany
GDR	German Democratic Republic
KPD	Communist Party of Germany
NATO	North Atlantic Treaty Organization
NGO	nongovernmental organization
NPD	National Democratic Party of Germany
SBZ	Soviet Occupation Zone
SED	Socialist Unity Party of Germany
SPD	Social Democratic Party of Germany
UAR	United Arab Republic
UN	United Nations
UNESCO	United Nations Educational, Scientific, and Cultural Organization
USSR	Union of Soviet Socialist Republics
VM	Valutamark (an East German currency unit, used exclusively for calculating the value of economic exchanges between the GDR and nonsocialist economies)
WHO	World Health Organization

GERMANY'S COLD WAR

Introduction

On the afternoon of March 30, 1960, Hasso von Etzdorf departed from Bonn on a most peculiar mission. Prussian aristocrats of the old school did not often venture into the interior of West Africa; top-ranking officials of the West German Foreign Ministry did not typically go chasing after foreign heads of state. Yet Etzdorf felt that his government could wait no longer to hear an answer from the president of Guinea, Ahmed Sékou Touré. Unfortunately Sékou Touré and his key advisers could not be reached in Conakry, the Guinean capital. Etzdorf resolved to follow them to Kankan, 700 kilometers inland, where the leaders of this African republic—independent only since the fall of 1958—were conferring on a revised economic program. Sékou Touré had kindly left his private plane at Etzdorf's disposal; but the plane's engines would not start, and the West German diplomat had no choice but to brave the nearly impassable roads. On April 3, 1960, Etzdorf finally held his long-anticipated conversation with the Guinean president. He returned to Bonn two days later satisfied that the crisis in relations with Guinea had passed. The West German press, which had followed the events with rapt attention, expressed relief at the favorable outcome.[1]

Although it was Etzdorf's "political safari" to Guinea that grabbed the headlines in Hamburg, Frankfurt, and Munich, another prominent German visitor had immediately preceded him: Alfred Kurella, a writer and candidate Politburo member in East Berlin. Etzdorf, the polished nobleman, and Kurella, the cultural functionary of the "workers' and peasants' state": Sékou Touré did not have to be deeply schooled in German affairs to realize that the two represented radically different, deeply antagonistic social and political orders. Their personal biographies followed two extremes in German history. Kurella had spent most of the 1930s and 1940s exiled in the Soviet Union, while Etzdorf spent the war as a diplomat with Nazi party affiliation—though he sympathized with the Stauffenberg resistance circle.[2] Why did the paths of Etzdorf and Kurella converge in Guinea? How did a small West African republic become a focal point for German attentions? A certain rivalry between the capitalists in Bonn and the communists in

East Berlin was only to be expected at the height of the Cold War, but why did the competition spill over into such a remote corner as Kankan, Guinea?

Observers at the time would scarcely have posed such questions, for the tussle over Guinea was simply the latest manifestation of a familiar dynamic: East Germany sought the world over to gain acceptance as a legitimate state, and West Germany sought to prevent this. Sékou Touré, professing neutrality in the Cold War, wished to maintain friendly relations with *both* German governments, but the polarized nature of the German Question militated against this. Bonn's diplomats insisted that the Guinean president make a choice. Ideologically, Sékou Touré felt greater affinity with East Germany. In March 1960 he was busy enacting a three-year plan that would lessen Guinea's dependence on Western Europe and introduce socialist methods of production and distribution. During his conversations with Kurella, Sékou Touré pleaded for time, promising that within a month, when Guinea's political situation had stabilized, he would establish diplomatic relations with the German Democratic Republic (GDR). Yet Etzdorf's lightning visit forced Sékou Touré to backtrack. The threats issued by the Federal Republic of Germany (FRG) were simply too intimidating. Etzdorf assured Sékou Touré of Bonn's eagerness to assist in the economic development of Guinea—so long as the government in Conakry refrained from recognizing the GDR. If Guinea were to establish diplomatic relations with East Germany, West Germany would respond with harsh countermeasures, up to and including the severing of diplomatic relations. Confronted with such a stark choice, Sékou Touré followed the example set by every other noncommunist leader before him, preferring Bonn over East Berlin. It was a banner victory for the Hallstein Doctrine, the controversial but crudely successful centerpiece of West Germany's isolation campaign against East Germany.

Although the situation in Guinea was particularly tense, scenarios such as this one played out time and again throughout the developing world in the 1950s and 1960s. As the larger and economically more potent of the two German rivals, the Federal Republic held the upper hand from the outset; yet this placed Bonn in the position of always fighting a defensive battle. From Bogota to Baghdad, from Addis Ababa to Phnom Penh, West German diplomats intervened to protest against the smallest gestures of kindness toward the GDR. Even the hoisting of the East German flag at an international trade fair could generate a forceful protest from Bonn. At the United Nations (UN), where the Federal Republic itself enjoyed only observer status, Bonn and its allies kept a tight watch to uphold the GDR's long-standing exclusion from international organizations and treaties. In effect, the Federal Republic sought to micromanage the behavior of other governments toward the GDR, a task that required constant vigilance and immense diplomatic energies. By the mid-1960s the West German Foreign Ministry was entirely consumed with this struggle: "We judge almost every foreign event primarily from the standpoint of whether it increases or diminishes the isolation of the Zone," acknowledged Karl Carstens, the second in command at the ministry, refusing even to refer to the GDR by name.[3]

For the dictatorship in East Berlin, the struggle was still more intense, as the stakes were immeasurably higher. Bonn's aggressive behavior was motivated by an abstract yet potent idea, the insistence that Germany must one day be reunited. The GDR, by contrast, was battling for its very right to exist. Soviet power alone had created and sustained the East German regime; veteran communist Walter Ulbricht had little meaningful support among the population he controlled. Plagued by this enormous deficit of legitimacy, Ulbricht and his colleagues faced an uphill struggle in trying to demonstrate to the East Germans that their government had substance and permanence. East Germany's leaders grasped for whatever evidence they could find of the GDR's credibility in the international arena, but such evidence was sadly lacking. A mere eleven countries, all communist, had recognized the GDR upon its founding in 1949. The remainder of the world turned a cold shoulder toward East Berlin. From the early 1950s through the late 1960s, the GDR labored to persuade even one noncommunist government to grant formal recognition. Such a precedent would, it was hoped, generate an avalanche of further recognitions and result in a more general acceptance of the GDR as an independent state. Little could be expected from the members of the North Atlantic Treaty Organization (NATO), given their commitments to West Germany. But what of the nonaligned world, the wide stretches of Africa, Asia, and Latin America that claimed no particular allegiance in the Cold War? By the early 1960s, politically reliable East Germans from many spheres of life—sports teams, youth leaders, union bosses, industrial and agricultural experts, and of course, communist functionaries—were plying the capitals of the Third World, seeking to win sympathy for the "other Germany." None of this sufficed to break the Federal Republic's monopoly position as acknowledged representative of the German people.

For nonaligned leaders, the "German-German" rivalry was a continual headache. They had to make decisions monthly about which German delegations to receive, how their representatives at the UN should vote, and whether, say, the local East German trade mission should be issued "consular corps" license plates. In countries with major communist constituencies, such as Ceylon, Tanzania, and Laos, the seemingly esoteric problem of German division could blow up into a domestic political crisis of the highest order. On the other hand, the situation also created opportunities. Public figures in Third World countries had ready access to medical treatment in East or West Germany—or both, so long as the trips were arranged separately.[4] Some statesmen and -women in newly independent countries relished their ability to command worldwide attention simply by issuing pronouncements on the German Question. More generally, the competition for favor in the Third World cast both German governments in the role of petitioners. In August 1961, when the West German ambassador in Baghdad pleaded for support at an upcoming conference, the conversation took "a somewhat odd turn": the Iraqi foreign minister listened "with a smile and a slight shaking of the head and finally remarked that it was an irony of world history that a great country like Germany must struggle to achieve self-determination, and that it seems to place such value in the good will of the Iraqi government."[5] Canny nonaligned leaders demanded material compensation for their favors; Presidents Kwame Nkrumah of Ghana, Gamal Abdul Nasser of Egypt, and Ahmed Sukarno of Indonesia proved particularly adept at this game. By the mid-1960s, Bonn and East Berlin were locked in bidding wars over these major nonaligned powers.

As the paragraphs above suggest, the fraternal German competition had implications for countries around the globe. This was, indeed, Germany's Cold War: a specifically German aspect of the worldwide confrontation between East and West. By exploring the nexus between Germany's internal partition and the larger course of the Cold War, this book aims to provide fresh perspectives on each. Scholars of the international system since 1945 will find in these pages a surprisingly active West Germany, one that became much more enmeshed in the Near East, South and Southeast Asia, and Africa than is commonly understood. Historians of postwar Germany will, in turn, discover unsuspected ways in which the heated contest overseas influenced affairs within both German states. Ideally, readers will come away with a deeper appreciation of the global reach of such Cold War conflicts as the German Question. Long before the term "globalization" came into fashion, the world was integrating in peculiar ways, making questions of German identity and representation a topic of concern as far away as Guinea—or even Guyana.

The chapters that follow are organized as a chronological narrative, for this offers the best means of highlighting the ever changing nature of East and West German strategy against the shifting context of the Cold War.[6] Rather than summarizing the chapters serially, then, I find it more appropriate to call attention to four layers of analysis running throughout the text. The first and foremost layer concerns relationships between the German states and the countries of the developing world. Questions of strategy stand in the foreground here: Which approaches worked, and which did not, as Bonn and East Berlin sought to guide the behavior of nonaligned governments? Both sides elaborated complicated theories about how the isolation campaign should be conducted (or stymied), yet in practice East and West German diplomats were constantly improvising. The Federal Republic's Hallstein Doctrine was no doctrine at all, merely an accumulation of emergency measures. Likewise, despite a penchant in the 1960s for "scientific planning," the East Germans could not chart their relations with the Third World according to a foreordained seven-year plan. On balance the learning curve in Bonn was steeper than contemporary observers guessed; West German diplomats not only held East German gains to a minimum for two decades, but they also managed to bring the political and financial burdens of the isolation campaign under control. The communist leadership in East Berlin, hampered by the misjudgments of an inexperienced diplomatic corps and the reckless optimism of the Marxist-Leninist worldview, consistently failed to turn promising openings into lasting successes. The GDR attained its final goal, worldwide recognition, only as a result of a sea change in West German politics in the late 1960s. East Germany did not "win"; its rival threw in the towel.

Correspondingly, the second key angle of this study concerns the domestic politics of the isolation campaign. Given the lack of open political debate in the GDR, attention here focuses primarily on West Germany.[7] If Bonn's Hallstein Doctrine generally worked well, as argued here, why did contemporaries frequently bemoan its rigidity and ineffectiveness? Part of the answer lies in the deliberate efforts of the West German Foreign Ministry (known as the Auswärtiges Amt, or Foreign Office) to depict its policy in stark, uncompromising terms. This strident tone, intended mainly for a foreign audience, alarmed many within West Germany. Especially troubling was the tendency of the campaign against East Germany to impede or overshadow efforts to normalize relations with Israel and with Eastern Europe. The term "Hallstein Doctrine" itself was coined in 1958 as a means of ridiculing the hard-line approach favored by Walter Hallstein, state secretary at the Foreign Office. In the ensuing years the term took on a life and content of its own; long after Bonn's diplomats had phased out Hallstein's methods, West German politicians continued to grandstand by arguing over the future of the Hallstein Doctrine. As late as 1969, a governing coalition in Bonn nearly buckled under the strain of a seemingly arcane point: whether to break diplomatic relations with Cambodia, which had just unexpectedly recognized the GDR. Such examples of controversy should not, however, obscure the high degree of consensus in Bonn about the nature of the regime in East Berlin. During the first two postwar decades nearly all public figures in western Germany could agree on the desirability of isolating the GDR and hindering its consolidation as a separate state.

This underlying consensus began to unravel in the second half of the 1960s, as a growing number of West Germans came to favor a modus vivendi with East Germany. Thus a third level of analysis considers the state of relations between the two German states. For the 1950s there is little to report: Konrad Adenauer, the Federal Republic's founding chancellor, steadfastly forbade any direct contacts between his government and the rival administration in East Berlin, lest they be construed as an implicit recognition of that regime. In the field, too, East and West German diplomats scrupulously avoided one another, lending the fight in the developing world a strangely impersonal character. Only third parties, like Nasser and Sékou Touré, actually communicated with representatives from each side. Yet an interaction of sorts can nevertheless be charted. In the course of their shadowboxing in Asia, Africa, and elsewhere, East and West Germans were constantly forced to respond to the other side's initiatives. Moreover, with the passing of time, some in the Federal Republic demanded a more open dialogue with the GDR. Was it not counterproductive, they argued, to seal off Ulbricht's regime so tightly that East and West Germans began to lose their sense of common identity? Such concerns played a key role in Bonn's decision to abandon the isolation campaign and "deal with the devil," a process that Mary Sarotte explores more thoroughly in her contribution to this series.[8] By the early 1970s, however, the alienation between East and West was all but irreversible. The "mental maps" of most West Germans were deeply etched with geographic horizons that placed Bonn much closer to Paris, London, and even Washington than to the dreaded East Berlin. Likewise, the rulers of East Germany had learned to fix their gaze on Moscow and the eastern bloc, even if the population of the "Soviet Zone" did cast sideways glances at the consumer paradise to the west.

Clearly, then, the ties between the two German states and their allies constitute a fourth and highly significant dimension of this study. Through-out this period, formal responsibility for the unification of Germany lay in the hands of the four principal victors of World War II: France, Britain, the United States, and the Soviet Union. It was these powers that initiated the struggle over the representation of Germany, for until the mid-1950s the Federal Republic and the GDR were too weak to assert themselves credibly in the international community. After this, Moscow's support for its East German client was surprisingly lukewarm; the Soviets sporadically at-tempted to promote the GDR's case among the nonaligned countries, but little energy went into this campaign until the late 1960s. This left Walter Ulbricht and his colleagues considerable leeway in pursuing their aims in the developing world, a freedom otherwise seldom seen in Soviet–East German relations. Coordination on the Western side was considerably tighter. Nonrecognition was a standard tool of Anglo-American diplomacy, and the United States proved particularly zealous in hindering East Ger-man accession to international life in the 1950s. France and Britain also assisted the Federal Republic routinely, albeit with less enthusiasm. To what extent did the campaign against East Germany become an unwel-come burden for the three Western Allies? Once they had settled on a course of détente with the Soviet Union, did they exert pressure on the Federal Republic to discard the Hallstein Doctrine? German writers long assumed that this was the case, but I argue below that Paris, London, and Washington continued to back Bonn's isolation campaign in order to assure West German cooperation in other projects of interest to the Allies.

The years 1969–72 saw the winding down of the global Cold War be-tween East and West Germany. In September 1973 both German states en-tered the UN simultaneously, a clear demonstration of their formal equality under international law. Afterward the Hallstein Doctrine had the aura of a failed strategy; experts on West Germany routinely contrasted the dy-namism of Chancellor Willy Brandt's Eastern policy after 1969 with the immobilism of his predecessors. In the writings of Waldemar Besson, Wolf-ram Hanrieder, Peter Bender, and many others, the isolation campaign figured primarily as an obstacle to Bonn's own maneuvering room vis-à-vis Eastern Europe and even the Western alliance.[9] Heinrich End treated the subject more broadly in his study *Zweimal deutsche Aussenpolitik*, but he, too, regarded the campaign against East Germany as an unfortunate bu-reaucratic fixation.[10] More differentiated judgments have come from the pens of Klaus Hildebrand and Hans Buchheim. Hildebrand, the foremost historian of German diplomacy, was among the first scholars to observe that the Hallstein Doctrine was designed as an elastic instrument of West German policy and that its meaning and use varied considerably over time. Along similar lines, Buchheim maintained that Bonn's efforts made sense in the 1950s, when the regime in East Berlin had not yet consolidated its power. Only later, when the GDR had grown in stability and prestige, did the Federal Republic's fight against East Germany become fruitless.[11]

Since the GDR's unexpected collapse, the proponents of Brandt's Eastern policy have come under fire themselves. Timothy Garton Ash has drafted the most balanced and trenchant critique: in seeking accommodation with the East German leadership, Brandt and his successors unwittingly prolonged the life of the GDR and the other communist regimes in Eastern Europe. Going one step further, some Christian Democratic partisans interpreted the events of 1989 as a vindication of Konrad Adenauer's "policy of strength," the theory that a powerful, prosperous West Germany would severely destabilize the East German state.[12] Was it a mistake, then, for Bonn to abandon its earlier efforts to isolate and stigmatize the GDR? Such questions have lingered in the background as a new generation of historians reassesses the Hallstein Doctrine. In a study synthesizing the available published evidence, Rüdiger Marco Booz highlighted the Federal Republic's remarkable success in blocking East German recognition for nearly two decades.[13] The view from East Berlin appears to corroborate this. In a perceptive sketch of the GDR's situation between 1965 and 1972, Alexander Troche noted that the republic's few international victories came only at tremendous cost. Michael Lemke, the most accomplished interpreter of East German policy, has stressed Ulbricht's pattern of failure—particularly when measured against his bold pretensions.[14]

Not all observers are quick to reverse received wisdom, however. One former West German diplomat, Werner Kilian, has recently depicted the "diplomatic war" between Bonn and East Berlin as a wasteful, futile, often picayune endeavor. Kilian's lengthy monograph on the Hallstein Doctrine, the first such volume to consider both East and West German archival documentation, restates the judgment of an earlier generation: the denial of East Germany's statehood was a meaningless target reflecting the impractical obsessions of the law professors dominating Bonn's Foreign Office.[15] The work at hand has benefited tremendously from Kilian's detailed case studies, along with other recent scholarship on the German-German conflict in such diverse arenas as Finland, Yugoslavia, Ghana, Zanzibar, and the Olympic Games.[16] Nevertheless, the present book differs markedly from its predecessors in approach, content, and conclusions. Rather than focusing narrowly on the Hallstein Doctrine, which was in itself little more than a diplomatic tool, this inquiry concerns "international dimensions of an intra-German conflict," much in the spirit of Heinrich End's classic study from 1973.[17] Understanding the "intra-German conflict" involved a close look at the records of four major political parties—the Christian Democratic Union (CDU), Social Democratic Party (SPD), Free Democratic Party (FDP), and Socialist Unity Party (SED)—as well as the personal papers of a wide range of German politicians. Analyzing the "international dimensions" required extensive use of British, French, and American sources. Aside from spelling out the views of the Allies on the isolation campaign, these records proved invaluable in assessing German diplomatic activity abroad and also in illuminating the internal decision-making process in Bonn.[18]

Until recently the archival work demanded by this project was simply not feasible; this applies not only to the documentation once locked behind the Berlin Wall but also—just as importantly—to the material in Western archives. Now that the thirty-year mark has passed, many records from the tumultuous 1960s are directly accessible to researchers. Others are being published under the auspices of a major declassification project sponsored by the Institute for Contemporary History in Munich.[19] This bountiful supply of new documents has made possible the present contribution to the "New Cold War History" and will doubtless continue to fuel the rewriting of German and international history during the Cold War era.

Chapter 1

Containing East Germany
in the Early 1950s

Konrad Adenauer, the newly elected chancellor of the newly created Federal Republic of Germany, faced a challenge to his position and to his very government on October 7, 1949. Four and a half months earlier the states of the three western occupation zones had adopted a provisional constitution, the Basic Law, providing the framework for a reconstituted German state.[1] Elections in the three zones in August 1949 yielded only the slimmest majority for the so-called bourgeois parties in the West German Bundestag: Adenauer's own centrist CDU, the right-liberal FDP, the nationalist German Party, and a smattering of other splinter groups. By a majority of just one vote, the Bundestag designated Adenauer as chancellor on September 15, 1949.[2] Adding to the instability of Adenauer's domestic position were the cantankerous dynamism of Kurt Schumacher, head of the opposition SPD, and the polemics of the small but vocal Communist Party (KPD). The communists never tired of depicting the chancellor as a mere client of the Western Allies—Britain, France, and the United States.[3] The charge was not entirely false. Although Adenauer was anything but subservient in his dealings with the Allies, the Occupation Statute of May 1949 left the final authority in West Germany squarely in the hands of the Allied High Commission. Adenauer's fledgling regime, housed in temporary quarters in a provincial town on the Rhine, was a decidedly humble successor to the German Reich of Otto von Bismarck and Adolf Hitler.

The proclamation of a rival government in Berlin on October 7, 1949, thus posed a threat to the institutions in Bonn. That was precisely the point of the hastily founded German Democratic Republic: it was intended to destabilize and delegitimize Adenauer's government and the Federal Republic as a whole.[4] Neither the Soviet Union nor its client regime in East Berlin had abandoned the goal of a unified Germany; the newly fashioned GDR was merely a platform for consolidating the strength of the SED so that it could win the allegiance of the working classes in western Germany. The SED-led regime, disguised as a "national front" of diverse political parties, claimed to speak not just for eastern Germany but for the German people as a whole; it saw itself as "the first independent all-German government."[5] Soviet and SED propaganda derided Adenauer as a separatist and a traitor to his nation. Meanwhile, to foster the illusion that the East German state was truly independent, the Soviets allowed the GDR to establish a Ministry of Foreign Affairs and to exchange ambassadors with the socialist states of Eastern Europe. On the surface, then, the authorities in East Berlin appeared to enjoy far more maneuvering room than their counterparts in Bonn.[6]

Politically aware Germans were not impressed. "Responsible Germans in the Western Zones, though somewhat disturbed at the establishment of this new 'government,' regard it with contempt," observed the Foreign Office in London.[7] If the cabinet members in Bonn lacked substance and authority, the credentials of their counterparts in East Berlin were no more appealing. Wilhelm Pieck, the GDR's president, and Walter Ulbricht, first secretary of the SED, had spent World War II exiled in the Soviet Union; this marked them as Moscow's puppets in West German eyes. Otto Grotewohl, the prime minister, had betrayed his Social Democratic colleagues in April 1946 by acceding to the creation of the SED in a "shotgun wedding" between the SPD and the KPD within the Soviet Zone that had led to the jailing and persecution of thousands of Social Democrats.[8] Three and a half years later the West German SPD still faced persistent East German efforts to infiltrate labor unions in the Ruhr industrial district.[9] All of this ensured that Kurt Schumacher, however blistering in his assessment of Adenauer, would reserve his sharpest barbs for the newly established SED administration. Among the broader public, too, the government in East Berlin had little credibility. Of those Germans in the American Zone who had heard of the GDR in November 1949, fully 76 percent regarded it as a tool of the Soviet authorities in Germany.[10]

Konrad Adenauer was thus squarely echoing the sentiments of the new West German political class when he dismissed the GDR as a product of Soviet fiat, created "with the participation of a small minority of subordinate Germans." The regime in East Berlin was no legitimate government, intoned the chancellor; in fact, the GDR was not even a genuine *state*. In making this argument to the Bundestag on October 21, 1949, Adenauer articulated what would remain the Federal Republic's basic statement of identity for the next two decades: Germany was a unique entity. There could be only one. Until that one Germany was restored as a unified state, the government of the Federal Republic—which alone had been elected in a free and democratic manner—would act as the sole legitimate representative of the German people.[11]

Adenauer's classic position linked two fundamental assertions: nonrecognition of the GDR, on one hand, and Bonn's exclusive representation of Germany, on the other. Neither was controversial in 1949. Indeed, with the GDR proclaiming *its* status as the only valid German government, there was nothing peculiar about Adenauer arrogating the same right for his administration. What did furrow the brows of some contemporaries was the highly abstract quality of the chancellor's standpoint. He was behaving as if the GDR did not exist—as if the Bundestag really did directly represent the 18 million Germans living in the Soviet Zone. Consequently, Adenauer refused to have any dealings whatsoever with the SED regime. Prominent Social Democrats and even members of Adenauer's cabinet quickly perceived that some interaction with the East German authorities would be necessary to coordinate everyday matters like exchanging mail. Trade might prove even more problematic: What if the GDR insisted on a formal treaty to regulate the exchange of goods between East and West Germany?[12] It was characteristic of Adenauer, with his unambiguous orientation toward Western Europe, that he did not lose much sleep over the problem of contact with Germans in the Soviet Zone. Just as characteristically, it was his nationalist critics, ever sensitive to the plight of their conationals in the East, who would later press for a greater openness between Bonn and East Berlin.[13]

Such questions did not invite passionate controversies at the height of the Cold War, however. Newspaper jargon faithfully reflected the dismissive attitudes of the West German mainstream. Rather than writing of a German Democratic Republic centered in Berlin, journalists referred to the "'so-called' GDR" or the "Soviet Zone" headquartered in "Pankow." Use of the term "Pankow"—a district of Berlin where many East German organs were in fact housed—served to deny any geographic coincidence with the historic seat of German government along Unter den Linden. "Soviet Zone" implied that the GDR was a fiction propagated by the Soviet occupiers of central Germany, not an independent regime with German nationals in charge. This Cold War cliché contained more than a whiff of truth in the early 1950s. The GDR remained under the direct sovereignty of the Soviet Union, just as the Federal Republic answered to the Allied powers at every turn. Adenauer would scarcely have had the authority to recognize the SED regime, even had he wanted to. West Germans, save a small and diminishing circle of communists, despised the upstart East German government and hoped to discourage its consolidation and international recognition, but they were powerless to influence such decisions.

Constructing the Diplomatic Blockade

Like Adenauer, the foreign ministers of France, Britain, and the United States quickly resolved to ignore the SED and to continue regarding the Soviet military administration as the authoritative voice in East Berlin. According to this view the proclamation of the GDR had not altered the legal situation in the slightest. "The existence of the eastern German government is not recognized as legitimate," observed one American official. "Therefore, the situation is as if it did not exist."[14] Meeting in Paris in November 1949, the three Western Allies agreed on a common line toward the GDR: they would neither recognize the SED regime de jure nor take any actions that might imply a de facto recognition. Moreover, they would encourage other countries to adopt a similar stance.[15] This uniform approach toward the GDR was all the more significant in light of the contrasting Western responses to the victory of Mao Tse-Tung's communist forces in mainland China. Chiang-kai Shek's Nationalists, banished to the island of Formosa, claimed still to represent the legal government of all China; the Truman administration chose to back this claim, at least for the time being, in order to work against worldwide recognition of Mao's government in Beijing. For the United States, the policy of "containment" offered a consistent rationale for disputing the legitimacy of communist gains around the globe, whether in China or eastern Germany. In London, Clement Attlee's government judged that British economic interests would be better served by acknowledging the reality of communist rule in China. It was also hoped that Mao's abrasive anti-imperialist rhetoric would mellow following Red China's integration into the international system. On January 5, 1950, the United Kingdom consequently recognized the People's Republic of China.[16] Similar arguments would one day be advanced to support recognition of the GDR. It was a political reality and an important market, and its international behavior might be modified by greater interaction with the West. In the winter of 1949–50, however, these considerations did not apply to the situation in the Soviet Zone of Germany. Paris, London, and Washington— themselves founders of a "client" state in Germany—perceived the emergence of a Soviet-backed regime in East Berlin as an unwelcome complication in their efforts to steer the fate of postwar Europe.

Although international law offered few hard and fast rules on questions of recognition, standards of conduct toward unrecognized regimes had been continuously refined in the nineteenth and twentieth centuries. Many precedents dated from the decade after 1917, when the countries of the League of Nations had contested the legitimacy of the Bolshevik revolution in Russia.[17] Little advance preparation was needed in late 1949 for the Western Allies, in consultation with Belgium, Luxembourg, and the Netherlands, to compose a list of acceptable and unacceptable forms of interaction with the regime in East Berlin.[18] Diplomatic relations were, of course, entirely out of the question; according to standard international practice, only governments that recognized one another could maintain diplomatic relations. Consular relations, too, were held to imply recognition. Also off-limits was the signing of any official agreement by cabinet-level ministers of the Western powers and the SED regime.[19] Instead, the Allies recommended that informal trade arrangements be worked out between nongovernmental bodies—by chambers of commerce, for example. Such measures had an artificial quality: for a country like the GDR, where economic decisions were increasingly subject to the will of the SED, the distinction between commercial and state representatives was often inconsequential. Nevertheless, contacts on the level of chambers of commerce allowed Western governments to maintain the formal requirements of nonrecognition without provoking an outcry from business interests.[20]

The Allies did not overtly publicize these resolutions, but they did undertake to inform countries outside the Western alliance about the terms of the diplomatic blockade. With an East German team en route to South America in December 1949, the United States hastened to spread the word in the Western Hemisphere; the United Kingdom took the nations of the Commonwealth into its confidence. European members of the Organization for Economic Cooperation and Development (Marshall Plan), such as Sweden, were also notified.[21] As the Allies had hoped, countries outside the Soviet bloc heeded the Western standpoint and refrained from establishing political relations with the regime in East Berlin. The one partial exception was Finland, which—after months of hesitation—signed a government-level trade agreement with the GDR. Yet the Finnish decision was hardly an unqualified triumph for the Soviet bloc, for Helsinki disavowed any intention of recognizing the SED government.[22]

Dilettantism and a lack of realism in East Berlin contributed to the effectiveness of the Allied blockade. Virtually all of the German Reich's veteran diplomats had fled to the western zones in the late 1940s, leaving behind only a handful of officials familiar with the workings of a foreign ministry. Like Soviet Russia after the revolution, the GDR had at its disposal articulate members of the labor "aristocracy," a working-class elite that wanted not for energy but still had much to learn about the fine airs of diplomacy.[23] Representatives of the new state phrased their demands in categorical terms, insisting that foreign governments recognize the GDR as a prerequisite for doing business. Foreign Minister Georg Dertinger, himself one of the few "bourgeois" members of the East German government, predicted in March 1950 that East Germany was "economically so important for the countries of the neutral realm . . . that in the long run they will be forced to pursue trade ties with the GDR out of their own self-interest."[24] According to this calculation, neutral countries such as Sweden and Switzerland could be pressured into declaring full recognition of the GDR, so the East Germans should not let them off the hook by accepting ad hoc relations on an unofficial basis. There was some basis for optimism. Bern worried about the fate of 5,000 Swiss citizens resident in the GDR, while Stockholm depended heavily on East German rail lines for access to European markets. Yet East Berlin's demands proved to be premature and overly blunt. Most European countries did not even have official relations with the larger and more populous Federal Republic, which in 1950 had no foreign service and only the rudimentary beginnings of a consular network in place.[25] In the absence of diplomatic relations with the Federal Republic, the governments of Sweden, Switzerland, and Finland showed no interest in arranging such ties with the GDR. Clearly, if the East German leadership wished to establish any sort of working relationship with its noncommunist neighbors, it would have to compromise on the question of diplomatic recognition. The 1950 trade agreement with Finland was a first step in this direction, but it remained a lone exception.

Surprisingly, the policy of suppressing East Germany practiced by the Allies actually predated their international engagement on behalf of West Germany. Despite their role in sponsoring the founding of the Federal Republic, the Allies did not initially endorse Adenauer's claim to speak on behalf of the entire German people. For one thing, they did not wish to question the Soviet Union's right to speak on behalf of the eastern zone of occupation. For another, they were not entirely sure whether to bill the Federal Republic as a state (as opposed to a mere government) under international law. Might this not make the Allies appear complicit in the division of Germany into two states?[26] Although the Allies were eager to promote West German membership in international bodies such as the

World Health Organization (who) and the International Labor Organization, the legal consequences concerned them. So, too, did the feared Soviet reaction: Soviet and East European delegations in the suborganizations of the un might storm out in protest against the presence of West German representatives, or they might well demand equal representation for the East Germans.[27] Despite the strong interest of the Allies in anchoring the Federal Republic within international institutions, they proceeded cautiously throughout the winter of 1949–50.

What transformed West Germany's prospects was the war in Korea. The North Korean invasion of its southern neighbor in June 1950 cast the European situation in a new light: What if the Soviet Union, believed to be the instigator in Korea, also pushed the East Germans to unify Germany by force? Now there was no question that Adenauer's government was a necessary partner in the defense of Europe.[28] Negotiations commenced in the fall of 1950 between the Federal Republic and the Allies regarding a West German military contribution to nato. Adenauer made the most of the situation, wringing political concessions and greater autonomy from the Allies in exchange for the planned recruitment of German soldiers.[29] One of the first gestures came on September 19, 1950, when the Allied foreign ministers announced in New York that they regarded Adenauer's government to be "the only German Government freely and legitimately constituted and therefore entitled to speak for Germany as the representative of the German people in international affairs."[30] The Allies abandoned their earlier reservations about promoting the independent status of West Germany; the path was clear for the Federal Republic to accede to a plethora of un-related organizations as the official representative of Germany.[31] On other levels, too, Adenauer's government quickly amassed a newfound weight. In March 1951 the Allies finally permitted the opening of a foreign ministry in Bonn; the chancellor restored the name "Foreign Office" (Auswärtiges Amt) in accord with a German bureaucratic tradition dating back to Bismarck. That same month West Germany's first ambassadors departed for posts in the Allied capitals.[32]

The Soviet Union did, of course, object to the Federal Republic's rapid rise in international esteem. Yet Soviet backing of the gdr in the international arena was halting and inconsistent; Moscow was apparently more intent upon unifying Germany on favorable terms than on securing a separate East German presence in global affairs.[33] At any rate, given the commanding majority enjoyed by pro-Western governments in the un and its subsidiary bodies, the communist states had little prospect of blocking the

Federal Republic's acceptance. By late 1952 the Federal Republic had been welcomed as a full partner in most UN-related institutions.[34] Only formal membership in the UN General Assembly seemed out of reach, thanks to the Soviet Union's veto in the Security Council on questions of membership. Meanwhile, the United States grew "progressively more stubborn" about "the slightest suggestion" of participation by the GDR in international organizations.[35] Now that acceptance of West Germany by the international community was assured, the Allies tried all the harder to ensure that East Germany was denied a comparable status. At times this meant the Federal Republic would have to wait. In October 1951 the State Department rejected a plan to enhance West Germany's status in the Economic Council of Europe (ECE), for fear that this particular organization—headed by a Swede of neutralist complexion, Gunnar Myrdal—would accord equivalent representation to East Germany.[36]

Why did the Allies take such pains to squelch the GDR's tenuous links with the noncommunist world? Aside from basic considerations of Cold War prestige, which dictated that each side must support its own client against the claims and propaganda of the rival government, the West found that denigrating the GDR served a useful function in assigning blame for the Cold War. The Allies dismissed the East German government as a product of Soviet administrative fiat; the Union of Soviet Socialist Republics (USSR) could pave the way for unification any time merely by withdrawing support for the SED administration and agreeing to hold free elections in eastern Germany.[37] In this way the Allies deflected attention away from their own plans for rearming West Germany, a project that promised to deepen the country's division still further by tying the Federal Republic politically and militarily to the West. In a decade when statesmen routinely described the unresolved German Question as a major threat to world peace, the Western Allies took considerable pains to convince the members of the UN that the Soviet Union was the primary obstacle to unification. In the fall of 1951, for example, the Allies proposed a UN investigation to determine whether free elections could be held throughout Germany. Predictably, the SED refused to allow the UN delegation to inspect conditions in East Germany.[38] At least until 1953 the United States also pursued a more offensive goal with respect to the GDR: hindering the consolidation of the SED regime.[39] In blocking East German successes on the international plane, the Western Allies denied the SED one important means of demonstrating to its own citizens its serious (and permanent) character.

In the early 1950s the Federal Republic was seldom equipped to fight its own battles. The Foreign Office in Bonn was too preoccupied with the expansion of its diplomatic network to concern itself with the sporadic international activity of its rival.[40] The self-assertion of West Germany took precedence over the denigration of East Germany. Hence Adenauer's government hastened to send delegates to address the UN in December 1951, even though East German spokesmen were accorded equal status there. This display of public showmanship left an unfavorable impression, though, even among Germany's allies.[41] It simply did not behoove the Federal Republic to take the spotlight during these years of lingering suspicion. The task of blocking East Germany's admission to international conferences fell to the Western Allies; West German delegations were instructed to offer no more than a few sentences of support in favor of positions argued by the American, British, or French delegates.[42] Significantly, East German observers considered American, not West German, influence to be the principal explanation for the tendency of Third World leaders to discriminate against the GDR.[43]

In some corners of the world, however, the Western Allies were in no position to offer the Federal Republic significant backing. In Helsinki, for example, American and British officials scrupulously avoided any semblance of pressure, in light of Finland's long, exposed border with the Soviet Union.[44] Finland remained the sole noncommunist country in Europe to shun recognition of Adenauer's government. Yet Finnish leaders distinguished their policies from those of the Soviet satellites by denying recognition to Ulbricht's government as well. For a country in Finland's geographic position, equally distant treatment of both German states was a sensible strategy. It satisfied East Germany's demand for equal status with West Germany while also conforming to Bonn's plea that Finland forswear diplomatic relations with East Germany. In the summer of 1953 the Finnish authorities took a key step toward stabilizing the situation by allowing both governments to open trade missions in Helsinki.[45] It galled the West Germans to be placed on a par with the East Germans, but the low level of representation made practical relations workable without raising any thorny questions about the diplomatic status of the rival German mission.

Another politically contested region, the Near East, saw the two German states squared off directly against each other as early as the winter of 1952–53. Allied influence in the region was slipping, particularly in Egypt, considered the voice of Arab opinion by most outsiders (and inevitably by the Egyptians themselves). The Germans, for their part, reaped a windfall of respect among the Arab countries for their defiance of France and Britain during the world wars. For those Arabs fixated on the conflict with Israel, the legacy of the Holocaust did not taint Germany's reputation; without actively trying to make political capital of this, the Federal Republic did send a considerable number of former Nazis as ambassadors to the Near East.[46] Quite independently of politics, German engineering was much sought-after in the region. These favorable conditions accrued to the Federal Republic first, thanks to the skill and energy of West German trade agents in Cairo.[47] Yet this promising start only heightened the Arab sense of betrayal when Adenauer signed a restitution treaty with Israel in September 1952 pledging delivery of DM 3 billion ($714 million) in goods over a span of fourteen years. At first the Arab League intimidated Bonn with the threat of an economic boycott designed to delay or block ratification of the accords between West Germany and Israel. By early 1953, though, Egyptian tactics had shifted to another obvious source of leverage: open flirtation with the GDR.[48]

Officials in East Berlin were slow to respond to Cairo's prodding. Negotiations with Switzerland had recently foundered over Bern's refusal to grant the GDR equal status with the Federal Republic. The Swiss had offered the East Germans an unofficial trade mission in Zurich, whereas the West Germans already maintained a diplomatic legation in Bern. In a fit of pique, the SED Politburo had expelled the Swiss delegation from East Berlin. All of this did not bode well for the future of trade ties with other capitalist countries.[49] Yet the GDR's Foreign and Trade Ministries came to see the situation in Cairo as a unique opportunity. In their view the new rulers of Egypt were serious about counterbalancing the influence of "imperialist" powers such as Britain and the United States. By arranging a barter deal with Egypt—cotton for finished goods—the GDR could promote its industrial exports while helping to wean Egypt from its former colonial masters.[50] A trade delegation departed for Cairo in February 1953 armed with instructions to negotiate and sign a government-level trade agreement with the Egyptian authorities. The instructions sounded a cautious note, pointing out that East Germans were venturing for the first time to a foreign capital where the West Germans had already planted an embassy. The GDR's diplomats would suffer all manner of discrimination at the hands of the Egyptians. This departure from the usual East German insistence on equal treatment was justified, however, for it would ultimately result in "a further breach" in the diplomatic blockade surrounding the GDR.[51] In other words, some international presence was better than none. In embracing this line of reasoning, the East Germans abandoned their earlier all-or-nothing standpoint, which had yielded few positive results, and laid the groundwork for a more gradual expansion of East Berlin's political and economic activity abroad.

Egypt, the first country to play the two German governments against each other, was also the first to experience the righteous indignation of the West Germans at this manipulative treatment. A top West German official, State Secretary Ludger Westrick of the Economics Ministry, was conducting negotiations in Cairo when the East German delegation turned up there. In the short run this transparent effort to pressure the Federal Republic backfired; Westrick stormed back to Bonn and urged that the parliament accelerate ratification of the West German–Israeli accord.[52] Within a few months, however, tempers had cooled, and the government of Gamal Abdul Nasser ended up with remarkably advanced relations with both German states. Adenauer's government dispatched a team of engineers to examine the technical and economic prospects of a dam at Aswan, Nasser's great hope for the modernization of Egypt.[53] For their part, the East Germans felt bold enough to establish a permanent trade mission in Cairo in late 1953—their first foothold outside Europe, save in the communist capitals of Beijing and Pyongyang. West Germany's Foreign Office was hardly pleased at this development, but it had no obvious recourse once the Egyptian authorities had earnestly promised not to entertain diplomatic or consular relations with the GDR and to sharply restrict the activities of all East German trade representatives in Cairo.[54] The basic ingredients for seventeen years of diplomatic wrangling were in place: East German pressure for improvements in the humble status of their trade mission, West German insistence that the GDR remain unrecognized by Egypt, and the readiness of Egyptian leaders to exploit this tension to win favors from each side.

By the end of 1953 Bonn was playing an increasingly active role in blocking the GDR's advances, particularly in regions where the Western Allies had little more clout than the Germans themselves. In December of that year Bonn undertook its own démarches in Lebanon, Syria, and other Near Eastern capitals to dissuade those countries from copying Egypt's example.[55] Even so, the Federal Republic lacked formal sovereignty over its internal and external affairs, leaving it heavily dependent on the continuing approval of France, Britain, and the United States. When Moscow and East Berlin launched a fresh drive to promote the recognition of an independent East German state in the spring of 1954, it was the Western Allies who seized the initiative once again. This time, however, the Federal Republic

CONTAINING EAST GERMANY

followed through with a global campaign of its own: its first step toward the construction of a specifically West German blockade of East Germany.

East German "Sovereignty" and the Western Response

Despite the recent successes in Egypt and Finland, the GDR's foreign presence remained all but negligible in early 1954, the fifth year after the state's founding. Whereas the Federal Republic had established diplomatic relations with fifty-three states by this time, the GDR could boast of similar ties with only eleven, all associated with the Sino-Soviet bloc.[56] Moscow and East Berlin could not afford to be complacent about this lack of international credibility, for it was one facet of a more profound crisis of legitimacy hovering over the GDR. In June 1953, workers' riots throughout eastern Germany had thrown into sharp relief the SED's unpopularity among the very class it was supposed to represent. Under the right circumstances, Stalin's successors in Moscow might have been willing to dispose of the troublesome GDR altogether, but they could not pursue any German policy successfully with a limp and disreputable client state.[57] At the Berlin Conference of February 1954, when the Soviets and the Allies sat down for yet another fruitless round of negotiations over Germany, Moscow focused its strategy on demonstrating the stability of the SED regime.[58] One month later the Soviets put forward a measure designed to enhance the authority of the rulers in East Berlin: a proclamation appearing to bestow sovereignty on the GDR.

The Soviet decree of March 25, 1954, promised that East Germany would be "free to decide on internal and external affairs, including the question of relations with Western Germany, at its discretion."[59] To West Germans the intended propaganda message was transparent enough. Whereas the Federal Republic remained under the thumb of the Western Allies, the GDR would now theoretically have the right to chart its own course. Even a cursory examination of the Soviet statement revealed a number of qualifying hedges, though. The document delicately avoided use of the term "sovereignty," suggesting that East Germany's elevation in status would have no precise legal connotations. The USSR reserved for itself "functions connected with guaranteeing security," indicating that Russian tanks would linger within striking distance of central Berlin. Who could doubt that the satellite relationship between the USSR and the GDR would persist? "At first sight it would appear that the altered status of the 'German Democratic Republic' will not make much difference to us," observed the Foreign Office in London, "unless the Soviet authorities particularly wish to twist our tails."[60] This assessment failed to appreciate that the decree of March 25, though laced with anti-Western propaganda targeted at the West German public, was designed primarily to sway governments outside the Western alliance. Moscow was asking countries around the world to reconsider their attitudes toward the GDR, thereby placing recognition of that government on the international agenda for the first time since 1949.

West German and American observers anticipated an immediate boost in East German fortunes among neutral and developing countries—Sweden and Switzerland, on one hand, and Egypt, Syria, and India, on the other. Statements from East Berlin indicated that the GDR was determined to extort recognition from states that did not offer it willingly. On March 30, 1954, Walter Ulbricht proclaimed that the European military missions in eastern Berlin would have to close; countries affected by this decision should establish proper embassies instead.[61] The U.S. High Commission in Bonn predicted that "the GDR has no intention of letting grass grow under its feet and is likely to follow up today's announcement by putting increasing pressure upon the most vulnerable and susceptible countries to establish formal relations."[62] Up to this point the State Department had hoped to play down the significance of the GDR's elevation in status, but on March 31 it proposed instead that France, Britain, and the United States meet the challenge through the application of Western pressure around the globe. As in previous years, Washington acknowledged the primary responsibility of the Western Allies in fending off potential gains in East Germany's international position. Nevertheless, this plan did foresee a limited degree of participation by the Federal Republic itself. West German ambassadors in the field might be urged to associate with the démarches of their Allied colleagues—or, at the very least, the Foreign Office could make its position clear to foreign ambassadors accredited in Bonn.[63]

French and British officials showed little enthusiasm for a worldwide initiative. The Quai d'Orsay put forward a more modest plan: the Allies should intervene in Sweden and Switzerland as well as among the dozen or so countries represented on the board of the UN's Economic and Social Council (ECOSOC).[64] In London the Foreign Office wondered why the West Germans could not simply undertake their own soundings in Stockholm and Bern.[65] From the standpoint of Paris and London, the Federal Republic no longer looked so vulnerable among the European neutrals or in the many countries of the developing world; West German exports were crowding into Near and Middle Eastern markets at an alarming pace.[66]

CONTAINING EAST GERMANY

Even so, formal responsibility for German affairs remained with the Western Allies, and a breakthrough by the GDR would hardly make negotiations with the Soviet Union any easier. The three partners settled on a mutually agreeable division of labor. On April 5, 1954, the State Department moved forward with its global diplomatic action, instructing U.S. diplomats to raise the nonrecognition issue informally with their host governments. Four days later the British Foreign Office followed suit, casting aside its earlier reservations.[67] France took the lead in crafting a concerted response by NATO. In public, though, the Allied High Commission delicately refrained from issuing any statements until after Chancellor Adenauer had spoken. Optically at least, this was the moment for West Germany to take center stage in the struggle against its eastern rival.

Adenauer's first instinct was to insist on a thorough examination of the Federal Republic's status under international law. This was entirely in keeping with the tone of West German policy in the early 1950s, when State Secretary Walter Hallstein, a professor of law, directed the activities of Bonn's Foreign Office. For the chancellor and his advisers, embedding the Federal Republic in a dense network of legally binding relationships offered the prospect of restoring Western confidence in German reliability. Nearly all of Bonn's diplomatic projects in 1950–55 involved contractual negotiations: with the Western Allies collectively, with France over questions like the Saar, and with France and the Benelux countries over coal and steel production. In confronting the latest challenge from East Germany, then, it was natural for the chancellor to place great stock in the persuasive powers of laws and constitutions. Conferring with his cabinet on March 31, 1954, Adenauer revealed his intention of using the Bundestag as a forum to "warn the world community, using statements grounded in international law (*völkerrechtlich*), against taking up diplomatic relations with the Pankow government."[68] Over the next several days the legal adviser in Bonn's Foreign Office, Erich Kaufmann, elaborated just such an argument. States having relations with the Federal Republic had implicitly acknowledged its status as the sole representative of Germany. If such countries were to recognize the GDR as well, Kaufmann suggested, this would mark a breach of contract; Bonn could rightfully view this as an "*acta peu amicale*"—an unfriendly act.[69]

Perhaps under the influence of the Western Allies, Adenauer refrained from using such pointed words in his address to the Bundestag on April 7, 1954.[70] Rather than insisting on the *obligation* of Bonn's diplomatic partners to reject the GDR, Adenauer delivered a morally based appeal. A freely constituted government ruled in Bonn, but in Berlin (or "Pankow"), an unwanted regime had been foisted on 18 million Germans. "No nation which respects the free political self-determination of each people over its form of government . . . will be able to recognize this communist regime of the German Soviet Zone as a sovereign state."[71] Having committed the Federal Republic to a strict observance of international norms, the chancellor felt justified in admonishing other countries to keep their distance from an illegitimate dictatorship like the one in East Berlin. Moscow's attempt to found a second state on German soil represented a violation of the Germans' will to remain united. "In its declaration, the Soviet Government tries to awaken the impression that the part of Germany it occupies is an independent entity on equal footing with sovereign states. Yet the Soviet declaration can do nothing to change the fact that there is, was, and will be only *one* German state, and that today it is exclusively the government of the Federal Republic of Germany that represents this never extinguished German state."[72] These words were met with stormy applause from the entire Bundestag.

More controversially, the chancellor extended his moral reasoning to the plane of relations between the two parts of Germany, restating his refusal to deal in any fashion with the regime in East Berlin: "We would dishonor ourselves and insult all the victims of the communist rule of terror if we were to acknowledge the authorities there as partners in working toward the reunification of Germany."[73] Such comments addressed what Adenauer perceived to be the greatest single danger of the Soviet declaration: that it would persuade naive West Germans to strike up direct contacts with the SED leadership, now being touted as a "proper government."[74] On the right, industrialists of the Rhein-Ruhr-Klub had recently hosted Hermann Rauschning, the former Nazi mayor of Danzig, who advocated direct talks between the German states as a means of defying *all four* occupying powers.[75] On the left, the SPD under chairman Erich Ollenhauer was stressing the need for a more active exchange between East and West, lest the division of Germany harden into permanency.[76] As in 1949, no serious West German politician advocated an outright recognition of the GDR, but Adenauer was inclined to doubt the political acumen of his fellow Germans even under the best circumstances. On March 31 the chancellor explained to the cabinet that "a debate in the Bundestag . . . must be avoided, so as not to allow comments by the opposition to jeopardize the unity and potency of the German standpoint." Adenauer's wish was fulfilled. He skillfully maneuvered the SPD into postponing a debate about the full implications of East German "sovereignty." Following the chancellor's statement on April 7, 1954, Bonn's parliamentarians passed a unanimous resolution affirming that "the communist regime in the Soviet-occupied zone of Germany exists only on the basis of force, and is no representative of the German people."[77] Such phrases effectively hung a moral stigma on all interaction with the SED regime, helping to discourage both foreign and West German interest in a normalization of relations with East Germany.

Adenauer's public pronouncements coincided with the Foreign Office's first major diplomatic counteroffensive against the GDR, launched on April 6–7, 1954. France, Britain, and the United States still acted as the final guarantors of West Germany's claims, but Bonn now asked for independent assurances from third countries. State Secretary Hallstein was, in effect, striving for a one-sided contract with the countries of the free world. He hoped that all four dozen countries entertaining diplomatic relations with Bonn would make a solemn commitment not to recognize the GDR and would permit a high degree of transparency in their informal dealings with East German officials.[78] This implied that *any* level of contact with East Germany was suspect. Without demanding an outright trade embargo of the Soviet Zone, these instructions hinted that Bonn would view the establishment of East German trade missions unfavorably, even if such missions exercised no consular or diplomatic functions.[79] Significantly, Hallstein's orders were virtually identical for NATO and non-NATO countries, indicating that he expected the same degree of cooperation from outside nations as from Bonn's close associates. All told, Adenauer's government had produced a model for a blockade far more stringent than the one imposed by the Western Allies.

How far would Bonn go to enforce this policy? Some in the government advocated the use of "any means, up to and including the breaking of diplomatic relations and trade war" to block the GDR's progress.[80] Such attitudes would eventually prevail in Bonn, but in the spring of 1954 Adenauer and Hallstein opted for a more cautious line. As noted above, the chancellor's address of April 7 contained admonitions but not threats. In those few cases where the Foreign Office did not anticipate ready compliance, it privately informed these governments that the nonrecognition problem was of such fundamental importance that Bonn would accept "no compromise." After all, the Federal Government wished "to avoid unfortunate effects on German public opinion, which might in turn also affect mutual relations." Although the factor of public opinion was introduced to mediate the threat, the strong language—*no compromise*—indicated clearly enough that recognition of the GDR in any form would work to the detriment of relations with the Federal Republic.[81] This was a threat, but a deliberately vague one.

Specific warnings hardly seemed necessary in light of the initial results of April's worldwide démarche. No countries outside the Soviet bloc stepped forward to recognize the GDR or grant it consular status. Many even offered written assurances of their position, committing themselves on paper to the view that the Federal Republic alone was the true Germany. By April 28 only six countries had responded in a manner that was "still unclear." All others could be categorized as "unambiguously positive" or "fundamentally in agreement with our position, but not yet committed."[82] Yet the six stragglers with "unclear" views—Egypt, Syria, India, Indonesia, Sweden, and Switzerland—proved impossible to pin down. Each of these governments had reasons to seek some limited degree of accommodation with the authorities in East Berlin, and they did not wish to tie their hands by making sweeping promises to Bonn. Sweden, for example, still fretted about transit rights through the GDR and considered inviting an East German technical representative to reside in Stockholm for the purpose of issuing visas.[83] Although the Foreign Office guessed that there was "no acute grounds for concern" about any Swedish recognition of the GDR, Bonn pressed Stockholm for clarifications. Would the Swedish government accord diplomatic or consular rights to the projected East German visa office in Stockholm? Why did Sweden persist in relativizing all pronouncements by stating that *for the time being* it would not grant de jure or de facto recognition to the Pankow regime?[84] The issue remained theoretical, since the Soviet embassy in Stockholm continued to issue visas on the GDR's behalf. Yet Stockholm refused to elaborate. The West Germans simply had to learn to live with a certain degree of ambiguity in the Swedish attitude.

Out of exasperation, desk officers in Bonn did consider using sharper measures in their efforts to block the spread of East German trading outposts. Yet the Foreign Office still had no clear conception of how to wield political or economic threats effectively to influence the behavior of neutral nations, as a dispute with the West German ambassador in New Delhi demonstrated. Bonn's orders to the ambassador on May 21, 1954, stated that Bonn would view the opening of an East German trade mission in India as a de facto recognition of the Pankow regime. India's cooperation on this issue was "an important prerequisite for the further satisfactory development of political relations and especially for the successful building of economic relations between the two countries." Behind this stilted bureaucratic language, the Foreign Office was trying to establish a link between New Delhi's behavior toward the GDR and West Germany's continuing participation in the industrial development of India.[85] Ambassador Ernst Wilhelm Meyer, a political science professor with Social Democratic leanings, refused to act on these orders. In a personal letter to his superiors, Meyer predicted that German attempts to couple economic favors with political preconditions would infuriate Indian prime minister Jawarlahal Nehru, who took great pride in pursuing an ethically based foreign policy independent of material considerations. Bonn's trade with the subcontinent could hardly be considered charity in any case; West German industry would profit immensely from the recent agreement to erect a massive steel complex at Rourkela.[86] Meyer might well have added that the Foreign Office's goals in 1954 were patently unrealistic. The Western Allies had concluded as early as 1949 that the exchange of nongovernmental chambers of commerce with the GDR was unobjectionable. Why, then, was the Federal Republic attempting to deny to India and Indonesia a privilege that Belgium and the Netherlands already enjoyed? By the fall of 1954 Bonn had bowed to the inevitable and accepted the opening of East German chambers of commerce in Jakarta, Bombay, and Calcutta. In accord with Western guidelines, these trade offices enjoyed neither consular nor diplomatic privileges, nor were the corresponding agreements signed at the government level.[87]

If Bonn's tactics were somewhat unrefined and its goals overly ambitious, the same was doubly true of East Berlin. Moscow's sovereignty declaration of March 1954 had convinced no one. East German hopes of strong-arming the Scandinavian countries into an exchange of diplomatic relations, "as befits the GDR as a sovereign state," were quickly disappointed.[88] Finland would not sign a long-term trade agreement at such a price. Sweden tried to sidestep the recognition problem by suggesting that East Germany establish a visa office in Stockholm. Stubborn pride kept the Foreign Ministry from even responding to this proposal.[89] As before, the GDR's all-or-nothing stance severely hindered its progress in Europe. Farther from home, though, a more flexible attitude was in evidence. Sheer distance implied that if East Germany's state enterprises were to find markets in South and Southeast Asia, some form of unofficial representation on the ground would be necessary. Without a commercial outpost in Jakarta, for example, the GDR would have been hard pressed to deliver on its contract with Indonesia to build a sugarcane factory at a bargain-basement price.[90] Rather than making diplomatic relations a *precondition* for trade relations,

East German officials—particularly in the Ministry for Intra-German and Foreign Trade—hoped to use targeted trade deals as a springboard for realizing the SED's political goals.[91] By the fall of 1954 this strategy appeared to have borne fruit in the Near East, where a high-profile industrial exposition in Cairo had piqued the interest of business leaders throughout the region. In mid-October the Lebanese foreign minister assented to the opening of a mission in Beirut analogous to the East German office in Cairo.[92] The triumph was short lived, however, for the Western Allies and the Federal Republic objected strenuously to the extension of East German influence in a basically pro-Western country. Lebanon's Council of Ministers, worried by the tone of the Western démarches, voted to disavow the earlier promise to East Berlin.[93]

Lebanon's behavior exemplified a difficulty faced by the GDR in most developing countries in the early 1950s: interest in deeper economic relations with the SED regime, though substantial, seldom outweighed the fear of alienating the West. Concepts such as the "free world," a blanket term embracing all noncommunist members of the UN, still had resonance; the sympathies of virtually all independent countries, from Thailand to Iraq to Brazil, lay with West Germany as a matter of course. Yet the momentum in the developing world lay with the self-proclaimed neutrals, countries such as India, Indonesia, and Egypt. These governments had already demonstrated a willingness to entertain low-level, practical relations with the GDR. As Burma's ambassador to Moscow remarked, his government was independent on principle and wished to deepen its ties with all countries, regardless of political orientation.[94] This refusal to view the world through a Cold War lens appeared to give the GDR an opening: Did not the logic of nonalignment demand that neutral countries establish equal diplomatic relations with *both* German states? The first step toward consolidating an organized nonaligned movement, taken at the Afro-Asian Conference in Bandung, Indonesia in April 1955, was greeted by East German officials with optimism. East Berlin's Trade Ministry vowed to "support the Asian and African peoples in their struggle for freedom" by prioritizing commercial relations with these continents.[95] Given the GDR's limited export capacity, this entailed a quiet shift away from South American markets, for these offered only a limited potential for political gains.[96]

For the time being, uncertainty over the future status of Germany continued to slow the GDR's acceptance. Jawarlahal Nehru, the most respected neutral statesman, characterized the division of Germany as an imminent danger to the peace; in his view German unification would diminish the

CONTAINING EAST GERMANY

threat of a third world war. For this reason Nehru insisted that India would refrain from any actions that would deepen the country's division—such as recognizing the GDR as a second German state.[97] On a more pragmatic level, nonaligned leaders doubtless saw little reason to antagonize Bonn over an issue that might soon be moot. If the Soviets and the Western Allies could agree on a plan for unifying Germany, then the GDR would likely disappear anyway. What would happen, though, if the status quo of a divided Germany began to harden, turning the SED regime into a permanent feature of European geography? As events in 1955 pointed increasingly in this direction, the Federal Republic found itself hard pressed to maintain the diplomatic blockade around its rival.

Chapter 2

Staving Off Collapse

"The Federal Republic of Germany has now won back its sovereignty, and with that its freedom," exulted Chancellor Adenauer in a radio broadcast on May 5, 1955.[1] The occasion marked a genuine high point in Adenauer's political career; since 1949 the attainment of full sovereignty for the Federal Republic had constituted an overriding goal of his foreign policy. At noon on May 5 the Paris Treaties went into effect, bringing about the dissolution of the Allied High Commission and the admission of West Germany into NATO as an equal partner. With certain restrictions—regarding Berlin, the problem of unification, and the manufacture of atomic, biological, and chemical weapons—the Federal Republic now enjoyed complete freedom in its internal and external affairs.[2]

After so many years of dependence on the Western Allies, however, neither Adenauer nor the government apparatus in Bonn felt quite at home making fundamental political decisions. The path was now clear for West Germany to establish ties with the states of Eastern Europe, above all the Soviet Union, yet the issue tormented the chancellor and his inner circle all summer without resolution. Could the Federal Republic establish a working relationship with the Soviet bloc without appearing to accept the legitimacy of communist rule in East Germany? The uncertainty in Bonn was magnified by the advent of another round of negotiations on the German Question: the Geneva summit conference of July 1955. Adenauer feared that the Western Allies might reach some form of accommodation with the Soviet Union, thereby acknowledging the status quo in Europe. Ironically, the *collapse* of the Geneva negotiations in November 1955 had a similar effect, for it signaled that the unification of Germany was further away than ever. With the Federal Republic now a member of NATO and the GDR incorporated into the newly founded Warsaw Pact, the situation in central Europe appeared to be frozen, both politically and militarily.

Not unreasonably, the SED anticipated a fundamental improvement in the GDR's international standing. After all, the East German state looked increasingly like an established fact of European geography. Surely the world's nonaligned leaders would now relent and establish relations with both German governments, just as the Soviet Union had done. Adenauer's government vowed to resist this eventuality, lest the bankruptcy of West German unification policy be made plain for all to see. After several months of disorientation, the Foreign Office called its ambassadors to Bonn in December 1955 to devise a more effective strategy for pursuing its isolation campaign. The end product was a surprisingly resilient and enduring formula later known as the Hallstein Doctrine.

A Shifting Landscape: Geneva and Moscow

For outside observers, Soviet foreign policy in 1955 was even more inscrutable than usual. Since the death of Stalin in March 1953, a small number of Politburo members had struggled for preeminence, but two years later it was still not clear who held the upper hand, Nikita Khrushchev or Nikolai Bulganin. It was, however, obvious that the Soviet leadership was rethinking its relationship with the West.[3] In April, Moscow surprised the Western Allies by agreeing to a peace settlement with Austria, allowing for the complete withdrawal of occupation forces and the permanent neutralization of that country. Was this, many wondered, a Soviet model for how to solve the German Question as well?[4] Another surprise came in June 1955, when the Soviet leadership invited Adenauer to Moscow to discuss a normalization of relations. For the next three months officials in Bonn, Paris, London, Washington, and doubtless elsewhere pondered the motives behind this stunning move. Were the Soviets still hoping to lure the Federal Republic away from the Western alliance? Or were they merely seeking to establish diplomatic relations with the Federal Republic, thus underlining the existence of two German states? These questions were all the more pressing in light of a parallel event planned for July: a conference of the top leaders of the Four Powers in Geneva. Two items were on the agenda: disarmament and German unification. Though it seemed unlikely, the prospect of a Four Power agreement on Germany could not be ruled out.

Despite Adenauer's reputation for caution and suspicion, his first reaction to the Soviet invitation was thinly disguised enthusiasm.[5] After all, a visit to Moscow would boost the prestige of the Federal Republic tremendously. It would show that the government in Bonn, a creation of the Western Allies, had been acknowledged as an independent political entity by the Allies' fiercest enemy. It would also help to assuage those in Adenauer's own ruling coalition who complained (accurately enough) that the chancellor had neglected relations with Germany's eastern neighbors.[6] As to what the journey might accomplish, in the spring of 1955 Adenauer even seemed favorably inclined toward establishing diplomatic relations with the Soviet Union. At one time he had feared that the presence of two German embassies in Moscow would imply a recognition of the GDR by the Federal Republic. By early 1955, though, the chancellor had discarded this concern.[7] As Adenauer explained to the Bundestag's Foreign Affairs Committee, he would merely have to express a formal reservation while taking up relations with Moscow, stating that the Federal Republic continued to deny the legitimacy of the Soviet-backed SED regime. "This problem is not grounds enough for us to ignore the great utility for Germany of establishing direct diplomatic relations," he concluded.[8]

Nevertheless, the chancellor intended to handle the question of relations with the Soviet Union as circumspectly as possible. It took the Federal Republic more than three weeks to compose an official reply to the Soviet note, and even this spoke only of exploratory conversations in Paris.[9] Thus Adenauer was deeply embarrassed by the forthrightness of Heinrich von Brentano, his newly appointed foreign minister, during a press conference on June 14, 1955. First Brentano intimated that the presence of an East German embassy in Moscow would not pose an insuperable obstacle to the founding of a West German embassy there. Then he described the situation in Helsinki, where both the Federal Republic and the GDR maintained trade missions without diplomatic status, as an arrangement that might also be tried in Moscow.[10] Upon reading press reports about these and other comments by the hapless minister, Adenauer very nearly demanded his immediate resignation.[11] At the Foreign Office, officials worked desperately to cover the effects of Brentano's gaffe, which had raised eyebrows in Vienna, Bern, and Helsinki. The Swiss Federal Council wondered whether Bonn had reconciled itself to dual German representation around the globe.[12] Far from it, warned a circular telegram sent by Hallstein to all West German missions on June 29, 1955. "The hypothetical remarks of the Minister referred exclusively to states within the Soviet sphere of power or, as the example of Finland shows, states in exceptional geographic and political dependence." Just for good measure, Hallstein specified that the "admission of GDR diplomatic representation in states with which we maintain diplomatic relations would unleash the sharpest resistance on the part of the Federal Government, and might possibly even lead to the withdrawal of our representatives."[13]

STAVING OFF COLLAPSE

Brentano's comments, and the subsequent confusion they touched off in many neutral countries, demonstrated the existence of an inescapable link between Bonn's attitude toward Moscow and its overall nonrecognition policy. If the Federal Republic *did* establish diplomatic relations with the Soviet Union, it appeared likely that several neutral powers would use this as an excuse to formalize economic and even political relations with the GDR.[14] "We have always taken the standpoint that we cannot allow two German ambassadors or legations in a single city," observed Baron Wolfgang von Welck, a leading director at the Foreign Office. "We have made an exception only in the case of Finland." But once the Federal Republic allowed two German representatives in Moscow, how could it stop other countries from following this pattern? "I can imagine that it was a primary goal [of the Soviets] to place us before this dilemma," Welck speculated.[15]

From Southeast Asia came further signs that Bonn's cordon sanitaire was in danger of slipping. Burma, like several other nations in the region, had been actively pursuing trade with eastern Germany; the SED regime had obliged by bartering industrial products for Burmese rice. In 1954 Burma copied Indonesia's example and permitted two delegates from East Germany's Chamber for Foreign Trade to reside in Rangoon.[16] These delegates persuaded the Burmese Foreign Ministry in June 1955 that granting official status to their mission, along with consular rights, would greatly facilitate trade. The GDR was angling to open a formal legation in Rangoon, reported the West German envoy there, "and is likely to succeed."[17] Hallstein responded by ordering the envoy, Wilhelm Kopf, to deliver the bluntest threat to date in defense of Bonn's nonrecognition policy. "Please seek out the foreign minister without delay and inform him that the granting of official status to the economic mission of the Soviet Zone would be regarded as an unfriendly act by the Federal Government, and could have serious consequences for relations between Burma and the Federal Republic. If Burma were to take up diplomatic relations with the so-called German Democratic Republic, we would have to consider breaking off diplomatic relations with Burma."[18]

Like Ambassador Meyer in New Delhi one year earlier, Kopf balked at his orders. "In accord with duty," he elaborated his "serious reservations" against threatening to break relations. Not only would the threat irritate the Burmese; it would not even be taken seriously by them, for they well knew the extent to which West Germany profited from its lucrative trade with Burma. A temporary coexistence of East and West German missions might even prove beneficial to the West, for the comparison would be instructive to the Burmese. At any rate, side-by-side competition would be preferable to a headlong retreat by West Germany in the event that the Foreign Office had to make good on its threat.[19] Kopf met with the acting foreign minister of Burma on June 29 but did not mention the possibility of a break in relations. The Burmese official promised to postpone a decision on the status of the East German mission until after the Geneva Conference in July.[20]

Kopf's telegrams anticipated a number of arguments that would recur throughout the long history of Bonn's isolation campaign. He identified West Germany's international standing with the success of its exports and welcomed open competition between the two German states. In rejecting this standpoint, Hallstein and the Foreign Office revealed the isolation of East Germany to be a central concern. Economic setbacks would have to be taken in stride, as Welck's reply to Rangoon on July 4 stated outright. Bonn's policy could not take account of particular local circumstances, such as the Burmese need to export rice; instead the threatened sanctions must apply to *any* noncommunist state that took up relations with the Pankow government. Welck's instructions for Kopf did represent a slight softening, though, for now the threatened sanction consisted of a "withdrawal" of the envoy rather than a complete break in diplomatic relations.[21] Still Kopf refused to act, demanding that he be recalled to Bonn for consultations. "The new political situation here created by the communist economic offensive demands an adjustment in our tactics," he cabled. Grudgingly, he consented to carry out the instructions of July 4 as a precondition for his return.[22] After this, Hallstein handled the affair in person through conversations with the Burmese chargé in Bonn. Only in late August did the government of Burma make a final decision: the mission of the GDR would have no diplomatic or consular status. Bonn's threats had paid off.[23]

As the summer progressed and the confrontation with Burma dragged on, the Foreign Office became ever less inclined to risk opening diplomatic relations with Moscow.[24] Writing in late June, Boris Meissner, head of the ministry's Soviet desk, acknowledged that once Bonn had taken up relations with the USSR, several countries were likely to send ambassadors to "Pankow."[25] Was this an acceptable loss? That all depended on the gains to be expected from relations with Moscow. Here the Foreign Office, and even more so Adenauer himself, began to have doubts. The Geneva Conference amounted to "a total victory for the Russians," the chancellor wrote on August 9 to U.S. Secretary of State John Foster Dulles. The Soviet leaders had demonstrated their complete antipathy to German unification.[26] This

34

apparently diminished the utility of a direct channel to Moscow in the chancellor's eyes. By mid-August the French chargé in Bonn detected a growing reserve about Adenauer's coming trip in political circles and within the government itself. On August 17 the government's foreign policy spokesman, Günter Diehl, stated that truly *normal* diplomatic relations could be established only between the Soviet Union and a single unified German state.[27] Clearly Diehl was trying to prepare the public for something short of full diplomatic relations with Moscow.

Meeting against the Alpine backdrop of Mürren, Switzerland, Adenauer and his top advisers reached consensus on August 23, 1955, about the limited goals of his Moscow trip. This was merely a first contact, they agreed; no concrete decisions could be expected in the course of a three- to four-day visit. Taking up full diplomatic relations with the Soviet Union was "inconceivable" without progress in the question of German unification and without the return of the remaining Germans in Soviet captivity— prisoners of war and other civilians deported from the Reich. In lieu of an exchange of ambassadors, the Federal Republic would propose the establishment of four mixed German-Soviet commissions to negotiate the fine points of mutual relations. If all the West German proposals were rejected by the Soviet leaders, Adenauer's delegation would depart, leaving behind only a provisional "diplomatic agent" so that not all contact with the Soviet government was lost.[28]

In adopting this plan, Adenauer's government attempted to avoid the unpleasant side effects of diplomatic relations with the Soviet Union—above all, the anticipated boost in the status of the East German government—by backing away from the problem entirely. As Adenauer commented at the end of August to Dulles's emissary, Livingston Merchant, "There could be no true normalization as represented by full diplomatic relations so long as the Soviet Union maintained the GDR."[29] In light of the intransigent Soviet position at the Geneva Conference, though, no one at the Foreign Office expected the Soviet leadership to drop the SED regime.[30] By setting a vague goal such as "progress on the question of German unification" as a prerequisite for diplomatic relations with the Soviet Union, the chancellor and his advisers were establishing a trip wire that would allow the negotiations in Moscow to collapse. What, after all, might constitute an adequate degree of progress on unification? Interpreted broadly, this might mean pinning the Soviets down on a date for the beginning of the unification process. Interpreted narrowly, this meant nothing more binding than the avoidance of a "sharp no" on the part of the Soviets toward unification.[31]

Shortly before the long-awaited departure for Moscow, the government cleared its negotiating position with the Western Allies and with key figures in the Bundestag. Washington was particularly sympathetic, as officials in the State Department also thought the Germans might be wise to hold back on full diplomatic relations with the Soviet Union. These American officials shared the concerns of Brentano and Hallstein, namely, that a German embassy in Moscow might make it more difficult for Bonn to keep third countries from recognizing the GDR.[32] In London, Sir Ivone Kirkpatrick, permanent under secretary at the British Foreign Office, "thought it a good thing for the Germans to hold up on the establishment of full diplomatic relations, as they planned, if they could manage this."[33] In explaining their position privately, West German leaders did not state categorically that they would refrain from diplomatic relations with the Soviet Union, but this was certainly the impression left by such conversations. This cautious stance was lauded by some parliamentarians; even Erich Ollenhauer, chairman of the SPD, agreed that the government should ensure that the policy of nonrecognition of the GDR did not begin to slip.[34]

In light of this carefully crafted and seemingly inflexible position, Adenauer's comportment in Moscow shocked the leadership of the Foreign Office. The West German–Soviet negotiations reached an impasse very quickly, reflecting the contradictory goals harbored by the two sides. The Federal Republic sought to obtain concessions from the Soviet leadership on the question of German unity, whereas the Soviets hoped to solidify the position of the SED by winning West German acknowledgment of the GDR. "Your attitude toward the German Democratic Republic is clear to us, but we cannot declare our agreement with this attitude," declared Khrushchev. "The German Democratic Republic is the future. It is the future, and not only of the German people alone."[35] Khrushchev and Bulganin refused to expand on the topic of unification, insisting that this was a matter for the Federal Republic and the GDR to discuss amongst themselves. Adenauer was just preparing to stage a theatrical early return to Bonn when the Soviets approached him with a blunt offer: the return of the last 10,000 German prisoners of war in exchange for the establishment of diplomatic relations between the Federal Republic and the Soviet Union. Such a barter did not live up to Adenauer's original goals for the trip, but the chancellor was too masterful a politician not to recognize the political benefits that might accrue from the final return of all POWs from the Soviet camps. Against the impassioned resistance of Brentano, Hallstein, and Grewe, the chancellor persuaded the West German delegation to accept the deal.[36]

STAVING OFF COLLAPSE

Adenauer was left with a paper-thin device to save face. Before leaving Moscow, he presented Soviet Minister-President Nikolai Bulganin with a letter expressing two German reservations: first, that the Federal Republic continued to view itself as the sole representative of the German people and, second, that the Federal Republic did not accept the postwar delineation of Germany's boundaries as final.[37] The Soviet leader declined to acknowledge the letter's contents, let alone express agreement. On the other hand, Bulganin did not refuse to receive the letter or expressly refute these interpretations of the meaning of the German-Soviet agreement.[38] As the chancellor assured the CDU Bundestag caucus upon his return from Moscow, this procedure guaranteed the continuing legal validity of West Germany's claims.[39] In a political sense, Adenauer may have been right, for this letter documented the failure of the Soviet leadership to persuade the West Germans to abandon their visceral rejection of the satellite regime in East Berlin. The question now was whether other countries would continue to share West Germany's views about the GDR. Foreign Minister Brentano, addressing the CDU Bundestag caucus immediately after the chancellor on September 15, saw "no grounds for celebration. A development has been set in motion, the control of which rests not alone in our hands, but in the course of events."[40]

Brentano's fatalistic attitude represented the "varying degrees of gloom" evident at the Foreign Office following the Moscow talks.[41] One week earlier the minister had explained to the Bundestag's Foreign Affairs Committee why it would be too dangerous to take up diplomatic relations with the USSR:

> Up to now we have adopted the standpoint that in every case and in every country with which we have diplomatic relations, only *one* German mission can be active in these countries. In every case when a country expressed the intention of taking up diplomatic relations with the GDR, we . . . have stated that taking up relations with the GDR would necessarily result in a break in the diplomatic relations to the Federal Republic. We would lose this very important political argument if we were to take up bona fide diplomatic relations [with the USSR] and hence allow other states to refer to this episode.[42]

As a result of Adenauer's Moscow decision, then, the Foreign Office had (in Brentano's terms) lost an important political argument; it would have to devise a new one. Now that two German ambassadors would reside in Moscow, why should other countries continue to shun a similar arrangement in their own capitals? On the return flight from Moscow, in a lively and egalitarian brainstorming session, the top officials of the Foreign Office puzzled out a plan for damage control.[43]

The solution, drawn up by Wilhelm Grewe on September 15, 1955, was to pretend that the Moscow decision did not matter after all. Grewe argued that the dual German representation in Moscow constituted a onetime exception to Bonn's general rule. According to Grewe's thesis, two considerations made the Moscow exception necessary: the return of the prisoners of war, and the role of the Soviet Union as one of the Four Powers with a say in the resolution of the German Question.[44] This latter point allowed the Federal Republic to depict the outcome in Moscow as a boon for unification, for now the West Germans were in a position to present their case directly to the fourth and most recalcitrant of the Four Powers. In conveying these arguments to foreign governments, the Foreign Office followed the procedure used in April 1954: a statement by Adenauer to the Bundestag, supported by worldwide action on the part of West German diplomats. Having already assured the Federal Republic's diplomatic posts on September 15 that "in the question of the recognition of the GDR, all previous instructions remain in force," Hallstein issued a template on September 21 for a standard aide-mémoire to be presented to all governments with which Bonn had relations. This document reproduced the text of Adenauer's letter to Bulganin and then pointed out that the Federal Republic had taken up diplomatic relations only with those states that had no diplomatic relations with the GDR. West Germany's relationship with the Soviet Union was a "singular situation" that should not lead to unwarranted generalizations on the part of other states.[45]

This line of argumentation contained a logical restriction on Bonn's own freedom of action, for if Moscow was to be the sole exception to the rule about no double representation, then the Federal Republic could not open embassies in Warsaw, Prague, or the other capitals of the eastern bloc. It may be that the chancellor intended the freeze in relations to Eastern Europe to apply only for a short time, until the waves set in motion by the Moscow decision had calmed.[46] On September 16 Adenauer glossed over the problem by remarking to journalists that he and Brentano had not yet considered the subject. Behind closed doors, though, Bonn's top officials made their point of view blatantly clear.[47] The U.S. embassy in Bonn concluded that further American planning "must be based on the assumption that the Federal Republic will not have diplomatic relations with Soviet satellite states in the foreseeable future."[48] Such long-term consequences might have been avoided had the Foreign Office prepared adequately for the Moscow trip. Instead, Brentano and his top advisers were caught off guard by Adenauer's decision. Their panicked reaction preserved the basic logic of Bonn's isolation policy but vastly complicated West Germany's future relations with Eastern Europe.

The Blockade Slips

In addressing the Bundestag on September 22, 1955, Adenauer's political imperative was to prove that his conduct in Moscow did not amount to a fatal capitulation to the Soviets. As the U.S. embassy observed, political circles in Bonn were "depressed and uneasy about the foreign policy implications of the chancellor's Moscow trip."[49] Christian Democratic parliamentarians had greeted the Moscow decision with mixed reactions. On September 15, when Adenauer appeared before the CDU/CSU (Christian Social Union) caucus to make his initial report, the group rose to its feet as a gesture of respect. Yet in a discussion of the Moscow events on September 21, the caucus leader, Heinrich Krone, rated the outcome as "not especially favorable." At length the CDU/CSU caucus accepted Krone's assessment that, in light of the extremely difficult circumstances in Moscow, the Federal Republic could not have secured a better deal.[50] At any rate, the citizens of West Germany showed much less concern than did political elites about the GDR recognition problem, judging it "a question for the Foreign Office expert." To the average German voter, the release of 10,000 prisoners of war from Soviet captivity represented an outstanding success. No doubt this high level of public approval facilitated the Bundestag's unanimous vote on September 22, 1955, to endorse the Moscow decision.[51]

In his official report to the Bundestag, Adenauer spoke with an unprecedented degree of harshness in order to convince skeptical parliamentarians of the firmness of West German policy. After explaining at length how his letter to Bulganin ensured the continuing validity of the Federal Republic's legal position, Adenauer delivered a stern warning to third countries. Those governments that had relations with Bonn should refrain from taking up relations with the GDR; such a step would be viewed by West Germany as an "unfriendly act, since it would serve to deepen the division of Germany." Before Adenauer had even finished this sentence, members of the government party burst out in applause, indicating their approval of a hard-line stance on the recognition issue.[52]

As noted above, Brentano had outlined an ever sharper version of Bonn's policy to the Foreign Affairs Committee before the Moscow trip; he spelled it out once more on September 21.[53] Yet the Foreign Affairs Committee met in tightly guarded secrecy, whereas now Adenauer ventured to define this standpoint loudly and publicly. Erich Ollenhauer, the SPD's caucus chairman, responded in the Bundestag plenum with a show of moral indignation. Had not the chancellor spoken many times about the long, difficult process of winning back the world's trust in the German people? The government must stay away from language that could only "reopen old wounds and endanger young friendships." Ollenhauer accepted the principle of intervening in third countries to discourage the recognition of East Germany; he merely urged that this happen "in a form more appropriate for us, by means of a friendly understanding." Regarding the internal implications of nonrecognition, Ollenhauer was still more critical. As more authority devolved to the Pankow regime, he argued, the West German government must overcome its reluctance to undertake practical dealings with East German officials. Recognition of the GDR was out of the question, but technical agreements, such as the regulation of traffic between the populations of East and West, must not collapse due to "problems of prestige and protocol."[54]

The SPD's calls for greater contact with East Germany reflected a recent change in the status of the satellite regime. On September 20, hard on the heels of the West German negotiations in Moscow, the Soviet government signed a treaty with the GDR bestowing formal sovereignty on the Pankow regime. Most of the reservations contained in the unilateral Soviet declaration of March 25, 1954, were lifted, giving the GDR a legal status identical to that of the Federal Republic.[55] With this step the USSR furnished the constitutional basis for the "two-state" theory. Abandoning all pretense of advocating the cause of unification, the Soviets moved to assist in the consolidation of East Germany's international position. States within easy reach of Moscow felt the pressure immediately. When Finland's president visited the Soviet Union in late September, Khrushchev delivered strong hints about recognizing the GDR.[56] In Yugoslavia, Josip Broz Tito leaned ever closer to the Soviet line on the German Question in order to underscore his reconciliation with the Kremlin. Experts at the Foreign Office judged that, were it not for Yugoslav hopes for war-related reparations from the Federal Republic, Tito would instantly accede to Soviet wishes and take up relations with the GDR.[57]

A number of states beyond Moscow's immediate grasp also reevaluated their views on Germany in the wake of September's events. Foreign diplomats showed annoyance or confusion at the arguments supplied by the

Foreign Office to explain the installation of a second German embassy in Moscow; some concluded that Bonn had revised its attitude toward the recognition of the GDR.[58] The Lebanese Council of Ministers acted accordingly, voting on October 12 to permit the opening of an East German trade mission in Beirut. Far away in Montevideo, the Uruguayan government commissioned an official trade representative to East Berlin.[59] Elsewhere, rumors circulated wildly about which countries were on the verge of recognizing the GDR outright.[60] Nonaligned countries began paying the Pankow government elementary courtesies—by having their ambassadors attend GDR-sponsored receptions in eastern bloc countries, for example.[61] Whereas the West German aide-mémoire of April 1954 yielded an outpouring of written assurances by third countries, the corresponding aide-mémoire of September 1955 was received almost without comment. In trying to estimate which countries might now be inclined to recognize the GDR, the Foreign Office found in late October that the number of problem cases had more than doubled.[62]

Capitalizing on the unstable situation, the Politburo in East Berlin resolved to bolster the top echelons of the Foreign Ministry, to recruit more diplomats into the East German foreign service, and to seek a higher profile in international organizations.[63] Of special significance was an initiative undertaken by Heinrich Rau, the trade minister, in late October 1955; he paid lengthy visits to New Delhi and Cairo, the two major capitals of the nonaligned world, thereby becoming the first East German cabinet member to travel beyond the bounds of the Soviet bloc. In India, Rau attended the opening festivities of an industrial exposition—the avowed purpose of his trip—but also found the doors open for a conversation with Prime Minister Nehru. Such a high-level reception naturally disturbed Bonn, though the Indian government refrained from granting any substantial concessions to the GDR. The Foreign Office could also take comfort in the fact that Rau was welcomed as a "distinguished guest" but not as an official representative of the East German regime.[64] In Cairo, by contrast, there was no disguising the cordiality of Rau's reception. Gamal Abdul Nasser, now Egypt's unchallenged leader, had concluded a major arms deal with Czechoslovakia in the second half of 1955, smoothing the path for a plum East German gain. Not only did Rau and his delegation sign a generous handful of government-level trade agreements with their Egyptian counterparts, but the two sides also pledged a mutual exchange of official trade missions with consular rights.[65] Thus Egypt was poised to defy two of Bonn's dictums: East German officials in Cairo would now enjoy the sort of consular privileges ordinarily reserved for sovereign, officially recognized states, and Nasser's government would double the damage by becoming the first noncommunist nation to open a government-level trade mission in East Berlin. In a much more public and dramatic way than in the case of Burma several months earlier, Egypt had crossed a line that demanded some response from Adenauer's government.

Even as the Federal Republic faced a rapid erosion of its nonrecognition policy, it found that French and British interest in maintaining the cordon sanitaire around East Germany had ebbed to a new low. Both the Quai d'Orsay and the Foreign Office reflected on the advantages of a tacit acceptance of the territorial status quo in Europe. Not coincidentally, both came out in favor of expanded intra-German contacts in order to make the human consequences of division more bearable.[66] France had never offered much assistance in support of the nonrecognition policy in the first place, but Britain turned down several West German requests for assistance in the fall of 1955.[67] At this point only the United States appeared to support West Germany's nonrecognition efforts energetically.[68] When the Soviet Union proclaimed the GDR's full sovereignty on September 20, this gave the Americans a welcome opportunity to reiterate the standard Western position on Germany. Meeting in New York on September 28, the foreign ministers of the three Western Allies issued a communiqué—over British objections—proclaiming once again that only Adenauer's government was entitled to speak on behalf of the German people and that the three governments had no intention of taking up relations with the so-called GDR.[69] The New York communiqué, followed by an American démarche in Helsinki in mid-October, impressed Finland enough to defer any immediate plans there for recognizing East Germany.[70] The continuing responsibility of the Four Powers for German unification gave the Allies a pretext to intervene against the GDR even after both German states had achieved formal sovereignty. In light of the anti-imperialist fervor of many nonaligned countries, though, and particularly in the wake of the Bandung Conference, the involvement of the Western Allies was hardly a guaranteed safety net for the Federal Republic.[71]

A further blow to West German credibility came in mid-November with the collapse of the Geneva Conference of Foreign Ministers. Soviet foreign minister Molotov brought the conference to a halt with a sudden, stinging rejection of the prospect of German unification through free elections.[72] The Western Allies had not expected substantial progress in Geneva in any

case, but they had envisioned a continuation of the conference the following spring in order to obscure the extent of disagreement among the Four
Powers.[73] Instead Molotov's intransigence forced a premature end to the
conference, revealing to all the near-impossibility of any agreements on
German reunification. As a corollary, West Germany could no longer point
to the ephemeral character of the East German regime. The unification of
Germany, which would bring in its wake the dissolution of the unpopular
regime in the Soviet Zone, appeared more distant than ever. Earlier in the
year the Federal Republic had asked wavering countries not to take any far-
reaching decisions regarding the GDR until after the Geneva Conference.[74]
Now that time was at hand. India, which had previously expressed its
desire to avoid any actions that might deepen the division of Germany,
began voting in favor of East German admission to international organizations.[75] Egypt and Yugoslavia followed suit. Though still unwilling to accord the regime in East Berlin de jure recognition, the world's leading
nonaligned powers were increasingly paying respect to the GDR as a distinct
state. Could the rest of the Third World be far behind?

Threatened with the unraveling of its isolation policy, the Adenauer
government never seriously considered abandoning it entirely. The failure
of the Geneva Conference had actually increased the domestic political
value of the campaign against East Germany. Both the Social Democrats
and the Free Democrats attributed the conference's failure less to Soviet rigidity than to a lack of creativity on Adenauer's part. FDP chairman Thomas
Dehler was clamoring for new approaches to Moscow, putting the governing coalition (to which the FDP still nominally belonged) under pressure to
demonstrate some activity on behalf of German unification.[76] Yet activism
for activism's sake was anathema to Adenauer. Fearful of awakening Western suspicions about the untrustworthiness of all Germans, the chancellor
rejected Dehler's demands for intensive political conversations with the
Soviet Union. Adenauer also called on the rebellious FDP to reaffirm its
allegiance to his general foreign policy line; but Dehler refused, and he led
his party into the ranks of Adenauer's parliamentary opponents soon thereafter.[77] While Adenauer was locking horns with Dehler, the Foreign Office
had scant room to maneuver in reasserting the credibility of the government's reunification policy. At the very least, Bonn could show that the
door to German unity remained open—that the GDR had failed to assert
itself as an autonomous and equal German state. Strong action against
East Germany's foreign pretensions might serve two purposes: it could halt

the progress of the GDR's bid for international respectability, and it could demonstrate vigorously the commitment of Adenauer's government to the cause of unification.

The Bonn Ambassadors' Conference

Within the Foreign Office, the top leadership resolved to counter the GDR's gains by raising the stakes in the recognition game. Adenauer's comments to the Bundestag on September 22, 1955, apparently did not constitute a sufficient deterrent. The chancellor had declared recognition of the GDR to be an "unfriendly act," which sounded ominous, but provided no indication of what consequences might ensue. How, precisely, did Bonn intend to punish the perpetrator of such an unfriendly act?[78] Hallstein and Brentano had long since concluded that Bonn could only react to an outright recognition of the GDR by breaking off relations with the offender, yet this standpoint was not widely known in foreign diplomatic circles or even within the Foreign Office. Karl Carstens, who had served as Wilhelm Grewe's deputy since September, first learned of this school of thought in early November.[79] If Bonn wished to deter third countries from unwanted dealings with the GDR, it would have to deliver its threats more openly. Meanwhile, West German officials and diplomats needed more explicit guidance about how to implement the nonrecognition policy. To work out a comprehensive approach to the problem of isolating East Germany, the Foreign Office summoned its leading ambassadors to Bonn for a major conference on December 8–10, 1955.

In the weeks before the Ambassadors' Conference, the Foreign Office defined the organizational framework for the Federal Republic's redoubled efforts. On November 24, Hallstein delegated authority on the nonrecognition problem to Wilhelm Grewe, whose Political Department now absorbed the "reunification" desk.[80] This move had important implications for Bonn's isolation strategy. Since April 1955 the reunification desk had worked under the auspices of the Countries Department (Länderabteilung), the division responsible for handling bilateral relations with nations around the world. This gave experts on individual countries a great deal of say in determining how Bonn's nonrecognition policy should be applied in specific local contexts. In shifting the problem to a department that handled concerns of a more general nature, Hallstein and Grewe sought to centralize and routinize decision making. As Grewe argued, "Our reaction to the GDR's efforts to establish diplomatic or consular footing in third countries cannot be determined from our bilateral relations with the country in question. Such a reaction follows rather from general principles in the realm of unification policy. Perspectives derived from bilateral relations with the said country can only be applied as a corrective, delaying and curbing the execution of the general principles, or hastening and intensifying them."[81] The lawyers at the Foreign Office, Hallstein and Grewe, were determined to coordinate the isolation campaign with careful attention to precedent.

For the West German diplomats and officials assembled in Bonn on December 8–10, 1955, the Ambassadors' Conference represented a supreme moment of self-assertion for West German diplomacy. Foreign Minister Brentano, who in recent weeks had just begun to step out from under Chancellor Adenauer's shadow, opened the conference with a defiant speech heralding the primacy of politics over economics.[82] Granted, it was a particular kind of politics: a highly moralistic, loudly intoned primacy of national interest (unification) above the private interests of individuals and industry. Brentano left the ambassadors in no doubt that no matter what the cost, he was prepared to break with any country that crossed the line in its dealings with the Pankow regime. "Of course it's clear to me that if it comes to this, in some case or other valuable and perhaps even irreplaceable ties for the German economy will be interrupted. But I believe that economic considerations must retreat behind basic political considerations, if we do not wish to give up our entire line of policy as carried out until now. The Federal Government as presently constituted is certainly not prepared to do that—least of all the chancellor and I myself."[83] Brentano added that this position should quell any rumors about Bonn taking up relations with the satellite states in Eastern Europe. For Brentano the trade benefits of an opening toward the East would hardly compensate for the damage to the nonrecognition policy. Here he spoke not only as foreign minister but as an impassioned Christian Democrat. Though he did not mention the FDP by name, his comments were obviously directed toward the CDU's mutinous coalition partner. After all, it was in the camp of the strongly pro-industry Free Democrats that one found the most vocal proponents for opening relations with the East.[84]

Brentano's speech set the tone for the remainder of the conference. Although his opening comments marked the boundaries of discussion— relations with Eastern Europe were clearly not on the agenda—he invited the diplomats to speak their minds freely, noting how pleased he had been with the frank and earnest objections raised by one German in the field earlier that year.[85] Brentano's central dictum was hardly new to Bonn insiders anyway; where the conference brought genuine innovation was in the realm of tactics. Two days of discussion at an oversized oval table stimulated a fruitful problem-solving atmosphere that spurred activity on several fronts.[86] Diplomats posted around the globe attested to the sensitivity of their host countries to precedents set elsewhere. The preferred metaphor for Bonn's nonrecognition policy was that of a dam: a breach in one place would weaken the entire structure and unleash a flood, sweeping nations from Sweden to Brazil in its wake.[87] Unanimous in their assessment of the seriousness of the problem, the conference participants resolved to act promptly and forcefully in response to overly friendly behavior toward the GDR. The diplomats also called for proactive measures to further widen the representation gap between the German states. In November, Bonn had scored a coup by striking up full diplomatic relations with Vienna; Austria, like Sweden, chose West Germany over its eastern rival despite professing a neutral posture in the Cold War.[88] The Ambassadors' Conference resolved to take another step forward by securing full West German membership in the UN-affiliated ECE.[89]

This newfound energy might well have dissipated without long-term effects were it not for the conference's success in delineating a conceptual framework for applying Bonn's policy. Wilhelm Grewe's comments led the way. After Brentano had identified the lengths to which West Germany would go if necessary, Grewe's tactical plan explored how the Foreign Office could achieve its aims without resorting to drastic measures. With the nonrecognition policy under siege from so many directions, Grewe noted, Bonn must weigh carefully when and how to apply pressure on foreign governments. Some degree of contact between third countries and the GDR must be tolerated, since "a state-like territory with a population of seventeen million cannot be treated as nonexistent by the rest of the world."[90] Problems of transit through East German territory, or nonpolitical issues such as trade relations, would inevitably lead to low-level contacts between the outside world and the authorities in East Berlin. The West Germans could not reasonably seek to forbid these contacts, especially in light of their own unofficial connections with the East Germans.

Where should West Germany draw the line, then, separating acceptable and unacceptable dealings between third countries and the GDR? Grewe explained that precedent in international law defined no hard and fast boundaries between acts that implied recognition and those that did not.[91] There were, of course, a few straightforward cases. Any country that took up diplomatic relations with East Berlin—whether on the level of ambassador, envoy, or chargé—had recognized the GDR as a new, independent state. Did this apply to consular relations as well? Grewe maintained that this case was ambiguous. Equally uncertain was the example of hosting a government-level delegation from East Germany.[92] Unofficial delegations, or trade agreements between private chambers of commerce, clearly did *not* imply recognition. Yet ominously enough, a string of isolated acts that did not in themselves entail recognition might nevertheless, taken as a whole, be construed as a tacit recognition.[93]

Grewe recommended that, since international law provided no definitive answers, the Federal Republic should take advantage of this ambiguity. There was no point in delineating publicly which actions the Foreign Office found intolerable and which steps it would reluctantly accept. Drawing a line in the sand would only tempt states to advance to this line. By keeping its pronouncements vague, the Federal Republic could more readily discourage steps that were *politically* undesirable but *legally* acceptable. Such a procedure also left open the possibility of a graceful retreat in cases where third countries could not be dissuaded from contacts with the GDR. Rather than inflating every attempted contact between third parties and the East Germans into a question of recognition or nonrecognition, Grewe concluded, the West Germans should judge each case by the circumstances.[94] Taken as a whole, Grewe's suggestions added up to a program of calculated ambiguity that would preserve maximum maneuvering room for the Federal Republic.

State Secretary Hallstein, in a follow-up statement, endorsed Grewe's flexible approach to the question of what constituted recognition. "It is not our intention to work out some kind of catechism for the GDR question, a tutorial that contains all eventualities," noted the state secretary.[95] Hallstein agreed with Grewe that the Foreign Office should refrain from blowing out of proportion every instance of contact with the GDR. "That means that we won't make cases out of situations that really *aren't* cases." He added, "But that doesn't mean that we can avoid the issue if the problem is concretely posed somewhere."[96] On this point Hallstein's views were far more stringent than Grewe's. Although it might be more convenient to look the other way, in some circumstances the Federal Republic would have no choice but to intervene against countries fostering questionable relations with the GDR. Referring to the situation in Egypt, Hallstein commented that the Foreign Office could not simply accept at face value the assurances of Nasser's government that it had not recognized the GDR. Two other sources of authority would decide whether that was the case: the objective precedents of international law and the subjective response of world opinion.[97] Appearances weighed heavily in Hallstein's estimation. Acts that *seemed* to imply a de facto recognition of East Germany could not go unanswered, lest other states follow suit.

In keeping with this concern for appearances, Hallstein and Brentano ensured that public statements on the outcome of the Ambassadors' Conference stressed the hard edge of Bonn's policy. On December 9, 1955, the Foreign Office proclaimed to the public for the first time that Bonn would, in fact, break relations with any country that recognized the GDR, and that similar reasoning would hold the Federal Republic back from seeking diplomatic relations with the satellite states. Spokesman Günter Diehl did not elaborate further, leaving the impression that West Germany's policy could be characterized by a single formula: "Whoever maintains diplomatic relations with us, maintains no diplomatic relations with the GDR."[98] This was the government's deterrent in its crudest form: any country committing the unfriendly act of recognizing East Germany would be asked to withdraw its embassy from West Germany. Rather than articulating such a peremptory threat directly to foreign governments via its ambassadors, the Foreign Office allowed the media to drive home the seriousness of Bonn's position.[99]

West Germany's leading newspapers did not doubt the severity of Brentano's intentions, but they expressed nearly universal condemnation of the resolute tone at the Foreign Office.[100] Some commentators objected on principle to the exercise of pressure on nonaligned powers: "The states of the Bandung Conference have become self-aware, and they don't let anyone talk to them in the tone of white colonial masters any more."[101] Others wondered whether the Federal Republic actually possessed the diplomatic leverage to make good on its threats.[102] A number of editorials agreed that it was foolish to broadcast Bonn's intentions in advance. Would it truly be in Bonn's interests to break relations in every case? wondered the *Frankfurter Allgemeine Zeitung*. These observers were especially aggrieved by the announcement that Bonn would not pursue relations with Eastern Europe.[103] As early as December 1955 the Foreign Office was confronted with the charges of dogmatism and inflexibility that would plague the isolation campaign throughout its history.

Wilhelm Grewe, appalled at the press response to the Ambassadors' Conference, took to the airwaves on December 11 in an attempt to set the record straight. In a radio interview approved by the foreign minister, Grewe denied the proposition that the nonrecognition policy was overly simplistic.[104] He explained that the Federal Republic would *not* automatically break relations in response to every affront against its nonrecognition policy. Since it was impossible to stipulate which actions implied recognition, the Federal Republic would view *any* intensification of relations with the SED regime as an unfriendly act. But one could respond to an unfriendly act with a graduated series of responses, ranging from recalling Bonn's ambassador to reducing the size of an embassy's staff; the severing of diplomatic relations would be a final step that would be taken "only after very careful consideration and in a very serious situation." Having thus affirmed the flexibility of Bonn's approach, Grewe admitted that if a third country tried to allow double representation of Germany in its capital, "we will probably have no choice but to draw very serious consequences."[105]

Grewe's radio interview provided a strikingly forthright depiction of the considerations that would guide the Foreign Office in the years to come. Continuous improvisation, not mechanical certainty, was the essential hallmark of Bonn's efforts to block East German advances. Yet Grewe's comments did not lend themselves to pithy summarization; the West German press tended to assume that Adenauer's government would *automatically* break relations with any country that recognized the GDR.[106] State Secretary Hallstein actively encouraged such oversimplifications. In several background conversations with the press in 1955 and 1956, he characterized Bonn's policy as severe and uncompromising.[107] Hallstein thus used the media in his quest to convey an image of West German firmness, taking in stride the many unflattering judgments that these journalists then formed about Bonn's policy, such as its rigidity, its inappropriate use of diplomatic pressure, and its neglect of Eastern Europe. The state secretary was repaid fairly for his cavalier treatment of the press in mid-1958 when a journalist appended his name to the nonrecognition policy, dubbing it the Hallstein Doctrine.[108]

"Managed Relationships" and the Isolation Campaign

Aside from the public elaboration of the Hallstein Doctrine in all but name, December 1955 saw another development of lasting import for Bonn's isolation policy: the formation of the Bonn Group, a bimonthly gathering of German and Allied officials in the West German capital. The initiative came from the Allied embassies in Bonn, which sought a standing forum for consultation on matters of mutual concern, above all problems regarding Berlin and transit through the GDR. This would ensure that none of the four governments inadvertently compromised the nonrecognition policy through unilateral arrangements with East German officials.[109] The meetings also lent a welcome measure of transparency to West Germany's dealings with East Germany and the Soviet Union.[110] For its part, the Foreign Office adeptly played up the link between the internal and external aspects of the recognition problem. In the first two meetings of the Bonn Group, the Allies raised the question of navigation permits for East German waterways, while the Federal Republic brought up the deepening of ties between Cairo and East Berlin.[111] Throughout the 1950s and 1960s these routine, working-level conversations addressed topics ranging from the GDR's efforts in Cambodia to contingency planning regarding Berlin to the granting of temporary travel documents to East Germans en route to NATO countries.[112] Meetings generally emphasized the exchange of information rather than in-depth discussion; nevertheless, the Bonn Group might well be characterized as the central inter-Allied coordinating body for the isolation of East Germany.

On other levels, too, the Allies began to concern themselves with the recognition question more intensively. At a closed meeting of NATO foreign ministers in Paris on December 16, 1955, Heinrich von Brentano reiterated his government's attitude toward countries that recognized the GDR, either de facto or de jure. British foreign minister Harold Macmillan endorsed Brentano's words "in letter and spirit," agreeing that "one must show firmness."[113] This surprisingly strong expression of British approval came only a week after another, more direct offer of support: the Foreign Office in London informed its West German counterpart that it was willing to intervene diplomatically in nonaligned capitals if Bonn so desired.[114] Mounting concern within NATO about the expansion of Soviet influence in the Middle East was redounding to West Germany's benefit. Bonn could argue with some plausibility that East Germany's gains in that region represented a problem for the Atlantic alliance as a whole.[115] Appeals to Western solidarity also effected a remarkable turnaround in the attitude of France, which had previously been cool to West German interests beyond the continent of Europe. In the spring of 1956 the Quai d'Orsay—prompted frequently by the French embassy in Bonn—initiated a number of actions to prop up the diplomatic blockade against East Germany.[116] Allied cooperation proved especially helpful in the realm of international organizations, since West Germany was still not an official member of the UN. In December 1955 the British government sponsored a resolution calling for West Germany's full admission to the ECE. Not only did this measure pass, despite the strong presence of neutral and eastern bloc countries in the ECE, but the Allies managed to fend off a corresponding petition by the GDR at the next session of the ECE in April 1956.[117] Such victories for West Germany had an important symbolic value, for they showed that even after the failure of the Geneva Conference, East Germany remained a pariah in Europe.

On the level of bilateral relations, the West Germans themselves played the dominant role in halting the GDR's diplomatic offensive. Turning to the nonaligned world with renewed vigor, the Federal Republic shored up the barriers to East German participation in international life. Treaties or special agreements with India, Egypt, and Yugoslavia brought noticeable improvements in West German relations with the world's three leading nonaligned powers. In January 1956 the Foreign Office received intelligence that the Soviet ambassador to East Berlin had castigated the SED for its overeager forays into the Near East; the Soviets reportedly complained that the GDR's efforts had yielded a sharp counterreaction on the part of the West, exemplified by the firm new line taken at the Bonn Ambassadors' Conference.[118]

What role did the Federal Republic's widely publicized threats play in the stabilization of its cordon sanitaire around East Germany? Was the policy later known as the Hallstein Doctrine responsible for this turnaround? State Secretary Hallstein, speaking before the Bundestag's Foreign Affairs Committee in early February 1956, averred that in the course of the "very harsh, very difficult, and very dogged" struggle against the tendency of third countries to grow soft toward East Germany, the threat of retaliation had proven its usefulness.[119] Hallstein went on to explain that, though accurate, the term "threat" was best avoided in describing Bonn's policy; speaking so frankly would only decrease the willingness of prestige-conscious governments to cooperate. Tactical considerations had led the Foreign Office to present its position in a more guarded form. In the interests of harmonious relations, the Federal Republic felt it important to call attention to the inevitable consequences of such a step as recognizing the GDR. "We do not say this with the intention of exercising pressure on your government's decision in an offensive, in an inadmissible, in an inappropriate manner. You are completely free to act in accord with your own considerations, to weigh the advantages and disadvantages."[120]

In short, the Federal Republic did not admit that it was pressuring other governments with a blunt threat, and these other governments did not admit that their subsequent behavior reflected an adjustment to that pressure. How, then, can the historian evaluate the significance of Bonn's hard line in blocking East German recognition? Perhaps the best clue is the extent to which the Foreign Office sought means other than verbal deterrents to solidify relations with nonaligned countries. With India, the Federal Republic focused on flattery and personal diplomacy. Vice-Chancellor Franz Blücher, who in October had postponed a trip to India on account of Adenauer's illness, toured the subcontinent in January 1956. On the advice of Ambassador Meyer, who understood that Prime Minister Nehru would not make any binding declarations about East Germany in any case, Blücher refrained from demanding any outright assurances about nonrecognition. Instead he played on Nehru's concerns about world peace, arguing that an Indian recognition of the GDR would heighten, not lessen, the tension in divided Europe.[121] By July 1956, when Nehru paid an official visit to Bonn, the Foreign Office had perfected its appeals to the prime minister's moral sensibilities.[122] An unspoken quid pro quo evolved between the two countries: India respected West Germany's wishes regarding the German Question, while the West Germans affirmed their ever growing interest in the industrialization of India—avoiding, of course, any hint that economics rather than ethics determined Nehru's stance.[123] This did not yet cost Adenauer's administration a great deal in financial terms, since the Indian government dealt directly with private West German firms.

Settling the situation in Yugoslavia required far more cash and far less politesse. Here there was nothing subtle about the quid pro quo: Josip Broz Tito, the capricious Yugoslav leader, made it plain that a generous restitution payment for the ravages of World War II represented the only chance of keeping relations between Yugoslavia and West Germany on a solid footing. As early as November 1955, Adenauer's cabinet concluded that the Federal Republic would have to offer hundreds of millions of marks to Yugoslavia. Ambassador Karl-Georg Pfleiderer, in defending this approach to the cabinet, suggested that Bonn might successfully tie the aid to Yugoslavia's behavior regarding East Germany.[124] The Foreign Office did indeed pursue this tactic throughout the negotiations and subsequently claimed that Yugoslavia's friendly stance on the German Question formed the contractual basis (*Geschäftsgrundlage*) for the aid and restitution treaty signed on March 10, 1956.[125] In this case, rather than relying solely on the deterrent effect of the threat to break relations, West German officials attempted to bind Yugoslavia contractually to nonrecognition of East Germany.

The most pressing crisis during these months concerned relations with Egypt. Once Nasser had taken a bold step forward, the governments of Syria, Sudan, and Lebanon followed his lead; this made it all the more imperative that West Germany quickly defuse the situation in Cairo.[126] For all the publicity given Brentano's threat at the Ambassadors' Conference, up to that point Bonn had handled the affair quietly by seeking a face-saving means for the Egyptians to rescind their promises to the East Germans.[127] Rather than recalling Ambassador Walter Becker immediately in an open display of anger, the Foreign Office instructed him to seek clarifications from the Egyptians first. What was the precise legal status envisioned for the East German trade mission in Cairo? Two arrangements were described as completely unacceptable to Bonn: that the East German mission should be called a consulate and that it should be issued an exequatur (a formal decree of empowerment). Either of these eventualities would signify a de facto recognition of the GDR.[128] In setting such boundaries, Brentano and his ministry implicitly showed a readiness to compromise. They would accept the presence of an official East German government office in Cairo and perhaps even look the other way if it exercised certain consular rights, so long as it did not outwardly resemble a consulate.[129]

West Germany and Egypt did eventually come to terms on this basis, but only after two months of irritation and tension. Ambassador Becker's initial soundings in Cairo yielded no satisfactory answers, and in early December 1955 he informed the Egyptian foreign minister, Mahmoud Fawzi, that he was being recalled to Bonn.[130] From the Ambassadors' Conference came the famous warning that Bonn would break relations with any country that recognized East Germany. Despite the negative press response this generated in Germany, some observers concluded that the naked threat, together with the recall of Ambassador Becker, had a sobering effect in Cairo.[131] Nasser himself obliged by declaring to a reporter of the *Frankfurter Allgemeine Zeitung* on December 15, 1955, that his government had no intention of taking up consular, let alone diplomatic, relations with the GDR; a recognition of East Germany was "out of study and out of question."[132] This welcome news led the Foreign Office to send Becker back to his post on December 21. Yet Nasser's sweeping statement dodged many details, and the Federal Republic still had no precise assurances about the character of the East German mission in Cairo.[133]

Such assurances were long in coming. Only in early February did the German embassy in Cairo learn that Nasser had postponed the establishment of Egypt's trade mission in East Berlin.[134] During this long interval the Egyptians exercised pressure on West Germany regarding trade issues and relations with Israel—in both cases by cleverly inverting Bonn's threats. On January 24, 1956, the Egyptian embassy in Bonn published a polemical broadside charging that the Federal Republic was deliberately stalling trade talks in order to discourage the intensification of relations between East Germany and Egypt. This effort to place the onus on Bonn for exerting unfair economic pressure was in its own right a questionable form of conduct; embassies do not generally engage in direct attacks on their host governments.[135] Was the Egyptian charge substantially correct? Even forty years later, the situation is difficult to assess. Many of the contentious points in the West German–Egyptian trade talks reflected the orthodoxy of Bonn's Economics Ministry, not the political wishes of the Foreign Office. Yet Foreign Minister Brentano did appear to link the issues in a conversation with the Egyptian ambassador on January 17.[136] Whatever the case, the Egyptian allegations created a stir among the nonaligned embassies in Bonn, alerting the Federal Republic to the potential dangers of using economic leverage overtly in the pursuit of its nonrecognition policy.[137]

Of greater long-term import was Cairo's success in using the East German question to block a deepening of relations between Bonn and Tel Aviv. Nothing in the basic logic of the Bonn isolation campaign required West Germany to abstain from diplomatic or other relations with Israel, a country that had virtually no dealings with the GDR.[138] Having weathered a massive protest in 1952–53 over restitution payments to Israel, though, West German officials were loath to take any steps that might touch off a new storm in relations with the Arab states. As early as 1954, Near Eastern experts in Bonn recognized that Arab nations saw a link between Bonn's attitude toward Israel and the Arab attitude toward East Germany. Rather than actively disavowing such a connection, these West German policy makers were predisposed to accept it. "It doesn't help that the Federal Republic refuses to recognize such a link. For the Egyptians it exists, and they will act accordingly," wrote one official fatalistically.[139] Nasser ventured to express the link openly in April 1956, explaining that "up to now we have refused to recognize the GDR and take up relations with it. A recognition of Israel by the Federal Republic would, however, sweep aside our reservations, since it would be an unfriendly act against the Arab states."[140] In the spring of 1956 the Foreign Office allowed such considerations to overshadow the course of normalization with Israel. At Israel's suggestion, Adenauer's government briefly considered founding a West German mission in Tel Aviv, but a conference of German ambassadors to the countries of the Middle East, held in Istanbul in April 1956, persuaded Brentano to drop the plan.[141] For the next nine years, Nasser's threat held political relations between West Germany and Israel in check.

As the three cases above demonstrate, West Germany relied on more than just stern warnings to hold the line on its nonrecognition policy. With India, Yugoslavia, and Egypt, Bonn developed what might be termed managed relationships. The Federal Republic made certain financial or political concessions in order to secure cooperation regarding the nonrecognition of East Germany. As we will see, these countries—and eventually a great many others in the developing world—learned to make use of such "managed relationships" to wring further concessions from the West Germans. In most cases, though, the tactics introduced at the Ambassadors' Conference in December 1955 proved admirably suited to the task at hand. By advertising its readiness to take strong measures in defense of its blockade against East Germany, Adenauer's government put an end to the uncertainty prevalent in the fall of 1955. Speaking to an assembly of West German diplomats fourteen months later, State Secretary Hallstein characterized the isolation policy as a display of sheer determination. "It is in fact one of the verifiable accomplishments of our foreign service that it has succeeded in preventing the recognition of Pankow. We must keep telling this to the German public, too, because it proves what one can do if one *wills* it. International politics does not develop according to natural laws—it is made by men and determined by human will."[142] As an act of self-assertion on the part of the Federal Republic, the Hallstein Doctrine combined a strong moral claim—Adenauer's government as the sole legitimate representative of the German people—with a stark dose of power politics. As the conflict with Yugoslavia in 1957 would show, Bonn's threat was not empty.

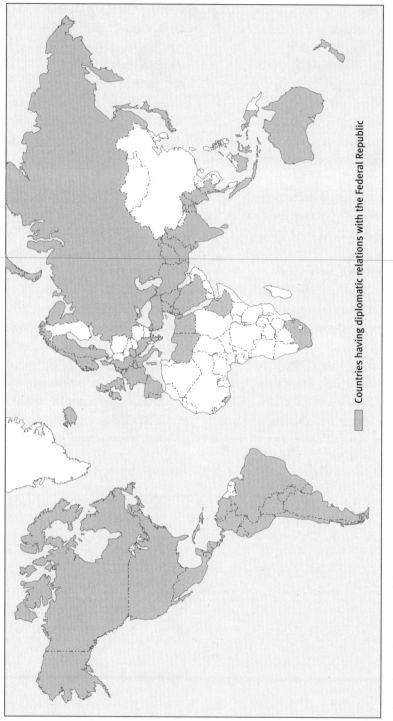

Countries having diplomatic relations with the Federal Republic

Map 1. West Germany's Diplomatic Network, December 1955

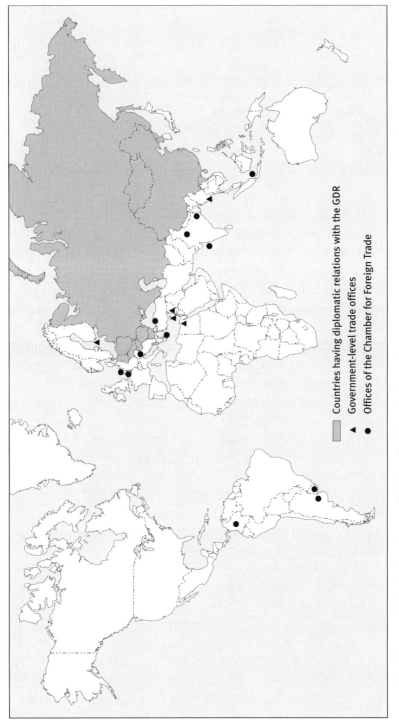

MAP 2. East Germany's Trade, Consular, and Diplomatic Network, December 1955

Chapter 3
Yugoslavia Crosses the Line

Only gradually in the winter of 1955–56 did the SED's leaders come to appreciate the extent of their continuing isolation. The hardening of the status quo in Europe had not led the nonaligned countries to embrace the GDR as a second state after all. Even those leaders most favorably disposed to the GDR, such as Nasser and Nehru, were still blatantly discriminating in favor of West Germany. Bitter protests about this injustice won East German diplomats few friends in the capitals of the developing world. Arduous local efforts to "ratchet up" the official status of East German missions had little effect on the GDR's overall position. Association with the Soviet Union was Ulbricht's one significant asset; nonaligned leaders courting Moscow's favor found it expedient to offer concessions to East Berlin. Yet even these cases did not automatically yield long-sought breakthroughs, for Soviet diplomats acted to restrain their East German colleagues. To a surprising extent, Moscow sympathized with the reluctance of African and Asian statesmen to provoke West Germany's ire.

Flush with success, officials on the Rhine began to regard the improvised threats of December 1955 as a long-term strategy for containing the GDR. Nevertheless, whenever the interests of Bonn's isolation campaign clashed with Adenauer's firm intention to expand West German political and economic influence in the developing world, the latter usually won. In Eastern Europe, too, the absence of relations with the "satellite" states was becoming a political liability. During the 1957 election campaign, the chancellor and others in his party hinted that the fall might bring a reevaluation of Bonn's policies toward Eastern Europe. West German diplomats held exploratory conversations with their Polish counterparts in Washington and Belgrade. In the midst of all the speculation about Adenauer's intentions, Marshal Tito of Yugoslavia concluded that he could safely recognize the GDR without fear of retaliation from Bonn.

This proved to be a serious miscalculation. Caught by surprise, Adenauer answered Tito's affront by severing diplomatic relations with Yugoslavia. The opposition parties in Bonn pleaded emotionally against this harsh response, predicting that it would cripple West German efforts at reconciliation with Eastern Europe. Yet this was a price the chancellor was willing to pay. In sacrificing its embassy in Belgrade, Bonn set a memorable precedent that impressed the nonaligned nations for many years to come. For the leadership in East Berlin, then, the triumph in Belgrade ended as a Pyrrhic victory. Rather than inspiring a wave of imitators, Yugoslavia's recognition of the GDR served as a warning to others tempted by the GDR's persistent overtures.

Grasping for Openings

From the standpoint of East Berlin, the fall of 1955 had brought a substantial deepening of ties with the nonaligned world. Trade Minister Heinrich Rau returned from his journey to Cairo and New Delhi convinced that the GDR now enjoyed a solid working relationship with both governments. Rau's was a gradualist vision: by demonstrating solidarity and economic partnership, without putting short-term political goals in the foreground, the GDR would eventually reap the diplomatic rewards it craved.[1] Rau and the members of his ministry thus took pains to downplay the recognition issue; in mid-1955 one East German trade representative in India was sacked for having raised the topic fecklessly with Prime Minister Nehru.[2] As the first Politburo member to tour the developing world, Rau learned firsthand about the priorities of leaders such as Nasser. The Egyptian president was completely preoccupied with the Aswan Dam, Rau observed; the Warsaw Pact nations would do well to get involved in that project. By financing the dam on the Nile, the Soviet Union and its allies could assist the Arabs in breaking their economic dependence on the imperialist West.[3] Much like Adenauer and Brentano, who saw themselves as working to uphold the position of "the West" in the developing world, Rau thought the GDR should play its part in advancing the reputation of the Soviet bloc among the Arab nations.

In light of this optimism about the GDR's improved standing and its potential contributions to the battle against "imperialism," SED leaders were jarred by fresh evidence of their regime's ongoing weakness in the nonaligned world. During his visit to New Delhi in January 1956, the West German vice-chancellor, Franz Blücher, was granted three private audiences with Prime Minister Nehru; Blücher also had the opportunity to propagate the Federal Republic's views in such public venues as India's Council on World Affairs. Although Nehru avoided any endorsement of Bonn's plans for German unification and even indirectly criticized the Federal Republic's decision to join NATO, the SED Politburo took great umbrage at the latitude the Indians had granted Blücher to "slander" the GDR.[4] More alarming still was Nehru's acceptance of an invitation by Blücher to visit Bonn in the summer of 1956. East German determination to talk Nehru out of this, or at the very least to persuade the Indian leader to visit East Berlin as well, foundered on Soviet resistance. From Moscow's perspective, the GDR had not yet done enough to make itself attractive to the Indians. Only the expansion of commercial, cultural, and scientific relations between East Berlin and New Delhi could smooth the path for a top-level exchange of visits.[5]

This guidance from Moscow did not, however, prevent the SED from venting its anger to Nehru. At times like this, Rau's moderate line was bypassed by the East German Foreign Ministry, which had an obvious institutional interest in expanding the GDR's diplomatic network. Months of prodding by Foreign Minister Lothar Bolz finally yielded Politburo approval of a strongly worded message to the Indian government, conveyed via the East German ambassador to Peking.[6] In this message, delivered orally, Bolz complained that the GDR's lack of diplomatic relations with India meant that the latter was hearing only one side of the story. Unintentionally, perhaps, India was supporting the line of the "imperialist forces in Germany" to the detriment of the "forces of peace and democracy." This was astonishing, in the SED's view, in light of the obvious commonalities between Indian and East German goals. Both countries were "against colonialism, for the preservation of the peace, against the formation of aggressive military blocks."[7] Such invocations of ideological solidarity would one day take on a routine, formulaic character, but the SED appears genuinely to have believed that its anti-imperialist rhetoric would be honored as an expression of the "spirit of Bandung." The reaction from New Delhi was disheartening. As before, recognition of the GDR was out of the question for Nehru; nor did the prime minister assent, however tentatively, to visit East Germany in the future.[8] Such a response made it painfully evident—even before Nehru's high-profile visit to Bonn in June 1956—that India's neutrality in the Cold War was not translating into an equal regard for the two rival governments in Germany.

Disappointment in New Delhi was tempered by a positive turn in Belgrade, and Yugoslavia swiftly eclipsed India as a focal point of East German aspirations. Since mid-1955 President Tito and Nikita Khrushchev had endeavored to heal the damaging rifts of the Stalin years. Tito's visit to Moscow in June 1956 marked a giant step toward reconciling the divergent strains of communism. Among the Yugoslav leader's many concessions was a near-reversal of his earlier stance on the German Question. Since 1951 Tito had maintained diplomatic relations with the Federal Republic alone. Now, speaking at Moscow's Dynamo Stadium on June 19, 1956, he remarked that it was necessary to view the process of German unification "realistically": "Two states now exist, West and East Germany, and it would be a mistake not to take this fact into account. It would be a mistake not to see that, besides West Germany, there is also an East Germany, where the internal process of development in social, political, cultural, and other affairs has run differently than in West Germany. Thus it would be a mistake not to recognize the individual state organism of East Germany."[9] On the following day Tito signed a joint communiqué with Khrushchev affirming that "at present, now that two sovereign states have been formed on the territory of postwar Germany, negotiations between the Federal Republic of Germany and the German Democratic Republic are necessary to reach the goal of unification."[10] This was an explicit endorsement of the SED's official program for German unity.

Although Tito stopped short of pronouncing his country's outright recognition of the GDR, East Berlin believed it had won an influential ally. The timing could hardly have been better, for Yugoslavia's star was on the rise within the nonaligned movement.[11] Tito's years of experience maneuvering between the two Cold War camps made him a natural European conversation partner for Nehru and Nasser, and the three arranged to meet in the Adriatic in July 1956 for a miniature nonaligned summit. From East Germany's standpoint, this marked a prime opportunity to achieve a long-awaited breakthrough. Surely Tito could persuade his visitors to join in acknowledging the existence of two German states. Ulbricht wrote the Yugoslav leader personally about the matter through Communist Party channels, arguing that the European questions of greatest urgency to the Bandung states—peace, disarmament, and German unification—could hardly be addressed so long as the GDR was denied its rightful place in Europe.[12] Coming just weeks after Tito's "conversion" in Moscow, Ulbricht's letter demonstrated a remarkable degree of confidence in Yugoslavia's readiness to support the GDR's cause. Later in July, Ulbricht went so far as to lecture the Yugoslav ambassador in Moscow about Belgrade's "international duty" to recognize his government.[13]

However faithfully Tito presented the East German case, he failed to sway Nehru and Nasser during their meetings on the island of Brioni. Both Egypt and India had achieved a delicate balance in relations with the Federal Republic, and they had little incentive to join Yugoslavia in underlining the existence of a second German state. The final communiqué from Brioni recommended ambiguously that the German Question "should be solved in conformity with the wishes of the German people by peaceful negotiated settlement."[14] Negotiations among *whom*? How were "the wishes of the German people" to be ascertained? The Brioni statement simultaneously hinted at both the central West German demand (free elections in the "Soviet Zone") and the opposing East German demand (negotiations between two equal German states) without backing either. More significantly, perhaps, the three leaders could agree on little else during their days in the Adriatic; Nehru reportedly found Nasser's course of confrontation with the West utterly distasteful.[15] The Brioni "summit" demonstrated that the nonaligned movement was too internally divided to serve as a useful vehicle for East German ambitions.

In the meantime Tito's own resolve had been shaken by the shrill tones emanating from Bonn. Addressing the Bundestag on June 28, 1956, a week after Tito's controversial speech in Moscow, Foreign Minister Brentano issued the most explicit warning to date in defense of Bonn's isolation campaign: the Federal Government "cannot but clarify once again that in the future, too, if a third state with which Bonn has diplomatic relations should establish diplomatic relations with the so-called 'GDR,' it must view this as an unfriendly act that would deepen and harden the division of Germany. In such a case, the Federal Government would have to reexamine its relations to the state in question."[16] Brentano still did not categorically threaten to break diplomatic ties with any state that recognized East Germany, but the final comment about reexamining relations came quite close. In the meantime the Foreign Office tugged at the levers of economic diplomacy, making use of the convenient fact that the Bundestag had not yet ratified the Yugoslav–West German restitution treaty of March 1956. State Secretary Hallstein hinted to parliamentarians that the government would prefer to see ratification postponed until Tito had clarified his intentions vis-à-vis East Germany.[17] The Bundestag actually exceeded Hallstein's expectations and suspended ratification until the new legislative period.[18] Tito did not gladly bow to this pressure; for nearly a month he put off requests by the West German ambassador to see him, further angering parliamentarians in Bonn. He finally received Bonn's ambassador, Karl-

Georg Pfleiderer, just days before the Brioni meetings to confirm that Yugoslavia would not establish relations with the GDR at present. Like so many other nonaligned statesmen, however, he refused to limit his future options.[19] Relations between Bonn and Belgrade reached a delicate state of equilibrium. West Germany expected its restitution agreement with Yugoslavia, disbursed in semiannual installments of DM 50 million ($11.9 million), to keep Tito in check; the Yugoslav president used the ever present possibility of recognizing East Germany as a means of exerting steady pressure on the West Germans.

The loser in such stalemates was inevitably the GDR. Bilateral relations between Belgrade and East Berlin had scarcely begun to thaw in 1956; Tito's new stance on the German Question had mainly to do with Yugoslav-Soviet relations.[20] The June speech in Moscow apparently accomplished all that the Soviet leadership had hoped for. Afterward, Soviet officials demonstrated sympathy for Belgrade's concerns about West German retaliation. Yugoslav diplomats explained that they "could not afford" to recognize the GDR, in light of the expected rupture in relations with the Federal Republic and the attendant economic damage.[21] The East Germans had to be content with vague promises that, over time, the Yugoslavs would gradually move from trade relations toward more formal ties with the GDR. The implied condition was, of course, economic cooperation. Ulbricht's government, itself scarcely on a stable financial footing, became the reluctant partner in a joint Soviet–East German investment project to expand Yugoslavia's aluminum industry.[22] Yet the Soviet intervention in Hungary in late October 1956, condemned sharply by Tito, put the aluminum project on ice for nearly a year; thus the one aspect of relations with the GDR that genuinely interested the Yugoslav president was deferred. In February 1957 Belgrade haughtily dismissed East Berlin's awkward bid to exchange government-level trade missions. Two months later a more perfunctory arrangement—chambers of commerce—finally won Yugoslav approval.[23]

As Yugoslavia's behavior demonstrated, the GDR was seldom the author of its own successes in the mid-1950s. Its fate remained closely tied to that of the Soviet Union and thus to the general ebbs and flows of the Cold War. Ulbricht's policy in the nonaligned world, like Khrushchev's, was opportunistic; the East saw openings wherever the West was in disrepute.[24] From this standpoint, the explosive situation in the Near East in 1956 looked promising indeed. Israel's purchases of French jets and military equipment, coupled with a series of preemptive strikes against neighboring territory, had driven Egypt and Syria to conclude various weapons deals with Czechoslovakia and the Soviet Union.[25] These developments could not help but raise the stock of other communist countries in Arab capitals such as Damascus. Syrian interest in the GDR was further stimulated by anger over Bonn's ongoing economic aid to Israel, which seemed particularly objectionable in the context of an accelerating Near Eastern arms race. When the well-traveled Heinrich Rau visited Damascus in May 1956, Syrian president Shukri al-Quwatli expressed his personal thanks for East Germany's refusal to grant Israel compensation for the Nazi genocide.[26] Shortly thereafter, the appointment of a left-leaning prime minister in Damascus brought another round of visits by Soviet and East German officials. In July Syria signed a cultural exchange treaty with the GDR. This was in itself a fairly innocuous arrangement, but the East German negotiators cleverly stipulated that the treaty must be ratified by each country's parliament—an act that would, in the view of legal experts, entail mutual recognition.[27] Leftist deputies in Syria's parliament circulated a petition calling for the establishment of normal diplomatic relations with the GDR, and the prime minister admitted privately that this step was under consideration.[28]

Bonn's ability to respond to the situation in Syria was sharply constrained by its alliance commitments. East Berlin's stridently pro-Arab rhetoric depicted the Near East conflict in straight Cold War terms: the Warsaw Pact was a patron of the Arab liberation struggle, while NATO (above all the Federal Republic) was the sponsor of Zionist aggression and imperialist oppression. To counter such allegations, the reunification desk in Bonn's Foreign Office planned an extensive démarche in the Arab capitals designed to highlight West Germany's neutrality in the Arab-Israeli conflict and its eagerness to intensify economic relations with the Arab countries.[29] This idea had to be jettisoned, however, for fear that France and Britain would take offense. In June 1956 the British government had already expressed reservations about a plan to invite Nasser to the Federal Republic.[30] The following month Cairo nationalized the assets of the Suez Canal, touching off a tense diplomatic crisis between the Egyptian president and the Western Allies. Under these circumstances, Bonn could scarcely make an overt profession of German-Arab friendship without appearing to repudiate its European partners.[31] At any rate, both the chancellor and his foreign minister sympathized strongly with the standpoint of Paris and London; Adenauer later characterized Nasser as a "little Hitler" whose nationalization policies represented an attack on international law and the prestige of Europe.[32] In mid-August, at a conference in London on the future of Suez, Brentano voiced support for a Western proposal calling for an international authority to run the canal. Faced with a choice between the Arabs and the West, Brentano wrote to Adenauer, "No doubts must arise about which side we stand on."[33] Given the strong opinions of the top leadership in Bonn, the Near Eastern hands at the Foreign Office had no choice but to ride out the crisis and hope to repair Bonn's relations with Arab nationalists at a later date.

In East Berlin the Ministry for Foreign Affairs gleefully exploited Bonn's dilemma. On August 26, 1956, it pledged the GDR's "respect for the sovereignty and independence of each nation" and endorsed Nasser's decision to reject international control of the Suez Canal.[34] The Egyptian government remained unmoved. This was in keeping with Moscow's wishes; in July, after Nasser had ventured to recognize Red China, the Soviet Foreign Ministry chose not to press him on the question of East Germany. "Nasser has enough domestic difficulties and cannot do everything at once," explained the head of the Near and Middle Eastern desk in Moscow.[35] Syria's government, though considerably less stable than Egypt's, showed greater boldness. In early October, Syria honored the GDR's anti-Zionist, pro-Nasser stance by agreeing to exchange consulates with the East Germans—the first such arrangement between any noncommunist power and the SED regime. This was, indeed, a step that Hallstein and Grewe had identified ten months earlier as possibly implying recognition. A strict interpretation of Bonn's policy could have resulted in an immediate break in relations. Yet the complexities of West German diplomacy in the developing world, particularly the Near East, demanded a more nuanced approach.

Damascus, but Not Warsaw

Word of Syria's decision reached Bonn through open channels. On October 9, 1956, a Syrian spokesman announced on public radio that consulates would be opening in both Damascus and East Berlin. The first reaction in Bonn was pessimism and resignation, for it seemed unlikely that the Syrians would back down from such a visible affront. Meeting at the Foreign Office later that day, Wilhelm Grewe and other midlevel officials considered what punishment, if any, would be appropriate.[36] Should the West German envoy be recalled to Bonn? Should diplomatic relations be severed entirely? The latter option seemed too risky, for it might provoke a sympathy response from the more radical Arab states. Even if the other Arab leaders remained passive, Bonn would still be vacating an important Near Eastern capital of its own volition, weakening the overall position of the

Western camp in Syria.[37] Breaking relations would also likely result in "heated polemics" from the opposition parties in West Germany, particularly the FDP, which had never ceased to advertise its disapproval of the hard line at the Foreign Office.[38] In light of these drawbacks to Bonn's advertised policy, the participants in this meeting suggested that the time had come for a drastic revision of the course laid out in December 1955. They judged it worthwhile to fire one last "warning shot" across Syria's bow, in the hopes that this might yet dissuade the Syrians from going forward with their plans. Should that go unheeded, the Foreign Office would acquiesce in Damascus and proceed to a more general revision of its isolation campaign. This ignoble retreat would be covered by a statement affirming that Bonn, having done everything in its power to convince Syria of the correctness of its standpoint, preferred to retain a presence in this important Near Eastern capital.[39]

One should not attribute too much significance to this conversation, for the top echelon of Bonn's foreign policy hierarchy—Adenauer, Brentano, and Hallstein—was not party to this freewheeling exchange. Nevertheless, the discussion's open-ended outcome suggests that ten months after the Ambassadors' Conference of December 1955, the stark either/or policy preferred by Brentano and Hallstein was still controversial. Outside the Foreign Ministry, members of Adenauer's government were even more skeptical. State Secretary Westrick of the Economics Ministry observed that harsh treatment of Syria might alienate key Arab oil-producing states, thereby endangering West German fuel supplies.[40] In Syria itself, the German Oil Corporation had recently signed two promising concessions for exploration and possible exploitation; members of the board wrote to Brentano urging him to tolerate the presence of an East German consulate in Damascus.[41] The Federal Republic's strong economic presence in the Near and Middle East was having an ambiguous effect on the German-German competition in these regions. On one hand, Bonn's preponderance over East Berlin in the realm of trade meant that only the most ideologically charged governments, like Syria's, would give preference to the GDR at the risk of antagonizing the Federal Republic. On the other hand, as East German diplomats were quick to point out, the West Germans would always be reluctant to jeopardize that lucrative trade by breaking relations.[42]

Hallstein and Brentano were not averse to *threatening* a break in relations, however. Bonn's warning shot, delivered on October 11, 1956, betrayed little of the uncertainty aired within the Foreign Office two days earlier. The instructions for the West German envoy in Damascus, Hans-joachim von der Esch, stated matter-of-factly that the Federal Republic could not accept dual representation of Germany in foreign capitals; "third states must decide whom they wish to recognize as the legitimate representative of Germany under international law." If the Syrians allowed an East German consulate to open in Damascus, and especially if they issued an exequatur to the East German consul, this would necessarily imply a recognition of the GDR—even if the Syrian government denied any intention of doing so. In this case, Foreign Minister Brentano's warning of June 28, 1956, concerning a "reexamination of relations" would surely apply.[43] The message actually delivered by von der Esch was even more direct: an East German consulate in Damascus would compel the Federal Republic to sever ties with Syria. Von der Esch went on to announce that he was being recalled to Bonn for consultations; he pleaded one last time for some sign that the Syrian decision might be reconsidered.[44]

Affecting great surprise at the ferocity of Bonn's reaction, Syrian leaders began to backpedal. There was no plan for an actual *consulate*, claimed the foreign minister. At most, the Syrians would allow the East German trade mission to exercise certain consular rights. There would be no consulate in East Berlin, either, just a small office handling commercial affairs.[45] Von der Esch carried news of these concessions to Beirut, where he conferred with Hallstein on October 13. Sensing a lack of resolve in Damascus, Hallstein sent the envoy back to Syria with instructions for a new, more forceful démarche.[46] President al-Quwatli met with von der Esch on October 15, revealing that he had intervened to restrain efforts by "certain circles" to bring about a recognition of East Germany. He went on to promise that Syria would hold strictly to the example set by Egypt: a trade mission with limited consular rights in Damascus and no office whatsoever in East Berlin. Syria's foreign minister proved more difficult to pin down. No written confirmation of al-Quwatli's verbal assurances was forthcoming.[47] Like Cairo the previous winter, Damascus was willing to set aside its signed agreement with the GDR but not to disavow the text entirely. This left a window of opportunity narrowly cracked for the East Germans. Might the Syrians yet be convinced to put the agreement into effect?

After waiting in vain for some definitive clarification, Brentano opted to bring the episode quietly to a close. Syria had been genuinely intimidated, at least for the time being, but it was best not to advertise this too loudly. As Brentano explained to the Bundestag's Foreign Affairs Committee, triumphalism in Bonn might well encourage the prestige-conscious Syrians to draw even closer to East Germany.[48] The logic of diplomacy compelled

Adenauer's government to downplay its successes in public. So, too, did the state of opinion in the Federal Republic, for press reports about West Germany's posture in Damascus had aroused great concern in industrial circles. Brentano and the Foreign Office took pains to underplay the intensity of the whole affair, claiming (misleadingly) that von der Esch had *not* threatened to break relations and that he had *not* been recalled for consultation.[49] That such doctored versions of events seemed necessary points to serious reservations within the CDU, many government ministries in Bonn, and even the Foreign Office itself about the merits of a punitive isolation policy. The desirability of containing the GDR was not in dispute, but not everyone accorded this goal such a high priority as did Hallstein. As an export-oriented country and a paragon of Western influence in the nonaligned world, could the Federal Republic abdicate its responsibilities just because the East Germans were making their presence felt?

Such considerations became more pronounced in the final months of 1956, when a serendipitous turn of events propelled the Federal Republic to the forefront of Western powers active in the region. Adenauer had long since identified the Near and Middle East as special areas of interest for West Germany. As early as 1954, speaking behind closed doors, he described the realm stretching from Turkey to India as "the future of our foreign policy power."[50] In February 1956 the chancellor suggested to a visiting American that the Federal Republic had a unique contribution to make in the battle against communism in the developing world, in light of the great respect the Germans enjoyed there. Yet he hesitated to commit his government to any independent financial initiatives in the Near East, citing a lack of investment capital.[51] What changed Adenauer's mind was the specter of Western impotence and disunity in the face of Soviet expansion. "Control of the Mediterranean basin by Soviet Russia would spell the end of Europe," he predicted in late November 1956, adopting the slightly hysterical tone that often pervaded his Cold War utterances.[52] French and British influence in the Near Eastern capitals had been crippled by their abortive military strike against the Suez Canal. This left the Federal Republic with a responsibility (in conjunction with the United States) to activate its economic policy in the region, so that "the Middle East countries are made economic partners with the West."[53] Putting to one side his distaste of Nasser and Arab nationalism more generally, Adenauer endorsed the Foreign Office's ambitious plans for deeper West German involvement in Iran, Turkey, Egypt, and beyond.[54]

By the spring of 1957 the results were quite dramatic. The summer of

1956 had already seen a parade of Third World statesmen passing through Bonn: President William Tubman of Liberia, President Sukarno of Indonesia, and of course Prime Minister Nehru of India. Now it was the turn of West German luminaries to pay their respects. As the U.S. embassy in Bonn later tabulated, "In a period of a few weeks in March and April 1957 Chancellor Adenauer was in Iran; Foreign Minister von Brentano in India; President Heuss, von Brentano and Defense Minister Strauss in Turkey; Vice-Chancellor Blücher in Pakistan; Justice Minister von Merkatz in Tunisia; and Refugee Minister Oberländer in Ghana."[55] Dealing with Egypt required more circumspection in light of Britain's recent humiliation. Ludwig Erhard, Bonn's rotund minister of economics, had to abandon plans to attend the opening of a West German industrial exposition in Cairo in March 1957.[56] Yet the exhibition went forward anyway, reminding Egyptians in attendance of the abundance and quality of imports from the Federal Republic. In more subtle ways, too, Bonn proved responsive to Egypt's interests. The Foreign Office maintained a healthy distance from King Faisal of Iraq, Nasser's greatest rival and anchor of the pro-British Baghdad Pact.[57] Meanwhile, Adenauer's government continued to shun diplomatic relations with Tel Aviv, arguing that the Federal Republic could best contribute to Israel's defense by inducing moderation among the Arab firebrands. If West Germany were to establish formal relations with Israel, this would lead several Arab countries to establish similar relations with East Germany, thus augmenting the strength of the Soviet bloc in the Near and Middle East.[58] Seen from this perspective, Bonn's active presence in Arab capitals—and absence from Tel Aviv—reinforced the isolation of East Germany while upholding the position of the Western camp more generally.

West German determination to pursue a constructive policy in the Near East required a measure of discernment on the fine points of nonrecognition. The Foreign Office remained vigorously opposed to all East German efforts to win consular rights for its trade missions.[59] On a day-to-day basis, however, West German diplomats could not undertake weighty démarches in response to every offense. East Germany's activities in the region were too manifold and varied for the West to register and protest each time. This redounded to the benefit of the East Germans, who were not averse to advancing in tiny increments. In February 1957 the GDR's designated consul in Syria, Eduard Claudius, turned up in Damascus; Syrian officials steadfastly refused to grant Claudius an exequatur, but he carried on a shadow existence in the Syrian capital anyway, surreptitiously distributing business cards with the title "Consul-General."[60] The East German trade mission routinely exceeded its competence in symbolic ways—by equipping the staff car with diplomatic plates, for example. When the West German envoy called attention to these petty attempts to disguise the GDR's real status, Syrian authorities did take action, insisting that the East German trade mission *call* itself a trade mission in official correspondence.[61] Yet it proved impossible to complain on every occasion, lest the Syrians become irritated by the constant badgering. At any rate, the Soviet Union's waxing influence in Damascus meant that the GDR had powerful protectors in the army and in the country's more radical political parties.[62] In June 1957 Syria officially ratified the cultural agreement it had signed with East Germany the preceding July. As Bonn's legal experts well knew, this act implied recognition, but it would hardly have been politic to seize upon such an obscure point as grounds for breaking relations. True to his general theory that political, not legal, criteria must be foremost in the execution of West Germany's isolation campaign, Wilhelm Grewe saw to it that the Syrians were let off with a simple warning.[63] Practical considerations, not doctrinal purity, guided Bonn's nonrecognition policy in the developing world.

Attitudes were entirely different vis-à-vis Eastern Europe. In dealing with the Warsaw Pact states, Adenauer and his colleagues showed much greater concern for the fate of the campaign against East Germany. They also demonstrated little enthusiasm about the possibility of establishing a West German presence in the region. On this point the Adenauer government found itself at odds with the press, the opposition parties, and even some members of the ruling coalition. Ever since word leaked out in the spring of 1956 about Khrushchev's "secret speech" denouncing Stalinism, media observers had speculated about a ripple effect of liberal reform across the satellite realm.[64] For these analysts the exhilarating "Polish October"—capped by the selection of Wladislaw Gomulka as first secretary of the Polish Communist Party—proved that the Soviet Union's grip on Eastern Europe was slipping. Liberalization in Budapest moved much more rapidly, but it was the events in Warsaw that captured the special attention of West Germans.[65] After the bloody suppression of the Hungarian uprising in early November 1956, Gomulka's regime stood alone as the great hope for substantial change in Eastern Europe. A broad spectrum of columnists, politicians, and policy makers agreed that the time had come for Bonn to normalize relations with Poland and perhaps with the other satellite states. In so doing, they argued, the Federal Republic would stiffen Gomulka's back against domestic foes and the Kremlin as well. Such a course might in good time redound to the benefit of Germany, since a gradual breakup of the satellite empire could lead the Soviet Union to rethink its opposition to German unification.

Adenauer and Brentano distanced themselves from such expectations, though they did move to improve economic relations. On November 16, 1956, Bonn signed an extensive trade agreement with Warsaw, allowing the Poles to run up considerable debt in German imports.[66] Yet this upswing in trade was not accompanied by any formalization of diplomatic or consular ties. Why did Adenauer's cabinet respond so hesitantly to the prospect of reform in the Soviet bloc? Scholars agree that Adenauer himself was quite indifferent to Poland. The chancellor remained fixated on the situation in the Kremlin and did not doubt Khrushchev's determination to hold on to the satellites at all costs.[67] He set no store in the possibility of a wedge strategy designed to divide Moscow from Warsaw and the other East European capitals.[68] Foreign Minister Brentano *did* take this prospect seriously, even to the point of overestimating the potential for German influence in Poland; yet by early 1957 he had concluded that precipitate moves toward Warsaw could well *hinder* rather than *help* Gomulka's efforts to assert some degree of autonomy from Moscow. West German embraces might be the kiss of death for Gomulka.[69] The Eisenhower administration likewise advised caution. Judging it unlikely that Warsaw would ever enjoy full autonomy in foreign affairs, the State Department set the more modest goal of lessening Poland's economic dependence on the Soviet Union. Toward this end, an intensification of trade between West Germany and Poland was certainly desirable, and Washington prompted Bonn to offer emergency loans to prop up Poland's ailing economy.[70] Remembering the fate of Hungary, though, American officials hesitated to give the Soviets any pretext for armed intervention. In March 1957 Secretary of State Dulles remarked that it would be premature for the Federal Republic to establish diplomatic links with Poland.[71] Such reservations on the part of West Germany's most important ally reinforced Adenauer's inclination to move slowly in initiating political contacts with Eastern Europe.[72]

Naturally, considerations of domestic politics also played a role. Adenauer wished to keep the Polish question out of the 1957 election campaign. Any steps toward reconciliation with Warsaw were likely to anger the "expellees," those millions of Germans who had been driven from territories now controlled by the satellite regimes, mainly Poland and Czechoslovakia. Having successfully split apart the League of Expellees and Disprivileged, an expellee political party, Adenauer wished to ensure that the

CDU/CSU cornered the votes of league supporters.[73] At any rate, the central thrust of the CDU's campaign was virtually incompatible with a strong emphasis on Eastern Europe. Proponents of an active Eastern policy, particularly within the FDP, inevitably borrowed some variation of the "bridge" metaphor, with Germany acting as a point of contact between East and West.[74] Adenauer's 1957 campaign, however, asked voters for an unambiguous endorsement of Western integration. Posters and leaflets played up the dichotomy between the social market economy of the West and the enslaving socialism of the East.[75] One should not assume that Adenauer's thinking was as rigid as his propaganda; the apostle of "no experiments!" knew very well how to entertain radical alternatives to his policies. As election time neared, he even dropped several hints—discussed in greater detail below—that fresh approaches to Poland might be in the offing soon. Anticipating little political capital from such ventures, though, the chancellor put these issues on hold until after his parliamentary position had been reaffirmed.

Historians commonly describe the Hallstein Doctrine as one of the key obstacles to any easing of tensions between Bonn and Warsaw.[76] Until the fall of 1957, however, Bonn's nonrecognition campaign did *not* constitute an insuperable obstacle to a West German presence in Eastern Europe. The phrase "Hallstein Doctrine" had not even been coined yet, and the content of this "doctrine" was by no means a matter of consensus within the Foreign Office itself. Brentano's views on the matter were well known; in June 1956 he had informed the Bundestag outright that establishing diplomatic relations with the satellite states would be tantamount to abandoning the dream of German unification.[77] His reasoning was familiar: since these states already had diplomatic relations with the GDR, the Federal Republic would implicitly be acknowledging that it was only one of two independent, sovereign German governments. This would encourage others to follow the example of the satellite states and maintain ambassadors from both German states, leading rapidly to full international recognition of the SED regime. To some in the Foreign Office, this anticipated chain of events had taken on the aura of inevitability. Was there any way to minimize the danger, though? The possibility was hotly debated throughout the winter of 1956–57 within the Foreign Office, where a sizable minority was not reconciled to West German inactivity in Eastern Europe.

One of the earliest and least convincing proposals for averting the recognition conundrum involved an extension of the Moscow precedent from 1955. Adenauer's government had justified its decision to establish relations with the Soviet Union by pointing to Moscow's special status as an occupying power in Germany. Might this exception also apply to Poland, which was presently "occupying" the Oder-Neisse territories?[78] Of all the countries in Eastern Europe, Poland clearly had the largest stake in the German Question, since German unification would necessarily raise questions about the unified country's borders. Yet it was a dubious exaggeration to describe Poland as a "fifth occupying power," since historically no Polish representatives had been admitted to the charmed circle of the four wartime allies. At any rate, the "fifth occupying power" argument did not leave open any avenues for relations with the *other* satellite states.[79] The suggestion continued to surface in planning papers at the Foreign Office, though, indicating the extent to which Poland alone remained the preoccupation of officials in Bonn.[80]

A more all-inclusive case for relations with Eastern Europe focused on chronology. Since the satellite states had been compelled by the Soviet Union to recognize the GDR at the moment of its creation in 1949, they could not be held accountable for committing an "unfriendly act" against the Federal Republic. Thus Bonn could initiate diplomatic relations with the satellite regimes without insisting that they break relations with the GDR first. At the same time, the Foreign Office could continue to warn third countries against any *new* recognitions of East Germany.[81] Ten years later a different West German administration would finally make use of this approach, dubbed the "birth defect theory," to justify an exchange of ambassadors with Romania. In the 1950s, however, many policy makers balked at the fine differentiations required; communist regimes would be permitted to have relations with both German governments, while nonaligned states would still have to choose one or the other. Nevertheless, the more optimistic proponents of a new Eastern policy thought that India and Egypt might be persuaded to accept this arrangement, which would suffice to keep the other nonaligned powers in check.[82]

One final scheme for skirting the nonrecognition issue involved the exchange of official trade missions rather than full embassies between Bonn and the satellite states. Because in this case no diplomatic relations were involved, the problem of East Germany would be avoided altogether. This initiative was promoted with particular energy by Wilhelm Grewe, who resolutely opposed any diplomatic exchange with Eastern Europe.[83] For a few brief months at the turn of 1956–57, the working levels at the Foreign Office agreed on the desirability of starting off with trade missions in the satellite capitals.[84] However, the idea found little support from Brentano, and some in the CDU also doubted whether trade missions would really offer the Federal Republic a useful political voice in the satellites. The party's leading experts on foreign policy concluded that "trade missions are probably not suitable for achieving what is supposed to be achieved, nor will they prevent what is supposed to be prevented."[85]

So long as no far-reaching consensus could be reached about the desirability of relations with Eastern Europe, West Germany remained frozen out of the region by default. In this sense the isolation campaign against East Germany—together with the electoral situation described above—did hinder the establishment of relations between the Federal Republic and Poland. Yet there are indications that both Adenauer and Brentano were softening their views during 1957. The foreign minister authorized discreet soundings of Polish diplomats in Washington, D.C., to determine what arrangements might be acceptable to Warsaw.[86] In the final weeks of the election campaign, the chancellor looked ahead to a more active Eastern policy in the near future. On July 12, 1957, Adenauer assured reporters that "the Federal Government is very carefully examining the question of whether and in what form permanent missions might be set up in the respective capitals." Three weeks later he noted further that following the election, his government would like to send a trade delegation to Warsaw.[87] In truth, no final decisions had been taken, nor were any likely so long as the CDU/CSU was campaigning and key figures in the Foreign Office were vacationing.[88] Nevertheless, Adenauer's comments are a useful reminder of the fluidity that still characterized Bonn's Eastern policy at this time. What ossified West German attitudes, at least within the cabinet and the Foreign Office, was the fateful train of events in September and October 1957.

A Failure of Deterrence

On October 15, 1957, the eventuality long feared in Bonn came to pass: a state outside the Sino-Soviet bloc dared to recognize the GDR and initiate diplomatic relations. That the offender in question was a zealous communist, Josip Broz Tito, did little to diminish the blow; after all, many nonaligned statesmen counted Tito as one of their own. In the context of the 1950s, with most of Europe sharply polarized along Cold War lines, Yugoslavia's recognition of East Germany breached the usual order in a spectacular way. Not surprisingly, then, scholars have often speculated about Tito's motives. Was ideological kinship with Walter Ulbricht grounds enough? Or was it the prospect of drawing capital investment and perhaps

YUGOSLAVIA CROSSES THE LINE

even reparations from the GDR that swayed Tito's decision? In the absence of documentation from Belgrade, all such arguments are necessarily inconclusive.[89] At any rate, the more interesting question is not why Tito might have wanted to recognize the GDR—many nonaligned statesmen shared this desire—but why he did not fear retaliation from West Germany. How is it that the severe warnings devised by Hallstein, Grewe, and Brentano two years earlier failed to achieve their purpose? The explanation, based on a close reading of the crisis, is simply that Adenauer's government allowed confusion over its Eastern policies to obscure the continuing earnestness of its position on East Germany.

To be sure, pressure from the Soviet bloc was intensifying. In July 1957 trilateral conversations on the Soviet–East German–Yugoslav aluminum project afforded the SED an opportunity to restate its position: in light of the "great sacrifice" demanded of the East German economy, "the necessity and advantage of such a sacrifice must be made clear to the population." In other words, before East Berlin could agree to any further negotiations with Belgrade on aluminum investments, "Yugoslavia must take a clear position on recognition of the GDR."[90] This ploy did not afford the East Germans much additional leverage, however, since Soviet officials preferred not to introduce such unilateral conditions into the already wearisome trilateral negotiations. Yugoslav diplomats bristled at such a blatant coupling of economic and political questions.[91] Not the SED's own efforts, but a more general rapprochement between Tito and Khrushchev caused Belgrade to relent. The warming of Soviet-Yugoslav relations, interrupted for long months by the Hungarian crisis, resumed apace following Khrushchev's expulsion of several old Stalinists from the Politburo in June 1957. In early August the two leaders met for a summit in Bucharest, where Tito apparently gave a firm promise to recognize the GDR in the near future.[92] From this point onward, Tito's government was "much like a man about to dive into a swimming pool," as Belgrade's ambassador to Washington observed. "At some point he dives."[93]

Tito did test the waters first. On September 10, 1957, during a visit by Gomulka, the Yugoslav president toasted his distinguished visitor's health—and the sanctity of Poland's borders. Coming at a time when the Adenauer government still considered many regions in western Poland to be German by right, Tito's statement was calculated to cause offense in Bonn. He compounded the insult by implying that German territorial claims on Poland constituted a threat to the very peace of Europe.[94] Tito was the first statesman outside the Soviet bloc to side with Warsaw and not

Bonn on the border issue, and Walter Hallstein expressed "shock and out-rage" to the Yugoslav chargé in Bonn. Yet the tone in West Germany—outside expellee circles, at any rate—was muted.[95] At the Foreign Office, observers feared that retaliatory measures, such as a suspension of the 1956 reparations treaty, might drive Yugoslavia to go further and recognize the GDR outright.[96] Adenauer himself displayed little concern. "I don't think we should take Tito all that seriously," he remarked to a visitor on September 26, adding that the Yugoslav president appeared to shift back and forth with each passing year.[97]

Bonn's calm response to this affront reassured Tito that he could safely proceed with a bolder move. On September 13, 1957, an East German emissary in Belgrade received word that Tito would soon be drafting a most satisfactory letter to Otto Grotewohl, the East German premier.[98] The outcome of West Germany's elections on September 15 provided a further impetus. Up to this point, the communists in Yugoslavia had tried to avoid any measures that might harm the Social Democrats at the polls.[99] As it happened, the German electorate delivered Adenauer his greatest victory yet; the CDU/CSU won an absolute majority of the votes cast (50.2 percent) and 270 of the 497 seats in the Bundestag. With the SPD out of power for another four years, Tito had no more reason to spare the Federal Republic a blow to its nonrecognition campaign. Now haste was of the essence, for there would be a tactical advantage to acting while Adenauer was still preoccupied with appointing a new cabinet. On October 3, 1957, Tito wrote to Grotewohl affirming that a "realistic policy in the German Question" entailed the "recognition of the existence of two German states." Therefore he was prepared to accept the East German proposal for an exchange of diplomatic representatives.[100]

Tito's decision was not yet known in the capitals of the West, though rumors abounded. Would stern warnings from the Federal Republic and its allies have made any difference at this point? It seems unlikely, yet it is nevertheless significant that the Western camp was largely reticent in the face of mounting evidence about Yugoslav intentions. The Quai d'Orsay, persuaded that Tito was sliding into the Soviet orbit, attempted to organize a démarche by the three Western Allies.[101] Washington and London dismissed the idea. Officials there interpreted Yugoslavia's recent gestures toward the Soviet Union as mere lip service, intended to deflect Soviet criticism of the budding Yugoslav-Polish friendship. Indeed, the State Department was doing all it could to foster positive relations between Tito and Gomulka, in the hopes that Belgrade's example might stimulate a spirit of nonconformity and economic reform in Warsaw.[102] During a high-level meeting on aid questions in early October, Secretary of State Dulles did warn a Yugoslav official that recognition of East Germany would "obliterate the last difference between the Yugoslav and the Soviet foreign policy lines." This, Dulles noted, would greatly anger Congress. Yet he did not threaten any specific sanctions, thereby signaling (albeit unintentionally) that the Eisenhower administration would not allow Yugoslavia's stance on the German Question to interfere with the provision of U.S. aid.[103]

If optimism about Eastern Europe colored views in Washington and London, this was even more true in Bonn. Debates about the future of Eastern policy reached a fever pitch in early October; the puzzle of Yugoslavia's recent behavior was subsumed beneath this larger rubric. At the Foreign Office, Baron Wolfgang von Welck drafted a lengthy petition advocating diplomatic relations with Eastern Europe, even at the cost of seeing states like Yugoslavia respond with a recognition of East Germany. Gaining representation in the Warsaw Pact capitals would, in Welck's judgment, more than counterbalance the opening of East German embassies in select nonaligned states.[104] More outspoken in public was Herbert Blankenhorn, Bonn's ambassador to NATO, who canvassed groups inside and outside the Foreign Office to embrace a fundamental revision of West German policy. Once the chancellor's closest adviser, Blankenhorn commanded enough independent authority to circumvent the disapproval of Foreign Minister Brentano. In his October 1957 notes and conversations, Blankenhorn pleaded for decisive action in Eastern Europe that would "burst the restraining corset of juristic constructions and, like a magnetic field, strengthen those forces in the satellite realm which slowly, step by step, are tending toward a closer orientation toward the West and thus toward freedom."[105] Among Blankenhorn's more sympathetic listeners were the chancellor's chief spokesman, Felix von Eckardt, and the president of the Bundestag, Eugen Gerstenmaier. An assembly of West German industrialists also resoundingly applauded his calls for closer ties with Eastern Europe.[106]

Blankenhorn's vision of Eastern policy harbored no small degree of romanticism. Still more passionate, even utopian in his perspective was Ambassador Pfleiderer. Like many of his colleagues in the FDP, Pfleiderer was a dedicated proponent of reconciliation between West Germany and Poland, and he had used his post in Belgrade to further this end.[107] With Brentano's reluctant blessing, Pfleiderer had attended the fateful reception for Gomulka on September 10, thereby witnessing firsthand Tito's remarks about the German-Polish border. Before returning to Bonn for consultations, Pfleiderer met secretly with Polish foreign minister Adam Rapacki, who affirmed Poland's interest in diplomatic relations with Bonn.[108] Upon his arrival in the West German capital, the ambassador expended the last of his energies drafting a controversial memorandum for the chancellor. The Federal Republic's Ostpolitik had reached a "dead end," wrote Pfleiderer. It was time to abandon the old tenets of unification policy, such as Four Power responsibility for German unity, the demand for free elections throughout Germany, and the claim that only the Federal Republic could speak for the German people. Rather than rigidly defending these positions, Bonn should attend to its more immediate interests. "We stand before the task of restoring our influence in Eastern, Central, and Southeastern Europe, of winning back prestige and trust, and of giving new value to the German name, which once played such a great role in the realms of intellectual, economic and even daily life." Such goals could only be achieved following the establishment of diplomatic relations between West Germany and the satellite states. This would, of course, lead to the international recognition of East Germany, but since unification was but a distant dream, that did not much matter.[109]

The optimism of Blankenhorn and Pfleiderer exceeded even that of the West German press, which had begun to criticize a wave of internal repression taking place in both Poland and Yugoslavia in early October.[110] By framing their ideas in such revolutionary terms, Blankenhorn and especially Pfleiderer managed to alienate the chancellor and his foreign minister. Neither Adenauer nor Brentano thought it wise to reverse abruptly the fundamentals of West German unification policy as practiced until September 15, 1957; they also doubted that a "new Eastern policy" could achieve all that Pfleiderer imagined.[111] On the afternoon of October 8, fifty-eight-year-old Pfleiderer delivered his final thoughts on the subject and then succumbed to stress and a weak heart. By the following day Adenauer had already rejected the deceased ambassador's concept and, with it, the prospect of anything more far-reaching than West German trade missions in the satellite states.[112] Brentano, as usual, framed his objections in terms of the recognition problem. Speaking privately to the CDU parliamentary caucus later on October 9, Brentano explained that he

> did not believe we could start in right away opening diplomatic relations with Poland and the satellite states. The Federal Government has the duty always to examine its policies to establish whether they further or harm Germany's cause, and in no case may it promote a development

which could in the end endanger Germany's reunification policy. Above all, we cannot ourselves contribute to the possibility that a future recognition of the GDR by Yugoslavia would be followed by other countries, for this could lead to a certain sense of normalcy about the existence of two German states.[113]

Brentano insisted that no final decisions had been taken; the government would consult the Bundestag, the new cabinet, and Germany's NATO allies before proceeding further. This statement was an attempt to share the political responsibility for his cautious line on Eastern policy, preempting any debilitating attacks from the opposition parties.[114] Brentano's stance had important consequences for press coverage of the government's plans. Rather than signaling a hard-line policy against those countries that had recognized the GDR, West Germany's newspapers reported in great detail about the opposing schools of thought within Adenauer's government. Eulogies for Pfleiderer stressed the ambassador's differences with many of his colleagues.[115] Meanwhile, the press division of the Foreign Office issued several corrections and clarifications to Brentano's October 9 comments, adding to the confusion about the government line. Readers would have been justified in concluding that amidst all this uncertainty, a recognition of the GDR might go unpunished by the Federal Republic.[116]

During these weeks of transition, the hesitant public leadership provided by Adenauer and Brentano strongly undermined the deterrent value of their nonrecognition policy. Throughout September and October 1957, in the midst of highly publicized debates about Eastern policy, officials in Bonn said nothing openly to affirm that the old rules might still apply—that the Federal Republic would continue to regard a recognition of the GDR as an unfriendly act meriting strong retaliation. Even more seriously, the Foreign Office neglected to convey a firm line in private diplomatic conversations. State Secretary Hallstein met with the Yugoslav chargé three times between mid-September and mid-October, but there is no indication that he commented even once on how Bonn might react if Belgrade sent an ambassador to East Berlin. Instead, Hallstein focused his displeasure on Tito's unwelcome endorsement of the German-Polish border.[117] On October 9, 1957, the Department of State reported confidentially to the U.S. embassy in Bonn that Yugoslavia was strongly tempted to recognize the GDR and that Belgrade did not anticipate any strong reaction on the part of the Federal Republic.[118]

Bonn's stance did not grow any firmer over the next few days, even as clues multiplied about Yugoslav intentions. The final West German appeal to Yugoslavia took place in Washington rather than Bonn or Belgrade, and it took the form of a plea rather than a warning. Using the State Department as an intermediary, Bonn asked Belgrade on October 11, 1957, to consider once more the future of Germany's Eastern policy. If Yugoslavia were to recognize East Germany, this would greatly hamper the course of reconciliation between West Germany and Eastern Europe.[119] This démarche in Washington would have been a fine opportunity to impress upon the Americans, if not the Yugoslavs, the firmness of West German intentions, but the German chargé remarked to his American interlocutors that he *did not know* how Bonn would respond to a Yugoslav recognition.[120] The chargé, a close friend of Blankenhorn's, may have willfully underplayed the possibility that Bonn might break with Belgrade. Yet even Hallstein's instructions for the démarche indicated that if the Federal Republic *did* decide to open relations with Poland, it was unclear how it would then respond to a Yugoslav recognition of East Germany.[121] Others in Bonn who favored a hard line expressed doubts about its continuing applicability. Weeks of indecision had sown confusion in the ranks.[122]

Under other circumstances this lack of resolution in Bonn might have been offset by vigorous action on the part of Washington, London, and Paris, but as noted above, the State Department and the British Foreign Office did not find Yugoslavia's recent behavior to be particularly worrisome. By the time an exasperated Quai d'Orsay undertook a unilateral démarche in Paris, the Yugoslav recognition of East Germany appeared a foregone conclusion.[123] In Washington the absence of Dulles left matters in the hands of the bureau chiefs, who apparently saw little point in linking American policy in Yugoslavia to Germany's. As requested by Bonn, on October 11, 1957, Deputy Under Secretary of State for Political Affairs Robert Murphy explained to the Yugoslav chargé the close connection between Bonn's interest in a softer Eastern policy and its need for a continuing diplomatic blockade of East Germany. Against the recommendation of his own staff, however, Murphy did not mention the possibility of American economic reprisals against Yugoslavia if it should recognize the GDR.[124]

In Belgrade, then, Tito had no special cause for concern about a costly Western reaction to an exchange of ambassadors with East Berlin. Neither the State Department nor the West German Foreign Office (nor, for that matter, the corresponding institutions in London and Paris) gave concrete indications about how they might punish Yugoslavia for recognizing East Germany. Bonn's sluggish response to the Tito-Gomulka communiqué made it appear unlikely that Adenauer's still-protean cabinet would re-act quickly to further provocations. Media reports of a coming change in Bonn's Eastern policy, including a revision of its harsh stance against recognition of the GDR by third parties, held out the prospect of escaping retaliation. Pfleiderer's own passionate commitment to improving relations with Poland, not to mention his openly vented exasperation with Hallstein's legalistic approach, must have impressed Tito, though perhaps not in ways the ambassador anticipated.[125] Finally, even after Adenauer had backed away from any radical change of direction on Eastern policy, he and Brentano failed to articulate a clear position.

A forceful, unambiguous warning to Yugoslavia may not have held back Tito from recognizing East Germany, but Belgrade might have been persuaded to choose a lower degree of formal ties, such as an exchange of consulates. In that case, Adenauer's cabinet would doubtless have accepted this blow without a damaging reprisal. Wilhelm Grewe, still the leading tactician of the nonrecognition campaign, judged that "in the worst case we can let anything pass that doesn't yet amount to the form of recognition and the formal establishment of diplomatic relations."[126] Tito did, in fact, attempt to sweeten the pill by initiating relations with the GDR on the level of legations (*Gesandtschaften*) rather than full embassies. Yet this half-hearted attempt to appease West Germany did nothing to diminish the gravity of the situation. The joint Yugoslav–East German communiqué of October 15 stated plainly that Yugoslavia and East Germany had agreed to establish "normal diplomatic relations."[127] If the Federal Republic wished to preserve the long-standing blockade of its eastern rival, it would have to act swiftly.

The Hallstein Doctrine

Tito's move had a wonderfully clarifying effect in Bonn. Adenauer and Brentano had shown considerable unease about the prospect of deeper ties with the Soviet bloc; the murky language of reconciliation with the East did not flow smoothly across the lips of the chancellor and the leading lights of the Foreign Office. Yugoslavia's precipitate action, however unwelcome, did at least restore the primacy of Cold War considerations. Adenauer's main concern was credibility. Tito had called Bonn's bluff, leaving the Federal Republic no choice but to make good on its earlier threats. A lame response would "awaken false impressions" about West Germany being resigned to the status quo in Europe. Bonn must impress its allies and foes alike with its "straight and firm stance," lest doubts arise about the seriousness of Western diplomacy.[128] Brentano, as usual, centered his arguments more narrowly on the preservation of the campaign against East Germany. A failure to punish Yugoslavia would touch off a chain reaction in the nonaligned world; by the end, some twenty-five to thirty additional countries might initiate relations with the GDR, effectively underlining the Soviet thesis that two independent, equal states existed in Germany. If the cabinet in Bonn were to observe passively while this scenario played out, it would give the lie to the government's habitual rhetoric about unification.[129]

For Adenauer and the top leadership of the Foreign Office, the decision was perfectly straightforward. As early as October 14, 1957, before the Yugoslav decision had even been announced in public, Hallstein was certain that the chancellor would opt for a break in diplomatic relations.[130] It took four days of consultations to build consensus for this course among Bonn's allies, the cabinet, and the Bundestag. The British government, having carefully nurtured its own relations with Yugoslavia, did not welcome the prospect of a strong West German reaction, but Secretary of State Dulles persuaded his British counterpart, Selwyn Lloyd, that a tepid response by the Federal Republic would damage the prestige of the entire Western camp.[131] French officials commented on the need to "stop the rot among the 'uncommitted nations'" regarding East Germany.[132] To the dismay of Blankenhorn, who was still pleading for a revived Eastern policy, Walter Hallstein found a positive echo when he explained his government's reasoning to the NATO Council in Paris on October 16.[133] In Bonn the post-election hiatus meant that the new parliament and cabinet had yet to be constituted, but a special session of the outgoing cabinet on October 17 produced another endorsement of the chancellor's intentions.[134] Finally, the following morning, Brentano met with representatives of all the major West German parties. Although he failed to convince the SPD and FDP deputies, and even many CDU leaders, of the wisdom of severing relations, these critics lacked the strength and numbers to halt the momentum.[135] On October 19, 1957, after a brief interview with Brentano, the Yugoslav ambassador in Bonn wistfully took his hat and departed.[136]

Despite appearances, the break was not nearly so complete as Brentano let on. The Yugoslav government, though indignant, showed a keen interest in salvaging as much of the relationship as possible. This left the West Germans considerable leeway in deciding whether to augment their diplomatic measures with economic reprisals. In his initial announcement of October 19, 1957, Brentano dodged any reference to such issues in order to convey the impression of a total rupture.[137] During the ensuing weeks, however, the Foreign Office took pains to accommodate Belgrade as much as possible. The argument for economic sanctions was compelling: if Yugoslavia did not suffer materially from its recognition of East Germany, the deterrent effect on other nonaligned countries would be weakened.[138] On the other hand, neither the Federal Republic nor its NATO allies wished to shove Yugoslavia completely into the arms of the Soviet bloc, and officials in Bonn worried that a trade war with Belgrade would harm German interests disproportionately, since Yugoslavia supplied 40 percent of the country's bauxite and was heavily indebted to West German firms. Adenauer's government settled on a rather mild economic sanction: the suspension of further government-subsidized export insurance for German-Yugoslav trade deals.[139] Of greater import was the fate of the reparations treaty of March 1956, which had earlier occasioned such acrimony between Bonn and Belgrade. When the treaty was signed, Hallstein had insisted that its "contractual basis" rested on Belgrade's agreement not to recognize East Germany. In the event, however, Brentano judged it inadvisable for Bonn to court accusations of callously tearing up its treaty obligations. Since the next installment was not scheduled for disbursement until the spring of 1958, the Foreign Office deferred any final decision on the matter.[140]

Yet another crucial decision concerned the problem of consular relations. If West Germany retained consulates in Belgrade and Zagreb, might this tempt other nonaligned countries to exchange consulates with East Germany?[141] While recognizing this danger, Adenauer's cabinet concluded in November 1957 that Bonn should keep the Zagreb consulate in service. This would uphold West Germany's extensive interests in the Yugoslav republic of Croatia while also preserving at least some maneuvering room for new initiatives in Eastern Europe.[142] Such considerations reveal the extent to which Adenauer's cabinet denied any essential link between its punishment of Yugoslavia and the future of Bonn's Eastern policy. In conversation with reporters, the Bundestag, and Bonn's allies, Brentano insisted that the path remained open for diplomatic relations with Poland at some future date.[143] It is on this point that the government differed most sharply with the opposition. Much like Pfleiderer before his death, the SPD and FDP adopted an either/or perspective. By severing diplomatic ties with Belgrade, the Federal Republic would effectively be "self-blockading" itself out of Eastern Europe. A number of West German newspapers also came out against a break with Yugoslavia, or at least—like many in the CDU—

expressed regret at having to take this unfortunate step.[144] When the break did come, the opposition parties and many columnists decried the government's inflexibility. Why had the Foreign Office backed itself into a corner by issuing such categorical threats two years earlier? Was it really worth preserving the isolation campaign against East Germany at the cost of relations with Eastern Europe?[145]

These critics proved to be more realistic than Brentano in assessing the ultimate cost of the rupture with Belgrade. The modest Eastern policy envisioned by the Foreign Office—trade missions, but nothing more formal—proved unacceptable to the Soviet bloc regimes in the late 1950s. Gomulka's Poland insisted on nothing less than full diplomatic relations.[146] Pressure to meet this demand came from several corners: the SPD and the FDP in the Bundestag's Foreign Affairs Committee, and the Quai d'Orsay and the State Department among Bonn's allies.[147] Each time the issue came to a head, though, Brentano and the CDU's foreign policy experts balked at the prospect of undermining their earlier positions. Since they had broken with Yugoslavia over the question of East Germany, it hardly made sense to establish diplomatic ties with *other* regimes that had long since recognized the GDR. Doing so might well appear to outsiders like a change in Bonn's standpoint and invite the nonaligned countries to reconsider the possibility of relations with the GDR. Thus, as Brentano remarked to Dulles in June 1958, "by recognizing Poland, the Federal Republic might set in motion a process that might be irreversible and undo all that ha[s] been done to achieve a solution of the reunification question."[148] A similar immobility dashed any chance that Yugoslavia and the Federal Republic might reconcile their differences in the near future. Bonn insisted that Belgrade would have to break relations with East Berlin, which the Yugoslavs pointedly refused to do. Over time, attitudes in both Bonn and Belgrade soured, and the relative politeness that prevailed in the winter of 1957–58 gave way to long years of mutual recriminations.[149] All told, the key decisions of late 1957—West Germany's avoidance of diplomatic relations with Eastern Europe, Yugoslavia's recognition of East Germany, and West Germany's break with Yugoslavia—could not easily be reversed.

Several months later, in July 1958, discontent over the government's rigid policies found a name. Joachim Schwelien, a reporter for the *Frankfurter Allgemeine Zeitung*, identified two major obstacles to a reconciliation with Poland: the Oder-Neisse border question and the "Hallstein-Grewe Doctrine."[150] Schwelien was not the first to identify Hallstein and Grewe as the foremost practitioners of the isolation campaign, but his ironic phrasing elevated their views to the level of dogmatic certainty. The term "doctrine" had a special resonance in the summer of 1958, when German newspapers were filled with critical stories about an American intervention in Lebanon—the first concrete application of Washington's "Eisenhower Doctrine," which held that the United States would intervene to fight the spread of communism in the Middle East.[151] By christening the Federal Republic's diplomatic dictum after two decidedly unpresidential figures, rather than Adenauer or even Brentano, Schwelien implicitly ridiculed the smallness of the government's vision. Conveniently, both Hallstein and Grewe had left Bonn in early 1958 for other posts, the former as commissioner of the European Economic Community (EEC) in Brussels, the latter as ambassador to Washington. Schwelien's phrase thus slyly hinted that any policy associated with Hallstein and Grewe was now hopelessly behind the times.[152] Contrary to Schwelien's expectations, though, his coinage—and the policy that had inspired it—remained a staple of West German diplomacy and politics into the late 1960s. For the sake of brevity, Grewe's name quietly fell away as the doctrine's name passed into everyday usage.[153]

From the start, then, the phrase "Hallstein Doctrine" was associated with the most negative aspect of the government's nonrecognition policy, the avoidance of diplomatic relations with Eastern Europe. What these critics failed to appreciate was that Bonn's move against Belgrade, however detrimental to the course of Eastern policy, provided a potent reinforcement of the Federal Republic's position throughout the developing world. In October 1957 one angry columnist wrote, "Let's talk in three years again and see how many states the Federal Republic has broken diplomatic relations with by then."[154] The sum total in October 1960, to everyone's surprise, was still one. By making an example of Yugoslavia, Adenauer's government had not merely stopped a "leak" in the "dam," as the era's common hydrological metaphor would have it. Instead, Bonn's tangible display of anger sharply boosted the deterrent effect of its earlier threats. The results were immediately apparent, for Tito's efforts to persuade other nonaligned statesmen to follow his lead came to naught.[155] Leaders in the Near East and Asia prudently waited to gauge Bonn's reaction, and that reaction proved to be harsh enough and rapid enough to dispel any thought of pursuing diplomatic relations with East Berlin. As early as October 24, 1957, Hallstein voiced his confidence that India and Egypt would refrain from recognizing the GDR; this would, in turn, suffice to keep Syria and the Southeast Asian nations in check.[156] In early 1959, documentation unexpectedly came to light confirming Hallstein's basic analysis. Burmese officials showed West German diplomats internal correspondence indicating that the prior government in Rangoon had been on the brink of recognizing East Germany in October 1957 but had postponed these plans indefinitely in the wake of Bonn's break with Belgrade.[157]

From the standpoint of East Berlin, the momentous events of late 1957 were bittersweet at best. At the moment of East Germany's greatest diplomatic achievement, the SED press had been obliged—at Tito's insistence—to report the events without elaborate fanfare.[158] Belgrade's last-minute decision to erect a diplomatic legation, not a full embassy, in East Berlin further blemished the advent of Yugoslav–East German relations. More generally, the Yugoslavs became sullen and even resentful about the sacrifices involved in establishing ties with the GDR. In the spring of 1958 another round of ideological bickering between Tito and Khrushchev put a further strain on the SED's relations with the "Yugocommunists."[159] In sum, East Berlin had not exactly gained a reliable partner in Belgrade, and it had inadvertently given the West Germans a powerful new tool for blocking East German progress throughout the nonaligned world. To all appearances the GDR was now further than ever from achieving international recognition as a second German state.

Such an outcome could scarcely have been predicted one year earlier, in the fall of 1956. Then, the Foreign Office had shown considerable flexibility in balancing the isolation campaign against Bonn's other foreign policy interests. Rather than withdrawing abruptly from Syria in the wake of East German encroachments there, West German diplomats considered it more advisable to maintain a presence in Damascus. Even in Syria, this pragmatic approach was beginning to give way by the following year; there is little doubt that an outright Syrian recognition of East Germany in the fall of 1957 would have yielded a response every bit as severe as in the case of Yugoslavia.[160] Yet it was Eastern Europe that provided the first significant testing ground of the Adenauer government's core values. Faced with Tito's recognition of East Germany, a frontal blow against the isolation campaign, the chancellor and foreign minister might well have opted to shift tactics and acquiesce in a more general international recognition of the GDR. Instead, Adenauer and Brentano made the recognition question a matter of basic doctrine—with lasting implications for the international role of both German states.

Chapter 4

Scrambling for Africa

However disheartening the setbacks of 1957, the SED was not about to cast aside its foreign ambitions. As before, turmoil in the Near East presented manifold opportunities for East German initiatives. Nasser's United Arab Republic (UAR), an amalgamation of Egypt and Syria, served as a laboratory for the cultivation of propaganda and influence-building techniques. East German diplomats also demonstrated remarkable agility in exploiting anti-imperialist sentiment in such diverse countries as Iraq and Guinea. These achievements were capped in January 1959 by a landmark voyage by Prime Minister Otto Grotewohl to Cairo, Baghdad, and New Delhi. Although the results of Grotewohl's trip fell short of expectations, West German observers had ample grounds for concern at this obvious boost in respectability for the GDR, particularly after Cairo became host to the first East German consulate beyond the communist realm.

Closer to home, the Federal Republic and its allies faced an acute challenge in Berlin. Nikita Khrushchev, hoping to stabilize the domestic position of the SED regime, attempted to drive the Western Allies from their occupation zones in the divided city. For several bleak months in the winter of 1958–59, it appeared that Khrushchev might succeed in forcing the Allies to recognize the East German regime, thereby rendering Bonn's isolation campaign irrelevant. As the Berlin Crisis stabilized, however, the Foreign Office turned to confront the stepped-up East German campaign in the nonaligned world. A dynamic public relations counteroffensive aimed at presenting West Germany as the true champion of "self-determination" coincided with the onset of breakneck decolonization on the continent of Africa. Bonn's timing was fortuitous; sixteen African states gained independence in 1960, but not a single one ventured to recognize the GDR. A curious struggle over the fate of Guinea showed that when forced to make a choice, even the most radical governments of the Third World preferred to side with the Federal Republic.

Otto Grotewohl's Journey

On October 19, 1957, the day West Germany broke relations with Yugoslavia, Heinrich Rau arrived in Cairo to cut the ribbon on an East German industrial exhibition, the second to be held there in four years.[1] Rau's weeklong stay provided the occasion for conversations with Nasser and the Egyptian ministers of trade, industry, finance, and foreign affairs. Rau pressed Nasser about the prospect of diplomatic relations and came away convinced that the Egyptian president was all in favor; it was "bourgeois" circles in Cairo that were urging restraint, lest Egypt face Western reprisals for taking bold advances toward the Soviet bloc. The solution, according to Rau, was to neutralize this "bourgeois" criticism and "awaken the demand for diplomatic relations among the population" by engaging the GDR in eye-catching trade and investment projects in Egypt and Syria. To achieve this, the volume of trade with these two Arab nations would have to shoot up dramatically, and the SED would also need to offer finance credits for the purchase of East German industrial goods—a sum in the range of 2.5 million Egyptian pounds ($7.2 million), with another 1.5 million pounds ($4.3 million) earmarked for Syria. Officials in East Berlin were unaccustomed to handling such large volumes of foreign currency; they ordinarily preferred to trade by barter. On November 2, 1957, the Politburo endorsed Rau's program on condition that the GDR's direct financial outlays be concentrated exclusively on Egypt and Syria. Deals pending with other Asian countries would have to be sacrificed.[2]

This was a short-term, high-risk strategy for the East Germans, for it carried the potential of alienating friends in New Delhi and Rangoon.[3] Nevertheless, the clarification of East Berlin's priorities allowed for a remarkable burst of activity in the target capitals. In December 1957 Nasser allowed the "Plenipotentiary of the Government of the German Democratic Republic to the Arab States," Ernst Scholz, to open a permanent office in Cairo. Given this city's centrality to Arab, African, and nonaligned politics in general, this granted the GDR a convenient base for undertaking inconspicuous, high-level contacts with Arab statesmen and with the leaders of various African liberation movements.[4] A further concentration of resources in Cairo followed the amalgamation of Egypt and Syria into a single state, the UAR, at the end of January 1958. This was a mixed blessing, for it marked the loss of East Germany's advanced position in Damascus.[5] Yet the years of creeping progress in Syria were not in vain, for some of the GDR's friends in Damascus were now taken into the state apparatus of the UAR—a vastly bigger prize.

Between them, the Plenipotentiary's Office and the trade mission in

Cairo were home to some twenty full-time propaganda and public relations agents by the spring of 1959.[6] They planted articles in the cash-hungry local press, issued invitations to Arab writers and cultural figures to visit East Germany, and doled out dozens of stipends for long-term study at universities in the GDR. They hosted receptions on any conceivable occasion so that Arabs could mingle with prominent East German visitors, ranging from trade unionists to sports figures to the mayor of Leipzig. Such occasions did not need to be overtly political; the point was rather to associate the GDR closely with the industrial and cultural achievements of the historical Germany, which many Arabs continued to hold in high esteem. By adopting ambiguous and misleading titles such as "Commercial Attaché of the Embassy of Democratic Germany," East German agents gave the impression that they were accredited diplomats of a recognized power. Richard Gyptner, plenipotentiary from 1958 through 1961, went around calling himself an ambassador. Such camouflage opened doors and helped to overcome whatever suspicion local "bourgeois" elements may have harbored about representatives of a communist regime.[7]

Though unnerved at this hectic barrage of East German activity, West German observers saw little likelihood that the UAR president would be persuaded to change his policy on the recognition question. From the vantage point of Moscow, Soviet experts also predicted no imminent change; they observed that Bonn's diplomats were wielding the Yugoslav example effectively in all the Arab capitals.[8] Ironically, the rise of Soviet influence in the UAR throughout 1958 worked to the detriment of the GDR, at least in the near term, for Nasser counterbalanced his deepening involvement with Moscow by courting Bonn as well. Ignoring the admonishments of Secretary of State Dulles, who considered the UAR a disruptive force in Arab politics, Adenauer guided the Federal Republic into a leading position among the Western powers in Cairo.[9] In May 1958 Bonn agreed to furnish nearly DM 400 million ($95.2 million) in credits for the purchase of industrial equipment, and later in the year Adenauer's government made a serious bid to assist in the construction of the Aswan Dam.[10] East Germany's humbler offer to Nasser of 7.5 million Egyptian pounds ($21.5 million) in credits, while already considerably higher than what the Politburo had approved in November 1957, went unanswered for several months.[11] Nasser did at least honor his promise—made in November 1955—to dispatch a permanent trade representative to East Berlin. Yet the sole occupant of this office limited himself strictly to commercial topics so that his mission in Berlin could not be construed as political.[12]

Most frustrating for the East Germans was the UAR's persistent refusal to codify the rights and status of their respective trade missions. This was not just a matter of rank and prestige; all sorts of practical difficulties arose from the anomalous situation. Two days before the trade mission's grandiose celebrations in Cairo commemorating the GDR's ninth anniversary (October 7, 1958), twenty boxes of relevant materials were still held up in customs, since the mission enjoyed no immunity from import duties.[13] The UAR's trade office in East Berlin had no authority to issue visas, which meant that the steady stream of East German visitors either had to apply through the UAR embassy in Prague or simply travel without visas—a risky proposition. As early as September 7, 1957, the Egyptian government had signed a protocol with the GDR regulating these questions. Yet Nasser postponed ratification of this protocol indefinitely, presumably because concessions of this magnitude—which would, in effect, bestow consular privileges on the East German trade mission in Cairo—would only be worth the risk if accompanied by significant incentives. The SED Politburo chafed at Nasser's stalling tactics and chastised Rau in September 1958 when he announced the conclusion of negotiations with the UAR concerning the credit offer of $21.5 million.[14] This sum now seemed inordinately large to the Politburo; it resolved that the republic's funds should not be disbursed until an effort had been made to win full diplomatic recognition from the UAR. At the very least, Nasser must ratify the "consular agreement" of September 1957.[15] The East German credit package, once envisioned as a goodwill gesture to soften Egyptian attitudes toward the GDR, was now being exploited as an instrument to extract immediate political concessions.

This hardening of hearts in East Berlin reflected not only impatience with Nasser but also a sense that the GDR was nearing a fundamental breakthrough. A wave of anti-imperialist sentiment coursed through the developing world in the summer and fall of 1958, putting the West on the defensive. In Iraq a military junta led by Abdul Karim Qassem toppled the Anglophile Hussein dynasty in July 1958. Scenes of agitated crowds storming the British embassy suggested a deeply held popular animus against "imperialism." When the United States and Britain responded with troop deployments in Lebanon and Jordan, respectively, many Arab commentators sharply condemned this Western intervention.[16] Adenauer kept a low profile throughout the crisis, in part due to his anger over the lack of prior consultation from his allies. Nevertheless, his government could not entirely escape Arab criticism, since the Federal Republic had served as a staging area for the American landings.[17] The GDR lost no time in lambasting Bonn for its collusion with the "imperialists," and within two weeks of the revolution a "Special Emissary" of Prime Minister Grotewohl was en route to Baghdad to raise the question of diplomatic relations with the new Iraqi regime. Qassem temporized; he insisted that Iraq wanted good relations with all countries, including East Germany, but for the time being his country relied on economic ties with West Germany.[18] In practice this meant that Qassem would align his policies on the German Question with the example set by Nasser: diplomatic relations with Bonn but substantial de facto connections with East Berlin. In November 1958 the GDR received permission to open a trade mission in Baghdad enjoying a status parallel to the one in Cairo.[19] This was springboard enough for the restless East Germans, and a swarm of special delegations descended on the Iraqi capital in the ensuing months. Alongside the UAR, a second front had now opened in the struggle for the Arab world.[20]

In Africa, too, the SED found a new partner in the fall of 1958. In late September the newly appointed leader of France, General Charles de Gaulle, sought to reorganize his country's African territories as a "French Community," which would provide a marginally greater degree of local autonomy. Voters in the colonies endorsed the plan by a margin of nine to one, save in the tiny West African colony of Guinea, where fully 97 percent voted *against* de Gaulle's proposal.[21] This blow to French aspirations was organized by the Parti Démocratique de la Guinée (Democratic Party of Guinea), a startlingly effective political machine; its leader, Ahmed Sékou Touré, went on to declare Guinea's independence on October 2, 1958. De Gaulle replied with vindictiveness, withdrawing from the former colony all French personnel, medical supplies, and office equipment. He also encouraged his Western allies not to recognize the independent sovereignty of Guinea for the time being.[22] With Guinea thus cut off from the Western world and desperately in need of basic supplies, the East Germans found a ready welcome in the Guinean capital, Conakry. A hastily dispatched delegation from East Berlin agreed on the spot to buy up the fall banana harvest, then in danger of rotting on the docks.[23] In mid-November East German emissaries signed protocols in Conakry regarding trade, cultural relations, and the exchange of trade missions—the first such agreements between Guinea and *any* foreign country. The GDR's relative isolation was proving to be an asset in wooing leaders such as Qassem and Sékou Touré. The SED had so few international commitments that it could respond rapidly and flexibly to opportunities as far-flung as those in Baghdad and Conakry.

Despite this promising start in Guinea, it would be some time before the

SED devoted serious attention to West Africa. Anticipation centered mainly around an upcoming visit by Prime Minister Grotewohl to leading capitals of the developing world: Cairo, Baghdad, New Delhi, and Rangoon. Grotewohl's itinerary was arranged as a series of stopovers on the way to Beijing and Hanoi, which were more typical destinations for an East German leader. This procedure allowed the nonaligned governments in question to receive Grotewohl as a private citizen rather than as a political representative of the GDR. No formal invitations were forthcoming; the prime minister had, after all, invited himself.[24] Nevertheless, the spectacular nature of the journey was hard to deny. The titular head of the East German government would be meeting one-on-one with Nasser, Qassem, and Nehru. Grotewohl, a former Social Democrat, had long since lost his influence within the SED, but this made him no less effective as an advocate of the GDR's drive for international respectability.[25] Party and state functionaries in East Berlin seized on the planned journey, scheduled for January 1959, as a rare opportunity to press home East German demands. Presumably to deflate the SED's pressure, Nasser finally relented in November 1958 and ratified the long-defunct protocol granting consular rights to the trade mission in Cairo.[26] This only served to whet appetites in East Berlin. A planning document from early December suggested that in the best-case scenario, Grotewohl's visit might bring offers of diplomatic relations with the UAR and Iraq and an exchange of consulates with India and Burma. At the very least Grotewohl could count on the opening of full consulates in Cairo and Baghdad.[27]

By mid-December 1958, when news broke internationally about Grotewohl's plans, Rangoon had been dropped from the itinerary; Burma's cautious new military administration preferred to abstain from such an open display of support for the GDR.[28] This particular setback was not widely reported, though, and Western press coverage predicted that Grotewohl's voyage would bring an enormous boost in East German prestige throughout the nonaligned world. The prime minister's arrival in Cairo was, indeed, an impressive occasion. The UAR's vice-president and several top ministers greeted him at the airport with an honor guard and the playing of the East German anthem.[29] The following day Grotewohl engaged in a two-hour conversation with Nasser followed by an elaborate dinner. "Aside from the question of ambassadors, Egypt's nonrecognition of the GDR is now nothing more than a fiction," remarked the French ambassador in Bonn.[30] In his private remarks to Grotewohl, Nasser acknowledged that expediency alone, not any question of principle, was holding him back from an outright recognition of the SED regime. The threat of sanctions by the Federal Republic and its allies was simply too overwhelming.[31] Nasser provided little room for hope that the situation would change any time soon. After much prodding, he did reluctantly agree to let the GDR open a consulate in Cairo, but he refused to confirm this in writing or in a joint press communiqué.[32]

Grotewohl, anxious to demonstrate some concrete gains from his visit, broke the news about the consulates during a press statement on January 7, 1959. No corroboration was forthcoming from the Egyptian side, however, and the accuracy of Grotewohl's claims was left in doubt.[33] Officials in Iraq, the next country on Grotewohl's route, were not impressed. Qassem had already bestowed consular privileges on the recently opened East German trade mission in Baghdad, and he showed no inclination to go further.[34] The warmth of Qassem's remarks about German-Arab friendship was not matched by any genuine change of heart on the question of recognition. The joint communiqué issued at the end of Grotewohl's sojourn in Baghdad spoke only of a willingness "to discuss [whether], when conditions are appropriate, diplomatic relations between the German Democratic Republic and the Republic of Iraq will be established and political representations exchanged."[35] Although the mention of diplomatic relations was music to the ears of East German leaders, all that Qassem had promised to do was hold a conversation on the topic in the future—a vague commitment at best.

Continuing eastward, Grotewohl alighted next in New Delhi, where the reception was markedly frostier. Prime Minister Nehru, animated by concern over Khrushchev's aggressive policies in Berlin, displayed a firm resistance to Soviet bloc views. Grotewohl's attempts to identify the SED with the cause of peace in Europe went awry; Nehru dismissed the argument that recognizing East Germany would contribute to a peaceful solution of the German Question.[36] Indian ministers also responded with annoyance to charges that their stance vis-à-vis the German states was "not objective."[37] Given the maladroit handling of these conversations, it is hardly surprising that the visit brought none of the hoped-for improvements to East Germany's status in New Delhi. In India, as elsewhere, the optical effect of Grotewohl's journey far outweighed any immediate substantive gains. Grotewohl, a man of sixty-four years and kindly demeanor, helped to make the GDR seem a more tangible, nonthreatening entity to observers in the nonaligned world. Other South and Southeast Asian nations later took India's cordial interactions with Grotewohl as grounds to deepen their own ties with the GDR.

The Politburo's capacity for self-deception was seldom more evident than in its summary analysis of the Grotewohl mission. To be sure, the "authority of the GDR" likely *had* increased in all three countries visited. In this sense the "exclusivity claims" of the Federal Republic had indeed suffered a "serious blow," as stated in a report adopted by the Politburo on February 10, 1959. To speak of an "extensive overlapping of views" with nonaligned leaders on major international questions was, however, hopelessly premature.[38] In devising practical measures to follow up on the January conversations, the Politburo employed what might charitably be described as willful optimism; noncommittal remarks were seized on as solemn promises. Thus planning for an East German consulate in Cairo proceeded at great haste despite Nasser's obvious misgivings.[39] As for Iraq, Grotewohl wrote to Qassem on April 30, 1959, suggesting that the upcoming Geneva Conference would be a suitable occasion for an exchange of ambassadors. No reply was forthcoming.[40] By grasping at straws like this, East German leaders repeatedly set themselves up for disappointment. Yet the GDR's leadership had every motivation to stay focused on positive, incremental gains. By projecting boundless confidence and by exaggerating the scope of their international successes, the East Germans could hope to impress outside parties, leading these, in turn, to deepen their associations with the GDR. Grotewohl had employed this technique during his conversations with Nasser, claiming—untruthfully—that the East Germans already operated a consulate in Helsinki, Finland.[41]

Perhaps unintentionally, these tactics had the greatest impact on observers in the Federal Republic. The international press took at face value Grotewohl's claims about consulates in Cairo and East Berlin, prompting a round of gloomy commentary in the major West German papers.[42] More broadly, the Grotewohl trip drew attention to the GDR's rapidly expanding propaganda apparatus in the nonaligned world: twenty public relations agents in Cairo, ten in Baghdad, ten in Jakarta, eight in Rangoon, and thirty-five total in four Indian cities.[43] Until the winter of 1958–59, such activities had not occasioned particular alarm in Bonn, since they did not seem directly pertinent to the question of diplomatic recognition. After all, the Foreign Office had long insisted that it had no objection to informal ties, such as trade and cultural exchange, between the GDR and other countries. This equanimity began to evaporate, however, in the wake of

Grotewohl's seeming accomplishments.[44] East Germany's gains were all the more ominous when seen in conjunction with Khrushchev's menace to Western positions in Berlin. In the long run, Adenauer's government would respond to these dual challenges by unleashing a concerted counteroffensive. In the early months of 1959, however, many in Bonn seemed more inclined to dispense with the isolation campaign altogether and acquiesce in the international acceptance of the GDR.

Doubts and Hesitations: The Berlin Crisis

The Berlin Crisis, touched off by Khrushchev in a speech of November 10, 1958, had an immediate and debilitating effect on the Federal Republic's international position. Relations between the Soviet Union and West Germany had been on the upswing before this; Soviet trade minister Anastas Mikoyan traveled to Bonn in April 1958 to sign a landmark agreement on trade and cultural exchange. For the first time since the establishment of diplomatic relations in 1955, Adenauer seemed prepared to converse seriously with the Soviet leadership about political questions.[45] Yet the moment passed, and—for reasons still fiercely debated by historians— Khrushchev turned on West Germany quite suddenly, identifying it as a country ruled by unbridled militarists who threatened the peace of Europe.[46] Perhaps most insultingly, Khrushchev brought his accusations directly to the Western Allies, thereby denying the Federal Republic an immediate role in the diplomacy of the Berlin Crisis.[47] After three and a half years of sovereignty in foreign affairs, Adenauer's government found itself reverting to a more passive role as the object of international diplomacy. The four victorious powers of World War II remained the true arbiters of Germany's fate.

In his speech of November 10, 1958, Khrushchev called on the Western Allies to surrender their sovereign rights in Berlin. The city's anomalous status as a ward of the Four Powers had outlived its usefulness, argued the Soviet leader; it was time to end the foreign occupation of the old German capital. If the Four Powers could not agree to act jointly, the USSR would move unilaterally to transfer its rights in Berlin to the East German authorities.[48] In the following weeks, Khrushchev broadened the scope of his demands, setting a six-month time limit on Allied deliberation and demanding that a peace treaty be signed with the two German states.[49] Why should these threats, delivered so brusquely, have placed the Western Allies in such a terrible dilemma? The explanation lies in the West's long-standing policy of not recognizing the GDR. If the Allies insisted on retaining their rights in Berlin, they would soon be confronted with the need to negotiate directly with the East Germans in order to secure passage to the landlocked city by air, river, and land. This would be tantamount to de facto recognition of the GDR as a second German state and would thereby strongly undermine the West's stance on German unification. On the other hand, abandoning West Berlin under duress was hardly an attractive option for the Allies, for it would smack of appeasement, potentially damaging the credibility of the NATO alliance. Yet either of these options was preferable to fighting a war, which could escalate into a nuclear exchange, over access to Berlin.[50]

Khrushchev's ultimatum succeeded in forcing French, British, and American leaders to reflect again on the rationale for their nonrecognition policy. Especially in the early months of the crisis, it appeared that one or more of the Allies would move toward a de facto acceptance of the GDR. Britain's line was the softest. As early as November 15, 1958, British foreign minister Selwyn Lloyd argued that the Allies should remain in Berlin but that they should be prepared to negotiate with the East German authorities in order to guarantee access. "I would not much mind if it ended up with the recognition of the DDR Government," Lloyd cabled to Paris and Washington. This standpoint came as a shock to French, American, and above all West German officials, who were alarmed at Britain's readiness to capitulate in the face of Soviet threats.[51] Yet even American secretary of state John Foster Dulles mused in public about whether Allied convoys could regard East German border guards as "agents" of the Soviet Union, thereby skirting the problem of recognition.[52] Only France, now led by the prestige-conscious Charles de Gaulle, made a show of rejecting any compromise with the Soviets; his hawkishness pleased Konrad Adenauer immensely.[53]

After deliberating throughout December 1958, the three Western Allies reached a common position: they denounced the form of Khrushchev's demands but proposed conversations with the Soviets on the problems of Berlin, Germany, and European security. In the spring of 1959, then, the Federal Republic once again faced the specter of negotiations in Geneva among the Four Powers. Repeated assurances by the United States and Britain failed to dispel Chancellor Adenauer's black mood. He followed every step of Allied diplomacy with embittered suspicion, fearful that at any moment the Western Allies might find some basis for an agreement with the Soviets that called into question his unification policy or the fundamentals of West German security.[54] While Adenauer underestimated the resolve of the West to resist Khrushchev, the planning for Geneva did place new and uncomfortable pressures on the Federal Republic to make concessions. Might the West Germans agree to intensify contacts with the East Germans? Or recognize the Oder-Neisse border between Germany and Poland? Or exchange declarations of nonaggression with the Warsaw Pact countries? Each of these ideas was explored at length in conversations between West German and Allied officials.[55] Since many of these proposals touched indirectly on the Hallstein Doctrine, it is hardly surprising that Bonn's policy of isolating the GDR was itself subjected to a reexamination.

On January 22, 1959, Adenauer aired his doubts to a small circle of reporters: "Sooner or later . . . we won't be able to get around a recognition of the GDR." The chancellor added in strict confidence that he considered three issues vital for the future of the Federal Republic: NATO, European integration, and controlled disarmament.[56] Reunification was conspicuously absent from the list. Khrushchev's threats had put Bonn completely on the defensive; a despairing Adenauer now felt that the best West Germany could hope for was a *stabilization* of the status quo. *Overcoming* the status quo, the stated goal of Bonn's reunification policy, appeared completely out of the question for the time being.[57] Adenauer spoke of the years ahead as a "pause for breath," a time when the West Germans might be able to offer humanitarian support to their East German compatriots but not hope for a rapid dissolution of the SED regime.[58] In this context, with the chancellor bracing himself for a provisional acceptance of the GDR, the nonrecognition campaign lost much of its urgency. As one journalist taken into Adenauer's confidence observed, "Previous positions—the Hallstein Doctrine, the relationship with the GDR, relations with the satellites—could be thrown overboard by Adenauer for reasons of realpolitik much more rapidly than many imagine."[59]

At the Foreign Office, too, the immediacy and danger of the Berlin Crisis overshadowed such long-term concerns as the international recognition of East Germany. Throughout the first half of 1959, the reunification desk was preoccupied with the Geneva Conference and had little opportunity to coordinate the isolation campaign.[60] At higher levels in the Foreign Ministry, Wilhelm Grewe and Walter Hallstein had departed for other posts, leaving behind a new leadership team with less personal stake in the struggle against East Germany.[61] Hallstein's replacement as state secretary, Albert Hilger van Scherpenberg, was a veteran of the Weimar-era foreign service; like many German diplomats of his generation, Scherpenberg showed a much stronger interest than his predecessor in problems of trade policy and Ostpolitik. His inclinations were bolstered by the creation of an entire division responsible for Eastern policy, led by Georg Ferdinand Duckwitz, an experienced diplomat with strong SPD ties.[62] This Eastern Department—which, significantly, assumed control over the reunification desk—had a certain institutional interest in pressing for a modification of the Hallstein Doctrine, in light of the difficulties that Bonn's nonrecognition policy presented for the establishment of relations with the Eastern Europe.

For opponents of the isolation campaign within the Foreign Office, early 1959 was a propitious time to advance counterarguments. In the wake of Grotewohl's much publicized trip to the Middle East and South Asia, both the SPD and the FDP called on the government to drop the Hallstein Doctrine, since it was clearly not doing much to block the GDR's international gains.[63] West Germany's most reputable newspapers soon followed with a rash of long opinion pieces complaining about Bonn's inflexibility and its overemphasis on the minutiae of diplomatic recognition.[64] Expanding on these criticisms, officials in the Foreign Ministry's Legal Department contemplated a redefinition of relations between East and West Germany that would allow Bonn to stop expending its "political capital" in an attempt to hinder the inevitable, the international acceptance of the GDR.[65] Albrecht von Kessel, a high-level official involved in the planning for Geneva, described the Hallstein Doctrine as an "ideological straitjacket" that led Bonn to overemphasize the weight of the Third World. Germany was a continental power with European interests, observed Kessel; it was folly for Bonn to isolate itself from one-half of the European continent just to block the advance of East Germany in the nonaligned world.[66]

It is difficult to ascertain how widespread these sentiments were within the Foreign Office—which, strained to the utmost by the Berlin Crisis, was "in a sad state of leaderless disarray, full of faction and intrigue."[67] One desk officer lamented privately that, in the absence of Hallstein and Grewe, "fundamentals of our policy, formulated a few years ago by clever people, are being abandoned today, yet without our receiving any new talking points or directives."[68] Outwardly Bonn stood by its previous position: "Formal recognition of the GDR by a state with which the Federal Republic entertains diplomatic relations would represent an unfriendly act; the government would have to draw [the] necessary consequences."[69] In April 1959 the West German ambassador to Ceylon, supported by an imposing array of Western diplomats, successfully persuaded the left-leaning prime minister to desist from plans to formalize ties with the GDR.[70] Certainly Foreign Minister Brentano did not propose any discontinuation of Bonn's efforts to block worldwide acceptance of the GDR. But neither Brentano nor

Scherpenberg enjoyed complete control over the Foreign Office, and in practice the exigencies of the Berlin Crisis took precedence over concerns about a consistent application of Bonn's isolation strategy.[71]

The lower priority accorded the Hallstein Doctrine was most evident in Bonn's handling of Yugoslavia. Throughout 1958, Belgrade rather than Bonn had pushed for a resumption of diplomatic relations, but in the wake of Khrushchev's ultimatum, the tables were turned. The Foreign Office hoped that Yugoslavia, still an influential presence in the nonaligned world, might be persuaded to support the Western position on Berlin.[72] As a program for reconciliation, Bonn secretly proposed a trade-off: first, the Federal Republic would supply a generous new installment of export credits to Yugoslavia; next, Belgrade would recall its envoy from East Berlin, but without breaking off diplomatic relations with the GDR entirely; finally, Bonn and Belgrade would exchange ambassadors once again.[73] Such an arrangement, had it been realized, would have marked a near-reversal of Bonn's stance in 1957 and sharply undermined the deterrent value of the Hallstein Doctrine. This option was never put to a test, however, since Tito's government refused these terms. Evidently Belgrade gambled that Bonn might be desperate enough to agree to an exchange of ambassadors unconditionally, without any Yugoslav concessions.[74]

In the Near East, too, the Berlin Crisis overshadowed Bonn's efforts to pursue the campaign against East Germany. When Grotewohl came forward in January 1959 with his report about a new consulate in Cairo, the working level of the Foreign Office adjusted swiftly to the prospect. As in the case of Syria years before, many desk officers concluded that the opening of a consulate would not imply recognition so long as it operated without an exequatur.[75] Foreign Minister Brentano reacted more severely; he recalled Bonn's ambassador for consultations and urged a group of West German parliamentarians to cancel their flight to Cairo. Since the delegation had intended to hold detailed conversations in the UAR about the Aswan Dam, a project of no small interest to Nasser, this postponement was a clear attempt to exert economic pressure on the Egyptian president.[76] These menacing tones were hardly backed by any consensus in Bonn, however. As recently as July 1958 Adenauer had characterized the Near East as "a suitable field in which to engage our political strength," and the chancellor gave no indication that the Grotewohl trip would lead him to scale back West Germany's presence in the region.[77] In the event, the Federal Republic was spared having to make any difficult choices in Cairo for the time being. A Spanish diplomat intervened on Bonn's behalf and learned that whatever

Nasser had agreed on with Grotewohl "is so vague that its implementation can be postponed ad infinitum."[78]

It was in the regions of least interest to the Federal Republic that the hard line prevailed. Alarmed at the GDR's progress in Guinea, the Foreign Office sent a delegation to Conakry in January 1959 to discuss commercial relations and to ascertain just how far the West African republic had already gone in its dealings with East Berlin. Sékou Touré assured Bonn's envoys that he had taken up neither diplomatic nor consular relations with the GDR. Unfortunately, the wording of the agreements between Guinea and East Germany was ambiguous, leading to a sharp divergence of opinion at the Foreign Office.[79] A majority argued that Sékou Touré, still inexperienced in foreign affairs, should not be judged too stringently; they advocated a rapid establishment of diplomatic relations, since the stationing of a West German chargé in Conakry would hinder any further deepening of relations between Guinea and East Germany.[80] At the reunification desk, officials took a sterner view, warning that the Guinean position must be studied more carefully. Why should the Federal Republic risk watering down the Hallstein Doctrine for the sake of an unimportant country like Guinea?[81] At length Bonn resorted to both a carrot and a stick. In March 1959 West German officials signed a "framework agreement" defining the rough contours of Bonn's future aid to Guinea. At the same time, Brentano made one last effort to pin down Sékou Touré's views on the German Question; he wrote to the Guinean president personally on March 4, 1959, pointing out in fairly direct language that nonrecognition of the GDR was a prerequisite for diplomatic relations with the Federal Republic.[82] Awkwardly enough, this letter went unanswered by Sékou Touré for months, so plans for the embassy in Conakry were put on hold. From the sidelines, the West German consul in Dakar, Senegal, reported frantically about the steady stream of Soviet bloc guns and Chinese rice heading toward Guinea. In a strained gesture of goodwill, Adenauer's government pledged to donate 5,000 tons of rice as well.[83] Finally in late July 1959, Sékou Touré, now interested in exploring what the Western powers had to offer, relented and gave Bonn permission to open a diplomatic legation in Conakry—a full six months after the founding of the East German trade mission there.[84]

In areas considered more vital to the Federal Republic's overall foreign policy, Adenauer's government could not afford to exhibit such doctrinal inflexibility. Most dramatically, both East and West German observers attended the Geneva Conference of 1959. It was the first occasion since 1951 when rival German delegations received equal treatment at an international meeting.[85] They did not sit at the main negotiating table in Geneva, and they most certainly did not sit together; from separate side tables, each German contingent observed and commented on proposals by the Four Powers regarding Berlin and the German Question. This direct access to the conference chamber was a welcome contrast to the 1955 Geneva sessions, when the West Germans had been forced to wait outside as the Four Powers deliberated. Yet it came at some cost, for the GDR derived a substantial propaganda bonus from its equal treatment at the Geneva Conference.[86] Chancellor Adenauer, fiercely resistant to deepening contacts between East and West German officials, strongly disapproved of this arrangement. Yet on this point, as on many others, the chancellor was politically isolated in the spring of 1959.[87] Foreign Minister Brentano, sensitive to the complaints of the Western Allies and the opposition parties that Bonn was too rigid on the question of contacts with East Germany, accepted the dual German presence in Geneva as a nod in the direction of some new, as yet undefined relationship between the two halves of the divided nation.[88]

If all sides involved were prepared to accept the continuing division of Germany, why did the Geneva Conference—which ran from May through August 1959—not lead to an outright recognition of the GDR? How is it that the isolation campaign against East Germany survived the challenge of the Berlin Crisis? The decisions did not all lie in West German hands, and only the briefest sketch of Allied motives can be presented here.[89] Most importantly, the Western Allies did not want to be maneuvered by Khrushchev into endorsing the division of Europe. By upholding their public insistence on free elections and the unification of Germany, the Allies retained the moral high ground and placed the onus on the Soviets for blocking the resolution of the German Question.[90] For tactical reasons, then, France, the United States, and even Britain took an extremely firm line against any degree of recognition for the GDR, arguing that Khrushchev had no right to terminate unilaterally the arrangements of the Four Powers on Berlin and hand over the Soviet rights to the SED regime. Khrushchev, for his part, refused to endorse the Allied presence in Berlin by negotiating a new contractual agreement.[91] In short, no progress was made in Geneva on the problems of Berlin or unification. Yet this stalemate produced just the result Adenauer had been hoping for: a stabilization of the status quo that did not overtly compromise the Federal Republic's long-term goal of German unity.[92]

During the Geneva Conference, Khrushchev's original six-month deadline quietly lapsed. The Berlin Crisis, though unresolved, lost its urgency for the time being. Now that the Western Allies had committed their prestige so unequivocally to the continuing nonrecognition of East Germany, Bonn no longer had to fear unpleasant surprises from Paris, London, or Washington on this count in the near future. Interest in experimental approaches to the German Question waned considerably; the brazen demeanor of East Germany's foreign minister, Lothar Bolz, at the Geneva Conference helped quash enthusiasm for increased contacts between the two German regimes.[93] In the realm of Eastern policy, too, Adenauer's government lost its stomach for grand gestures, prompting the resignation of Albrecht von Kessel from the Foreign Office in September 1959.[94] The departure of Kessel, the Hallstein Doctrine's most vocal in-house critic, was emblematic of a more general shift of mood within the Foreign Office. As uncertainty about the future of its nonrecognition policy lifted, Bonn turned its attentions again to the problem of containing East Germany's advances in the developing world.

Bonn's Counteroffensive

Initially the Federal Republic's concern was simply to match the range and intensity of the Soviet bloc's rhetoric. Confronted with a "broadly deployed propaganda campaign to defame the Federal Republic," West German officials resolved to answer with a corresponding campaign of their own: a massive public relations effort to counter Moscow's charges and to persuade nonaligned countries to support the West's position on the German Question.[95] One such effort had already been mobilized to inform world opinion about Berlin. In January 1959 the government's Press and Information Office launched a six-month "Berlin Action" that involved visits by special press agents to the most important nonaligned countries, world tours by eminent Germans, and gratis trips to Berlin for select foreign businessmen and politicians.[96] Under the auspices of this program the lord mayor of Berlin, Willy Brandt, appeared in Rangoon, Burma, to explain the plight of his city—surely one of the most unlikely speaking engagements of the Cold War.[97] Once funding for the "Berlin Action" ran dry, the Foreign Office and the Information Office collaborated in setting up a more permanent and extensive public relations network overseas. This involved significant expenditures in industrialized nations as well as the Third World; sensing that Americans were growing weary of the German Question, Adenauer's government founded a well-staffed German Information Center in New York.[98] In the developing world, the government concentrated on assigning press attachés to embassies throughout Asia and Africa—not just obvious choices such as Jakarta and Baghdad, but a broad sampling of other capitals such as Tunis, Accra, Colombo, and Lagos. These attachés produced local newsletters, planted articles in major foreign newspapers, and distributed pamphlets explaining Bonn's standpoint on key international issues.[99]

In late 1959 West Germany's public relations program coalesced around a powerful leitmotiv: "self-determination." This Wilsonian catchword, adopted widely by anticolonial activists in the Third World, proclaimed the right of all peoples to choose their form of government.[100] In applying the concept of self-determination to the German Question, the Foreign Office likened the GDR to a colony. Did not the population of this region, like the colonized lands of Asia and Africa, possess the right to cast off the unjust oppression of the Soviet Union? This argument hit the Soviets at a weak point in their own public posture, since Moscow generally billed itself as the patron of national liberation movements. Emphasizing a universal principle such as self-determination also promised to generate more resonance abroad than a specific German demand like reunification.[101] At the same time, it aligned German vocabulary with the Cold War rhetoric of the United States; indeed, American analysts such as Henry Kissinger drew a connection between the Third World and the German situation even before most Germans did.[102]

Bonn's official unification policy had long since been predicated on the demand for free elections in both parts of Germany. The new emphasis on self-determination did, however, mark a major shift in the Federal Republic's approach to the continent of Africa. Prior to 1959, Bonn had conspicuously avoided use of the self-determination argument, so as not to alarm its allies with colonial holdings—that is to say, most of Western Europe. Indirectly, Adenauer's government was even subsidizing the position of France and Belgium in Africa; under the terms of the Treaty of Rome in 1957, West Germany paid $200 million to a fund of the EEC dedicated to building infrastructure in overseas territories.[103] In switching to invoke the right of self-determination for Germany in late 1959, the Federal Republic was implicitly siding with the African colonies in their quest for independence. Fortunately, neither France nor Britain—two of the three defenders of West Berlin—objected to Bonn's reversal on the colonial question, presumably because both powers were adjusting to the inevitability of a hasty decolonization in sub-Saharan Africa.

Indeed, the problem of rhetorical support for self-determination paled in comparison with a much larger challenge, the establishment of a substantial West German presence across the African continent. Until recently Bonn had regarded much of North and West Africa as a French sphere of influence, and East Africa as a zone of British paramountcy. As late as April 1959, two years after Tunisia had won its liberty from France, German embassy officials in Tunis worried "that an independent German policy toward Tunisia might do more harm than good if it were at the expense of Franco-German friendship."[104] With the crumbling of the European colonial empires, however, the Soviet Union, Czechoslovakia, and the GDR were striving to secure footholds across Africa. For West German officials, the basic imperative was straightforward enough: *get there first*.[105] After all, the GDR's six-month head start in Guinea had allowed the East Germans to become quite entrenched there. Determined to avoid a repetition of this scenario, West German officials elaborated a procedure for ensuring a smooth transition as each colony gained its independence. Bonn would declare its recognition of the new state at once and immediately establish a working mission in the capital. The mission's head, whether an envoy or a full ambassador, could be appointed later, after the necessary formalities had been worked out with the new government.[106] This strategy played on Bonn's one great advantage over East Berlin: Bonn's allies controlled the administration of these colonies until the moment of independence. The European powers could thus bar the travel of East German officials to the colonies while giving the West Germans an opportunity to strike up direct contacts with the designated leaders of the soon-to-be-independent countries.[107] In this way Bonn succeeded in hindering the appearance of East German dignitaries at a formative moment in the emergence of each new country, the lavish independence celebrations that accompanied the assumption of formal sovereignty.[108]

West Germany's plans for an active role in Africa took shape during the a weeklong Ambassadors' Conference in October 1959. The very choice of meeting place—Addis Ababa, Ethiopia—served as a striking indication of Bonn's intention to address the problems of that continent seriously. The tone of the proceedings was pragmatic rather than ideologically charged. West German diplomats already at work in Africa confirmed that communist influence was growing rapidly but warned against panicky counter-propaganda. Several speakers emphasized that the West would benefit the most by granting aid to the new African governments according to economic criteria, without making it conditional on each government's political orientation.[109] As for Bonn's particular interest in hampering East Germany's progress, many officials took the position that positive incentives were necessary, not just threats along the lines of the Hallstein Doctrine. "Simple arguments about legitimacy are not enough to counter the GDR's efforts in Africa," remarked Hasso von Etzdorf, head of the division responsible for policy toward this continent. "We must achieve more than [the GDR], and achieve it faster."[110] While acknowledging that Bonn would have to increase its aid to Africa, though, State Secretary Scherpenberg expressed skepticism about the value of expensive prestige projects that made little economic sense. Instead of large-scale capital aid, the Foreign Office proposed to expand its modest programs of technical aid, aimed at educating the workforce of the developing countries. Partnership and personal contact were judged to be more important than the sheer *amount* of aid flowing from Bonn.[111]

The Addis Ababa conference showed that the Hallstein Doctrine in its strictest sense—that is, the threat to break relations—was playing a diminishing role in Bonn's overall approach toward the developing world. In September 1959 Nasser had finally forced Brentano's hand by allowing the East German consulate to open in Cairo. UAR officials proved disconcertingly evasive when questioned about the exact legal status of the new consulate, which aggravated suspicions in Bonn. True to form, Brentano recalled the West German ambassador, but his sharp reaction was a bluff; just as in January 1959, the Adenauer government was not prepared to retaliate against the UAR in any serious way.[112] Within a week the dust had settled, and Bonn and Cairo met in the middle. The Egyptian government agreed to issue to the East German consul a limited exequatur explicitly stating that it should not be interpreted as an implied recognition of the GDR by the UAR.[113] This arrangement allowed the East German consulate to function normally in Cairo without technically compromising Bonn's requirements for nonrecognition. The Federal Republic could continue to claim that Nasser's government, like all other noncommunist governments around the world, refused to acknowledge the legitimacy or statehood of the regime in East Berlin.[114]

If the new arrangement with Cairo had long been anticipated by the Foreign Office, the outcome nevertheless seemed an important (and welcome) novelty to outside observers. "This kind of thing could not have taken place three years ago," remarked one British official cheerily in early October 1959, congratulating the Foreign Office on its "perfectly logical and practical" change of policy.[115] However expedient it may have seemed at the time, though, the compromise with Nasser greatly complicated the diplomacy of the isolation campaign in subsequent years. The details of Bonn's arrangement with Cairo were too arcane to be easily communicated to other states. In August 1960, when both Indonesia and Burma allowed the opening of East German consulates in their capitals, West German diplomats had to scramble to ensure that the wording of the exequaturs remained on a par with Nasser's example.[116] The line between recognition and nonrecognition as defined by Bonn was growing exceedingly narrow. Everything now hinged on the precise form of a legal document whose very existence was not commonly known, even to well-educated West Germans.

What other means of persuasion could the Federal Republic employ, then, in trying to hamper East German activities in the Third World? Increasingly, Bonn concerned itself with symbols. One such area, the nomenclature of the other German state, had long been an obsession for German diplomats; the Federal Republic intervened, albeit not always successfully, against East German vendors who posted the name "German Democratic Republic" above their stands at international trade fairs.[117] In UN publications, too, Adenauer's government ensured that the designation "GDR" never appeared, even in the most obscure statistical publications. Instead, Bonn preferred "Soviet Zone of Occupation," "the so-called GDR," or "eastern Germany."[118] After October 1959, when the SED regime unfurled a "national" flag of its own, the struggle over symbols intensified. West German officials quickly ruled that their country's sportsmen could not participate in international events where East German teams displayed the new hammer-and-compass insignia on their uniforms.[119] The flying of the East German flag on any occasion—even at the GDR's own trade missions abroad—inevitably provoked a complaint from the local West German embassy. Bonn also watched carefully to ensure that the GDR did not enjoy those courtesies ordinarily reserved for recognized countries: the use of diplomatic license plates, for example, or the inclusion of East German officials in a foreign capital's formal list of the diplomatic or consular corps.[120]

By cataloging East German abuses and registering complaints with local governments, West German diplomats hoped to demonstrate earnestness without invoking any heavy-handed threats about breaking diplomatic relations. Even so, there was a danger that host governments might tire of these frequent petitions about relatively minor incidents.[121] In addition, registering and responding to the myriad East German endeavors often taxed the organizational capacities of the Foreign Office unduly. Nor was there any guarantee that this defensive activity would, in the final analysis, slow the spread of East German prestige and influence. At best, the inter-

ventions of West German diplomats might persuade well-meaning governments to better regulate the GDR's activities. Yet Bonn found that it had few
solid arguments against the spread of East German trade, cultural, and
even consular ties to more nonaligned countries. On the level of diplomatic
relations, the Federal Republic retained a monopoly, even among the nonaligned countries of decolonizing Africa, but below this level the GDR was
increasingly making its presence felt in the late 1950s and early 1960s.
Carried *ad absurdum*, Third World governments could have any degree of
association they wished with the GDR, so long as the East German mission
did not bear the name "embassy." Uncertain how else to proceed, West
German officials grew more tolerant of the GDR's international presence.
Bonn's monthlong quarrel with Guinea in the spring of 1960 only confirmed this trend.

Guinea: The Exception That Proved the Rule

In the other German capital, too, foreign policy experts were intensely
preoccupied with the future of Africa. Initially Guinea had seemed like a
sideshow, but during 1959 the GDR invested heavily in this West African
republic, making it the true advance post of the recognition campaign.
Certain features of Sékou Touré's regime seemed especially promising.
Aside from the president's own background in French communist labor
politics, Guinea was now organized as a one-party state under the leadership of a body known as the Politburo.[122] As early as February 10, 1959, the
East German Politburo identified Guinea as the "basis of the struggle of
progressive forces in Africa." Enhancing Guinea's independence vis-à-vis
the West would therefore have "direct consequences for the struggle of all
African peoples against imperialism."[123] In Marxist terms, this was justification enough to start arming and outfitting Guinea's security forces.
Czechoslovakia supplied the arms and ammunition, while the GDR sent
military advisers and a free shipment of radio equipment.[124] Propaganda
was another area of East German activity. The East Germans promised to
sell a complete state publishing house—albeit on terms that the Guineans
later found to be onerously burdensome.[125] By mid-1959, planning experts
in East Berlin were fashioning a more comprehensive program of economic
support for Conakry, reasoning that "if we succeed in delivering effective
aid to Guinea in the immediate future, this aid will not go unnoticed in
the neighboring countries that gain their independence in the next few
years."[126] This was nothing more than a restatement of the strategy the
GDR had long pursued in the developing world. By concentrating trade

and economic incentives on a few socialist "showcases," the financially strapped authorities in East Berlin could generate maximum impact at a minimum cost.

The political fruits of this engagement were long in coming. In the fall of 1958 Sékou Touré had confidentially promised that Guinea would establish diplomatic relations with the GDR in the immediate future or, at the very latest, simultaneously with the Federal Republic.[127] Much to the annoyance of the SED, the Guinean president broke his word in the late summer of 1959 by allowing a West German legation (a form of diplomatic representation) to open in Conakry without granting the East Germans a similar privilege.[128] More insultingly, Sékou Touré accepted an invitation to Bonn but declined a similar offer from East Berlin. A series of heavy-handed efforts to change Sékou Touré's mind only produced irritation in Conakry.[129] Significantly, Moscow refused to back the East German démarches; Soviet diplomats accepted the Guinean argument that their country's delicate geopolitical position precluded strong gestures of sympathy for the GDR. After all, Guinea stood virtually alone as the beacon of liberty in West Africa, and France was looking for every excuse to undermine and overthrow the obstreperous Sékou Touré.[130] In Guinea, as in the UAR, deepening Soviet involvement—signaled in August 1959 with the offer of a loan worth 140 million rubles (ca. $35 million)—was not working to East Germany's immediate advantage. With major promises in hand from Moscow, Prague, and East Berlin, Sékou Touré was eager to see what Washington, London, and Bonn might offer.

Chancellor Adenauer, no great admirer of African statesmen, received the Guinean president only reluctantly.[131] French diplomats begged that Sékou Touré not be given too grand a welcome, lest this encourage other African politicians to seek independence from the French Community. Nevertheless, West German officials "went out of their way to give M. Sékou Touré all the honors due to the head of a foreign state," as the British embassy in Bonn reported; he was awarded the Federal Republic's highest honorary medal, the *Bundesverdienstkreuz*, and held conversations with such West German dignitaries as Federal President Heinrich Lübke, Bundestag President Eugen Gerstenmaier, Brentano, and—briefly—Adenauer himself.[132] Officials at the Foreign Office prepared an aid package for Guinea that represented the state of the art in West German assistance: stipends for Guineans to study in the Federal Republic and funds for West German economists, engineers, doctors, and veterinarians to undertake surveys and scientific studies in Guinea.[133] Though impressed by the Mercedes wagons he inspected, Sékou Touré showed less enthusiasm for West German ideas on aid. His conversations with President Dwight Eisenhower proved even more disappointing. The Guinean president balked at signing an aid agreement with the United States, claiming that it would compromise African sovereignty to grant special rights and protections to American aid workers in Guinea.[134]

Convinced now that the Soviet camp was more serious than the West about assisting his country financially, in the winter of 1959–60 Sékou Touré took several steps to align Guinea's economy with the socialist bloc. With this came a belated attempt to redress the problem of relations with East Germany. In December 1959, when Bonn upgraded the status of its diplomatic mission in Conakry from legation to embassy, Guinean officials sought to use the occasion to grant the GDR a similar status.[135] Insisting that the West German standpoint was "untenable in the long run," Sékou Touré pleaded for Bonn to make a special exception for Guinea just as it had for the Soviet Union in 1955. After all, if Conakry was to maintain a neutral stance in the Cold War, should it not logically maintain diplomatic relations with both German states?[136] In a frantic reply from Bonn, State Secretary Scherpenberg retorted that many other neutral states, such as Sweden, Switzerland, and even Finland, refused to recognize the GDR. The Soviet Union was a valid and singular exception in light of its special role in German affairs. Scherpenberg went on to invoke his government's latest public relations catchword, arguing that Germans living under Soviet domination should be granted the right to self-determination. Finally, he authorized the German ambassador to utter the following threat "if absolutely necessary": "The example of Yugoslavia shows unmistakably that the Federal government views the assumption of diplomatic relations with the SBZ [Soviet Occupation Zone] to be such a serious matter that the rupture of our own diplomatic relations with the state in question can become necessary."[137]

The vigor of Scherpenberg's reply held Sékou Touré at bay, but only briefly. March 1960 brought a significant lurch to the left in Guinean domestic and foreign policies. The Guinean leader withdrew his country from the franc zone in West Africa and established a new currency backed by massive influxes of Soviet aid.[138] France was the immediate target, but the Federal Republic suffered from guilt by association. The Guinean representative at the UN circulated an inflammatory text accusing the West Germans of assisting France financially and technologically in the testing of atomic bombs in the Sahara.[139] Even as Sékou Touré was disavowing this statement, the East German news service ADN broadcast the following report on the afternoon of March 5, 1960: "The governments of the GDR and the Republic of Guinea have agreed to take up diplomatic relations and to exchange ambassadors. GDR ambassador Karl Nohr is already on his way to Conakry. The ambassador of Guinea to the GDR, Dr. Seydou Conté, was received Saturday [March 5] by President Wilhelm Pieck at his official residence in the Niederschönhausen Palace in Berlin."[140] Guinea had just become the first noncommunist nation in the world to recognize and establish diplomatic relations with the SED regime.

Or had it? The events in East Berlin caught Sékou Touré off guard. Undoubtedly he was planning an exchange of ambassadors with the GDR in the immediate future, but this does not appear to be what he had in mind in sending Seydou Conté, Guinea's ambassador in Moscow, to the East German capital on March 5.[141] Either the diplomat exceeded his orders, or he was ambushed by aggressive SED officials hoping to generate a fait accompli. In any event, the resulting confusion fueled a month of intense wrangling in Bonn, Conakry, and East Berlin.

"In my view there is only one response," Brentano wrote to Adenauer upon hearing the ADN report. "If we swallow such an impudent affront from a country like Guinea, then we can be certain that our policy will be no longer be seen as consistent or credible. Then, according to the rule that bad examples corrupt good morals, others will do the same; and we'll have tied our own hands."[142] Adenauer was alarmed at Sékou Touré's seeming readiness to throw in his lot with world communism. In off-the-cuff remarks to foreign journalists on March 7, he growled that the obvious solution was to cut off Western aid to Guinea.[143] At the Foreign Office, officials saw this as a welcome opportunity to demonstrate the severity of Bonn's policy toward the newly independent African nations. For the time being, the government announced two concrete measures: the recall of the West German ambassador from Conakry and the cancellation of a "goodwill" mission scheduled to depart the following week.[144]

This readiness to punish Guinea found its parallel in the West German press; many columnists viewed Sékou Touré's behavior as an unprovoked insult deserving retaliation.[145] Erich Ollenhauer, the SPD's conscientious but uninspiring chairman, reiterated in party circles his opposition to the Hallstein Doctrine: "Breaking relations with Guinea would be problematic. We must not offend the young states in Africa."[146] Yet the SPD was in the throes of a fundamental reorientation, triggered in part by the Berlin Crisis and in part by a sense that its Marxist premises were failing to attract middle-class votes. On problems such as Western integration and German unification, the Social Democrats were drawing ever closer to the Adenauer line.[147] Addressing the topic of Guinea on March 7, 1960, a spokesman for the SPD Executive Committee embraced the basic logic of the Foreign Office, arguing that a strong reaction against Conakry might deter other African countries from recognizing East Germany. With a summit conference of the Four Powers scheduled for Paris in May 1960, this was hardly the time to let down Bonn's guard and lend support to the GDR's claims to be an internationally recognized German state.[148] Meanwhile, Adenauer's administration assuaged SPD concerns by clarifying what, precisely, the Hallstein Doctrine entailed. Government spokesman Felix von Eckardt assured the press that there was nothing "automatic" about Bonn's response to the situation in Guinea. The government's decision would depend on the circumstances—though Eckardt acknowledged that Sékou Touré's action appeared to be a "very unfriendly act," hinting that a break in diplomatic relations was being considered.[149]

Reports from the German ambassador in Conakry, Herbert Schroeder, soon complicated the picture for decision makers in Bonn. In an hourlong conversation with Schroeder, Sékou Touré insisted that he had merely sent Conté on a fact-finding mission to East Berlin. He refused to issue a public denial of the ADN report, however, as he did not wish to make any binding declarations on the matter.[150] In East Berlin, Conté persisted in consorting with East German party officials. Did Conakry have diplomatic relations with East Berlin, or did it not? Guinea's ambassador to the Federal Republic—who resided in Paris, inconveniently enough—professed no knowledge of the situation. Absent any official response from Guinea, the West German cabinet authorized Brentano to sever relations—unless Sékou Touré's government could declare authoritatively within a very short time that it had *not* recognized the GDR. As initially conceived, Bonn's query to Conakry had the character of an ultimatum, with a public response demanded from Sékou Touré within two to three days.[151] Brentano and Scherpenberg softened this time limit, however, lest the ultimatum cast West Germany in an unsympathetic light.[152]

Anticipating a break between the Federal Republic and Guinea, the SED drafted a press release criticizing Bonn's bullying behavior; clearly the Adenauer government was "not prepared to respect the independence of other states" in reaching foreign policy decisions.[153] In the meantime, East German functionaries fanned out through the developing world seeking to capitalize on Guinea's pathbreaking example. The GDR's top Middle East expert, Wolfgang Kiesewetter, met with Qassem on March 9 but heard only vague platitudes. His superiors in East Berlin ordered him to stay in Baghdad until something more affirmative materialized.[154] From Ghana, which was, after Guinea, the most pro-Soviet of the independent African states, East German diplomats learned that President Kwame Nkrumah had no intention of seconding Sékou Touré's move. Nkrumah was, in fact, quite upset with his Guinean counterpart for failing to coordinate their policies on Germany more closely.[155] All of this activity suggested that Guinea's isolated decision would not, as hoped, touch off a landslide of recognitions of East Germany. More alarmingly, the Guinean government released no statements in Conakry confirming the ADN report about diplomatic relations. Karl Nohr, the ambassador-designate in Conakry, sat restlessly in the Guinean capital awaiting his accreditation. Was Sékou Touré having second thoughts? On March 15 the SED Politburo commissioned one of its candidate members, Alfred Kurella, to seek an explanation in person. He was authorized to make additional offers of a cultural or economic nature if the situation called for it.[156]

Sékou Touré, hoping to avert West Germany's wrath, used an interview in *Der Spiegel* to signal that he would "deeply regret" a break in relations with Bonn. He acknowledged that Guinea had erred in consorting too closely with the GDR and expressed hope that West Germany would show understanding for a "young state without diplomatic experience."[157] However, in his official reply to the West German quasi-ultimatum, he refused to comment on his future intentions and even stated that under "normal circumstances" his country would proceed to recognize East Germany. Senior officials at the Foreign Office, hoping to bring the episode to a close, were prepared to overlook these qualifications. They scrambled to find a face-saving compromise that would allow Bonn to retain diplomatic relations with Guinea. Perhaps the GDR and Guinea might agree on the opening of a consulate rather than a full embassy?[158] From across the Atlantic, however, Brentano, who was touring the United States, dismissed Sékou Touré's reply as unsatisfactory. A barrage of painstaking questions was fired off to Conakry on March 18: What was the precise nature of Seydou Conté's mission to East Berlin? Which "normal circumstances" might lead Guinea to opt for diplomatic relations with the GDR? This time Brentano was less shy about issuing an ultimatum; he demanded an answer within three days.[159]

Much to the frustration of Adenauer's government, Sékou Touré stalled for time. Playing masterfully on his country's perceived weaknesses, he used Guinea's rudimentary communications network as an excuse for delay. The problem worsened after the president and virtually his entire government departed for the interior at the end of March, assembling in Guinea's second city, Kankan, for a major conference of the country's ruling party.[160] From Moscow and East Berlin, hints about an exchange of ambassadors between Guinea and the GDR continued to filter into Bonn, yet at the same time Sékou Touré wrote a personal letter to President Eisenhower averring that he had not recognized the regime in East Berlin.[161] By now the Guinean president, well aware of the deep differences of opinion in Bonn, expected to avert a catastrophe on the West German side. The question was whether the East Germans could be persuaded to accept a postponement gracefully. After keeping Alfred Kurella, the Politburo emissary, waiting in Conakry for more than a week, Sékou Touré promised to commence the establishment of diplomatic relations in three or four weeks' time.[162] Satisfied with this timetable, Kurella returned home but left behind a functionary charged with negotiating further aid packages for Guinea.[163]

Sékou Touré's promise may well have been uttered in good faith. After all, he had originally sent Seydou Conté to East Berlin for the purpose of initiating diplomatic relations in the near future, and he encouraged Karl Nohr, the East German ambassador-designate, to remain in Conakry until he could be formally accredited.[164] Nevertheless, Guinea's leader was swayed by West Germany's last-ditch effort, which took a strikingly humble form. A high-level official from the Foreign Office literally chased after Sékou Touré to solicit further assurances. Wiring from Tokyo on March 30, Brentano dispatched the head of the Political Department, Hasso von Etzdorf, to seek out the Guinean president in remote Kankan.[165] Etzdorf's mission took on an epic quality, as he was forced to make the 700-kilometer journey from Conakry to Kankan by car along nearly impassable roads. Finally, on April 3, 1960, Sékou Touré and Etzdorf met to clarify the central points of concern. Sékou Touré repeated his comments to Ambassador Schroeder of a month earlier, explaining that Seydou Conté had presented East German officials with a letter of introduction, *not* official credentials as ambassador to East Berlin. Guinea did not recognize the GDR or have diplomatic relations with it, a statement that Sékou Touré now agreed to issue officially and publicly.[166] The substance of his declaration contained not a word about Guinea's future plans, but Adenauer's government opted to take what it could get and celebrated the Guinean communiqué as a stunning victory. On April 8, 1960, Brentano interrupted a session of the Bundestag to present the good news that Bonn would be keeping its embassy in Conakry. His announcement drew applause from the entire house.[167]

Brentano's concluding remarks on the Guinean crisis resonated well in the West German capital: "Not acting too hastily has turned out to be the right decision."[168] Politicians and columnists across the political spectrum embraced this interpretation, praising the remarkable patience demonstrated by the Foreign Office throughout the affair. Etzdorf's journey into the wilderness seemed to point to a more personal touch in West German relations with the Third World, a stance that accorded well with the astounding popularity of development aid during 1960, the year of African independence.[169] The harmonious outcome in Guinea proved to be enormously influential in shaping attitudes toward the isolation campaign, both in the public sphere and within Adenauer's government. For many in the SPD, the government's mixture of firmness and moderation toward Sékou Touré helped bring about a reconciliation with the Hallstein Doctrine. What young SPD activists such as Hans-Jürgen Wischnewski wanted most was for West Germans to challenge the East Germans head-to-head in the Third World.[170] A strict application of the Hallstein Doctrine could only lead to Bonn's progressive retreat from the more radical nonaligned capitals, yet now the Foreign Office seemed determined to fight on in those countries where the GDR was gaining a foothold. By the mid-1960s Wischnewski, a burly trade-union figure with close ties to the Algerian liberation movement, would become one of the most active liaisons for Bonn's isolation campaign throughout the Middle East and Africa.[171] More support from the left came as the central West German trade union organization, the German League of Unions, began to take aim at the international propaganda efforts of the East German Free Trade Unions.[172] As the Foreign Office decreased its reliance on the classic instruments of diplomacy in pursuing its isolation campaign, more and more sectors of West German society became involved in the effort. On balance, noted the American embassy in Bonn, "the satisfactory resolution of the crisis [over Guinea] . . . permitted Bonn to preserve its Hallstein Doctrine intact and to avoid any 'agonizing reappraisal' of that policy."[173]

Ironically, while spared a thorough reexamination of its nonrecognition campaign, the Foreign Office drew much the same conclusion from the Guinean crisis as the SPD and the West German press: Bonn must use positive incentives to win the confidence and trust of the developing world. As Etzdorf had observed the preceding year at the conference in Addis

the very moment when the FDP, the Hallstein Doctrine's most consistent foe, rejoined Adenauer's governing coalition. From late 1961 through early 1963, the Foreign Office found no easy formula for transforming development aid into a lever to block East German gains; with little financial expenditure, the GDR widened its consular network in key developing countries. Frustrated at the difficulties of keeping unpredictable countries like Ghana, Iraq, and Indonesia in line, West German leaders became increasingly vocal in their insistence that their generosity be repaid with cooperation in the campaign against East Germany.

Bonn's Billion-Dollar Aid Program

In August 1958 Adenauer could still write that the Federal Republic was a "poor country" compared with France and Britain. Aid should be given in modest amounts, with the sole purpose of achieving foreign policy credit.[1] Such attitudes governed West German behavior throughout the 1950s; when Adenauer's cabinet did approve aid payments, the point was to bolster the Federal Republic's reputation as a responsible member of the world community and to secure its place as the exclusive representative of Germany within UN organizations.[2] Multilateral forms of aid were preferred, in order to protect the Federal Republic from direct financial accountability for expensive and risky foreign undertakings. Initially the sums involved were quite small: DM 1 million ($238,000) to the UN Children's Fund in December 1955, for example. Bonn's pledge in 1957 to provide DM 160 million ($38 million) annually to the EEC's overseas development fund dwarfed all its previous multilateral efforts.[3] Starting in 1958, though, the United States pressed Adenauer's government to shoulder a greater proportion of the West's efforts in the developing world, and German loans to the International Monetary Fund and the World Bank mushroomed in the late 1950s. West Germany also signed on to major international consortia assisting Greece, Turkey, and India.[4] The case of India provides a glaring example of Bonn's caution about taking on bilateral aid commitments. Large-scale public West German assistance to New Delhi commenced only after the Indian government was on the brink of defaulting on its obligations to private West German firms.[5] Only in Egypt did Adenauer's government pursue a relatively independent aid agenda; in May 1958 Bonn furnished nearly DM 400 million ($95.2 million) in credits for Nasser's government to purchase industrial equipment, and later in the year Brentano contemplated making an offer to assist in the construction of the Aswan Dam. The Soviet Union's decision to finance the entire first stage of the dam put an end to these plans but heightened Bonn's determination to maintain a strong economic presence in the UAR.[6]

Where Bonn did see fit to offer bilateral aid in the years before 1960, this usually came in the form of technical assistance programs. Confident in Germany's image as a technologically innovative society, Adenauer's government offered scholarships for training in Germany's factories and vocational schools and, in some cases, even built and staffed industrial training centers in developing countries. To West German officials, technical assistance appeared to be a suitable means of advancing the Third World toward economic self-reliance.[7] Such programs were also relatively inexpensive; the annual budget for technical aid totaled DM 50 million ($11.9 million) in the fiscal years 1956–58 and DM 70 million ($16.7 million) in 1959.[8] By the mid-1960 the Federal Republic had opened trade schools or workshops in thirty-one cities throughout the developing world, including Cairo and Aleppo in the UAR, New Delhi and Madras in India, and Colombo in Ceylon.[9] These were sites of intense competition with the GDR. Yet a large proportion of the Federal Republic's technical aid flowed to Turkey, Greece, and Iran, countries that, by virtue of their alliances and domestic political situations, were extremely unlikely to consort with the SED regime.[10]

A third form of development aid, at least as Bonn defined it, came in the form of "Hermes" credits and guarantees. This was a mixed government and private-sector institution that provided, in the first instance, insurance for exports to non-Western countries. Private insurance companies were unwilling to cover the political and economic risks associated with exports to unstable parts of the world; the West German government did so according to a system that was largely self-financing (through fees paid by the exporters) but guaranteed in the last resort by federal appropriations.[11] Aside from this insurance mechanism, the Hermes system also extended credits to certain developing countries, thereby enabling them to pay for German imports. These credits were essentially medium-term loans with a redemption period of four to five years and interest rates at market levels. Bonn's financial role was indirect; the private lenders of the Hermes consortium provided the credits, with the government simply acting as the guarantor. However, political circumstances often influenced the granting of Hermes credits and guarantees. After breaking diplomatic relations with Yugoslavia in October 1957, Adenauer's government put a block on any further insurance guarantees to that country, a measure that would have seriously dampened trade between West Germany and Yugoslavia had it not been lifted some eighteen months later.[12] In the late 1950s

DEVELOPMENT AID

the Foreign Office promoted a looser distribution of Hermes credits for Egypt, Iraq, India, and other developing countries. With the Eisenhower administration constantly admonishing Bonn to offer more aid, Adenauer's government hoped that the Hermes system might serve as the focal point of a commercially sound yet propagandistically effective development aid program.[13]

Officials in Washington were not convinced, however, and by 1960 many observers in Bonn also acknowledged the inadequacy of West German aid. Compared with the financial assistance provided by either the United States or the Soviet Union, the interest rates on Hermes credits were staggeringly high and the redemption period too short.[14] In Amman, for example, the Jordanian government was using "soft" American aid to repay the "hard" Hermes credits taken out to purchase West German goods. Essentially this meant that American taxpayers were subsidizing the Federal Republic's exports to Jordan, a situation the State Department found intolerable.[15] Meanwhile, India's debt to Germany was just a few years from maturity—nearly DM 1 billion ($238 million) in Hermes credits at 6.3 percent interest, a tremendously costly burden that scarcely qualified as aid.[16] The prime beneficiaries of the credits were, after all, the Federal Republic's own export industries, as both the SPD and the FDP observed.[17] During the Bundestag's first in-depth debate on development aid, held in June 1960, Economics Minister Ludwig Erhard announced that Bonn would soon be providing a new, more generous form of assistance to the developing world: bilateral capital aid. Erhard explained that without access to long-term credits at artificially low interest rates, the governments of the Third World could not hope to finance the infrastructural projects—roads, bridges, dams, and harbors—that represented the first step toward industrialization.[18] Controversy lingered in government circles about how the expensive new program should be financed and whether the American demands for amounts reaching DM 3-4 billion (nearly $1 billion) per annum could be met.[19] Despite this lack of agreement about the level of funding, West Germany's capital assistance program started operation in December 1960 under the direction of an interministerial committee that also assumed control over technical assistance. The Hermes system remained in place as a supplementary source of credit.

Bonn's hastily improvised program rested on a basic consensus in the Federal Republic about the need to give more freely. Development aid was "in." Charitable groups such as the Friedrich Ebert Foundation organized conferences on aid, while the Bundestag sponsored an "Africa Week" featuring parliamentarians from that continent.[20] Although humanitarian concern undoubtedly motivated some West Germans, public discussions usually mixed Malthusian projections with Cold War fears. Poverty in the Third World, combined with explosive population growth, appeared to make the entire region vulnerable to communist propaganda. "Without a rise in social and economic conditions there can be no lasting freedom in this part of the world," warned SPD parliamentary deputy Helmut Kalbitzer.[21] What if the Soviet Union, deceptively waving the banner of national liberation, succeeded in turning the great mass of humanity in Africa and Asia against the West? As Brentano remarked to U.S. secretary of state Christian Herter in March 1960, "The Germans concurred with the American view that the cold war might well be decided in the developing countries."[22] Konrad Adenauer found the danger less worrisome, but he still identified the "fight against communism" as the only sensible reason for aiding the Third World. "I don't feel conscious of any moral guilt toward a colored person," he quipped privately; "I didn't give him the color."[23]

Curiously, the very prevalence of Cold War motives led West German elites to adopt an aid strategy that deemphasized ideology. According to this reasoning, it would be a mistake for the Federal Republic to demand political favors in return for its aid, since this would surely backfire. The prestige-conscious leaders of the Third World guarded their independence jealously and resented outside attempts to influence their foreign policy.[24] Leaders in Bonn's government and parliament proclaimed piously that the Cold War must be kept out of Third World affairs. West German aid, as Brentano assured the Bundestag, came free of political strings.[25] This standpoint was somewhat disingenuous, since Bonn clearly anticipated that its assistance would be reciprocated with goodwill. Yet in the early 1960s, Adenauer's government did consciously refrain from using political criteria to judge the recipients of its aid. The Federal Republic gave assistance just as readily to radical regimes (Ghana, Guinea, and Mali) as to moderates (Tunisia and Thailand) or to reactionaries (Iran). This represented a marked contrast to France, which explicitly favored cooperative regimes and punished uncooperative ones.[26] The universal nature of Bonn's aid reflected a positive assessment of the nonaligned movement; like their American counterparts at the beginning of the 1960s, West German leaders argued that Western interests would be served by the mere existence of aggressively independent noncommunist regimes in the Third World.[27] Refusing to aid neutralist regimes would be counterproductive; it would only drive them into the arms of the Soviet Union.[28]

In the course of less than two years, from late 1960 to mid-1962, the Federal Republic committed billions of marks to countries in Asia and Africa and signed aid agreements with thirty-five countries.[29] To maximize the favorable publicity, West German dignitaries preferred to announce new aid agreements during extended tours to the affected regions. In January and February 1961, cabinet member Hans-Joachim Merkatz (replacing Brentano, who had just broken his arm) toured Southeast Asia, showering Burma, Thailand, Indonesia, and Ceylon with multimillion-mark packages offering a combination of long-term loans, technical assistance, and Hermes credits.[30] Bonn's most eager traveler was Federal President Heinrich Lübke, who embarked on a tour of Africa in early 1962 and of India and Pakistan later that year. Lübke's passion on the subject of rural development was genuine, but during his state visits he liked to give away aid almost like candy, offering checks to schools and social institutions during his travels.[31] Other prominent West Germans were hardly better on this count. Bundestag President Eugen Gerstenmaier made an impromptu, unauthorized offer of DM 4 million ($1 million) to the government of Cameroon during his visit there in early 1961.[32] Despite these flourishes of interest in even the smallest, poorest developing countries, the lion's share of West German aid still flowed to India and the UAR. In July 1961 Economics Minister Erhard signed a landmark treaty with UAR trade minister Abdel Latif Boghdadi offering DM 650 million ($162 million) in long-term loans and DM 400 million ($100 million) in Hermes credits. Following in the footsteps of the Soviet Union, which had assumed sole responsibility for the dam at Aswan, the Federal Republic committed itself to planning and building a dam on the Euphrates River in the Syrian portion of the UAR.[33] Now Bonn, too, was in the business of directly financing prestige projects.

In the midst of this initial flush of enthusiasm, the isolation campaign against East Germany played but a secondary role in the conception and execution of Bonn's new program. Certain of the regions singled out for special attention—Southeast Asia, for example—were chosen in order to balance out the GDR's prior successes.[34] Yet the Foreign Office had devised no precise mechanism for using aid to influence the foreign policies of developing countries; moreover, decisions about aid levels to various countries were made by an interministerial Steering Committee, or Lenkungsausschuß, composed largely of economic and financial experts.[35] Bonn hinted strongly to perennial offenders, such as the UAR and Indonesia, that West German aid was contingent on nonrecognition of East Germany. These were exceptional cases, however. Both Nasser and Sukarno had already wrestled with Bonn over the issue of East German consulates, and there was no compelling need for delicacy. On other occasions West German diplomats avoided bringing up aid and the German Question in the same breath, lest this be interpreted as an attempt to exert undue pressure.[36] In most cases, policy makers in Bonn simply operated under the unstated assumption that the new capital aid program would win sympathy among the recipients for the Federal Republic and its quest for unification.

Such high expectations invited disappointment, and during 1961 Adenauer's government gradually learned that its standing in the developing world was not so exalted after all. Even as Bonn's aid program was getting under way in 1960–61, the states of Africa and the Middle East were dividing into mutually antagonistic groupings. This reflected the strain of two major conflicts, the civil war in Congo and the Algerian war of independence against France.[37] The more radical countries, such as Ghana, Guinea, and Mali, tended to support Soviet or Chinese positions on Cold War questions, and they saw little reason to make an exception when it came to Germany. Although the Federal Republic described itself as a foe of imperialism and a champion of national self-determination, its close alliance with *all* the leading colonial powers in Africa—France, Britain, Belgium, Italy, and Portugal—undermined this claim. The All-African Peoples' Congress, a leftist organization that convened in Cairo for its third conference in April 1961, ranked the Federal Republic among the "main perpetrators of neocolonialism."[38] Closer to home, African students in Bonn adopted contemporary Marxist vocabulary in taunting the local police as "assassins, Nazis, fascists."[39] These views were far to the left of the mainstream in Africa; most newly independent countries retained close ties with their former colonial metropoles. Still, the Hallstein Doctrine could be compromised by even a small group of strongly pro-Eastern states in the developing world. In early and mid-1961 the GDR continued its advance. Ceylon and Mali accepted permanent East German trade missions in April and May 1961, respectively, while in mid-1961 President Nkrumah of Ghana invited an East German delegation to take part in Ghana's independence day ceremonies. In accord with Bonn's guidelines, the West German ambassador stayed home from the event in retaliation.[40]

The Federal Republic was not the only disillusioned party. Having been promised millions of marks in long-term, low-interest loans, Third World governments were annoyed to learn in subsequent months that these funds were not immediately forthcoming. The large numbers bandied about in West German aid agreements had little practical meaning; they represented only the *maximum* value of loans and credits that the Federal Republic was willing to provide.[41] Unlike other Western donors, Bonn disbursed its loans exclusively on a project-by-project basis. Upon being offered, say, DM 20 million in aid, a receiving country had to draft a series of proposals about how these funds were to be used. The Steering Committee in Bonn then examined each petition for feasibility and economic rationality. This procedure severely taxed the limited technical expertise of many Third World governments; some regimes had difficulty even devising a "wish list."[42] Attention to economic viability was, of course, in everyone's long-term interest. Moreover, some aspects of Bonn's approach were quite liberal. West German aid was not tied to imports from the Federal Republic, which meant that loans from Bonn could be used to finance contracts with any competent Western engineering firm, be it French, Swedish, or American.[43] Nevertheless, the delays inherent in West Germany's cumbersome approval process inevitably generated friction between Bonn and Third World capitals, particularly if a government felt that the delays were politically motivated.[44]

In the early phases of Bonn's capital aid program, such political interference was genuinely absent from West German thinking about assistance to the Third World. Given the large sums involved, though—as much as DM 3.5 billion ($875 million) annually, or some 1 percent of the country's gross domestic product—it is not surprising that the Bundestag eventually demanded some measure of accountability.[45] For all those from Adenauer on down who took the fight against communism to be the prime goal of this expensive undertaking, that measure could only be a recipient's posture in the Cold War. At the Belgrade Conference of nonaligned powers in September 1961, it became painfully obvious that a sizable number of developing countries shared the Soviet Union's standpoint on the German Question. This realization prompted Adenauer's government to adjust its aid strategy to focus on the more coercive task of supporting the isolation campaign.

The Shock of the Belgrade Conference

The gulf between East and West German capacities was wider than ever during the early 1960s. Even as the Federal Republic was asserting itself as a major creditor to the Third World, the GDR found itself on the verge of financial collapse. In large part the disaster was self-generated. The SED had alienated farmers with a shock program of collectivization in the spring of 1960, triggering a flight from the land—and to the Federal Republic through the open borders of Berlin. Farmers were joined by even greater numbers of artisans and skilled workers. A total of 199,000 East Germans emigrated to the West in 1960, seriously undermining the GDR's production goals.[46] Meanwhile, the SED found its socialist partners unable to supply the foodstuffs and consumer products necessary to maintain East Germany's standard of living; it was forced to import these goods from the West using short-term credits that soon placed the GDR in an untenable economic position. At length the Soviet Union stepped in to pick up the slack, extending millions of marks in loans to bail out the SED from 1960 to 1962.[47]

Under the circumstances, East Berlin could hardly contemplate the export of capital to the Third World in the form of development aid. In mid-1962 the Politburo actually had to beg Egypt to postpone the credits proffered in 1958, since the GDR was in no position to make the promised deliveries.[48] Where East Germany gained ground in the early 1960s, it did so through the skillful use of rhetoric—the proclamation of solidarity in the struggle against imperialism. Privately the regime's ideologists dismissed the nonaligned movement; after all, the Third World should be aligning itself explicitly with the socialist camp rather than staking out some middle ground between capitalism and socialism.[49] Nevertheless, a number of events in the first half of 1961 provided convenient opportunities for grandstanding. The SED was quick to accuse the United States (and by implication its West German ally) of complicity in the assassination of Congolese leftist Patrice Lumumba in February 1961. Lumumba was instantly canonized in the GDR as an "African freedom fighter."[50] The aborted U.S. invasion of Cuba in April provided further evidence of imperialist aggression. So, too, did the ongoing French war in Algeria.[51] It was this constellation that gave East German representatives such ready access to leaders in the more radical Third World states such as Mali, Ghana, and Ceylon in 1961. Clear-sighted observers in East Berlin could not help but notice, however, that nonaligned states *also* consorted with the GDR in order to put pressure on the Federal Republic.[52]

The flow of refugees out of East Germany continued unabated in the first half of 1961. The GDR's weakness was again a matter of high politics; attention turned once more to Berlin, the Achilles' heel of the SED regime. Khrushchev renewed his earlier threat to sign a separate peace treaty with the GDR if the Western Allies did not terminate their occupation of Berlin by the end of 1961.[53] The Kennedy administration met this Soviet challenge with a determination not to yield ground. In West Germany, Adenauer and his advisers looked on helplessly as the superpowers seemed to drift toward nuclear war; in East Germany, fears of imminent disaster only accelerated the flight to the West.[54] Plugging the leak in Berlin offered the surest solution to the GDR's immediate crisis of legitimacy. On the morning of August 13, 1961, the SED addressed the problem with barbed wire, cordoning off the Western sectors of Berlin and securing the border with machine guns. Construction of a reinforced concrete version of this "anti-fascist protective wall" commenced within a matter of weeks.[55] Erecting the wall stanched the flow of refugees, but in the near term this step was regarded by many in Bonn and Washington as an *escalation* of the crisis. Standoffs between American and Soviet tanks at "Checkpoint Charlie" continued into the fall of 1961, lending a hair-trigger atmosphere to the situation in Germany.[56]

Preoccupied with these momentous events, the Western powers paid little heed to plans by Yugoslavia, India, and the UAR to call a conference of nonaligned states in Belgrade for September 1961. The purpose of this summit gathering—the first of its kind since the Bandung Conference of 1955—was to canvass and express the views of Asia and Africa on the great political questions of the day. More ambitiously, the organizers hoped to transform the nonaligned movement into "a basic factor for the preservation of peace and international security."[57] One month before the conference it was still unclear just who would be attending and what the invited leaders would discuss. Yet certain decisions by the organizers restricted the circle of invitations to a small core of nonaligned countries. First, in contrast to Bandung, the members of Western- or Eastern-led military alliances were not eligible to attend, disqualifying China and North Korea but also Turkey, Thailand, Iran, and Japan. Second, by inviting the Algerian provisional government, Tito and Nasser ensured that nearly all of France's former colonies—still associated with the French Community—would not be able to attend.[58] Despite these indications that pro-Western moderates would be outnumbered at the conference, American officials adopted a wait-and-see attitude. Conceding that "we are likely to take a beating on some issues—colonialism, foreign bases, etc.," they took comfort in the thought that "the USSR is as uncertain as we are as to what might come out of this bag of eels."[59] The conference's location offered some grounds for optimism. The American ambassador in Belgrade, historian and diplomat George F. Kennan, anticipated that although Tito's views on Berlin and Germany diverged sharply from those of the West, the "Yugoslavs have it in their power to be distinctly helpful at [the] Belgrade conference, and would in principle like to do so."[60]

Although the Federal Republic had no diplomatic representation in Belgrade, it, too, took a relatively sanguine view of the approaching conference. "In the long run," predicted the Foreign Office, the recent stirrings among the neutral countries "might well be more dangerous for Soviet communism than for the free world."[61] Nor did Adenauer's government respond vigorously when it learned that the nonaligned powers intended to discuss the German Question in Belgrade. The king of Morocco and the emperor of Ethiopia had to prompt Bonn to supply memoranda explaining the West's positions on Berlin and Germany.[62] In mid-August the swiftly moving events in Berlin wrought a sense of malaise and helplessness in Bonn. What could the West Germans say about the moral bankruptcy of the East German regime that was not already expressed by the horrible blemish of the Berlin Wall?[63] Only in the last week of August, shortly before the conference began, did the Federal Republic court the twenty-five designated conference participants with the same intensity as the Soviet bloc. Adenauer addressed a note to each invited head of state and enclosed two memoranda, one on reunification ("self-determination for Germans, too") and one on Berlin. No one thought to distribute pictures of the loathsome wall or even of the refugees who had poured into West German reception centers during June, July, and the first twelve days of August.[64]

Bonn's stiffly written texts were no substitute for the personal diplomacy practiced by East German activists throughout the turbulent summer of 1961. "Special ambassadors" were dispatched from East Berlin with messages from Ulbricht or Grotewohl underscoring the GDR's dedication to world peace. Among the more skillful was Paul Scholz, a deputy prime minister who visited with Nkrumah in early July. By calling attention to West German support for Togo, Ghana's neighbor and rival, Scholz was able to sharply differentiate the Federal Republic's imperialism from the GDR's genuine interest in the liberation of Africa.[65] Other fortunate choices included Professor Kurt Hager of the Humboldt University, who traveled to India and Indonesia in August 1961. Hager had spent much of World War II in exile in London, where he had made the acquaintance of influential Indians such as Krishna Menon, Nehru's minister of defense.[66] Exploiting the general nervousness about a world war, Hager argued in New Delhi that the Federal Republic was intensifying the crisis with its militarist posture and its efforts to undermine the stability of the GDR. The logical solution was for India to support Khrushchev's efforts to settle the status quo in Europe. Hager reported from New Delhi that Nehru was likely to speak out in Belgrade on behalf of a compromise solution to the Berlin

DEVELOPMENT AID

Crisis: the Western powers should recognize the GDR in exchange for guaranteed Allied rights in the western sectors of the city.[67]

When the Belgrade Conference opened on September 1, 1961, however, all bets were off. The Soviet Union marked the occasion by detonating a thermonuclear bomb in Central Asia, putting an end to the unofficial testing moratorium that Britain, the United States, and the USSR had observed since 1958.[68] Khrushchev's timing can hardly have been coincidental. The explosion signaled emphatically that no matter what the nonaligned leaders resolved in Belgrade, the world's power would still be concentrated in the hands of the Eastern and Western alliances.[69] Apparently this heavy-handed gesture intimidated the conference participants; rather than censuring Moscow's action, most speakers passed over it in embarrassed silence. Marshal Tito reportedly took steps behind the scenes to play down the importance of the Soviet action.[70] In his own speech to the conference on September 3, Tito justified the Soviet test as a response to the nuclear policies of France. With regard to the German Question, too, Tito followed a strongly pro-Soviet line, contrasting the positive social model of East Germany with the "typically capitalist social system" of West Germany, "fraught and interwoven with remnants of fascist and revanchist conceptions." Tito complained that the Western Allies had irresponsibly promoted the rearmament of West Germany, leading to a revival of German militarism: "Who can guarantee that this danger will not assume, again, tomorrow, proportions liable to inflict new miseries upon mankind?"[71] Contrary to Kennan's expectations, Tito was not restraining the radical Third World regimes in Belgrade; he was egging them on.[72]

Although other statesmen at the Belgrade Conference refrained from such vehement attacks against the Federal Republic, the proceedings revealed with devastating clarity just how few of the prominent nonaligned leaders shared the West's views on German unification. Before the conference, West German ambassadors had asked the participating heads of state to address the crisis in Germany under the rubric of "self-determination," implying that the root of the problem lay in the refusal of the Soviet and East German authorities to permit free elections in the "Soviet Zone of Occupation."[73] Instead, most speakers—appalled at the saber rattling in both Cold War camps in the summer of 1961—treated the German Question as a special application of the "peaceful coexistence" they wished to see develop between the East and West. Indonesian President Ahmed Sukarno set the tone in a speech on September 1 by laying out a program for German unification with great appeal to the nonaligned countries: "Formalize or legalize existing conditions; remove all possibility of a spread of hostilities; accept the difference in social outlook; avoid every single act which might provoke greater mistrust and suspicion; withdraw all interference from outside; let the Germans themselves decide on their future destiny. Let them initiate talks in a serious endeavor to reach understanding. Let them take initial steps, however small, towards the creation and strengthening of regular forms of contact."[74] This line of reasoning strongly echoed the official East German stance on unification, which emphasized the need for the two German governments to sit down together to sort out their differences. Coming three weeks after the East Germans had strung barbed wire across the city of Berlin, Sukarno's words could only infuriate the West German public, which was less inclined than ever to contemplate discussions with the machine-gunning SED regime.

Worse still, the idea of peaceful coexistence with the GDR implied that it should be granted some degree of recognition. Sukarno attempted to soften this demand by speaking of a "recognition of the temporary *de facto* sovereignty of two Germanies," but others were more direct. President Nkrumah of Ghana asked that there be no "hypocrisy" on this count: "Everyone knows that there are two Germanies. . . . The nations of the world should therefore recognize the existence of these two States to enable them to co-exist peacefully."[75] President Modibo Keita of Mali and Prince Norodom Sihanouk of Cambodia expressed similar views. Even Nehru, regarded by so many West Germans as an important friend, insisted that there were "two independent entities, powers, countries" in Germany. "This is a fact of life: it is not a matter of my or anyone else's liking or disliking it; it is a fact that has to be recognized."[76] Tito did his utmost to ensure that these views were enshrined in the conference's final communiqué. Behind closed doors, he implored the assembled leaders to ignore Bonn's threats, claiming that Yugoslavia had not suffered materially after West Germany broke diplomatic relations in 1957; trade flowed normally as before.[77] In the committee responsible for drafting the communiqué, eight or nine governments spoke in favor of a passage taking note of "existing realities" in Germany, including the presence of two states.[78] Though such a declaration would not bind the conference participants to recognize the GDR, it would certainly give them carte blanche to do so.

Adenauer's government faced the most serious challenge to its isolation campaign yet—in Belgrade, a capital where it was in no position to influence the course of events.[79] Brentano made the best use he could of the West German media to circulate Bonn's standard threats. More explicitly than usual, the Foreign Office let it be known that a recognition of the GDR would almost certainly lead the Federal Republic to break diplomatic relations with the state in question.[80] However, these indirect warnings may not even have reached the statesmen in Belgrade. West Germany's position on the ground was defended by a most unlikely champion: Egyptian president Gamal Abdul Nasser. On the level of principle, several considerations led Nasser to resist any formal recognition of the GDR by the nonaligned world. As an advocate of Arab unity, he wished to maintain public support of German unity as well; as a vociferous hater of Israel, he wished to avoid sanctioning the territorial status quo in Germany and elsewhere, for his government still aimed at the elimination of Israel as a state.[81] On a more cynical level, Nasser likely calculated that if the nonaligned countries succeeded in collectively bringing down the Hallstein Doctrine, his government would lose a lucrative source of leverage against the Federal Republic.[82] Whatever his motives, Nasser led the Arab countries represented in Belgrade to vote against any inclusion of Soviet bloc positions on Germany in the communiqué. The final document, released on September 6, 1961, noted innocuously that the conference participants "call upon all parties concerned not to resort to or to threaten the use of force to solve the German question or the problem of Berlin."[83]

The Belgrade meeting adjourned without a landslide of recognitions of East Germany, but the danger was not yet past. Rumors abounded that a group of states had pledged to take up diplomatic relations with the GDR shortly after the conference. Adenauer's government set to work to hinder this eventuality with a series of stern démarches.[84] In the case of Indonesia, this involved a surprise call on Sukarno in Vienna by Hans-Joachim Merkatz, who had led the West German delegation to Jakarta in February 1961. Sukarno showed no willingness to depart from the views he had expressed in Belgrade, but he did at least promise not to take any initiative toward a de jure recognition of the GDR.[85] A similar response came from Mali and Ghana. Both African governments reiterated their standpoint that two German states now existed, but they indicated that relations with the Federal Republic were too important for them to risk formalizing ties with East Germany.[86] Nehru posed a more difficult problem. As always, the Indian leader attempted to define his foreign policy according to principles rather than material considerations. Since he had concluded that neither the Western Allies nor the Soviet Union wished to see a united Germany, the only argument still holding Nehru back from recognizing the GDR was his view that this would, in the near term, exacerbate the crisis over Berlin.[87]

How long Nehru or the others might hold off was uncertain, but Bonn's démarches in September 1961 do appear to have stalled whatever momentum might have existed for group action on recognition.

Particularly worrisome for Adenauer's government was the pragmatic argument employed by Tito in his backroom conversations: that Yugoslavia had not truly suffered from the absence of diplomatic relations with the Federal Republic. This was a potent claim that threatened to undermine the deterrent value of the Hallstein Doctrine.[88] Bonn's response—aside from a series of punitive economic measures against Yugoslavia—was to introduce a new dimension to its standard warnings.[89] Since 1955 Adenauer's government had maintained that if another country committed the "unfriendly act" of recognizing the GDR, the Federal Republic reserved the right to respond as the circumstances warranted. However, reactions other than a break in diplomatic relations were seldom mentioned. This changed on September 6, 1961, when a government spokesman announced for the first time that the Federal Republic would almost certainly cut off development aid to any country that recognized the GDR. Without fanfare, Adenauer's government had taken a first step toward the politicization of aid and a noteworthy intensification of the Hallstein Doctrine.[90]

Linking development assistance with particular political objectives was not, of course, a novel or revolutionary idea, but it did imply a revision of Bonn's claim to be giving aid without any strings attached.[91] In the aftermath of the Belgrade Conference, this approach seemed quite natural to many in the Federal Republic. Leading newspapers reported with great precision which countries had spoken out in support of West Germany's "right to self-determination" (Somalia and Cyprus) and which had endorsed Khrushchev's call for a peace treaty sealing the status quo in Germany (Ghana and Yugoslavia).[92] It did not take West Germans long to begin demanding that Bonn's development aid be distributed accordingly. Erich Mende, chairman of the FDP, contended that Bonn should redirect its aid away from countries such as India, Indonesia, and Ghana, since they were "harming German interests" with their attitudes toward the GDR.[93] This suggestion was all the more striking coming from the FDP, a traditional foe of the Hallstein Doctrine. When Mende insisted in the same breath that the Hallstein Doctrine was "no longer a useful instrument" of German diplomacy, he was referring exclusively to the situation in Eastern Europe. More and more of the doctrine's former opponents now viewed it as indispensable as a means of hindering the SED regime's quest for legitimacy in the Third World.[94]

At the UN, the Federal Republic canvassed friendly regimes to give brief statements in support of Germany's "right to self-determination." Karl Carstens, the state secretary of the Foreign Office, assigned cardinal importance to this effort; he asked to be given daily reports on what was said about Germany and Berlin in the General Assembly.[95] The numbers were on West Germany's side in the fall of 1961: of 101 members of the UN, 38 spoke out in a manner consistent with Bonn's standpoint, while 18 took the opposite stance.[96] This practice became an annual ritual, with Bonn sending out a démarche each summer in advance of the General Assembly asking friendly regimes to speak out on behalf of German unification. The point of this somewhat artificial exercise was to keep alive the idea that the free world overwhelmingly supported Bonn's views on the German Question. But every fall from 1962 through 1964, the number of states explicitly endorsing the West German standpoint in the UN fell; a slight rise in 1965 hardly had an impact on the overall downward trend.[97] What one reporter observed in the wake of the Belgrade Conference was undoubtedly accurate: for most nonaligned countries, there were now, in fact, two German states. Adenauer's government could continue to stave off recognitions of the GDR with economic measures, "but in the future it will only be a question of money."[98] In September 1961 the Foreign Office implicitly took this into account by publicly linking development aid with the problem of unification. At the very moment when the building of the Berlin Wall demonstrated the moral weakness of the Ulbricht regime, Adenauer's government found its own moral claims going unheeded. More and more, the isolation campaign was dominated by considerations of high finance.

Experiments in Economic Leverage

Voters in the elections of September 17, 1961, did not turn out Adenauer's party, but the CDU/CSU lost its absolute majority in the Bundestag. The SPD, led by its appealing chancellor candidate Willy Brandt, enjoyed a marked upswing at the polls, yet the election's real victor was the FDP, which saw its share of votes rise from 7.7 percent to 12.8 percent in the four years since 1957.[99] Most importantly, all of the smaller West German parties failed to gain representation in the new Bundestag, leaving the FDP in the fortunate position of being the CDU's only potential coalition partner.[100] Reaching agreement between these parties was not easy. Negotiations dragged on until November, and Bonn was bereft of a working government for much of the fall. The FDP did not manage to dislodge Adenauer from his post as chancellor, which was an embarrassment for the party; it had run an emphatically anti-Adenauer campaign.[101] To compensate, the party sought to prove its mettle in the realm of foreign policy. Since 1956 the Free Democrats had taken strong exception to Adenauer's lack of interest in Eastern policy, and they had made opposition to the Hallstein Doctrine one of their most identifiable credos. How could the FDP now submit to the foreign policy of Adenauer and Brentano without losing face?

Throughout October the CDU and FDP haggled over a "coalition agreement," an informal contract outlining the bases of common policy for the new government. Brentano, seeking to preserve absolute continuity in the ream of foreign relations, put forward a three-page paper outlining what he described as "the fundamentals of the foreign policy of the past 12 years." The more controversial passages related to Bonn's relationship with the GDR. Brentano insisted that there could be no government-level contacts with the regime in East Berlin, for this would lead to a recognition of the GDR and the definitive division of Germany: "We also cannot allow that, through a recognition of the SBZ, the German Question slowly but surely disappears from world public opinion as an open political problem. The basic principle that we can maintain no diplomatic relations with third states which have recognized the 'GDR' as a sovereign state brooks no exception. This point is important as a warning to states that are toying with the idea of acknowledging or signing a separate peace between the Soviet Union and the GDR."[102] At the FDP's insistence, these words were struck from the coalition agreement. However, the document did not repudiate the Hallstein Doctrine outright, so the Foreign Office was free to carry on as before.[103] Nor did the FDP insist on the establishment of diplomatic relations with Eastern Europe as a central feature of the coalition agreement, even though this was one of the party's perennial election planks. Instead the Free Democrats focused on getting their people in the right places in the new government.[104] In this they were only modestly successful. Brentano flatly rejected efforts to create a third state secretary post within the Foreign Office for a prominent FDP politician. This left the Free Democrats scurrying to find some other cabinet post with foreign policy relevance for Walter Scheel, the party's most senior ministerial candidate. Scheel was willing to serve as either minister for European affairs or minister for development aid; neither ministry existed, so one would have to be created for the occasion. The latter option was deemed less objectionable by the Foreign Office, though Economics Minister Ludwig Erhard made a futile threat to resign over the issue. On November 24, 1961, Adenauer called into being the Ministry for Economic Cooperation, which

DEVELOPMENT AID

was granted a limited degree of authority in the coordination of Bonn's aid programs.[105]

Scheel's appointment as development minister did not entirely satisfy the FDP caucus, however; the party, flushed with a sense of power after its success at the polls, insisted on a more pronounced break in continuity from the preceding cabinet. Its final target was a negative objective—the fall of Foreign Minister Brentano.[106] Although Adenauer resisted this demand until the end of October, he did not show particular energy in defending his minister. Brentano finally lost his temper in the face of the FDP's malice and the evident ambition of several CDU politicians to succeed him. On October 28 the nervous, chain-smoking bachelor tendered his resignation.[107] Despite his poor health, Brentano did not retire into obscurity; he returned to the Bundestag to serve as chairman of the CDU/CSU's parliamentary caucus, the same function he had exercised from 1951 to 1955. In this post Brentano continued to wield influence as a "watchdog" over the government's foreign policy until his death in 1964.

Brentano's successor, Gerhard Schröder, had much greater appeal for the Free Democrats. Schröder was a north German Protestant, which set him apart from the predominantly Catholic leadership of the CDU/CSU. Schröder, who had served as interior minister from 1953 to 1961, inspired respect if not warmth with his elegant attire and imposing air.[108] Above all, Schröder strove to appear modern, expressing enthusiasm for contemporary authors such as Mary McCarthy and Henry Miller.[109] Such reading habits, shocking enough to conservative Bavarian Catholics, were less controversial than his stance on Berlin. From the start, the new minister sympathized with American and British efforts to resolve the crisis peacefully, even if this involved some compromise over the status of the divided city.[110] This was in line with the chancellor's own preferences; in the winter of 1961–62, Adenauer and Schröder gave their blessing to a series of negotiations between the United States and the Soviet Union that were deeply unpopular in Germany. Yet it was Schröder rather than Adenauer who caught the political fallout for this endorsement. The foreign minister never enjoyed the full support of the CDU's Bundestag caucus, now in the hands of the increasingly dogmatic Brentano.[111]

If the FDP's leaders believed that the new minister would also take a softer line on the Hallstein Doctrine, they were mistaken. In public Schröder maintained a low profile on the subject, but the government's first foreign policy address in late November 1961 left no doubt that Bonn would continue to regard the opening of diplomatic relations with the GDR as an unfriendly act.[112] In political terms, Schröder had every reason to stand firm on the question of nonrecognition, in order to appease the CDU's discontent over his Berlin policies. However, much of the continuity in the isolation campaign can be attributed to the influence of Karl Carstens, Schröder's immensely capable state secretary. One of the few Foreign Office leaders whom Adenauer respected, Carstens was a career outsider who had raced up the Foreign Ministry's bureaucratic ladder in just a few short years.[113] In mid-1960 he was appointed junior state secretary alongside the ailing Hilger van Scherpenberg; a year later Scherpenberg departed, leaving Carstens at the helm. A lawyer by training, Carstens waged the Federal Republic's nonrecognition campaign with rigorous precision. Particularly in the wake of the Belgrade Conference, Carstens strove to shake the Foreign Office out of its seeming fatalism regarding East German gains in the Third World. Since the opening of the GDR's consulate-general in Cairo in September 1959, Bonn had not found any compelling arguments to stop other countries from following this example. The Federal Republic was to have still more unpleasant experiences in this regard in 1962–63, but rather than despairing, Carstens led the Foreign Office in a relentless effort to halt the erosion of West Germany's position in the Third World.[114]

As noted above, Adenauer's government was increasingly prepared to use aid as a lever in defense of the Hallstein Doctrine. Walter Scheel, in his capacity as development aid minister, tried to resist this trend. He viewed dispensing aid as a unique task that could not simply be subordinated to foreign policy goals. Interviewed by *Der Spiegel* in May 1962, Scheel insisted that "our development aid bears no relation to the political role of Pankow around the world."[115] Ironically, though, the creation of Scheel's new ministry accelerated the trend toward an instrumental view of aid in Bonn, for his organization drew away the more idealistic functionaries from the Foreign Office and the Economics Ministry, leaving behind the cynical ones.[116] Moreover, the two older ministries managed to retain most of their responsibilities in the realm of aid, leaving Scheel's organization with little power. The interministerial Steering Committee remained the central decision-making authority on development aid.[117] Now that the Foreign Office and the Economics Ministry had a common institutional rival, the two began to vote together in the Steering Committee in favor of aid projects that were explicitly political. As early as October 1961, representatives of Erhard's Economics Ministry were showing a newfound sensitivity to the isolation campaign; they urged that Morocco be granted DM

40 million ($10 million) in capital assistance as soon as possible in light of that country's favorable stance at the Belgrade Conference.[118]

More commonly, the Federal Republic manipulated its aid not to reward its friends but to keep less friendly countries in line. In the winter of 1961–62, Ghana was an ambitious test case for this approach. At the Belgrade Conference and again during a visit to Moscow, President Nkrumah had fully endorsed the Soviet Union's views on Germany, though without proceeding to a formal recognition of the GDR. To hold Nkrumah back from this final step, the West German ambassador to Ghana recommended that Bonn provide aid in discrete portions, starting with DM 20 million ($5 million)—not so little as to anger Nkrumah, but not so much as to satisfy him completely.[119] The Foreign Office also worked to insert a political "security clause" into its aid agreement with Ghana. In practice this amounted to a trivial-sounding reference in the preamble noting that the agreement was an expression of the friendly relations between the two countries; this would, in theory, give Adenauer's government some moral grounds to withhold aid payments if the friendliness of the relations deteriorated.[120] Some form of this clause was, in fact, accepted by Nkrumah, perhaps because he had already agreed to a similar arrangement with the United States. However, the Steering Committee was reluctant to establish this as a general procedure, since it was too obvious an example of attaching political strings to aid.[121]

In March 1962 Cambodia's decision to initiate consular relations with the GDR prompted Bonn to undertake another untried form of aid-related pressure. Since the Federal Republic itself had no diplomatic or consular relations with Cambodia, the new consulate was a noteworthy coup for the GDR. Now East Germany would be the sole representative of the German people in the Cambodian capital, Phnom Penh.[122] Damage control was not easy without any West Germans on the ground; Heinrich Bassler, head of the Southeast Asia desk in Bonn, flew to Phnom Penh to negotiate directly with Prince Sihanouk. Bassler's mission was to obtain clarification from the Cambodians that accepting an East German consulate did not imply a recognition of the GDR. Initially he came armed only with a threat: if Cambodia did not comply, the Federal Republic would cancel its offer of aid (a paltry DM 1.5 million). He could not, after all, threaten to break diplomatic relations, since these had never been established.[123] Once in Phnom Penh, Bassler realized that he would have to up the ante and cabled Bonn for permission to offer a loan of DM 15 million ($3.75 million). After some hand-wringing by the Finance Ministry, the Steering Committee agreed to this emergency request. Bassler negotiated hard in Phnom Penh, insisting on an open and published confirmation of Cambodia's nonrecognition of the GDR. Prince Sihanouk finally gave his consent, despite massive Soviet and East German pressure not to restrict the legal position of the GDR's consulate.[124] Sihanouk's government got its revenge, though. Cambodian negotiators in Bonn later talked the Federal Republic into an even more generous aid package, involving DM 5.5 million in technical aid and a loan of DM 20 to 25 million at an extremely low interest rate.[125]

Without the instrument of aid, Bonn's exacting standards regarding consuls and exequaturs were becoming difficult to enforce. In mid-1962, when the government of Abdul Karim Qassem in Iraq opened consular relations with the GDR, Bonn found that it had almost no leverage over Baghdad.[126] As in the case of Cambodia, Bonn dispatched envoys to the scene to obtain, as American diplomats put it, "a quotable statement by the Iraqi Government to the effect that Baghdad was not giving diplomatic recognition to East Germany."[127] Unfortunately, Qassem found this tactic of sending special agents from Bonn to be an egregious example of interference in Iraq's internal affairs; he would not receive them or make any statements whatsoever about the nature of Iraq's consular arrangements with the GDR. Eventually the West German officials were asked to leave the country.[128]

For observers in Bonn, the snub from Iraq was humiliating, and Konrad Adenauer did not disguise from reporters his impatience with the Hallstein Doctrine. Around the same time, relations with Ceylon were also deteriorating, in no small part due to irritations stemming from the isolation campaign. Adenauer seemed inclined to favor a tactical retreat on the question of East German consulates in order to avoid these continuing diplomatic run-ins.[129] However, the Foreign Office resisted this move, arguing that Bonn could not simply stand by idly while the GDR expanded its consular network.[130] As a result, Bonn continued to suffer through major and minor crises over formalistic matters such as exequaturs. In November 1962 the Indonesian foreign minister deliberately omitted the nonrecognition clause when he issued an exequatur to the new East German consul in Jakarta. In the context of a more general slump in relations between West Germany and Indonesia, this move set off warning bells in Bonn, and State Secretary Carstens insisted on a public declaration by Sukarno that Indonesia did not recognize the government of East Germany.[131] The disagreement was temporarily smoothed over by a conversation at the highest levels: Schröder met with Sukarno for a hastily arranged discussion in Bangkok, Thailand. But relations did not improve substantially until the spring of 1963, when the Steering Committee finally agreed to fund some of Sukarno's economically senseless pet projects.[132] In this case, the Indonesians found Bonn's sensitivity to issues such as exequaturs to be a useful lever in extorting aid. This was not how the link between aid and the Hallstein Doctrine was supposed to work.[133]

Admittedly, these were exceptional cases. Other Western countries were just as powerless in Iraq and Indonesia; these were rogue regimes that had alienated most of their neighbors as well as the major European powers. In certain instances, Bonn's aid appeared to function smoothly enough as "hush money." Mali, Guinea, and Syria, countries that had once flirted ostentatiously with the GDR, remained conspicuously quiet in 1962–63. Mali was promised military aid from the Federal Republic; Guinea, capital assistance; and Syria, the Euphrates Dam.[134] But these examples, too, showed that Bonn's nonrecognition policy was now much less cost-effective than in the early years. Grewe and Hallstein had devised their policy as a *universal* deterrent, making the nonrecognition of East Germany a precondition for relations with West Germany. With large countries such as Yugoslavia, India, and Egypt, the Federal Republic had always been forced to negotiate over the terms of nonrecognition, and from an early date this involved financial arrangements as well as political agreements. But with the advent of Bonn's global aid program, even weak countries like Cambodia had an opportunity to set a price for conforming to West German requirements. The isolation campaign was splintering into an array of individual "managed relationships" between the Federal Republic and the countries of the Third World. The efforts of Adenauer's government to politicize its aid relationships only exacerbated the problem.

The government did not stop experimenting, however. By the second half of 1962, the idea of harnessing aid in the service of the Hallstein Doctrine was common currency in Bonn. In August, Foreign Minister Schröder and Ernst Majonica, a leading foreign policy expert of the CDU, both warned that Bonn was prepared to throttle development aid to any country that agreed to sign a separate peace treaty with the GDR.[135] This was not a novel position, as similar warnings had surfaced the preceding September; but it touched off a fresh debate in West Germany about the merits of politically tied aid. Quite a number of commentators approved. "Why shouldn't the West make use of such an effective instrument?" wondered Robert Strobel, a regular at Adenauer's press teas. The *Rheinischer Merkur* praised the clarity of the government's stance, which it summarized in the simple phrase, "whoever recognizes Pankow will get nothing more from us."[136] The left-liberal press raised its usual reservations, and the FDP's chairman, Erich Mende, protested bitterly at the new round of threats against the developing world; yet the affair merely highlighted once more the FDP's near-irrelevance on foreign policy questions.[137] Other West Germans found more convenient uses for aid—as a bargaining chip for obtaining landing rights for Lufthansa in East Africa, for example.[138] A much larger initiative came in the fall of 1962, when the EEC was negotiating new association agreements with select African countries. Adenauer's government informed the community's representatives in Brussels that it would veto any EEC aid agreements with an associated government that recognized the GDR.[139] This standpoint would effectively have turned the EEC into an accomplice of the Hallstein Doctrine in Africa. A cool reception from the other five EEC members led Bonn to back away from its proposal, but not before the project had been leaked to the press, impressing several African governments yet again with the seriousness with which Bonn regarded the question of recognition.[140]

After envisioning economic sanctions on behalf of its nonrecognition policy for more than a year, Adenauer's government was almost relieved to have a chance to execute them in early 1963. Quite unexpectedly, Cuba recognized the GDR on January 11. In many ways this was only a formality; Castro's revolutionary Cuba had long since enjoyed better relations with East Berlin than with Bonn. But the definitive recognition of East Germany by Cuba gave West Germany an opportunity to unleash the full force of the Hallstein Doctrine. As in 1957, Bonn sounded out the views of the Western Allies before taking action, but there was never any doubt about the Federal Republic's decision. On January 14 Carstens presented the Cuban chargé with a note announcing that Bonn was breaking diplomatic *and* consular relations, with all the attendant economic consequences.[141] In the following weeks, the Foreign Office—ever mindful of its prior leniency toward Yugoslavia—sought with grim determination to make the break with Havana as thorough as possible. Since Bonn had not sponsored any aid programs in Cuba, attention focused on trade relations, and Adenauer's government moved to suspend a shipping and trade treaty dating back to 1953. Not only would there be no trade between the Federal Republic and Cuba, but a legal framework for such transactions would be lacking entirely.[142] Cuban attempts to soften the blow by opening a trade mission or consulate in Hamburg were sharply rebuffed.[143]

Bonn's strike against Cuba was a message to all those countries that had been swayed by Tito's reassurances at the Belgrade Conference. It was applauded by both the CDU and the SPD, while the FDP, as a partner in government, had only limited maneuvering room in criticizing the action.[144] West Germany's insistence on punishing Cuba harshly marked the beginning of a genuine radicalization within the Foreign Office on the nonrecognition question. In the following years, the Foreign Ministry—along with substantial portions of the government apparatus—sought ever new means of perfecting the deterrent effect of the Hallstein Doctrine. The days of freely given development aid were past. The Federal Republic continued to aid regimes of all political stripes, but it no longer expected that non-aligned governments would respect Bonn's stance on the German Question as a matter of courtesy. From 1963 onward, the element of compulsion in relations with the Third World mounted continuously.

Chapter 6
The Perils of Détente

By 1963 both German governments were long accustomed to a state of high tension among the major world powers. The Berlin Crisis had, it was true, reinforced the central role of the Four Powers in deciding the fate of Germany, but Ulbricht and Adenauer enjoyed a strong enough position within their respective alliances to veto any arrangements they found unacceptable. What neither side was prepared for was a genuine warming of relations between Washington and Moscow. Yet the showdown over missiles in Cuba in October 1962 proved to be a watershed; the main Cold War protagonists, sobered by the experience, edged toward a series of agreements to help regulate the worldwide conflict.[1] Further complicating the international environment was a partial breakdown of cohesion within each alliance. Just as Beijing drifted ever further from Moscow's orbit, so Paris under President Charles de Gaulle promoted the creation of a "European Europe" that was less dependent on Washington's security guarantees. Within the Federal Republic, the growing distance between France and the United States produced a sharp split between "Atlanticists" and "Gaullists" in the ruling coalition, creating serious complications for Adenauer's successor, Ludwig Erhard.

The advent of détente transformed the landscape in Europe, and Bonn and East Berlin raced to exploit the opportunities while avoiding the pitfalls inherent in the situation. The easing of tensions in Europe allowed the Federal Republic to initiate closer relations with Poland, Hungary, and other East European states, raising the distinct possibility that the GDR could be isolated in its own "backyard." Yet, to the advantage of the GDR, the new circumstances appeared to solidify the status quo in Europe. Ulbricht accordingly demanded an intensification of efforts to "break through" the Hallstein Doctrine once and for all. Erhard's administration, in turn, redoubled its campaign against the GDR. In the spring of 1964 West German officials effected a major tightening of the isolation strategy by linking economic reprisals not only to *recognition* of East Germany but also to any other gestures that enhanced its status. The strategy appeared to be succeeding, but the immense diplomatic effort was exhausting. By the winter of 1964–65, when the Federal Republic's Middle Eastern policy disintegrated into a morass of contradictions, Erhard could not muster the will to respond coherently. Out of exasperation, President Nasser—by turns one of Bonn's greatest allies and greatest enemies in containing the GDR—dealt the Hallstein Doctrine a blow from which it never fully recovered.

De Gaulle, Détente, and the "Policy of Movement"

Konrad Adenauer's treaty with Charles de Gaulle in January 1963 took all sides by surprise. For the chancellor, who had made reconciliation with France the central mission of his last year in office, the Elysée Treaty, which provided for regular consultation and cooperation between the two governments, established the institutional basis for a powerful Franco-German entente.[2] But the reaction in Bonn showed that Adenauer had overshot the mark. Detractors worried that this exclusive bilateral relationship with France would wreck the larger project of building the EEC; that it would alienate Britain, which had just been rejected by de Gaulle as a prospective new entrant to the EEC; and that it would anger the United States, which was increasingly at odds with France.[3] Ludwig Erhard, the highly popular minister of economics, spoke out vehemently against the treaty. Adenauer's heavy-handed attempts to stifle Erhard's criticisms only generated further sympathy for the portly, cigar-smoking minister. On April 24, 1963, the CDU/CSU parliamentary caucus voted 159-47 (with 19 abstentions) in favor of Erhard as chancellor designate, with the understanding that Adenauer would step down in the fall.[4] Soon thereafter the Bundestag voted almost unanimously to attach a preamble to the Franco-German treaty, emphasizing that it did not supersede Bonn's commitments to the Atlantic community.[5] This was more than just a repudiation of the treaty's essential political meaning; it marked the end of Adenauer's real influence over West German foreign policy.

The immediate winner of the power struggle within the CDU/CSU was Foreign Minister Gerhard Schröder, who guided Bonn's diplomacy during the long months of transition from Adenauer to Erhard. Although Schröder had signed the Elysée Treaty and urged the Bundestag not to repudiate it, he regarded the United States as a more reliable ally than France on the basic problems of European defense and German unification. He wholeheartedly endorsed negotiations toward a multilateral nuclear force, an

American-sponsored plan for sharing nuclear responsibilities with NATO members without actually letting West Germans have their own atomic weapons.[6] On détente, Schröder's views were pragmatic; he recognized that Bonn could not afford to speak out openly against the warming of relations between Washington and Moscow, for this would only give ammunition to Soviet propagandists seeking to brand the Federal Republic as a "militarist," "revanchist" power. Consequently, Schröder introduced a "policy of movement" aimed at reducing suspicions of West Germany in Eastern Europe.[7] In March 1963, nearly seven years after the idea had first surfaced in the Foreign Office, West Germany and Poland settled on the establishment of a permanent trade mission in Warsaw. Similar agreements followed with Hungary, Romania, and Bulgaria.[8]

Schröder's policy of movement did not generate much resistance within the CDU/CSU from the standpoint of the isolation campaign. The Foreign Office carefully circumscribed the powers of the new trade missions in Eastern Europe, ensuring that they exercised no diplomatic functions and only limited consular powers. This allowed West German diplomats to assert that Bonn's opening toward Eastern Europe was fully compatible with the Hallstein Doctrine.[9] Indeed, Schröder often billed the policy of movement as an *offensive* step designed to weaken the GDR's standing among its own allies. "Every improvement in our relations to [the satellite states] means on the other side a worsening of their relations to Ulbricht," predicted the foreign minister.[10] This was a somewhat inconsistent standpoint, since the trade missions were so weak in stature that they could hardly be expected to play a political role in the Warsaw Pact capitals. Yet an entirely different problem unnerved critics in the CDU/CSU. Several deputies complained that the interests of West Berlin had not been properly secured in the arrangements with Warsaw. For the more suspicious members of the caucus, such as the chairman, Heinrich von Brentano, Schröder's vague handling of the "Berlin clause" demonstrated the dangers of an overly hasty détente: the government was in such a rush to improve its standing in Eastern Europe that it was neglecting the defense of Bonn's "legal position."[11]

Unfortunately for Schröder, the Kennedy administration startled the Federal Republic with a measure that appeared to confirm the link between détente and the sacrifice of vital German interests. On July 26, 1963, the United States, Britain, and the Soviet Union initialed the Limited Test Ban Treaty outlawing above-ground nuclear testing. Bonn was, of course, aware of the negotiations in Moscow, but it had expected that the treaty

would apply only to the three principal signatories. Instead these governments opened the treaty for participation by "all states."[12] Not only would
West Germany and the other members of NATO be expected to sign, but this
formulation left open the possibility of East German adherence. Indeed,
the United States *desired* the GDR's signature on the treaty, as it did also
China's. For American officials, concerns about nuclear testing and pro-
liferation overrode considerations about a possible indirect recognition of
the signatories.[13] China, France, and India all indicated that they would
not sign, but Walter Ulbricht proclaimed the GDR's adherence to the Moscow agreement and expressed his hope that the Federal Republic would
follow suit.[14]

The Test Ban Treaty was deliberately anti-German in content as well as
form, being designed to reassure the Soviets that the Federal Republic
would not gain control over nuclear weapons.[15] However, it was the "upgrading" (*Aufwertung*) of the GDR as a signatory to a major international
treaty that most upset political elites in Bonn. Adenauer, then in the lame-
duck phase of his chancellorship, was tempted to resign in protest; his shrill
reaction was seconded by Brentano and by Franz-Josef Strauss, chairman
of the Bavarian CSU.[16] The Federal Republic waited more than two weeks
before announcing its intention to sign the treaty. In the meantime, West
German and American officials scrambled to work out a few devices to
minimize the legal implications of East Germany's signature. Secretary of
State Dean Rusk read aloud a special statement during ratification hear-
ings in the Senate explaining why the GDR's adherence to the treaty did not
enhance its status: "We do not recognize, and do not intend to recognize,
the Soviet occupation zone of East Germany as a state or as an entity
possessing national sovereignty, or to recognize the local authorities as a
government. Those authorities cannot alter these facts by the act of sub-
scribing to the test ban treaty."[17] This standpoint allowed the United States
to disavow any indirect recognition of the GDR while finessing the delicate
question of whether East Germany would be bound by the treaty's stipu-
lations regarding nuclear testing. However, the GDR's participation was
bound to be a recurring problem in further steps toward détente, since no
meaningful arrangements could be struck between NATO and the Warsaw
Pact that exempted the territory of the GDR.[18]

"We are the victims of America's policy of détente," noted Heinrich
Krone in his diary on August 5, 1963.[19] Krone, one of Adenauer's closest political associates, expressed the sense of betrayal felt by many in
the CDU/CSU in the summer of 1963. Just one month after the German

public had jubilantly received John F. Kennedy, a seeming high point in German-American relations, the Kennedy administration had effected a major breakthrough in East-West relations without informing the West Germans ahead of time.[20] Schröder felt personally compromised by this lack of consultation and vented his anger quite freely in Washington, but he continued to advocate détente in both government and party circles in Bonn.[21] Yet the Test Ban Treaty galvanized suspicion of the United States among a small but growing faction in the CDU/CSU: the Gaullists. If the United States had resigned itself to the status quo, might not an exclusive partnership with France offer the best remaining hope for overcoming the division of Europe?[22] Whether German unity was truly within de Gaulle's power or design was almost beside the point; the Gaullist position was above all an expression of distrust in America, just as the Atlanticists had been called to arms by Adenauer's overtly pro-French tilt in early 1963.[23]

The swearing in of a new chancellor helped to smooth the internal differences in the CDU/CSU for several months. Erhard's term began auspiciously with a warmly received inaugural address to the Bundestag on October 18, 1963. Remarking on the successful course of postwar reconstruction in West Germany, Erhard admonished the parliament and the people not to fall into the apathy of individualistic consumption: "We must consider the whole and measure our actions against common goals." In effect, Erhard was arguing that more visible displays of patriotism were necessary to demonstrate the Germans' "sense of belong[ing] together."[24] It was the duty of the West Germans to remind the world over and over of the injustice and even dangers inherent in the country's ongoing division. Without directly criticizing the course of détente, Erhard pointed out that "the German Question is one of the main causes of tension in the world, and one can't hope to put aside these tensions so long as the German Question remains unsolved." The Soviet Union must be persuaded that it was a mistake to perpetuate the unnatural division of the German nation. In the meantime, the West Germans should work to improve the lot of their fellow Germans in the East, but under no circumstances would his government adopt measures sanctioning the status quo or improving the international standing of the regime in the "Soviet Occupied Zone."[25]

Erhard's speech was short on specifics, but it indicated clearly enough that the new government would pursue new initiatives toward unification and would be less tolerant of gains by the GDR. He warned against any "upgrading" of the status of Ulbricht's regime, a term that could refer to any deepening of relations with East Germany, whether on the diplomatic,

THE PERILS OF DÉTENTE

consular, or commercial level.[26] Here Erhard's approach differed considerably from his predecessor's. Adenauer had, of course, helped to author the Federal Republic's early strategy against East German recognition, but he seldom expressed much interest in the narrower details of the Hallstein Doctrine. In conversations with the press, Adenauer even mocked the Foreign Office for its rigidity, setting himself off as a more pragmatic thinker than the lawyers in Bonn's foreign service.[27] Erhard, incapable of such distance and cynicism, assigned vastly more significance to the mechanics of the isolation campaign. He and his cabinet began to lose perspective on the entire project.

The new chancellor's optimism and idealism resonated well in Bonn, marking a welcome contrast to Adenauer's more calculating style.[28] Not only did Erhard enjoy tremendous personal cachet among the voting public, but the other parties in the Bundestag found much to laud in his ideas on domestic and foreign policy. Erhard's strident rhetoric on unification and Schröder's modest opening toward Eastern Europe suited the Free Democrats quite well and helped to integrate the FDP more reliably into the governing coalition. The departure of Adenauer cleared the way for the FDP's chairman, Erich Mende, to assume a high-profile role in the cabinet as vice-chancellor and minister for all-German affairs. A pattern of constructive cooperation also characterized the Social Democrats, who sought to convince voters of their seriousness and responsibility by emphasizing the party's "commonality" with the present administration. Fritz Erler, leader of the SPD caucus in the Bundestag, heartily endorsed Schröder's foreign policy on all counts—the policy of movement, the preference for America over France, and the quest for German participation in a multilateral nuclear force. Indeed, the SPD caucus in the Bundestag backed Erhard so consistently that FDP politicians mocked it for neglecting the proper functions of an opposition party.[29]

Despite this broad base of general support—one could even call it "tripartisan"—Erhard and Schröder still found it difficult to pursue a constructive foreign policy. The FDP and SPD repeatedly called on Erhard to expand intra-German contacts, yet voices in the CDU/CSU, particularly among the Gaullists, cautioned against any steps that might compromise Bonn's "legal position." These conflicting impulses came to the fore in the winter of 1963–64, when Willy Brandt, mayor of West Berlin and the SPD's most visible national leader, improvised a hasty deal with the East Germans to allow Christmas visits across the Berlin Wall. The arrangement called for stationing East German visa officers in West Berlin, a situation that many in the government found appalling.[30] Nevertheless, the holiday visits were a popular success, and Erhard defended the outcome to the CDU/CSU caucus in his usual clichéd vocabulary: the 1.2 million visits to East Berlin during the Christmas season "proved to the world the Germans' sense of belonging together."[31] To guard against any further undermining of Bonn's nonrecognition policy, the Foreign Office worked in tandem with the authorities in West Berlin to secure different terms for the next round of visits, scheduled for the Easter holiday of 1964. The East German negotiators responded to this stiffer attitude by pulling out of the negotiations. For some observers, this merely proved that the Ulbricht regime was abusing the visits to achieve an indirect recognition from the West Germans.[32] However, a different lesson could be drawn from this turn of events, namely, that it was Bonn's excessive legalism on the recognition question that was responsible for blocking progress toward free mobility between East and West.[33]

With the problem of East German recognition at the core of so many current issues in West Germany, from détente to the Berlin visits, the isolation campaign took on a political weight in 1963–64 that it had not previously known. However much the SPD, FDP, and CDU/CSU differed on the details of technical contacts with the Ulbricht regime, all agreed on the desirability of blocking East Germany's progress in the developing world.[34] At the same time, the most notorious and unwelcome side effect of the Hallstein Doctrine, the absence of official contacts with Eastern Europe, had been defused temporarily by Schröder's policy of movement.[35] The one related problem that still excited heated debate in Bonn was the Arab-Israeli conflict. One group of parliamentarians in the CDU/CSU and the SPD pleaded with the government to establish full diplomatic relations with Israel and to ban the employment of German scientists in Egypt's defense industry.[36] Another group, also crossing party lines, shared the standpoint of Schröder and the Foreign Office, namely, that any normalization of relations with Israel would disrupt the traditional German-Arab friendship and even drive the Arab states to recognize the GDR. Material aid to Israel, in the form of economic support, would have to substitute for conventional diplomatic ties.[37] Tellingly, even the advocates of diplomatic relations with Israel generally endorsed the Hallstein Doctrine as a tool of West German diplomacy; they merely disputed the right of the Arab leaders to interfere with the warming of relations between the Federal Republic and Israel.[38] In other words, the debate over Israel was *not* carried out as a discussion of the merits of the Hallstein Doctrine itself. Carlo Schmid, one of the SPD's

THE PERILS OF DÉTENTE

senior parliamentarians, was virtually alone in calling outright for the doctrine's abolition.[39] As the course of events in 1964 and 1965 would show, the Bundestag was more likely to criticize any perceived *lapses* in the campaign against East Germany than to speak out against excesses. The domestic political constellation strongly favored a tightening of Bonn's isolation policy.

Planning the Breakthrough

For Ulbricht, too, the waning of tensions between the United States and the Soviet Union required a change of course. Sealing off West Berlin with a wall was hardly an elegant solution to the GDR's crisis of legitimacy; in the year and a half after August 13, 1961, the East German leader pushed relentlessly for a more formal settlement of the German Question. A peace treaty stipulating the neutralization of West Berlin and the withdrawal of Allied soldiers from the city remained the ultimate goal of East German and Soviet policy. In the absence of agreement among the Four Powers, Ulbricht urged Khrushchev to sign a separate peace treaty with the GDR. Such a treaty would not be directly binding on the Western Allies, but if enough nonaligned countries could be persuaded to endorse the separate peace, the division of Germany would enjoy a more solid foundation under international law.[40] Consequently, the major thrust of East Berlin's diplomacy in 1961 and 1962 did not directly concern the question of recognition. Instead, East German diplomats and "special ambassadors" canvassed neutral leaders for promises to add their signatures to a future East German–Soviet peace treaty. Unfortunately, few addressees in the Third World expressed anything more than polite interest; even Tito remained wary of the endeavor.[41] Khrushchev himself backed away from his bold words on the topic during the course of 1962 for fear that a separate peace would further exacerbate the strains in Soviet relations with the Western Allies. Yet a provocative move also seemed ill advised once Washington and Moscow began to reach agreement on major European issues in the first half of 1963. The GDR was going to have to do without a peace treaty.[42]

Absent a victory on this more fundamental Cold War question, Ulbricht returned to the familiar problem of recognition. The GDR had made sporadic progress since the construction of the Berlin Wall and the Belgrade Conference. Two East German consulates opened in 1962 (Cambodia and Iraq), and one consulate and one trade mission followed in the spring of 1963 (Yemen and Algeria, respectively). This was not a terribly vigorous pace, however, and consular relations were hardly a satisfactory substitute for diplomatic relations.[43] East German diplomats were able to reap "declarations of sympathy and promises, but not tangible improvements," confessed State Secretary Otto Winzer, the Foreign Ministry's guiding figure, in June 1963.[44] The opening of an East German embassy in Havana was no consolation, for Cuba's obvious drift into the Soviet camp made it unlikely that nonaligned powers would consider emulating this example. At any rate, West Germany's sharp reaction had underscored once again the potential severity of the Hallstein Doctrine. The diplomatic balance between East and West Germany was positively humbling. In mid-1963 the GDR enjoyed consular relations with seven noncommunist states: Egypt, Syria, Yemen, Iraq, Burma, Cambodia, and Indonesia. Official, government-level trade missions could be found in a further ten countries: Finland, Guinea, Ghana, Mali, Morocco, Algeria, Lebanon, Sudan, India, and Ceylon. On an informal level, seventeen states, mainly in Latin America and Europe, tolerated the presence of East German chambers of commerce within their borders.[45] Nearly three dozen noncommunist governments around the world were thus willing to deal with East German authorities in some fashion. In addition, the GDR enjoyed full diplomatic relations with thirteen communist nations. It would almost have sounded impressive, were it not for the Federal Republic's numbers: diplomatic relations with ninety states at the beginning of 1963 and with ninety-eight by the end of the year.[46] For all the GDR's efforts, the gap was widening, not narrowing.

This trend was particularly upsetting now that the Federal Republic, through Schröder's policy of movement, was establishing a foothold in Eastern Europe. The danger was all too clear: a West German presence in capitals such as Warsaw threatened to weaken solidarity among the socialist powers and isolate the GDR within its own camp. One of the Politburo's first concerns was thus to step up East Germany's own political, economic, cultural, and public relations work in Eastern Europe.[47] Another priority was to ensure that the GDR's Warsaw Pact allies did not make things too easy for Bonn. The Federal Republic was obviously trying to avoid establishing anything so formal as consular or diplomatic relations with the states of Eastern Europe. This approach would allow Bonn to achieve its aims without simultaneously undermining the basic principles of the Hallstein Doctrine. The Politburo accordingly demanded that its allies publicize the trade missions as a first step toward diplomatic relations and that they grant West Germany consular rights only in the form of published treaties. If all went well, the GDR would be able to use these precedents to advance its own efforts to gain consular and diplomatic representation elsewhere in the world.[48] Such hopes were not to be fulfilled; Poland, Hungary, Bulgaria, and Romania all acquiesced in the Federal Republic's desire to establish the most rudimentary trade missions possible. Only Czechoslovakia met East German expectations by refusing to accept Bonn's formulas.[49] The policy of movement did not boomerang back against the Federal Republic after all.

Since the financial and economic turbulence of the early 1960s, the East Germans had relied almost exclusively on declamatory diplomacy to curry favor in the nonaligned world. This pattern continued in April 1963 with Ulbricht's new Seven Point Plan of Wisdom and Good Will, intended to form the basis for agitation and propaganda throughout the spring and summer. The basic thrust was, as usual, to contrast the GDR's interest in disarmament with the Federal Republic's aggressive drive to acquire nuclear weapons.[50] Such arguments fit easily into the image the East Germans had been painting since 1961, or even 1958—that of West Germany as the chief troublemaker in Europe. Now that the danger of war had diminished substantially, however, it was harder to argue that nonaligned governments would be striking a decisive blow for peace by recognizing the socialist regime in East Berlin. With the advent of détente, the GDR's pacific jargon was bringing diminishing returns. As many as 1 million brochures outlining the Seven Point Plan were printed in East Berlin and distributed worldwide, but the contents were instantly forgotten.[51] Even those leaders who responded enthusiastically to East German rhetoric, such as Nkrumah of Ghana and Modibo Keita of Mali, showed extreme caution when it came to formalizing ties with the SED regime. In April 1963 Nkrumah agreed to open a Ghanaian office in East Berlin, but he adamantly refused to endow it with consular status. In the face of East German insistence that something grander than a mere trade office was called for, Ghana's leaders settled on the formula "economic and trade mission," a nearly intangible enhancement.[52] After five years of engagement in sub-Saharan Africa, the GDR had yet to plant a single consulate there.

One solution was, of course, to find more effective propaganda themes. Ulbricht's seventieth birthday was celebrated on a lavish scale; flatterers in East Berlin characterized the receptions in countries such as Syria, Cambodia, Burma, and Indonesia as knockout successes.[53] Nevertheless, the putative cult of personality surrounding Ulbricht offered no compelling reason why leaders in these countries should embrace the GDR to the detriment of relations with the Federal Republic. Negative advertising offered more potential. In July 1963 the SED implemented a boycott on trade with

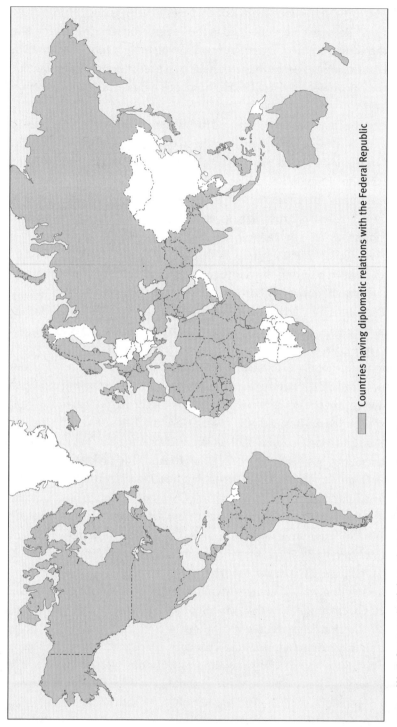

■ Countries having diplomatic relations with the Federal Republic

MAP 3. West Germany's Diplomatic Network, December 1963

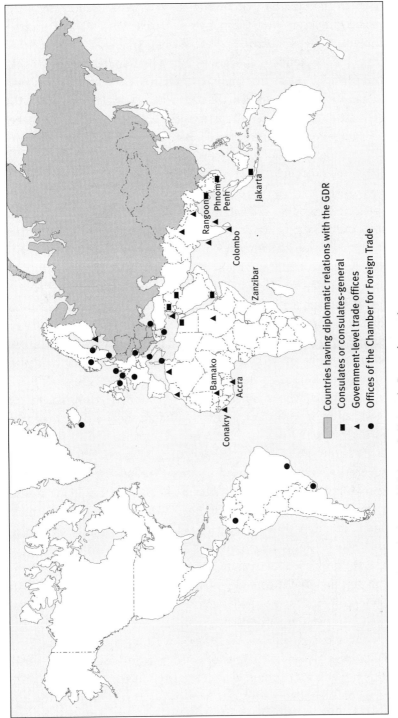

Countries having diplomatic relations with the GDR

■ Consulates or consulates-general

▲ Government-level trade offices

● Offices of the Chamber for Foreign Trade

Rangoon
Phnom Penh
Jakarta
Colombo
Zanzibar
Bamako
Accra
Conakry

MAP 4. East Germany's Trade, Consular, and Diplomatic Network, December 1963

South Africa—an otherwise promising market—in order to mount a more convincing attack on West Germany's extensive ties with the apartheid government. By September 1964, East German propagandists had cleverly synthesized their standard allegations into a pseudodocumentary booklet charging that the revanchist, militarist, racist West German government was cooperating with Pretoria in the production of nuclear weapons.[54] Still more effective (and more accurate) was the East German drive to expose West German–Portuguese military cooperation. In light of Portugal's ruthless suppression of the national liberation movements in Angola and Mozambique, the GDR could count on an African audience whenever it aired such topics.[55]

Increasingly, though, officials in East Berlin expressed doubts about the GDR's exclusive reliance on proclamations of solidarity with the Third World. Blanket propaganda campaigns were easily mounted but did not speak to the interests and ambitions of individual leaders.[56] Ulbricht, impatient at the ongoing discrimination his government had to endure, prodded party and state circles in East Berlin to think more systematically about how to "break through" the Hallstein Doctrine. The Foreign Ministry proposed singling out two countries in each major grouping—Latin America, sub-Saharan Africa, Asia, and the Arab countries—for special attention. This seemed unrealistic to Hermann Axen, chairman of the SED's foreign policy commission, who commented that "our strength is insufficient" for a head-to-head fight with West Germany in more than two or three states worldwide.[57] At length the Foreign Ministry narrowed its choice of "main points of concentration" to four: Ghana, Brazil, Ceylon, and the East African Federation. The list betrayed a marked preference for new targets rather than familiar scenarios; by this point the GDR's diplomats understood very well that a country like Egypt was in no hurry to establish diplomatic relations. It was easier to place hope in previously untested waters—Uganda, Kenya, and Tanganyika, for example, which had all just received their independence from Britain and were reportedly poised to form an anti-imperialist confederation in East Africa.[58] Algeria, liberated from France in 1962 after a vicious colonial war, seemed almost as promising to many East German observers. In late September 1963 the SED's foreign policy commission ranked Algeria with Indonesia, Burma, Egypt, and Finland as "secondary points of concentration"—sites where further attention might lay the groundwork for "partial successes" in the future.[59]

These conversations were laced with constant references to the GDR's economic weakness vis-à-vis the Federal Republic. The Foreign Ministry

THE PERILS OF DÉTENTE

noted in all frankness that East Germany's trade volume with Indonesia amounted to a mere 4 percent of the West German figure; in Burma, too, the West German trade position seemed unassailable. If Ceylon qualified as a "main point of concentration," this had as much to do with the Federal Republic's declining trade volume there as with the political tenor of the government of Sirimavo Bandaranaike.[60] To many discussants, the obvious procedure was to coordinate East Germany's efforts with the other East European countries; in Algeria, for example, the GDR could undertake initiatives in conjunction with the Soviet Union's recent credit offer. If France, Britain, and the United States continued to assist the Federal Republic in upholding the Hallstein Doctrine, surely the GDR's allies could play a similar role in *opposing* the doctrine in designated target countries.[61] Here again, Hermann Axen played the pessimist, observing that the Warsaw Pact—and even its economic counterpart, the Council for Mutual Economic Assistance—lacked the proper mechanisms for coordinating economic relations beyond the socialist world. Gerhard Weiss, deputy minister of trade, cited a comment by Ulbricht to the effect that one should not exaggerate the degree of common interests among the socialist countries.[62] By early 1964, East German functionaries had concluded that any further progress toward "smashing" the Hallstein Doctrine was contingent on the GDR's own financial sacrifices in the Third World.

The prospect of lending millions of marks in development aid was slightly less daunting now that the GDR's economy had begun growing again. Two years after the Berlin Wall had locked East Germany's population in place, the internal situation was stable enough to allow for the return of long-term planning. Ulbricht's New Economic System of Planning and Direction, introduced in June 1963, encouraged functionaries to map out the GDR's economic development through 1970.[63] Within this larger framework, nearly 1 billion Valutamarks (VM, an East German accounting unit worth slightly less than one DM in the 1960s) could be set aside for the pursuit of Ulbricht's foreign policy goals.[64] This was an enormous leap beyond the scale of East Berlin's earlier possibilities and marked the onset of its first serious capital aid program.

The new approach was first deployed in Southeast Asia. Bruno Leuschner, a top planning expert and deputy prime minister, toured the region in January and February 1964 as Ulbricht's personal emissary. Leuschner's mission was to wield government credits in a manner that achieved political gains—the elevation of East Germany's status—while also serving the GDR's economic interests. Ideally, the target countries would use the credits to pay for industrial equipment, helping to secure markets for East Germany's steel and metal exports. The recipients would later repay the loan with whichever foodstuffs and raw materials were of greatest utility to East Germans. In the best-case scenario, these two goals would mesh harmoniously. The GDR's credits would finance the construction of processing plants in the developing world that produced goods of particular interest for the GDR.[65] These aspirations represented little more than wishful thinking; but the utilitarian nature of the Politburo's reasoning is noteworthy, for it marks an effort to prove that the millions about to be spent undermining the Hallstein Doctrine would not diminish East Germany's economic well-being.

Leuschner's itinerary brought him to five countries. In each case he made offers in strictest secrecy: VM 30 million to Cambodia, VM 60 million to Burma, VM 120 million to Indonesia, VM 200 million to India, and VM 200 million to Ceylon.[66] The sums were largely theoretical, contingent on a long series of future negotiations about the projects to be funded. East Berlin had an interest in dragging out the process as much as possible so as to extract a number of political concessions along the way. Given the rigidity inherent in the East German concept—the credits were, after all, tied to a narrow palate of industrial offerings from the GDR—India and Indonesia did not signal much interest. For the less populous countries on the list, however, Leuschner's offers compared favorably with the levels of aid made available by West Germany.[67] Ceylon, as one of East Berlin's prime "points of concentration," received the most lavish attention. Sirimavo Bandaranaike, the world's first woman prime minister, had been making friendly comments about the GDR almost since she came to power in 1960. During a tour of Warsaw Pact capitals in October 1963, she affirmed repeatedly that "two states exist in the territory of Germany."[68] Up to this point, the GDR's presence in Ceylon had been limited to a trade mission, so Bandaranaike was widely expected to greet Leuschner with the news that an East German consulate would now be welcome in the capital city, Colombo.

In itself, the opening of yet another East German consulate was nothing spectacular. For East Berlin, though, it marked a triumph for the notion that the GDR could advance steadily by focusing a package of financial incentives on carefully chosen "main points of concentration" such as Ceylon. This was surely a comforting notion for an elite that lived and ruled by means of painstaking, centrally dictated plans. Thus it was quite ironic that, even as Leuschner's visit was still under way, the GDR landed an even greater victory in a place where no East German diplomats had set foot before January 1964. The setting was Zanzibar, the "spice island" just off the shores of Tanganyika in East Africa. In mid-January, one month after Britain had bestowed independence on the colony, Chinese-backed revolutionaries overthrew the government of Zanzibar and established a radical republic. Although the island's explosive social tension was largely ethnic in nature, outside parties interpreted the revolution in Cold War terms.[69] The United States and West Germany, conscious of Britain's reservations, hesitated to recognize the new government, which had, in fact, bloodily eliminated the ruling class left in place by the departing British colonialists. Authorities in East Berlin, having fewer reservations about such matters, instantly welcomed the new regime. Their gesture was reciprocated on January 28, 1964, when the government of Zanzibar established diplomatic relations with the GDR.[70] The East Germans were finally to get an embassy in a country that, while leftist, was not explicitly communist. Here was an island nation on such a small scale—the population numbered no more than 300,000—that East German aid could transform it into a showcase of socialist benevolence. In the most unlikely of places, a breakthrough had come at last.

"New Measures" in Ceylon and Zanzibar

The coincidence of East German gains in Ceylon and Zanzibar touched off an unusual reaction in Bonn. The Ceylonese ambassador in Bonn had predicted, reasonably enough, that Bonn would "grumble" about an East German consulate in Ceylon but would undertake no serious measures in response.[71] Comments by West Germany's departing ambassador in Colombo, Theodor Auer, substantiated this view; in December 1963 Auer had remarked that a consulate "would not constitute a major problem" so long as no formal exequatur was issued to the East German consul.[72]

It was Bandaranaike's misfortune that her decision came when the Foreign Office was training its sights on the GDR's international activities with greater precision and zeal than ever before. In the spring of 1963, Schröder and Carstens had comprehensively reorganized the Foreign Office, grouping all the desks pertaining to the Third World in a single department. Under the direction of Josef Jansen, a fiercely anticommunist Catholic, and Alexander Böker, his deputy, the Countries Department had become the chief vehicle for prosecuting the isolation campaign.[73] "The defensive battle against the SBZ constitutes the very daily bread of my entire department," wrote Jansen proudly in late 1964. "In truth everyone here, especially the younger colleagues, is eagerly working to prevail in this struggle."[74] Such fire did not, however, diminish the sense of pessimism and desperation in Bonn. On the contrary, the more exhaustively West Germany could monitor its rival's progress, the more daunting seemed the task of staving off its recognition.[75] In February 1964 the desk officers of Jansen's Countries Department sketched some rather bleak pictures about what might happen if Leuschner got his consulate in Ceylon. His next stop after Colombo was New Delhi; might India, too, relent and establish consular relations with the GDR? Zanzibar's recognition of East Germany—which West German diplomats were still scrambling to reverse—placed further pressure on the Foreign Office. A failure to act against Ceylon just might "set off unpredictable chain reactions throughout the nonaligned world," read one memorandum signed by Jansen. At any rate, Ceylon, unlike India, was an easy target that Bonn could strike without measurable economic risk.[76]

State Secretary Rolf Lahr, Carstens's junior colleague at the Foreign Office, was remarkably candid in conveying this reasoning to Ceylonese officials on February 7, 1964, the day Leuschner was due to arrive in Colombo. "For a long time, the Federal Government has observed with growing concern the attempts of the SBZ to extend its position abroad," Lahr pointed out. "A continuation of this trend would damage the interests of the German people most seriously." Bandaranaike's plan for an East German consulate in Colombo was deeply objectionable, since "the example of Ceylon could lead other states to allow SBZ consulates as well. . . . The Federal Government is determined not to tolerate such an unfriendly act by Ceylon, and reserves the right to respond accordingly."[77] By this point, though, Bandaranaike had long since made up her mind, and Lahr's strongly worded telegram did not faze her. The GDR's consulate opened as expected on February 14, 1964.

In the meantime, the situation in Zanzibar went from bad to worse. On the weekend of February 6–7, a junior West German diplomat had struck a deal with the new regime in Zanzibar. The Federal Republic would ignore any earlier comments about recognizing the GDR and establish diplomatic relations with the revolutionary government forthwith. The one prerequisite was that no East German missions be allowed on the island.[78] This "calculated risk" on Bonn's part, an improvised "bulge" in the Hallstein Doctrine designed to accommodate the confusing situation on the island, quickly turned sour.[79] On February 12 Erhard's government publicized the guarantees it had received from the Zanzibari government and indicated that it would soon become the first Western country to take up relations with the People's Republic of Zanzibar—an announcement that raised eye-

THE PERILS OF DÉTENTE

brows in London but was welcomed in Washington.[80] Yet Zanzibari leaders refused to confirm these arrangements and allowed an East German ambassador to present his credentials.

On February 19 Erhard's cabinet opted to backtrack. Even as the United States and Britain were preparing to follow Bonn's lead in establishing relations with Zanzibar, the Federal Republic announced that it would not do so after all. The State Department showed considerable annoyance at Bonn's reversal, insisting that the situation in Zanzibar was not yet irretrievable. Officials in Washington recalled the example of Guinea in March 1960, when West Germany's measured diplomacy had averted a recognition of the GDR by Sékou Touré.[81] Coincidentally, Bonn's man in Tanganyika—and for a brief period the designated ambassador to Zanzibar as well—was Herbert Schroeder, the very ambassador to Guinea who had pleaded with Brentano to be patient in 1960. This time, however, Schroeder counseled firmness. In rejecting formal relations with the island regime, Erhard's government hoped to make the boundaries of West German tolerance clear.[82] However, this was scarcely a satisfactory or intimidating punishment, given the absence of West German commitments to the island. True to form, the GDR exploited its window of opportunity by showering Zanzibar with aid and special deliveries, thereby earning favor with the revolutionary leaders and entrenching itself quite deeply in just a few short months.[83]

Ceylon's transgression was less weighty than Zanzibar's, and the Foreign Office immediately ruled out a break in diplomatic relations. Attention focused instead on economic reprisals—the freezing of West German aid. Bonn's chargé in Colombo warned against any spectacular moves to slash aid programs, since this was likely to touch off an emotional counterreaction in Ceylon. The State Department provided similar advice based on its own recent experiences.[84] Yet the Foreign Office was no longer judging the situation in Colombo on the level of German-Ceylonese relations. If Bonn's measures antagonized the Bandaranaike government and drove it to recognize the GDR, so be it: "The price of a break with Ceylon would not be too high, if thereby a further expansion of the SBZ's influence could be prevented," wrote Jansen.[85] As matters stood, the appearance of an East German consulate in Colombo provided West Germany with a sterling opportunity to part with precedent and to apply economic sanctions—"our strongest political weapon"—in a new way. The reprisals against Ceylon could serve as the foundation of a new, more comprehensive Hallstein Doctrine.[86] Though Erhard's cabinet did not take a position on these far-reaching implications, it adopted the recommendations of the Foreign Ministry on February 19, proclaiming that development aid to Ceylon would be terminated at once.

The amount in question was not overwhelming. Most of the DM 40 million ($10 million) in capital aid that Bonn offered Ceylon in 1961 had already been disbursed, and the Foreign Office considered it inadvisable to halt those technical assistance programs that were still under way. This left the capital aid agreement of November 1963, worth DM 6 million ($1.5 million) in long-term financial support, as the only program available for immediate liquidation.[87] Even for a poor island nation, this was hardly a princely sum, but it was the *principle* that the Federal Republic found so compelling, and Ceylon so upsetting. With good reason, Bandaranaike's government saw itself as the victim of discrimination. Bonn was treating Ceylon differently from the other nonaligned countries entertaining consular relations with East Berlin.[88] Certain West German newspapers, while welcoming the government's show of vigor, also expressed reservations at this seeming double standard.[89] Erhard's government presented two main arguments in defense of its new approach. First, the building of the Berlin Wall had revealed the true character of the SED regime more clearly than before; thus Bonn had greater cause to be angry with governments that drew closer to the GDR after August 1961.[90] Second, on a more general plane, Bonn asserted its right to respond as each case demanded: "Circumstances are so differentiated in each locale that there is no patent formula. . . . Each case requires thorough analysis and a consideration of those measures which are specially suited and necessary."[91] These words by a government spokesman on February 19, 1964, do not have a particularly revolutionary ring, but they marked a fundamental departure in the practice of the Hallstein Doctrine. Bonn was attempting to deny the role of precedent in the pursuit of its isolation policy.

Thinking in terms of precedents came naturally to jurists like Hallstein, and indeed the doctrine itself was built around the desire to avert the creation of unwanted precedents. The Foreign Office worked under the assumption—almost certainly justified—that if Bonn allowed one country to recognize the GDR, others would insist on doing so. In resisting such a development, the Federal Republic made constant use of argument by precedent. West German diplomats pointed out that not a single noncommunist country had ever dared to recognize East Germany, so there was little to be gained by being the first. Yet precedent had proved to be a double-edged sword, for whenever a leader (most commonly Nasser) had moved one step closer to recognition of the GDR, the Federal Republic had found itself unable to deny others the same privilege. It was this dynamic that the Foreign Office sought to transform in an energetic burst of planning and discussion in the spring of 1964.[92] It was a liberating moment for West German officials; they sketched out the contours of the new approach with a haste that testified to pent-up frustration.[93] The rejection of precedent meant that the Hallstein Doctrine would no longer be universal in its application. Different regions would be held to different standards. What Egypt could do, Ceylon could not. Quite arbitrarily, the desk officer for sub-Saharan Africa suggested that Bonn set an even stricter standard for his region: the opening of East German *trade missions* should be occasion for West German countermeasures.[94] Later in 1964, State Secretary Carstens took this principle still further and sought to dissuade Cyprus from accepting an office of the East German chamber of commerce, regardless of the fact that such offices could be found in both Greece and Turkey, Bonn's NATO allies in the region.[95]

Coupled with the departure from precedent came efforts to adopt a new scale of punishments. Except in the case of Cuba, which involved a full recognition of the GDR, the Federal Republic had never actually carried out economic reprisals against countries that moved closer to the GDR. On the contrary, countries that flirted with East Germany tended to draw *more* West German aid, not *less*—a pattern that officials in Bonn registered privately with some dismay.[96] Once the Erhard cabinet had broken the ice with its economic countermeasures against Ceylon, however, activists at the Foreign Office hastened to forge an entire "arsenal of economic-political weapons."[97] Alexander Böker came forward with some truly extreme proposals. What if Bonn encouraged its citizens to boycott certain imports from the country in question? Or used its influence with the EEC or the World Bank to damage that country's interests? Or aided and abetted ethnic or separatist movements within that country?[98] Böker did not expect the Federal Republic to resort to any of these draconian punishments; he merely envisioned issuing new threats that would genuinely intimidate most leaders in the developing world. Though Böker's suggestions were quickly set aside, other ideas that might at one time have seemed drastic—such as interference with trade by cutting back Hermes credits or abrogating trade treaties—were now discussed calmly as appropriate countermeasures against upgrading the status of the GDR.[99]

In a circular instruction to West German diplomatic missions in June 1964, Carstens outlined the "new measures" being prepared in defense of

Bonn's "claim to sole representation" of Germany. Carstens predicted that the measures in question would widen Bonn's maneuvering room while ensuring a more rational distribution of development aid.[100] For all their theoretical promise, however, the new measures only further complicated the prosecution of West Germany's isolation campaign in the Third World. Bonn's move against Ceylon soon hardened into a precedent in its own right, one that impelled the Erhard government to take a firmer line in the next crisis over consular relations. Under other circumstances, the news from East Africa in late April 1964 would have produced an ecstatic reaction in Bonn. Julius Nyerere's government in Tanganyika had negotiated a hasty political federation with Zanzibar in an effort to preempt the ominous activities of the GDR and China on the wayward island.[101] The new United Republic of Tanganyika and Zanzibar—later christened Tanzania— was to be headed by Nyerere, one of Bonn's closest partners in the developing world. Nyerere had requested West German assistance in outfitting and training Tanganyika's air force and sea patrol; this appeared to give Erhard's government outstanding leverage in securing the abolition of the lone East German embassy in all of Africa.[102] Yet the outcome was messier, thanks to the refusal of either German state to back down.

At first Nyerere anticipated no problem in demoting the East German embassy on Zanzibar to the status of a trade mission; this was a position generally acceptable to Bonn's Foreign Office, though officials such as Böker still hoped for a complete elimination of the GDR from the island.[103] However, Nyerere found that the East Germans had forged deep ties with Zanzibari president (and now Tanzanian vice-president) Abeid Karume. Throughout May 1964 Karume and the East Germans resisted all efforts to close the GDR's embassy on the island, demonstratively signing a "friendship treaty" and otherwise carrying on as if Zanzibar remained an independent, sovereign state. Nyerere, concerned lest the very union itself founder on the problem of German representation, suggested a compromise solution: the GDR would retain a consulate on the island with authority extending throughout the united Tanzania.[104] Just a few months earlier, this solution might have been accepted grudgingly by the Federal Republic, particularly since Nyerere expressed his intention of restricting the consul's powers along the lines of the "Cairo model." Having made an example of Ceylon, though, Erhard's government refused to sanction the appearance of an East German consulate in united Tanzania.[105] In late June, Nyerere disregarded Bonn's objections and decreed the transformation of all embassies on Zanzibar into consulates. From Dar-es-Salaam, a livid Ambassador Schroeder cabled back to Bonn that it was time to pull the plug on military assistance to Nyerere's government. This would probably not change Nyerere's mind, added the ambassador, and it might even result in a break with Tanzania; but at least this would hold back other African leaders from a similar upgrading of the GDR.[106]

Erhard's government refrained from acting on this rash advice, thanks to the sobering spectacle of its rival's behavior. The East German representatives on Zanzibar refused to comply with Nyerere's decree, provoking the leader's wrath. An editorial ghostwritten by Nyerere himself accused the GDR of trying to "buy" the foreign policy of Zanzibar through aid, and of sabotaging the union of Zanzibar and Tanganyika for its own selfish reasons.[107] Awed by the extent to which Karume had been "bewitched by the East Germans," Nyerere nevertheless considered the situation too delicate to insist on anything less than consular status for the GDR in united Tanzania.[108] Nyerere's appeals for patience met with sympathy among high-level West German officials; they saw an opportunity to seize the moral high ground by showing understanding for the difficulties faced by the fledgling union. Carstens agreed that the final determination of East Germany's status could be deferred until the spring of 1965, when the union would celebrate its first anniversary.[109] The problem of Tanzania did not disappear entirely in West Germany; politicians and the press expressed concern about the continuing anomaly of a GDR "embassy" on Zanzibar.[110] Nyerere ameliorated matters somewhat by warning other African leaders about the dangers of dealing with the East German regime. Yet the disadvantages of *West* German aid were also becoming clear to Tanzania's neighbors, and the newly independent republic of Zambia turned down an offer of financial assistance from Bonn rather than accept the political strings attached.[111]

The struggle over Zanzibar revealed just how intense the competition between the rival German states had become. A decade earlier, officials in Bonn had spoken of the Hallstein Doctrine as a "dam" erected to avert an elemental "flood" or "wave" of recognitions. But in the five years since 1959, the GDR had expanded its network of missions considerably, bringing East and West German diplomats into a situation of heated rivalry in many Third World capitals. Military metaphors now seemed best suited to describe the situation. "We're fighting here. We're at the front, and we feel like we're under siege," intoned the West German press attaché in Lagos, Nigeria.[112] Officials spoke of gaining or losing "terrain" or "positions" vis-à-vis the GDR. Foreign Minister Schröder himself favored these military analogies; he characterized the West German representatives in the Warsaw Pact capitals as combatants maneuvering across "completely mined terrain."[113] In many ways the adoption of new measures for the enforcement of Bonn's isolation policy was merely a tactical adjustment to the perception of close combat with the other side's diplomats. Rather than allowing the East Germans to advance into the "approach" (*Vorfeld*) of recognition, the Federal Republic would undertake preemptive strikes.[114] In July 1964 the Foreign Office organized its most ambitious effort yet to catalog and routinize Bonn's deterrence measures. Appropriately enough, the schema bore a military appellation: the mobilization plan.[115]

The Apex of West German Vigilance

During most of 1964, one event on the diplomatic horizon provided a focal point for West German energies in the Third World: the Second Non-Aligned Conference, to be held in Cairo in early October. For officials in Bonn, such conferences were inherently unnerving.[116] No matter how smoothly the Hallstein Doctrine functioned, it simply did not offer any serious protection against the possibility that a group of states might jointly decide to recognize the GDR. Would the Federal Republic truly decide to break relations with a large handful of neutral states at once? Few in the Foreign Office thought so.[117] Scarred by memories of the Belgrade Conference in 1961, when Indonesia, Ghana, and a few other states seemed poised to recognize the GDR in unison, West German officials worked tirelessly to anticipate and forestall a similar challenge at the Cairo Conference. Bonn's position in 1964 seemed even less favorable than before, for now *three* countries—Yugoslavia, Cuba, and Zanzibar—could be counted on to proselytize on behalf of the GDR. An assortment of other states, including Ceylon and Algeria as well as perennial suspects Ghana, Mali, Indonesia, and Burma, constituted a pool of likely candidates for upgrading the status of the GDR in a unitary action.[118] A preconference meeting held in Colombo, Ceylon, passed without incident, but Indian officials advised the Federal Republic that the German Question would probably appear on the final agenda in Cairo.[119] Defensive preparations for the showdown in October overshadowed all of the Erhard government's positive initiatives toward reunification; more so than ever before, the nonrecognition campaign moved to the center of West German diplomacy.

Bonn's narrow focus on the GDR problem afforded the Western Allies a mercifully cost-effective means of demonstrating their continuing loyalty. Larger issues such as German unification were becoming an embarrassment to the Allies, particularly the Johnson administration. In January 1964 Erhard and Schröder had attempted to launch a "Germany Initiative" designed to place the problem of unity back on the international agenda.[120] Quadripartite discussions in Washington between the Federal Republic and the Western Allies dragged on throughout the spring without result. Secretary of State Dean Rusk saw no point in raising the German Question with the Soviets. At best it would get nowhere, thanks to Moscow's intransigence; at worst it would risk a renewed crisis over Berlin.[121] French officials assumed that the German initiative was driven by domestic politics and was thus a low priority for the alliance. On this count at least, Bonn's Foreign Office managed to convince the Quai d'Orsay otherwise during bilateral consultations in March 1964. West German officials explained what was really at stake: if the Allies did not make a show of activity on the German Question, the trend toward recognition of the GDR would accelerate.[122] Perhaps without even realizing it, the Foreign Office had reversed its earlier priorities. Previously, the West had discouraged others from recognizing the GDR in order to keep the German Question open; now Bonn seemed to be keeping the German Question open in order to maintain the sanctity of its isolation campaign. Small wonder, then, that both France and Britain showed renewed vigor in their support of the Hallstein Doctrine in the mid-1960s.[123] Cooperation with Bonn in this area could help generate goodwill on questions of greater interest to London and Paris— without their getting entangled in something so vague and risky as a "Germany Initiative."

The occasion for a demonstrative Allied gesture came in June 1964, when the Soviet Union and the GDR signed a treaty of "friendship, mutual support and cooperation."[124] This document cautiously avoided challenging Allied rights in Germany or Berlin; in this sense, it marked the last word on the Berlin Crisis touched off by Khrushchev's ultimatum of November 1958. It certainly contained vastly less than the separate peace treaty Ulbricht had once clamored for.[125] So far as Western analysts could ascertain, the treaty's principal aim was to enhance the GDR's prestige on the eve of the Cairo Conference. This coincided with other reports that the Soviet Union was prepared to redouble its efforts in support of the GDR's international pretensions.[126] For the Western Allies, the reiteration of their standpoint on the German Question came as a reflex action. Two days *before* the signing of the Soviet–East German treaty, they undertook a joint démarche in Moscow stating that they stood by their rights in Germany and that free elections were the only acceptable path to reunification. It was the

French government that first hit on the idea of publicizing the text of this démarche as a public affirmation of Allied unity on Germany.[127] On June 26 the final, amended Allied text was released, stating in all clarity that the government in Bonn was the "only German government freely and legitimately constituted and therefore entitled to speak for the German people in international affairs. The Three Governments do not recognize the East German regime nor the existence of a state in eastern Germany."[128]

On a rhetorical level, then, the Allies supplied a ringing endorsement of Bonn's unification policy, including the demand that the "principle of self-determination" be applied to Germany. Erhard's government hastened to circulate the text to its diplomatic partners around the world under the pompous title "Germany Declaration of the Three Powers."[129] For their part, the Allies undertook a supporting démarche of their own in Africa; energetic French appeals reached twenty-one francophone statesmen on July 15 and 16, immediately before the opening of a summit meeting of the Organization of African Unity.[130] In early September the Allies extended the range of their démarches to Asia and Latin America, strongly cautioning the fifty-plus leaders invited to the Cairo Conference against any steps toward a direct or indirect recognition of the East German regime. The task of coordinating these démarches fell to the quadripartite group in Washington, the same institution that had spent so mainly fruitless hours debating Erhard's "Germany Initiative" earlier in the year. Here, too, the constructive yet elusive goal of unification yielded to the more immediate, negative task of blocking East German gains.[131]

Naturally, Moscow and East Berlin did not remain passive in the months leading up to the Cairo Conference. Aside from circulating numerous memoranda elaborating East German views on world events—typically attacks on the Federal Republic for supporting Portuguese imperialism, South African apartheid, or the nuclear arming of the Bundeswehr—the SED regime launched an impressive number of goodwill missions to neutral countries during September 1964.[132] Unbeknownst to Bonn, however, planners in East Berlin set fairly modest goals for the upcoming conference. As early as May 1964, the SED's foreign policy commission had concluded that it would be unrealistic to expect dramatic events in Cairo such as a collective decision to recognize the GDR.[133] State Secretary Otto Winzer observed three months later that, compared with 1961, the German Question no longer seemed a danger to world peace, so nonaligned leaders were less inclined to take a position on the matter. "On top of this, West Germany's pressure on the neutrals has significantly increased," Winzer noted laconically.[134]

Consequently, East German diplomats and "special ambassadors" concentrated their efforts on achieving a verbal victory—getting a few key SED concepts, like the existence of two German states and the necessity of German-German negotiations, accepted in the final communiqué of the Cairo Conference.[135]

Bonn's approach was rather more aggressive. As usual, the Foreign Office found it difficult to field a sizable number of special emissaries, despite elaborate plans to mobilize a wide circle of Bundestag deputies, journalists, and academics in support of the Hallstein Doctrine.[136] In the realm of propaganda, though, Bonn put out a vast amount of material intended to discredit the GDR. One circular released intelligence on the internal behavioral guidelines of East German missions abroad in order to draw attention to "the enforced collective lifestyle and the systematic eavesdropping" characteristic of the GDR.[137] Even so, the real thrust of West German preparation for the Cairo Conference lay in smoothing over relations with key nonaligned countries. As so often in the past, this involved a fresh round of bribes to those countries that were *most* friendly toward the GDR.

By this perverse logic, Yugoslavia, the archenemy of the Hallstein Doctrine, was first in line for concessions from the Federal Republic. Since early 1963, Tito's government had been clamoring for a new round of restitution payments from Bonn for victims of Nazism; it also demanded restrictions on the activities of Croatian émigré groups in the Federal Republic. Belgrade threatened that if Bonn were not forthcoming, it would initiate a worldwide smear campaign against the Federal Republic, including a drive to encourage nonaligned governments to recognize the GDR.[138] Officials in Washington, hoping to prevent an acrimonious feud, restrained Tito for much of 1963. By the spring of 1964, however, the State Department began to sympathize with the Yugoslav standpoint, and Secretary of State Rusk wrote personally to Schröder in April encouraging friendly overtures toward Belgrade.[139] West German officials fumed at the idea that Bonn should offer reparations to a government that was inciting Ceylon and other countries to deepen relations with the GDR.[140] Yet Allied officials saw little evidence of a concerted Yugoslav campaign in the Third World, and Tito's government hotly denied these charges. Pressure from the United States, together with fears about the havoc that Yugoslavia could potentially wreak at the upcoming Cairo Conference, finally led the Foreign Office to take a softer line.[141] On July 16, 1964, the Federal Republic signed an agreement in Belgrade regulating trade and economic relations between the two countries. The text did at least contain a "good-behavior" clause admonishing both sides to "avoid political disturbances," and State Secretary Lahr visited Belgrade discreetly in early September to hear assurances that Yugoslavia would remain inactive at the Cairo Conference.[142] Even so, the signs of rapprochement between West Germany and Yugoslavia touched off "bewilderment and confusion" among those in Bonn who wondered why Erhard's government was showering kindnesses on Belgrade.[143]

In the case of Algeria, too, the Federal Republic rewarded a country suspected of harboring ill intentions. West German relations with the newly independent Algeria had been amicable enough in 1962 and 1963, thanks in no small part to the personal diplomacy of SPD emissary Hans-Jürgen Wischnewski.[144] President Ahmed Ben Bella began drifting to the left, however, and he returned from a trip to Moscow in mid-1964 convinced of the need to move closer to the GDR. One of Ben Bella's close associates published an editorial demanding an outright recognition of the SED regime; the president reportedly wrote to his counterparts in Guinea, Mali, the UAR, and a few other states urging that "something be done" at the upcoming Cairo Conference about the problem of East Germany.[145] West German officials also noted with some concern that the GDR sought the opening of a consulate in Algiers. Bonn's first response was to issue warnings: if Ben Bella acted to upgrade the GDR, the Federal Republic would speak out against further EEC-funded development projects in Algeria.[146] As the nonaligned conference drew nearer, though, Erhard's government dangled positive incentives before the Algerians. In early October Bonn concluded an agreement with Algiers on the implementation of DM 70 million ($17.5 million) in capital aid, destined for an irrigation project of questionable feasibility. The Foreign Office was pleased with this outcome in light of the assurances provided by Ben Bella's officials: no East German consulate in Algiers, and a good-behavior clause in the text of the aid agreement.[147]

In financial terms, Bonn's handling of Egypt was considerably more measured. As was only to be expected, the Federal Republic lavished considerable attention on Nasser. With Cairo serving as the diplomatic fulcrum of Africa and Asia, the Foreign Office wished to ensure that the atmosphere in the Egyptian capital remained friendly to West German interests. Arab experts in Bonn did not anticipate any direct challenge from Nasser, who had taken a moderate line on the German Question since the Belgrade Conference in 1961.[148] They recognized, however, that Cairo expected to be rewarded for its discretion; Egyptian government and industry representatives discussed their "wish lists" openly with visiting West Germans. Yet Erhard's government coyly refrained from making any immediate commitments to Egypt's second five-year plan, indicating only a general willingness to open negotiations *following* the Cairo Conference.[149]

Bonn's main concessions to Egypt were political rather than economic. In June 1964 Erhard remarked informally that Nasser would be welcome to visit Bonn in the first half of 1965. For the Egyptian leader, who had not yet been received in any West European capital, this represented a flattering mark of recognition.[150] Nor was this Erhard's only act of deference toward Nasser. Since early 1963 the Israeli government had been urging Bonn to pass a law prohibiting the participation of German scientists in Egypt's missile program. With an eye toward the Cairo Conference, however, Erhard's cabinet suspended consideration of a draft law put forward by the pro-Israel factions in the CDU and FDP.[151] In addition, the Foreign Office vetoed plans for a meeting between Erhard and Israeli prime minister Levi Eshkol any time before the nonaligned summit.[152] This steady stream of pro-Arab decisions throughout 1964 might have provoked a furious reaction in Tel Aviv were it not for Bonn's secret program of military aid to Israel—a scheme undertaken to compensate the Israelis for the lack of formal political relations. The program dated back to 1962, but in June 1964 Erhard's administration undertook a steep escalation of its military involvement in the Middle East, acquiescing in a U.S.-Israeli scheme to ship 150 American-built tanks via Italy to Israel.[153] These top-secret deliveries represented a remarkably foolhardy endeavor. They were not of any practical use in defusing public pressure for a normalization of relations with Israel, and if discovered, they left Bonn open to Arab charges of double-dealing in its Middle Eastern diplomacy. The Hallstein Doctrine was not, of course, responsible for the poor judgment exercised in Bonn regarding military aid to Israel. The decisions of mid-1964 reflected a more fundamental disarray in the top echelons of Erhard's administration.[154] However, it was Bonn's overriding interest in isolating the GDR that led it to court Nasser so assiduously and, therefore, to prefer only the most clandestine measures in support of Israel.

Whatever the costs, Erhard's government did at least succeed in discouraging the adoption of unwelcome resolutions at the Second Non-Aligned Conference. In the "Program for Peace" drafted by the forty-seven official delegations, the following passage represented the sole commentary on the topic of divided countries: "The Conference considers that one of the causes of international tension lies in the problem of divided nations. It expresses its entire sympathy with the peoples of such countries and upholds their desire to achieve unity. It exhorts the countries concerned to seek a just and lasting solution in order to achieve the unification of their territories by peaceful methods without interference or pressure."[155] There was little overt support here for Bonn's program for unification, based on "self-determination" through free elections in eastern Germany; moreover, the phrase "without interference" might call into question the responsibilities of the four wartime allies for German unity. Yet the text deftly avoided speaking of "two states" in Germany or elsewhere, and it did not explicitly advocate negotiations between Bonn and East Berlin—thereby falling short of the GDR's principal goals for the conference. According to later West German investigations, only Cuba, Ghana, and Mali had urged the adoption of East German formulations, and President Nkrumah was persuaded by his advisers to speak publicly of "two Germanies" rather than "two German states."[156]

Significantly, Alexander Böker's lobbying in Cairo during the conference itself exerted little influence over the deliberations, since the Egyptian government kept the conference delegations as sequestered as possible.[157] Even without extensive cues on the scene from West German diplomats, the nonaligned leaders in Cairo produced a statement that respected Bonn's admonitions against recognizing the SED regime in any form. The rash of West German and Allied démarches in the summer of 1964 had worked.[158] So, too, had Bonn's recent generosity toward potential troublemakers Algeria and Yugoslavia. The ebbing of the Berlin Crisis also played a role, for now there was little incentive for Third World leaders to seek acclaim by taking a strong position on the German Question; the problems of German unification and European security were becoming increasingly tangential to the nonaligned movement.[159] Bonn stood to gain from a shift in focus from East-West to North-South issues. When economics rather than Cold War ideology shaped the terms of debate, the Federal Republic could easily prevail over the GDR. Kenneth Kaunda, leader of the newly independent Zambia, chose to recognize the People's Republic of China and the Federal Republic because of their preponderant populations relative to Taiwan and the GDR—an eminently pragmatic argument.[160]

The Foreign Office took a less sanguine view. Alexander Böker returned from Cairo fuming about the bloated East German staffs there; some 120 to 130 midlevel and senior officials of the SED regime were active at the East German trade mission, the consulate, and the office of the special plenipotentiary to the UAR. By contrast, only 25 such officials served in Bonn's embassy in Cairo, and the political affairs desk there was operated by one lone diplomat.[161] The outcome of the Cairo Conference—which Böker acknowledged was "unexpectedly favorable"—certainly provided little lasting satisfaction for West German diplomats. For one thing, the next major Third World gathering was already in the planning stages; a second Bandung Conference, sponsored primarily by Indonesia and China, was scheduled to take place in Algiers in the spring of 1965. As 1964 drew to a close, Sukarno's Indonesia moved to the top of Bonn's "danger" list, and it seemed unlikely that the opening of an Indonesian consulate in East Berlin could long be averted.[162] In many cases, however, the pessimism in Bonn reflected a shift in perspective rather than a qualitative improvement in the GDR's international presence. Having trained their eyes on the task of blocking *any* East German gains, even those far below the level of diplomatic relations, West German officials found themselves confronting a daunting array of challenges. In Zambia and Dahomey, the Federal Republic intervened against the prospect of East German trade missions. In Kenya, the West German ambassador protested against the propaganda activities of an East German correspondent, hinting that Bonn's aid to Kenya might be jeopardized.[163] Even on the island of Cyprus, where ethnic clashes had led to the stationing of a UN peacekeeping force, Bonn did not step gingerly. When the government of Archbishop Makarios signed an agreement with the GDR providing for a trade mission in Nicosia, the Foreign Office sent a special emissary to browbeat Makarios into downgrading the East German status there.[164] In previous years, none of these episodes would have produced such a fierce reaction; the events of 1964 had done much to radicalize West German attitudes.

For officials in this frame of mind, there was always more that the Federal Republic could be doing. Carstens recommended a stepped-up rotation of high-profile visits to the Third World by West German leaders.[165] Böker called for a more selective staffing of Bonn's embassies in Africa and Asia, with a preference for "younger, energetic and convincing personalities." He also insisted that trade and development aid "must, more so than before, be placed in the service of our unification policy."[166] Rolf Pauls, deputy director of the Foreign Office's Trade and Development Department, came forward in January 1965 with proposals to streamline Bonn's aid practices so that the Federal Republic could respond to diplomatic crises more rapidly and more flexibly. Aid should no longer be tied to particular projects, argued Pauls, and credit terms must be loosened. Most importantly, the trend toward a reduction in Bonn's overall aid program should be reversed.[167] These proposals for intensifying the Hallstein Doctrine reflected a perception that Erhard's government was already backing down from the gritty determination displayed in early 1964. In one celebrated example from late October 1964, the cabinet decided to provide export guarantees for the construction of a cement factory in Puttalam, Ceylon. While acknowledging that export insurance did not, strictly speaking, constitute development aid, the reunification desk and the Countries Department predicted that this gesture would demolish the credibility gained through Bonn's initial retaliation against Ceylon.[168] In a telling indication of the passions involved, Böker wrote to his superior, Josef Jansen, that the government's decision "is causing me sleepless nights here, and has generated shock, demoralization and to some extent outrage among my colleagues."[169]

Ironically, the very adamance of the Foreign Office was beginning to undermine support within Erhard's cabinet for material and political sacrifices in the service of Bonn's isolation policy. In October 1964 the finance minister wrote to Schröder warning against the overpoliticization of development aid; the Economics Ministry seconded this opinion.[170] After the Cairo Conference had already produced one round of expensive preemptive aid agreements, the cabinet was hardly pleased to see three more emergency requests in January 1965, pertaining to Ghana, Indonesia, and Egypt.[171] Walter Scheel of the FDP, head of the Development Aid Ministry, took especially strong exception to the projects being financed in Indonesia. The steel works at Lampong was guaranteed never to produce a profit, given its unfavorable location and the unavailability of raw materials.[172] Key voices outside the cabinet also began to question the tactic of using development aid to "buy" friends or "buy off" opportunistic regimes. At a mixed government and private-sector meeting in January 1965, State Secretary Lahr warned that without a drastic increase in aid funding, the Hallstein Doctrine was in danger of collapsing. Hermann-Josef Abs of the Deutsche Bank replied that the question of German unity would not be decided in the developing countries anyway; that it was typically a country's *overall* position in the Cold War, not the amount of aid it received from one side or other, that determined its attitude toward the GDR; and that the Hallstein Doctrine itself was ripe for reexamination.[173]

These expressions of impatience with Bonn's isolation program came at a critical juncture. For much of 1964, the Foreign Office had subordinated many foreign policy interests to the one objective of securing a favorable outcome at the Cairo Conference. In the aftermath of that conference, the

Erhard government now addressed these other, long-neglected problems—above all, Israel. Pressure for some improvement in relations between West Germany and Israel could no longer be ignored. Bonn's reparations payments were scheduled to end in 1966, thus removing the formal raison d'être of the Israeli purchasing mission in Cologne. March 1966 thus served as a deadline; by that time, the Federal Republic would have to place its ties with Israel on a new basis so that relations did not come to a standstill.[174] A complete absence of official contacts with Israel was simply not acceptable to most West Germans, especially now that the war crimes trials of the 1960s were calling renewed attention to the Holocaust. On this count, another deadline loomed, for after May 1965 the Federal Republic's statute of limitations would prohibit the prosecution of suspected war criminals.[175] Nor had the problem of German rocket experts in Egypt's defense industry completely disappeared. The challenge for Erhard's government at the turn of 1964–65 was to reach some new understanding with Israel on these issues without alienating the leading Arab states.

This task became immensely more complicated in late October, when news leaked of West Germany's secret military assistance to Israel. Although government spokesmen in Bonn refused to confirm these stories, neither did they deny the reports. Henceforth the Federal Republic's credibility throughout the Arab world would be deeply compromised.[176] Neither the Chancellor's Office nor the Foreign Office undertook much to assuage Arab concerns in the following weeks; this mission fell to a relative outsider, Bundestag President Eugen Gerstenmaier, who enjoyed a reputation as a friend to both Israel and the developing world. After meeting with Nasser in Cairo on November 23, Gerstenmaier put forward a three-point "package deal" designed to stabilize West Germany's position in the Middle East: Bonn must cancel all further arms deliveries to Israel immediately, grant substantial new sums in capital and technical assistance to the Arab states, and establish consular, but not diplomatic, relations with Israel.[177]

Whether Gerstenmaier's package deal would have satisfied Arab and Israeli politicians is impossible to say. Nevertheless, if the Erhard government had continued to give top priority to the Hallstein Doctrine, it would certainly have acted more promptly on these proposals, for the reports from Bonn's Middle Eastern posts were truly alarming. The Foreign Office predicted that unless Erhard terminated the military assistance to Israel without delay, the Arab states would retaliate by recognizing the GDR. In Cairo, representatives of the Arab League were already drafting such a resolution.[178] Nasser's government dropped a few hints of its own, first by signing a long-term lease for exhibition space at the GDR's premier trade fair in Leipzig, then by granting permission for an East German cultural institute to open in Cairo.[179] Although the West German ambassador in Cairo tried to pique Nasser's interest with promises of sizable contributions to Egypt's second five-year plan, these carrots remained all too intangible, for they were not backed by any firm plans in Bonn. By contrast, the GDR pledged solid numbers to Egypt at the end of 1964: VM 200 million (nearly $50 million) in government credits and VM 130 million in commercial credits.[180] Erhard did at least renew his invitation to Nasser to visit the Federal Republic in mid-1965, which the latter gladly accepted, but the chancellor was seriously in error if he believed that a resolution of Bonn's Middle Eastern dilemma could wait until Nasser's journey to Bonn.

In the meantime, the question that mattered most—the ongoing flow of tanks to Israel—continued to fester. To some extent this simply reflected the preoccupation of Erhard and Schröder with other issues in the final months of 1964. In November both came under heavy fire from Gaullists in the CDU/CSU for neglecting relations with Paris; in December they struggled to keep afloat the idea of a multilateral nuclear force within NATO.[181] Yet even the decision makers in Bonn who *were* following the situation in the Middle East steadfastly refused to contemplate an abrupt cancellation of the shipments to Israel. Ludger Westrick, head of the Chancellor's Office, remarked that "one cannot simply abrogate treaties unilaterally."[182] Karl Carstens took a similar line, reasoning that the government did not dare breach the contracts signed between Bonn's Defense Ministry and weapons manufacturers in Britain and North America.[183] There was little grand idealism at work here; Westrick and Carstens did not expound any historic duty of the Germans to assist in the defense of the Jewish homeland. But their concern with demonstrating German reliability is nonetheless significant, considering how easily the government could have wriggled out of its commitments. The original agreements with Israel dated back to the era of Adenauer and Strauss and had been sealed with only a peremptory hint of parliamentary approval.[184] Only much later, after the damage had already been done to Bonn's position in the Arab world, did Erhard's government use these excuses to modify the terms of its deliveries to Israel.

The period from November 1964 through January 1965 appears in retrospect to mark the beginning of the end of the Hallstein Doctrine. Without intentionally letting down their guard, leaders in Bonn stopped allowing the nonrecognition campaign to dictate every detail of their policy in the Middle East. This unusual display of West German indifference toward

Arab concerns finally drove Nasser to an act of calculated retaliation.[185] On January 24 the Egyptian press reported that a distinguished visitor would be arriving shortly in Cairo: Walter Ulbricht, first secretary of the SED and chairman of the GDR's State Council. For the first time, the "enemy number one of German unity" would travel outside the Soviet bloc, enjoying the honor and respect accorded other major international figures.[186] Now it was no longer just West Germany's Middle Eastern policy that was in shambles; the entire edifice of its isolation strategy seemed ready to buckle. The memorable headline "Stalingrad on the Nile," published in the conservative *Christ und Welt* on February 5, 1965, foretold a bitter defeat—a turning point in Bonn's arduous campaign against East Berlin.[187]

Chapter 7

The Peculiar Longevity
of a Discredited Doctrine

"After a visit by Ulbricht to Cairo," remarked Foreign Minister Schröder in late January 1965, "the world will look different than it did before."[1] Across West Germany, public figures shared this view, regardless of whether they cheered or lamented the demise of the Hallstein Doctrine. Surprisingly, though, the end was not as nigh as many assumed. Erhard's cabinet handled the Middle Eastern crisis ineptly, leading to a humiliating West German retreat from the region in May 1965. In the Arab world, the old rules of the Hallstein Doctrine no longer applied, since Bonn could not threaten to break diplomatic relations. Yet the global confrontation with East Germany persisted and indeed intensified further as the GDR's economy entered a period of rapid growth. Remarkably, Ulbricht and the SED failed to build on the success in Cairo, proving that Bonn's loss was not automatically East Berlin's gain. At the West German Foreign Office, the "new measures" of 1964 evolved into an offensive program for scaling back the GDR's presence in key nonaligned countries. Nevertheless, continuing success in this arena was not the same as progress toward unification, and Erhard's lack of concrete ideas on this topic became glaringly obvious during 1966. An anxious mood gripped West Germany's political elites, exacerbated by the onset of the republic's first major postwar recession. Erhard's administration was swept away, and with it many of the assumptions about the German Question that had guided Bonn since 1949.

The Debacle: West Germany's Expulsion from the Arab World

For West Germans active in public life, Nasser's invitation to Ulbricht in January 1965 was no mere provocation; it was a dance with the devil himself. Of all the East Germans Nasser might have chosen to consort with, Ulbricht was far and away the most vilified in the West. "Ulbricht is a symbol of everything we reject about the SBZ," observed Franz Krapf, head of the Foreign Office's East-West Department.[2] For this symbol to be seen parading through Cairo was without a doubt the GDR's greatest foreign policy victory since 1949. But did this imply an outright recognition of East Germany on the part of Egypt? Nasser insisted that it did not; but he added that if the flow of weapons to Israel continued, he would not hesitate to pronounce a final, definitive recognition of the GDR.[3] The ambiguous legal implications of Ulbricht's visit and the bluntly menacing pose adopted by Nasser left the members of Erhard's cabinet sharply at odds over how to respond. Should the Federal Republic appease the Egyptian leader in the hope of achieving a postponement or cancellation of the scheduled visit? Or should Bonn instead make an example of Nasser by applying economic and political sanctions? Throughout February, Erhard's administration lurched aimlessly between these two extremes.

Given the agitated state of West German elite opinion, an abject appeasement of Nasser seemed out of the question. Bonn's ambassador in Cairo sent cables imploring the Foreign Office to offer substantial new aid packages and to halt the arms to Israel at once, but the cabinet was hardly inclined to reward Egypt's impudence in this way.[4] The mood in Bonn tended toward defiance. Virtually all political commentators interpreted Nasser's behavior as a form of blackmail.[5] Critics of the Hallstein Doctrine quickly generalized this observation, arguing that Third World statesmen were now routinely playing East and West Germany against one another in order to win more aid from each side.[6] For mainstream politicians, this was no grounds for dispensing with the Hallstein Doctrine altogether. The trick was, rather, to distribute West German aid more discriminatingly, so that it rewarded only those countries that respected the Federal Republic's standpoint. Karl Mommer, a Social Democratic deputy from Berlin, proclaimed that "the Bundestag will not approve one penny in development aid to countries that receive as a guest the divider of the German nation."[7] Franz-Josef Strauss, chairman of the CSU, took a similar line, remarking that the government should save its aid for Bonn's true friends.[8]

Schröder was more cautious. His main concern throughout February was to keep the crisis from spiraling out of control. If Bonn failed to reach an understanding with Nasser, the Egyptian president just might proceed with a full recognition of the GDR, leaving the Federal Republic with two uncomfortable alternatives: breaking relations with Egypt or letting the Hallstein Doctrine collapse. In Schröder's view, it would be folly for West Germany to break with Egypt; this might well lead other Arab states to break with Bonn (or recognize the GDR) out of solidarity with Nasser. "We cannot let ourselves be pushed out of this region," remarked Schröder to the CDU/CSU caucus on February 9. "Every bit we give up there will be occupied *a tempo* by Pankow."[9] For the Foreign Office, then, the key imperative was to play down the importance of the Ulbricht visit and ensure that Nasser kept the affair as quiet and insignificant as possible. Here Schröder's approach meshed well with that of the FDP; this party, traditionally hostile to the Hallstein Doctrine, urged the government to avoid a showdown with Egypt.[10] Walter Scheel, the minister for development aid, argued that Bonn's Middle Eastern quandary proved the obsolescence of the old doctrine, but he acknowledged that it would be a foreign policy disaster for the government to abandon it under duress. The best solution was to ride out the current crisis without putting Egypt to the test.[11]

Placating Nasser meant halting the weapons deliveries to Israel, a solution that Schröder favored from the outset.[12] On January 27 Erhard's cabinet resolved just the opposite: it agreed that Bonn would not conclude any further agreements for military aid to Israel but that current obligations would be honored. In effect, this decision entailed sending another DM 150 million ($37.5 million) in equipment to Israel, including at least ninety tanks.[13] Yet shortly thereafter critics of the arms program began to wear down the chancellor's resistance.[14] Erhard, fair-minded by nature, wondered if perhaps the Israelis might accept cash payments in lieu of the remaining deliveries; Eshkol's government could use the money to buy tanks wherever it pleased.[15] Eshkol promptly rejected the idea. Nevertheless, Erhard's position hardened in the following days, as it became clear that Nasser was successfully rallying Arab opinion to his side. Nasser's ruling party even vowed to break diplomatic relations with the Federal Republic over the weapons issue.[16] Erhard, Westrick, and the CDU/CSU's foreign policy circle concluded that Bonn could not continue arming the Israelis under any circumstances. Erhard wrote to Eshkol on February 11 assuring him that Israel would be compensated in other ways and pointing out that it really was in everyone's best interests if the Federal Republic retained its presence in the Arab capitals.[17]

The suspension of deliveries to Israel did yield a temporary modus vivendi with Nasser, who agreed—via a Spanish intermediary—to receive Ulbricht with as little ceremony as possible. As far as Egypt was concerned, the crisis was over.[18] Unfortunately, neither Nasser's government nor the Spanish diplomat handled the matter discreetly, and the episode ended in a public relations disaster for Erhard's government. It appeared, based on reports from Cairo, that Bonn had capitulated to Arab blackmail on two counts: in halting the weapons shipments to Israel and in promising not to establish diplomatic relations with Tel Aviv.[19] The latter charge prompted vehement denials from State Secretary Carstens, who swore to the Bundestag that Bonn had made no binding commitments to the Arab states about its future relations with Israel. This was at best a half-truth, and it came back to haunt the government in early March; but it stilled the critics for the time being.[20] More troubling to many was the impression that Erhard had sacrificed Israel's defense in order to save the Hallstein Doctrine. Pro-Israel circles protested that the government's move obliterated the moral credit that West Germany had so painstakingly amassed since World War II.[21] Such sentiments could also be heard across the Atlantic. In a full-page advertisement in the *New York Times*, the Jewish War Veterans of the U.S.A. lambasted the Federal Republic for "the callous disregard of its treaty obligations in connection with military aid, which it arbitrarily 'canceled' at the demand of the Egyptian dictator, Nasser."[22] Ominously, several North American firms moved to boycott West German goods and services. Quaking with fear and resentment at the specter of an international campaign of "world Jewry" against the Federal Republic, ministers in Bonn begged the United States to intervene on Bonn's behalf in Tel Aviv.[23]

For a government prone to swerving, the next move was, predictably enough, to dispel the impression that it was being "soft" toward Nasser. Up to this point Bonn had stated with deliberate imprecision that the Ulbricht visit, should it take place, would "not be without consequences" for relations between Egypt and West Germany.[24] In comments to the CDU caucus and to the Bundestag on February 16 and 17, Erhard specified for the first time that his government would answer the visit by suspending all economic aid to Egypt. Political measures might follow as well, depending on how cordially Nasser treated his guest.[25] The envisioned punishments were hardly novel and accorded with what the Bundestag had been demanding all along; but articulating the threat in public was a grave tactical error, for it invited Nasser to respond with face-saving gestures of his own.[26] Nor did it help that, in an attempt to mollify the more moderate Arab leaders, Alexander Böker slipped off to Amman and Beirut to herald West Germany's deeply felt friendship with the Arab people.[27] Such maneuvers only heightened Arab solidarity with Egypt, particularly once Nasser had informed them about the true extent of Bonn's military aid to Israel. On February 23 the Arab League vowed to adopt a unitary stance vis-à-vis the Federal Republic in light of its recent behavior toward Israel.[28] This afforded Nasser a considerable degree of diplomatic cover as he proceeded to defy West Germany's request—seconded by France, Italy, and the United States—to keep the Ulbricht visit as low-key as possible. On the morning of February 24, Ulbricht was received in Alexandria and Cairo with the East German flag hoisted high, the "national anthem" blaring, and a twenty-one-gun salute. Although Nasser carefully described the occasion as a "friendship visit," the reception had all the trappings of a formal state visit.[29]

By this time Erhard's government was hopelessly divided and under fire from every conceivable direction. The din of newspaper editorials heralding the "death" of the Hallstein Doctrine continued unabated, with some journalists betraying a glimmer of schadenfreude and others lamenting Erhard's carelessness for endangering the doctrine in the first place.[30] SPD caucus leader Fritz Erler, who had stood behind the government's foreign policy for the preceding year and a half, now lashed out against Erhard for failing to block the Ulbricht visit and, more generally, for allowing the Federal Republic's position in the Middle East to crumble.[31] On the right, Gaullist commentators in the CDU/CSU did not want to blacken their own party's chancellor too directly, as parliamentary elections were due in the fall. Instead they vented their anger against the United States for originating the tanks-to-Israel scheme and then leaving the West Germans hanging out to dry. Columnists in respected newspapers went even further, speculating that Washington had deliberately leaked information about Bonn's aid to Israel in order to infuriate the Arabs and bring down the Hallstein Doctrine. "Seeing the Hallstein Doctrine founder is the secret wish of all those who wish to pursue a policy of détente at any price, without reference to German interests," proclaimed a front-page editorial in the *Frankfurter Allgemeine Zeitung*.[32] George McGhee, the American ambassador in Bonn, reported that Washington's passivity during the crisis was seriously eroding West German confidence in America's commitment to unification. "A German-American dispute about the Hallstein Doctrine could be blown into disastrous proportions in a German electoral year," warned McGhee.[33]

Bonn confessed its desperate situation to the Western Allies in no uncertain terms. Its isolation campaign was being sorely tested not only in the Middle East but in Indonesia and Tanzania as well. Sukarno was still considering opening an Indonesian consulate in East Berlin and reportedly also weighing an invitation to Ulbricht.[34] In Tanzania, President Nyerere had agreed to let the GDR open a consulate in Dar-es-Salaam in exchange for closing its embassy on the island of Zanzibar. Nyerere insisted that this was a downgrading of East Germany's presence in the country, but Erhard's government interpreted the shift as an upgrading of the GDR's presence on the mainland of sub-Saharan Africa.[35] Carstens informed the Allies of the planned West German countermeasures—in all cases, the severing of development aid—and asked for advice. This was, in effect, an effort to sound out the commitment of the Allies to the Hallstein Doctrine.[36] London had little to offer, save in Dar-es-Salaam, where it promised vigorous support of Bonn's position. In Paris, the Quai d'Orsay understood very well what Bonn was after and proposed a series of regular bilateral consultations on the problem of containing East Germany. As for the immediate crises, French officials warned against any strong actions versus Tanzania.[37] Finally, in Washington, Secretary of State Rusk expressed regret that Cairo, Jakarta, and Dar-es-Salaam were capitals where American influence had dwindled to insignificance. However, Rusk promised to "draw a considerable amount of heat away" from the Federal Republic in the Middle East. In the following days, Washington acknowledged publicly for the first time that it had helped instigate the secret tank deal. Soon thereafter an American envoy departed for Israel to discuss new alternatives for Israeli defense.[38]

While Bonn nervously awaited Ulbricht's arrival in Cairo, the government gladly seized an opportunity to act on another front. The victim was Tanzania, which officially announced the opening of the East German consulate in Dar-es-Salaam on February 19. Erhard's cabinet voted to cancel Bonn's military aid to Tanzania while leaving other aid programs intact. On February 28, 1965, West Germany's air force training units in Dar-es-Salaam startled the Tanzanians by abruptly departing for Europe.[39] The effect of this forceful display was instantly undermined, however, by a brilliant gesture on the part of Nyerere: he proclaimed that since the Federal Republic was so insistent on abusing its military aid for political ends, his country would forgo *all* forms of West German aid. With nearly DM 130 million ($32.5 million) in projects at stake, Nyerere's announcement resonated as an example of principled resistance to foreign manipulation.[40] Political elites in Bonn largely shared Erhard's impatience with Nyerere but found the timing of the countermeasure embarrassing. Even West German diplomats acknowledged a link between the government's difficulties in the Middle East and its resolute punishment of the smaller, weaker Tanzania.[41]

Once Ulbricht finally sailed from Alexandria harbor on March 2, Bonn could no longer defer the issue of countermeasures against Egypt. Shortly before Ulbricht's trip, East German negotiators had pulled out all the stops, boosting the original offer of vm 200 million in government credits by an additional 50 percent to vm 300 million (approx. $75 million).[42] As a reward, Ulbricht carried home even more political concessions than the Foreign Office had anticipated. Aside from signing treaties concerning economic, scientific, and cultural cooperation with the GDR, Nasser uttered a firm promise to open an Egyptian consulate in East Berlin and to pay Ulbricht a return visit to the GDR.[43] There could be no doubt that Nasser's courteous treatment of the East German head of state implied a de facto recognition of the GDR. Under these circumstances, Erhard felt that a simple termination of West German economic aid was not harsh enough.[44] His top foreign policy adviser, along with several cabinet ministers and the chairmen of both the CDU/CSU and the CSU (Adenauer and Strauss, respectively) favored a complete break in relations with Egypt. The Hallstein Doctrine's namesake, Walter Hallstein himself, slipped back to Bonn to prod Erhard in the same direction.[45] Yet there was unyielding resistance within the cabinet from the usual corners: the economics minister, the foreign minister, and all the FDP cabinet members. Schröder, following the reasoning of his Middle Eastern experts, worried about the unpredictable phenomenon of pan-Arabism. If Bonn broke with Cairo, would this lead a series of other Arab states to cut ties with Bonn?[46] The State Department, fearing a sudden loss of West Germany's presence throughout the Middle East, cautioned Erhard in the strongest imaginable terms against any precipitate action. The Quai d'Orsay offered the same advice in more moderate language.[47] By the evening of March 5, after two wearying days of deliberation in the cabinet, only a handful of top party and government leaders still saw any possibility of applying the Hallstein Doctrine in all its severity.

Erhard, still insistent on taking some strong action, seized upon a different plan: an exchange of embassies with Israel. This idea had been floated several times over the past several weeks as a constructive means of retaliation against the Arabs; Rainer Barzel, Brentano's replacement as CDU/CSU caucus leader and a rising star in West German politics, returned from a trip to the United States with this solution in mind.[48] In the abstract, the establishment of full diplomatic relations between the Federal Republic and Israel was clearly a desirable goal, for the anomalous lack of formal relations was beginning to take a serious toll on the course of German-Jewish reconciliation. However, the timing and circumstances of Erhard's decision left much to be desired. At the end of a weekend of tortuous conversations at his vacation home on the Tegernsee, Erhard and a handful of CDU/CSU leaders—foremost among them Barzel—reached the decision on Sunday, March 7.[49] Schröder was consulted, but only a short while before the news broke; the rest of the Foreign Office was caught completely by surprise.[50] Kurt Birrenbach, a West German emissary on his way to Israel to sort out the thorny problem of the weapons deliveries, received a new mission after his arrival in Tel Aviv: to sound out Eshkol's government about Israel's conditions for exchanging embassies with the Federal Republic.[51]

Erhard's impulsive decision destroyed the last vestiges of West German credibility in the Arab world. For months Bonn had been reassuring Arab leaders quietly that the Federal Republic would certainly not establish diplomatic relations with Israel before the Bundestag elections in September 1965. These assurances, made via diplomatic channels, reflected an honest assessment of the government's thinking at the time, but now it appeared that the Federal Republic had misled the Arabs. In Baghdad and Taiz, Yemen, angry crowds set fire to the West German embassies. On March 14 the member states of the Arab League vowed to break diplomatic relations with the Federal Republic if it took up diplomatic relations with Israel—a sort of reverse Hallstein Doctrine.[52] Having committed itself in public, though, Erhard's government could scarcely back down without inviting a terrifying backlash in Israel, in the Western democracies, and in West Germany itself. Hoping that Arab tempers would cool, Bonn did not rush its negotiations with Tel Aviv.[53] From mid-March through mid-May, West German emissaries plied the capitals of the Middle East, seeking to pacify Arab leaders with secret offers of additional aid should diplomatic relations be retained.[54] However, only three states enjoying particularly close ties with Bonn—Morocco, Tunisia, and Libya—proved willing to ignore the directives of the Arab League. On May 12, 1965, the Federal Republic sent its first ambassador, Rolf Pauls, to Tel Aviv. Ten Arab states immediately proclaimed a break with Bonn: Algeria, Lebanon, Jordan, Syria, Saudi Arabia, Yemen, Iraq, Kuwait, Sudan, and of course, Egypt.[55]

The outcome could conceivably have been worse. In many respects Israel counted for more internationally than all the Arab states combined. For the Federal Republic in particular, reconciliation with Israel was absolutely vital for retaining the trust and support of its most important ally, the United States. The Erhard government's behavior in early 1965—its initial refusal to renew the statute of limitations for Nazi-era crimes and its cancellation of arms deliveries to Israel—had seriously tarnished West Germany's public image in the United States. Although the State Department did not explicitly encourage Erhard to initiate diplomatic relations with Israel, Erhard's decision arrested an ominous deterioration in German-American relations. Domestically, too, the chancellor's action was applauded by many as a welcome act of statesmanship. Some, though not all, of the damage that Erhard's reputation had suffered during the long indecisive weeks of February was now repaired. Even in the Middle East, there was a glimmer of hope. The ten states that broke with Bonn did *not* proceed to recognize the GDR. Despite their outrage, the Arab leaders did not burn all of their bridges with the Federal Republic.

Even so, the crisis of 1965 dealt a major blow to West German prestige. An aura of helplessness pervaded the government's every move during these desperate weeks. Bonn's use of a Spanish intermediary in Cairo, a representative of Francisco Franco's dictatorship, occasioned befuddlement at home and abroad. At NATO headquarters in Paris the West German delegate made vague appeals to alliance solidarity in facing Nasser's challenge, without stating how the other Western powers might be of assistance.[56] All of this suggested that Bonn was in over its head—that it lacked the fortitude to play an independent role in the diplomacy of the Middle East or elsewhere. As the State Department had predicted back in December, Erhard's cabinet ended up turning to the United States to bail it out of its predicament; the Johnson administration supplied to Israel the tanks that West Germany would no longer deliver.[57] Perhaps most humiliatingly, the Foreign Office now had to rely extensively on other Western diplomats, usually French or Italian ambassadors, to curb East German inroads into the Arab countries where the Federal Republic was no longer represented.[58] Influencing the behavior of governments in the Near and Middle East would be vastly more complicated now that there were no diplomatic relations left to break. In effect, the Hallstein Doctrine had been rendered inoperative in this part of the world.

The Contest Goes On

Without actually saying so in public, the Foreign Office drew one central conclusion from its tribulations in the Middle East: Hallstein's old tool of diplomacy was now obsolete. More precisely, Bonn could still threaten to break relations, but it could not afford to make good on that threat. Journalists had long complained that the Hallstein Doctrine pushed the Federal Republic into a state of "self-isolation," since whenever Bonn severed relations with a country, it lost all hope of influencing events there. An abrupt departure of West German representatives from a nonaligned country in-

A DISCREDITED DOCTRINE

evitably left the GDR in a position to act as the sole voice of Germany there.[59] Schröder employed precisely this reasoning in early 1965 when he argued against a break with Cairo. "Every place which the Federal Republic vacates will be taken by Pankow. A German flag will be hoisted, a separatists' flag to be sure, but in [the] eyes of the people there a German flag nonetheless. For this reason we must fight for every centimeter with all acceptable means."[60] As Schröder's rhetoric attests, the Ulbricht visit to Cairo intensified feelings of rivalry with the GDR as never before. Neither he nor any other major figure in Erhard's government wished to let the isolation campaign wane. During the next year and a half, the parties of the governing coalition quarreled often about the Hallstein Doctrine, but the differences of opinion concerned tactical details rather than strategic goals.

Planners in Bonn proceeded along the conceptual path opened by the "new measures" one year earlier. In 1964 the Foreign Office had resolved to supplement its standard punishment of breaking diplomatic relations with a wider range of reprisals, applicable in cases where other countries had not yet established full diplomatic relations with East Germany. Now several officials were prepared to dispense with Bonn's ultimate sanction altogether. Even where another state recognized the GDR outright, wrote one expert, severing diplomatic ties was the one countermeasure Bonn should *not* consider. Punish the offender in every other way, support its rivals and enemies, but keep diplomatic relations intact.[61] This standpoint marked a sharp departure from the original logic of Bonn's isolation campaign. Since the early 1950s, the Federal Republic had insisted that it alone bore the right to represent the German people in international affairs. For this reason, the one situation it refused to countenance was the simultaneous presence, in any capital save Moscow, of two equally ranked German representatives, one from the East and one from the West. Writing in March 1965, however, State Secretary Carstens wondered whether it might be preferable to retain a West German presence even in international organizations that the East Germans had managed to join.[62] What Carstens saw in both the sphere of multilateral diplomacy and many capitals of the Third World was not a recognized Federal Republic confronting a nonrecognized GDR but, rather, a dogged struggle between the two sides. West Germany had the upper hand, yet the gap between the rivals was narrowing. Resisting the GDR's advances would require laborious efforts and generous outpourings of aid in one nonaligned capital after another. In Carstens's analysis, the concept of deterrence by example—one standard means of limiting costs—played almost no role; he noted bitterly that Bonn's countermeasures against Ceylon had failed to deter Tanzania from accepting an East German consulate.[63]

Despite these pessimistic assessments, there was no need yet for Bonn to disavow the Hallstein Doctrine in broad daylight. Erhard's government had nothing to lose by reiterating its traditional stance, now largely a bluff, in the hope that this would continue to ward off overt recognitions of East Germany. Speaking to the Bundestag on March 10, 1965, Schröder cited the two foundational texts of the Hallstein Doctrine: Adenauer's declaration of September 22, 1955, and Brentano's follow-up on June 28, 1956. The imprecision of both passages suited Schröder's purposes very well. They prescribed only a "reevaluation" of Bonn's relations with any country that recognized East Germany, leaving the government with considerable maneuvering room in deciding how to respond. "We will realize our sole right to represent all of Germany and defend our country's vital interests with the most suitable, most emphatic means available," remarked the foreign minister in closing.[64] For the many publicists and government officials who advocated flexibility, these comments signaled a readiness to dispense with the rigidity commonly associated with the Hallstein Doctrine.[65] By associating himself with the key policy statements of 1955–56, however, Schröder hoped to shield himself from right-wing criticism that he was undermining the very doctrine of which he spoke. Baron Guttenberg, the csu's top foreign policy expert and an implacable rival of the foreign minister, understood very well that Schröder was advocating a "presence doctrine" that held that Bonn should hold its ground even in situations where East Berlin was also present in force. In Guttenberg's view, this approach could only accustom world leaders to the existence of two German states.[66] Schröder deflected this accusation, which Guttenberg aired in the Bundestag in mid-May, by affirming once again that the Adenauer and Brentano statements remained the basis of Bonn's policy.[67]

Schröder's comments apparently dispelled whatever speculations may have arisen in the wake of the Middle Eastern crisis about a softening of West German resolve. Until 1969 not a single nonaligned state called Bonn's bluff by recognizing the GDR. This spared the Federal Republic from facing the dilemma of either breaking diplomatic relations or allowing the credibility of its threat to evaporate. As in previous years, the battleground between the two rivals lay in the approach to recognition. In keeping with the radical tone predominant at the Foreign Office since early 1964, country experts there continued to devise new measures to contest even the most minor East German gains. In early 1966 the Latin America desk proposed an embargo of Colombian coffee in response to the opening of an East German chamber of commerce office in Bogota.[68] This plan was eventually dismissed as "too harsh," but other spheres of West German economic activity were drawn into the isolation campaign during this period. As the official East German airline, Interflug, began to cast out a fledgling network of international flights to Third World capitals, Erhard's government pressed a number of governments not to grant the airline overflight privileges or landing rights.[69] At times this required the active collaboration of West Germany's state-owned airline, Lufthansa. Although Lufthansa's original charter directed it to establish only air routes that would be commercially profitable, the Foreign Office urged the cabinet to make special subsidized exceptions in situations where this would enable Lufthansa to squeeze out Interflug.[70]

Despite its ambitions, the Foreign Office faced a number of new political barriers in pursuing its isolation campaign. FDP leaders, gearing up for the fall elections in 1965, broke coalition discipline in March and polemicized openly against the Hallstein Doctrine.[71] This entailed much more than the perennial demand for diplomatic relations with Eastern Europe. Now the FDP ministers in Erhard's cabinet flatly refused to sanction punitive countermeasures in defense of Bonn's claim to sole representation of Germany. The first test of this stance came in July 1965, when Egypt opened its long-anticipated consulate in East Berlin. The Foreign Office could identify only one possible reprisal: the forced closure of Egypt's consulates in Frankfurt and Hamburg.[72] Yet FDP chairman Erich Mende, who presided over the relevant cabinet meetings in his capacity as vice-chancellor, persuaded the ministers to postpone a decision until after the elections. By the time the idea of a reprisal came up again in November, it no longer seemed timely.[73]

From the political right came pressure of a different order. Several activists in the CDU/CSU insisted on an orthodox interpretation of the Hallstein Doctrine that ruled out the establishment of diplomatic relations with Eastern Europe. Schröder's views on the subject were well known; he hinted several times that he thought the time was almost ripe for an exchange of ambassadors with the satellite states.[74] The Foreign Office was now largely behind him on this, seeing an opening to the east as a constructive means of restoring dynamism to the isolation campaign after the debacle in the Middle East.[75] After Erhard's victory in the elections of September 1965, however, Schröder's enemies in the Bavarian CSU attempted to cement a rigid, uncompromising version of the Hallstein Doctrine into the government's program. They also persuaded President Heinrich Lübke to use his powers of appointment to block Schröder's reinstatement as foreign minister.[76] Erhard clung loyally to his minister but showed distress at evidence that Schröder had been conspiring behind his back to establish diplomatic relations with the Warsaw Pact nations. Such a move would be "completely wrong," Erhard remarked to Carstens; it would entail "giving up the Hallstein Doctrine."[77] Carstens assured the chancellor that Schröder did not view the problem of diplomatic relations as "acute," and indeed the foreign minister's ardor on the subject did cool noticeably after CSU obstruction had nearly cost him his job.[78]

Fiscal considerations also limited Bonn's maneuvering room. Since the early 1960s, the amount budgeted for new development aid commitments had shrunk drastically; for fiscal year 1965, only DM 600 million ($150 million) in appropriations was available, and of this nearly two-thirds was already earmarked for major consortia.[79] The amount of aid actually flowing out of the Federal Republic did not fall as quickly, since much of the capital promised in earlier years was only then being supplied to the recipients. Nevertheless, this limited capacity to make new offers blunted one of the principal instruments of Bonn's nonrecognition policy. The situation did ease pressure on the Foreign Office from one corner: out of a combination of expediency and conviction, the Development Aid Ministry softened its critique of the Hallstein Doctrine. Officials at the aid ministry now concluded that the isolation campaign did *not* monopolize West German aid distribution after all.[80] In pitching appeals to the cabinet and the Bundestag in the winter of 1965–66, the Development Aid Ministry joined forces with the Economics Ministry and the Foreign Office in stressing the intimate connection between aid levels and Bonn's foremost goal, unification. "If we do not show understanding for the problems of the developing countries through an appropriate amount of aid, we cannot expect any understanding from them regarding our German needs," argued a draft paper for the cabinet.[81] In early January 1966, the cabinet did approve 1.275 billion marks ($318 million) in appropriations—provided that some half-billion of the newly promised aid did not have to be paid out before 1969.[82] In the following months, though, West Germany's economy lumbered into recession, necessitating budget cuts across the board. Special emergency requests, such as the Foreign Office's plea for DM 50 million ($12.5 million) to be donated to the UN relief organizations working in Palestine, did not stand a chance.[83]

Lastly, the Foreign Office did not have a free hand to pursue its isolation campaign in the Middle East, as relations with Israel took top priority.

Officials in the Foreign Ministry desperately wished to restore diplomatic relations with the Arab states, beginning with the more moderate ones, in order to provide some insurance against East German inroads there. Wary of the endemic problem of blackmail, Erhard's government took a firm line in public: the Arab states must make the first move, and they should not expect the Federal Republic to provide any financial incentives.[84] However, the cabinet's decision to retain certain development aid programs did give Bonn a limited degree of leverage in Sudan and Jordan, and in the winter of 1965–66 both countries expressed interest in the resumption of diplomatic ties.[85] What scuttled these efforts was a generous new capital aid agreement signed between the Federal Republic and Israel in March 1966, providing DM 160 million ($40 million) in loans each year at 3 percent interest. This renewal of Bonn's commitment to the Jewish state, which was really just an extension of German restitution payments under the rubric of development aid, touched off another wave of denunciations by the Arab League. As a consequence, Jordan and Sudan lost their nerve.[86] For want of other alternatives, the Foreign Office resorted to the politics of small symbols in resisting East German encroachments in the Middle East. In the summer of 1966, Bonn withdrew from official participation in the Algiers Trade Fair rather than tolerate the display of East German flags on the fairgrounds.[87] Via its Italian trustees in Yemen, Bonn protested against the use of diplomatic plates on the car of the East German consul. The point of these exercises was to show that Bonn was watching carefully and that the Federal Republic was *not* becoming reconciled to the existence of a second German state.[88] Interventions on minor issues also helped to distract attention from the cabinet's disinclination to adopt truly severe countermeasures in defense of its nonrecognition policy.

Considering the Federal Republic's vulnerability, the SED regime made distressingly slow progress in the Near and Middle East. The more radical countries in the region were lost to Bonn, but they were not yet won for East Berlin. Clearly the Arab leaders expected more from the GDR than denunciations of Israel and proclamations of solidarity with the Arab people. Most of the region's leaders were still quite suspicious of communism, though "goodwill diplomacy"—frequent visits by Foreign Minister Otto Winzer and free trips to East Berlin for Arab officials—provided some potential for influence building. Stipends and scholarships helped as well. When the son of Iraq's minister of culture was studying gratis at the University of Leipzig, no one thought it strange that the red-baiting Iraqi government promoted cultural exchanges with the communist half of Germany.[89]

Even so, only the region's most politically "progressive" governments—Egypt, Syria, and Yemen—took steps to upgrade their relations during this period by opening consulates in East Berlin. All had received material incentives in the form of long-term government credits: VM 300 million (approx. $75 million) to Egypt, promised on the eve of Ulbricht's visit; VM 100 million ($25 million) to Syria; and VM 22 million ($6.5 million) to Yemen.[90]

If this was the going price for consulates in Berlin, what, then, would the GDR have to pay for diplomatic relations? Like the West Germans five years earlier, the East Germans now discovered one unfortunate dynamic of development aid: once it was available in large quantities, nonaligned countries began demanding ever more of it as the price for cooperation. At the Belgrade Conference in 1961, several Third World countries appeared inclined to recognize the GDR for "free," out of the conviction that this would advance the cause of peace in Europe. Now that East Berlin had promised indulgent aid packages to certain nonaligned powers, however, other states held out for similar rewards. Algeria, one of the GDR's chosen "points of concentration," proved particularly elusive. The Politburo envisioned offering credits of VM 100 million (approx. $25 million), to be repaid with high-quality Algerian oil. Expectations on the other side were considerably more inflated: $80 to $100 million in hard currency, with wine and iron ore as the principal goods for repayment.[91] By early 1967 a compromise sum of $45 million was in sight, but the East Germans balked at offering the Algerians a lower interest rate and a longer loan period than they had previously granted Egypt and Syria. More importantly, the GDR still had no clear indication of what political concessions would be forthcoming; Algeria's foreign minister rejected any explicit link between the credit agreement and an exchange of consulates.[92] At this point the Politburo, disappointed by Algeria's opportunistic behavior, backed away from the talks. Large offers of aid were no "miracle weapon" for the SED, even in a region where the GDR's anti-Israeli stance had garnered considerable sympathy.

Outside the Arab world, East Germany fared even worse. From the spring of 1965 through the fall of 1966, the GDR actually lost ground in several African and Asian "points of concentration." Voters in Ceylon threw Bandaranaike from office in March 1965, at least in part because of her tendency to alienate Western economic partners such as the Federal Republic. Bonn seized the opportunity to swap capital aid for a scaling back of the GDR's presence on the island.[93] Stanley Senanayake, the new Ceylonese prime minister, did not downgrade the East German consulate to a trade mission, as many West Germans had hoped, but he did reduce the number of the consulate's personnel by two-thirds. He also issued a statement affirming that Ceylon did not recognize the GDR in any form.[94] Similar cutbacks followed in Tanzania. In mid-1966 Julius Nyerere mandated that the staff of the East German consulate in Dar-es-Salaam drop from ten to six.[95] Nyerere was likely responding to news from Ghana, where alarming details about East German activities had come to light. Officers leading a coup against Nkrumah in February 1966 uncovered a secret school where experts from the famed Stasi, the GDR's state security organ, were training African counterparts in the ways of intelligence, surveillance, and political control. The new regime in Ghana expelled all East Germans from the country, including the personnel of the trade mission in Accra.[96] Nor were Bandaranaike and Nkrumah the only friends of East Germany to fall from power during this period. Upheavals in Indonesia—a communist uprising followed by a bloody crackdown—led to the ouster of Ahmed Sukarno in the fall of 1965.[97] The SED's International Relations Department, appalled at the string of unpleasant surprises, called for a more "systematic, prognostic, theoretical" approach to foreign policy. Instead of "judging situations spontaneously based upon superficial appearances," the Foreign Ministry, in consultation with East German research institutes, was to arrive at "an exact political analysis of the class situation in the most important countries."[98] Such resolutions hinted at a deep-seated frustration in East Berlin over the unpredictability of international affairs. So much of the effort put into Ghana, Ceylon, and Indonesia had been for naught. One consolation was that the capital assistance once set aside for Nkrumah and Bandaranaike could now be used to make new offers elsewhere.[99]

One of East Germany's more embarrassing defeats was entirely self-generated. At Ulbricht's initiative, the GDR took a gamble on February 28, 1966, by submitting an application to join the United Nations. This was unlikely to get very far, since membership questions were the prerogative of the UN Security Council, where France, Britain, and the United States enjoyed veto power. For similar reasons—the Soviet Union's veto—West Germany had never applied for UN membership, limiting itself to an observer function and participation in the specialized suborganizations. Most likely Ulbricht was hoping to achieve a status comparable to that of West Germany, which had effectively monopolized the German voice in intergovernmental associations such as the UN Educational, Scientific, and Cultural Organization (UNESCO) since the early 1950s.[100] Secretary General

U Thant, Burmese by nationality, was known to favor the admission of an East German observer to the UN. Why, then, did the GDR submit an application for full membership? The step was "not very appropriate," remarked U Thant privately, echoing the feelings of many nonaligned countries. Since the application was destined for failure, its purpose was too obviously propagandistic.[101] As early as March 3, 1966, the Western Allies circulated a note arguing that the GDR was ineligible for membership because it was not an independent state. This made it clear that the East German application would not even make it onto the Security Council agenda, so the Soviet Union and its allies refrained from putting the subject up for a vote. Instead they tried to keep the East German question in conversation as long as possible within the corridors of the UN. Meanwhile, the GDR undertook the usual steps to garner sympathy abroad: a goodwill delegation traversed Southeast Asia, and Foreign Minister Winzer trekked off to Mali. Despite these efforts, not a single neutral state came forward with a letter endorsing East German membership in the UN.[102]

These developments were still not comforting to West German observers. They would have preferred a more dramatic showdown—a devastating rejection of the East German application by the Security Council, perhaps.[103] Throughout the mid-1960s, the momentum appeared to lie with the GDR in its quest to join multilateral conferences and organizations. Given the universal humanitarian mission of such UN subgroups as the WHO, the Federal Republic was having a difficult time explaining why East German participation would be harmful.[104] If this were true on the level of *inter*governmental organizations, where the Foreign Office had the possibility of exerting diplomatic influence, this was doubly true of *non*governmental organizations (NGOs). Specialized international congresses of geophysicists, art critics, or even lawyers accepted the presence of separate "national" delegations from the GDR without much fuss. Often the West German delegations—composed of private citizens rather than government officials—did not even bother to protest. As of February 1966, the Foreign Office counted 1,470 NGOs worldwide, with West Germans represented in 1,121 and East Germans in 252.[105] Most NGOs, being obscure, did not provide many propaganda opportunities anyway. In the realm of sports, however, the SED regime concentrated all its efforts on fielding separate teams wearing the GDR's distinctive insignia. In the summer of 1965 the Foreign Office fought and lost a crucial battle on this terrain. The International Olympic Committee pronounced its recognition of the East German Olympic Committee. During the 1968 games in Grenoble and Mexico City, television audiences would see athletic proof of the existence of two competing German states.[106]

Assessing the GDR's position in the world had always been an exercise in reading water in a glass: was it half-empty or half-full? State Secretary Karl Carstens thought the glass was half-empty and falling quickly. In January 1966 he drafted a lengthy memorandum warning that the "erosion" of Bonn's isolation policy was "progressing unstoppably." Bonn had no choice but to continue the struggle, since every partial victory made the SED regime even more aggressive. Nevertheless, "we must realize that we are expending the greater part, perhaps most of our foreign policy energy on this fundamentally thankless and unsatisfying defensive action."[107] By October 1966 his vision was even darker. "Hardly a day goes by" without the hoisting of the East German flag somewhere or the friendly reception of a GDR delegation in some nonaligned country, Carstens wrote. The Federal Republic's record was "astonishing" in many respects, and it had indeed "won back lost terrain" in Ceylon, Ghana, and Indonesia; yet "a gradual advance of the SBZ in third countries and in international organizations" was inevitable.[108] Naturally, from the perspective of East Berlin, the situation was not nearly so promising. SED functionaries felt themselves hemmed in by their government's "partial isolation and discrimination at the hands of other states."[109] But Carstens's sense of foreboding was no longer centered strictly on the problem of East Germany's international recognition. In a broader sense, he argued, West Germany had entered a state of deep crisis. "The will to reunify is diminishing," he lamented; "the ongoing separation is leading to an inner alienation between the two halves of our people."[110] Carstens, like many of his contemporaries, was beginning to doubt the efficacy of the unification program introduced by Adenauer in 1949 and perpetuated by Erhard—at least until his sudden downfall in the fall of 1966.

Unification Hysteria and Erhard's Political Demise

Ludwig Erhard was completely unprepared for the storm that rolled over him. In October 1965 he had been reelected by a comfortable margin, and his coalition of CDU/CSU and FDP commanded 294 of 496 seats in the Bundestag. With the election season past, however, pending issues could no longer be deferred. Unification in particular was on the agenda—thanks in no small part to expectations the chancellor himself had aroused during his first two years in office. Polls in 1965 suggested that among the major concerns of West Germans, the problem of unity had moved to the top of the list.[111] "After the election, however it turns out, the German Question will become the dominant theme," wrote one CDU foreign policy expert to Henry Kissinger in April 1965. "Thinking in the Federal Republic is in flux. . . . Strange as it sounds, the annoyance with Egypt over the Ulbricht visit has helped push in this direction. The feeling has grown that the German position is vulnerable."[112] This prediction by Johann Baptist Gradl proved accurate. The postelection period yielded an explosion of publications along the lines of W. W. Schütz's *Rethinking German Policy*, which called on West Germans to undertake genuine sacrifices for the sake of national unity. The British ambassador was unimpressed by the agitated discussion in Bonn: "Most of it is no more than froth."[113] But it was Erhard's inability to keep up with the rapidly shifting debate that branded his administration as hopelessly wooden and behind the times.

At the root of West German anxieties lay a shift in perspective about the staying power of Ulbricht's regime. With the New Economic Program running in high gear, the GDR was experiencing robust growth on the order of 5 percent per annum. Some spoke of a "second economic miracle" on German soil parallel to the Federal Republic's rapid expansion in the 1950s.[114] In light of the crass exploitation this portion of Germany had earlier suffered at the hands of the Soviet occupiers, the GDR's record seemed all the more impressive. Erich Mende, Bonn's minister for all-German affairs, remarked on several occasions that the recent progress in the GDR "has led the people there to take pride in their constructive accomplishments— which could well develop into a sense of separateness or at least an acceptance of the regime."[115] This was precisely what many in Bonn feared. Could it be that the population of East Germany was coming to terms with the SED dictatorship? If so, what did this entail for West Germany's long-heralded goal of unification? Was the German Reich fashioned by Bismarck just a passing historical episode, one that could never be re-created through the adjoining of East and West Germany?[116] Journalists and publicists speculated that the GDR might one day be seen as a foreign entity that happened to share certain cultural traits with the Federal Republic—much like Austria and Switzerland.

For the generation then dominant in Bonn, which attached great significance to the goal of national unity, these were truly appalling scenarios. Leaders across the political spectrum demanded creative new approaches to revive a sense of community among all Germans. Willy Brandt envisioned a modus vivendi between "the two territories" of Germany—albeit one that was "qualified, regulated, and temporally limited." Hans Dichgans, a Christian Democrat with strong ties to industry, called for a West

A DISCREDITED DOCTRINE

German program to finance residential and hospital construction in the GDR.[117] To a surprising extent, the East German side acted as a catalyst. A state secretary for all-German questions was appointed in East Berlin, and the SED initiated a dialogue with the SPD in early 1966. With the SED posing, however implausibly, as a champion of German unity, public figures in the West insisted that the time was ripe for a *"geistige Auseinandersetzung"* with East Germany.[118] This vague, untranslatable buzzword suggested that Bonn should defend its social and political model aggressively in an open exchange of views with East German representatives. Free traffic in theater ensembles, films, books, and newspapers across the borders would help diminish the creeping alienation of the divided German population.[119] Such proposals rapidly exceeded the boundaries of what East Berlin could tolerate; the SED had no interest in exposing East Germans to a stream of West German influences. Yet many in the CDU/CSU were nearly as uncomfortable at the prospect of allowing "murderers" from the East German Politburo to agitate freely in the Federal Republic.[120] At length the Bundestag passed a special law granting temporary immunity to SED visitors so that they would not be subject to prosecution when they crossed over onto West German soil. Albert Norden, the SED's chief ideologist, retorted that "citizens of our state . . . are being treated in West Germany like criminals," and he used the occasion to call off a previously scheduled exchange of speakers between the SPD and the SED.[121]

For all his rhetorical bombast, Norden had a point. Erhard's administration continued to regard the SED as the primary obstacle to unification and adamantly refused to initiate any contacts with the East German authorities that might imply a recognition of the GDR. Whatever Erhard and his cabinet wished to undertake on behalf of German unity would have to be done without the cooperation of East Berlin. As one CDU activist explained, "Our interest lies in making Ulbricht an anachronism in Eastern Europe."[122] By shunning the SED regime while embracing reformed communists elsewhere in Eastern Europe, the Federal Republic could intensify the GDR's isolation and eventually force positive changes in the "Soviet Zone of Germany." With this in mind, Erhard and Schröder circulated a "peace note" on March 25, 1966, expressing West Germany's rejection of war and offering nonaggression pacts with the states of Eastern Europe. Governments in the West and in the Third World responded favorably to the tone of Bonn's peace note, but recipients in Eastern Europe answered with polemics.[123] If anything, the note lent credibility to East German and Soviet charges of revanchism, since it gave no indication that Bonn would accept the finality of the Oder-Neisse border with Poland. Nor did the peace note call for the establishment of diplomatic relations between the Federal Republic and Eastern Europe, since these governments had diplomatic relations with the GDR. On both counts, Erhard had scarcely moved beyond the positions drawn up by Adenauer and Brentano ten years earlier.[124]

To many West Germans, the peace note symbolized the bankruptcy of Erhard's approach. The release of a "white book" documenting Bonn's prior initiatives on the German Question did little to dispel this impression.[125] By the late spring of 1966, when the FDP, SPD, and CDU/CSU held a series of emergency sessions on the topic of national unity, the Chancellor's Office was providing no coherent leadership. Erhard acknowledged that Bonn's policies had not brought unification any closer, but he added that at least "we have managed to uphold the claim to exclusive representation of Germany. And a formation like the Zone must ask itself how long it can actually keep on going as a pseudo-state formation unrecognized by the world."[126] Such comments invited mockery from FDP deputies, who could scarcely imagine that Ulbricht's regime would simply give up in despair at its pariah status.[127] For the time being, none of the mainstream parties in West Germany was willing to endorse the opposite tack: abandoning Bonn's claim to represent all of Germany and acquiescing in the recognition of the GDR as a second German state. Throughout the excruciating "summer of discontent," the Foreign Office had the authority to carry out its isolation campaign as before.[128] But the absence of diplomatic relations with Eastern Europe seemed a greater liability than ever in light of the acidic propaganda emanating from the region. The SPD pleaded for a "differentiated application" of the Hallstein Doctrine with respect to Eastern Europe. The FDP, for what must have seemed like the thousandth time, insisted that the doctrine be repudiated altogether.[129] With his typically poor sense of timing, Erhard finally resolved in October 1966 to pursue diplomatic relations with Romania. A year earlier this would have seemed courageous, but by this point nothing could restore faith in the chancellor's decision-making abilities.[130]

The onset of recession hollowed out the last vestiges of Erhard's popularity. Having built his reputation as an economic miracle worker, the chancellor was particularly vulnerable once West Germany slid into its first major downturn since 1950.[131] Yet foreign policy failures played a central role in the unraveling of Erhard's chancellorship. As a champion of close relations with the United States, Erhard was humiliated when President Lyndon Johnson refused to honor the chancellor's friendship by accepting a postponement of West Germany's "offset" payments.[132] Meanwhile, in early October 1966 the American president signaled a major shift in American policy. Echoing the line taken by de Gaulle since the beginning of 1965, Johnson emphasized that German unification could take place only within the larger context of European unification. Johnson's New York speech did not even mention standard positions such as Four Power responsibility for Germany, free elections in the GDR, or nonrecognition of the SED regime. Clearly the American president was determined to pursue a wide-ranging "peaceful engagement" with Moscow without reference to the problems of divided Germany.[133] This left the Federal Republic isolated in its resistance to détente. State Secretary Carstens painted a bleak picture to the cabinet on October 14, stressing that Bonn's policy on unification had no serious backing from the Allies and in a sense compromised West German security by provoking the implacable hostility of the Soviet Union.[134] Erhard had no response save to beg the members of his cabinet to remain silent about Carstens's prognosis. Word leaked to the press anyway, and the weekly magazine *Der Spiegel* concluded that Erhard's administration had reached a dead end. Few disagreed save Erhard himself, who clung to power tenaciously even after the FDP withdrew from the cabinet on October 27, 1966.[135]

Erhard's fall from grace marked a major caesura in postwar German history. So many of the former chancellor's positions—and those of his long-serving predecessor, Adenauer—were now open to question. Was it time to embrace détente in Europe, even if this worked to solidify the political division of Germany? Could Bonn continue to avoid direct conversations with East Berlin? Should the Federal Republic persist in its long-running campaign to isolate the GDR internationally? Was it still meaningful to describe Bonn as the sole legitimate voice of the German people? Erhard's critics offered a wide variety of answers to these questions; finding any sort of consensus in the late 1960s and early 1970s would prove excruciatingly difficult. But the floundering image Erhard had presented during the Near Eastern crisis of 1965 and throughout the summer and fall of 1966 gave influential West Germans a clear idea of what they did *not* want: a Federal Republic bound so tightly to the defense of received wisdom that it lacked the capacity to respond creatively.

Chapter 8

Of Two Minds

The Grand Coalition and
the Problem of Recognition

Erhard was replaced not by one leader but by two. Kurt Kiesinger of the CDU/CSU and Willy Brandt of the SPD joined forces to form a "Grand Coalition," a limited partnership intended to stimulate the economy, reform the party system, and break new ground in foreign relations. The coalition's "new Eastern policy" marked a valiant attempt to embrace the cause of détente without abandoning hope for an eventual reunification. Thus, even as Bonn moved to normalize relations with Eastern Europe, it continued to block the recognition of East Germany by outside parties. This aroused the intense ire of the Soviet Union as well as the GDR, which endeavored to shut down the new Eastern policy and force through the international recognition of Ulbricht's regime once and for all. After all, by the time Bonn had established diplomatic relations with Romania and reestablished them with Yugoslavia, there was not much logic remaining to the old rules of the Hallstein Doctrine. Yet the GDR still did not exploit these contradictions successfully. The radical Arab states, though more pro-Soviet than ever in the wake of the Six Day War in June 1967, made their attitude toward East Germany contingent on financial and military assistance on a scale the GDR could not provide.

The instability of the Grand Coalition finally provided an opening for the East Germans. Unnerved by Moscow's hostility, which seemed all the more dangerous in the wake of the Warsaw Pact invasion of Czechoslovakia, the SPD and the CDU/CSU drew opposite conclusions about how to achieve a more lasting peace with the Soviet bloc. The Christian Democrats edged away from détente, even as the Social Democrats came to favor a comprehensive modus vivendi with the Soviet Union, Poland, and the GDR. These contrasting programs very nearly split the coalition. The showdown came in May 1969, when Cambodia unexpectedly recognized East Germany. Brandt and the SPD abjectly refused to break relations with this Southeast Asian republic, signaling the political death of the Hallstein Doctrine. Yet even this did not pave the way for the GDR's worldwide recognition; five Arab governments did establish diplomatic relations, but Ulbricht's government then ran out of funds. Twenty years after its founding, the GDR remained on the fringes of international life.

The Ulbricht Doctrine

Kurt Georg Kiesinger, younger and leaner than Erhard, assumed the chancellorship on December 1, 1966. His party, the CDU/CSU, retained a numerical edge in the new cabinet, but the SPD joined the coalition with fresh perspectives and a sense of forward momentum. This was, after all, the SPD's first taste of political power at the national level since the decline of the Weimar Republic. The administration enjoyed a staggering majority in the Bundestag; the Free Democrats, occupying a mere one-tenth of the seats, sat alone in opposition. Ironically, governing with such an enormous parliamentary backing proved to be unwieldy, for the more extreme elements in both the CDU/CSU and the SPD felt little pressure to heed party discipline and abide by the compromises worked out at the center. Nor did the cabinet itself often speak with one voice, for it suffered from an excess of talented, ambitious politicians.[1] Influential foreign policy advisers included Willy Brandt as foreign minister; Herbert Wehner, the SPD's master strategist, as minister for all-German affairs; Gerhard Schröder, who moved to the Defense Ministry; and CSU chairman Franz-Josef Strauss as minister of finance. Kiesinger himself entered office with a reputation as a foreign affairs expert, though his prolonged absence from Bonn—he had served as minister-president of the southwest German state of Baden-Württemberg since 1958—left him without any clearly defined contours on the issues of the day. This worked to Kiesinger's advantage in healing the breach between Gaullists and Atlanticists within the union parties.

Early on, Kiesinger's administration did articulate a distinctive and coherent response to the country's worrisome political isolation. Most importantly, the coalition embraced the cause of East-West détente: "The will to peace and to reconciliation among peoples is the first word and the foundational goal of this government," proclaimed Kiesinger during his inaugural address on December 13, 1966.[2] The new coalition pledged to contribute actively to the lessening of tensions between NATO and the Warsaw Pact via a new Eastern policy. Addressing the Soviet Union and the states of Eastern Europe, Kiesinger renewed the offer—first extended in Erhard's peace note of March 1966—to exchange declarations of nonaggression. Regarding the old question of diplomatic relations, the chancellor proclaimed the government's eagerness to establish political ties "wherever circumstances allow" as well as to improve economic and cultural relations with Eastern Europe. Kiesinger even appropriated certain Soviet political slogans, speaking out in favor of a "European peace order" that would span East and West.[3] Taken as a whole, the coalition's program signaled a closer alignment of Bonn's views with those of Washington, London, and especially Paris.

One feature of the new cabinet's program remained troublingly ambiguous: the relationship between Bonn's new Eastern policy and its reunification agenda. Kiesinger and Brandt consciously toned down West German rhetoric about unification, eschewing Erhard's pathos about national unity being the Federal Republic's highest goal. Without peace and a lessening of tensions in Europe, they argued, German unification would never come about.[4] The coalition officially retired the polemical designation "Soviet Occupation Zone" for East Germany, though without approving official use of the term "German Democratic Republic" either. Euphemisms like "the other part of Germany" or "the other side" prevailed in the diction of the CDU/CSU and SPD.[5] Kiesinger's government retained the perennial West German hostility to the person of Walter Ulbricht; some officials saw the new Eastern policy as a means to brand the SED regime as an anachronistic, Stalinist holdover among the socialist nations of Eastern Europe.[6] Even so, Bonn now took pains to refute Soviet charges that the Federal Republic was bent on undermining and annexing the GDR. As Kiesinger explained to the French ambassador in March 1967, the West Germans demanded free elections in eastern Germany for *humanitarian* reasons, not out of some nationalist or expansionist vision. If the Germans in the GDR were to vote to remain a separate entity from the Federal Republic, Bonn would respect this expression of self-determination.[7] Though a purely hypothetical position—no one seriously expected the SED to allow free elections—this standpoint reflected an important reinterpretation of Bonn's claim to sole representation of Germany. Self-determination was no longer considered to be synonymous with reunification.

To the new Social Democratic leadership at the Foreign Office, certain facets of the isolation campaign seemed downright counterproductive. Previously, Bonn had tried to hinder the appearance of separate East German delegations at international cultural and scientific gatherings or at sporting events. Since the SED regime prohibited the formation of joint delegations, this West German standpoint had indirectly stymied foreign travel by East German scholars and athletes. This struck Brandt and the SPD officials he brought with him from Berlin, Egon Bahr and Klaus Schütz, as needlessly punitive to the citizens of the GDR. "It cannot be in the German interest to insist on isolating these people," Brandt proclaimed to his British, American, and French colleagues in December 1966.[8] Following a train of thought already pursued by Karl Carstens two years earlier, officials on the planning staff considered how the Federal Republic might uphold its claim as the sole legitimate representative of Germany and yet still accept or even encourage East German participation in select international organizations.[9] Most at the Foreign Office still shunned the idea of direct, high-level political contacts between East and West Germans, fearing that this would imply a recognition of the GDR. Yet Egon Bahr promoted that idea relentlessly, arguing that the only path to unification lay in "embracing" the GDR.[10] Kiesinger himself displayed a willingness to experiment in the field of German-German contacts, engaging in a brief exchange of letters with the GDR's prime minister, Willi Stoph, in mid-1967.[11]

Where did these activities leave the Hallstein Doctrine? In general, given the Grand Coalition's readiness to grant the GDR a limited degree of international respectability, Bonn's isolation efforts in the Third World were now of secondary importance to policy makers. The best reason the Foreign Office could give for retaining the Hallstein Doctrine was that it still worked. The GDR had to contend with a markedly inferior international status thanks to its dearth of formal recognition.[12] Officials in Bonn began to regard the Hallstein Doctrine as a form of leverage over the GDR, a "trump card" that could be bargained away in exchange for concrete arrangements with the SED regime—perhaps solid guarantees regarding transit to Berlin.[13] In the near term, it made sense for Bonn to continue enforcing the isolation policy with the accustomed rigor so that its advantageous position did not just slip away gradually. Thus the West German ambassador to Mali undertook a curt démarche in May 1967, complete with a personal appeal from President Lübke, in order to protest against Mali's plans to erect a trade mission in East Berlin.[14] Bonn also resisted East German efforts to open *any* form of mission in Singapore, fearing that the city-state's geographic position would offer outstanding propaganda opportunities for the GDR in Southeast Asia.[15] For many diplomats in the field, the instincts honed during the long years of German-German competition remained active. Alexander Böker, who stayed on as the coordinator of Bonn's political relations with the developing world through early 1968, continued to describe the rival regime as the Soviet Occupation Zone.[16]

Chancellor Kiesinger needed the Hallstein Doctrine above all as a political cover for his new Eastern policy. Many elements in the CDU/CSU remained suspicious of détente, though the problem was somewhat lessened by Kiesinger's clever decision to coopt the CSU's leading Gaullists into government service.[17] Conservatives in the union parties had long resisted the establishment of diplomatic relations with Eastern Europe for fear that the Hallstein Doctrine would collapse. Once the Grand Coalition exchanged ambassadors with Romania in January 1967, Kiesinger had to prove the doomsayers wrong.[18] The Federal Republic undertook a worldwide démarche explaining the basis of the coalition's foreign policy, supported by individual démarches from French, British, and American diplomats. In each case the basic argument was the same: the Grand Coalition's opening toward Eastern Europe was a step toward détente; it would help lessen suspicions between East and West and thus reduce the likelihood of war. Those countries that favored détente ought to welcome Bonn's new Eastern policy and not take advantage of the situation by recognizing the GDR or upgrading its status.[19] Naturally, Kiesinger's government did not neglect to wield the old "birth defect" argument, pointing out that Romania's decision to recognize the GDR had taken place under duress back in 1949, so it need not be viewed as an unfriendly act against the Federal Republic.[20]

Bonn's "covering operation" of January 1967 ran even more smoothly than anticipated. Not a single country moved to establish diplomatic relations with the GDR in the following months. In the Middle East, Bonn actually gained back some lost terrain by reopening its embassy in Amman, Jordan, in late February.[21] It was not the Hallstein Doctrine but the new Eastern policy itself that ran aground in the spring of 1967. In Moscow, Warsaw, and East Berlin, the ruling parties responded with white-hot fury to the Grand Coalition's approach. For one thing, it appeared that Bonn was trying to split apart the Soviet bloc by exploiting Romania's maverick tendencies. The strategy appeared to be working; Hungarian and even Czech party leaders responded positively to the overtures by Kiesinger and Brandt.[22] Perhaps more disturbingly, the West Germans were talking of peace while continuing to reject the status quo of a divided Germany. Détente on this basis was plainly unacceptable to the Soviets.[23] In February 1967 Bonn's bitterest foes—Poland and the GDR—moved to enforce discipline within the Soviet bloc. The foreign ministers of the Warsaw Pact (save Romania) met in the Polish capital and agreed that further diplomatic cooperation with West Germany would be contingent on several conditions: Bonn must recognize the GDR, recognize Poland's Oder-Neisse border, renounce any ambitions regarding nuclear weapons, and stop claiming West Berlin as an integral component of West German territory.[24] In effect, so long as the Kiesinger government refused to endorse the status quo in Europe, the Federal Republic would be barred from further political gains in Eastern Europe. Pundits soon devised an ironic appellation for the Warsaw Pact's hard line: the "Ulbricht Doctrine."

Jarred into action, the Soviet leadership vowed that the socialist states must evince deeper solidarity with the GDR in its quest for worldwide recognition. This aroused visions in East Berlin of a coordinated financial effort by the Warsaw Pact to buy off nonaligned governments, but what the Soviets had in mind was straightforward political pressure.[25] In March 1967 Moscow directed a memorandum to select nonaligned leaders, arguing that the Federal Republic was bent on smashing socialism and restoring capitalism in East Germany. If the addressees—including Egypt, Syria, Algeria, Yemen, and Tanzania—were serious about the causes of national liberation, progress, and socialism, they had an obligation to support the GDR. Soviet ambassadors were instructed to expose the "neocolonial" nature of Bonn's Hallstein Doctrine: "It is an expression of great power policy. . . . It is the same conception as in the time of the German Kaisers and of Hitler-fascism." Bonn's threatened sanctions were hollow, anyway, and in the unlikely event of concrete West German reprisals, the Soviet bloc would consider balancing them out.[26] Moscow's hints about economic assistance were apparently too vague to have much impact, however; Foreign Minister Winzer found little readiness for a change of course during his tour of "progressive" Arab capitals in May 1967. Despite their generally friendly attitude toward the SED regime, they continued to balk at the idea of carrying on relations with the GDR alone. Asked whether he might prefer a simultaneous opening of relations with East *and* West Germany, Nasser demurred, presumably because of his reluctance to contemplate restoring diplomatic ties with Bonn.[27] The one bright spot was Syria, which—anticipating bountiful rewards—pressed urgently for a visit by Walter Ulbricht. Yet the GDR was not about to sell Ulbricht's prestige short. East German diplomats made it clear that the heroic proletarian leader could not leave Damascus with anything less than an exchange of full diplomatic relations.[28] This was a perfectly sensible position; but it slowed the pace of negotiations between East Germany and Syria, for it encouraged the Syrians to ensure that they received an adequately high price for trading in their last bit of leverage over the GDR.

As so often before, East Germany's fortunes appeared to turn with a shift in the political—and military—terrain. During the Six Day War of June 1967, Israel administered painful blows to Arab armies on all fronts, capturing substantial chunks of territory from Egypt, Syria, and Jordan. The renewed outbreak of hostilities polarized the Near East along Cold War lines more sharply than ever. Before the fighting had even ceased, Prime Minister Stoph dashed off a message to Egypt and Syria offering East German medical and logistical support.[29] East Berlin's gesture resonated widely in the Near and Middle East; flattering Arab officials remarked that the GDR had outshone even the Soviet Union in its reflexive solidarity with the region.[30] Hoping to capitalize on this glowing sentiment, Ulbricht sent a personal emissary in early July to inquire where things stood with diplomatic relations. Nasser promised to move forward with a formal recognition of the GDR "as soon as the military and moral position" of the Arab camp was restored.[31] In Syria the ruling Ba'ath Party passed a motion in favor of recognizing East Germany; establishing diplomatic relations was thus no more than a "procedural question." Yet Damascus made it plain that Syria expected concrete assistance in the form of fighter aircraft and pilots.[32] Ulbricht, by now accustomed to such extortionate behavior, shared the following analysis with Soviet party secretary Leonid Brezhnev: the "progressive" Arab states were using the "question of normalizing relations to the GDR as a ransom (*Faustpfand*) in order to obtain a maximum of military aid and political and economic support from the USSR, the GDR, and the other socialist states."[33]

However tempted Ulbricht may have been to buy recognition in this form, he abided by Moscow's cautious line. Providing jets was one thing; the GDR promised ten Soviet-made MiG fighters to Syria and fifty to Egypt. But commissioning East German pilots would signify a more direct form of involvement that could, in Ulbricht's words, be construed as favoring a "military solution" to the problem of Israel—the annihilation of the Jewish state.[34] Having assumed a sort of hegemony among the radical Arab states, the Soviet bloc now felt a certain responsibility to restrain their clients for the sake of peace. Rather than placing all its hopes in military cooperation, the GDR sought to deepen ties in the realms of education, commerce, and propaganda by replacing "bourgeois" Western advisers with East German experts. Another promising avenue of influence came via the exchange of delegations between the SED and its supposed "brother parties" in the Near East—the Ba'ath in Syria and the Arab Socialist Union in Egypt.[35] There was no doubt now that these two countries and perhaps other Arab states would recognize the GDR without first trying to reorder their relations with the Federal Republic. Yet the asking price remained out of reach. Negotiations in early 1968 broke down after Syria refused to budge from its demand of $50 million in credits at 0.5 percent interest. Soviet diplomats on-site urged the East Germans to pay up or even to make an outright gift to the Syrians, but the SED Politburo resisted such obvious expedients.[36] As desperately as Ulbricht wished to achieve diplomatic relations with *some* noncommunist country, pride—and the GDR's limited financial capacities—counseled patience. Caving in to Syria's exorbitant demands would only lead other Arab states to expect similar treatment.[37]

By January 1968 the SED was looking for help from an unexpected corner. Bonn's new Eastern policy, once a source of panic in East Berlin, now presented a most tantalizing prospect: the Federal Republic was on the verge of reestablishing diplomatic relations with Yugoslavia. This was a natural move for the Grand Coalition, which hungered for new successes in Eastern Europe. Eastern policy was, after all, one of the principal hallmarks of the governing alliance between CDU/CSU and SPD. Now that Bonn's ambitions among the Warsaw Pact states had been thwarted, Yugoslavia was the next logical candidate. Tito's regime was considerably more pro-Western than the members of the Warsaw Pact, and there were a number of bilateral issues—such as Yugoslav guest workers in Germany or German bathers on the Adriatic coast—that made the lack of formal relations seem onerous. As early as March 1967, Willy Brandt set his sights on a restoration of diplomatic ties with Belgrade before the end of the calendar year.[38] Kiesinger moved more cautiously. Once the Federal Republic had mended fences with Tito, the perpetrator of the original "unfriendly act," what would remain of Bonn's classic deterrent? Foreign observers, like many in the CDU/CSU, predicted a wave of recognitions of the GDR in the wake of a reconciliation between Bonn and Belgrade.[39] This, of course, is precisely what the SED was hoping for. Was the end of the Hallstein Doctrine nigh?

Tito certainly hoped so; he assured Otto Winzer that Yugoslav diplomats would assist the GDR in exposing the arbitrary, contradictory nature of Bonn's threats, particularly in the Arab capitals.[40] Kiesinger, for his part, faced pressure once again to prove that the new Eastern policy was not harmful to Bonn's long-term interest in unification. During a tour of Southeast Asia in November 1967, the chancellor discussed the issue at length with the leaders of India, Pakistan, Ceylon, and Burma. He couched his plea in terms of domestic opposition to détente: if Bonn's opening to Yugoslavia led to a collapse of the Hallstein Doctrine, then the CDU/CSU was likely to turn against the Grand Coalition's policy of peaceful reconciliation with Eastern Europe.[41] In reply, Indian prime minister Indira Gandhi made no specific promises about Yugoslavia, but she did state that India's policy toward Germany would remain unchanged. Similar responses came from the other Asian leaders consulted.[42] Persuaded that Bonn's position in the developing world was strong enough to withstand any possible complications, Kiesinger's cabinet officially reestablished diplomatic relations with Yugoslavia on January 31, 1968.

Once more, as one year earlier, a covering operation by Bonn helped to stave off any immediate reaction in the developing world. Egyptian officials were quick to point out the illogic of Bonn's position. If Belgrade—still one of the world's foremost nonaligned capitals—was allowed to host two German embassies, then surely Cairo should be able to as well.[43] Yet countries around the Third World continued to show remarkable reserve toward the GDR, despite the increasingly arbitrary permutations of the Hallstein Doctrine propagated by the Grand Coalition. To some extent this flowed from a favorable international constellation. After all the conferences and grandstanding from 1961 to 1965, the nonaligned movement remained dormant in the second half of the decade.[44] Bonn had also neutralized one classic incentive for developing countries to upgrade their relations with the GDR. They could no longer be certain that it would stimulate fresh offers of aid from the Federal Republic. In the view of Hans-Jürgen Wischnewski, now serving as development aid minister, nervous attempts to influence a country's behavior via emergency aid measures only left the Federal Republic vulnerable to blackmail. Speaking to the Bundestag in October 1967, Wischnewski asserted that "if individual countries should attempt . . . to exploit Germany's division and use it against us, the Federal Government will react calmly and will not let itself be forced into making concessions."[45] The lessons of the disastrous Near Eastern crisis in 1965 had been learned. This did not, of course, mean that Wischnewski and his colleagues had dismissed the possibility of *negative* economic sanctions. Bonn routinely hinted to Algeria and Mali that their dealings with the EEC could be jeopardized if they allowed East German consulates (let alone embassies) into their countries.[46]

By 1968 it seemed unlikely that the GDR would ever win substantial international recognition on its own strength. Only a handful of countries in the nonaligned world sympathized with Ulbricht's regime, and these were unabashedly mercenary about their material expectations. A vote in the WHO, an intergovernmental subsidiary of the United Nations, offered a high-resolution snapshot of East Berlin's weak position. Only 19 countries voted in favor of the GDR's application for admission to the WHO in May 1968; 59 voted against, 27 abstained, and an additional 15 were absent from the vote. This was not necessarily a glowing success for the Federal Republic either, for it had not managed to rally a majority of the organization's members to endorse its viewpoint. Yet outright support for the GDR remained confined to the usual corners: the communist members plus Mali, Burma, Cambodia, and several Arab states.[47] Ulbricht's state was not uniquely vilified on account of the Berlin Wall or its lack of political and cultural freedoms; far more distasteful regimes enjoyed the respect of the international community. Under ordinary circumstances, most governments—in the West as well as in the nonaligned world—would have long since established diplomatic relations with the GDR as a matter of course. Yet the circumstances were far from ordinary so long as West Germans continued to assert their opposition to East German recognition. Germany's Cold War would draw to a close only when the Federal Republic was prepared to accept the GDR as a fact of international life.

The Coalition "Cambodes"

Soviet pressure on the Grand Coalition intensified in 1968. Bonn's international behavior—resumption of West German–Yugoslav relations and resistance to East German membership in the WHO—confirmed the Soviet government's worst suspicions about the new Eastern policy of the Kiesinger-Brandt cabinet.[48] In Soviet terms, the Federal Republic continued to pursue a revanchist agenda aimed at overturning several elements of the postwar settlement. First, Bonn continued to insist that the final boundaries of the unified German state could only be drawn at a peace conference. Second, the West Germans kept pressing for modifications in the draft of the nuclear nonproliferation treaty to ensure that a joint West European nuclear force would not be prohibited. Third, Kiesinger's cabinet refused to accept the existence of the GDR or to consider its territory as a foreign country. These issues boiled down to a single overarching question: Was the Federal Republic prepared to accept the status quo in Europe and, in particular, the perpetuation of a weakened, divided Germany? Only on this basis was the Soviet Union prepared to honor Bonn's new Eastern policy.[49]

The Soviets and their allies drove this point home in uncomfortable ways. On a rhetorical level, the fulminations of Moscow and East Berlin reached new heights in 1967 and 1968. More so than ever, they claimed, the Federal Republic was in the hands of former Nazis and Nazi sympathizers. A highly organized defamation campaign branded President

Lübke as a *"KZ-Baumeister,"* a specialist in the construction of concentration camps during the Third Reich.[50] The charges against Chancellor Kiesinger were more founded: he had never denied joining the Nazi party as early as 1933 and serving as a propagandist in the Foreign Ministry during World War II. The rise of the right-radical National Democratic Party (NPD) provided further grist for the mill; the party gained representation in seven state parliaments between November 1966 and April 1968.[51] External pressure from the Warsaw Pact dovetailed with internal criticisms by a student movement increasingly prone to question the democratic character of the Grand Coalition. When the coalition parties controlled 90 percent of the seats in the Bundestag, what effective checks remained on the government's power? The burgeoning "extra-parliamentary opposition" grew alarmed at the coalition's plans to pass a series of laws regulating some future state of emergency; in the hysterical atmosphere of the late 1960s, these laws appeared to herald a return to the police state of yesteryear.[52] For the first time, East Germany's favorite leitmotivs were finding an audience both within West Germany and in the wider international community. The "good" Germany, the GDR, had eliminated the root causes of fascism in its territory and now worked to uphold the peace in Europe; the "bad" Germany, the Federal Republic, was once again in the hands of dangerous militarists who were aching to reverse the outcome of World War II. To be sure, critical students and intellectuals were more prone to revere guerilla communists such as Che Guevara than bureaucrats like Ulbricht. Yet the critique of West German institutions hit home, as countless flyers from 1968 indicate.[53]

The Soviet bloc supplemented these verbal barrages with a series of overtly menacing acts. In April 1968, authorities in the GDR announced that they would bar all West German cabinet members and other top officials from traveling through East German territory. They followed this up in June by demanding passports, visas, and transit fees from *all* German travelers passing between the Federal Republic and Berlin—a sobering reminder of West Berlin's precarious position.[54] Soviet notes to the Kiesinger government referred bluntly to Articles 53 and 107 of the UN charter, which gave the victors of World War II the authority to intervene in defeated countries such as Germany.[55] In August 1968 a different, brutal intervention *did* take place—against Czechoslovakia, where the "Prague Spring" had taken on dimensions of cultural autonomy that appeared to threaten the primacy of the Communist Party. Though the links between Bonn's new Eastern policy and events in Prague were indirect, the incident confirmed to West German leaders that their efforts at reconciliation with Eastern Europe could only succeed if Moscow gave its approval.[56]

Faced with this intense Soviet pressure to acknowledge the status quo, the two coalition partners tended increasingly to give opposite answers. For a year and a half the CDU/CSU and SPD had managed to cooperate amicably in the pursuit of a new Eastern policy, but Kiesinger's policy statement of December 13, 1966, was growing more dated with every passing month. One wing of the SPD, swayed in part by the antiauthoritarian, antiwar anthems of the student movement, came to favor dramatic conciliatory gestures toward Moscow and Warsaw. The FDP showed the way; alone in opposition, this small party had reinvented itself as a font of reformist, nonconformist impulses.[57] In April 1967 the Free Democrats waged a bitter internal debate over the German-Polish border at their party congress in Hanover; in March 1968 the Social Democrats followed suit at their Nuremberg congress. Neither party could agree on an unequivocal recognition of the Oder-Neisse line, but Brandt—in his capacity as SPD chairman—pledged to respect the present border with Poland until a peace treaty could be negotiated.[58] It was a compromise that Egon Bahr, Brandt's chief of planning at the Foreign Office, found completely inadequate to calm Polish fears. As it was, though, the SPD resolutions in Nuremberg went far beyond what the CDU/CSU leadership, including Kiesinger himself, wished to endorse.[59]

Tentatively, some in the SPD began to consider what might responsibly be sacrificed to achieve a calm, productive dialogue with Ulbricht's regime. At issue was not the isolation campaign as such; so far as the leadership of the SPD was concerned, the Hallstein Doctrine was nothing more than an afterthought. The debate now turned upon a more fundamental problem: Should the Federal Republic *itself* recognize the GDR? Brandt resisted such a step, not because of its likely effect on the GDR's international standing, but because it might deepen the gulf between East and West Germany. In the foreign minister's words, the GDR was "not a foreign country."[60] Others in the party embraced the reasoning of journalists such as Peter Bender, who published a pamphlet titled *Ten Reasons to Recognize the GDR* in 1968. Student organizations and "youth" sections of all the mainstream parties came forward with resolutions demanding recognition of the SED regime as the only sensible means of settling German affairs.[61] In April 1969 the Social Democrats—following the FDP's lead—expressed their readiness to engage in negotiations with the East German government "without any sort of discrimination," so long as the SED showed a constructive attitude.[62]

The SPD and FDP were now finding common ground on many issues, it seemed; the two parties even cooperated in the selection of Gustav Heinemann, one of Adenauer's fiercest critics, as the third president of the Federal Republic. Significant groups in both parties were evidently steering toward the creation of a Social-Liberal coalition after the fall elections.[63]

Politicians in the CDU/CSU responded to the leftward drift of its two main rivals by inching to the right. Electoral calculations played a role; the rise of a right-wing competitor, the NPD, drove the CDU/CSU to assert its patriotic credentials more forcefully.[64] On a more basic level, a backlash against the new Eastern policy set in among the union parties in the months following the Prague tragedy, reflecting a deep discomfort with the recent actions of the governing coalition. Kiesinger had long encountered resistance from such venerable figures as Heinrich Krone, a former confidante of Adenauer's, who predicted that the coalition's policies would lead to a "hardening, even a sanctioning of the current status of a divided Germany."[65] As early as October 1967, the chancellor had seen fit to cover his back by railing against the "party of recognition"—the West German media—which, he claimed, irresponsibly promoted the full recognition of the GDR.[66] Kiesinger's own preference was to hold the line, clinging to whatever positions could still be held in the contest of wills between the Federal Republic and the Soviet Union. He and the party's other leading lights on foreign policy, Franz-Josef Strauss and Gerhard Schröder, had essentially given up on the prospect of achieving renunciation of force agreements with Moscow. Brandt's ongoing dialogue with the Soviet ambassador came to seem downright reckless, and rumors about secret contacts between Egon Bahr and the Italian Communist Party raised further questions within the CDU/CSU about the reliability of the SPD as a coalition partner.[67] The union parties came to the election season of 1969 in a demoralized state, unenthused about Kiesinger and his Grand Coalition yet lacking viable alternatives.[68]

A showdown over Eastern policy was clearly in the cards. The Western Allies scrambled to keep out of the way, lest they be dragged into the electoral contest. Internally, many British and American diplomats shared the CDU/CSU's concerns about the SPD line. For much of the 1960s, London and Washington had encouraged greater West German openness toward the Soviet bloc, but by the end of 1967 they began to fear that Bonn's dialogue with Moscow might end up compromising Allied rights in Berlin.[69] They hoped that the West Germans could find a means of increasing human contacts with East German citizens *without* a formal recognition of the SED regime; once the GDR was accepted internationally as a sovereign state, they reasoned, it would be nearly impossible to justify the Allied presence in the former German capital.[70] In Paris, officials were more welcoming of Brandt's ideas, perhaps because de Gaulle himself toyed with the idea of normalizing relations with East Germany. The GDR was, after all, interesting as an export market for European industrialists, and French leaders were relatively open in their preference for seeing two German states rather than one.[71] As it happened, the installation of new presidents in Paris and Washington—Georges Pompidou and Richard Nixon, respectively—facilitated the Allied efforts to keep a low profile in the spring of 1969. Only *after* West Germany's fall elections would the extent of Allied reservations vis-à-vis Brandt's Eastern policy become evident.

Despite many obvious signs that the Grand Coalition was crumbling, no one would have dared predict that its most trying test would arise over a threadbare issue such as the Hallstein Doctrine. For much of the spring, monetary policy divided the cabinet. The German mark had long been undervalued with respect to other currencies, but the SPD could not persuade the CDU/CSU cabinet members to adjust the mark's value upward. With elections just a few months away, the parties had more to gain from posturing than from compromise.[72] The same considerations applied on a larger scale when the coalition faced the scenario once so feared in Bonn: a "wave" of recognitions of East Germany. Iraq, now ruled by the revolutionary command of the Ba'ath Party, announced on April 30 that it would establish diplomatic relations with the GDR. A similar statement followed from Cambodia on May 8. The CDU/CSU and the SPD leaped to the barricades, pitting chancellor against foreign minister in a sharply partisan feud. As an instrument of policy, the Hallstein Doctrine had long since lost its luster at the Foreign Office, but the doctrine retained a symbolic value in West German politics that could not help but manifest itself during an election year.

Since Iraq had severed diplomatic relations with the Federal Republic back in 1965, the Foreign Office could identify no practical means of punishing Baghdad's "unfriendly act." Bonn's aid programs in Iraq were quite modest, and there was little appetite for a ban on the import of Iraqi oil.[73] Attention in Bonn thus focused on the kingdom of Cambodia. For most of the 1960s, Prince Sihanouk had enjoyed considerable leeway in his relations with the two German states, granting West Germany a status only marginally superior to that of East Germany. Until 1967 this meant that both states entertained only consular relations with Cambodia, though the

West German office in Phnom Penh bore the title *représentation*, suggesting a diplomatic presence. In July 1967 Prince Sihanouk agreed to designate the East German office as a *représentation* as well, leading to a frantic West German intervention.[74] The issue was resolved in November of that year when the Federal Republic and Cambodia established full diplomatic relations, giving Bonn a clear lead over East Berlin again. This solution had murky implications for the Hallstein Doctrine; but the affair drew little publicity at the time, and Bonn's quiet, pragmatic handling of the issue represented a mark of sympathy for Cambodia's precarious geographic situation.[75] In striking up diplomatic relations with the GDR in 1969, then, Prince Sihanouk was merely restoring the balance on German issues that he felt his country's neutral position demanded. Was this grounds for harsh retaliation by the Federal Republic?

Many in the CDU/CSU thought so, invoking the old argument that a failure to act against Cambodia would embolden other countries to follow its bad example.[76] Chancellor Kiesinger, not noted for being a "Hallstein-Doctrinaire," gave the matter no special urgency. Government spokespersons labeled Sihanouk's move an unfriendly act but showed reserve in discussing possible countermeasures. In the cabinet, Kiesinger expressed a preference for strong action, but when confronted with Brandt's firm resistance, the chancellor urged that the subject be postponed until the West German ambassador had returned to Bonn for consultations and the Cambodian ambassador to the Federal Republic (who resided in Paris) had appeared in Bonn to clarify his government's position.[77] Kiesinger then departed for a state visit to Japan, which left the foreign minister a free hand to seek a diplomatic solution to the crisis.

Brandt responded quite emotionally to the situation. Having worked for years to diminish the role of the Hallstein Doctrine in West German foreign policy, he recoiled at the prospect of breaking diplomatic relations with Phnom Penh. As far as Brandt was concerned, the real issue was not Cambodia but the overall state of the isolation campaign. He and his top advisers—within both the SPD and the Foreign Office—hoped to create a new precedent proving that Bonn had weaned itself from the Hallstein Doctrine.[78] With each passing day the foreign minister articulated his standpoint with greater clarity: Bonn's policy did *not* require an automatic severing of relations with countries that recognized the GDR. In some cases it might make more sense for Bonn to hold its ground rather than walk away, leaving the East Germans alone to represent the German people in a foreign capital.[79] Under some circumstances, Brandt reasoned, a recognition of the

OF TWO MINDS

GDR by an outside party might not even qualify as an unfriendly act. For the time being, the SED regime's "intransigent and malicious stance" on questions of German-German relations meant that Bonn must still react with displeasure to recognitions of the GDR. But Brandt could envision an end to the isolation campaign, a time when the two German governments engaged in cooperation rather than confrontation.[80]

Unfortunately for Brandt, relations with Phnom Penh had already suffered irreparable damage. Prince Sihanouk professed grave offense at Bonn's handling of the situation and accused the Federal Republic of "great power chauvinism." He had no intention of letting the Cambodian ambassador travel to Bonn just to "click his heels and say Heil Hitler." Sihanouk's latter remark was suppressed in the Cambodian record of the press conference, but Kiesinger learned of it anyway, and this—together with the ambassador's failure to appear in Bonn—constituted an unpardonable slight in the chancellor's eyes.[81] Word that the Cambodian foreign minister was en route to East Berlin compounded the anger in Bonn. Kiesinger returned from Tokyo on May 23, even as Brandt departed for an official visit to Ankara. Circles around the chancellor demanded retaliation against Sihanouk; Günter Diehl, the government's top spokesman, hinted that a break in relations might be forthcoming.[82] Meanwhile, in the final days of May, an anti-Western military coup in Sudan yielded one more recognition of the GDR. Here, as in Iraq, the Federal Republic was powerless to react, which only increased the temptation to move against Cambodia. Brandt, who learned of the chancellor's increasingly hostile views while still in Turkey, returned to Bonn spoiling for a fight.[83] Brandt's resolve was bolstered by Egon Bahr, his longtime adviser and chief of planning at the Foreign Office, who insisted that the SPD was arguing from a position of strength within the coalition and must not let itself be bullied by the CDU/CSU.[84]

Seven hours of debate in the cabinet meeting of May 30, 1969, brought no decisions on Cambodia. Brandt, disgusted at the spectacle, threatened to resign if the cabinet chose to break with Phnom Penh.[85] The issue was then referred to the coalition's informal clearing station, the "Kressbonn Circle," which deliberated on June 2 until deep into the night. A year's worth of accusations flew across the table in what proved to be a remarkably cathartic session. As a compromise between extremes, the group opted to "freeze" diplomatic relations with Cambodia—whatever that meant. Would Bonn's embassy in Phnom Penh close down, or would it remain open?[86] The government's official statement of June 4 specified only that its ambassador would be recalled permanently, that diplomatic activity at the embassy would cease, and that no new treaties of economic cooperation would be signed.[87] West German pundits coined a new verb to describe the coalition's muddled response: *kambodschieren*, "to cambode." It must have come as a relief to many when Prince Sihanouk ended the charade by unilaterally breaking diplomatic ties with the Federal Republic on June 11.[88]

Did the wrangling over Cambodia mark the end of the Hallstein Doctrine? Brandt certainly did not think so at the time; he returned home from the Kressbonn Circle meeting of June 2 utterly crestfallen, furious that his SPD colleagues had not supported him more wholeheartedly in his efforts to repudiate the doctrine once and for all.[89] Indeed, it was Herbert Wehner of the SPD who devised a formula allowing the coalition to postulate the continuity of its isolation campaign. At Wehner's suggestion, the cabinet resolved that when an outside country committed the "unfriendly act" of recognizing the GDR, Bonn's "attitude and response would depend upon the circumstances and upon the interests of the entire German people."[90] On the surface, this standpoint scarcely deviated from the line presented by Adenauer and Brentano in 1955–56. As before, Bonn reserved the right to punish those who transgressed against its nonrecognition policy. Yet the emphasis had shifted perceptibly. Instead of serving as a declaration of principle that justified harsh measures, Wehner's formulation was designed to explain away Bonn's reluctance to act in cases such as Cambodia's. The Grand Coalition lacked the political will to take irrevocable measures. Its more dynamic half, the SPD, was well on the way toward conceptualizing a new relationship with East Germany that would allow the GDR complete access to international life. Remarkably, these signals from Bonn had little immediate impact overseas. Even in the absence of the old-style Hallstein Doctrine, Ulbricht's regime found itself clawing for recognition just as before.

A Qualified Breakthrough

Prior to Iraq's surprise announcement on the last day of April, the East German leadership had gone for more than a year without substantial gains. This grew more exasperating with each passing day, for October 7, 1969—the twentieth anniversary of the GDR's founding—was rapidly nearing. Ulbricht and his party comrades were anxious to turn the obligatory pompous celebrations into a milestone of international respect for the SED's achievements.[91] Yet the regime's ongoing isolation threatened to undermine the effect. Negotiating partners in the Middle East must have sensed East Berlin's desperation, for they held out for top dollar in the spring of 1969. Egypt, the focal point of Ulbricht's ambitions, dodged Soviet and East German pressure by assenting to a new intermediate step: the exchange of "diplomatic missions." Despite the promising name, these missions were defined by Nasser as a stage *prior to* diplomatic relations.[92] Syria's price for recognition remained unchanged from February 1968: $50 million in aid projects at 0.5 percent interest. As of late April 1969, the SED Politburo was still reluctant to drop below 1.75 percent.[93] Meanwhile, Iraq, now moving to the forefront of the "progressive" Arab states, was still articulating far-fetched proposals in the final days of April. Baghdad expressed disdain for the GDR's project-oriented aid programs and insisted on receiving loans of some £40 million ($96 million) in hard currency. The Iraqi regime also hinted broadly that it expected "gestures of solidarity" from the East Germans, such as the delivery of small arms and uniforms. On April 29, 1969, Winzer gloomily observed that his scheduled trip to Iraq seemed ill timed and superfluous.[94] Against this background, Iraq's reversal, billed as a May Day gift, pleased the East Germans immensely. Nevertheless, it represented nothing more than a change of tactics. The Iraqis were clearly hoping that their fait accompli would shame the East Germans into writing a massive check.[95]

In Cambodia, too, the decision to initiate diplomatic relations caught the GDR's leadership off guard. During a visit to Phnom Penh in February 1968, Winzer had failed to sway Prince Sihanouk to advance mutual relations beyond the level of *représentation*.[96] What had changed in the intervening fifteen months? East German diplomats on the scene had seen no prior indications of a change of heart. Skeptical officials pondered Sihanouk's motives and began to doubt whether the Cambodian leader would follow through on his bold announcement of May 8, 1969.[97] Not wishing to over-analyze this gift horse, however, the East Germans put their concessions on the table. The Cambodians would receive an embassy building and ambassador's residence in Berlin free of charge, a loan of VM 50 million (ca. $11 million) in capital assistance, and a technical training school at no cost.[98] Sihanouk graciously accepted these offerings but did not hesitate to exploit his stance on Germany in order to pry more aid from the Soviets. In early June, after Bonn had "frozen" relations and withdrawn an offer of $1 million in aid to an international dam project, Sihanouk demanded that this sum be replaced by the USSR. Otherwise, he hinted, he might have to repair his ties with the Federal Republic at the expense of the GDR. Only after receiving Moscow's word about the $1 million did Cambodia move to break diplomatic relations with West Germany.[99]

As pleased as the East Germans were over their unforeseen successes in Baghdad and Phnom Penh, these cases provided no obvious lessons about how concerted East German pressure might be used to bring about further recognitions. On the level of propaganda, naturally, the Politburo undertook a major new offensive in mid-May highlighting Cambodia and Iraq as heroic examples for the nonaligned world.[100] Within the Arab community, however, Baghdad's unexpected move actually complicated the GDR's position, for neither Egypt nor Syria wished to give the impression of riding Iraq's coattails. Nasser admitted his embarrassment openly, noting that he had always expected to be the first Arab leader to recognize the GDR.[101] In many ways Sudan's decision to establish diplomatic relations on May 28 continued the string of ambiguous successes; East Germany's most solid supporters appeared to lie on the periphery rather than in the mainstream of the developing world.[102] By early June the financial pressure on East Berlin was intensifying. Clearly Iraq and Sudan would have to be rewarded, yet vast sums would also be required to win the cooperation of Syria and the most-sought-after prize, Egypt.

Wild rumors abounded in all the major Arab capitals. West German agents—representatives of the Federal Intelligence Service—were allegedly making vastly inflated offers in order to stave off further recognitions of the GDR.[103] Some reports contained an element of truth: Hans-Jürgen Wischnewski, Bonn's longtime contact with the Arab world, did clandestinely offer to help finance Egypt's wheat imports with a commercial credit worth $25 million. Officials in Bonn had no interest in sparking another bidding war with the GDR; but Wischnewski's proposal was billed as a humanitarian gesture, and leaders of the Grand Coalition hoped to see the chain of recognitions of East Germany come to a halt sooner rather than later.[104] Arab diplomats embellished considerably in their conversations with East German representatives, magnifying the sums fivefold and sometimes fabricating West German promises outright. The point was, of course, to underscore the virtue of the Arabs in turning down these overtures from Bonn—and to hint that East Berlin ought to show its gratitude by producing comparable amounts.[105] Ulbricht's regime could not hope to match the Federal Republic's actual aid and trade figures, let alone these imaginary sums, but Baghdad and Khartoum did land significant prizes—as much as $84 million and 5,000 rifles for Iraq and some $11 million for Sudan.[106] On June 5, 1969, Winzer finally signed an agreement in Damascus regarding

OF TWO MINDS

the long-mooted loan of $50 million, marking the onset of diplomatic relations with Syria. South Yemen was next in line. Its recognition of the GDR on June 30 was rewarded with an aid package promising more than $7 million.[107]

Nasser relented on July 10, 1969. Until early July, Egypt continued in public to deny its intention of recognizing East Germany; Foreign Minister Winzer's June stopover in Cairo yielded no discernible progress.[108] Nasser's final decision apparently resulted from Soviet pressure in conjunction with a pending arms sale. As usual, the GDR's own position was a direct function of the Soviet Union's relative standing in foreign capitals.[109] It was, of course, understood that the East Germans would renew their aid commitments to Egypt—on the order of $75 million in government credits and a further $37 million on commercial terms over 1970–75.[110] By this point the GDR's aid fund was hopelessly overburdened; from now on the "recognition wave" would have to move forward on its own momentum. Surely Egypt's decision would have a signal effect on other nonaligned powers, amplifying the wave into a flood? Such a contingency, long feared by the authors of the Hallstein Doctrine, did not come to pass. Certain governments outside the Arab world did adjust their relations with the GDR in minor ways. Guinea raised the level of East German representation in Conakry from trade mission to consulate. India moved forward with a project postponed since 1966, the opening of a state trading office in East Berlin.[111] Yet the number of noncommunist states entertaining diplomatic relations with East Germany halted at six for the rest of the calendar year. Nasser's decision marked the last ripple of the recognition wave of 1969.

Lingering fears about West German reactions surely played a role here. Bonn's response to the Syrian and Egyptian transgressions was relatively passive, since the Federal Republic had long ceased funding aid projects in these countries. South Yemen was in a more vulnerable position, however, and it paid a price. The Grand Coalition repeated its Cambodia formula by freezing diplomatic relations and canceling its projected financial assistance.[112] A country such as India, so dependent on West German largesse, was reluctant to risk a similar response, however unlikely Bonn was to exact sanctions against such a major trading partner. Uncertainty about the future of East and West German relations was further grounds for reserve. Outside observers could see clearly that important voices in the Federal Republic were angling toward some de facto acceptance of the GDR as a second German state. In the long run, then, the isolation campaign against East Germany would draw to a close. What was the point in antagonizing

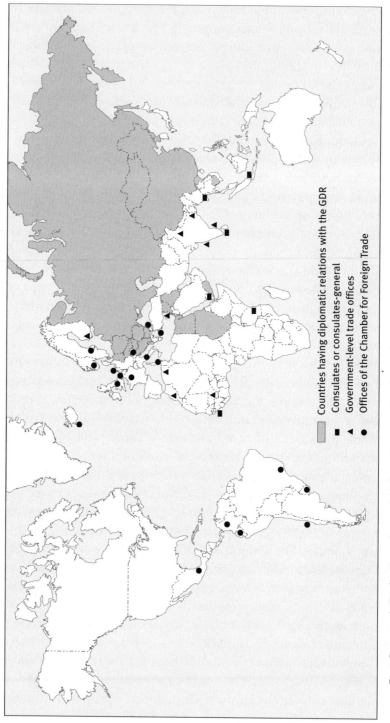

Countries having diplomatic relations with the GDR

■ Consulates or consulates-general

◀ Government-level trade offices

● Offices of the Chamber for Foreign Trade

MAP 5. East Germany's Trade, Consular, and Diplomatic Network, December 1969

the Federal Republic now, when in two years—or even two months—recognition of the GDR would go unpunished?[113] The GDR generously offered to make good any fiscal shortfalls occasioned by West German retaliation, but such guarantees were scarcely credible in light of the depleted state of East Germany's treasury. The SED regime could ill afford to buy more friends. Indeed, shortly after the pompous twentieth-anniversary celebrations in October 1969, consumers in the GDR faced shortages of such basic supplies as coal and potatoes. Ulbricht's investments in technology—symbolized by Berlin's newly operational television tower—had failed to resolve East Germany's more fundamental economic problems.[114] It is little wonder that newspapers in the GDR reported so sparingly about the millions of marks promised to foreign governments in the pursuit of Ulbricht's prestige project, international recognition. The six recognitions of 1969 had not put bread on the table of East German workers. With winter approaching, the Politburo opted to delay formal negotiations with Egypt on the new credit package.[115]

Despite all this, the GDR's long-term outlook was promising. By mid-1969, Finland was energetically promoting the idea of a European security conference, the framework later known as the Helsinki process. Although the Finnish government continued to postpone formal recognition of East (and West) Germany, the European conference project demanded equal participation by both German states. Détente in this form would thus mark the GDR's final acceptance into the community of Europe by all sides: the Warsaw Pact states, the neutrals, and the NATO powers.[116] Such a prospect had long been anathema in Bonn, but the elections of September 1969 brought forward a new Social-Liberal coalition, a partnership of SPD and FDP. With Willy Brandt as chancellor and Walter Scheel as foreign minister, the stage was set for a more comprehensive Eastern policy that proceeded from the territorial realities of postwar Europe. In November 1969 Egon Bahr, now Brandt's top foreign policy adviser in the Chancellor's Office, charted Bonn's next moves in strict secrecy: first, a renunciation of force agreement with Moscow; second, a similar arrangement with Warsaw; third, a modus vivendi with East Berlin; and finally, the accession of East Germany to normal diplomatic life.[117] East Germany's international recognition was coming, and it would arrive with West Germany's blessing.

In the fall of 1969, however, that time was not yet at hand. Brandt and the members of his cabinet, for all their impatience with the isolation campaign, accepted its functional utility as a means of keeping up the pressure on Ulbricht and his regime.[118] In accord with positions first articulated by

Brandt in May 1969, the Social-Liberal coalition vowed to contain the GDR's foreign presence until the East German leadership had demonstrated sufficient cooperation in the regulation of East-West affairs. Foreign Minister Scheel served as the principal spokesman for this holding operation, subsequently known as the "Scheel Doctrine."[119] The entire endeavor was a coda to the original Hallstein Doctrine. Third parties found the West German standpoint somewhat contradictory. On one hand, Brandt described Germany as consisting of "two states within one nation"; on the other hand, the Federal Republic continued to discourage other countries from dealing with the GDR as a normal state.[120] The coalition's policy was not without teeth. When Ceylon—once again under the leadership of Sirimavo Bandaranaike—recognized the GDR in the spring of 1970, the Brandt-Scheel cabinet retaliated by refusing to sign four recently negotiated aid agreements.[121]

If the Federal Republic kept imploring "not yet," the GDR answered with a broad campaign demanding "recognition now!" This was nothing more than a struggle for tactical gain. The SED leadership hoped that by forcing through the GDR's international recognition, its bargaining position vis-à-vis the Federal Republic would be enhanced. By the early 1970s, sympathizers across Europe had planted GDR recognition societies; citizens' movements (funded largely via East German front organizations) were particularly strong in Britain, Belgium, the Netherlands, and the Scandinavian countries.[122] For the first time since the early 1950s, the GDR's aspirations focused squarely on the continent of Europe. Yet success was confined to the developing world. The Republic of Congo (Brazzaville), Somalia, the Central African Republic, and the Maledive Islands all established diplomatic relations in the spring of 1970. A more tangible partner, Algeria, finally consented to recognition in May of that year, thanks to an East German aid package reportedly topping $142 million.[123] In no case did the Federal Republic break diplomatic relations. Yet by and large, nonaligned states as well as Western countries respected West German wishes.

The final breakthrough came only after Bonn had concluded its long-anticipated Basic Treaty with East Berlin, a modus vivendi that laid the groundwork for practical cooperation between the two German states on cross-border issues.[124] In the days immediately before and after the treaty's signing on December 21, 1972, the floodgates of recognition opened; twenty-one states established diplomatic ties with the GDR in December 1972 alone. The precise order mattered only for an instant. Belgium's recognition of the GDR on December 27, the first such proclamation by a NATO member, was considered a bit premature by its allies, but France and the United Kingdom had followed suit by February 9, 1973. The United States, hoping to pressure East Germany into paying restitution to Israel, held out until September 1974.[125] As satisfying as each of these milestones must have been for the SED leadership, the landslide of recognitions should not be construed as a defeat for the Federal Republic. The East German regime had remained on the fringes of international life precisely as long as West Germans wanted it to.

Conclusion

By the mid-1970s, East Germany had emerged as a recognized and moderately respected member of the international community. More than 130 states eventually exchanged diplomatic relations with East Berlin, and the GDR's reputation as a friend to "national liberation" movements in the 1960s blossomed into a series of intimate relationships with African and Middle Eastern countries in subsequent decades. Former East German diplomats, unexpectedly forced into retirement by the events of 1989–90, take pains to highlight the constructive role played by the GDR in world politics during the 1970s and 1980s.[1] From a Western perspective, the East German legacy seems less halcyon; after all, the Stasi helped to prop up such unsavory dictators as Mengistu Haile Mariam in Ethiopia. Regardless of one's standpoint, though, the GDR's significance as a Cold War actor—working in close affiliation with, but not slavish dependence on, the Soviet Union—can scarcely be doubted.[2]

For the SED leadership, such obvious successes did not dispel the trauma of years in isolation. Ulbricht's successor as party and state leader, Erich Honecker, inherited the complexes of his predecessor; achieving world-wide diplomatic recognition did not satisfy Honecker's craving for respect. The quest for formal recognition graduated into a more nebulous pursuit of international renown as a model socialist society. Hundreds of East German athletes paid the price, participating—some knowingly, some not—in steroid-boosting regimens that enhanced their Olympic performances but continue to exact a physiological toll. Honecker himself sought to augment his prestige with state visits to once-inaccessible Western capitals. Whereas Ulbricht had to settle for "friendship visits" to Cairo and Belgrade, Honecker was welcomed in Rome, Paris, and Bonn. The GDR had finally arrived, it seemed—just a few short years before the bottom fell out.

The isolation campaign left lasting scars in East Berlin; a position of relative inferiority haunted East German policy makers throughout the republic's history. West Germans, by contrast, betrayed few lingering symptoms after disengaging from the fraternal German-German rivalry in the early 1970s. Perhaps the most lasting reflex in Bonn was a tendency to *depoliticize* relations with unfriendly regimes. In the 1980s the Federal Republic promoted a policy of dialogue with revolutionary Iran and brushed aside pressure from Washington to hang an embargo on pipeline sales to the Soviet Union. West Germans now showed a distinct unwillingness to participate in politically motivated isolation strategies. With the Hallstein Doctrine repudiated, trade policy moved to the center of Bonn's foreign policy toward the socialist camp and the developing world.

The global campaign against East Germany did, in the end, outlive its usefulness. But for two decades, from 1949 through 1969 and even a bit thereafter, the West's isolation program was a prominent feature of the Cold War landscape in Germany, in the United Nations, and around the developing world. In this volume I have considered the history of this remarkable struggle from several vantage points. The introduction spelled out four key sets of relationships: between the German states and the nonaligned world, between the German states and the Four Powers, between the two German states themselves, and between the leaders and politically interested public within West Germany. In this concluding section I will recapitulate the book's principal arguments according to a different schema. The first section concerns problems of strategy and tactics—the nuts and bolts of the Germans' interaction with the nonaligned world. The second section analyzes the interaction between the isolation campaign and the broader Cold War. The third and final section explores the function of the fraternal German rivalry as a contribution (or obstacle) to the politics of German unification.

The Halting Progress of a German Sisyphus

The GDR's basic strategy for attaining recognition changed only once, very early in the game. In the first months after the founding of the republic in October 1949, the inexperienced yet ambitious leadership of the Ministry of Foreign Affairs expected to garner recognition from the GDR's near neighbors as a matter of course. The SED thus treated diplomatic relations as a precondition for *all* forms of interaction and refused to do business with countries that evaded outright recognition. As early as 1950, Finland's hesitation led to a compromise of this iron principle; the East German authorities signed a trade agreement with the Finnish government after Helsinki made it clear that it would not recognize either German state. The GDR nevertheless persisted through the mid-1950s in maladroit attempts to extort recognition from European neutrals such as Switzerland and Sweden. Any interest that Central and Western European countries had in treating with the GDR was more than counterbalanced by East Germany's own economic needs, however, and eventually the SED abandoned the fiction that capitalist countries would regard the two German states as equals. West Germany enjoyed diplomatic relations with the key European countries, while East Germany had to be content with trading on an unofficial level—contracts negotiated between industrial conglomerates or chambers of commerce. In Europe, and particularly among the NATO countries, the GDR had no choice but to adjust to the rules established by France, Britain, and the United States.

Increasingly, then, the SED turned to the world beyond Europe. The crystallization of a nonaligned movement, spearheaded by Yugoslavia, Egypt, and India, offered the distinct possibility that leaders impatient with the West would embrace East Germany as a means of asserting independence in world affairs. As early as 1953, an East German trade mission opened in Egypt, and soon thereafter India, Burma, and other developing countries had opened their doors to commerce with the GDR. They did not express any immediate intention of recognizing the SED regime, but East German officials held out hope that a progressive deepening of ties might eventually lead to full-fledged diplomatic relations. This gradualist strategy would serve as the basis of all the GDR's recognition efforts from the mid-1950s onward. East German diplomats proved remarkably adept at ratcheting up their status. The heads of trade missions described themselves as "consuls," while the plenipotentiary to the Arab states in Cairo assumed the personal title "ambassador." Aside from these fictitious designations, the real status of East German representation did improve over time. Officials posted to trade missions won the right to import personal effects from Germany duty-free, and permission to transmit ciphered messages sometimes followed. By the late 1950s, East German trade missions were giving way to formal consulates in several Arab and Southeast Asian capitals, which greatly simplified logistical problems such as the procurement of visas. Nonaligned governments were also becoming more tolerant of aggressive public relations techniques, including the defamation of West Germany as a "neo-imperialist" power and the celebration of socialist achievements in the GDR. Without a doubt, the SED's shift to a gradualist approach made possible a formidable array of activities in the nonaligned world.

Nevertheless, East Germany's ultimate goal remained out of reach. The regime's emissaries were engaged in a Sisyphean task, as West German pressure kept rolling the East German boulder back down the slope. More often than not, Nasser, Nkrumah, and other Third World leaders rescinded or postponed earlier promises made to East German representatives. Such reversals were all the more embarrassing in light of the SED's boastful tendencies, shown in all their folly in March 1960, when East Germans broke the news of diplomatic relations with Guinea a trifle prematurely. Sékou Touré's retreat exposed the fundamental limitations of East Berlin's gradualist strategy. No matter how many incremental advances the GDR achieved in Cairo or Conakry, the gap between intimate informality and de jure recognition remained unbridgeable. Nonaligned heads of state refused to alienate West Germany by defying the sacred rule of the Hallstein Doctrine: no diplomatic relations with East Germany. Did this matter, since the GDR already enjoyed extensive de facto relations with important developing countries such as India and Indonesia? Indeed it did, so long as Walter Ulbricht and his colleagues placed such a premium on assuming their rightful place among the community of states. Not only did the perpetual isolation offend Ulbricht's vanity; it placed substantial barriers on the GDR's freedom to maneuver. Absence from the UN, international trade conferences, and most nonaligned capitals (not to mention *all* Western capitals) marked East Germany as an anomaly, a pariah. Most importantly, this absence was a glaring reminder that the German Question, although scarcely open by the late 1960s, had not yet been solved according to the Eastern model of two German states. Ultimately, such a solution could only be realized with West German cooperation.

With this in mind, I have constructed the narrative in the chapters above with the Federal Republic rather than the GDR as the principal subject. Ulbricht's regime was, in effect, the *object* of a highly successful isolation campaign orchestrated by the Federal Republic and the Western Allies. West Germans did not always appreciate this at the time; they tended to see themselves as occupying a reactive position. Paul Frank, a state secretary in the 1970s, compared Bonn's foreign service to a fire brigade rushing about the globe desperately to extinguish the flames set by crafty East German diplomats.[3] Frank's metaphor does colorfully express the exhaustion felt by key troubleshooters such as Rolf Lahr, Alexander Böker, and Frank himself at the peak of the isolation campaign. Yet the comparison breaks down when the responses of foreign leaders are taken into account. Forests in California are not impressed by the firefighting prowess of rangers in Montana, but nonaligned heads of state could and did take careful note of how Bonn handled challenges half a world away. Understandably, West Germans fretted over certain tactical advantages enjoyed by East Germany, such as its ability to select a few promising points of concentration, or its opportunistic embrace of revolutionary situations in Iraq and Zanzibar. But scholars peering into the internal record of conversations in East Berlin can now appreciate the perpetual frustrations faced by party and state leaders there. By the late 1960s, the unflagging optimism once displayed by Ulbricht and his Politburo had been superseded by a deep cynicism about the allegiances of nonaligned leaders such as Nasser and Sihanouk.

Naturally, one should not exaggerate the wisdom and foresight of the political leadership in Bonn. On the advice of the Foreign Office's legal experts, Chancellor Adenauer insisted that the GDR lacked the qualities of a proper state—a standpoint that strained the patience of even the most sympathetic observers by the late 1960s. Yet Walter Hallstein and Wilhelm Grewe displayed a keen sense of realpolitik when they elaborated the essential features of Bonn's isolation strategy in 1954–55. Experience suggested that West Germany could not hope to block all forms of contact between third countries and East Germany; Bonn would have to distinguish between those forms of association that did not imply recognition (trade and cultural ties) and those that did (consular and diplomatic relations). With the articulation of the Hallstein Doctrine—in spirit if not in name—in December 1955, the Foreign Office fielded an admirably efficient system of deterrence. The initial costs were minimal. By threatening to break relations with any state that recognized the GDR, Grewe and Hallstein effectively made cooperation on this point a nonnegotiable prerequisite for diplomatic relations with the Federal Republic. Unfortunately, Adenauer's ambiguous and indecisive attitude toward Eastern Europe in the fall of 1957 cast doubt on the credibility of Bonn's threats, at least in the mind of President Tito. Yugoslavia's recognition of East Berlin necessitated a strong reaction like breaking diplomatic relations, as Adenauer, Brentano, Hallstein, and Grewe all understood. For other political observers in Bonn, the dark side of the isolation campaign came as an unpleasant surprise. Yet many of the sharpest critics of Bonn's policy later endorsed the implicit trade-off. By sacrificing relations with Yugoslavia, the Federal Republic bought peace on other fronts, for now the deterrent value of Bonn's threats was powerful indeed.

Over time, more subtle drawbacks of the Hallstein-Grewe line became manifest. Verbal deterrence had never been adequate in handling major nonaligned powers such as India, Egypt, and (until October 1957) Yugoslavia. Instead, Bonn fell into a pattern of "managed relationships" in order to guarantee cooperation on the German Question. With India this was

CONCLUSION

seldom onerous, since the Federal Republic had sufficient cultural and commercial interests on the subcontinent to justify an active financial involvement. In the case of Egypt, though, Bonn made concessions that were costly both politically and economically: extreme caution in the formalization of relations with Israel, long-term Hermes credits to Egypt, and massive technical and capital assistance programs. Nasser learned to tweak Bonn with sporadic but deliberate steps closer to a de jure recognition of the GDR, such as the 1959 opening of an East German consulate in Cairo. Such incremental audacities inevitably drew more assistance from Bonn, the argument being that it would be even more dangerous to stand by idly while Egypt slid headlong into complete dependency on Moscow and East Berlin. Other enterprising nonaligned leaders also found that flirtation with the GDR paid off in terms of attention from the Federal Republic. In the early 1960s, with a new East German consulate opening every six months or so, more and more of Bonn's relations with Third World countries devolved into managed relationships.

The advent of large-scale West German aid only exacerbated this tendency. Rather than giving Bonn additional leverage, the wide distribution of long-term loans allowed the more daring recipients to set a price for their cooperation. By 1964, though, the Foreign Office had finally worked out a new tactical approach that promised to link aid and the Hallstein Doctrine more effectively. If the earlier threat of breaking relations could be considered a kind of "massive retaliation," to use the vocabulary of the day, then the natural counterpoint was a system of "flexible response."[4] Like a nuclear first strike, the severing of diplomatic relations was too cumbersome a weapon to be used except in moments of absolute necessity. One answer lay in setting forth a new scale of reprisals, generally involving the revocation of development aid, in response to offenses that did not quite entail full recognition of the GDR. Bonn's "new measures" of 1964, first tested against Ceylon, helped to restore the primacy of deterrence in the isolation campaign. In the long run, though, West German resistance to blackmail played a more significant role in returning balance to Bonn's worldwide efforts. Now it was East Germany that faced constant pressure to dole out massive loans. The more it gave, the more others expected of it.

By the late 1960s, the original content of West Germany's Hallstein Doctrine had been hollowed out almost entirely. This had little to do with Bonn's decision to open diplomatic relations with Romania. An active Eastern policy had never been incompatible with the Hallstein Doctrine; Adenauer's tendency to ignore Eastern Europe was a political choice, not the inevitable product of the iron logic of some doctrine. What marked the end of the Hallstein Doctrine as a diplomatic lever was Bonn's obvious reluctance to use it. As early as 1965, Schröder and many others in the coalition scorned the idea of severing relations with Egypt. In January 1968, Kiesinger and Brandt reversed an earlier use of the doctrine by reestablishing relations with Yugoslavia. Finally, in the spring of 1969, the Grand Coalition "camboded" rather than undertake a complete rupture in relations with Phnom Penh. The Hallstein Doctrine had lost its teeth. Yet the nonaligned world did not race to establish embassies in East Berlin, as panic-stricken West German officials had once predicted. Bonn's threats had ceased to determine the attitude of third countries toward the GDR; East Germany's own lack of merits weighed far more heavily.

A War within a War

Very often Germans on both sides were preoccupied by their Cold War *en miniature*, yet the global contest between Bonn and East Berlin was inescapably intertwined with the larger East-West conflict. This interaction worked in two directions. The intense rivalry drove both regimes to establish a more active presence in developing countries than they might otherwise have fielded, with implications for the overall strength of the Eastern and Western camps in those countries. Likewise, the general direction of the Cold War could have a direct bearing on the standing of the two German states in world affairs. It was, after all, the Western Allies who first hung the curtain of isolation around the GDR in the early 1950s, when Adenauer's cabinet was in no position to enforce its claim to speak on behalf of the entire German people. France, Britain, and the United States cooperated in ensuring that the Federal Republic occupied the vacant German seat in various international organizations and in the capitals of the "free world." Blocking East German access to these institutions was a matter of basic prestige for the three powers. Conveniently enough, the Soviet Union offered little substantive backing for the SED regime in the early 1950s, granting the Federal Republic an enormous head start.

In 1955 the Soviet leadership dropped all interest in seeing a unified Germany; henceforth it would insist on a two-state solution to the German Question, with the GDR as an equal to the Federal Republic in the international sphere. This put the West on the defensive. Whereas the Soviets now accepted the existence of the Federal Republic, and even held conversations with Adenauer in Moscow, the members of NATO had to justify their continuing rejection of Ulbricht's regime. Countries associated with the nonaligned movement showed less inclination to follow Western guidance on international questions. At this dangerous juncture, Adenauer's government stepped forward to assume control of the ongoing isolation campaign against East Germany. Nonaligned countries responded favorably to West Germany's new assertiveness. In many capitals the Federal Republic enjoyed more sympathy than France, Britain, or the United States, particularly in the wake of the aborted Śuez Canal intervention in late 1956. Rising Soviet influence in the Near and Middle East did not automatically accrue to East Germany's advantage; Nasser's Egypt balanced a deepening military relationship with Moscow by courting *West* Germany. In Cold War terms, the Federal Republic enjoyed a considerable advantage over the GDR in the 1950s. West Germany was often perceived as a natural, even neutral choice of diplomatic partners. East Germany, by contrast, bore the stigma of Stalinism. Nonaligned states had good reason to fear that, if they trafficked too intimately with the GDR, they might be branded as partisans of the Soviet camp. The behavior of African leaders in 1960 brought this point home: among the sixteen colonies that received independence in that year, all of them opted for exclusive relations with the Federal Republic.

By this time, Khrushchev's Berlin ultimatum had returned the German Question to the center of world attention. Once again the Western Allies were forced to grapple with fundamental issues such as reunification, access to Berlin, and the status of the GDR. Whatever their initial inclinations, Macmillan, Eisenhower, and de Gaulle all concluded that they could not afford to compromise under duress. For nearly four years, then, the Allies devoted a staggering amount of energy to arcane calculations about how to maintain a presence in Berlin without tacitly recognizing East Germany's transit authorities. In the end, Khrushchev failed to dislodge the Allies and failed also to secure international recognition of the GDR. The strains of the Berlin Crisis did nevertheless influence the terms of debate in the nonaligned world. In the winter of 1958–59, Nehru regarded Khrushchev's blustery threats as the principal obstacle to peace in Europe. Two and a half years later, fears of a third world war animated a rather different analysis at the Belgrade Nonaligned Conference. Nehru and other speakers castigated *both* Cold War camps for their saber rattling over Berlin. There were two German states in Europe, argued Nehru; it was only logical to acknowledge the existence of both. The conference participants did not immediately act on these convictions, thanks to Bonn's array of carrots and sticks, including development aid and the Hallstein Doctrine. After the fall of 1961, however, East Germany's absence from international venues seemed increasingly artificial.

The waning of the Berlin Crisis in 1962–63 allowed the Western Allies to adopt a more relaxed view of the GDR, at least within the context of European security. Nevertheless, they accepted the need to maintain the diplomatic blockade against East Germany in the Third World. The GDR's enduring isolation underscored the supposed openness of the German Question; just as importantly, it kept one of the Soviet bloc's most zealous regimes from making too much mischief in the name of Karl Marx and Vladimir Lenin. Support for Bonn's global campaign also allowed France, Britain, and the United States, competitors for West Germany's affections, to demonstrate goodwill on a matter that the Erhard government took very seriously. Sharp disagreements over tactics did arise. The Allies frowned on Bonn's readiness to sever ties with countries that drew too close to the GDR. In 1964 and 1965 the United States attempted (with limited success) to forestall West German retaliation against Ceylon, Tanzania, and Egypt. Some West German commentators intimated that the Allies wished to see the Hallstein Doctrine fail, but if there was any truth to this charge, it applied only to the narrow definition of the doctrine as a threat to break diplomatic relations. More than ever, the Allies valued West Germany's presence in the nonaligned world as a bulwark against the influence of the Soviet bloc, and for this reason they wished to see Bonn stand its ground whenever possible.

After the disastrous collapse of its Middle Eastern policy in the spring of 1965, the Federal Republic lost its most significant power base in the developing world. For the rest of the decade, the vagaries of the Cold War largely dictated the relative standing of Bonn and East Berlin. In 1965–66 the Federal Republic profited unexpectedly from coups in Ghana and Indonesia and elections in Ceylon; meanwhile, the absence of major nonaligned conferences saved Bonn from the possibility of a group recognition of the GDR. In the late 1960s, though, the SED reaped a windfall from regional conflicts in the Middle East and Southeast Asia. After the Six Day War of June 1967, Egypt and Syria stepped up their military ties with the Soviet Union. A radicalization of Arab sentiment brought to the fore blisteringly anti-Western regimes in Iraq and Sudan, both of which established diplomatic relations with the GDR shortly after coming to power in the spring of 1969. Meanwhile, America's war in Vietnam ground on, with dire and unpredictable effects for nearby Cambodia. Many developing countries no longer bothered to profess nonalignment; those that looked to Moscow's leadership now had fewer qualms about adopting unambiguously pro-Soviet stances on issues such as the German Question. Even if such governments had still taken the Hallstein Doctrine seriously, the possibility of a break with Bonn could scarcely have fazed them. The Arab countries that recognized the GDR in 1969 were essentially lost causes for the West, at least until Egypt turned away from the Soviet Union in 1972. Bonn had no Cold War role to play in such an environment.

Within Europe, too, the character of the East-West conflict was changing. Détente in the 1960s had skirted the German Question; détente in the 1970s was achieved precisely *because* of agreements on Germany. The Helsinki process gave the GDR nearly everything it wanted—but at the price of establishing a working relationship with the Federal Republic. It was the final service of the isolation campaign to stave off the GDR's definitive recognition until after the SED had signed off on a series of agreements regulating intra-German exchanges. The Basic Treaty of December 1972 did not, in the end, live up to West German expectations; alienation between the citizens of East and West deepened with each passing year. Yet it is unclear whether the cabinets in Bonn could have resisted this trend more effectively by letting go of the isolation campaign sooner. The root problem was not the Hallstein Doctrine but, rather, East German opposition to unification and the lack of practical ideas in West Germany about how to overcome this.

The Hallstein Doctrine and German Unity

Konrad Adenauer had bold, cunning visions about how to bind the Federal Republic's destiny to Europe and to the broader Atlantic community. Unfortunately, all of his projects pointed away from the realization of national unity. Military integration into NATO and economic integration into a Europe of Six could not help but widen the gulf between the Federal Republic and its eastern counterpart. In the early 1950s, Social Democrats and assorted nationalists within the governing coalition challenged Adenauer's priorities; given a choice, they would have promoted unity at the expense of Western integration. The chancellor responded by placing the onus for Germany's division on Moscow's shoulders. Treating the SED regime as an unrecognizable, foreign element on German soil absolved Adenauer from any responsibility for dealing with the national question. According to this line of reasoning, there was no point in holding conversations with a traitor like Ulbricht. In the context of relations with East Berlin, then, Adenauer's approach was essentially passive. This heightened the appeal of inter-nationalizing the German-German struggle; it gave the West Germans an opportunity to strike a more activist pose. In political terms, then, the Hallstein Doctrine's function was to make Western integration more palatable to skeptical nationalists by involving West German diplomats in a grand struggle to keep the German Question open.

Adenauer's rivals outside the CDU/CSU were seldom prepared to accept the isolation campaign as a substitute for more direct initiatives. It was the FDP, the smallest and most nationalist of the three major West German parties, that criticized Bonn's strategy most consistently. In the mid-1950s, Thomas Dehler's demands for a more constructive unification program led to friction with Adenauer and the FDP's withdrawal from the governing coalition. From the banks of the opposition, Free Democratic deputies formulated a number of objections to the Hallstein-Grewe line. They argued that it made no sense to break relations and thus withdraw from countries that had recognized the GDR. They also complained vehemently that Brentano's dogmatism was an impediment to the unfolding of relations between West Germany and the countries of Eastern Europe. Although later stylized into a pathbreaking call for reconciliation with the victims of World War II, the FDP's stance on Poland was motivated largely by business interests and by the conviction that dialogue with the Soviet bloc would somehow advance the cause of German unity. Karl-Georg Pfleiderer, the Free Democratic deputy who served as ambassador to Yugoslavia, was virtually alone in arguing that Bonn's Eastern policy should proceed from the realization that Germany had, in fact, lost the Eastern provinces as a result of Hitler's aggression. Tellingly, the FDP's passion on the question of Eastern Europe did not extend to Israel; the party's affiliates in the commercial realm were unabashedly pro-Arab.

The SPD's relationship to the isolation campaign was altogether more complex. Kurt Schumacher's intense hatred of the Moscow-trained SED functionaries continued to resonate among Social Democrats well after his death in 1952. Three years later the SPD was nevertheless pleading for "technical" contacts with East German officials in order to keep some channels of communication open. The party's short-lived Germany Plan of 1959 followed along similar lines. In the international sphere, SPD chair Erich Ollenhauer questioned the appropriateness of an isolation strategy based on threats of retaliation. Not surprisingly, Social Democrats recoiled with horror when Adenauer actually broke relations with Yugoslavia in 1957. What historians have failed to appreciate is the party's abrupt reversal in the early 1960s. The strain of the Berlin Crisis and anxiety over East Germany's gains in the nonaligned world led Fritz Erler, Hans-Jürgen Wischnewski, and other prominent Social Democrats to cooperate with the Foreign Office in forging ties with politicians and union bosses in Africa and the Middle East. Within the Bundestag's Foreign Affairs Committee, SPD politicians discussed the mechanics of the isolation strategy approvingly and with remarkable expertise. Given the FDP's continuing discomfort with the Hallstein Doctrine, SPD support of the government line was particularly important in providing Ludwig Erhard with the parliamentary basis for an intensification of the campaign against East Germany.

Much like his predecessor, Erhard promoted the Hallstein Doctrine as a substitute—albeit a weak one—for achieving actual progress toward unification. Erhard's cabinet could claim that by staving off recognition of the GDR, it was keeping the path clear for reunification on Western terms. The more remote the likelihood of achieving forward motion on the German Question, the more fiercely the Foreign Office endeavored to block East German gains in the developing world. However, Erhard was readier than Adenauer to assign an independent value to the Hallstein Doctrine. Adenauer was flexible enough to contemplate—in strict confidence—other, novel forms of relations between the two German states: an "Austrian solution" involving neutralization of the GDR, or a ten-year truce on the German Question. During moments of profound uncertainty, such as January 1959, the old Rhinelander considered dropping the isolation campaign altogether. For Erhard, by contrast, and even more so for President Lübke, the Hallstein Doctrine counted as an inviolable component of Bonn's foreign policy. Even as the Foreign Office was reformulating its tactics and backing away from the policy of breaking relations, conservatives in the CDU/CSU held fast to a reified version of the Hallstein Doctrine: no diplomatic relations with Eastern Europe, and no tolerance for the planting of East German embassies abroad.

The sterility of Erhard's approach to the German Question helped to cost him the chancellorship. His successors, Kurt-Georg Kiesinger and Willy Brandt, devised a more conciliatory approach toward both Eastern Europe and, more reluctantly, the GDR itself. Now that the CDU/CSU and the SPD, the parties of the Grand Coalition, were demonstrating creativity in foreign policy, the domestic function of the Hallstein Doctrine shifted. The government no longer needed a fig leaf to conceal its inactivity; instead, Kiesinger simply had to prove to conservatives in his own party that the "new Eastern policy" would not inadvertently result in the worldwide recognition of East

Germany. By and large he succeeded. The Grand Coalition reinterpreted several aspects of the Hallstein Doctrine without unleashing a torrent of recognitions. In the meantime, Brandt and his chief foreign policy adviser, Egon Bahr, had convinced the rank and file of the SPD that the isolation campaign was counterproductive and should gradually be dismantled. In Bahr's view, Bonn had erred in forcing the SED into a defensive posture, thereby justifying the communists' efforts to seal off the East Germans from their West German counterparts. Bahr's solution was to seek a more open dialogue with the SED and to phase out Bonn's strictures against East German cultural, scientific, and athletic interaction with the world at large.

As late as 1969, alas, the coalition's new Eastern policy had generated no discernible softening in East Berlin. Ulbricht actually strove for a more rigid delimitation (*Abgrenzung*) of East Germans from their western neighbors by introducing such innovations as a separate citizenship law for the GDR. Moscow, too, responded negatively to the Kiesinger-Brandt line. This left the coalition with a classic dilemma: should it offer *more* cooperation or *less*? The CDU/CSU favored a retreat from détente, even as the SPD demanded a more consistent and heartfelt Eastern policy that proceeded from an acknowledgment of the status quo. Against this background, the decision by Cambodia and a handful of Arab countries to recognize the GDR touched off a remarkably heated debate in Bonn. Whereas Brandt, Herbert Wehner, and others in the SPD assumed that the Hallstein Doctrine was long since passé, Kiesinger insisted on answering Cambodia's "unfriendly act" in customary style by severing diplomatic relations. Were it not election season, the issue might not have flared up into a major crisis. Yet the seemingly obscure issue of how to punish Cambodia reflected profound disagreements over the meaning of Germany's division. Should the Federal Republic preserve the openness of the German Question by denying the permanence of the GDR, or should it embrace the status quo in the hopes of one day overcoming it? The latter course, Bahr's "change through rapprochement," demanded a dialectical optimism that exceeded the imaginative capacity of CDU/CSU grandees. Yet the Christian Democrats had exhausted their own limited supply of suggestions as to how to restore German unity; clinging to the Hallstein Doctrine only emphasized the party's lack of constructive alternatives. The Social Democratic line at least had the advantage of novelty.

Brandt's SPD won the argument over Cambodia and—after a fashion— the 1969 elections too. Ironically, Brandt and Bahr found it expedient to perpetuate the isolation of East Germany under a different name. The existing isolation structures, a routine element of international life for twenty years, were simply too useful as a source of leverage over the SED regime. Like the Hallstein Doctrine before it, the "Scheel Doctrine" worked remarkably well, not as a serious program for unification in its own right, but as means of underlining the special character of the German Question. The normalcy that Ulbricht and Honecker strove to acquire for the GDR came only after the two German states had negotiated a treaty highlighting the uniqueness (hence, *abnormality*) of their relationship. In the decades remaining to them, the SED's guiding figures would vainly attempt to distance themselves from the very notion of Germanness, but Brandt's formula of two states in one nation continued to resonate beyond the Berlin Wall. Worldwide recognition, the obsession of Walter Ulbricht and a whole generation of East German leaders, proved to be a hollow and short-lived achievement. West Germany's insistence on the indivisibility of the nation, the concept underlying both the isolation campaign and the new Eastern policy that followed, retained a strong appeal. However estranged the populations of East and West, however artificial and constructed German national identity may have appeared by 1990, the prospect of a free and independent East Germany seemed even *more* dubious. Seldom has an internationally recognized state vanished so swiftly and so unmourned.

NOTES

Citations of archival and published documents generally appear in the following format: details about the document *itself* appear before the colon; details about the document's *location* appear after the colon. For example, the following citation indicates that the October 1949 memorandum from Kirkpatrick to Bevin is found in *Dokumente zur Deutschlandpolitik*, vol. 2, part 2, page 681: "Kirkpatrick, memorandum for Foreign Minister Bevin, Oct. 14, 1949: *DzD* II/2, 681."

Given my extensive use of diplomatic dispatches from various foreign services, I developed a shorthand for denoting the British, French, American, and German embassies in different countries. For French and German embassies, I use the actual telegraph codes of the time: AF for "Ambafrance," DG for "Diplogerma"; for those of the United Kingdom and United States, the initials UK and US. Readers will thus find such abbreviations as AF Damascus, DG Khartoum, US Bonn, UK Belgrade, etc. Because the GDR usually did not have diplomatic representation in foreign capitals, I have tried to be more specific, listing the author and status of the sender for East German dispatches. Where an East German embassy did exist, I list the city after the governmental abbreviation DDR, i.e., DDR Moscow, DDR Warsaw, etc.

ABBREVIATIONS

AA	Auswärtiges Amt (Foreign Office, Bonn)
AAPD	*Akten zur auswärtigen Politik der Bundesrepublik Deutschland*
Abt.	Abteilung (department)
ACDP	Archiv für christlich-demokratische Politik
ADL	Archiv des deutschen Liberalismus
AdsD	Archiv der sozialen Demokratie
AF	Ambafrance (French embassy dispatches)
ANF	Alpha-Numeric Files
Aufz.	Aufzeichnung (memorandum)
Ausw. Aus.	Auswärtiger Ausschuß des Deutschen Bundestags
B	Bestand (collection)
BAK	Bundesarchiv Koblenz
BAL	Bundesarchiv Berlin-Lichterfelde
BA-SAPMO	Stiftung Archiv der Parteien und Massenorganisationen der DDR im Bundesarchiv
Bd.	Band (archival volume in Germany)
Bl.	Blatt (numbered page within archival volume)
BMG	Bundesministerium für gesamtdeutsche Fragen
BMZ	Bundesministerium für wirtschaftliche Zusammenarbeit
BPA	Presse- und Informationsamt der Bundesregierung
BT/PA	Parlamentsarchiv des Deutschen Bundestages

CDF	Central Decimal Files
DARDDR	*Dokumente zur Außenpolitik der Regierung der Deutschen Demokratischen Republik* (later published as *DADDR*, *Dokumente zur Außenpolitik der DDR*)
DDF	*Documents diplomatiques français*
DDR	German Democratic Republic
DG	Diplogerma (Federal Republic embassy dispatches)
DepSta	Department of State (used to denote instructions issued from Washington)
dpa	deutsche presse-agentur
DzD	*Dokumente zur Deutschlandpolitik*
FAZ	*Frankfurter Allgemeine Zeitung*
fdk	*freie demokratische korrespondenz*
FO	Foreign Office, London (used to denote instructions issued from London)
FRG-FA	Federal Republic of Germany: Foreign Affairs (microfilm collection)
FRG-IA	Federal Republic of Germany: Internal Affairs (microfilm collection)
FRUS	*Foreign Relations of the United States*
G-FA	Germany: Foreign Affairs (microfilm collection)
GDR-IA	German Democratic Republic: Internal Affairs (microfilm collection)
HICOG	U.S. High Commission in Germany
IfZ	Institut für Zeitgeschichte, Munich
MAE	Ministère des Affaires Étrangères
MAI	Ministerium für Außenhandel und Innerdeutsche Handel (Ministry for Foreign and Intra-German Trade, East Berlin)
MfAA	Ministerium für Auswärtige Angelegenheiten (Ministry for Foreign Affairs, East Berlin)
NARA	National Archives and Records Administration
NL	Nachlaß (personal papers)
PA/AA	Politisches Archiv des Auswärtigen Amts
PRO	Public Records Office
Quai	Quai d'Orsay (used to denote instructions issued from Paris)
Ref.	Referat
RG	Record Group
SecSta	Secretary of State (used to denote instructions issued from Washington)
StBKAH	Stiftung Bundeskanzler-Adenauer-Haus
Sten. Ber.	*Stenographische Berichte der Verhandlungen des Deutschen Bundestages*
UK	United Kingdom embassy dispatches
US	United States embassy dispatches
USSR-FA	Soviet Union: Foreign Affairs (microfilm collection)
WP	Wahlperiode
ZK	Zentralkommittee (Central Committee of the SED)

INTRODUCTION

1. On Etzdorf's mission, see Dieter Schröder, "Herrn von Etzdorfs hochpolitische Safari," *Süddeutsche Zeitung*, Apr. 11, 1960; and Peter Scholz's contribution in Blasius, *Hasso von Etzdorf*, 95–96.

2. On Etzdorf's colorful political career, see Döscher, *Verschworene Gesellschaft*, 112–13, and Blasius, *Hasso von Etzdorf*. This characterization of Kurella is drawn from the obituary published in the *Munziger-Archiv*, Oct. 4, 1975.

3. Carstens, Aufz., "Vorschläge zur Deutschlandpolitik," Mar. 10, 1965, 8: PA/AA, B 150, Bd. 48. The term "Zone" used by Carstens is shorthand for "Soviet Occupation Zone," a designation that implied that the GDR was not a proper state. Terminology played a vital role in the competition between the two German states, and to some extent Cold War usages linger on: in scholarly literature, West Germany is regularly denoted as the "Federal Republic," not the "FRG," while East Germany is more diminutively labeled "the GDR." I have retained this usage (Federal Republic vs. GDR), mainly because to my ears "FRG" sounds hopelessly awkward.

4. The Ghanaian foreign minister made a habit of taking month-long hospital "holidays" in the GDR and the Federal Republic by turns. Kilian, *Hallstein-Doktrin*, 71–73.

5. DG Baghdad (Bargen) 252, Aug. 24, 1961: PA/AA, B 12, Bd. 46.

6. For a stirring defense of historical narrative as a complex explanatory model, see Gaddis, "History, Theory, and Common Ground," 82–84.

7. I do not mean to suggest that the GDR was a space devoid of competing political conceptions; within the exalted circles of party and state leadership, the conduct of the recognition campaign could be quite contentious. Examples of this appear in the chapters below. Nevertheless, there was never an opportunity for a critical public to take issue with the basic priorities set by the SED.

8. Sarotte, *Dealing with the Devil: East Germany, Détente, and Ostpolitik, 1969–1973*. In a sense, the present volume serves as a prelude to the developments spelled out in Sarotte's work.

9. Besson, *Die Außenpolitik der Bundesrepublik*, 199; Hanrieder, *Germany, America, Europe*, 170–209; Bender, *Die "Neue Ostpolitik" und ihre Folgen*, 50, 105–18, 138–54.

10. End, *Zweimal deutsche Außenpolitik*, 43.

11. Buchheim, *Deutschlandpolitik 1949–1972*, 129–33; Hildebrand, *Von Erhard zur Großen Koalition*, 329–31. Hildebrand's interpretation relies heavily on the memoirs of Wilhelm Grewe, one of the isolation campaign's earliest practitioners; see Grewe, *Rückblenden*, 231–64.

12. Garton Ash, *In Europe's Name*. On the post-1989 debate, see Smith, "'Ostpolitik' since Reunification." As Jim McAdams observes, the mud-flinging has been fairly restrained among top party leaders, for nearly all West German politicians sought personal contacts with East German leader Erich Honecker in the 1980s. McAdams, "Revisiting the *Ostpolitik* in the 1990s." See also Cary, "Reassessing Germany's *Ostpolitik*."

13. Booz, "*Hallsteinzeit*," 165–74, esp. 170–71. This work was a very fine master's thesis completed in Bonn under Klaus Hildebrand's guidance; Booz did not conduct archival research, but he did piece together a compelling narrative based on memoirs, secondary sources, and extensive newspaper clippings.

14. Troche, *Ulbricht und die Dritte Welt*; Lemke, "'Doppelte Alleinvertretung'"; Lemke, "Der Nahe Osten, Indien und die Grotewohlreise von 1959."

15. Kilian, *Hallstein-Doktrin*. Kilian brings the eye of a trained diplomat to his sources; I have found his readings of certain episodes to be quite insightful. Unfortunately, Kilian restricted his archival research to the foreign ministries of East and West Germany, which is a rather narrow basis for reaching broader conclusions about the "diplomatic war between the FRG and the GDR." In particular, East German policy can scarcely be understood without reference to the files of the SED.

16. Putensen, *Im Konfliktfeld zwischen Ost und West*; Anic de Osona, *Die erste Anerkennung der DDR*; Engel and Schleicher, *Die beiden deutschen Staaten in Afrika*; Schneppen, "Eine Insel und zwei deutsche Staaten"; Geyer, "Der Kampf um nationale Repräsentation."

17. This is in fact the subtitle of End's book, *Zweimal deutsche Außenpolitik* (1973).

18. Virtually every leading policy maker in Bonn, it seems, had a conversation partner in at least one of the three Allied embassies. Some of these information sessions were undoubtedly tuned for foreign listeners, but one can nevertheless encounter remarkable details about personal and institutional rivalries that the West German informants might never have committed to paper themselves. I regret not having similar access to Soviet records. Soviet documents do abound in the East German archives—often in the form of unsigned, unattributed notes in Russian conveying "recommendations" to the SED leadership. For the most part, however, my understanding of Soviet policy is reliant upon the work of scholars such as Gerhard Wettig, who have managed to transcend the usual obstacles to working on German topics at the Foreign Ministry archive in Moscow.

19. Published volumes of *Akten zur auswärtigen Politik der Bundesrepublik Deutschland* (*AAPD*) are available covering the years 1949–52 and 1963–70; further records declassified in the course of this project can be consulted in PA/AA, B 150.

CHAPTER ONE

1. On the deliberations of the Parlamentarischer Rat, see Benz, *Die Gründung der Bundesrepublik*, 118–30.

2. The coalition parties controlled 208 of 402 seats in the Bundestag, but only 202 had voted for Adenauer on September 15. Ritter and Niehuss, *Wahlen in Deutschland*, 100–101; Benz, *Die Gründung der Bundesrepublik*, 144.

3. See, for example, the witty comments by the communist deputy Heinz Renner in the Bundestag on October 21, 1949; he described Adenauer as pursuing "policy in the spirit of Wall Street." *DzD* II/2, 224–28 (quote from 225). See also Major, *Death of the KPD*, 111–12. One month later, Kurt Schumacher—in a passing comment—called Adenauer the "chancellor of the Allies," which caused much more of an uproar coming from a democratic parliamentarian. Merseburger, *Der schwierige Deutsche*, 462–64; Todt, *Anfangsjahre der Bundesrepublik Deutschland*, 20–21.

4. Staritz, *Die Gründung der DDR*, 185–87; Badstübner, "Die sowjetische Deutschlandpolitik im Lichte neuer Quellen," 127–29.

5. Quote from a set of talking points dated September 8, 1949, prepared for use in an official declaration by the future prime minister of the GDR. *DzD* II/2, 448–50; note esp. points 2, 3, 11, 16. See also Lemke, "'Doppelte Alleinvertretung,'" 533–35.

6. On October 2, 1949, SED chairman Walter Ulbricht revealed his plans for the

founding of the GDR to the Polish military observer in Berlin. In his report back to Warsaw, the Pole considered the erection of an East German Ministry for Foreign Affairs (MfAA) to be Ulbricht's greatest coup. *DzD* II/2, 492.

7. Kirkpatrick, memorandum for Foreign Minister Bevin, Oct. 14, 1949: *DzD* II/2, 681.

8. On the forced union of the KPD and SPD, see Faulenbach and Potthoff, *Sozialdemokraten und Kommunisten nach Nationalsozialismus und Krieg*.

9. Indeed, this was still a major source of concern in the mid-1950s; see p. 4 of the meeting of the SPD Parteivorstand, Sept. 16, 1955, in AdsD.

10. Merritt and Merritt, *Public Opinion in Semisovereign Germany*, 56. It should be remembered that many Germans had adopted a profoundly apolitical attitude as a response to war and privation; in the poll cited here, only 58 percent interviewed in November 1949 had actually heard about the GDR's founding. Tellingly, the proportion in heavily politicized West Berlin was vastly higher, at 88 percent; and of them, 88 percent considered the SED regime to be a puppet state.

11. Deutscher Bundestag, 13. Sitzung, excerpted in *DzD* II/2, 213–14.

12. See Carlo Schmid's remarks on this point during a meeting of the SPD's Parteivorstand, Oct. 22–23, 1949: *DzD* II/2, 708.

13. For an important and comprehensive study of Adenauer's nationalist opponents, see Gallus, *Die Neutralisten*.

14. Memorandum by a State Department legal adviser, July 13, 1950, printed in *DzD* II/3, 873.

15. US Paris (Acheson) to Truman and Acting Secretary Webb 4716, Nov. 11, 1949, secret: *FRUS* 1949/III, 305–6.

16. Martin, *Divided Counsel*, 86–93.

17. Precedents from the post-1917 decade are scattered throughout Peterson, *Recognition of Governments*.

18. These internal guidelines were adopted by the Brussels Pact—a nearly superfluous organization founded as NATO's immediate predecessor, comprising Britain, France, and the Benelux countries—on December 15, 1949. For a summary, see DepSta, Circtel, Feb. 10, 1950, secret: *FRUS* 1950/IV, 942–44.

19. For a useful discussion of the elaborate rules of nonrecognition, see Peterson, *Recognition of Governments*, esp. the top of 99, where he presents a summary of situations that unambiguously imply recognition.

20. The point of coordinating Allied and Benelux policies via the Brussels Pact was, indeed, to ensure that none of the governments in question was tempted to go too far in independent dealings with East Berlin. Exporters in the Netherlands and Britain had a strong interest in the East German market. See a telegram from the Commonwealth Relations Office, Nov. 12, 1949, printed in *DzD* II/2, 783–84; also Becker, *DDR und Großbritannien*, chap. 3.

21. On December 9, 1949, the Department of State advised U.S. missions in Latin America to be on the alert for a small delegation of East German visitors lobbying for recognition. The missions were to submit an aide-mémoire to their host governments outlining Allied policy toward the GDR. *FRUS* 1949/III, 544–45. For a summary of the individual British, American, and French démarches in Stockholm, see Scholz, "Östen Undén und die DDR," 398–99.

22. Putensen, *Im Konfliktfeld zwischen Ost und West*, 51–56.

23. On the social and political backgrounds of the East German foreign service in these years, see Muth, *DDR-Außenpolitik*, 153–58. In his memoirs, Horst Grunert identifies only two officials with relevant experience: Ferdinand Thun (aristocratic heritage) and Gerhard Kegel (service as a communist mole in Hitler's foreign ministry). Grunert, *Für Honecker auf glattem Parkett*, 102, 133–35. For an indication of the organizational chaos during these years, see Dertinger's comments to the ministry's leading officials, Sept. 29, 1950: MfAA, LS-A 2, Fiche 2, Bl. 99.

24. Comments by Dertinger to the Foreign Affairs Committee of the Provisional Volkskammer, Mar. 22, 1950: *DzD* II/3, 641–42. The GDR's uncompromising attitude was endorsed by Moscow: see Ackermann to Ulbricht, Apr. 26, 1950: BA-SAPMO, NY 4182, Bd. 1314. For an indication of how dismally this approach worked in the case of Switzerland, see Schueller, Vermerk, "Stellung der Schweiz zur Bundesrepublik und zur Ostzonenregierung," Oct. 6, 1950: PA/AA, B 11, Bd. 356.

25. Maulucci, "Creation and Early History of the West German Foreign Office," 185–89.

26. See the memorandum by the head of the German Political Affairs desk in Washington, Ellwood Williams III. "German International Relations," Oct. 11, 1949, confidential: NARA, RG 59, Lot 57 D 417, Box 5, folder "International organizations, German participation in."

27. See the comments by Bidault in the American record of an Allied foreign ministers' meeting, Nov. 9, 1949: *DzD* II/2, 745. Also instructive is the report by the Inter-Government Working Group of Nov. 1, 1949: *DzD* II/2, 730–33.

28. Wiggershaus, "Die Entscheidung für einen westdeutschen Verteidigungsbeitrag 1950."

29. The classic account here is Baring, *Außenpolitik in Adenauers Kanzlerdemokratie*, which depicts the chancellor as a clever old fox. An important corrective is Rupieper, *Der besetzte Verbündete*; here it is the Allies who are getting their way by promising to revise the Occupation Statute.

30. Ruhm von Oppen, *Documents on Germany Under Occupation*, 518.

31. DepSta (Webb) to HICOG, Sept. 5, 1950, secret: NARA, RG 59, CDF, 300.162A.

32. On the retention of the name "Auswärtiges Amt," see Müller, *Relaunching German Diplomacy*, 56.

33. On Soviet policy during this period, see Wettig, *Bereitschaft zu Einheit in Freiheit*, 205–27; and Mastny, *Cold War and Soviet Insecurity*, 134–38.

34. A chronological table of the FRG's accession to various organizations appears in Dröge et al., *Federal Republic of Germany and the United Nations*, 84.

35. German Political Affairs (Williams) to UN Political Affairs (Taylor), June 5, 1951, secret: NARA, RG 59, Lot 57 D 417, Box 5, folder "International organizations, German participation in."

36. DepSta (Acheson) to Paris Secrep 38, Oct. 11, 1951: FRG-IA 50–54, reel 30, frames 742–43 (762A.02).

37. The standard Western demand for free elections in all of Germany dated back to early 1950, when U.S. High Commissioner John J. McCloy first raised this possibility as a means of countering East German propaganda about "Germans at one table." Rupieper, *Der besetzte Verbündete*, 218–19.

38. Pawelka, *Die UNO und das Deutschlandproblem*, 55–69.

39. On American policy toward the GDR in this period, see Ingimundarson, "The

Eisenhower Administration, the Adenauer Government, and the Political Uses of the East German Uprising of 1953"; also Ostermann, "'Die Ostdeutschen an einen langwierigen Kampf gewöhnen.'"

40. On the "growing pains" of the Auswärtiges Amt, see Maulucci, "Creation and Early History of the West German Foreign Office," chap. 4.

41. An analysis by the State Department's UN Affairs division in March 1952 noted that the West Germans had lambasted the East Germans "without displaying a modicum of humility," while the East Germans had added nothing new to the Soviet litany. FRG-IA 50–54, reel 14, frames 381–85; quote from 381–82.

42. For Hallstein's explicit orders on this point (concerning a UNESCO conference at The Hague), see the note by Trützschler, "Sowjetzone und UNESCO," Apr. 21, 1954: PA/AA, B 10, Bd. 297, Bl. 202–3.

43. See a draft of negotiating instructions for a delegation to Egypt, prepared in late January 1953: BAL, DL 2, Bd. 1702, Bl. 7–11, p. 2, bottom.

44. For British and American views about the need to step gingerly, see US Helsinki (Cabot) 153, Apr. 3, 1950, secret; and DepSta's reply of Apr. 10, 1950: FRG-IA 50–54, reel 30, Bl. 581–83 (762A.02).

45. Putensen, Im Konfliktfeld zwischen West und Ost, 56–60.

46. Examples from the first half of the 1950s include the envoys (Gesandten) in Beirut and Baghdad, Herbert Nöhring and Wilhelm Melchers, respectively. Maulucci, "Creation and Early History," 425–32. Sven Olaf Berggötz, in his excellent study Nahostpolitik in der Ära Adenauer, manages to sidestep this issue when discussing the continuity question; he analyzes the retention of personnel from the Weimar era and the Third Reich but without indicating which of the diplomats had once been Nazi Party members (105–13). Several diplomats who were sharply attacked in the early 1950s for their Nazi past later found posts in the Near and Middle East; see Döscher, Verschworene Gesellschaft.

47. Berggötz, Nahostpolitik in der Ära Adenauer, 175–79.

48. See the analysis in Trimbur, De la Shoah à la réconciliation?

49. On the Swiss proposal for a Zurich trade mission, see AF Bern (Chauvel) no. 1576/EU, July 16, 1952: MAE, EU 44–60, All 681, 133–36. For the East German retaliation, see the Politbüro resolution of October 31, 1952 (which was not, however, put into force until the end of the year): BA-SAPMO, NY 4182, Bd. 1322, Bl. 4–6. See also Gerber, "Zwischen Neutralitätspolitik und Anlehnung an den Westen," 331–35.

50. Documentation prepared by the Trade Ministry and the Ministry for Foreign Affairs in BAL, DL 2, Bd. 1702, Bl. 1–13.

51. Ibid., quote on Bl. 7.

52. US Bonn (West) Air Pouch 2439, Feb. 17, 1953, confidential: FRG-FA 50–54, reel 6, frames 159–61 (662A.86). See also Hünseler, Die außenpolitischen Beziehungen, 57–60.

53. On Bonn's promise regarding the engineers, see US Cairo (McClintock) Air Pouch 1750, Feb. 27, 1953, secret: FRG-FA 50–54, reel 5, frame 962 (662A.74).

54. Because this mission was operated by East Germany's Ministerium für Außenhandel und Innerdeutschen Handel, not the Kammer für Außenhandel, this Egyptian model transgressed the guidelines set by the Brussels Pact powers in 1949. To emphasize the nondiplomatic nature of this mission, Nasser's government did insist that the East German officials must deal with the Egyptian Ministry of Economics rather than

its Foreign Ministry. Abteilung V, Aufz., "Kontakte zwischen der Bundesrepublik und der Sowjetzone," undated (but almost certainly March 1954), 3: PA/AA, B 80, Bd. 236.

55. US Beirut (Hare) 513, Dec. 9, 1953, confidential: NARA, RG 59, CDF, 462B. 83A31. Commercial circles in Syria and Lebanon were showing particular interest in the East German market; see the MAI document "Plan für die Durchführung der handelspolitischen Richtlinien für die Jahre 1953 und 1954," Aug. 8, 1953, 4: BAL, DL 2, Bd. 1534, Bl. 14–17.

56. These were the Soviet Union, Poland, Czechoslovakia, Hungary, Romania, Bulgaria, Albania, the People's Republic of China, North Korea, North Vietnam, and Mongolia. *Außenpolitik der DDR: Drei Jahrzehnte sozialistische deutsche Friedenspolitik*, 388–89. In the United Nations, Ukraine and Belarus were represented independently of the Soviet Union, giving the GDR two additional votes in UN-affiliated institutions. The Federal Republic's tally is calculated from Auswärtiges Amt, *40 Jahre Außenpolitik der Bundesrepublik Deutschland*, 733–50.

57. Lavrentia Beria, the most powerful of Stalin's immediate successors, had a particularly disdainful view of the GDR; yet this may well have provoked his downfall in the summer of 1953. At the very least, Beria's loathing of the SED state bolstered the determination of others in Moscow to keep the GDR alive. Mastny, *Cold War and Soviet Insecurity*, 178–90. See also Ostermann, *Uprising in East Germany, 1953*.

58. Katzer, *"Eine Übung im Kalten Krieg,"* 276.

59. Ruhm von Oppen, *Documents on Germany Under Occupation*, 597–98; German text in *Beziehungen DDR-UdSSR 1949 bis 1955*, 639–41.

60. Foreign Office minutes (P. F. Hancock), Mar. 26, 1954, quoted in Becker, *DDR und Großbritannien*, 104–5. For a similar assessment by the State Department, urging that the Soviet decree be played down, see DepSta (Dulles) to US Bonn 2715, Mar. 27, 1954, secret: *FRUS 1952–54/VII*, 1678–79.

61. US Bonn (Conant) to DepSta 3039, Mar. 30, 1954, secret, priority: GDR-IA 50–54, reel 5, frames 467–68 (762B.02).

62. Ibid. For the purposes of smooth reading, "the" was inserted before "most vulnerable."

63. DepSta to London 5081 and Paris 3410, Mar. 31, 1954, confidential: *FRUS 1954*, VII/1682–83.

64. Quai to AF Washington and London, Apr. 8, 1954: MAE, EU 44–60, All 682, 56–58. The telegram noted that ECOSOC was expected to discuss the question of East German membership in the Economic Council of Europe (ECE) in April.

65. AF London (Massigli) tel. 1514–17, Apr. 9, 1954: MAE, EU 44–60, All 682, 61; US London (Aldrich) 4339, Apr. 2, 1954, confidential: GDR-IA 50–54, reel 6, frame 475 (762B.02).

66. For an example of French concern over Bonn's success (and lack of solidarity with the West) in the region, see AF Bonn (François-Poncet) No. 865/EU, Apr. 26, 1954: MAE, EU 44–60, All 693, 15–18. For a useful table comparing German, American, and British exports to select Near Eastern countries, see Hünseler, *Die außenpolitischen Beziehungen*, 94. As early as 1954, the Federal Republic had surpassed Britain's market share in Iran and Turkey; in Egypt, the lead enjoyed by Britain was rapidly narrowing.

67. DepSta Circtel 350, Apr. 5, 1954, official use only; US London (Aldrich) 4477,

Apr. 9, 1954, confidential: both GDR-IA 50–54, reel 5, frames 481–82, 475, 495 (762B.02).

68. Bundeskabinett, 27. Sitzung (Mar. 31, 1954): *Kabinettsprotokolle* 7:132.

69. Kaufmann, Aufz., Apr. 5, 1954: PA/AA, B 10, Bd. 298, Bl. 3–8.

70. Adenauer conferred with the three Allied high commissioners on April 5, 1954. For the German summary, see BAK, NL Blankenhorn, Bd. 30a, Bl. 259–63; see also Becker, *DDR und Großbritannien*, 106–7.

71. Deutscher Bundestag, 2. WP, 23. Sitzung (Apr. 7, 1954): *Sten. Ber.*, 794C–795C.

72. Ibid.

73. Ibid.

74. Adenauer's comments to the British high commissioner, Sir Frederick Hoyer Millar, Apr. 2, 1954, quoted in Becker, *DDR und Großbritannien*, 105–6.

75. Rauschning spoke on "Deutschlands Rolle in der Weltpolitik" on March 24, 1954. The CDU's most important foreign policy discussion group, Arbeitskreis V of the CDU parliamentary caucus, resolved to intervene with the Rhein-Ruhr-Klub in the wake of Rauschning's speech. Rhein-Ruhr-Klub, "Verzeichnis der Vorträge aus den Jahren 1949–1961," undated: ACDP, NL Birrenbach, I-433-008/1; Arbeitskreis V, Sitzung, Apr. 6, 1954: ACDP, VIII-06-1/1.

76. See Ollenhauer's comments to the Bundestag during its 26. Sitzung, Apr. 29, 1954: *Sten. Ber.*, 1083–85.

77. *Sten. Ber.*, 795–96. On Adenauer outmaneuvering the SPD, see Auswärtiger Ausschuß, 13. Sitzung (Apr. 6, 1954), 13–15: BT/PA, Ausw. Aus., 2. WP, Bd. 2.

78. For the text of Hallstein's instructions, see PA/AA, B 10, Bd. 297, Bl. 54–56. Hallstein's contractual approach is illustrated vividly in the case of Egypt. In May, the Foreign Office ordered the West German chargé to draw up an aide-mémoire reiterating West Germany's views and also quoting *selectively* from comments made privately on April 8 by a high-level Egyptian official. The purpose of this aide-mémoire was "to make it more difficult for the Egyptian government to back away" from the views its official had expressed on April 8. Trützschler to DG Cairo, May 11, 1954: PA/AA, B 10, Bd. 297, Bl. 164–65.

79. The telegrams of April 6–7 gave mixed signals on this point, contained in the phrase "zunächst nur Handelsmissionen." "Only" trade missions implies that they were essentially not a problem, while "for the time being" indicates an expectation that the GDR would use trade missions in third countries as a foothold to win consular and diplomatic concessions.

80. This recommendation appeared in a memorandum produced in the Federal Ministry for All-German Affairs (BMG). Münchheimer, Aufz., "Materialien zu einer Stellungnahme der Bundesregierung . . . ," Apr. 1, 1954, p. 7: BAK, B 137, Bd. 1404.

81. Hallstein to the German missions in Jakarta, Cairo, Beirut, Damascus, Baghdad, Addis Ababa, and Bangkok, Apr. 7, 1954: PA/AA, B 10, Bd. 297, Bl. 58–59.

82. Ref. 202 (Jansen), Aufz., Apr. 28, 1954: PA/AA, B 10, Bd. 298.

83. US Stockholm (Abbott) Courier Pouch 1080, Apr. 15, 1954, confidential: GDR-IA 50–54, reel 5, frames 512–16 (762B.02).

84. AF Stockholm (du Chayla) 521/EU, June 8, 1954: MAE, EU 44–60, All 682, 213–19; for the quote, see Grewe, Aufz., "Schwedische Politik gegenüber der DDR," May 13, 1954: PA/AA, NL Grewe, Bd. 47.

85. Trützschler to DG New Delhi, May 21, 1954: PA/AA, B 10, Bd. 298, Bl. 164–65.

86. Meyer to Trützschler, June 14, 1954: PA/AA, B 10, Bd. 299, Bl. 92–96.

87. In the case of Indonesia, the East German trade representative was only gradually allowed to turn his mission into a fixed office; see DG Jakarta (Allardt) Ber. 1119/54, Dec. 30, 1954, vertraulich: PA/AA, B 12, Bd. 95. On India, see DG New Delhi (Richter), Apr. 1, 1955: PA/AA, B 12, Bd. 94.

88. MAI, "Begründung zum Abschluß eines langfristigen Handelsabkommens zwischen der DDR und der Republik Finnland," Oct. 4, 1954: BAL, DL 2, Bd. 4061.

89. Scholz, "Östen Undén und die DDR," 410–11 (drawing on records from the East German and Swedish foreign ministries).

90. This plant went on to become an embarrassing white elephant for the GDR. The initial selling price proved to be far too low to cover costs, leading the East Germans to press Jakarta for higher payments. See Rau to Ulbricht, May 24, 1957: BA-SAPMO, NY 4182, Bd. 1331.

91. This thinking is implicit in the "Plan für das politische Auftreten der Handelsdelegation der Deutschen Demokratischen Republik in Indien," Aug. 26, 1954, 3: BA-SAPMO, NY 4090, Bd. 493.

92. DG Beirut (Nöhring) 45, Oct. 16, 1954: PA/AA, B 12, Bd. 119.

93. See Trützschler, Plurex, Nov. 15, 1954: PA/AA, B 12, Bd. 119. This telegram summarized the events in Beirut for the benefit of West German diplomats in other neutral capitals.

94. Conversation between Rudolf Appelt, the East German ambassador in Moscow, and his Burmese counterpart, Feb. 15, 1954: BAL, DL 2, Bd. 1715, Bl. 89–90.

95. Sterna (head of the Trade Ministry's Near Eastern desk), Aufz., "Beschlußprotokoll über die Auswertung der Bandung-Konferenz," May 11, 1955: BAL, DL 2, Bd. 1533, Bl. 272. On the Bandung conference itself, the most insightful discussion is surely Jansen, *Nonalignment and the Afro-Asian States*, 182–226.

96. As early as March 1955, the GDR had defaulted on its trade commitments to Uruguay; East Berlin could not cover the value of its imports with corresponding exports. DG Montevideo (Schwarz) Ber. 218/55, Mar. 21, 1955: PA/AA, B 12, Bd. 113.

97. For a summary of Nehru's comments to the Indian parliament on November 23, 1954, see Jansen, Runderlaß, Dec. 2, 1954: PA/AA, B 12, Bd. 138. Bonn's haste in circulating Nehru's comments to West German diplomatic posts around the world suggests how welcome the Indian standpoint was to West Germany.

CHAPTER TWO

1. Ansprache des Bundeskanzlers Adenauer im Sender Freies Berlin, May 5, 1955: *DzD* III/1, 12.

2. On the Federal Republic's status after the Paris Treaties had come into force, see Walter Schwengler's comments in Abelshauser and Schwengler, *Anfänge westdeutscher Sicherheitspolitik*, 330–51.

3. Zubok, "Soviet Policy Aims at the Geneva Conference, 1955," 57–59.

4. Gehler, "Österreichs außenpolitische Emanzipation und die deutsche Frage 1945–1955," 253–65; Bischof, "Making of the Austrian Treaty and the Road to Geneva," 144–47.

5. For a complaint from the Foreign Office about Adenauer's apparent haste to accept the offer, see Welck to Blankenhorn, June 12, 1955: BAK, NL Blankenhorn, Bd. 41a, Bl. 264–66.

6. Kosthorst, *Brentano und die deutsche Einheit*, 58.

7. Otto Bräutigam, head of Unterabteilung 35 (Osteuropa) at the Foreign Office, told an American official that "the chancellor at about the turn of the year had remarked that he would not be concerned by the existence of a GDR mission in Moscow if the Federal Republic should establish a mission there, since it would be only a very short time before the Soviets would be giving all their attention to the Federal Republic mission." Bräutigam said that Hallstein had recently confirmed this view. US Bonn (O'Shaughnessy) Air Pouch 1883, Mar. 4, 1955, confidential: USSR-FA 55–59, reel 4, frames 254–55 (661.62A).

8. Auswärtiger Ausschuß, 34. Sitzung (Feb. 7, 1955), 71: BT/PA, Ausw. Aus., 2. WP, Bd. 5. When the issue first came up in the cabinet on June 8, 1955, Minister for All-German Affairs Jakob Kaiser spoke out against any sort of relations with the Soviet Union so long as Germany remained divided. Adenauer contradicted this view, commenting that now that the Federal Republic was sovereign, world opinion would not understand a flat denial by West Germany to take up relations with the USSR. *Kabinettsprotokolle* 8:354.

9. West German note of June 30, 1955: *DzD* III/1, 123.

10. For a summary of Brentano's remarks, see Kosthorst, *Brentano und die deutsche Einheit*, 53.

11. To be sure, Adenauer's main objections to the Brentano conference focused on points other than the ones addressed here. See the exchange of telegrams printed in Baring, *Sehr verehrter Herr Bundeskanzler!*, 147–57.

12. DG Bern (Holzapfel) Ber. 1086, July 2, 1955: B 12, Bd. 122. Speculations in the Austrian press led Brentano to send off these hasty orders to the German trade representative in Vienna: "The Federal Government expects now as before that states with which it has diplomatic relations not allow representatives of the GDR. . . . The acceptance by the Austrian government of a diplomatic mission from the GDR would unleash the sharpest resistance on the part of the Federal Government." Brentano to the German consulate in Vienna, June 21, 1955: PA/AA, B 12, Bd. 125. It should be noted that the Federal Republic itself did not yet have diplomatic relations with Austria.

13. Hallstein, Runderlaß, June 29, 1955: PA/AA, B 80, Bd. 235; see also Welck, Runderlaß 19 Multex, June 20, 1955: PA/AA, B 12, Bd. 136.

14. This was true even of some of Bonn's new allies. One Dutch official remarked that if West Germany established an embassy in Moscow, the Netherlands might well open a mission in East Berlin. After all, one could not expect the Dutch to be "holier than the pope." This official, director of the Central European division, referred to pressure from Dutch businessmen. DG The Hague (Mühlenfeld) Ber. 1738, June 15, 1955: PA/AA, B 80, Bd. 236.

15. FDP-Bundeshauptausschuß, Bonn, July 2, 1955: ADL, Bd. A12-19, pp. 5–6. Welck was the head of Abteilung 3, the Countries Department, which coordinated the Federal Republic's bilateral relations with individual states.

16. See the note from the Burmese Foreign Ministry to the GDR's temporary representative, Helmut Kindler, July 12, 1954: BAL, DL 2, Bd. 1715, Bl. 29.

17. DG Rangoon (Kopf) 34, June 18, 1955: PA/AA, B 12, Bd. 90. As early as February, the Burmese Foreign Ministry had vaguely envisioned the opening of a "Büro des Handelsrats" in Rangoon; see the note of Feb. 27, 1955, in BAL, DL 2, Bd. 1719.

18. Hallstein to DG Rangoon 35, June 23, 1955: PA/AA, B 12, Bd. 90. This final sentence was added to the draft by Hallstein personally; see Referat 411 (Kiderlen), Aufz., June 29, 1955, in the same volume.

19. DG Rangoon (Kopf) 35, June 26, 1955: PA/AA, B 12, Bd. 90.

20. DG Rangoon (Kopf) 38, June 29, 1955: PA/AA, B 12, Bd. 90.

21. Furthermore, the legate was instructed to state (if asked) that the Burmese legate could remain in Bonn even after the West German representative had departed from Rangoon. This represents a sanction much less severe than the breaking of diplomatic relations. Welck to DG Rangoon 30, July 1, 1955 (sent July 4): PA/AA, B 12, Bd. 90.

22. DG Rangoon (Kopf) 41, July 14, 1955; and DG Rangoon (Kopf) 42, July 21, 1955: PA/AA, B 12, Bd. 90.

23. Welck, Aufz., Aug. 31, 1955: PA/AA, B 12, Bd. 90. The East German records suggest that the Burmese government had not made extensive promises to the GDR in the first place; see the MAI's instructions for August negotiations: BAL, DL 2, Bd. 1719, Bl. 7–9.

24. As early as July 29, Foreign Minister Brentano remarked to the French ambassador that he hoped nothing more would be exchanged with the Soviet Union than missions led by chargés. AF Bonn (François-Poncet) tel. 2983–3006, July 29, 1955: *DDF* 1955, II:156. During these months, a consensus also emerged within Bonn's Countries Department (Länderabteilung) that it would be too risky to take up official relations with Israel.

25. Ref. 350 (Meissner), Aufz., "Voraussetzungen für die Aufnahme diplomatischer Beziehungen mit der Sowjetunion," June 27, 1955, geheim: PA/AA, B 2, Bd. 4, Bl. 55–59. He predicted that at least Bonn's friends would stand firm, provided the Foreign Office took care to advertise its continuing claim to sole representation of Germany.

26. Letter printed in Adenauer, *Erinnerungen*, 2:478–80. See also Conze, "No Way Back to Potsdam," 207–9.

27. AF Bonn (Margerie) tel. 3250–63, Aug. 18, 1955, réservé: *DDF* 1955, II:261–63; Pressekonferenz, Aug. 17, 1955, p. 5: ACDP, NL Eckardt, I-010-008/2.

28. Note (attributed to Grewe) for Hallstein, Blankenhorn, and Maltzan, Aug. 23, 1955: PA/AA, B 2, Bd. 3, Bl. 134–35. This sharply limited agenda for Moscow had been anticipated by the government's reply of August 12 to the Soviet note of August 3. *DzD* III/1, 262–63.

29. Merchant, conversation with Adenauer, Aug. 31, 1955, secret: *FRUS* 1955–57/V, 569.

30. Ref. 354 (Fechter), Aufz., "Die Frage der Wiedervereinigung in Moskau," Aug. 9, 1955, geheim: PA/AA, B 2, Bd. 3, Bl. 59–65.

31. The first suggestion appears in Grewe, Aufz., "Notwendige Vorbehalte bei der Aufnahme diplomatischer Beziehungen," undated (but enclosed in the conference portfolio prepared for the trip in September 1955): PA/AA, B 2, Bd. 2. In the cabinet meeting of August 31, Adenauer himself spoke of the need to avoid a "sharp no" in Moscow. *Kabinettsprotokolle* 8:479 and 485 (there is a discrepancy in the use of the phrase "kein schroffes Nein" between the summary protocol and the verbatim record of the meeting).

32. In a conversation with Albrecht von Kessel (counselor of the German embassy

in Washington), Coburn Kidd (a key American adviser on Germany) suggested a few alternative arrangements: a German trade mission in Moscow, or a diplomatic mission without embassy status, or an embassy staffed by a chargé rather than a full ambassador. Kidd assured Kessel that, in terms of America's own interests, the State Department would have no objection to seeing a full-fledged West German embassy in Moscow. Kessel, Vermerk, Aug. 12, 1955: PA/AA, NL Kessel, Bd. 6.

33. Merchant, conversation with Kirkpatrick, Sept. 1, 1955, secret: *FRUS* 1955–57/V, 571. Kirkpatrick was commenting to Merchant on views expressed by Blankenhorn that morning.

34. Notes by Wilhelm Grewe of a *Fraktionsbesprechung* (an informational session for representatives from all the Bundestag caucuses), Sept. 2, 1955, p. 5: PA/AA, NL Grewe, Bd. 62.

35. Speeches from the first two days of the negotiations (Sept. 9 and 10, 1955) are published in *DzD* III/1, 302–28; quote on 328.

36. Important discussions of the Moscow negotiations appear in Kosthorst, *Brentano und die deutsche Einheit*, 63–77; Köhler, *Adenauer*, 873–89; and Schwarz, *Adenauer. Der Staatsmann* (hereafter *Staatsmann*), 207–22. In his memoirs, Grewe claims that his objection to the Soviet offer was of "tactical, not fundamental nature"—that he (and, he presumes, Hallstein and Brentano) simply wanted the German delegation to hold out for a better deal. Grewe, *Rückblenden*, 250. By contrast, the documentation I consulted appears to show that the top officials at the Foreign Office wanted to avoid diplomatic relations with Moscow under any circumstances.

37. For the text of Adenauer's letter of September 13, 1955, see *DzD* III/1 [misdated as Sept. 14], 337.

38. The Soviet news agency TASS did, however, issue a statement on September 14 reiterating the Soviet government's viewpoint that the Federal Republic and the GDR were both parts of Germany and that the border question had been resolved by the Potsdam Treaty. *DzD* III/1, 341–42.

39. CDU-Fraktion, Sept. 15, 1955, p. 22: ACDP, VIII-001-1007/2. Henning Köhler's assessment is probably closer to the mark. After describing the roundabout way in which Adenauer finally managed to send his letter to the Soviets, Köhler labels this method of preserving Germany's legal position "plum-soft." Köhler, *Adenauer*, 887–88.

40. CDU-Fraktion, Sept. 15, 1955, p. 26: ACDP, VIII-001-1007/2.

41. UK Bonn (Allen) No. 513, Sept. 14, 1955, secret, immediate: PRO, FO 371/118182.

42. Auswärtiger Ausschuß, 49. Sitzung (Sept. 7, 1955), 7–8: BT/PA, Ausw. Aus., 2. WP, Bd. 6.

43. Peckert, *Zeitwende zum Frieden*, 72–73.

44. Grewe, "Entwurf einer Note an alle Regierungen, mit denen die B-rep D-land diplomatische Beziehungen unterhält," Sept. 15, 1955: PA/AA, NL Grewe, Bd. 47.

45. Hallstein, Runderlaß Multex 33, Sept. 15, 1955: PA/AA, B 2, Bd. 3, Bl. 300; Hallstein, Runderlaß Multex 35, Sept. 21, 1955: PA/AA, B 12, Bd. 137.

46. Precisely this reasoning was employed by the Foreign Office in discussing the problem of German representation at the Geneva Conference. On October 10, at a meeting of the quadripartite (French, British, American, West German) working group preparing for the conference, Wilhelm Grewe explained that the Federal Re-

public could not tolerate the participation of the GDR at the conference on equal terms with the FRG. A German delegation member subsequently commented that this stance reflected primarily concern over the effects of the Moscow trip; the Federal Republic "might reverse its position at later date when danger was past." US Paris (Dillon, from Beam) to SecSta 1654, Oct. 10, 1955, secret: *FRUS 1955–57/V*, 549–51.

47. See, for example, Hallstein's instructions for a conversation with Yugoslav officials, contained in DG New York 83, Sept. 27, 1955: PA/AA, B 12, Bd. 138. For Adenauer's remarks, see his press conference of Sept. 16, 1955, p. 16: ACDP, I-010-008/2.

48. This assessment followed from a conversation with Otto Bräutigam, head of the East European subdepartment. US Bonn (Conant) 1220, Oct. 17, 1955, confidential: FRG-FA 55–59, reel 1, frame 232 (662A.00). For the purposes of smooth reading, the following words implied in the source text have been filled in: "the" before assumption, "that the" before Federal Republic, "the" before "foreseeable future."

49. US Bonn (O'Shaughnessy) Air Pouch 731, Oct. 11, 1955, confidential, p. 1: USSR-FA 55–59, reel 4, frames 586–98 (661.62A).

50. CDU-Fraktion, Sept. 21, 1955, p. 32: ACDP, VIII-001-017/2. One dissident at this meeting was Gerd Bucerius, publisher of the highbrow weekly *Die Zeit* and the magazine *Stern*, who demanded to know why the chancellor had agreed to diplomatic relations after the public had been prepared "systematically from the highest sources" for a different outcome (ibid., 33–34).

51. Polls taken at the time of Adenauer's death showed that, among his accomplishments during fourteen years as chancellor, his success with the POWs was rated most highly. Schwarz, *Staatsmann*, 207. For the quote, see US Bonn Air Pouch 731 (cited above in n. 49), p. 13.

52. Deutscher Bundestag, 2. WP, 101. Sitzung (Sept. 22, 1955): *Sten. Ber.*, 5647A; also *DzD* III/1, 389.

53. Asked precisely what consequences the Federal Republic would foresee in response to an "unfriendly act," Brentano pointed to the Burmese case from the summer of 1955 (without mentioning the country's name). Auswärtiger Ausschuß, 50. Sitzung (Sept. 21, 1955), 49–50: BT/PA, Ausw. Aus., 2. WP, Bd. 6. Because this was a joint meeting involving both the Auswärtiger Ausschuß and the Gesamtdeutscher Ausschuß, along with many representatives from the Bundesrat, some eighty to ninety parliamentarians heard Brentano's comments.

54. Deutscher Bundestag, 2. WP, 102. Sitzung (Sept. 23, 1955): *Sten. Ber.*, 5656C–5657B; also *DzD* III/1, 397–98. The chancellor responded to Ollenhauer's complaints by reading aloud one more time the operative paragraph of the September 22 threat, containing the "unfriendly act" phrase.

55. For the treaty text and related documentation, see *Beziehungen DDR-UdSSR 1949 bis 1955*, 2:992–1001.

56. US Helsinki (Morgan) Air Pouch 187, Sept. 30, 1955, confidential: NARA, RG 59, CDF, 660E.62A.

57. Ref. 304 (Knoke), Aufz., Sept. 22, 1955: PA/AA, B 12, Bd. 138. East German observers reached the same conclusion; see Rau to Ulbricht and Grotewohl, Nov. 17, 1955: BAL, NY 4182, Bd. 1235.

58. Switzerland responded with annoyance, Pakistan with confusion. A leading Swiss official rejected Bonn's thesis that recognizing the GDR constituted an "un-

friendly act," pointing out that the Federal Republic had just taken up diplomatic relations with the USSR, a leading offender. From Karachi, the German ambassador reported that the Pakistani government was convinced that the Moscow decision spelled a change in Bonn's policy. US Bern (Melbourne) 365, Oct. 11, 1955, confidential: GDR-FA 55–59, reel 3, frame 1042 (762B.02); DG Karachi (Podeyn) Ber. 2642, Nov. 9, 1955: PA/AA, B 12, Bd. 120.

59. In Beirut, the Lebanese minister-president claimed that Adenauer's Moscow turnaround had strongly influenced the Lebanese cabinet in its decision to accede to the GDR's wishes. DG Beirut (Nöhring), Oct. 15, 1955: PA/AA, B 12, Bd. 119. The Uruguayan decision set off the usual flurry of West German attempts to clarify the precise status of the mission. See, for example, the conversation in Bonn between West German officials and the Uruguayan ambassador: Ref. 306, Aktenvermerk, Dec. 22, 1955: PA/AA, B 12, Bd. 113.

60. The following documents describe rumors circulating in Italy, concerning Italy or Switzerland: dpa-Spezial, "Adenauers Moskaureise in italienischem Licht," Sept. 17, 1955: PA/AA, B 12, Bd. 117; US Rome (Luce) to SecSta 1131, Oct. 5, 1955, confidential: GDR-FA 55–59, reel 3, frame 1039 (762B.02); DG Rome (C. von Brentano) Ber. 3985, Oct. 14, 1955, vertraulich: PA/AA, B 12, Bd. 122.

61. On October 7, 1955, the GDR's anniversary reception in Moscow drew the following foreign dignitaries: the ambassadors of India, Burma, Yugoslavia, and Egypt; the minister of the Lebanese embassy; and representatives from the Finnish and Indonesian embassies. AF Moscow (Le Roy) tel. 3262, Oct. 8, 1955: MAE, EU 44–60, All 684, 103. On this copy of the telegram, the name of each country is underlined in red, indicating that the Quai d'Orsay was paying close attention to these affairs.

62. Hallstein found to his dismay that Germany's diplomatic posts had to be prompted for a report on how the aide-mémoire was received. Brückner, Aufz., "Aufnahme der Demarche von Multex Nr. 35 (21. September 1955)," Oct. 18, 1955: PA/AA, B 12, Bd. 120. For overviews of the expected future stance of each of West Germany's diplomatic partners, see Abteilung 3, Aufz., Sept. 28, 1955, and Welck, Aufz., Nov. 21, 1955, streng vertraulich: both in PA/AA, B 12, Bd. 138.

63. Politbüro, Protokoll Nr. 46/55, Sept. 27, 1955, Anl. 1: BAL, DY 30/J IV 2/2, Bd. 443.

64. This distinction was spelled out plainly in the *Bonner Rundschau* in an editorial that appears to have been officially inspired. AF Bonn (Margerie) 1506/EU, Nov. 4, 1955: MAE, EU 44–60, All 694, 18–19. The one noteworthy Indian concession was the transfer of the head office of the East German Chamber for Foreign Commerce from Bombay to New Delhi. *DARDDR* III, 650–52.

65. Curt-Heinz Merkel, Aufz., "Nachanalyse zu den Abkommensverhandlungen mit Ägypten über das langfristige Handel," o. D., p. 6: BAL, DL 2, Bd. 1838, Bl. 18–24. Rau first publicized this Egyptian promise in a press conference at Berlin's Schönefeld Airport upon his return on November 13. *DARDDR* III, 622–23.

66. As early as July 1955, the Quai d'Orsay concluded that French interests would be served by encouraging coexistence between the two Germanies. Quai to Bonn, undated [handwritten: July 4 (?), 1955], secret; MAE, EU 44–60, All 684, 58–59. Other compelling documentation on the French attitude appears in Lohse, *Östliche Lockungen und westliche Zwänge*, 181–84. British concerns about West German rigid-

ity in dealing with East German officials are mentioned in a conversation between J. J. Reinstein and an official from the British embassy in Washington, Oct. 29, 1955, secret: *FRUS* 1955–57/XXVI, 544–55.

67. After learning in November of the GDR's efforts to open a liaison office in Sudan, the British Foreign Office judged that it would not be able to intervene in Khartoum. Also in November, London refused for a second time to support West Germany's bid to gain full membership in the UN-affiliated ECE. The first such refusal came in July 1955. On Sudan, see DG London (Herwarth) 883, Nov. 9, 1955: PA/AA, B 12, Bd. 107; on the ECE, DG London (Herwarth) 407, July 2, 1955: PA/AA, B 30, Bd. 25; also DG London (Herwarth) 939, Nov. 26, 1955: PA/AA, B 30, Bd. 27.

68. On September 15 the State Department sent out a circular to its diplomatic posts explaining why Adenauer's Moscow decision did not imply any change in West Germany's (or America's) nonrecognition policies. DepSta (Hoover), Circtel 170, Sept. 15, 1955, official use only: GDR-FA 55–59, reel 3, frames 1029–30 (762B.02).

69. On the British objections, see Kidd to Reinstein, Oct. 17, 1955: *FRUS* 1955–57/V, 614–15. Sir Frederick Hoyer Millar, the British ambassador in Bonn, was among those who thought it best "not to bind our hands in this respect or to make statements which we might subsequently be accused of disowning." UK Bonn No. 437, Sept. 27, 1955, secret, immediate: PRO, FO 371/118246.

70. DG Helsinki (Koenning) Ber. 2299, Oct. 23, 1955: PA/AA, B 12, Bd. 88. One should note, however, that the Federal Republic itself took a sharply drawn position in Helsinki that the British ambassador considered quite effective: if Finland recognized the GDR, the Federal Republic would withdraw its trade mission. US Helsinki (Morgan) Air Pouch 197, Oct. 12, 1955, confidential: NARA, RG 59, CDF, 660E.62B.

71. In the case of Lebanon, the Foreign Office advised against involving the American and British ambassadors. Welck to DG Beirut 26, Oct. 7, 1955: PA/AA, B 12, Bd. 119.

72. Molotov's statement of November 8, 1955, was published already in the following day's issue of *Pravda*. For the German text, see *DzD* III/1, 610–15. Dulles cabled Eisenhower describing Molotov's statement as "one of the most cynical and uncompromising speeches which I have ever heard." The conference limped along for another week before its complete dissolution. Dulles to DepSta Dulte 60, Nov. 8, 1955, secret: *FRUS* 1955–57/V, 725–26.

73. On the morning of November 8, experts from the three Allied powers still anticipated wrapping up the discussion of German unity *for the time being* and then returning to it the following spring. *FRUS* 1955–57/V, 705 (comments by Harrison and Margerie).

74. Hallstein to DG Rangoon 28, June 23, 1955: PA/AA, B 12, Bd. 90.

75. On November 9, the Indian representative to UNESCO voted in favor of East Germany's membership application; on December 7, its representative to ECOSOC voted for East German acceptance in the ECE. Confronted about the first of these votes, an Indian official referred explicitly to the failure of the Geneva Conference. DG New Delhi (Meyer) 130, Nov. 17, 1955: PA/AA, B 12, Bd. 94.

76. For Dehler's interpretation of the Geneva Conference, see Klingl, *Das ganze Deutschland soll es sein!*, 228–30. In the foreign policy debate of December 2, 1955, it was the SPD rather than the FDP that presented the sharpest criticism of the West's stance at Geneva; Erich Ollenhauer pleaded for a constructive dialogue with the Soviets. *DzD* III/1, 760–72.

77. Adenauer to Dehler, Nov. 22, 1955, printed in Adenauer, *Erinnerungen*, 3:80–82. Adenauer insisted to the cabinet that this was not merely a personal showdown with Dehler, explaining that it was "vitally important for Germany that the West not have any doubts about its [Germany's] foreign policy orientation." Bundeskabinett, 108. Sitzung (Nov. 30, 1955): *Kabinettsprotokolle* 8:709–10.

78. In mid-November, when the Pakistani Foreign Ministry posed this question rather casually, Bonn responded guardedly that "the Federal Government would be forced to revise fundamentally its relationship to this state." Welck to DG Karachi 97, Nov. 19, 1955: PA/AA, B 12, Bd. 120.

79. Carstens, Vermerk, Nov. 8, 1955: BAK, NL Carstens, Bd. 336. The attendance lists from the Auswärtiger Ausschuß meetings of September 7 and 21, 1955, where Brentano expressed this standpoint quite clearly, show that Carstens did not number among the observers sent by the Foreign Office (though Grewe did). Hallstein remarked to Carstens that he had described Bonn's likely reaction several times in conversations with foreign diplomats. Carstens, interoffice memo (draft) to Abteilungen I, 3, and 6, Nov. 21, 1955: BAK, NL Carstens, Bd. 336.

80. Grewe specifies this date in a note to Welck, Dec. 20, 1955: PA/AA, NL Grewe, Bd. 47. From 1955 onward, the desk's basic function remained the same, but its designation changed with every reorganization within the Foreign Office: from Referat 354 to Referat 201 (Dec. 1955) to Referat 700 (mid-1958) to Referat II 1 (Feb. 1963) to Referat II A 1 (Sept. 1965). The Referat retained the name "Wiedervereinigung" until 1967, when it was dubbed "Außenpolitische Fragen der gesamtdeutschen Angelegenheiten." End, *Zweimal deutsche Außenpolitik*, 196 n. 11.

81. Grewe, Aufz., "Organisatorische Zugehörigkeit des Referats Wiedervereinigung," Nov. 28, 1955, p. 2: PA/AA, B 12, Bd. 254.

82. The collapse of Adenauer's health for seven weeks in October and November 1955 had given the foreign minister a chance to step forward as the authentic interpreter of Adenauer's views; Brentano represented the government in the Bundestag's foreign policy debate of December 1, 1955. On Adenauer's sickness, see Schwarz, *Staatsmann*, 237. On Brentano's uneasy relationship with the chancellor, see Kosthorst, *Brentano und die deutsche Einheit*, 30–77; and Baring, *Sehr verehrter Herr Bundeskanzler!*, 147–72.

83. Brentano, "Eröffnungsrede," p. 11: PA/AA, B 2, Bd. 92, Bl. 12–24. Later that morning, during a discussion round, Brentano vented his scorn for "certain circles of our German industry which think only in terms of the bottom line, and have no concept of politics." Botschafterkonferenz (unedited transcript), Teil I, pp. 6–7: BAK, NL Blankenhorn, Bd. 41a. Blankenhorn's papers contain the entire transcript of the first day of the conference; Bd. 92 of B 2 contains select speeches.

84. In April 1954, FDP deputy Karl Georg Pfleiderer called upon the Foreign Office to remedy its neglect of the "blank spot, a veritable terra incognita in our foreign policy" stretching from Warsaw via Moscow to Peking. Deutscher Bundestag, 2. WP, 23. Sitzung (Apr. 7, 1954): *Sten. Ber.*, 818–19. Pfleiderer had since been appointed ambassador to Belgrade, but his place as an advocate of an opening to the East was soon filled by the FDP's Max Becker. See, for example, Becker's comments in Auswärtiger Ausschuß, 50. Sitzung (Sept. 21, 1955), p. 30: BT/PA, Ausw. Aus., 2. WP, Bd. 6.

85. Brentano explained, "I couldn't concur with his opinion, I had to act against his views for political reasons. But I took special occasion to thank him for representing

his opinion with a stubbornness that—I must tell you openly—appealed to me very much." Brentano may well have been referring to Wilhelm Kopf's refusal to threaten the Burmese government, which was a fairly spectacular case of defying orders. Brentano, "Eröffnungsrede" (cited in n. 83 above), p. 13.

86. A photograph of the conference in session appeared in the *Neue Zürcher Zeitung*, Dec. 12, 1955, 3. On the quality of discussions, see the opposing judgments in End, *Zweimal deutsche Außenpolitik*, 42–43; and Grewe, *Rückblenden*, 255–56.

87. See, for example, the comments by Müller-Graaff regarding Austria, in which he refers specifically to earlier statements by the ambassadors to Brazil and Sweden. Botschafterkonferenz, V. Teil, p. 8: BAK, NL Blankenhorn, Bd. 41, Bl. 76–103.

88. Brentano's visit to Vienna in November 1955 culminated in an announcement that the two countries would exchange ambassadors. Austria's foreign minister justified this stance in a closed meeting of Austrian officials by pointing out that Vienna could afford to wait until other neutral states had recognized the GDR. Word of this standpoint leaked to dpa, a West German press service, shortly before Brentano's trip to Austria. Ref. 304 (Knoke), Aufz., Nov. 12, 1955: PA/AA, B 1, Bd. 15.

89. At the urging of Felix von Eckardt, Adenauer's former (and future) press spokesman, the conference adopted a plan to press the British to support West Germany's application to the ECE. Eckardt predicted that this step, if successful, would greatly demoralize the East Germans. Botschafterkonferenz, Teil IV, pp. 9–10: BAK, NL Blankenhorn, Bd. 41a, Bl. 54–75; Ref. 203 (Overbeck), Aufz., "Antrag der britischen Regierung bei ECOSOC," Dec. 9, 1955: PA/AA, B 30, Bd. 27.

90. Grewe, Aufz., "Die Politik der 'Nicht-Anerkennung' der DDR," Dec. 7, 1955, p. 5: PA/AA, B 2, Bd. 92, Bl. 25–31. Excerpts from this document appear in Grewe, *Rückblenden*, 252–53 and endnotes. For a German author's very able explication of Grewe's views, see Booz, *"Hallsteinzeit,"* 19–27.

91. As if to underscore this point, the legal adviser to the Foreign Office, Erich Kaufmann, spoke after Grewe and produced a slightly different list of acceptable and unacceptable behaviors with respect to the GDR. In the summary of the Ambassadors' Conference that was circulated to all West German missions abroad, Prof. Kaufmann's talk was excluded, indicating that Grewe's views were considered more authoritative. Hallstein, Runderlaß, Jan. 16, 1956, vertraulich: PA/AA, B 2, Bd. 92, Bl. 5–11 and attachments; Kaufmann, Aufz., Dec. 7, 1955: PA/AA, B 80, Bd. 236.

92. Grewe's complete list of actions that might or might not imply recognition ran as follows: taking up consular or limited consular relations without an exequatur, sending or receiving a government-level trade delegation, issuing visas in GDR passports, tolerating the GDR's participation in multilateral conferences, tolerating the GDR's signing of multilateral treaties, and admitting the GDR to international organizations. Grewe, "Die Politik der 'Nicht-Anerkennung,'" p. 7. Grewe's inclusion of these last three items is striking in light of West Germany's dogged efforts to exclude East Germany from UN organizations, conferences, and treaties. This seems a particularly good example of Grewe's assertion that certain forms of East German diplomatic activity were undesirable for political reasons, regardless of the legal implications.

93. Ibid., 6–7.

94. Ibid., 7.

95. Hallstein, "Erläuterungen zu den Referaten von Prof. Kaufmann und Prof. Grewe," p. 2: PA/AA, B 2, Bd. 92, Bl. 141–46.

96. Ibid., 4.

97. Ibid., 6.

98. This was the summation offered by the *Frankfurter Allgemeine*, which reported (accurately) that Brentano himself had expressed this standpoint during his opening speech on December 8. "Anerkennung Ostberlins bedeutet Bruch mit Bonn," *FAZ*, Dec. 10, 1955, 1. For Diehl's curt remarks, see the press conference of Dec. 9, 1955, p. 1a: ACDP, NL Eckardt, I-010-008/2.

99. Officials at the Foreign Office told the American embassy that Diehl's comments exceeded the scope of his brief; however, they may have simply chosen to make Diehl a scapegoat following the unfavorable reception of the December 9 press conference. Hallstein himself offered a similarly blunt description of Bonn's policy in a background conversation with journalists twelve days later. US Bonn (O'Shaughnessy) Air Pouch 1261, Dec. 15, 1955, confidential: FRG-FA 55–59, reel 1, frames 108–12; Hallstein, Informationsgespräch, Dec. 21, 1955, pp. 22–23: ACDP, NL Eckardt, I-010-008/2.

100. Given the preponderance of local party–affiliated newspapers in West Germany in the 1950s, some papers naturally voiced support for Brentano's hard line. See, for example, "Pseudorealismus," *Kölner Stadt-Anzeiger*, Dec. 13, 1955. Among the independent newspapers—a better judge of elite opinion in West Germany—condemnation of the principles elaborated by Diehl is quite consistent. The editorials cited in this paragraph can be found in Abteilung Pressedokumentation of the Bundespresseamt.

101. Hans Henrich, "Der forsche Ton," *Frankfurter Rundschau*, Dec. 14, 1955. In a similar vein, Peter Cassel pointed out that neutral countries, be they in Europe or Asia, disliked being told what to do. "Irreale Politik," *Frankfurter Neue Presse*, Dec. 12, 1955.

102. Giselher Wirsing, "Diplomatie oder Deklamation?," *Die Welt*, Dec. 17, 1955; Walter Hück, "Wie stark sind wir?," *Die Rheinpfalz* (Ludwigshafen), Dec. 10, 1955.

103. "Grundsätzlich," *FAZ*, Dec. 10, 1955, 1; "Die Beziehungen zum Osten," *Stuttgarter Zeitung*, Dec. 12, 1955; "Porzellan der Außenpolitik," *Süd-West Rundschau* (Freiburg im Breisgau), Dec. 12, 1955.

104. On Brentano's approval, see Grewe, *Rückblenden*, 253.

105. Grewe interview, Dec. 11, 1955, printed in *Außenpolitik der Bundesrepublik Deutschland*, 229–30.

106. Even West German ambassadors occasionally tripped up on this point. When the ambassador to Denmark, Hans Berger, reported having used the term "automatic" in conversation with a Danish official, the Foreign Office notified him that his wording was inaccurate. DG Copenhagen (Berger) Ber. 331/60, Mar. 28, 1960: PA/AA, B 12, Bd. 93.

107. In addition to the background conversation of December 21, 1955, cited above, Hallstein commented a few weeks later: "You know that in case of a recognition of the GDR by a third country we've threatened a break in diplomatic relations. That was no empty threat. There have been cases where we were close to making good on this threat." In mid-1956, Hallstein affirmed that "there is no way we can compromise on this question." Hallstein, Informationsgespräch, Jan. 10, 1956, pp. 14–15: PA/AA, B 2, Bd. 30, Bl. 155–80; Hallstein, Informationsgespräch, July 12, 1956, p. 13: ACDP, NL Eckardt, I-010-009/2.

108. On the naming of the Hallstein Doctrine, see Chapter 3. Daniel Kosthorst, taking note of Brentano's strong pronouncements at the Bonn Conference, suggests that the foreign minister originated the policy of breaking relations—perhaps even independently of Hallstein. Kosthorst, *Brentano und die deutsche Einheit*, 91–93. Brentano does appear to have taken this line from a very early date, as shown in his comments to the Foreign Affairs Committee on September 7 and 21. The feud with Burma, the first occasion when Bonn considered wielding this threat, took place shortly after Brentano assumed office. Until more classified documents from 1955 are available, however, it is impossible to reach any final conclusions about the precise contributions of Grewe, Hallstein, and Brentano.

109. So U.S. Ambassador James B. Conant argued to Brentano in a conversation on December 6. A specific concern of the Americans was that the GDR might throttle traffic to Berlin in an attempt to extort recognition from the Western Allies. Such eventualities called for careful contingency planning. On U.S. motives, see Merchant to Hoover, Dec. 7, 1955, confidential: FRG-IA 55–59, reel 3, frames 486–88 (762A.00). For the Brentano-Conant conversation, see Brentano, Aufz., "Ost-West-Verhandlungen und Berlinfrage," Dec. 7, 1955: PA/AA, NL Grewe, Bd. 32.

110. This motive was underlined by the French chargé in Bonn, whose report to the Quai d'Orsay reflects some apprehension about the pending arrival of the first Soviet ambassador to the Federal Republic, Valerien Sorin. AF Bonn (Margerie) tel. 4776–82, Dec. 13, 1955: MAE, EU 44–60, All 684, 134.

111. UK Bonn (Hoyer Millar) No. 362, Dec. 8, 1955, secret: PRO, FO 371/118254; AF Bonn (Margerie) No. 1822, Dec. 23, 1955: MAE, EU 44–60, All 684, 154–58.

112. The files of the reunification desk contain the nearly complete minutes for the Bonn Group's meetings in 1956, part of 1957, and 1962: PA/AA, B 12, Bde. 150–51, and PA/AA, B 38, Bd. 40. For other years, the protocols appear to be classified *vertraulich* (confidential), and only fragments are available. The Foreign Office called these meetings *Konsultationsbesprechungen*, or "consultation meetings"; this seemingly redundant designation referred back to the Paris Treaties, which had included provisions for joint Allied-German consultation regarding Berlin, and regarding the issue of Germany as a whole.

113. DG NATO (Blankenhorn), reports of Dec. 17 (p. 3) and Dec. 18 (p. 2), 1955: copies in BAK, NL Blankenhorn, Bd. 58, Bl. 52–54 and 45–49. For public consumption, the NATO ministers adopted a resolution affirming the Federal Republic's status as the sole legitimate representative of the German people.

114. The British Foreign Office was responding to a West German appeal for advice about how to resolve its difficulties in Cairo. The Quai d'Orsay's initial stance showed much more reserve: "There is indubitably a disturbing tendency toward recognition of Pankow among a number of states which are, by virtue of their geographic position in Europe or their membership in the Bandung Group, oriented toward a certain neutralism. One must recognize that in practice it will not be easy for us to exercise pressure on the governments of these states. We understand, however, very well that for its part the government of the Federal Republic may take all measures which it deems useful to check this tendency." AF London (Chauvel) tel. 5294, Dec. 10, 1955, and Quai (Crouy) to AF Bonn tel. 4948, Dec. 9, 1955: MAE, EU 44–60, All 684, 131 and 126.

115. An especially clear presentation of this West German argument appears in AF Bonn (Joxe) tel. 187–90, Jan. 18, 1956: *DDF* 1956, I:56–57.

116. In early January 1956, the Quai d'Orsay considered intervening in Helsinki, though it established after consultation with the State Department and Foreign Office that this was unnecessary. In April the Quai instructed the French ambassador to Sudan to maintain close contact with the West German envoy regarding Soviet Zone affairs and to support him as necessary. On Finland, see AF London (Chauvel) tel. 19–20, Jan. 3, 1956, and AF Washington (Couve de Murville) tel. 9–10, Jan. 4, 1956: MAE, EU 44–60, RDA 23, 2 and 3. On Sudan, see Carstens to DG Khartoum 29, Apr. 23, 1956: PA/AA, B 12, Bd. 92. For an example (regarding Egypt) of prompting from the French embassy in Bonn, see AF Bonn (Margerie) No. 1804/EU, Dec. 22, 1955, p. 3: MAE, EU 44–60, All 441, 217–19. In this case the embassy referred specifically to a Bonn Group meeting, which suggests that the formation of this group played a role in mobilizing French action on the East German problem.

117. The success of the December initiative was by no means a foregone conclusion; the Foreign Office worried that the one-sided measure might provoke retaliation by the Soviets. The French were concerned as well, though in the end "pleasantly surprised" by the outcome. DG New York (Pauls) 167, Dec. 10, 1955, citissime; and DG Paris (Maltzan), Dec. 19, 1955: both in PA/AA, B 30, Bd. 25. On the April ECE conference, see Michael L. Hoffmann, "U.N. Unit Rejects German Red Bid," *New York Times*, Apr. 7, 1956, 3.

118. Voigt to the German embassies in Cairo, Damascus, Addis Ababa, Beirut, and New Delhi, Jan. 7, 1956, streng vertraulich: PA/AA, B 12, Bd. 138. The same report indicated that Ulbricht had accused Rau of lying about Nasser's readiness to recognize the GDR; Rau, backed by the Soviet ambassador to East Berlin, insisted that Nasser had capitulated to strong West German pressure. Voigt acknowledged that this report was unconfirmed.

119. Karl Mommer (SPD) had inquired of Vice-Chancellor Blücher whether his conversations with Nehru were overshadowed by the threat announced by Bonn in December. Blücher dissembled, but Hallstein stepped in a few minutes later in response to Mommer's use of the term "threat." Auswärtiger Ausschuß, 55. Sitzung (Feb. 1, 1956), 43–44, 45–47: BT/PA, Ausw. Aus., 2. WP, Bd. 7.

120. Ibid., 45–47.

121. UK Bonn (Hoyer Millar) 45, Feb. 4, 1956, confidential, para. 7: PRO, FO 371/124531. For an example of Ambassador Meyer's views, see Meyer to Hallstein, Jan. 24, 1956, p. 4: PA/AA, B 2, Bd. 16, Bl. 231–36.

122. Hallstein emphasized these tactics in his background press briefing of July 12, 1956, pp. 22–24: ACDP, NL Eckardt, I-010-009/2.

123. In private, Adenauer was quite sarcastic about the alleged philosophical basis of India's foreign policy. See Buchstab, *Adenauer: "Wir haben wirklich etwas geschaffen,"* 927.

124. Bundeskabinett, 107. Sitzung, Nov. 23, 1955: *Kabinettsprotokolle* 8:700, esp. n. 21.

125. Hallstein's conversation with Yugoslav State Secretary Brkic on March 7, 1956, shows that the Foreign Office had only limited justification for making this claim. PA/AA, B 12, Bd. 581.

126. The Sudanese minister-president assured the West German envoy that his government would follow the example of Egypt and the other Arab states. DG Khartoum (de Haas) 20, Nov. 19, 1955: PA/AA, B 12, Bd. 107. In the case of Syria, it was the FRG that set up Egypt as a benchmark; see Grewe to DG Damascus 34, Dec. 14, 1955: PA/AA, B 12, Bd. 100.

127. At the Ambassadors' Conference, Brentano congratulated Becker on his low-key handling of the issue, saying that Becker was quite right to explain to the Egyptians that West Germany had no interested in turning Egypt into a "test case" for the severity of its nonrecognition policy. Botschafterkonferenz, Teil III, pp. 16–17: BAK, NL Blankenhorn, Bd. 41a, Bl. 29–53.

128. Bonn's instructions to DG Cairo of Dec. 1, 1955, have not yet been declassified, but a later memo by the international law desk contains a reference to these two conditions. Ref. 500, Aufz., Jan. 31, 1956, p. 2: PA/AA, B 80, Bd. 236. Further details about Bonn's assessment of the situation (based on a December 1 conversation between Welck and representatives of the three Allied embassies) appear in AF Bonn (Margerie) tel. 4644–51, Dec. 2, 1955: MAE, EU 44–60, All 441, 215–16.

129. As the Foreign Office's leading Middle East expert, Hermann Voigt, phrased it: "As long as the posts of the GDR abroad sail under the flag of 'trade mission' and trade forms the bulk of their activity, it will be in our interest not to clear away from the countries in question, but to hold out there as long as possible." If the Federal Republic were to depart in anger from a given country, that would only increase the GDR's influence in that country, leading to the very situation Bonn wanted to avoid: a recognition of the GDR. Ref. 308 (Voigt), Aufz., Dec. 17, 1955, p. 3: PA/AA, B 12, Bd. 89.

130. To hint at the possibility of a lengthy absence, the Foreign Office arranged for the previous second-in-command of the Cairo embassy, Baron Dietrich von Mirbach, to return to Cairo as Becker's stand-in. Becker, Aufz., Dec. 12, 1955, regarding conversations with Fawzi on Dec. 3 and 4: PA/AA, B 12, Bd. 89.

131. Adalbert Weinstein (on location in Cairo), "Kairo befürchtet Gegenmaßnahmen Bonns," FAZ, Dec. 14, 1955, 4. The Egyptian ambassador to Sweden at least predicted that Brentano's comments would be helpful: DG Stockholm (Siegfried) Ber. 409/55, Dec. 14, 1955: PA/AA, B 12, Bd. 89.

132. Adalbert Weinstein, "Kairo erkennt Ost-Berlin nicht an," FAZ, Dec. 16, 1955, 1. An editorial on the same page, "Wichtige Klärung," pointed out that if Nasser had not come to this decision, West Germany would have stood before a difficult decision, "whose costs would have been borne above all by German exporters. They have been spared this, thus bringing one victory for the 'hard' policy of the Foreign Minister."

133. This was evident to the Foreign Office, but it opted to send Becker back in order to resolve the remaining points as soon as possible. Ref. 308 (Voigt), Aufz., Dec. 17, 1955, pp. 1–2: PA/AA, B 12, Bd. 89.

134. DG Cairo (Becker) Ber. 1112/56, Mar. 8, 1956: PA/AA, B 12, Bd. 89.

135. West German spokesmen pointed out that such behavior contradicted "international diplomatic customs" and asserted that the question of an Egyptian trade mission in East Berlin played no role in the trade talks in Cairo. Pressekonferenz, Jan. 25, 1956, pp. 11–12: ACDP, NL Eckardt, I-010-009/1.

136. PA/AA, B 12, Bd. 89. After the Egyptian ambassador complained about the lack of progress in the trade talks, Brentano noted that the Egyptian government had

not yet clarified its position toward the Soviet Zone of Germany. On the trade issues at stake, see Hünseler, *Die außenpolitischen Beziehungen*, 101–2.

137. This controversy is surely what led Hallstein to make his remarks to the Foreign Affairs Committee about the inadvisability of using the term "threat" to describe Bonn's stance, as described above. A conversation between the Foreign Office's Near East expert, Hermann Voigt, and a Japanese embassy official in Bonn provides a window into the attitudes of the nonaligned Asian embassies there. The Japanese official commented that many Asian diplomats believed the Egyptian charges—but that many were themselves not averse to closer relations with the GDR. He noted that these issues were hotly debated among the Asian missions in Bonn, and that all eyes were on the Foreign Office to see what it let Egypt get away with. Voigt, conversation, Jan. 31, 1956: PA/AA, B 12, Bd. 89.

138. In *Divided Memory*, Jeffrey Herf describes the GDR's deliberate neglect of Israel. Angelika Timm links this pattern to the GDR's efforts to win recognition from the Arab states in *Hammer, Zirkel, Davidstern*.

139. Abraham Frowein, Aufz., Sept. 28, 1955. In a memorandum of June 1, 1954, Hermann Voigt remarked that the Arabs had hinted at such a relationship but had not yet expressed it directly. Both documents are cited in Trimbur, "La question des rélations germano-israeliènnes (1949–1956)," 398 and 396 n. 151.

140. "Nasser warnt die Bundesregierung," *Die Welt*, Apr. 4, 1956, 1. Nasser was no doubt hoping to impress the West German diplomats assembled in Istanbul (see the following note). Already in Brentano's conversation with the Egyptian ambassador on January 17, the latter implied a connection between Israel's mission in Cologne and Egypt's handling of the GDR. PA/AA, B 12, Bd. 89.

141. In March 1956, Grewe encouraged Brentano to offer the Israelis a dilatory response and await the outcome of the Ambassadors' Conference in Istanbul. This gathering, chaired by Hallstein from April 3 to 9, 1956, recommended that Bonn not risk any level of official relations with Israel, lest it provoke the Arab states into recognizing East Germany. Grewe to Brentano, Mar. 6, 1956: PA/AA, NL Grewe, Bd. 47. Grewe's position appears to have been strongly influenced by an intelligence report (mentioned in Grewe's letter) that said the Czech-Egyptian weapons purchase agreement from the fall of 1955 had included a secret clause in which Egypt agreed to recognize the GDR. From the Ambassadors' Conference, see the comments by the chiefs of mission in Syria (Esch) and Egypt (Becker): PA/AA, B 2, Bd. 94, p. 101 and pp. 143–46 of the conference protocol.

142. Protocol of the Ambassadors' Conference in Tokyo, Feb. 18–23, 1957, pp. 35–36: PA/AA, B 1, Bd. 259.

CHAPTER THREE

1. Rau, Aufz., "Berichte und Maßnahmepläne zur Auswertung der Reise der Regierungsdelegation in die Republik Indien und Ägypten," Dec. 1955: BAL, DL 2, Bd. 66, Bl. 2–3.

2. Aside from being removed from the Trade Ministry, the official in question was given a "stern reprimand" on his personal dossier and banned from all foreign travel for two years. BA-SAPMO, NY 4090, Bd. 493.

3. Rau to Ulbricht, Nov. 25, 1955: BA-SAPMO, NY 4182, Bd. 1335. In this letter, Rau emphasized the need for Soviet leadership of such an initiative. Ulbricht duly passed

along Rau's letter to Moscow on December 1: see BA-SAPMO, DY 30, Bd. 3664. It would be intriguing to learn whether Rau's suggestion played any role in the eventual Soviet decision to go forward with the financing of the Aswan Dam.

4. Politbüro, Protokoll Nr. 9/56, Mar. 13, 1956, Anl. 7: BA-SAPMO, DY 30/J IV 2/2, Bd. 463.

5. The Soviet document, like all others of its type, gives no precise information about where it originated; only the date—February 1, 1956—is indicated. BA-SAPMO, NY 4090, Bd. 493, Bl. 36.

6. For an early indication of Bolz's feelings on this point, see Bolz to Grotewohl, Jan. 23, 1956: BA-SAPMO, NY 4090, Bd. 493. It is worth noting that Bolz himself was not a member of the Politburo, and thus was not terribly influential within the East German leadership.

7. Bolz to Richard Gyptner, undated [May 1956]: BA-SAPMO, DY 30/J IV 2/2, Bd. 477, Bl. 74–79; quotes from pp. 3–4 of the memo.

8. DDR Peking (Gyptner) 316, June 26, 1956, dringend: BA-SAPMO, NY 4090, Bd. 467, Bl. 153.

9. *Izvestia*, June 20, 1956, 2.

10. *Izvestia*, June 21, 1956, 1. For a German translation of this and the previously cited speech, see *DzD* III/2, 481–83.

11. Rubinstein, *Yugoslavia and the Nonaligned World*, 49–70.

12. Ulbricht to Tito, July 5, 1956: BA-SAPMO, DY 30, Bd. 3641.

13. Micunovic, *Moscow Diary*, 92.

14. Frankland and King, *Documents on International Affairs 1956*, 72.

15. DG Washington (Krekeler), Aug. 1, 1956: PA/AA, NL Kessel, Bd. 7.

16. *DzD* III/2, 513–14. Brentano discusses the purpose of Bonn's nonrecognition policy here at great length.

17. Hallstein's reluctance to state this outright during a meeting of the Bundestag's Foreign Affairs Committee made for a rather convoluted conversation. Auswärtiger Ausschuß, 60. Sitzung (June 26, 1956), 46–53: BT/PA, Ausw. Aus., 2. WP, Bd. 8.

18. See the CDU caucus meetings of July 3 (pp. 287–89), July 4 (pp. 293–94), and July 5 (p. 295): ACDP, VIII-001-1007/2.

19. DG Belgrade (Pfleiderer) 140, July 14, 1956, cito: PA/AA, B 12, Bd. 581.

20. For a contrasting evaluation, see Lorenzen, "Die Jugoslawien-Politik der DDR," 59–61. Lorenzen is impressed by the exchanges of party delegations between the SED and the League of Yugoslav Communists in the late summer of 1956, but very little warmth shows through the official records.

21. See pp. 7–8 of the Soviet document entitled "Zu den Ergebnissen der sowjetisch-jugoslawischen Verhandlungen im Juni 1956," handed in translation to the East Germans on July 18, 1956: BA-SAPMO, DY 30, Bd. 3641. On the absence of Soviet pressure, see also Micunovic, *Moscow Diary*, 65, 71.

22. The agreement, signed in early August 1956, had been in the works all summer. See the Soviet note of May 31, 1956, calling East German attention to the situation and suggesting that the GDR send a delegate to the Soviet-Yugoslav negotiations: BA-SAPMO, DY 30, Bd. 3641.

23. On the February debacle, see the note from the SED's Abteilung Binnen- und Außenhandel to Ulbricht, Feb. 6, 1957: BA-SAPMO, NY 4182, Bd. 1235. On the opera-

tions of the Yugoslav chamber of commerce office in East Berlin, see the SED's Abteilung Handel, Versorgung und Außenhandel to Florin, Apr. 25, 1957, in ibid.

24. One striking example of East German opportunism that I have not otherwise worked into the narrative involves Sudan, where teams of East German scientists went around searching for water—and uranium—in the mid-1950s. Schwanitz, "Wasser, Uran, und Paktfreiheit."

25. Ramet, *Soviet-Syrian Relationship*, 15–17.

26. DG Damascus (Esch) 19, May 15, 1956: PA/AA, B 12, Bd. 100. On the GDR's calculated refusal to acknowledge any moral debt to Israel, see Herf, *Divided Memory*, esp. chap. 6; Timm, *Hammer, Zirkel, Davidstern*.

27. Ref. 500 (Meyer-Lindenberg), Aufz., "Kulturabkommen zwischen Syrien und der sog. DDR," Aug. 23, 1956: PA/AA, B 12, Bd. 100.

28. On the petition, see the conversation between Grewe and the Syrian envoy in Bonn, Istuani, on July 19, 1956: ibid. For the comments by top Syrian officials, see US Damascus (Moose) 141, July 18, 1956, confidential: GDR-FR 55–59, reel 3, frame 1079 (762B.02).

29. Ref. 201 (Ruete), Plurex (draft), Aug. 11, 1956: PA/AA, B 12, Bd. 138.

30. Brentano to Welck, June 7, 1956: PA/AA, B 1, Bd. 20. Brentano was dissatisfied with this British response, and he suggested appealing over their heads to Washington. Adenauer did mention the possible Nasser invitation to Dulles on June 12, 1956, but in a fashion that suggested that his government had already dropped the matter. *FRUS* 1955–57/XXVI, 118.

31. For Ref. 201's acknowledgment of this, see the memorandum of Aug. 15, 1956: PA/AA, B 12, Bd. 138. See also Carstens's handwritten comments on the draft of Aug. 11, cited above.

32. Adenauer to the CDU-Bundesvorstand, Sept. 20, 1956, in Buchstab, *Adenauer: "Wir haben wirklich etwas geschaffen,"* 1027–28.

33. Brentano to Adenauer (then vacationing in Cadenabbia, Italy), Aug. 14, 1956: StBKAH, Bd. A40.

34. *DARDDR* V, 27.

35. Conversation König/Saizev, July 31, 1956, p. 6: BA-SAPMO, DY 30, Bd. 3664.

36. Grewe's memorandum about the meeting (PA/AA, B 12, Bd. 100) does not indicate who was in attendance, but it is safe to assume that no one there ranked higher than Grewe.

37. The Foreign Office also raised these concerns with the Western Allies; see UK Bonn (Barnes) to C. M. Anderson, Oct. 16, 1956: PRO, FO 371/124552.

38. On the FDP's likely accusation that Bonn was "sacrificing friendly relations with other states for the sake of a theory," see p. 2 of Grewe's memorandum cited in n. 36 above.

39. Ibid.

40. Ref. 416, Aufz., Oct. 16, 1956: PA/AA, B 12, Bd. 100.

41. Deutsche-Erdöl-Aktiengesellschaft to Brentano, Oct. 12, 1956: PA/AA, B 12, Bd. 100.

42. See, for example, the exchange between a visiting East German dignitary, Ernst Scholz, and Syrian foreign minister Bitar, Feb. 16, 1957, p. 4: BA-SAPMO, NY 4090, Bd. 495.

43. Grewe to DG Damascus 51, Oct. 11, 1956, geheim, citissime: PA/AA, B 12, Bd. 100.

44. US Damascus (Strong) 820, Oct. 13, 1956, confidential: NARA, RG 59, CDF, 602.62B83.

45. DG Damascus (Esch) 60, Oct. 11, 1956, citissime: PA/AA, B 12, Bd. 100.

46. AF Bonn (Couve) 3184–86, Oct. 15, 1956: MAE, EU 44–60, RFA 30, 30.

47. DG Damascus (Esch) 64 and 67, Oct. 15 and 26, 1956: PA/AA, B 12, Bd. 100

48. Auswärtiger Ausschuß, 64. Sitzung (Nov. 9, 1956), 10–12: BT/PA, 2. WP, Bd. 8.

49. See the doctored summary of the Syrian crisis prepared by Ref. 201 for distribution in the Foreign Office's own information service. Ref. 201, Aufz., Nov. 6, 1956: PA/AA, B 12, Bd. 100. A similar line is taken in Brentano's reply to the Deutsche-Erdöl-Aktiengesellschaft of Oct. 31, 1956, found in the same archival volume.

50. Adenauer to the CDU Bundesvorstand, Apr. 26, 1954. "There is no point in speaking publicly about these things," he admonished the group; until tensions subsided in Europe, the Germans would have to wait quietly. Buchstab, Adenauer: "Wir haben wirklich etwas geschaffen," 154.

51. Adenauer to Under Secretary of State Herbert Hoover Jr., in a conversation of February 4, 1956. Commenting on Germany's lack of capital, Adenauer had the nerve to inquire whether private American groups might be in a position to fund "German" aid efforts in the Near and Middle East. FRUS 1955–57/XXVI, 75.

52. CDU Bundesvorstand meeting of Nov. 23, 1956, in Buchstab, Adenauer: "Wir haben wirklich etwas geschaffen," 1111.

53. Gruenther (Supreme Commander, Allied Forces, Europe) to Goodpaster (Eisenhower's Staff Secretary), Nov. 19, 1956, secret: FRUS 1955–57/XXVI, 175. Gruenther was conveying here a personal message from Adenauer to Eisenhower, transmitted via Adenauer's confidante in Paris, Herbert Blankenhorn.

54. These Foreign Office plans were shared with NATO at the North Atlantic Council meeting in December 1956; see US Bonn (Trimble) Air Pouch 200, July 29, 1957, confidential, pp. 23–27: FRG-FA 55–59, reel 2, frames 698ff (662A.80). See also Berggötz, Nahostpolitik in der Ära Adenauer, 399–403.

55. US Bonn Air Pouch 200 (cited in the previous note), 9.

56. See comments by both Brentano and Dulles during their conversation of Mar. 4, 1957: FRUS 1955–57/XXVI, 206–7.

57. Welck, Aufz., "Einladung des irakischen Königs Faisal," Jan. 23, 1957: PA/AA, B 1, Bd. 20.

58. Brentano to Ollenhauer, Mar. 6, 1957: AdsD, NL Ollenhauer, Bd. 412.

59. See, for example, Carstens's instructions to DG Cairo, Sept. 9, 1957: PA/AA, B 12, Bd. 89.

60. DG Damascus (Ringelmann), July 10 and 22, 1957: both PA/AA, B 12, Bd. 100.

61. DG Damascus, Aug. 5, 1957: PA/AA, B 12, Bd. 100.

62. For evidence that Grewe was alive to the danger of irritating the Syrians, see his telegram to DG Damascus, Aug. 3, 1957: PA/AA, B 12, Bd. 100. On the rapid growth of Soviet influence in Syria, see Ramet, Soviet-Syrian Relationship, 19–23.

63. Grewe to DG Damascus, July 25, 1957: PA/AA, B 12, Bd. 100. See also Ref. 201 (Ruete) to Ref. 500, Aug. 27, 1957: PA/AA, B 12, Bd. 119.

64. See, for example, the telling headline by Jürgen Petersen in Die Zeit of May 10,

1956: "What's Happening in Poland's Communist Party? / The Turn from Stalin Has Touched Off an Avalanche."

65. *Die Zeit* all but ignored developments in Hungary until the moment of the Soviet crackdown; its columns in October 1956 were devoted to such articles as Gösta von Uexküll, "Wunder in Polen," Oct. 25, 1956, 1. More than four decades later, the "Polish October" still evoked nostalgia among West German journalists; see Klaus Harpprecht, "Als alles möglich schien," *Die Zeit*, June 18, 1998, 45.

66. Spaulding, *Osthandel and Ostpolitik*, 426–32; Anderson, *Cold War in the Soviet Bloc*, 164–66.

67. Stehle, "Adenauer, Polen, und die deutsche Frage," 83; Bingen, *Polenpolitik*, 23; Schwarz, "Vortasten nach Warschau."

68. "There is no way that a German or even another foreign ambassador in a satellite state can do anything to remove this country from Moscow's control," remarked Adenauer to the Bundestag on January 23, 1958; see Jacobsen and Tomala, *Bonn-Warschau 1945–1991*, 89. In November 1956, the chancellor briefly displayed some optimism about Poland's developing in the direction of freedom and complete sovereignty; but he soon returned to his usual view that satellites were satellites. *DzD* III/2, 875; Blankenhorn to Kessel, Jan. 12, 1957: PA/AA, NL Kessel, Bd. 8. See also Altmann, *Konrad Adenauer im Kalten Krieg*, 182–86, 198–204.

69. See Brentano's comments to John Foster Dulles on Mar. 4, 1957, in *FRUS 1955–57/XXVI*, 211. Earlier that year he had even considered it too risky to publish a New Year's statement to the Polish people; Kosthorst, *Brentano*, 186. For similar concerns expressed by Adenauer, see Adenauer, *Teegespräche 1955–58*, 201.

70. See memos from C. Douglas Dillon to Dulles of Mar. 28 and Apr. 16, 1957: *FRUS 1955–57/XXV*, 606–7, 615–16. A comparison of these documents shows that the Poles rejected an American proposal to have the sale of surplus American farm products financed by the Federal Republic. See also Marchtaler, Aufz., Apr. 11, 1957, geheim, pp. 1–2: PA/AA, NL Grewe, Bd. 34.

71. Conversation Brentano/Dulles, Mar. 4, 1957, in *FRUS 1955–57/XXVI*, 212.

72. See Adenauer's remarks to Dulles in their conversation of May 4, 1957: *FRUS 1955–57/XXVI*, 239.

73. For the definitive study of the expellees' impact on German policy, see Ahonen, "Expellee Organizations and West German Ostpolitik," esp. 200–201, 206–13.

74. On the FDP's bridge-building policy in this period, see Engelmann and Erker, *Annäherung und Abgrenzung*.

75. On the CDU's 1957 campaign, see Granieri, "America's Germany, Germany's Europe," 287–95; Thränhardt, "Wahlen und Wiedervereinigung"; and the classic account in Kitzinger, *German Electoral Politics*.

76. Bender, *Die "Neue Ostpolitik,"* 50; Kleßmann, *Zwei Staaten, eine Nation*, 94–96.

77. *DzD* III/2, 515–16.

78. This suggestion first surfaced outside government circles; see Gösta von Uexküll, "Die fünfte Besatzungsmacht," *Die Zeit*, May 17, 1956, 1–2.

79. Grewe, Aufz., June 26, 1956, 1: PA/AA, NL Grewe, Bd. 34.

80. See, for example, Welck, Aufz., "Lage in den Satellitenstaaten und Gestaltung unserer Beziehungen zu ihnen," Oct. 18, 1956, geheim, pp. 8–10: PA/AA, NL Grewe, Bd. 34.

81. In December 1956, Brentano himself made suggestions along these lines in a conversation with editors of the *Frankfurter Allgemeine*. Kosthorst, *Brentano*, 184.

82. Ref. 201 (Fechter), Aufz., May 22, 1956, geheim: PA/AA, NL Grewe, Bd. 34.

83. Grewe, *Rückblenden*, 262–65. Grewe's account emphasizes the forward-looking nature of his Ostpolitik; however, in the context of 1956–57, his standpoint was rather conservative.

84. Grewe, Aufz., Jan. 8, 1957, geheim, pp. 4–5: PA/AA, NL Grewe, Bd. 64; Abteilung 3, Aufz., Jan. 28, 1957: PA/AA, NL Grewe, Bd. 34.

85. Summary protocol of the meeting of Arbeitskreis V, Nov. 13, 1956: ACDP, VIII-006-1/1; Kosthorst, *Brentano*, 182–83.

86. See Kessel to Brentano, Jan. 23, 1957: BAK, NL Brentano, Bd. 165, Bl. 166–74; also Kessel, Aufz., June 19, 1957, streng geheim!: PA/AA, NL Kessel, Bd. 8.

87. US Bonn (O'Shaughnessy) Air Pouch 98, July 15, 1957, and Air Pouch 258, Aug. 7, 1957: both NARA, RG 59, CDF, 648.62A.

88. For comments along these lines by Ungern-Sternberg of the Foreign Office's Countries Department, see the second telegram cited in n. 87 immediately above.

89. For an argument featuring economic pressure as the main motive, see Ihme-Tuchel, "Das Bemühen der SED"; for a focus on ideological solidarity, see Lorenzen, "Die Jugoslawien-Politik der DDR."

90. Politbüro, Protokoll Nr. 28/57, July 9, 1957, Anl. 5 (beschlossen July 11 im Umlauf): BA-SAPMO, DY 30/J IV 2/2, Bd. 548.

91. Kerber (of the East German Foreign Trade Ministry), "Bericht über die Verhandlungen in Moskau . . . über den Aluminium-Kombinat," July 22, 1957, pp. 3–4: BAL, DL 2, Bd. 3489.

92. DG Moscow (Northe), Sept. 11, 1957: PA/AA, B 12, Bd. 97. Here Northe was reporting information passed along by the French chargé in Moscow. For an indication of the improved atmosphere between Yugoslavia and the USSR, see Micunovic, *Moscow Diary*, 287–90.

93. The words of Ambassador Mates on October 21, 1957, paraphrased by Robert Murphy in conversation with German ambassador Heinz Krekeler the following day: *FRUS* 1955–57/XXVI, 314.

94. For the text, see *DzD* III/3, 1597. Lorenzen concurs that Tito's statement was designed to test the waters. Lorenzen, "Die Jugoslawien-Politik der DDR," 62.

95. Hallstein, conversation with Jovic, Sept. 11, 1957: PA/AA, B 12, Bd. 97. Hallstein still hoped the issue could be played down in the West German media; see his comments to journalist Joachim Schwelien in a background conversation of Sept. 10, 1957: ACDP, I-010-010/2. For a lengthy discussion of the toast and the reaction in Bonn (drawing mainly on media sources in Bonn and Belgrade), see Anic de Osona, *Die erste Anerkennung*, 28–41.

96. AF Bonn (Couve) tel. 2322–25, Sept. 17, 1957: MAE, EU 44–60, Ygsl 167, 88. On September 12, the reunification desk proposed that Pfleiderer undertake one last démarche before leaving, warning that a Yugoslav recognition of the GDR would have consequences for the reparations treaty; but these draft orders were canceled. Ref. 201 to Belgrade (cessat), Sept. 12, 1957: PA/AA, B 12, Bd. 97.

97. Adenauer, *Teegespräche 1955–1958*, 234; he criticized the Foreign Office for taking Tito's comments "much too tragically." See also Adenauer's comments to the cabinet on Sept. 18, 1957: *Kabinettsprotokolle* 10:378.

98. See Georg Handke's report of Sept. 17, 1957: BA-SAPMO, DY 30, Bd. 3642.

99. This consideration, mentioned by a Polish diplomat to an East German counterpart in late August, rings true: the Yugoslav communists had cordial relations with many leading Social Democrats in West Germany, and the SPD's foreign policy platform had much more appeal to Yugoslavia than that of the CDU. Winzer to Ulbricht, Sept. 21, 1957, with attachments: BA-SAPMO, NY 4182, Bd. 1235. See also Ihme-Tuchel, "Das Bemühen der SED," 700.

100. Politbüro, Protokoll Nr. 42/57, Oct. 8, 1957, Anl. 3: BA-SAPMO, DY 30/J IV 2/2, Bd. 562.

101. AF Washington (Alphand) tel. 5870–85, Sept. 27, 1957, réservé: MAE, EU 44–60, Ygsl 168, 1–2.

102. Deputy Assistant Secretary of State for European Affairs (C. Burke Elbrick) to Dulles, "Preliminary Analysis of Polish-Yugoslav Talks," Sept. 20, 1957, confidential: NARA, RG 59, CDF, 648.68/9-2057.

103. Dulles, conversation with Yugoslav State Secretary for Finance Avdo Humo, Oct. 2, 1957, confidential: FRUS 1955–57/XXVI, 782.

104. Welck, Aufz., Oct. 7, 1957, geheim, pp. 2, 5–7: PA/AA, NL Grewe, Bd. 34.

105. Blankenhorn, Aufz., Oct. 4, 1957, p. 4: BAK, NL Blankenhorn, Bd. 79, Bl. 113.

106. Blankenhorn diary, Oct. 4, 1957: BAK, NL Blankenhorn, Bd. 79, Bl. 109. See also Hahn, Wiedervereinigung, 205–10, 238–41, 253–58.

107. For an overview of Pfleiderer's views before he assumed his post in 1955, see Schlarp, "Alternativen zur deutschen Außenpolitik 1952–55."

108. On the meeting with Rapacki, see AF Belgrade (Broustra) tel. 1017–27, Sept. 15, 1957, réservé, pp. 2–3: MAE, EU 44–60, Ygsl 167, 85–87. Upon learning that Pfleiderer had seen the text of Tito's Trinkspruch before the September 10 reception, Hallstein upbraided Pfleiderer for attending. Pfleiderer replied that had he canceled his appearance at the last minute, this would have merely demonstrated the "complete isolation" of Bonn's Ostpolitik. DG Belgrade 153, Sept. 12, 1957: PA/AA, B 12, Bd. 97.

109. Pfleiderer, Aufz. (Rohentwurf), "Neugestaltung der deutschen Ostpolitik," Oct. 8, 1957, esp. 2, 5–6, 10: StBKAH, Bd. A40. A thorough summary appears in Schwarz, Die Ära Adenauer. Epochenwechsel (hereafter Epochenwechsel), 33–35.

110. In Yugoslavia, Milovan Djilas, already in prison, was sentenced to a further ten years for his book The New Class; in Poland, the government banned the leading voice of reform, Po prostu, triggering an uproar among students in the capital. Such events received front-page attention in German newspapers, with Die Welt featuring the following headlines on October 4: "Tumulte in Warschau / Miliz gegen Studenten / Mit Tränengas und Gummiknüppeln." See also Immanuel Birnbaum, "Tito macht es uns schwer," Süddeutsche Zeitung, Oct. 8, 1957, 1.

111. Brentano to Adenauer, Oct. 8, 1957, persönlich/vertraulich: StBKAH, Bd. A40. The chancellor's reaction can be read from a number of points jotted down on the last page of Brentano's letter.

112. Ibid. See also Schwarz, Epochenwechsel, 35–36.

113. CDU-Bundestagsfraktion, Oct. 9, 1957, pp. 2–3: ACDP, VIII-001-1007/4.

114. This motive is spelled out explicitly in Brentano's letter to Adenauer of Oct. 8, 1957 (cited in n. 111 above), p. 3.

115. Georg Schröder, "Neuer Kurs der Ostpolitik ist noch nicht geklärt," Die Welt,

Oct. 12, 1957, 1. Schröder appears to have received much inside information from within the Foreign Office, probably from Blankenhorn himself.

116. US Bonn (Bruce) 1174, Oct. 11, 1957, confidential: FRG-FA 55–59, reel 2, frame 71 (662A.61). For a mocking FDP commentary, see "Futurum oder perfekt? Zwei Versionen zur neuen Bonner Ostpolitik," *fdk*, Oct. 10, 1957, 5–6.

117. Hallstein/Jovic, Sept. 11, 1957: PA/AA, B 12, Bd. 97; Hallstein/Jovic conversation, Oct. 5, 1957: PA/AA, B 12, Bd. 585; for the third conversation, see Anic de Osona, *Die erste Anerkennung*, 58–59.

118. DepSta to Bonn 982, Oct. 9, 1957, confidential: NARA, RG 59, CDF, 662B.68. This information was designated "FYI and not to be communicated to Germans." However, the embassy was instructed to find out from Adenauer himself how the Federal Republic would respond. It got no further than Hallstein, who appeared determined to recommend a break. US Bonn (Bruce) 1155, Oct. 10, 1957, secret, priority: ibid.

119. Hallstein to DG Washington 855, Oct. 11, 1957, described in Anic de Osona, *Die erste Anerkennung*, 106–7. As Daniel Kosthorst points out, this argument was somewhat disingenuous, since Brentano and Adenauer had already decided against diplomatic relations with Poland; but Hallstein likely anticipated that this standpoint would be well received at the State Department. Kosthorst, *Brentano*, 198.

120. Conversation Murphy/Kessel, Oct. 10, 1957, confidential: NARA, RG 59, Lot Files, Entry 3088, box 1, folder 2.4.5. See also their conversation of Oct. 11, 1957, confidential: GDR-IA 55–59, reel 3, frames 1083–84 (762B.02).

121. Hallstein to DG Washington 855, cited in n. 119 above. Kessel had, after all, been Brentano's conduit for conversations with Polish diplomats earlier in 1957. During the October crisis, Kessel suggested that Yugoslavia might be restrained with the following bargain: Bonn would promise to open relations with Warsaw if Belgrade promised to abstain from relations with East Berlin. Such thinking naturally presumed Yugoslav goodwill toward Bonn's Ostpolitik. DG Washington (Kessel), Oct. 11, 1957, streng geheim, citissime: PA/AA, NL Kessel, Bd. 8. See also Kessel's devastating critique of the "diplomatic-technical handling" of the conflict with Yugoslavia, dated Oct. 18, 1957, in the same archival volume.

122. Remarks by Carstens to an official in the French embassy (Puaux) on Oct. 12, described in Carstens, Aufz., Oct. 14, 1957, geheim/unter Verschluß: PA/AA, B 12, Bd. 97.

123. Pineau to London, Washington, Bonn, and Rome, Oct. 13, 1957, réservé, priorité: *DDF* 1957, II: 538–39. Another French official remarked that the Quai d'Orsay "at least had [the] satisfaction of anticipating [an] unpleasant event and of making its views known in strong terms before Yugoslav recognition of [the] GDR took place." US Paris (Houghton), Oct. 14, 1957, confidential: NARA, RG 59, CDF, 662B.68/10-1457.

124. Office of Western Affairs to Murphy, Oct. 11, 1957, secret: NARA, RG 59, CDF, 662B.68; Conversation Murphy/Primozic, Oct. 11, 1957, confidential: GDR-FA 55–59, reel 3, frames 1085–87 (762B.02). Further indications about Murphy's attitude can be found in a penciled note at the bottom of p. 2 of an uncleared memcon between Murphy and Kessel, Oct. 14, 1957: ibid., frames 1098–99.

125. As early as mid-1956, one American diplomat observed that "Pfleiderer has apparently been about as frank with Yugoslavs about his exasperation [over] Hall-

stein as he was with me." US Belgrade (Hooker) to DepSta 16, July 4, 1956, confidential: FRG-FA 55–59, reel 2, frames 543–44. Historians continue to find it puzzling that Adenauer should have entrusted the Belgrade embassy to an FDP politician whose views on German unification scarcely accorded with those of the government. Anic de Osona, *Die erste Anerkennung*, 50; Kosthorst, *Brentano*, 201.

126. Grewe, Aufz., "Zur Frage der Ostpolitik der neuen Bundesregierung," Oct. 8, 1957, geheim, p. 8: PA/AA, NL Grewe, Bd. 34.

127. *DARDDR* V, 348–49.

128. Grewe's notes of the October 17 cabinet meeting: PA/AA, NL Grewe, Bd. 64.

129. Brentano, Informationsgespräch, Oct. 16, 1957, 9–10: PA/AA, B 12, Bd. 585.

130. US Bonn (Bruce) to 1197, Oct. 14, 1957, secret, niact: NARA, RG 59, CDF, 662B.68/10-1457. See also Krone, *Tagebücher 1945–1961*, 267.

131. Conversation Dulles/Lloyd, Oct. 15, 1957, secret: *FRUS* 1955–57/XXVI, 787–88. For earlier British reserve, see FO to Bonn 1708, Oct. 15, 1957, confidential: PRO, FO 371/130723. For a revealing outline of American thinking, see Elbrick to Dulles, Oct. 14, 1957, secret: NARA, RG 59, Lot Files entry 3088, box 1, folder 2.4.5.

132. The words of Laloy, director of the European department at the Quai d'Orsay, as reported by the British ambassador. UK Paris (Gladwyn Jebb) tel. 312 Saving, Oct. 15, 1957, confidential: PRO, FO 371/130577. The Allied standpoints were presented to the West Germans during consultations on October 16 and 17, 1957. AF Bonn (Puaux) tel. 2486–95, Oct. 16, 1957, réservé, priorité: *DDF* 1957, II: 543–45. See also Puaux's follow-up telegram 2499–2502, Oct. 17, 1957: MAE, EU 44–60, Ygsl 168, 39.

133. For the text of Hallstein's statement (and Blankenhorn's reaction), see BAK, NL Blankenhorn, Bd. 79, Bl. 21–23, and Bd. 80, Bl. 294. The day before, Blankenhorn had gone behind the back of the West German Foreign Office in seeking out his British counterpart at NATO, Sir Frank Roberts. Blankenhorn urged Roberts to have the British embassy in Bonn say a restraining word to Adenauer and Brentano. UK NATO (Roberts) No. 295, immediate, secret, Oct. 15, 1957: PRO, FO 371/130723.

134. *Kabinettsprotokolle* 10:395–96.

135. For a thorough depiction of the discussions in Bonn that week, see Anic de Osona, *Die erste Anerkennung*, 183–237.

136. Brentano's notes on the conversation can be found in PA/AA, B 1, Bd. 128. A photograph of the Yugoslav ambassador taking his hat can be found in Birke, *Nation ohne Haus*, 453.

137. For the text of Brentano's memorandum announcing the break in relations, see *DzD* III/3: 1768–74. For the tactical thinking behind this memorandum, see US Bonn (Bruce) 1208, Oct. 15, 1957, secret, niact: NARA, RG 59, CDF, 662B.68/10-1557.

138. This was the first reaction of Baron von Welck at the Foreign Office: there should be no half-measures. Reporting from Japan, Hans Kroll—who had served as ambassador to Yugoslavia from 1951 to 1955—warned that the Japanese and other foreign observers would be much less impressed if economic relations (especially the reparations treaty) remained intact. An Indonesian diplomat in West Berlin made a similar observation. Welck, Aufz., Oct. 14, 1957: PA/AA, B 12, Bd. 583; DG Tokyo to AA 192, Oct. 22, 1957: PA/AA, B 12, Bd. 97; US Berlin (Hillenbrand) 456, Oct. 21, 1957, secret: GDR-FA 55–59, reel 3, frame 1118 (762B.02).

139. Because some 70 percent of West German exports to Yugoslavia relied on export insurance ("Hermes" guarantees, described in Chapter 5), this was a measure

that promised to dampen German-Yugoslav trade in the long run. Scherpenberg, Aufz., Dec. 18, 1957: PA/AA, B 12, Bd. 97. On Yugoslavia's inherent advantages in case of a trade war, see Welck, Aufz., Nov. 4, 1957, p. 3: PA/AA, B 12, Bd. 583. For Allied views, see Dulles's remarks in Secretary's Staff Meeting, Oct. 24, 1957, secret: *FRUS* 1955–57/XXVI, 794–95; and comments by Laloy reported in DG Paris (Jansen), Nov. 29, 1957: PA/AA, B 12, Bd. 583.

140. Hallstein, Informationsgespräch, Nov. 12, 1957: PA/AA, B 12, Bd. 585.

141. This concern was voiced by the West German envoy in Damascus. US Bonn (Bruce) 1375, Oct. 30, 1957, confidential: NARA, RG 59, CDF, 648.62A. Also of interest is Grewe to DG Damascus 59, Nov. 12, 1957: PA/AA, B 12, Bd. 100.

142. For an overview of the pros and cons of keeping consular relations, see Welck's memo of November 4, cited in n. 139 above. Yugoslavia, for its part, kept open its consulates in Hamburg and Munich.

143. See Brentano's Informationsgespräch of Oct. 16, pp. 10–11 (cited in n. 129 above); AF Bonn (Couve) 2522–28, Oct. 19, 1957, réservé: *DDF* 1957, II: 561–63; Grewe's notes of the Oct. 17 cabinet meeting, cited in n. 128 above; and Brentano's comments in a public press conference of Oct. 19, 1957, in which he stressed that Yugoslavia was an "individual case" that would not necessarily affect relations with Poland: *DzD* III/3, 1775–76.

144. Among nonpartisan regional newspapers, the following published editorials supporting a break with Yugoslavia: *Frankfurter Neue Presse*, Oct. 15; *Der Mittag* (Düsseldorf), Oct. 15; *Berliner Morgenpost*, Oct. 16; *Christ und Welt*, Oct. 17. The following printed editorials advised against a break: *FAZ*, Oct. 15; *Die Welt* (Essen), Oct. 15; *Münchner Merkur*, Oct. 16; *Hannoversche Allgemeine Zeitung*, Oct. 16; *Bremer Nachrichten*, Oct. 16; *Kölner Stadt-Anzeiger*, Oct. 16; *Die Rheinpfalz* (Ludwigshafen), Oct. 17. One could hardly draw quantitative conclusions from this sample, culled from Abteilung Pressedokumentation of the Bundespresseamt, but the sharp tone of many of these editorials is striking.

145. Hans Zehrer, "Im Gatter der Tabus," *Die Welt*, Oct. 19, 1957; Jürgen Tern, "Deutsche und Slawen," *FAZ*, Oct. 19, 1957; Werner Friedmann, "Moskau—der lachende Dritte," *Süddeutsche Zeitung*, Oct. 22, 1957. The concern of *Der Spiegel* over the barriers to Ostpolitik is evident in the questions posed to Kurt-Georg Kiesinger (CDU) in a SPIEGEL-Gespräch of Oct. 30, 1957, p. 22. Marion Gräfin Dönhoff of *Die Zeit* endorsed the government's step vis-à-vis Yugoslavia, while nevertheless calling for diplomatic relations with Poland; see "Abbruch der Beziehungen," Oct. 24, 1957, 1.

146. On the plan submitted by the Foreign Office to the cabinet, see US Bonn (Schwartz) Air Pouch 2270, June 23, 1958, confidential: NARA, RG 59, CDF, 648.62A. For a contrary reading of Polish intentions, see Bingen and Wec, *Die Deutschlandpolitik Polens*, 62–65.

147. On the discussions in the Bundestag's Foreign Affairs Committee in the spring of 1958, see Kosthorst, *Brentano*, 203–9; on the activities of the SPD's most formidable friend of Poland, see Weber, *Carlo Schmid*, 598–603.

148. Conversation Brentano/Dulles, June 5, 1958, p. 3: NARA, RG 59, CDF, 648.62A. It is worth noting that Dulles had reversed his position since the previous fall. Compare DepSta (Dulles) to Bonn 1204, Oct. 30, 1957, secret, limdis; DepSta (Dulles) to Bonn 3049, May 26, 1958, confidential; US Bonn (Trimble) 3536, June 2,

1958, confidential, priority: all NARA, RG 59, CDF, 648.62A. See also the memoranda by Herbert Dittmann, May 19 and 30, 1958: PA/AA, B 1, Bd. 128.

149. Abteilung 7, Aufz., "Wiederaufnahme der diplomatischen Beziehungen zu Jugoslawien," Aug. 31, 1958: PA/AA, B 12, Bd. 586.

150. Schwelien, "Bleibt Polen offen?", *FAZ*, July 5, 1958, 2.

151. Aside from the temporal coincidence, there is a striking connection between the "Eisenhower Doctrine" and the "Hallstein Doctrine" in the person of Albrecht von Kessel, the German counselor in Washington. Kessel's dispatches to Bonn critiquing the Eisenhower Doctrine echo many of the points he later made against the Hallstein Doctrine; in the late 1950s Kessel quit the foreign service to become a journalist highly critical of Adenauer's Eastern policy. Kessel to Welck, Jan. 30, 1957: PA/AA, NL Kessel, Bd. 8; DG Washington to AA, Oct. 14, 1957, vertraulich: BAK, NL Blankenhorn, Bd. 79, Bl. 45–49. It is quite possible that Kessel and Blankenhorn shared their complaints about Hallstein's legalistic foreign policy with Schwelien.

152. Even while introducing the doctrine, Schwelien remarked that its "fall must be expected sooner or later," that although the principle may have been useful at the time of its conception in 1955, it was now a liability for the Federal Republic. Schwelien, "Bleibt Polen offen?," col. 2.

153. For Grewe's comments on the paternity of the "Hallstein Doctrine," see Grewe, *Rückblenden*, 254.

154. Jürgen Tern, "Deutsche und Slawen," *FAZ*, Oct. 19, 1957, 1.

155. Via the Norwegian ambassador, the American embassy in Belgrade learned that Tito had met with the Indonesian ambassador on October 18 and tried to persuade him to recognize the GDR. US Belgrade (Marcy) 707, Oct. 24, 1957, confidential: GDR-FA 55–59, reel 3, frame 1123 (762B.02).

156. US Bonn (Bruce) 1312, Oct. 24, 1957, secret, priority: NARA, RG 59, CDF, 648.62A. If Hallstein had earlier been worried about India and Egypt, this may have followed from persistent rumors that Tito had discussed his intentions with Nasser and Nehru ahead of time (though the same reports stressed that both leaders had expressed approbation). AF Belgrade (Broustra) tel. 1200, Oct. 19, 1957, réservé: MAE, EU 44–60, Ygsl 168, 47.

157. DG Rangoon (Randow) Ber. 218/59, Mar. 18, 1959: PA/AA, B 12, Bd. 90.

158. US Berlin (Gufler) 435, Oct. 17, 1957: GDR-IA 55–59, reel 3, frame 1113 (762B.02); Tito's letter of Oct. 3, in the Politbüro minutes of Oct. 8, 1957 (cited in n. 100 above).

159. Kilian, *Hallstein-Doktrin*, 58–60.

160. Brentano stated this outright in his letter to Adenauer of Sept. 27, 1957: Baring, *Sehr verehrter Herr Bundeskanzler!*, 217–21.

CHAPTER FOUR

1. AF Berlin No. 365/EU, Nov. 19, 1957: MAE, EU 44–60, RDA 30, 50–53.

2. Politbüro, Nov. 2, 1957, agenda point 4 and Anl. 2: BA-SAPMO, DY 30/J IV 2/2, Bd. 567.

3. In the fall of 1958, the East Germans backed out of an agreement to build a film factory in India at the very last minute. This information appears on p. 3 of a formless document (likely passed along by Soviet authorities in Berlin) marked "Information

über den Aufenthalt des Ministers für Wirtschaft der DBR Erhardt [sic] in Indien": BA-SAPMO, NY 4090, Bd. 493, Bl. 119–21.

4. Ulf and Schleicher, *Die beiden deutschen Staaten in Afrika*, 92.

5. The West German embassy in Damascus (now downgraded to a consulate) gloated prematurely about the "fiasco" of East Germany's efforts there; DG Damascus Ber. 404/58, Feb. 25, 1958: PA/AA, B 12, Bd. 100.

6. Bundespresse- und Informationsamt, "Memorandum über den Ausbau der deutschen Informationsarbeit im Ausland," Apr. 16, 1959: BAK, B 136, Bd. 6527.

7. These various details about East German activities in Cairo are elaborated in DG Cairo (Becker), Betr.: "Sowjetzonale Betätigung in Ägypten," Aug. 23, 1958: PA/AA, B 12, Bd. 840. See also Duckwitz, "Werbetätigkeit der SBZ im Ausland," June 20, 1958: PA/AA, B 12, Bd. 1388.

8. Kiesewetter, conversation with Saizev (head of the Near East desk at the Soviet Foreign Ministry), drafted Jan. 25, 1958, p. 10: BAL, DL 2, Bd. 3310.

9. Conversation Dulles/Krekeler, Nov. 4, 1957, secret: FRG-FA 55–59, reel 2, frames 690–91 (662A.74). Adenauer was likely heartened by Nahum Goldmann's assurances that Israel would welcome German initiatives to develop Egypt's economy; see Adenauer's note to Brentano of Jan. 27, 1958: StBKAH, Bd. A40.

10. US Cairo Air Pouch 1133, May 19, 1958; US Bonn (Tasca) Air Pouch 815, Nov. 24, 1958: both confidential, both in FRG-IA 55–59, reel 5, frames 88–92, 127–29. See also Berggötz, *Nahostpolitik in der Ära Adenauer*, 349–56.

11. Grotewohl to Nasser, Jan. 21, 1958: BAL, DL 2, Bd. 3489.

12. The UAR's ambassador to Prague, Tarazi, pointed out expressly that any political conversations between the GDR and the UAR should take place either in Cairo or Prague; the trade representative in East Berlin was not to be involved. Kiesewetter, Vermerk, Nov. 4, 1958: BA-SAPMO, NY 4090, Bd. 497, Bl. 135–36.

13. For a description of the conversation between Richard Gyptner, the plenipotentiary in Cairo, and an Egyptian official on Oct. 5, 1958, see pp. 2–6 of the lengthy compilation dated Oct. 27, 1958, in BA-SAPMO, NY 4182, Bd. 1335.

14. Politbüro, Protokoll Nr. 40/58, Sept. 23, 1958: BA-SAPMO, DY 30/J IV 2/2, Bd. 612. Although Rau is not mentioned by name here, it seems telling that on the following day he wrote to all the members of the Politburo explaining the background of the credit negotiations with the UAR. BAL, DL 2, Bd. 3310, Bl. 49–50.

15. Politbüro, Protokoll Nr. 40/58, Sept. 23, 1958: BA-SAPMO, DY 30/J IV 2/2, Bd. 612. See also Politbüro, Arbeitsprotokoll Nr. 41/58, Sept. 30, 1958: BA-SAPMO, DY 30/J IV 2/2A, Bd. 656.

16. Karabell, *Architects of Intervention*, 166–68; Dann, *Iraq under Qassem*.

17. For an outstanding analysis of West German responses to this crisis, see AF Bonn (Leduc) No. 1389, Aug. 8, 1958: MAE, EU 44–60, All 1256, 298–303. On the chancellor's personal reaction, see Berggötz, *Nahostpolitik in der Ära Adenauer*, 408–14.

18. Wandel, Bericht an das Politbüro, Aug. 13, 1958, p. 9: BA-SAPMO, DY 30/IV 2/20, Bd. 2, Bl. 323–34.

19. Politbüro, Protokoll Nr. 45/58, Nov. 11, 1958, Anl. 1: BA-SAPMO, DY 30/J IV 2/2, Bd. 617.

20. The SED's increased concern with public relations abroad is evident in the "Maßnahmeplan" adopted at the meeting of November 11 (Anl. 2 of the meeting cited in n. 19 above).

21. Andereggen, *France's Relationship with Subsaharan Africa*, 43.

22. US Paris (Lyon) to DepSta 1360, Oct. 15, 1958, secret: *FRUS* 1958–60/XIV, 672–73.

23. Report 223/58 by the West German consul in Dakar (Reichhold), Oct. 23, 1958, p. 1: PA/AA, B 34, Bd. 87.

24. DG New Delhi (Melchers), Dec. 15, 1958: PA/AA, B 12, Bd. 103. Although it had not issued an invitation, the Indian Foreign Office did promise a "friendly atmosphere" for Grotewohl's visit; see Schwab to Grotewohl, Nov. 10, 1958: BA-SAPMO, NY 4090, Bd. 493, Bd. 122–23.

25. On Grotewohl's lack of influence from 1953 onward, see Jodl, *Amboß oder Hammer?*, 233–49.

26. Weiß to Rau, Nov. 27, 1958: BAL, DL 2, Bd. 3310, Bl. 1–4.

27. Schwab, Vorlage für das Aussenpolitische Kommission, Dec. 2, 1958: BA-SAPMO, DY 30/IV 2/20, Bd. 2, Bl. 422–27.

28. Schwab to Grotewohl, Dec. 9, 1958: BA-SAPMO, DY 4090, Bd. 492.

29. DG Cairo (Becker) 11, Jan. 5, 1959: PA/AA, B 12, Bd. 103.

30. AF Bonn (Seydoux) 19/20, Jan. 5, 1959: MAE, EU 44–60, RDA 30, 69.

31. Lemke, "Der Nahe Osten, Indien und die Grotewohlreise," 1036.

32. Kilian, *Hallstein-Doktrin*, 113–14.

33. Among those skeptical of Grotewohl's version of the conversations in Cairo was the UAR trade representative in Cairo, Hamdy; see Winzer to Ulbricht, Jan. 28, 1959: BA-SAPMO, NY 4182, Bd. 1335.

34. DG Baghdad (Richter), Nov. 27, 1958: PA/AA, B 12, Bd. 96.

35. Joint declaration by Grotewohl and Qassem, Jan. 11, 1959, printed in *DARDDR* VII, 369–70. The formulation in German is extremely slippery: the leaders agreed "zu erörtern, daß bei entprechender Lage diplomatische Beziehungen . . . hergestellt . . . werden." Syntactically this makes no sense. The German phrasing appears designed to exaggerate the degree of certainty attached to this decision. Until the last moment, Qassem had favored a still weaker formulation: agreement to *study* to problem.

36. Lemke, "Der Nahe Osten, Indien und die Grotewohlreise," 1037–38.

37. Conversation between Foreign Minister Lothar Bolz (who joined Grotewohl in New Delhi for these talks) and India's minister of defense, Krishna Menon, Jan. 13, 1959: BA-SAPMO, NY 4182, Bd. 1324, Bl. 55–58.

38. Politbüro, Protokoll Nr. 7/59, Feb. 10, 1959, Anl. 2: BA-SAPMO, DY 30/J IV 2/2, Bd. 631.

39. Politbüro, Protokoll Nr. 8/59, Feb. 17, 1959, Anl. 2, pp. 2–3: BA-SAPMO, DY 30/J IV 2/2, Bd. 632.

40. For the text of Grotewohl's letter, see BA-SAPMO, NY 4090, Bd. 494. Qassem's failure to reply is raised in Politbüro, Arbeitsprotokoll Nr. 4/60, Jan. 26, 1960, Anl. 3: BA-SAPMO, DY 30/J IV 2/2A, Bd. 736.

41. Conversation Grotewohl/Nasser, Jan. 4, 1959, p. 13: MfAA, A 12574, Bl. 191–204; see also Kilian, *Hallstein-Doktrin*, 112–14.

42. For press commentary on January 8, 1959, the day following Grotewohl's announcement, see N. B., "Eine Stufenleiter?", *FAZ*; "Nassers Flirt mit Grotewohl," *Süddeutsche Zeitung*; and "Grotewohls Reise," *Die Welt*.

43. Bundespresse- und Informationsamt, "Memorandum über den Ausbau der deutschen Informationsarbeit im Ausland," Apr. 16, 1959: BAK, B 136, Bd. 6527.

44. See, for example, Meissner, Aufz., "Begegnung der politischen, wirtschaftlichen und kulturellen Aktivität der sowjetischen Besatzungszone Deutschlands im afro-asiatischen Raum," Apr. 14, 1959: PA/AA, B 12, Bd. 800.

45. On Mikoyan's visit and Adenauer's designs for Ostpolitik more generally, see Spaulding, *Osthandel and Ostpolitik*, 449–58; also Siebenmorgen, *Gezeitenwechsel*, 141–56.

46. Among the many theories about why Khrushchev initiated the Berlin Crisis, two have received the most attention. More typically, historians point to the Soviet premier's interest in stabilizing the GDR and forcing its international recognition; see, for example, Wettig, "Die sowjetische Politik während der Berlinkrise." In the 1990s, Marc Trachtenberg developed an alternative explanation that focused on Khrushchev's efforts to block the arming of the German military with nuclear weapons. Trachtenberg, "The Berlin Crisis," in *History and Straegy* (1991), now further elaborated in his book *A Constructed Peace* (1999).

47. The Soviet Union did initially address notes to the Federal Republic; these contained accusations against the *Western Allies* for *their* conduct in Berlin! See, for example, the Soviet note to the Federal Republic of November 27, 1959: *DzD* IV/1, 178–91. Such transparent attempts to turn the Federal Republic against the Allies did not get very far, however, and the diplomacy of the Berlin Crisis turned entirely upon the Soviet notes to the Allies.

48. For the Russian and German texts, see *DzD* IV/1, 3–24.

49. The six-month ultimatum came in a Soviet note to the Allied governments of November 27, 1958; the proposal for a peace treaty followed on January 10, 1959. The Russian and German texts appear in *DzD* IV/1, 151–77, 545–66.

50. These three options—"(a) abandoning Berlin; (b) resorting to force; (c) staying in Berlin but dealing with and, if necessary ultimately recognising the D.D.R."—were identified immediately by the Foreign Office in London; quoted here is a dispatch to the British embassy in Washington of November 15, 1958. For the next four years, the diplomacy of Berlin revolved around these three possibilities. Mauer, "Macmillan und die Berlin-Krise 1958/59," 233–34.

51. Lloyd cited in Gearson, *Harold Macmillan and the Berlin Wall Crisis*, 38. On the reactions of Britain's allies, see Burr, "Avoiding the Slippery Slope," 187–88; Lee, "Perception and Reality: Anglo-German Relations during the Berlin Crisis," 51–52.

52. Burr, "Avoiding the Slippery Slope," 182–89; Burr also offers a clear explanation of why the State Department soon abandoned the "agents" theory.

53. Conze, *Die gaullistische Herausforderung*, 79–87; Buffet, "De Gaulle et Berlin."

54. In January 1959, Adenauer made a desperate, ridiculous attempt to block a meeting between the Soviet trade minister, Anastas Mikoyan, and President Eisenhower. Even more worrisome to Adenauer was the "voyage of discovery" to the Soviet Union undertaken by British prime minister Harold Macmillan in February 1959. Köhler, *Adenauer*, 1015, 1022; Gearson, *Harold Macmillan and the Berlin Wall Crisis*, 56–78.

55. On the planning for Geneva, see Kosthorst, *Brentano*, 269–87.

56. Adenauer, conversation with six journalists, Jan. 22, 1959, as described in a letter dated January 23 by one of the participants, Max Nitzsche; published by Küsters in "Kanzler in der Krise," 748–52.

57. See Adenauer's groundbreaking comments to a session of the Bundestag's CDU-Fraktionsvorstand on Mar. 16, 1959, pp. 8–9: ACDP, VIII-001-1503/2.

58. These ideas, aired by the chancellor in the January 22 meeting cited in n. 56 above, soon formed the basis for a top-secret "Globke Plan" for unification, named after the controversial state secretary in the Chancellor's Office. Schwarz, *Adenauer. Der Staatsmann* (hereafter *Staatsmann*), 479–87.

59. Memorandum by Georg Schröder marked "Vertrauliche Information," Jan. 23, 1959, published in Küsters, "Kanzler in der Krise," 752–54; quote on 752.

60. By mid-1959, the reunification desk (renumbered from 201 to 700 in mid-1958) was desperate for more personnel. See Ref. 700 (Forster), Aufz., June 18, 1959: PA/AA, B 12, Bd. 254. Another indication of Ref. 700's strained situation can be seen in the following reversal: in mid-1958, Ref. 700 complained that other desks were encroaching on its territory; in late 1959 it begged those same desks to stop burdening it with routine questions on the application of the isolation strategy. Ref. 700 (Ruete) to Refs. 600 and 709, June 4, 1958: PA/AA, B 12, Bd. 95; Ref. 700 (Forster), Vermerk, Nov. 11, 1959: PA/AA, B 12, Bd. 254.

61. Grewe served as ambassador to Washington (1958–62) and to NATO (1962–68). In January 1958, Hallstein was selected as the first commissioner of the European Economic Community, a post he held for ten years.

62. Scherpenberg had most recently served as director of the Foreign Office's Trade Policy Department. His keen interest in problems of Ostpolitik is quite evident in his correspondence with Brentano in 1959. See, for example, his letters to the foreign minister of Jan. 24 and Oct. 27, 1959: BAK, NL Brentano, Bd. 179, Bl. 70–76 and Bl. 63–66. On the creation of the Ostabteilung, see C. Müller, *Relaunching German Diplomacy*, 118–23. Duckwitz had won renown following the war for his role in the escape of thousand of Jews from Denmark.

63. The SPD-Pressedienst thundered, "What is the use now of this doctrine which Bonn is staking so much upon? It was thought up as an iron-clad protection against a repetition of Belgrade's act of sin, but it's now showing itself to be a trap in which Bonn itself has fallen." *Die Welt*, Jan. 9, 1959, 2. The SPD-owned press printed editorials with titles like "Hallstein-Doktrin widerlegt" (*Lübecker Freie Presse*, Jan. 10, 1959).

64. Junius, "Politik im Schmollwinkel," *Süddeutsche Zeitung*, Jan. 15, 1959, 1; Jürgen Tern, "Flexibilität," *FAZ*, Jan. 28, 1959, 1. Tern's article specifically called for the reestablishment of relations with Yugoslavia.

65. Horst Blomeyer-Bartenstein, Aufz., Feb. 26, 1959: excerpt in *AAPD* 1967, 393–94 n. 9. Blomeyer's proposal was particularly radical, but others in the legal affairs department also pondered ways in which Bonn might accept the GDR as a de facto government while still holding back from a formal recognition. Such discussions led the legal department to prepare a memorandum on "International Legal Aspects of the American Civil War." Berger, Aufz., May 26, 1959: PA/AA, B 80, Bd. 297.

66. Kessel, Aufz., "Die Hallstein-Doktrin," June 1, 1959: PA/AA, B 12, Bd. 137. Kessel's skepticism about the "Hallstein-These" is also apparent in an undated thinkpiece he drafted in the fall of 1958. "Möglichkeiten und Grenzen der deutschen Außenpolitik," pp. 66–74: PA/AA, NL Kessel, Bd. 10.

67. Assistant Secretary of State Foy Kohler to Secretary of State Christian Herter,

Aug. 21, 1959, secret: *FRUS 1958–60/IX*, 5–7. Kohler elaborated: "Various schools of thought propound their own views and attempt to manipulate their acceptance, cutting each other's bureaucratic throats in the process. Foreign Minister von Brentano has lost the respect of his staff and has shown an incapacity for having his views accepted by the chancellor or doing anything effective in support of them."

68. Herbert Müller-Roschach (the former chargé in Belgrade, who, after Pfleiderer's death, handled the break with Yugoslavia), cited in a letter from Erich Strätling to Josef Jansen, May 10, 1959: ACDP, NL Jansen, I-149-3/2. For a more neutral assessment of the change in leadership style from Hallstein to Scherpenberg, see the recollections of Lothar Lahn in Loth, *Walter Hallstein*, 30–31.

69. Dittmann to DG Moscow 139, Apr. 27, 1959. It is telling that the ambassador in Moscow had felt it necessary to ask in the first place; see DG Moscow (Kroll) 318, Apr. 24, 1959. Both telegrams in PA/AA, B 12, Bd. 124.

70. In the span of just a few days, the ambassadors to Ceylon from the following countries advised the Ceylonese prime minister not to recognize the GDR: Britain, the United States, Canada, Australia, India, Italy, Switzerland, the Netherlands, and, of course, West Germany. DG Colombo (Auer) Ber. 280/59, Apr. 24, 1959: PA/AA, B 12, Bd. 104.

71. On the weak leadership of Brentano and Scherpenberg, see Adenauer's complaints to Federal President Theodor Heuss on July 8, 1958, and again on April 6, 1959, in *Adenauer-Heuss: Unter vier Augen*, 273–74, 299.

72. On Yugoslav feelers in 1958, see Dittmann, Aufz., "Wiederaufnahme der diplomatischen Beziehungen zu Jugoslawien," Aug. 31, 1958: PA/AA, B 12, Bd. 586. On the impact of the Berlin Crisis, see US Bonn (Schwartz) Air Pouch 1425, Mar. 19, 1959, confidential: FRG-FA 55–59, reel 2, frames 647–48 (662.68).

73. These terms were cited by a Yugoslav official to the American embassy in Bonn several months after the fact. US Bonn (Tyler) Air Pouch 376, Sept. 10, 1959, confidential: FRG-FA 55–59, reel 2, frames 655–59.

74. This, at least, was the speculation of the American embassy in Bonn; see Air Pouch 1425, cited in n. 72 above.

75. Ref. 500 (Meyer-Lindenberg), Aufz., Jan. 7, 1959: PA/AA, B 12, Bd. 103.

76. On the recall of Ambassador Becker, see comments by the Foreign Office spokesman, Karl-Günther von Hase, in the press conference of Jan. 9, 1959, pp. 2–6: ACDP, NL Eckardt, I-010-012/1. On the parliamentarians, see DG Beirut 6, Jan. 9, 1959, supercitissime; Brentano to DG Beirut, Jan. 9, 1959, citissime mit Vorrang: both in PA/AA, B 12, Bd. 103.

77. For the quote, see Adenauer to Brentano, July 1, 1958: StBKAH, Bd. A40. See also Adenauer's remarks about Egypt's importance, made to the president of the World Bank, Eugene Black, on July 2, 1959: PA/AA, B 58, Bd. 215.

78. DG Madrid (Welck) 34, Jan. 24, 1959: PA/AA, B 12, Bd. 103. More details on this peculiar Spanish intervention can be found in Gray, "Hallstein Doctrine," chap. 4.

79. On Sékou Touré's assurances, see the report by Erich Korth, Jan. 19, 1959: PA/AA, B 12, Bd. 93. Unbeknownst to the Guinean president, Korth's team had managed to procure the text of the confidential Guinean–East German protocols— either through bribery or via the French intelligence services. For a legal analysis of these documents, see Abt. 5 to Abt. 3, Feb. 2, 1959: ibid.

80. Abt. 3 (Etzdorf), Aufz., Feb. 3, 1959: PA/AA, B 12, Bd. 93.

81. Ref. 700 (Fechter), Feb. 22, 1959: PA/AA, B 12, Bd. 93.

82. Brentano to Sékou Touré, Mar. 4, 1959: PA/AA, B 12, Bd. 93. Further documentation in this volume shows that the letter was hand delivered on March 12.

83. AF Bonn (Leduc), Apr. 30, 1959: MAE, EU 44–60, All 1258, 230–31; US Bonn (Bruce) Airgram G-656, June 16, 1959, confidential: NARA, RG 59, CDF, 601.62A70B; DG Dakar (Reichhold) Ber. 149/59, June 19, 1959: PA/AA, B 12, Bd. 93. For German-American conversations about the provision of rice and other staples to Guinea, see the telegrams between DepSta and US Bonn of June 1959 in FRG-IA 55–59 (II), reel 4, frames 998–1002 (862A.0070B).

84. DG Conakry (Poensgen), Aug. 4, 1959: PA/AA, B 12, Bd. 93.

85. In December 1951, the Federal Republic and the GDR both sent spokesmen to the United Nations to testify on the topic of all-German elections. The two delegations appeared on different days, however, so they were never in the same room together. Further details appear in Chapter 1.

86. For an example of how the GDR made propagandistic use of its presence at Geneva, see the Foreign Ministry's declaration on "the interference of the German Federal Republic in the internal affairs of the United Arab Republic," Sept. 14, 1959; it states outright that the Western Allies had recognized the GDR de facto by assenting to the participation of East German representatives. *DARDDR* VII, 124.

87. On the chancellor's lack of close, trusted advisers in early 1959, see Schwarz, *Staatsmann*, 477–78. Adenauer's political isolation only worsened in the wake of a fiasco during April–June 1959, when the chancellor identified himself as a candidate for the office of federal president. Schwarz, *Staatsmann*, 502–26; Köhler, *Adenauer*, 1025–49.

88. Kosthorst, *Brentano*, 255–87.

89. For a helpful overview of the course of the negotiations, see Hans Herzfeld's contribution to Cornides et al., *Die internationale Politik 1958–1960*, 585–99.

90. For a sample of American concern about not appearing to be the "co-dividers" of Germany, see US Paris (Lyon) 3196, Mar. 4, 1959, secret: *FRUS 1958–1960/VIII*, 417–19.

91. Especially clear examples of the basic tactics of the Allies and the Soviets can be seen in the American records of the formal negotiating sessions of May 28 and 30, 1959, secret: *FRUS 1958–60/VIII*, 773–81, 792–97.

92. Even in conversation with Prime Minister Harold Macmillan, whom Adenauer intensely distrusted, the chancellor suggested on March 12, 1959, that the West aim for a five-year freeze on the status quo in Berlin. Macmillan pressed the point home by asking whether the Germans would be able to bear another five years of division, to which Adenauer responded in the affirmative. Gearson, *Harold Macmillan and the Berlin Wall Crisis*, 82–83.

93. Eckardt to Adenauer, Aug. 17, 1959: StBKAH, Bd. III/24. Eckardt wrote that the decision to accept the presence of the East German delegation (approved unanimously by the Bundestag's Foreign Affairs Committee) was "surely a mistake," but he went on to comment that "the artless tactics of the GDR delegation on this unfamiliar stage helped to compensate for the Federal Republic's unfavorable position" (ibid., 2).

94. Pressekonferenz, Sept. 4, 1959, pp. 4–5: ACDP, NL Eckardt, I-010-013. Kessel went on to become a columnist for *Die Welt*, the flagship of the famous Springer concern.

95. Comments by Franz Thedieck, state secretary in the Ministry for All-German Questions, in an interministerial meeting of Mar. 17, 1959: BAK, B 136, Bd. 6527.

96. See the report by Felix von Eckardt to the foreign policy working group of the CDU Bundestag delegation, Oct. 13, 1959: ACDP, Arbeitskreis V, VIII-006-1/1.

97. On Brandt's trip to Burma, see Ref. 702 (Meissner), Aufz., Apr. 14, 1959, p. 16: PA/AA, B 12, Bd. 800.

98. By the time the German Information Center opened in 1960, the Berlin Crisis was hardly the Federal Republic's only public relations problem in the United States. On the wave of anti-Semitic incidents that occurred throughout West Germany in early 1960, see Schwarz, *Epochenwechsel*, 208–11.

99. Ref. 711, Aufz., Oct. 27, 1959: PA/AA, B 12, Bd. 254. The West German legation in Rangoon, which in previous years had despaired at the flow of Soviet bloc propaganda, regained its confidence after the arrival of a press attaché. In the three months from November 1, 1959, to January 31, 1960, the embassy produced 214 publications in 21 different English and Burmese-language newspapers, as compared to 186 publications by the GDR in 11 papers. DG Rangoon (Randow), Feb. 13, 1960: PA/AA, B 12, Bd. 90.

100. For an overview of how the term "self-determination" was used during the period of decolonization, see Emerson, *From Empire to Nation*, 295–359.

101. Both of these advantages are listed in a note by Karl Heinrich Knappstein to Adenauer, Nov. 11, 1959: PA/AA, B 12, Bd. 3. As Knappstein's note explains, Adenauer had lamented that world public opinion appeared to be tiring of the German Question; the chancellor suggested that the Foreign Office find some means of relating Germany's situation to other world problems, such as the civil wars in Laos, Vietnam, and Korea. Knappstein responded by putting forward the concept of self-determination.

102. In a letter of April 28, 1959, Kissinger wrote the following to CSU deputy Baron Karl Theodor von und zu Guttenberg: "I think it would be extremely dangerous to recognize the East German regime. To do so would strike me as such a moral defeat for the West that all our claims to stand for self-determination would ever afterwards ring hollow. It would also confirm the impression of the underdeveloped countries that this is the age of Communism and thereby increase the pressures against us all." BAK, NL Guttenberg, Bd. 63, Bl. 228.

103. This sum stretched over a period of five years, from 1958 to 1962. Bonn had fiercely resisted this feature of the Treaty of Rome, for even in 1957 it had no desire to be associated so directly with colonialism. In February 1957, Adenauer finally chalked up this rather expensive gift to France and its empire as the price for reaching agreement with Paris on the founding of the EEC. Küsters, *Die Gründung der Europäischen Wirtschaftsgemeinschaft*, 384–92; Carstens, *Erinnerungen und Erfahrungen*, 210–13.

104. US Tunis Air Pouch 773, Apr. 22, 1959, confidential, p. 1: FRG-FA 55–59, reel 2, frames 679–84 (662A.72).

105. See the memorandum by the head of the AA's personnel office, Georg von Broich-Oppert, "Errichtung von Vertretungen in Afrika," Sept. 7, 1959: PA/AA, B 2, Bd. 97, Bl. 99–103.

106. Büro Staatssekretär (Gehlhoff), Aufz., Oct. 19, 1959, vertraulich: PA/AA, B 2, Bd. 97, Bl. 347.

107. For example, in July 1960, Adenauer wrote a personal letter to the heads of

four French colonies that were about to celebrate their independence—the Ivory Coast, Upper Volta, Niger, and Dahomey. For a draft of this letter, see DG Abidjan Ber. 244/60, June 29, 1960: PA/AA, B 12, Bd. 139a.

108. One near miss occurred in Congo; see Frank, *Entschlüsselte Botschaft*, 185–213.

109. See, for example, comments by Herbert Schröder (p. 56) and Horst Dumke (p. 306) in the protocol contained in PA/AA, B 2, Bd. 96.

110. Etzdorf, report on "Afrika in der Weltpolitik," 32–42; quote on 42. Etzdorf's department, "West II," covered bilateral relations with various European nations; it is all too telling that the desk for sub-Saharan Africa should have been grouped in this department until 1963.

111. See the conversation on economic and trade policy (pp. 330–44) in the protocol cited in n. 109 above. Also of interest is the French analysis of the conference, conveyed in AF Bonn (Seydoux), Nov. 14, 1959, pp. 3–5: MAE, EU 44–60, All 1258, 246–51. A more systematic discussion of West German aid policy appears in Chapter 5.

112. In fact, the Foreign Office, not wishing to provoke the Egyptians, had been opposed to recalling the West German ambassador in the first place; this was Brentano's personal decision. AF Bonn (Seydoux) tel. 2572, Sept. 17, 1959, réservé, confidentiel: MAE, EU 44–60, RDA 30, 90; AF Bonn (Seydoux) tel. 2574, Sept. 18, 1959, réservé: MAE, EU 44–60, All 1256, 339. See also the foreign minister's comments in a letter to Adenauer, Sept. 18, 1959, p. 2: BAK, NL Brentano, Bd. 157, Bl. 264–66. The deputy chief of the Eastern Department informed American officials that "even if exequatur issued, unlikely FedRep would sever relations with UAR." US Bonn (Bruce) 558, Sept. 17, 1959, confidential: NARA, RG 59, CDF, 602.62B86B.

113. Kilian, *Hallstein-Doktrin*, 115–19.

114. At the Ambassadors' Conference in Addis Ababa, West German officials and diplomats responded quite enthusiastically to Nasser's position, regarding it as an excellent example for other Third World leaders. They were especially pleased that Nasser had stated publicly that his government did not recognize the GDR. PA/AA, B 2, Bd. 96, pp. 19–21 of protocol.

115. Comments by a British official in the bimonthly Allied embassy consultation talks with the West German Foreign Office, cited verbatim in US Bonn (Bruce) Airgram G-148, Oct. 2, 1959, confidential: NARA, RG 59, CDF, 602.62B86B. The French embassy also regarded Bonn's position as a "softening" of the Hallstein Doctrine. AF Bonn (Seydoux) tel. 2567–68, Sept. 17, 1959: MAE, EU 44–60, RDA 30, 89.

116. At length the Burmese agreed not to issue *any* exequatur to the East German consul, while the Indonesians followed the Egyptian precedent and devised a restricted exequatur. Also, neither country moved to open a consulate-general in East Berlin, again in line with Nasser's example. On Burma, see AF Bonn (Seydoux), Sept. 1, 1960: MAE, EU 44–60, RDA 31, 171–72; on Indonesia, see US Jakarta (Jones) 622, Sept. 1, 1960, confidential: NARA, RG 59, CDF, 662B.98.

117. For examples in Casablanca, Tunis, and Paris, see DG Rabat 21, May 7, 1957, cito; Ref. 201, Aufz., May 13, 1957: both in B 12, Bd. 106; Ref. 204 (Böker), Oct. 15, 1958: PA/AA, B 1, Bd. 19; DG Paris (Maltzan), July 23, 1958: PA/AA, B 12, Bd. 92.

118. In early 1958, Bonn persuaded the secretariat of the United Nations to issue regulations barring the use of "German Democratic Republic" in UN publications

and endorsing "Eastern Germany" as the UN-approved designation. DG UN (Broich-Oppert) to Ber. 391/58, Apr. 25, 1958: PA/AA, B 80, Bd. 236.

119. Meeting of the so-called "SBZ-Referate," Jan. 19, 1960: PA/AA, B 12, Bd. 86. On this problem more generally, see Geyer, "Der Kampf um nationale Repräsentation."

120. For examples of complaints regarding the GDR's "*Spalterflagge*," see DG Jakarta (Mirbach) Ber. 826/60, Sept. 20, 1960: PA/AA, B 12, Bd. 95; DG Rabat (Müller-Roschach) 115, Apr. 26, 1962: PA/AA, B 38, Bd. 343. For a typical West German complaint about license plates, see Duckwitz to DG Cairo, June 8, 1960: PA/AA, B 80, Bd. 373.

121. For warnings along these lines, see DG Rabat, Sept. 20, 1959: PA/AA, B 12, Bd. 106; also DG New Delhi (Melchers) 90, Mar. 16, 1960: PA/AA, B 2, Bd. 84, Bl. 118–19.

122. On Sékou Touré's ideology and the Guinean constitution, see Rivière, *Guinea*, 89–96.

123. Politbüro, Protokoll Nr. 7/59, Feb. 10, 1959, point 5: BA-SAPMO, DY 30/J IV 2/2, Bd. 631.

124. On the mission of the GDR's advisers and the "Geschenksendung" of radio equipment, see the report by a member of the Interior Ministry (Schönherr), June 5, 1959, streng vertraulich: BA-SAPMO, DY 30, Bd. 3633.

125. A report by Dr. Friedrich Gut of the Hochschule für Planökonomie, July 16, 1959, refers on p. 3 to East German intentions to build a "national publishing house" for Guinea. BA-SAPMO, DY 30/IV 2/20, Bd. 384, Bl. 9–18. A formal contract regarding the sale was signed on March 11, 1960; see the letter from the Guinean planning minister, Feb. 11, 1963, attached as Anl. 8 to Politbüro, Protokoll Nr. 9/63, Apr. 2, 1963: BA-SAPMO, DY 30/J IV 2/2, Bd. 873.

126. Report by Dr. Friedrich Gut (cited in n. 125 above), p. 2.

127. Georg Stibi, "Erster Bericht über die Reise nach Guinea," o. D. [November 1958], p. 15: BA-SAPMO, NY 4090, Bd. 499.

128. See Grotewohl's letter to Sékou Touré, approved by the Politburo in its meeting of Oct. 20, 1959, Anl. 3: BA-SAPMO, DY 30/J IV 2/2, Bd. 672.

129. The SED's invitation had, in fact, been issued first; for the details, see Scherpenberg to DG Conakry 10, Sept. 1, 1959, citissime mit Vorrang: PA/AA, B 34, Bd. 86. On Guinean irritation, see DDR Prague, Nov. 30, 1959: BA-SAPMO, NY 4182, Bd. 1328, Bl. 40.

130. An unmarked document from the Soviet embassy in East Berlin dated Nov. 5, 1959, explains the situation: BA-SAPMO, DY 30, Bd. 3633.

131. For Adenauer's skeptical reaction to the invitation, which had been issued without his approval, see his marginal note to Globke on a memorandum from the Foreign Office's protocol desk (Braun) to the Bundeskanzleramt, Oct. 5, 1959; and the note from Franz-Josef Bach to Adenauer, Oct. 12, 1959: both in BAK, B 136, Bd. 2071. For a sample of Adenauer's doubts about the ability of Africans to govern themselves, see his conversation with Israeli prime minister David Ben Gurion, Mar. 14, 1960, printed in differing German and Israeli versions in *Vierteljahrshefte für Zeitgeschichte* 45, 2 (April 1997): 340, 341.

132. UK Bonn (Steel) No. 327, Nov. 26, 1959, confidential, p. 1: PRO, FO 371/145771. Ambassador Seydoux raised the French request directly with Adenauer; see Ref. 307, Vermerk, Oct. 30, 1959: PA/AA, B 34, Bd. 86.

133. Etzdorf, Aufz., "Staatsbesuch des Präsidenten der Republik Guinea," Nov. 23, 1959: PA/AA, B 34, Bd. 86.

134. This continued to plague efforts at U.S.-Guinean cooperation in 1960; see Dillon to Riddleberger (director of the International Cooperation Administration), Mar. 3, 1960, confidential: *FRUS 1958–60/XIV*, 707–8.

135. In December 1959, Sékou Touré informed a visiting East German delegation, "We are prepared to receive an ambassador from you if you wish." The occasion is described in Anl. 3 of Politbüro, Arbeitsprotokoll Nr. 4/60, Jan. 26, 1960: BA-SAPMO, DY 30/J IV 2/2A, Bd. 736.

136. These arguments were brought to the new West German ambassador by Guinea's acting foreign minister on Sékou Touré's behalf; see DG Conakry (Schroeder) 76, Dec. 26, 1959: PA/AA, B 2, Bd. 78, Bl. 71.

137. Scherpenberg to DG Conakry, Dec. 28, 1959, vertraulich: ibid., Bl. 72–73.

138. Schroeder viewed the currency decision as the onset of a "second revolution" in Guinea; see DG Conakry Ber. 144/60, Mar. 7, 1960: PA/AA, B 34, Bd. 149.

139. French atomic testing in the Sahara was a sensitive issue across sub-Saharan Africa, as West German officials learned during travels in early January 1960. US Bonn (Tyler) Air Pouch 1147, Jan. 22, 1960, confidential, p. 3: NARA, RG 59, CDF, 662A.70. Guinea's accusations in the UN thus amounted to rather venomous slander, and—for many in the Foreign Office—already grounds for reprisals against Sékou Touré. Etzdorf to DG Conakry 11, Mar. 5, 1960, citissime: PA/AA, B 34, Bd. 149.

140. Cited in Ndumbe, *Was will Bonn in Afrika?*, 113.

141. See Schwab to Ulbricht et al., Mar. 14, 1960, which includes the text of telegram 3393 from the East German trade mission in Conakry, dated Mar. 12: BA-SAPMO, NY 4182, Bd. 1328, Bl. 56–59.

142. BAK, NL Brentano, Bd. 158, Bl. 25–26; portions in Baring, *Sehr verehrter Herr Bundeskanzler!*, 284–85. See also Brentano's comments to the Bundestag Foreign Affairs Committee on Mar. 10: BT/PA, Ausw. Aus., 3. WP, Bd. 7, p. 45.

143. Asked whether the Allies should stop aiding Guinea, Adenauer replied, "I sure wouldn't give him anything more, that Sékou Touré!" Pressed by American reporter Flora Lewis to say whether this referred to countries besides West Germany, Adenauer answered more carefully, "That's for them to decide." Adenauer, *Teegespräche 1959–61*, 222.

144. On the "welcome opportunity," see the report from the American embassy in Bonn, which cited an official in the Eastern division to this effect. The report noted that the Foreign Office was nearly unanimous in advocating a break. US Bonn (Dowling) 1695, Mar. 7, 1960, confidential, priority: NARA, RG 59, CDF, 662B.70B.

145. The following independent papers voiced support for a strong action by Bonn: *Die Welt* (Georg Schröder, "Sékou Touré," Mar. 7, 1), the *FAZ* (Alfred Rapp, "Giftpfeil aus Guinea," Mar. 9, 1), the *Süddeutsche Zeitung* ("Enttäuschung über Guinea," Mar. 7, 3, and "Bonner Quitting für Guinea," Mar. 10, 3), and *Die Zeit* (Fritz René Allemann, "Querschuß aus Guinea," Mar. 11, 1). Less prestigious right-leaning papers expressed their anger at Sékou Touré in alarmingly racist tones, prompting a thoughtful rebuttal by the editor-in-chief of the *Hamburger Echo*, Dr. Hans Henrich—a column entitled "Herrenvolk in der Hallsteinzeit" (Mar. 12, 1960).

146. SPD-Parteivorstand, Mar. 12, 1960, p. 4: AdsD, SPD-PV, Jan.–June 1960.

147. The classic account of this reorientation appears in Klotzbach, *Der Weg zur Staatspartei*.

148. These SPD arguments are summarized in "Das Kabinett befaßt sich mit der Brüskierung durch Seku Ture," *FAZ*, Mar. 8, 1960, 1; see also "Guinea und die Hallstein-Doktrin," *Süddeutsche Zeitung*, Mar. 8, 1960, pp. 1–2. This stance caught a number of newspapers by surprise; on the morning of March 7, most SPD-affiliated papers had printed editorials attacking the Hallstein Doctrine.

149. Pressekonferenz, Mar. 7, 1960, 12:00 P.M., pp. 10–11: ACPD, NL Eckardt, I-010-014. On March 14, Eckardt made similar comments about the Hallstein Doctrine at a press luncheon in New York City; there, too, reporters appeared to find Eckardt's standpoint reassuring. DG UN (Dankwort), Mar. 15, 1960: PA/AA, B 12, Bd. 93.

150. Baudissin, Vermerk, telephone conversation with Schroeder, Mar. 7, 1960: PA/AA, B 34, Bd. 149; also DG Conakry 19, Mar. 7, 1960: PA/AA, B 12, Bd. 93.

151. Eckardt's comments at a press conference of Mar. 9, 1960, p. 5: ACDP, NL Eckardt, I-010-014.

152. See two separate notes by Baudissin and Scherpenberg, Mar. 11, 1960: PA/AA, B 34, Bd. 149. Scherpenberg's note, approved by Brentano, warned that a German ultimatum might lead world opinion to sympathize with Guinea.

153. Schwab to Ulbricht, Mar. 10, 1960: BA-SAPMO, NY 4182, Bd. 1328, Bl. 51.

154. A second note from Schwab to Ulbricht, Mar. 10, 1960: BA-SAPMO, NY 4182, Bd. 1333.

155. Ghanaian officials made this plain to both German camps. On the East German side, see Tel. 3393 from Conakry of Mar. 12, sent by Schwab to Ulbricht, Mar. 14, 1960: BA-SAPMO, NY 4182, Bd. 1328, Bl. 56–59. On the West German side, see DG Accra (Stein) 19, Mar. 11, 1960: PA/AA, B 12, Bd. 105.

156. Politbüro, Arbeitsprotokoll Nr. 11/60: BA-SAPMO, DY 30/J IV 2/2A, Bd. 743. On Kurella's authority to make deals, see his comments to Sékou Touré in their conversation of Mar. 25, 1960, p. 9: BA-SAPMO, DY 30, Bd. 3633.

157. "Jeder macht mal Fehler," *Der Spiegel*, Mar. 16, 1960, 16. The basic content of this interview, held in Conakry on Mar. 10, was communicated to the Foreign Office on the same day.

158. Baudissin, Aufz., Mar. 14, 1960: PA/AA, B 12, Bd. 93. Via his interviewer, Engelmann, Sékou Touré suggested that perhaps the GDR should be granted a position in Guinea akin to Israel's mission to West Germany. Ref. 307 (Steltzer), Aufz., Mar. 15, 1960, p. 2: ibid. On the willingness of Foreign Office leaders to compromise, see US Bonn (Timberlake) 1796, Mar. 17, 1960, confidential: NARA, RG 59, CDF, 662B.70B. See also the protocol of the German-Allied consultation, Mar. 17, 1960: PA/AA, B 34, Bd. 149.

159. For a summary of the West German note, see US Bonn (Tyler) Air Pouch 69, July 14, 1960, confidential, pp. 2–3: NARA, RG 59, CDF, 662A.70B. This dispatch presents a comprehensive (and quite critical) analysis of Brentano's handling of the crisis with Guinea.

160. This conference of the Parti Démocratique de la Guinée drew up the country's first Three-Year Plan. Rivière, *Guinea*, 110–11.

161. For one such clue from Moscow, see DG Moscow (Kroll) 516, Apr. 1, 1960, citissime: PA/AA, B 34, Bd. 150. On Sékou Touré's letter to Eisenhower, see DepSta

Instruction CA-8822 to US Bonn, Apr. 25, 1960, confidential: NARA, RG 59, CDF, 662B.70B.

162. Conversation Kurella/Sékou Touré, Mar. 30, 1960: BA-SAPMO, DY 30, Bd. 3633. In their conversation of March 23 (same archival volume), the two had agreed that the Federal Republic was unlikely to break relations with Guinea.

163. True to form, however, this functionary was instructed not to *sign* any of the negotiated agreements; this would be the prerogative of the East German ambassador once diplomatic relations were finally established. Politbüro, Arbeitsprotokoll Nr. 15/60, Apr. 5, 1960, point 7: BA-SAPMO, DY 30/J IV 2/2A, Bd. 747.

164. Conversation Sékou Touré/Kurella, Mar. 30, 1960, p. 3.

165. Brentano remarked that Etzdorf's mission would show that "we take this country and its political importance just as seriously as others." Brentano, Informationsgespräch, Apr. 2, 1960, pp. 23–24: ACDP, NL Eckardt, I-010-014. For an indication of Etzdorf's goals, see his memorandum of Mar. 30, 1960: PA/AA, B 34, Bd. 149; also Blasius, *Hasso von Etzdorf*.

166. Guinea published the Etzdorf–Sékou Touré communiqué in the April 8 edition of the official government bulletin. DG Conakry 38, Apr. 8, 1960, citissime mit Vorrang: PA/AA, B 34, Bd. 149. For the most complete background information on the Etzdorf–Sékou Touré conversation, see US Bonn (Dowling) Airgram G–588, Apr. 20, 1960, confidential: NARA, RG 59, CDF, 601.62A70B.

167. Deutscher Bundestag, 3. WP, 110. Sitzung (Apr. 8, 1960): *Sten. Ber.*, 6123A.

168. Ibid.

169. For the extremely positive news coverage, see Dieter Schröder, "Herrn von Etzdorfs hochpolitische Safari," *Süddeutsche Zeitung*, Apr. 11, 1960; "Touré berichtigt," *Die Zeit*, Apr. 14, 1960, 3.

170. Tellingly, Wischnewski's original take on the Guinea crisis was entitled "Nicht die Flagge streichen—sondern kämpfen!," SPD-Pressedienst, Mar. 7, 1960 (P/XV/55).

171. As the SPD's point man on development aid during the 1960s, Wischnewski often criticized the government for its lack of zeal in blocking East German advances. As early as 1960, though, Wischnewski was reportedly receiving Foreign Office subsidies for trips to Ghana, Guinea, and the Congo. AF Berlin (Chalvron) No. 495/EU, Oct. 24, 1960, p. 2: MAE, EU 44–60, All 1258, 318–20. This is not how Wischnewski tells the story in his memoirs; there he laments the central role of the isolation campaign in Bonn's relations with the developing world. *Mit Leidenschaft und Augenmaß*, 40.

172. During the Ambassadors' Conference in Addis Ababa, some West German diplomats had lamented that the German League of Unions showed so little interest in foreign policy matters: PA/AA, B 2, Bd. 96, Bl. 23–31.

173. US Bonn Air Pouch 69, p. 1, cited in n. 159 above.

174. On Bonn's far-reaching trade treaty with Guinea, see DG Conakry (Schroeder) Ber. 423/60, July 11, 1960: PA/AA, B 12, Bd. 93. On the diesel locomotive, see Morrow, *First American Ambassador*, 58.

175. "In closing, he [Guevara] remarked that, all the same, he personally was of the opinion that this is all a somewhat artificial game." Baumann/Guevara conversation, Sept. 16, 1960: PA/AA, B 12, Bd. 111.

CHAPTER FIVE

1. Adenauer to Erhard, Aug. 28, 1958: *Briefe 1957–59*, 150.

2. Czempiel, *Macht und Kompromiß*, 41–46; Eckardt, *Ein unordentliches Leben*, 424–25.

3. On the EEC's overseas development fund, see Chapter 4.

4. On American policy, see NSC 5803, Feb. 7, 1958, secret: *FRUS 1958–60/IX*, 643. On the increased contributions to the International Monetary Fund and the World Bank, see Bellers, *Außenwirtschaftspolitik*, 208–9. Regarding Turkey, Adenauer actually pushed Dulles to take action; see the chancellor's comments to Federal President Heuss, July 8, 1958, *Adenauer-Heuss: Unter vier Augen*, 270. Bonn's share in the multilateral programs in Greece and Turkey came largely in the form of Hermes credits (discussed below); the U.S. was soon pushing for a more direct German contribution. DepSta to US Bonn 1805, Feb. 19, 1960, confidential: NARA, RG 59, CDF, 033.62A11.

5. Bodemer, *Entwicklungshilfe*, 29.

6. For thorough details, see US Cairo Air Pouch 1133, May 19, 1958; US Bonn Air Pouch 815, Nov. 24, 1958; and the conversation between Assistant Secretary of State C. Thomas Mann and Dr. Paul Leverkuhn, chairman of the Bundestag's Subcommittee on Development Aid, Mar. 27, 1959: all confidential, all in FRG-IA 55–99, reel 5, frames 88–92, 127–29, 130. See also Berggötz, *Nahostpolitik in der Ära Adenauer*, 349–60.

7. According to Horst Dumke, the Foreign Office's leading theorist on aid, the most general aim of technical assistance was to inculcate "an understanding of work and savings, for the discipline of the work process and for the preservation of capital." PA/AA, B 2, Bd. 96, Bl. 305.

8. Dennert, *Entwicklungshilfe geplant oder verwaltet?*, 31–32. As Dennert explains, the technical assistance program was a slow starter: even as the 1958 budget was under discussion, only DM 6 million of the DM 100 million appropriated for 1956–57 had been spent.

9. For the total number, see Brentano's comments in the Bundestag, 3. WP, 118. Sitzung (June 22, 1960): *Sten. Ber.*, 6820A; for a brief description of the projects mentioned here, see US Bonn Air Pouch 1369, Mar. 10, 1959, pp. 2–5: FRG-IA 55–99, reel 4, frames 694–98 (862A.00).

10. From 1957 to early 1959, of 1,315 industrial trainees sent to the Federal Republic on special programs, 401 hailed from the UAR, 229 from India, 173 from Turkey, 138 from Greece, 101 from Iran, and 100 from Italy. These six countries supplied 87 percent of the trainees in this program. US Bonn Air Pouch 1369, Mar. 10, 1959, p. 7: FRG-IA 55–99, reel 4, frames 694–98. On West German development projects in Turkey, see Gürbey, *Türkei-Politik*, 197–201.

11. Bellers, *Außenwirtschaftspolitik*, 117–21.

12. Scherpenberg, Aufz., "HERMES-Bürgschaften und -Garantien für neue Ausfuhrgeschäfte nach Jugoslawien," Dec. 18, 1957: PA/AA, B 12, Bd. 97; Krapf, Aufz., "Verschlechterung der deutsch-jugoslawischen Beziehungen," Mar. 18, 1962, p. 1: PA/AA, B 12, Bd. 588.

13. Details about the West German attempt to refashion the Hermes credits into development aid appear in the speech by Kurt Birrenbach (CDU) to the Bundestag during the debate of June 22, 1960: *Sten. Ber.*, 3. WP, 6815C–6816B.

14. See comments by Under Secretary of State C. Douglas Dillon to Brentano on March 15, 1960, in *FRUS* 1958–60/IX, 675.

15. Conversation between Dillon and Brentano in Bonn, Nov. 21, 1960, confidential: NARA, RG 59, Lot Files Europe—Entry 3090, box 13, "Jordan."

16. As of February 1958, Bonn had supplied DM 660 million at 6.3 percent interest, due March 31, 1961; see US Bonn (Bruce) 2706, Feb. 28, 1958: FRG-IA 55–59, reel 5, frame 207 (862A.0091). In the following two years the amount of the credits shot up considerably.

17. See the argument between Helmut Kalbitzer (SPD) and Kurt Birrenbach, as cited in n. 13 above; also comments by Walter Scheel (FDP) during the same debate: *Sten. Ber.*, 6824A–C. In September 1960, Brentano made a similar observation during an Ambassadors' Conference in Rio de Janeiro; see p. 39 of the protocol in PA/AA, B 1, Bd. 70.

18. Deutscher Bundestag, 3. WP, 118. Sitzung (June 22, 1960): *Sten. Ber.*, 6804B–6807C.

19. Bodemer, *Entwicklungshilfe*, 33–42.

20. See Krone, *Tagebücher 1945–1961*, 429. For a program of the Friedrich-Ebert-Stiftung's weekend conference about development aid held on January 16–17, 1960, see ACDP, NL Birrenbach, Bd. 2/2.

21. *Sten. Ber.*, 3. WP, 6811C.

22. Conversation Herter/Brentano, Mar. 15, 1960, confidential: *FRUS* 1958–60/IX, 675. In April 1960, CDU politician Kai-Uwe von Hassel argued that development aid should be discussed under the rubric of "security" at the CDU congress. Buchstab, *Adenauer: ". . . Um den Frieden zu gewinnen*," 903. See also Danckwortt, *Zur Psychologie der deutschen Entwicklungshilfe*, 34.

23. Quotes from a press tea, Mar. 2, 1961: Adenauer, *Teegespräche 1959–61*, 482–83. See also Adenauer's comments to Eisenhower on Mar. 15, 1960: *FRUS* 1958–60/IX, 666–67.

24. Brentano to Adenauer, Dec. 12, 1960: PA/AA, B 1, Bd. 137.

25. *Sten. Ber.*, 6818C (June 22, 1960); 9218A (159. Sitzung, May 5, 1961). For quotes of a similar nature by SPD politicians, see Dennert, *Entwicklungshilfe geplant oder verwaltet?*, 19–22.

26. This attitude is quite evident from the reporting of the French embassy in Bonn, which consistently criticized West German friendliness toward authoritarian, one-party regimes like those in Guinea and Mali. See, for example, AF Bonn (Seydoux) tel. 376–79, Jan. 19, 1962: MAE, EU 61–70, RFA Z215.

27. See the comments by the head of the desk for sub-Saharan Africa, Hans Steltzer, to an Ambassadors' Conference in Entebbe, Uganda, Oct. 29, 1962, 16–18: PA/AA, B 1, Bd. 260. For an interpretation of how the United States came to admire or at least tolerate the variants of neutralism espoused by Tito, Nehru, and Nasser, see Brands, *The Specter of Neutralism*.

28. A telegram signed by Dillon makes this case succinctly regarding Guinea and Mali: "Dept cannot lightly contemplate possibility [of] two West African states almost exclusively dependent [on the] Soviet Bloc for technical and advisory personnel, economic assistance, export markets." DepSta to USUN, Nov. 30, 1960, confidential: *FRUS* 1958–60/XIV, 245.

29. For the number of countries, see Abt. 3 (Sachs), Aufz., Nov. 7, 1961, p. 1: PA/AA, B 58, Bd. 215. During one typical journey undertaken by a Foreign Office functionary, Kurt Schlitter, Adenauer's government offered the following sums: Ivory Coast, DM 30 million; Senegal, DM 25 million; Upper Volta, Niger, and Dahomey, DM 15 million each. Lenkungsausschuß, 7. Sitzung, Feb. 7, 1961: BAK, B 213, Bd. 1516.

30. Abt. 7, Aufz., "Südostasien: Die Reise Merkatz," Mar. 21, 1961: PA/AA, B 12, Bd. 124. See also the vivid account in Diehl, *Zwischen Politik und Presse*, 256–79. The "Merkatz-Zusage" to Indonesia consisted of DM 100 million in long-term, low-interest loans and a like amount of Hermes credits. Ref. 411 to Ref. 803, Aug. 16, 1961: PA/AA, B 58, Bd. 215.

31. Lübke's plans to visit Africa for a second time in late 1962 were canceled by the Foreign Office, which did not want to give the impression of undue attention toward that continent. US Bonn (Dowling) A-1267, Apr. 14, 1962, secret: NARA, RG 59, CDF, 662A.70. On Lübke's role in promoting development aid, see Morsey, *Heinrich Lübke*, 369–75. See also notes by Carstens of Nov. 27, 1961, and Aug. 24, 1962: PA/AA, B 2, Bd. 88 Bl. 33 and Bd. 87 Bl. 270.

32. AF Bonn (Seydoux) tel. 889–92, Feb. 25, 1961, confidentiel: MAE, EU 61–70, RFA, Z215.

33. The "Boghdadi Agreement" of July 1961 contained the following provisions: DM 500 million for the Euphrates Dam (redemption over 20 years; 3.75 percent interest; 6-year grace period); DM 150 million for other infrastructural projects (12–16 years' redemption time, 3 percent interest); DM 150 million for special long-term Hermes guarantees (10 years' redemption); and DM 250 million for medium-term Hermes guarantees (5 years' redemption). Entwicklungsausschuß, 6. Sitzung, May 17, 1962, pp. 40–50: BT/PA, 3. WP, Bd. 1.

34. Ref. 709 (Döring) to Ref. 112, Dec. 19, 1960, p. 2: PA/AA, B 1, Bd. 18.

35. On the composition of the Steering Committee, see Dennert, *Entwicklungshilfe geplant oder verwaltet?*, 40–41. The Foreign Office, Economics Ministry, Finance Ministry, and Ministry for Economic Cooperation (after its creation in late 1961) were the most important ministries represented there, but until 1964 participation was also accorded the Ministries of Agriculture, Family, and others. Observers from the Kreditanstalt für Wiederaufbau (which handled Hermes credits) and the Deutsche Bank also joined the meetings.

36. Regarding a Brentano visit to India, see Abt. 7 (Duckwitz), Aufz., Mar. 7, 1960, pp. 12–13. On the Merkatz trip to Burma the following year, see Abt. 7, Aufz., Mar. 21, 1960, pp. 10–11. Both in PA/AA, B 12, Bd. 124.

37. Mortimer, *The Third World Coalition in International Politics*, 12–13.

38. US Bonn (Burns) Air Pouch 1657, May 10, 1961, confidential: NARA, RG 59, CDF, 662A.70.

39. AF Bonn (Seydoux) tel. 763–64, Feb. 20, 1961: MAE, EU 61–70, RFA, Z215. This exchange of unpleasantries occurred when a small demonstration dissolved into an altercation with the Bonn police. The "assassins" comment refers to the murder of Congolese leader Patrice Lumumba (the subject of the demonstration), which the Soviets and many Africans imputed to Western malfeasance.

40. Carstens to DG Colombo 50, Apr. 26, 1961: PA/AA, B 12, Bd. 124; Duckwitz, Aufz., "Beziehungen Mali-SBZ," May 10, 1961: PA/AA, B 12, Bd. 110; US Bamako 402, May 19, 1961, confidential, priority: NARA, RG 59, CDF, 662A.70E/5-1961. On the

independence day ceremonies in Ghana, see AF Bonn (Grousset) No. 474/AL, July 7, 1961: MAE, EU 61–70, RDA F185.

41. This was known as a "framework agreement" (*Rahmenabkommen*). The Federal Republic's practice in this regard was remarkably similar to the techniques of the Soviet Union, and the reasons for this are not difficult to surmise: in the early 1960s, both were in a hurry to impress the developing countries with their readiness to give magnanimously. On Soviet aid, see Stevens, *The Soviet Union and Black Africa*, chap. 3.

42. US Tunis Air Pouch 773, Apr. 22, 1959, confidential, p. 2: FRG-FA 55–59, reel 2, frames 679–84. For SPD criticism of these "framework agreements," see Wischnewski's speech in the Bundestag, 4. WP, 49. Sitzung (Nov. 16, 1962): *Sten. Ber.*, 2172–73.

43. "Untied" aid corresponded to the economic interests of the Federal Republic in the early 1960s: Adenauer's government did not *want* its development aid to be spent on contracts for West German goods and services, for fear that this would have inflationary consequences. In addition, the net outflow of capital helped ease the huge and rapidly growing surplus in the Federal Republic's current-accounts balance.

44. Even the strongly pro-German president of Togo, Sylvanus Olympio, grew impatient with the delays; see US Lomé Airgram G-250, June 9, 1961: NARA, RG 59, CDF, 662A.70D. West German ambassadors often reported that the slow fulfillment of Bonn's aid promises was harming their standing with their host governments. DG Conakry (Schroeder) 103, Sept. 22, 1961, citissime: PA/AA, B 12, Bd. 111; DG Mogadishu (Kopf) 92, Oct. 8, 1961: PA/AA, B 12, Bd. 106.

45. Bundeskanzleramt, Aufz., Jan. 6, 1962: ACDP, NL Vialon, I-475-015/11. According to these figures for the fiscal year 1960, the Federal Republic devoted 1.06 percent of its GDP, or 6.17 percent of its budget, to development aid. For the United States, the figures were 0.82 and 4.79 percent, respectively; for the Netherlands, 2.6 and 11.65 percent.

46. Staritz, *Geschichte der DDR*, 189–91.

47. On the use of short-term credits in this period, see "Konzeption für die Entwicklung der Kreditbeziehungen der DDR gegenüber dem Ausland im Perspektivzeitraum" (pp. 52–54), approved in the Politburo meeting of Aug. 16, 1966: BA-SAPMO, DY 30/J IV 2/2, Bd. 1072, Anl. 3. On the bailout, see Lemke, *Berlinkrise*, 58–69.

48. Politbüro, Protokoll Nr. 27/62, June 19, 1962, Anl. 5: BA-SAPMO, DY 30/J IV 2/2, Bd. 834. Interestingly, the Trade Ministry had called for a unilateral abrogation of the agreement, but the Foreign Ministry had warned sharply against such a procedure; the 1958 agreement had, after all, been officially ratified by both sides in 1960, making it a valid treaty under international law.

49. Florin, "Gedanken zur Einschätzung der internationalen Lage," undated [June 1960], p. 3: BA-SAPMO, DY 30/IV 2/20, Bd. 7, Bl. 125–29.

50. "Bericht des Komitees der DDR für Solidarität mit den Völkern Afrikas über seine Tätigkeit im Jahre 1961," o. D., p. 1: BA-SAPMO, DY 30/IV 2/20, Bd. 55, Bl. 191–202.

51. On Congo and Algeria, see Ulbricht's "Grußtelegramm" to the Third All-African Peoples' Conference held in Cairo, Mar. 25–30, 1961: *DARDDR* IX, 307–8. On Cuba, see Grotewohl's telegram to the chairman of the Political Committee of the UN General Assembly, Apr. 18, 1961: ibid., 368.

52. See p. 3 of the report sent by the consul general in Jakarta on Feb. 15, 1961,

excerpted in a note by Abteilung Information of Mar. 6: BA-SAPMO, NY 4182, Bd. 3125.

53. For a general overview of the crisis, see Tusa, *The Last Division*, chap. 8. On the Kennedy administration, see Schertz, *Die Deutschlandpolitik Kennedys und Johnsons*.

54. Schwarz, *Adenauer. Der Staatsmann* (hereafter *Staatsmann*), 653–54. For a useful breakdown of the number of East Germans making an appearance at West German intake centers from 1949–61, see Heidemeyer, *Flucht und Zuwanderung aus der SBZ/DDR*, 338–39.

55. Vivid accounts appear in Wyden, *Wall*. On East German planning during the summer of 1961, see Harrison, "Ulbricht and the Concrete 'Rose,'" 42–45; and Lemke, *Berlinkrise*, 161–66.

56. Trachtenberg, *History and Strategy*, 222; Costigliola, "The Pursuit of Atlantic Community," 42–43; Smyser, *From Yalta to Berlin*, 167–78.

57. Official communiqué issued after a preparatory conference held in Cairo, June 5–12, 1961, printed in *Conference of Heads of State*, 15–16. On the conference's origins, see Rubinstein, *Yugoslavia and the Nonaligned World*, 105.

58. Mortimer, *The Third World Coalition in International Politics*, 12–14.

59. The first quote is from McGhee to Johnson, Aug. 14, 1961, secret, p. 2; the second is from Arthur Schlesinger Jr., "Memorandum for the President," Aug. 3, 1961, secret, p. 1. See also the very detailed memo by J. Barrow of the Near Eastern Affairs desk, Aug. 23, 1961, confidential. All in in NARA, RG 59, CDF, 396.1-BE.

60. US Belgrade (Kennan) 115, July 31, 1961, secret, priority: *FRUS* 1961–63/XVI, 198.

61. Duckwitz, Runderlaß, Aug. 18, 1961, p. 19: PA/AA, B 12, Bd. 46.

62. DG Rabat (Müller-Roschach) 209, Aug. 14, 1961: PA/AA, B 12, Bd. 46; US Addis Ababa 80, Aug. 18, 1961: NARA, RG 59, CDF, 396.1-BE. Morocco's request was met by the Foreign Office's Legal Department with a dry ten-page memorandum utterly lacking in political appeal. Abt. 5 (Haeften) to DG Rabat, Aug. 19, 1961: PA/AA, B 12, Bd. 46.

63. For a discussion of how the Berlin Wall represented a moral defeat for the SED regime (and was accompanied by a series of other repressive measures), see Staritz, *Geschichte der DDR*, 198–202. A vivid portrait of Adenauer and Brentano's disorientation after the building of the wall can be found in Poppinga, *"Das Wichtigste ist der Mut,"* 314–22.

64. For the texts of the two Foreign Office memos, see *Bulletin*, Aug. 29 and 31, 1961; the latter one, on Berlin, is also published in *DzD* IV/7, 203–5. The texts were described as "sterile and anemic" by one West German observer; see Peter von Zahn, "Denkschrift ad acta," *Die Welt*, Sept. 1, 1961, p. 3. The lack of photos was criticized by the German ambassador to Burma, who pointed out that the United States Information Service had managed to stage an entire *exhibit* on Berlin in its Rangoon office. DG Rangoon (Randow) Ber. 734/61, Aug. 17, 1961: PA/AA, B 80, Bd. 295.

65. Conversation Scholz/Nkrumah, July 1, 1961: BA-SAPMO, NY 4182, Bd. 1326, Bl. 102–6. Scholz appealed to the Ghanaian leader's vanity by disclosing Humboldt University's plan to award Nkrumah an honorary doctorate; Nkrumah did in fact make a brief stopover in East Berlin for this occasion on August 1, 1961.

66. AF New Delhi (Garnier) 881, Aug. 16, 1961, passed along to the Foreign Office: PA/AA, B 12, Bd. 114.

67. Dispatch from the trade mission in New Delhi Nr. 6486, Aug. 25, 1961, dringend, streng geheim!: BA-SAPMO, NY 4182, Bd. 3125.

68. Beschloss, *The Crisis Years*, 294–95, 306.

69. Rubinstein, *Yugoslavia and the Nonaligned World*, 107–9.

70. US Belgrade (Kennan) 377, Sept. 3, 1961: *FRUS 1961–63/XVI*, 202–3.

71. *Conference of Heads of State*, 157. For the most recent of many Soviet statements along these lines, see the communiqué published by the Soviet government on Aug. 30, 1961: *DzD* IV/7, 290–92.

72. Kennan remarked that Tito's "passage on Berlin contains no word that could not have been written by Khrushchev." US Belgrade 377, cited in n. 70 above. Kennan sent this telegram unclassified (it was later upgraded to "official use only"), suggesting that it was intended to be leaked.

73. AF Addis Ababa tel. 474–76, Aug. 19, 1961, réservé, très urgent: MAE, EU 61–70, RFA Z215.

74. *Conference of Heads of State*, 36. Sukarno's views are quite similar to those described as typical of South India in a dispatch by the German consul in Bombay, Sept. 20, 1961: PA/AA, B 12, Bd. 139a.

75. *Conference of Heads of State*, 101.

76. Ibid., 214 (Keita), 186 (Sihanouk), 112 (Nehru). Before the conference, many Germans had looked to Nehru as a moderating influence; see Hans Walter Berg, "Nehru und die deutsche Frage / Indiens Premier wäre ein idealer Vermittler," *Die Zeit*, Aug. 11, 1961; and Jürgen Tern, "Die Blockfreien und Berlin," *FAZ*, Sept. 1, 1961, 1.

77. Krapf, Aufz., "Verschlechterung der deutsch-jugoslawischen Beziehungen—Das Heranrücken Jugoslawiens an die Sowjetunion," Mar. 18, 1962, pp. 3–4: PA/AA, B 12, Bd. 588.

78. US Belgrade (Kennan) 407, Sept. 5, 1961, confidential: NARA, RG 59, CDF, 396.1-BE.

79. One West Berliner was on hand with certain credentials to speak with delegation leaders: Ulrich Biel, a personal envoy sent by Mayor Willy Brandt. Biel conversed with Nehru about the details of West Berlin's plight and the political failure of the Ulbricht regime; see US Belgrade (Kennan) 387, Sept. 4, 1961, confidential: NARA, RG 59, CDF, 396.1-BE; and Scherpenberg, Vermerk, Sept. 4, 1961: PA/AA, B 12, Bd. 46.

80. "Brentano: 'Hallstein-Doktrin gilt nach wie vor,'" *Hamburger Abendblatt*, Sept. 5, 1961; "Hallstein-Doktrin soll bleiben," *Süddeutsche Zeitung*, Sept. 6, 1961.

81. These motives were spelled out before the conference by an Egyptian media official in Belgrade known to have contacts with high-level UAR officials. This prognosis proved to be a very accurate summary of Nasser's position. US Belgrade (Kennan) 274, Aug. 26, 1961: NARA, RG 59, CDF, 396.1-BE.

82. On the 1961 "Boghdadi Agreement," see n. 33 above. During the negotiations over this agreement, Nasser placed additional pressure on Bonn by allowing an East German consulate to open in Damascus. As the American embassy in Bonn pointed out, the Federal Republic really had no means to prevent this, since "it was unwilling [to] use economic pressure and realized that breaking diplomatic relations would play into Soviet hands." US Bonn (Morris) Airgram G-1401, June 17, 1961, confidential, p. 2: NARA, RG 59, CDF, 602.62B86B. Interestingly, one of Brentano's reasons for wanting to push ahead with the "Boghdadi Agreement" in June 1961 was the fear that

otherwise Nasser might speak out against Bonn at the nonaligned conference. Brentano to Adenauer, June 19, 1961: BAK, B 136, Bd. 2075.

83. *Conference of Heads of State*, 261. On Nasser's role, see the West German analysis reported in US Bonn (Dowling) A-358, Sept. 20, 1961, confidential: NARA, RG 59, CDF, 396.1-BE.

84. Among the alleged conspirators were Ghana, Mali, Guinea, Indonesia, Ceylon, and Burma. The Foreign Office presumed Burma's innocence, however, and took no action against it. US Bonn A-358, as in n. 83 above.

85. AF Bonn (Seydoux) tel. 4145–49, Sept. 12, 1961: MAE, EU 61–70, RFA Z211.

86. DG Bamako (Schlegl) 64, Sept. 12, 1961: PA/AA, B 12, Bd. 110; on Ghana, see US Bonn A-358, cited in n. 83 above. Both Nkrumah of Ghana and Keita of Mali passed over invitations by Bonn to visit the Federal Republic in the fall of 1961. AF Bonn (Seydoux) 4610–11, Apr. 4, 1961: MAE, EU 61–70, RFA Z215.

87. Abt.7 (Northe), Aufz., "Änderungstendenzen der indischen Deutschland-politik," Sept. 28, 1961: PA/AA, B 1, Bd. 132. This remained Nehru's position a year later; see Carstens to Schröder, Oct. 5, 1962: PA/AA, B 2, Bd. 84, Bl. 561.

88. Abt. 7 (Northe), Vermerk, Sept. 5, 1961: PA/AA, B 12, Bd. 730.

89. Restrictive trade measures against Yugoslavia were decreed by Carstens and approved by the Bundestag's Trady Policy Committee. Ref. 705 (Krafft), Aufz., Feb. 19, 1962; Abt. 4 to Abt. 7, Apr. 17, 1962: both in PA/AA, B 12, Bd. 588.

90. "Bonn an die Blockfreien: Anerkennung der Zone würde sich auch auf die Entwicklungshilfe auswirken," *Süddeutsche Zeitung*, Sept. 7, 1961.

91. Shortly before the Belgrade Conference, the linking of aid with political positions had found some supporters in the Foreign Office; see Ref. 418, Aufz., "Berlinkrise und Entwicklungshilfe," Aug. 25, 1961: PA/AA, B 58, Bd. 115.

92. As the French embassy observed, the West German media—typically sympathetic to African regimes—was becoming ever more critical of Ghana's government and foreign policy. AF Bonn (Seydoux) tel. 4431–32, Sept. 26, 1961: MAE, EU 61–70, RFA Z215. The following spring, the German ambassador to Jakarta remarked that West German public opinion had turned sharply against Indonesia since the Belgrade Conference. US Jakarta 1848, Apr. 13, 1962, confidential: NARA, RG 59, CDF, 662B.98.

93. "Mende lehnt Hallstein-Doktrin ab," *Die Welt*, Sept. 8, 1961, 2; for the list of which countries Mende had in mind, see AF Bonn (Seydoux) tel. 4145–49, Sept. 12, 1961, p. 2: MAE, EU 61–70, RFA Z211.

94. J. T., "Unfreundlicher Akt," *FAZ*, Sept. 7, 1961, 1. In 1957, Tern had characterized the Hallstein Doctrine as "leather-jacket diplomacy." Now he took issue with the "foolish schadenfreude" of those who took delight in the troubled state of the Hallstein Doctrine. Among Tern's obvious targets was Wolfgang Schollwer of the FDP; see Schollwer's essay "Quittung der Belgrader Konferenz: Fiasko der Hallstein-Doktrin," *fdk*, Sept. 5, 1961, 7–8.

95. Carstens to Puttkamer, Sept. 23, 1961: PA/AA, B 2, Bd. 76, Bl. 274.

96. Carstens, Runderlaß, "Deutschland- u. Berlin betreffende Fragen in der XVIII. UN-Vollversammlung," Aug. 9, 1962: PA/AA, B 38, Bd. 12.

97. Abt. 3 (Müller-Roschach), Nov. 27, 1962: PA/AA, B 33, Bd. 287; Jansen, Aufz., Dec. 21, 1963: PA/AA, B 38, Bd. 12; Puttkamer, Runderlaß, Mar. 12, 1965: PA/AA, B 38, Bd. 365; Puttkamer, Runderlaß, Nov. 25, 1965: ibid.

98. Peter Grubbe, "Die Angst bestimmt das Deutschlandbild," *Die Welt*, Sept. 6, 1961, 3; Hans Ulrich Kempski, "Beim Abschied krähen schon die Hähne," *Süddeutsche Zeitung*, Sept. 7, 1961, 3.

99. The CDU/CSU's share fell from 50.2 to 45.3 percent; that of the SPD rose from 31.8 to 36.2 percent. In the Bundestag, this left the CDU/CSU with 242 seats (down from 270), the SPD with 190 seats (from 169), and the FDP with 67 seats (from 41). See the tables in Braunthal, *Parties and Politics in Modern Germany*, 55, 57.

100. Schwarz runs through all conceivable alternative configurations at great length in *Die Ära Adenauer. Epochenwechsel*, 225–32.

101. Schwarz, *Staatsmann*, 678–79.

102. Brentano, Aufz., "Grundlagen der Außenpolitik der vergangenen 12 Jahren," Sept. 30, 1961: ACDP, NL Gerstenmaier, I-210-017/1. See also Brentano's comments to the CDU's Bundestag caucus, Oct. 12, 1961: ACDP, VIII-001-1009/1.

103. See the FDP's draft paper of Oct. 12, 1961, and the Koalitionsvereinbarung of Oct. 20, 1961: ACDP, NL Gerstenmaier, I-210-017/1 and ACDP, VIII-001-290/2. Neither paper included phrasing explicitly supporting or rejecting the Hallstein Doctrine, which greatly angered the FDP's firebrand speaker and former chairman Thomas Dehler. FDP-Bundeshauptausschuß, Oct. 21, 1961, p. 16: ADL, A12-38, A12-39.

104. See the remarks by Siegfried Zoglmann in the FDP's caucus meeting of Oct. 19, 1961, ADL, A040-739, p. 8.

105. Dennert, *Entwicklungshilfe geplant oder verwaltet?*, 51–52. On the Foreign Office objections to a Europe ministry, see Brentano to Adenauer, Oct. 21, 1961: Baring, *Sehr verehrter Herr Bundeskanzler!*, 357–61. For Erhard's threat, see CDU-Fraktionsvorstand, Nov. 3, 1961, pp. 1–2: VIII-001-1503/4; also Hentschel, *Ludwig Erhard*, 382–83.

106. See the discussions of the FDP-Fraktion on Oct. 20 and Oct. 25, 1961, both in ADL, A040-738. By the latter date, many in the caucus rejected the CDU's offer of keeping Brentano but installing an FDP man in the Foreign Office as a third state secretary.

107. Brentano to Adenauer, Oct. 28, 1961, in Baring, *Sehr verehrter Herr Bundeskanzler!*, 363–66. For an account of the events leading to Brentano's resignation, see Schwarz, *Staatsmann*, 689–93.

108. Seydoux, *Dans l'intimité franco-allemande*, 43–44.

109. Joachim Besser, "Die Politik als Schachspiel. Gerhard Schröder tut nur überlegte Züge," *Kölner Stadt-Anzeiger*, Aug. 29, 1964.

110. For CDU concerns about Schröder's alleged softness on Berlin, see the meeting of the CDU-Fraktion, Nov. 2, 1961: ACDP, VIII-001-1009/1. President Lübke attempted to block Schröder's nomination; see Krone, *Tagebücher 1945–1961*, 549.

111. For an example of serious CDU attacks against Schröder's Berlin policy, see the summary of a meeting of the Bundestag's Foreign Affairs Committee, Apr. 19, 1962: BAK, NL Brentano, Bd. 159, Bl. 194–204. By the summer of 1962, Adenauer himself was quite unhappy with Schröder; see Globke to Krone, July 27, 1962: ACDP, NL Krone, I-028-011/3.

112. Regierungserklärung, Nov. 29, 1961, printed in *DzD* IV/7, 1015–16. Ludwig Erhard, vice-chancellor and minister of economics, read the speech aloud to the Bundestag. "In the Soviet-occupied zone, the overwhelming majority of the people reject not only the regime, but also the existence of a separate German rump state," read Erhard—words that brought applause from the entire house.

113. On Carstens's rapid climb within the Foreign Office, see "Sprung nach vorn," *Der Spiegel*, July 20, 1960, 13–15 (where he is identified as a "Hallstein-Doktrinär"). As early as September 1959, Adenauer and Brentano were planning to phase out other top officials so Carstens could move up. Adenauer to Brentano, Sept. 29, 1959: BAK, NL Brentano, Bd. 157, Bl. 268.

114. Kilian also emphasizes the centrality of Carstens; see *Hallstein-Doktrin*, 361–65.

115. "Milliarden in den Busch?," *Der Spiegel*, May 16, 1962, 29. Klaus Bodemer (*Entwicklungshilfe*, 106) observes that this was wishful thinking on Scheel's part. Scheel's interviewers were equally skeptical.

116. The most important defection from the Foreign Office was Horst Dumke, the sole desk officer for development aid from 1958 to 1961. For an example of the more instrumental view prevailing in the Foreign Office after Dumke's departure, see Abt. 8 (Sachs), Aufz., Nov. 7, 1961: PA/AA, B 33, Bd. 215.

117. Dennert, *Entwicklungshilfe geplant oder verwaltet?*, 51–55. The ministry's two principle functions were to manage Bonn's technical aid programs and to chair the sessions of the Steering Committee.

118. Letter from the Economics Ministry to the members of the Steering Committee, Oct. 12, 1961: BAK, B 213, Bd. 1517. The Foreign Office had even tried to get the amount raised from DM 40 million to DM 80 million for foreign policy reasons, but this suggestion met the determined objection of the Finance Ministry. Lenkungsausschuß, 25. Sitzung, Sept. 29, 1961: ibid.

119. See the conversation between Carstens and Bonn's ambassador to Accra, Karl Heinz Lüders, Oct. 10, 1961: PA/AA, B 2, Bd. 88, Bl. 113. The total amount envisioned by the Foreign Office in the near term was closer to DM 90 million.

120. This idea, too, originated with Ambassador Lüders; see his comments to the Lenkungsausschuß, 32. Sitzung, Jan. 23, 1962, p. 1: BAK, B 213, Bd. 1518.

121. Lenkungsausschuß, 38. Sitzung, Apr. 17, 1962, pp. 6–8: BAK, B 213, Bd. 1519.

122. In the spring of 1961, Cambodia had invited the Federal Republic to establish a consulate in Phnom Penh; yet Adenauer's government had not acted on this, since Cambodia refused to give assurances that it would decline to accept an East German consulate in the future. DG Bangkok (Lankes) 41, Mar. 16, 1962: PA/AA, B 38, Bd. 351.

123. The figure of DM 1.5 million was raised in the conversations of the Steering Committee, cited in n. 124 below. The nature of Bassler's threat is clear from a handwritten note from Ref. 700, Mar. 20, 1962: PA/AA, B 38, Bd. 351.

124. For Bassler's reports, see telegrams from DG Saigon of Apr. 7 and 9, 1962, in PA/AA, B 38, Bd. 351; and from DG Bangkok, Apr. 25, 1962, citissime: PA/AA, B 38, Bd. 354. See also Lenkungsausschuß, 38. Sitzung, Apr. 17, 1962, pp. 2–3: BAK, B 213, Bd. 1519; also BMZ (Klamser), Aufz., Apr. 16, 1962: ibid. Bassler did *not* raise the offer of DM 15 million during his conversations with Sihanouk; this was discussed in lower-level conversations. This helped disguise the blatant nature of the bribe.

125. The Cambodian delegation in Bonn expressed astonishment that they had come all this way to discuss a *loan* of DM 15 million; they insisted that Bassler had promised them a *gift* of that amount! For a summary of the negotiations, see Bundesministerium für Wirtschaft, Bericht, July 9, 1962, and Lenkungsausschuß, 44. Sitzung, July 13, 1962: both in BAK, B 213, Bd. 1520.

126. Although the Federal Republic was one of Iraq's most important oil cus-

tomers, Adenauer's government avoided exploiting this as a means of exerting pressure, so as not to antagonize West German industry. US Baghdad A-358, June 26, 1962, confidential: NARA, RG 59, CDF, 662B.87.

127. US Bonn (Dowling) A-1556, June 21, 1962, confidential: NARA, RG 59, CDF, 602.62B87. For purposes of smooth reading, the implied words "the" and "was" were inserted before "Iraqi" and "not giving," respectively.

128. On the particular reasons for Qassem's annoyance, see DG Baghdad (Bargen), Sept. 29, 1962, vertraulich: PA/AA, B 2, Bd. 86, Bl. 415–16. At long last Bargen did receive assurances from the Iraqis that *no* exequatur would be issued to the East German consul; word of this leaked to the West German press, despite Bargen's promise to keep it confidential. Bargen to Carstens, July 12, 1962: ibid., Bl. 383–86.

129. The record of Adenauer's press tea with ten German journalists on June 18, 1962, does not show the chancellor explicitly advocating this solution. However, two press articles the following day indicated that high-level government sources were considering a reversal on the question of consular relations. These articles otherwise reflect precisely the points raised by the chancellor about Iraq, Ceylon, and Dahomey. Adenauer, *Teegespräche 1961–63*, 217–18; "Hallstein-Doktrin als Ballast," *Weser-Kurier* (Bremen), June 19, 1962; "Überprüft Bonn die Hallstein-Doktrin?," *Der Mittag* (Düsseldorf), June 19, 1962.

130. Abt. 5 (Haeften), Aufz., July 9, 1962: PA/AA, B 80, Bd. 365.

131. Carstens, Vermerk, Nov. 9, 1962: PA/AA, B 2, Bd. 87, Bl. 284; Carstens to DG Jakarta, Nov. 19, 1962: PA/AA, B 80, Bd. 374.

132. On the Schröder-Sukarno meeting, see DG Bangkok 208, Nov. 24, 1962: PA/AA, B 80, Bd. 374. On the conversations in the Steering Committee in March 1963, see BAK, B 213, Bd. 1522.

133. Even in the early 1960s, this problem was evident to critics of the Hallstein Doctrine. See, for example, the letter from Marcel Schulte (editor-in-chief of the *Frankfurter Neue Presse*) to Brentano, June 18, 1961: PA/AA, B 1, Bd. 118a.

134. Syria had withdrawn from the UAR in October 1961; it immediately "demoted" the East German consulate in Damascus to a trade mission. Ref. 708, Aufz., Nov. 23, 1961: PA/AA, B 12, Bd. 120. A minor incident with Mali arose in early 1963 when the East German trade mission began issuing visas for travel to the GDR; the Foreign Office decided to pass over this quietly. See PA/AA, B 38, Bd. 108.

135. Ernst Majonica, "Der Spaltervertrag und die Neutralen," *Deutschland-Union-Dienst*, Aug. 7, 1962, published in *DzD* IV/8, 908–10; Gerhard Schröder, interview with dpa, Aug. 8, 1962, in *DzD* IV/8, 916–17.

136. Strobel, "Die Schröder-Doktrin," *Deutsche Zeitung* (Köln), Aug. 9, 1962; "Klare Verhältnisse," *Rheinischer Merkur*, Aug. 17, 1962.

137. Eberhard Bitzer, "FDP über die Äußerungen Schröders verstimmt," *FAZ*, Aug. 10, 1962. See also Karl Hermann Flach, "Schröder-Doktrin," *Frankfurter Rundschau*, Aug. 15, 1962, and Wolfgang Schollwer, *FDP im Wandel*, 65. For a summary of the CDU's response, see "FDP-Kritik an Schröder zurückgewiesen," *Stuttgarter Nachrichten*, Aug. 10, 1962.

138. Fritz Erler, chairman of the SPD caucus, wrote to Scheel on September 14, 1962, asking whether development aid might be used in this way. By this date, the Foreign Office was already expressing its opposition to this plan; see Schröder to Heinrich Windelen, Sept. 14, 1962. Both in AdsD, NL Erler, Bd. 58.

139. DG Brussels/EEC (Harkort) 1339, Nov. 14, 1962: PA/AA, B 10, Bd. 652. Thanks to Jeffrey Vanke for this document. Interestingly, the SPD's point man on development aid, Hans-Jürgen Wischnewski, strongly supported the Foreign Office's position; see "Anerkennung und EWG-Assoziierung," *SPD-Mitteilung für die Presse*, Nov. 20, 1962.

140. State Secretary Lahr, who had unveiled this policy in Brussels, admitted that the point was merely to deter associated African governments from imprudent behavior toward the GDR; he did not expect that Bonn's threat would need to be carried out in practice. AF Bonn (Margerie) tel. 5907–10, Nov. 22, 1962, réservé, and tel. 5975–79, Nov. 28, 1962: both in MAE, EU 61–70, RFA Z215. On the German retreat, see DG Brussels/EEC (Harkort) 1500, Dec. 10, 1962: PA/AA, B 2, Bd. 75, Bl. 519–22.

141. For the note, see *DzD* IV/9, 16–17. The responses of the Allies were identical to those of 1957: France and the United States strongly encouraged a break in relations, while Britain said it would *understand* such a step, and would not advise against. DG Washington (Knappstein) 106, Jan. 11, 1963; DG Paris (Blankenhorn) 71, Jan. 12, 1963; DG London (Etzdorf) 36, Jan. 12, 1963: all in PA/AA, B 33, Bd. 354.

142. Initially, several desks at the Foreign Office and the Economics Ministry wanted to abrogate the treaty without notice; but such a unilateral action would have had no legal basis, and it was decided that Bonn should give six months' notice in accord with the terms of the treaty. See PA/AA, B 33, Bd. 354. Some $4 million in German property was confiscated by Cuba following the termination of the treaty; see Ref. I B 2, Aufz., Feb. 29, 1964: ibid., Bd. 355.

143. Spreti to Carstens, Feb. 11, 1963: PA/AA, B 33, Bd. 355.

144. The position of the SPD is especially noteworthy: Franz Barsig, the party's spokesman, observed that "It would be in the mutual interest of the Federal Government and the Social Democratic opposition to undertake all appropriate preventive measures jointly in order to prevent a diplomatic upgrading of the Pankow regime." *SPD-Mitteilung für die Presse*, Jan. 15, 1963, 1–2.

CHAPTER SIX

1. In recent years, many scholars have identified the Cuban Missile Crisis and its aftermath as a crucial turning point, heralding the end of Cold War confrontation over the status quo in Europe. See Gaddis, *We Now Know*; Trachtenberg, *A Constructed Peace*; Wenger, "Der lange Weg zur Stabilität."

2. Schwarz, *Adenauer. Der Staatsmann* (hereafter *Staatsmann*), 814–16.

3. Washington and London did, in fact, respond with dismay. Conze, *Die gaullistische Herausforderung*, 266–75; Hölscher, "Krisenmanagement in Sachen EWG"; Schwarz, *Staatsmann*, 816–26.

4. Koerfer, *Kampf ums Kanzleramt*; Lappenküper, "'Ich bin wirklich ein guter Europäer.'"

5. On the preamble, see Schwarz, *Die Ära Adenauer. Epochenwechsel*, 295–96.

6. Hoppe, *Zwischen Teilhabe und Mitsprache*, 132–33.

7. Although the opening to Eastern Europe was undertaken with the blessing of the Kennedy administration, Schröder's policy did not merely ape the American line on détente. Instead, his "policy of movement" more closely resembled the older American "wedge" strategy of playing off the satellites against Moscow. Even Schröder's choice of terms—with the emphasis on *movement*—represented a mild rebuke of

the seeming American willingness to accept a hardening of the status quo in Europe. This is quite evident from Schröder's words to Secretary of State Dean Rusk on Sept. 20, 1963: *AAPD* 1963, 1158–73 (esp. 1159). See also Eibl, *Politik der Bewegung*, 415–18.

8. Lindemann, "Anfänge einer neuen Ostpolitik?"

9. See Schröder's remarks on this point during an interview with dpa, Mar. 7, 1963, in Jacobsen and Tomala, *Bonn—Warschau 1945–1991*, 118. For a fuller exposition of the Foreign Office arguments, see Krapf, Runderlaß, Dec. 11, 1963: PA/AA, B 38, Bd. 34.

10. The Schröder quote comes from an internal "Arbeitsbesprechung über Fragen der deutschen Politik gegenüber den osteuropäischen Volksdemokratien am 23./24. Juli 1964" (drafted Aug. 5), vertraulich, p. 2: PA/AA, B 150, Bd. 34. He had already made a similar point to the CDU Bundestag caucus on Mar. 10, 1964: ACDP, VIII-001-1009/3, pp. 307–8.

11. Brentano to Schröder, July 10, 1963: ACDP, NL Birrenbach, Bd. 11/2.

12. Text of the Limited Test Ban Treaty in *Department of State Bulletin* 49, no. 1259 (Aug. 12, 1963): 239–40. The "all states" clause was especially upsetting to the West Germans in light of their difficult experiences in the United Nations. Soviet bloc nations and also many nonaligned countries sought to open multilateral treaties, organizations, and conferences to "all states," while the West preferred the more restrictive clause "member states and members of special organizations" in order to keep out nonrecognized states like the GDR and the People's Republic of China. Trying to persuade nonaligned states not to vote in favor of the "all states" clause had become a major preoccupation of West German officials in intergovernmental organizations. See, for example, evidence of Bonn's annoyance with Egypt for voting to open the Vienna Consular Convention to "all states": Abt. V (Haeften), Aufz., Apr. 1, 1963: PA/AA, B 80, Bd. 373.

13. This point can be inferred from Washington's efforts to ensure that the GDR could be considered legally bound by the treaty, even as the United States publicly insisted that East Germany (as a nonstate) could not join. See DepSta to US London 996, Aug. 12, 1963, confidential, immediate: NARA, RG 59, ANF 63, Box 3898 (Pol 16 E Ger); also comments by the State Department's legal adviser during the Adenauer-Rusk conversation of Aug. 10: *AAPD* 1963, 976–85, esp. 982–84.

14. See Ulbricht's statement to the Volkskammer, July 31, 1963: *DzD* IV/9, 589.

15. Trachtenberg, *A Constructed Peace*, 383–87.

16. Pautsch, "Im Sog der Entspannungspolitik," 130–31, 151. On the chancellor's threat to resign, see Schwarz, *Staatsmann*, 849.

17. Rusk statement of Aug. 12, 1963, published in *Department of State Bulletin* 49, no. 1262 (Sept. 2, 1963): 353. By this time a long string of U.S. officials had rushed to Bonn, including Secretary of Defense Robert McNamara and Rusk himself. Pautsch, "Im Sog der Entspannungspolitik," 131–39, 141–46.

18. In the fall of 1963, the Soviets were pushing for a nonaggression treaty between NATO and the Warsaw Pact. Also under consideration was an exchange of ground observation posts in the front-line countries, designed to reassure each side about the impossibility of a surprise attack. See *AAPD* 1963.

19. Krone, "Aufzeichnungen zur Deutschland- und Ostpolitik 1954–1969," 178. This phrase has been picked up repeatedly in the writings of Hans-Peter Schwarz.

20. Presently it is unclear whether the United States deliberately withheld infor-

mation from the Federal Republic regarding the shape of the Test Ban Treaty. This would hardly have been surprising; on an earlier occasion (in April 1962) the Adenauer government had shown a penchant for leaking to the press American proposals that it did not like. Mayer, "Adenauer and Kennedy," 93–95 (which tends to be harder on Kennedy than on Adenauer).

21. See Schröder's comments to McGeorge Bundy, the U.S. national security adviser, on Sept. 20: *AAPD* 1963, 1150–51.

22. One of the first open confrontations within the CDU caucus on this topic came in the meeting of October 2, 1963, with Schröder defending the policy of détente and Karl Theodor von und zu Guttenberg (CSU) calling for a "power center in Western Europe" independent of both the United States and the Soviet Union. Marcowitz, *Option für Paris?*, 163–64.

23. "The Americans are pursuing to some extent a downright devious course," wrote Guttenberg to Alois Mertes, a "Gaullist" posted to the West German embassy in Moscow, on Aug. 14, 1963: BA, NL Guttenberg, Bd. 68, Bl. 213. For a sample of Mertes's views, see his letter to Josef Jansen on Sept. 26, 1963: ACDP, NL Jansen, I-149-5/1.

24. Deutscher Bundestag, 4. WP, 90. Sitzung: *Sten. Ber.*, 4192–4209; quotes from 4193 and 4194–95. Erhard did not directly praise "patriotism" as a worthy value; he used a more cautious vocabulary, speaking of "community" (*Gemeinwesen*) and "the whole" (*das Ganze*).

25. This portion of the speech appears in *DzD* IV/9, 793–96.

26. Since the early 1960s, the term "Aufwertung" (which literally means "the adding of value to") had occasionally been used in diplomatic traffic to describe the GDR's efforts to obtain some form of greater prestige short of outright recognition. However, the term first leapt to the forefront of the government's political lexicon in late July and early August 1963, during the controversy over the Test Ban Treaty.

27. See especially Adenauer's comments in his press tea of June 18, 1962: *Teegespräche 1961–63*, 217–18; see also Werner Kilian's perceptive reading of this conversation in *Hallstein-Doktrin*, 323–24.

28. On the reception of Erhard's speech, see Hildebrand, *Von Erhard zur Großen Koalition*, 48–50.

29. Soell, *Fritz Erler*, pt. 8; remarks by Siegfried Zoglmann (FDP), November 1964, cited in Bouvier, *Zwischen Godesberg und Großer Koalition*, 214.

30. Carstens, Aufz., Dec. 18, 1963, geheim: *AAPD* 1963, 1656–58; Carstens, Vermerk, June 9, 1964, geheim: PA/AA, B 150, Bd. 30. As these memoranda show, the Foreign Office tended to focus its attention mainly on formal questions, such as the precise nature of the signatures on the agreements.

31. Erhard in the CDU-Fraktionsvorstand, Jan. 7, 1964, p. 2: ACDP, VIII-001-1504/2. Six weeks later, however, Erhard was complaining that the December 1963 arrangements with East Berlin had gone too far. CDU-Fraktion, Feb. 18, 1964: ACDP, VIII-001-1009/3, p. 265.

32. This attitude was reflected in, among other places, the many cartoons depicting the holiday passes as a "Trojan horse" that Ulbricht was riding to recognition. See, for example, the cartoons from the *Süddeutsche Zeitung*, *Die Welt*, and the *Deutsche Zeitung*, reprinted in *Der Spiegel*, Mar. 11, 1964, 26, 29, 30.

33. Karl-Hermann Flach, "Politik der Schwäche," *Frankfurter Rundschau*, Mar. 4, 1964, in *DzD* IV/10, 317–18; Brandt, *Begegnungen und Einsichten*, 101–7.

34. See the Allensbach poll data from January 1963, showing that 44 percent of West Germans agreed with the principle that Bonn should break diplomatic relations with any country that recognized the GDR, while only 20 percent disagreed. This pattern extended across party lines. US Bonn Airgram A-2375, May 9, 1963: NARA, RG 59, ANF 63, Box 4140 (Pol W Ger).

35. In a meeting of the FDP-Fraktion on Feb. 12, 1964, Oswald Kohut tried to persuade his colleagues to "say that the Hallstein Doctrine is senseless [*Unsinn*], that diplomatic relations should be renewed with the East bloc states, and that good diplomats should be sent there to win friends for Germany." Others in the caucus advised against this plan, and it took more than a year for FDP chairman Erich Mende to strike up a new initiative for diplomatic relations with Eastern Europe. ADL, A040-763.

36. Leading advocates of diplomatic relations with Israel included Bundestag President Eugen Gerstenmaier (CDU); Franz Böhm (CDU); Karl Mommer (SPD); and Chancellor Adenauer himself. For samples of their activities in 1962–63, see Vogel, *Der deutsch-israelische Dialog*, 216–52.

37. Blasius, "Geschäftsfreundschaft statt diplomatischer Beziehungen. Zur Israel-Politik 1962/63."

38. See Franz Böhm to his CDU colleague Ferdinand Friedensburg, Feb. 7, 1963: ACDP, NL Birrenbach, I-433-010/1. Böhm remarked that if Egypt recognized the GDR in retaliation for an exchange of West German and Israeli ambassadors, Bonn should respond by breaking relations with Egypt. Thus Böhm embraced the basic logic of the Hallstein Doctrine.

39. During a Bundestag debate on May 8, 1963, Schmid called upon Schröder to abandon the Hallstein Doctrine and establish diplomatic relations with Israel and the states of Eastern Europe. This was an abrupt deviation from the SPD's foreign policy line, and Schmid's statements received no backing from his colleagues. "Schröder verteidigt Hallstein-Doktrin," *Die Welt*, May 9, 1963.

40. For the fullest account of East German policy in 1961–62, emphasizing Ulbricht's differences with Khrushchev, see Lemke, *Berlinkrise*, chap. 4.

41. For East German hopes about setting off "a world movement" in favor of a peace treaty, see the protocol of the SED ZK's Außenpolitische Kommission, Aug. 31, 1961: BA-SAPMO, DY 30/IV 2/20, Bd. 8, Bl. 350–52.

42. Lemke, *Berlinkrise*, 207–15.

43. Algeria's behavior was particularly disappointing; the East Germans had hoped for diplomatic relations. Politbüro, Protokoll Nr. 6/63, Mar. 12, 1963, Anl. 5: BA-SAPMO, DY 30/J IV 2/2, Bd. 870. As for Yemen, the status of the consulate remained rather sketchy for most of the year. Bierbach, Leitungsvorlage, Sept. 17, 1963: MfAA, LS-A 23, Bl. 212–13.

44. "Thesen für den mündlichen Bericht des Genossen Staatssekretärs Winzer vor dem Staatsrat am 10. Juni 1963," June 7, 1963: MfAA, A 14819, Bl. 105–7.

45. Auswärtiger Ausschuß, 4. WP, 42. Sitzung (Nov. 27, 1963), 6: BT/PA. These numbers vary a bit from the information provided in Appendix 19 of Muth, *DDR-Außenpolitik*; in their statistics, East German diplomats tended to blur the line be-

tween government-level trade missions and chambers of commerce when classifying the offices in Latin America.

46. These numbers are calculated from Charts 20 and 21 of Auswärtiges Amt, *40 Jahre Außenpolitik der Bundesrepublik*.

47. Politbüro, Protokoll Nr. 27/63, Aug. 13, 1963, Anl. 1, pp. 3–4: BA-SAPMO, DY 30/J IV 2/2, Bd. 891.

48. Ibid., 6–9.

49. Admittedly, Prague's refusal had more to do with the "Berlin clause" than the question of the formal status of the trade mission. Lindemann, "Anfänge einer neuen Ostpolitik?," 73–96.

50. Politbüro, Protokoll Nr. 9/63, Apr. 2, 1963, Anl. 3: BA-SAPMO, DY 30/J IV 2/2, Bd. 873

51. For a general description of publicity events undertaken to advertise the Seven Point Plan, see the report by the Arbeitsgruppe Auslandsinformation, Aug. 20, 1963: BA-SAPMO, DY 30/IV A 2/20, Bd. 3.

52. Conversation Winzer/Botsio, Apr. 9, 1963: BA-SAPMO, DY 30/IV A 2/20, Bd. 795.

53. See the report by the Arbeitsgruppe Auslandsinformation, Aug. 20, 1963, cited in n. 51 above.

54. Schleicher and Schleicher, *Die DDR im südlichen Afrika*, 4–22, 36–44.

55. For details on West German–Portuguese military cooperation, see Carstens, Vermerk, Oct. 3, 1963, geheim: *AAPD* 1963, 1274–75; for Foreign Office attempts to explain this away in dealing with African leaders, see Ref. III A 1 (Keller), Runderlaß, Aug. 19, 1963: ibid., 1045–47.

56. For an indication of the Foreign Ministry's growing awareness of the need for targeted appeals, see the note from Kundermann to Neugebauer, June 28, 1963: MfAA, LS-A 21, Bl. 153.

57. Handwritten notes of the meeting of the Außenpolitische Kommission (des ZK der SED), July 5, 1963: BA-SAPMO, DY 30/IV A 2/20, Bd. 2, Bl. 8. On Ulbricht's prompting, see the protocol of the Leitungssitzung, July 10, 1963: MfAA, LS-A 21, Bl. 87.

58. Winzer, Aufz., "Durchbrechung der Hallstein-Doktrin," o. D. [Sept. 1963], p. 1, 36–39: BA-SAPMO, DY 30/IV A 2/20, Bd. 3. For a time the Foreign Ministry was enamored of an even more obscure target, British Guyana; see the Leitungsvorlage of the 2. Außereuropäische Abteilung, Aug. 7, 1963: MfAA, LS-A 22, Bl. 164–69. In all fairness, it should be noted that West German Foreign Office also considered British Guyana to be a promising venue for East Germany; see the documentation in PA/AA, B 38, Bd. 109.

59. Außenpol. Kommission, Protokoll der Beratung, Sept. 20, 1963: DY 30/IV 2/2.115, Bd. 4, Bl. 16–19.

60. Winzer, Aufz., "Durchbrechung der Hallstein-Doktrin," cited above: pp. 24–27, 30, 33.

61. Ibid., pp. 3, 39–40; on Algeria, see the handwritten notes of the meeting on Sept. 20, 1963: DY 30/IV A 2/20, Bd. 3, esp. the comments by Florin.

62. Meeting of Sept. 20, cited in n. 61 above.

63. Staritz, *Geschichte der DDR*, 211–17; Kopstein, *Politics of Economic Decline in East Germany*, 45–51.

64. This sum was calculated from a memo by the Staatliche Plankommission, Abt. Außenhandel, dated Feb. 19, 1965: BA-SAPMO, DY 30, Bd. 3665.

65. Politbüro, Protokoll Nr. 1/64, Jan. 7, 1964, Anl. 2: BA-SAPMO, DY 30/J IV 2/2, Bd. 916.

66. These figures derive from the Staatliche Plankommission document of Feb. 19, 1965, cited in n. 64 above. The delicacy of Leuschner's offers is indicated by the unwillingness of East German officials to put anything in writing. See p. 3 of the Leitungsvorlage of June 27, 1964: MfAA, LS-A 29, Bl. 580–88.

67. Harkort, Teilrunderlaß, May 3, 1966: IfZ, NL Böker, Außenpolitik. This document shows that in February 1965, Ceylon concluded a credit deal with the GDR worth $42.2 million, roughly equivalent to Leuschner's original offer of VM 200 million. Burma, too, eventually received its promised VM 60 million ($13 million) in an agreement signed in January 1966.

68. Kilian, *Hallstein-Doktrin*, 163.

69. For a general overview explaining the ethnic situation, see Clayton, *The Zanzibar Revolution and Its Aftermath*.

70. Case studies on the Zanzibar issue abound. See Engel and Schleicher, *Die beiden deutschen Staaten in Afrika*, 151–80; Schneppen, "Eine Insel und zwei deutsche Staaten"; and Kilian, *Hallstein-Doktrin*, 171–87.

71. DG Colombo (Ramisch) 23, Feb. 12, 1964, citissime mit Vorrang: PA/AA, B 80, Bd. 373.

72. For this quote (in English), see DG Colombo (Ramisch) Ber. 171/64, Feb. 27, 1964, p. 6: PA/AA, B 38, Bd. 112. Auer hotly disputed the Ceylonese version of his comments; he maintained that during his December conversations in Colombo, he had explained that the "consulates" in Cairo and Jakarta were not really consulates, since they lacked an exequatur. DG Hong Kong, Mar. 3, 1964: ibid.

73. The "reunification desk," introduced in Chapter 2 above, did not simply disappear; it remained responsible for *coordinating* the overall isolation campaign. By the mid-1960s, however, much of its attention was devoted to other issues, such as the Christmas and Easter passes to East Berlin. Useful organization charts of the Foreign Office appear at the back of *AAPD* 1963.

74. Jansen to Mertes, Dec. 9, 1964, p. 1: ACDP, NL Jansen, I-149-VI/1.

75. For this reason, Carstens judged in April 1963 that it would be counterproductive to circulate to the Bundestag's Foreign Affairs Committee a Foreign Office memorandum surveying all the GDR's foreign missions. Ref. II 1 (Oncken), Aufz., "Tätigkeit von Referat II 1 in der Zeit vom 5.-20. April," Apr. 20, 1963: PA/AA, B 38, Bd. 73.

76. Jansen, Aufz., "Maßnahmen der Bundesregierung im Falle der Zulassung eines SBZ-Generalkonsulats in Ceylon," Feb. 14, 1964, p. 3: PA/AA, B 38, Bd. 112. For examples of warning signs from India (which Ambassador Duckwitz himself did not take all that seriously, although the Foreign Office did), see DG New Delhi 54, Feb. 3, 1964, vertraulich: PA/AA, B 150, Bd. 22.

77. Lahr to DG Colombo, Feb. 7, 1964, citissime: PA/AA, B 38, Bd. 112. Although the instructions were signed by Lahr, this copy shows several corrections and additions in Carstens's handwriting.

78. On these terms, which were retroactively approved by the Foreign Office, the Chancellor's Office, and President Lübke (who held formal responsibility for appointing new chiefs of mission), see US Dar-es-Salaam (Leonhart) 1115, Feb. 8, 1964,

confidential, priority: NARA, RG 59, ANF 64–66, Box 3043 (Pol 16 Zan); also Jansen, Aufz., Feb. 11, 1964, geheim: *AAPD* 1964, 188–89.

79. Both phrases originated with Bonn's ambassador to Tanganyika, Herbert Schroeder. US Dar-es-Salaam (Leonhart) 1137, Feb. 10, 1964, confidential: Box 3043, cited in n. 78 above.

80. Duncan Sandys at the Foreign Office remarked that it was "very naughty of them but they always take a special interest in ex-German territories." US London 3941, Feb. 14, 1964, confidential. For the "highly favorable" reaction in Washington, see DepSta to Bonn 2240, Feb. 17, confidential. Both in Box 3043, cited in n. 78 above.

81. DepSta to Bonn 2300, Feb. 21, 1964, confidential, immediate: Box 3043, cited in n. 78 above. On the February 19 cabinet meeting, see Osterheld, *Außenpolitik*, 72.

82. Osterheld to Erhard, Feb. 17, 1964: BA, B 136, Bd. 6290. For Schröder's advice, see DG Dar-es-Salaam 51, Feb. 19, 1964, geheim, citissime mit Vorrang: PA/AA, B 150, Bd. 23.

83. East German housing experts arrived in Zanzibar within two weeks of the revolution to discuss construction projects on the island. Ref. I B 3, Vermerk, Feb. 4, 1964: PA/AA, B 150, Bd. 22.

84. DG Colombo (Ramisch) 28, Feb. 17, 1964, vertraulich: PA/AA, B 150, Bd. 23; DepSta to US Bonn 2276, Feb. 19, 1964, confidential, priority: NARA, RG 59, ANF 64–66, Box 506 (Aid [Ger W] Ceylon). Ramisch and the State Department both pointed ahead to the 1965 elections in Ceylon, noting that a strong West German presence would help serve as a moderating influence.

85. Jansen, Aufz., Feb. 14, 1964, cited in n. 76 above. State Secretary Carstens seemed a bit more hesitant about this in comments to U.S. ambassador George McGhee on Feb. 17; but Carstens, too, remarked that he did not see how West German aid could continue under these circumstances. US Bonn 2940, Feb. 18, 1964, confidential: NARA, RG 59, ANF 64–66, Box 2205 (Pol Ger E—Cey).

86. For the quote, and these ideas on how to supplement (*ergänzen*) the Hallstein Doctrine, see Ref. I B 4 (Dröge, Schlagintweit, Hofmann), Aufz., "Maßnahmen gegen eine faktische Aufwertung der SBZ," Feb. 17, 1964: PA/AA, B 38, Bd. 3.

87. Abt. III (Pauls), Aufz., "Wirtschaftsbeziehungen zu Ceylon; hier: Möglich-keiten der Einschränkung der Handelsbeziehungen und der Entwicklungshilfe," Feb. 18, 1964: PA/AA, B 38, Bd. 112.

88. The Ceylonese ambassador raised this objection as early as Feb. 12, when he learned of Bonn's démarches in Colombo. Jansen, Vermerk, Feb. 12, 1964: ibid.

89. "Doppelte Moral?," *Frankfurter Rundschau*, Feb. 20, 1964. On the media re-action more generally, see AF Bonn (Margerie) tel. 1533–38, Feb. 20, 1964: MAE, EU 61–70, RFA Z211.

90. See the official statement published by the Bundesregierung on Feb. 19, 1964: *DzD* IV/10, 260–61. This argument, repeated endlessly by West German diplomats in the following two years, glossed over the fact that Cambodia, Iraq, and Yemen had *also* initiated consular relations with the GDR since 1961.

91. Comments by the government's deputy spokesman (Krueger), Feb. 19, 1964, pp. 13–14: BPA, Pressemagazin, Jan.–June 1964.

92. In many ways, though, Bonn's treatment of Cuba in early 1963 presaged this line of thinking. As described at the end of Chapter 5, the Foreign Office deliberately treated Cuba more harshly in 1963 than it had Yugoslavia in 1957. At the time, the

Countries Department prepared a draft statement arguing that the Belgrade precedent was irrelevant; but the Legal Department suggested use of the term "parallel" rather than "precedent." Abt. V (Meyer-Lindenberg) to Abt. I, Mar. 14, 1963: PA/AA, B 33, Bd. 354.

93. Meeting of the "SBZ-Referate," Feb. 19, 1964: PA/AA, B 80, Bd. 372. Bonn informed the Allies right away of its plans for augmenting the Hallstein Doctrine; see AF Bonn (Margerie) tel. 1672–77, Feb. 27, 1964, réservé: MAE, EU 61–70, RFA Z211. The French embassy was quite underwhelmed by the actual measures taken against Ceylon.

94. Ref. I B 3 (Steltzer) to Ref. II 1, Apr. 16, 1964: PA/AA, B 33, Bd. 561. Since East German trade missions already existed in Ghana, Mali, and Sudan, this was a difficult resolution to enforce.

95. Carstens to DG Nicosia 103, Oct. 22, 1964, vertraulich, citissime: PA/AA, B 150, Bd. 39.

96. See, for example, the note from a junior official at the Southeast Asia desk (Fröwis) to the deputy director of Abt. II (Reinkemeyer), Mar. 13, 1964: PA/AA, B 38, Bd. 3.

97. Ref. I B 4, Aufz., "Maßnahmen gegen eine faktische Aufwertung der SBZ," Feb. 17, 1964, p. 3, cited in n. 86 above.

98. Böker, Vermerk, Mar. 3, 1964: PA/AA, B 38, Bd. 3. (This is a draft for part 3 of a circular explaining Bonn's new approach.)

99. For the rejection of Böker's suggestions, Abt. III (Pauls), Aufz., Mar. 11, and Abt. III (Sachs) to Abt. II, Mar. 26, 1964, pp. 1–2: both PA/AA, B 38, Bd. 3.

100. Carstens, Runderlaß, "Alleinvertretungs-Politik der Bundesregierung; hier: neue Maßnahmen zu ihrer Durchsetzung," June 18, 1964: *AAPD* 1964, 688–91. The switch from the designation "nonrecognition" (*Nichtanerkennung*) to "sole representation" (*Alleinvertretung*) was Schröder's cosmetic contribution: he wanted a more positive term to describe Bonn's policy. For the same reason, he avoided use of the term "Hallstein Doctrine." See his comments during the Ambassadors' Conference on the afternoon of April 21, 1964: *AAPD* 1964, 465; also Schröder's instructions as conveyed by Krapf, July 16, 1964: PA/AA, B 38, Bd. 34.

101. Clayton, *The Zanzibar Revolution and Its Aftermath*, 112–15.

102. Frightened at the possibility of an invasion from Zanzibar, which was receiving Soviet bloc weaponry, Nyerere pleaded for West German military assistance in early April. Abt. I (Jansen), Aufz., "Tanganjikische Besorgnisse über politische Entwicklungen in Sansibar," Apr. 7, 1964, geheim: *AAPD* 1964, 392–94.

103. On the acceptability of a trade mission, see Carstens to Schröder, Apr. 30, 1964, geheim: PA/AA, B 150, Bd. 27. The argument against a trade mission, elaborated by the sub-Saharan Africa desk (Ref. I B 3), warned that this would set a bad example for other governments of East Africa. Böker, Aufz., May 4, 1964, vertraulich: PA/AA, B 150, Bd. 28.

104. Nyerere first broached this officially with the West German ambassador in late June, though the idea had been floating around for at least a month. US Dar-es-Salaam 2187, May 27, 1964, confidential: NARA, RG 59, ANF 64–66, Box 2204 (Pol 16 Ger E); DG Dar-es-Salaam 182, June 25, vertraulich, citissime mit Vorrang: PA/AA, B 150, Bd. 31.

105. In conversations with Tanzania's foreign minister in Bonn in early May, offi-

cials made it clear that nothing more formal than an East German trade mission would be acceptable. Böker, Plurex 1738, May 6, 1964, geheim, citissime: PA/AA, B 150, Bd. 28.

106. On both the fait accompli and Schroeder's advice, see DG Dar-es-Salaam 183, June 26, 1964, vertraulich, citissime: PA/AA, B 150, Bd. 31.

107. This article appeared in the English-language newspaper *The Nationalist*, which acted as the semiofficial voice of Nyerere's government. The authorities on Zanzibar reacted to this stinging editorial by banning *The Nationalist* on the island— an edict that Tanganyikan security forces overruled. This episode demonstrates the extent to which the German Question had become a vehicle of the rivalry between Nyerere and Karume. DG Dar-es-Salaam 185, June 29, 1964, citissime: PA/AA, B 34, Bd. 511.

108. The quote (in English) came during a conversation with Hans Steltzer, head of Bonn's sub-Saharan Africa desk. DG Dar-es-Salaam 187, July 3, 1964, geheim, citissime: PA/AA, B 150, Bd. 32.

109. See Carstens's instructions for Ambassador Schroeder, Aug. 11, 1964, vertraulich: *AAPD* 1964, 957–58.

110. US Bonn (Mouser) Airgram A-388, Aug. 21, 1964, confidential: NARA, RG 59, ANF 64–66, Box 2227 (Pol Ger W—Tanzan). This report cites articles in the *FAZ*, the *General-Anzeiger*, and *Die Welt*.

111. Specifically, Bonn had demanded that no East German delegation be invited to Zambia's independence celebrations. DG Salisbury (Ringelmann) 51 and 53, Aug. 21 and 22, respectively: PA/AA, B 38, Bd. 105.

112. "Mit der Gießkanne," *Der Spiegel*, Dec. 1, 1964, 47–65 (quote from 59); Bodemer, *Entwicklungshilfe*, 112.

113. Schröder made this analogy during a conference with the heads of West Germany's trade missions in Eastern Europe. "Arbeitsbesprechung über Fragen der deutschen Politik gegenüber den osteuropäischen Volksdemokratien am 23./24. Juli 1964" (drafted Aug. 5), p. 1: PA/AA, B 150, Bd. 34.

114. The concept "Vorfeld der Anerkennung" was first introduced in the spring of 1964. Playing on this analogy, Ambassador Duckwitz criticized Bonn's new tactical approach at an Ambassadors' Conference in late April: there are situations "where one should give up the approach, if this helps one maintain the main battle line all the better." Protocol of the discussion on the morning of April 21, 1964, geheim, p. 6: PA/AA, B 150, Bd. 27.

115. Abt. II, Aufz., "Gegenmaßnahmen im Falle der Herstellung von Beziehungen zwischen dritten Ländern und Pankow (sog. Mob.-Plan)," July 17, 1964, vertraulich: *AAPD* 1964, 856–62.

116. Abt. I (Jansen), Aufz., "Internationale Konferenzen der Entwicklungsländer und die Deutschland-Frage," July 20, 1964: PA/AA, B 1, Bd. 219.

117. US Bonn Airgram A-1855, Apr. 17, 1964, confidential: NARA, RG 59, ANF 64–66, Box 2207 (Pol 1 Ger W), pp. 9–10. This document provides a fourteen-page evaluation of the Hallstein Doctrine drafted by Jim Sutterlin and Robert Davis of the U.S. embassy's political division.

118. Hausbesprechung, "Die kommende Neutralisten-Konferenz," Apr. 23, 1964 (protocol by Ref. I B 4 from May 8): PA/AA, B 38, Bd. 187. Which particular states fell into the "dangerous" category varied slightly from month to month.

119. DG New Delhi (Duckwitz) 127, Mar. 27, 1964, geheim: PA/AA, B 150, Bd. 25.

120. For background on Erhard's unification policy in this period, see Kosthorst, "Sowjetische Geheimpolitik in Deutschland?," 260–64.

121. During an in-house conversation on the "Germany Initiative," Rusk "noted with some resignation that he had been trying to get Berlin and Germany off the front pages for over three years and now that we had succeeded the Germans seem to want to put it back." Conversation of Apr. 21, 1964, secret: *FRUS* 1964–68/XV, 63. See also Abt. II (Krapf), Aufz., Apr. 17, 1964, geheim: *AAPD* 1964, 439–45.

122. See the protocol of the working-level German-French consultations (the institution created by the Elysée Treaty of January 1963), Mar. 18, 1964, geheim: *AAPD* 1964, 355–65, especially Jansen's comments about Ceylon and Zanzibar. See also Jansen's letter to Knappstein, Mar. 24, 1964: ACDP, NL Jansen, I-149-VI/1; and DG Paris (Klaiber) 514, Mar. 24, 1964, vertraulich: PA/AA, B 150, Bd. 25.

123. The turnaround was most visible in London, where Harold Macmillan had once shown considerable exasperation with the question of East German recognition. Henning Hoff dates this reorientation to February 1963, when British leaders concluded that West German support was crucial in order to gain entry to the EEC; see Hoff, "Großbritannien und die DDR," 204–5. The Labour Party's change of heart was especially noteworthy, for as recently as 1961 the party had demanded a de facto recognition of the GDR. By the time Harold Wilson came to power at the head of a Labour cabinet in October 1964, he had been convinced by SPD caucus chairman Fritz Erler of just how strongly the leading West German parties felt about maintaining East Germany's isolation. See Erler to Christopher Emmett, Apr. 11, 1963: AdsD, NL Erler, Bd. 156; and Brandt and Erler comments in the SPD-Parteivorstand, Sept. 30, 1963, pp. 8–9: AdsD, SPD-PV.

124. Text in *DADDR* 1964, 1021–25; also *DzD* IV/10, 717–20.

125. For contemporary observations on this point, see US Berlin (Calhoun) 1591, June 13, 1964, priority, limited official use: NARA, RG 59, ANF 64–66, Box 2206 (Pol 21 Ger E—USSR); also DG Washington (Knappstein) 1820, June 16, 1964, geheim, cito: *AAPD* 1964, 684–87.

126. US Moscow (Kohler) 3755, June 13, 1964, vertraulich; US London (Jones) 6380, June 23, 1964, confidential: both in Box 2206, cited in n. 125 above); see also Abt. II (Reinkemeyer), Chi-Brief Betr.: "Sowjetische Pläne zur Aufwertung der SBZ in afro-asiatischen Ländern," Mar. 12, 1964, vertraulich: PA/AA, B 150, Bd. 24.

127. Quai (Puaux) to AF Washington tel. 13124, June 15, 1964, immediat: MAE, EU 61–70, RDA F146.

128. *Department of State Bulletin* 51, no. 1307 (July 13, 1964): 44–45.

129. Krapf, Runderlaß Dipex 3, June 30, 1964: PA/AA, B 38, Bd. 101.

130. Quai to AF Washington 15401, July 17, 1964: MAE, EU 61–70, RDA F111.

131. On the outcome of the German and Allied démarches, see Ref. II 1 (Oncken), Aufz., "Reaktion dritter Staaten auf Deutschland-Erklärung der Drei Mächte," Oct. 30, 1964, vertraulich: *AAPD* 1964, 1201–3. Especially interesting is the tabulation attached to the document, available in PA/AA, B 150, Bd. 39.

132. Abt. II (Krapf), Aufz., "SBZ-Aktivität im afro-asiatischen Bereich; hier: Reisen prominenter Vertreter des Regimes seit Januar 1964," Sept. 29, 1964, vertraulich: PA/AA, B 150, Bd. 37.

133. Außenpolitische Kommission, Protokoll Nr. 6/64, May 22, 1964, p. 3: BA-SAPMO, DY 30/IV 2/2.115, Bd. 5, Bl. 232–36.

134. Winzer, Vorlage für die Außenpolitische Kommission, "Weiteres Vorgehen der DDR bei der Vorbereitung und Durchführung der 2. Konferenz nichtpaktge-bunedener Staaten," Aug. 18, 1964, p. 3: BA-SAPMO, DY 30/IV 2/2.115, Bd. 6, Bl. 300–303.

135. See the two memoranda dated Sept. 4, 1964, distributed by the GDR to the conference participants: *DADDR* 12, 592–601, esp. 597–98.

136. See pp. 3–4 of the Abt. II memo of Sept. 29, 1964, cited in n. 132 above. For protocols of planning sessions for the Cairo Conference on July 1, July 29, and Sept. 3, see B 38, Bd. 136.

137. Abt. II (Krapf), Runderlaß: "Hausordnungen der SBZ-Vertretungen," July 16, 1964: PA/AA, B 80, Bd. 372. The details had been supplied by Argentina, which closed down the East German chamber of commerce office in Buenos Aires in September 1962.

138. US Belgrade (Kennan) to SecSta 1098, Feb. 19, 1963, confidential, priority: NRA, RG 59, ANF 63, Box 4145 (Pol W Ger). In conveying this information to Kennan, the Yugoslavs were essentially manipulating the United States to place pressure on West Germany.

139. Rusk to Schröder, Apr. 9, 1964: NARA, RG 59, ANF 64–66, Box 2231 (Pol Ger W-Yugo). American efforts to encourage a softer West German line toward Yugoslavia dated back to the fall of 1962, when congressional hostility toward Belgrade tied the hands of the Kennedy administration in its dealings with Tito. See, for example, DepSta (Rusk) to US Bonn 1469, Dec. 28, 1962, confidential, priority: NARA, RG 59, CDF, 662A.68.

140. Schröder to Rusk, Apr. 22, 1964, vertraulich: *AAPD* 1964, 470–74. According to West German information, Ceylonese politicians had been heavily lobbied by the Yugoslav government during the 1963 conference of the International Parliamentary Union, held in Belgrade. US Colombo 601, Apr. 9, 1964, confidential: NARA, RG 59, ANF 64–66, Box 2204 (Pol 16 Ger E).

141. "Anti-German propaganda by the Yugoslavs at the planned neutralist conference could damage us considerably," warned Abt. II (Krapf) in a note to Abt. V on Feb. 19, 1964, p. 4: PA/AA, B 150, Bd. 23. However, Krapf and most other officials hoped that progress on the Croatian émigré organizations would be enough to placate Belgrade.

142. Lahr/Nikezic conversation, Sept. 8, 1964, geheim: *AAPD* 1001–3.

143. Quote from "Lahrs geheime Mission," *Christ und Welt*, Sept. 11, 1964; see also "Warum gleich Lahr?," *Münchner Merkur*, Sept. 8.

144. On Wischnewski's close ties to the Algerian liberation movement, see his *Mit Leidenschaft und Augenmaß*, 105–23.

145. DG UN (von Braun), June 27, 1964, geheim: PA/AA, B 150, Bd. 31. See also US Bamako 11, July 2, 1964, confidential, and US Algiers 130, July 13, 1964, confidential: both in NARA, RG 59, ANF 64–66, Box 2204 (Pol 16 Ger E).

146. See Lahr's conversation with Wischnewski, July 31, 1964, and Carstens's conversation with an Algerian official on August 5: *AAPD* 1964, 908–10, 945–47.

147. For details on the agreement in the Steering Committee meeting, see Oct. 14,

1964, pp. 9–10; on the limited economic utility of the project, see Lenkungsausschuß, June 24, 1964, p. 17: BA, B 213, Bd. 1528 and Bd. 1527, respectively.

148. The Foreign Office was especially pleased at Nasser's reserve during Khrushchev's visit to Egypt in May 1964. See the discussions in the North Atlantic Council on this point, described in DG Paris/NATO (Sahm), June 10, 1964, vertraulich: PA/AA, B 150, Bd. 30. However, there was an additional layer of complexity to Nasser's German policy: he appeared to make use of Egypt's hegemonic position in Yemen to test the firmness of Bonn's nonrecognition policy from time to time. DG Taiz (Steffen) Ber. 274/64, May 1, 1964: PA/AA, B 38, Bd. 116.

149. Böker, Aufz., "Erwartungen der VAR-Regierung gegenüber der Bundesregierung im Zusammenhang mit der Neutralistenkonferenz," Sept. 28, 1964, vertraulich: PA/AA, B 150, Bd. 37. For a useful overview of Bonn's aid policies toward Egypt in 1963–64, see BMZ, Aufz., "Ägypten: Fortsetzung der Entwicklungshilfe," Nov. 24, 1964: BA, B 213, Bd. 1529.

150. For Erhard's invitation, see Referat Protokoll, Vermerk, June 18, 1964: PA/AA, B 150, Bd. 31.

151. On the cabinet's decision, see Böker, Plurex 1590 (to various German missions), Apr. 24, 1964, vertraulich: PA/AA, B 150, Bd. 27. By the late spring, the top party leaders in the Bundestag shared the government's view that there should be no public debates on Israel until after the Cairo Conference. See comments by Rainer Barzel in the CDU-Fraktion, May 25, 1964: ACDP, VIII-001-1009/3, p. 338; and by Fritz Erler in the SPD-Fraktion, June 9, 1964, in Weber, Hölscher, and Potthoff, *Die SPD-Fraktion im Deutschen Bundestag*, 3:473–74.

152. Carstens, Vermerk, "Zusammenkunft zwischen dem Bundeskanzler und dem israelischen Ministerpräsidenten Eshkol im Juni in den USA," Apr. 1, 1964, geheim: PA/AA, B 150, Bd. 26.

153. For details on the West German arms deliveries, see Abt. III (Pauls), Aufz., "Sonderprojekt der Ausrüstungshilfe 'Frank./Kol.,'" Oct. 21, 1964, streng geheim: *AAPD* 1964, 1164–67. On the origins of military cooperation between Bonn and Tel Aviv in 1961–62, see the notes by Carstens compiled for Schröder on Jan. 4, 1965: *AAPD* 1965, 6–12.

154. "Erhard and Schroeder don't even talk together," noted one State Department expert on Germany. "Memorandum for the Files: A German Government," May 27, 1964, confidential: NARA, RG 59, ANF 64–66, Box 2207 (Pol 1 Ger).

155. *Conference of Heads of State*, 346.

156. AF Bonn (Margerie) 6895–99, Oct. 20, 1964: MAE, EU 61–70, RDA F112.

157. See Böker's complaints to Fawzi on this score during their conversation of Oct. 9: *AAPD* 1964, 1144.

158. On the success of the démarches, see Ref. II 1, Aufz., Oct. 30, 1964, as cited above. The Foreign Office thanked *seventeen* governments for strongly supporting Bonn's position during the debate on "divided countries." Of these, more than half were Arab countries. Carstens, Drahterlaß 3733 Plurex, Oct. 28, 1964: PA/AA, B 80, Bd. 590.

159. On the marginality of the German Question at the Cairo Conference, see DG Cairo (Federer), Oct. 15, 1964: PA/AA, B 34, Bd. 563. The UN Conference on Trade and Development, which had met in Geneva earlier in 1964, helped set the tone for Cairo. In Geneva, the less developed countries had formed a loose grouping known as

the G-77, reflecting a strong "north-south" polarization. Mortimer, *Third World Coalition in International Politics*, 15–20.

160. Abt. II (Luedde-Neurath), Vermerk, Oct. 31, 1964: PA/AA, B 38, Bd. 106. This note shows that Carstens was not entirely sure how to greet this line of reasoning.

161. Böker, Aufz., Oct. 29, 1964, geheim, p. 4: PA/AA, B 150, Bd. 39.

162. Ref. I B 5, Aufz., Dec. 28, 1964: PA/AA, B 38, Bd. 115. Bonn warned Jakarta that a consulate in East Berlin would lead the Federal Republic to reexamine its relations with Indonesia. As usual, though, positive reinforcement came in the form of promises of more aid. By early 1965, the Foreign Office had concluded that Sukarno's days were numbered and that it would be best to appease him until his regime lost power. See the protocol of the second Hausbesprechung "Aktionsprogramm Indonesien," Jan. 11, 1965 (drafted Mar. 4): PA/AA, B 38, Bd. 114.

163. On Dahomey, see Böker's conversation with President Apithy, reported in DG Cairo 917, Oct. 10, 1964, vertraulich: AAPD, 1150–53. On Zambia, see Jansen to DG Lusaka, Oct. 7, 1964, vertraulich, cito: PA/AA, B 150, Bd. 38. On Kenya, see the reports by US Nairobi (Attwood) 922 of Oct. 9, 1964; 1051 of Oct. 24; and 1357 of Nov. 20: all confidential, all in NARA, RG 59, ANF 64–66, Box 2204 (Pol 16 Ger E).

164. A report by the emissary, Baron Dieter von Mirbach, reveals a shockingly overbearing negotiating style. See DG Nicosia 98, Nov. 30, 1964, vertraulich, citissime mit Vorrang: AAPD 1964, 1414–17.

165. Carstens to various Referate, Dec. 10, 1964, vertraulich: PA/AA, B 150, Bd. 42.

166. Böker, Aufz., Oct. 31, 1964, vertraulich, pp. 8–9: PA/AA, B 150, Bd. 39.

167. Abt. III (Pauls), Aufz., "Verhältnis von Außen- und Wirtschaftspolitik," Jan. 16, 1965: PA/AA, B 34, Bd. 628.

168. Abt. I (Jansen), Aufz., "Grundsatzentscheidung über Wiederaufnahme der deutschen Wirtschaftshilfe an Ceylon; hier: Testfall Zementfabrik Puttalam," Oct. 26, 1964: PA/AA, B 80, Bd. 373; Abt. II (Luedde-Neurath), Aufz., "Alleinvertretungspolitik gegenüber Ceylon," Oct. 26, 1964, vertraulich: PA/AA, B 150, Bd. 39.

169. Böker to Jansen, Oct. 28, 1964: AAPD 1964, 1195–97. Böker was writing from the hospital; his illness might well have arisen in connection with the strain of lobbying in Cairo earlier in the month.

170. Bodemer, *Entwicklungshilfe*, 120. A letter by Schröder triggered this reaction; see Schröder, Rundschreiben, "Internationale Konferenzen der Entwicklungsländer und die Deutschlandfrage," Sept. 4, 1964: AAPD 1964, 993–97.

171. On the confluence of the three requests, see Bodemer, *Entwicklungshilfe*, 121.

172. Scheel, Vermerk, Jan. 18, 1965: ACDP, NL Vialon, I-475-016/3. As early as 1963, Scheel had described the Lampong steel works as a "classic case" of the Hallstein Doctrine's pernicious effects. Meeting of the Bundestag's Development Aid Committee, Oct. 17, 1963, p. 5: BT/PA, Entwicklungsausschuß, 4. Wahlperiode, Bd. 2.

173. Meeting of the Beirat für Entwicklungshilfe, Jan. 27, 1965, as recorded in a memo of the BMZ, Feb. 17, 1965, p. 3: BA, B 213, Bd. 1329. Another indication of impatience with Bonn's development aid appeared in *Der Spiegel*, which ran a sharply critical cover story on Dec. 1, 1964.

174. On the 1966 "deadline," see the deliberations in the Bundestag's Foreign Affairs committee, Dec. 16, 1964, esp. p. 4a: BT/PA, Ausw. Aus., 4. WP, Bd. 9.

175. For an introduction to these issues, see Lavy, *Germany and Israel*, or in more detail, Deutschkron, *Israel und die Deutschen*.

176. Abt. I (Jansen), Aufz., "Arabische Reaktion auf deutsche Waffenlieferungen nach Israel und deutsche Gegenmaßnahmen," Nov. 4, 1964, geheim: PA/AA, B 150, Bd. 40.

177. For details on the Gestenmaier/Nasser conversation, DG Cairo (Federer) 1053, Nov. 23, vertraulich, cito, and DG Cairo 1067, Nov. 25, geheim (nur für Staatssekretär), citissime: AAPD 1964, 1374–79, and PA/AA, B 150, Bd. 41, respectively. Gerstenmaier also called for a law banning all future West German weapons sales outside of NATO; but this "radical solution" was discounted by both parliamentarians and policy makers, who were convinced of the value of Bonn's military aid to several sub-Saharan nations. AAPD 1964, 1515–17.

178. Ref. I B 4 (Schirmer), Aufz., "Arabische Reaktion auf das Bekanntwerden der Waffenlieferungen an Israel," Dec. 9, 1964, vertraulich: PA/AA, B 150, Bd. 42.

179. Böker, Vermerk, Dec. 22, 1964, geheim: PA/AA, B 150, Bd. 43.

180. Präsidium des Ministerrats, "Beschluß zur Verwirklichung der Beziehungen der DDR zu den afrikanischen Staaten bis 1970," July 3, 1964, p. 22: BA-SAPMO, DC 20 I/4, Bd. 967. This sum consisted largely of new credits, but it did include ca. VM 40 million left over from the 1958 credit treaty. On the lack of concrete West German plans, US Bonn (McGhee) 2203, Dec. 8, 1964, confidential: NARA, RG 59, ANF 64–66 E, Box 507 (Aid Ger W 9 UAR).

181. Hoppe, Zwischen Teilhabe und Mitsprache, 211–14, 219–26.

182. Westrick conversation with Felix Shinnar, head of Israel's mission in Cologne, Jan. 29, 1965 (memorandum prepared by the Chancellor's Office, Feb. 2): PA/AA, B 150, Bd. 46.

183. Carstens, Vermerk, "Kabinettsvorlage zu den Waffenlieferungen an Israel," Jan. 4, 1965, streng geheim: PA/AA, B 150, Bd. 44. On Dec. 9, Jansen and the Countries Department had drafted a cabinet resolution calling for an immediate halt to the deliveries, but Carstens overruled this. The final version of the draft resolution, approved by the cabinet on January 27, was laughably vague: "Weapons deliveries to Israel are to be halted, except where prior and binding commitments are to be carried through."

184. Moreover, it was only after mid-January 1965 that the press reported in detail on the tank arrangements made by Erhard's government; until then, the focus had been much more on the Adenauer-Strauss deals. A surprising amount of background was provided by Erhard himself during his comments to the Bundestag on the afternoon of February 17, 1965; see DzD IV/11, 205–9.

185. As Rainer A. Blasius has recently demonstrated, Nasser had agreed already in August 1964 to receive Ulbricht in Cairo. Blasius, "'Völkerfreundschaft' am Nil." Nevertheless, Nasser did not follow through on this plan for many months thereafter; and it is quite likely that if West Germany had acted more promptly to disavow its agreements with Israel, the Ulbricht visit would never have come to pass.

186. The quote, rather a cliché of the time, is from Karl Mommer (SPD); see Deutscher Bundestag, 160. Sitzung, Jan. 29, 1965: Sten. Ber., 4. WP, 7877D.

187. Hildebrand, Von Erhard zur Großen Koalition, 116–17.

CHAPTER SEVEN

1. Schröder to the Bundestag's Foreign Affairs Committee, Jan. 28, 1965, cited verbatim in a memorandum of the Ministry of All-German Affairs, p. 4: BAK, B 137,

Bd. 5851. Curiously, the official protocol of the meeting records Schröder as saying the opposite: the world will look "exactly as it did before." This version seems at odds with the overall tenor of the foreign minister's remarks. Auswärtiger Ausschuß., 71. Sitzung (Jan. 29, 1965) 55: BT/PA, Ausw. Aus., 4. WP, Bd. 9.

2. Abt. II (Krapf), Aufz., Jan. 27, 1965, streng geheim: *AAPD* 1965, 201–2.

3. See Nasser's comments to Federer on Jan. 31, reported in DG Cairo 101, Feb. 1, geheim, citissime mit Vorrang: *AAPD* 1965, 227–30.

4. DG Cairo (Federer) 81 for Carstens, Jan. 28, 1965, geheim, citissime; and Westrick's response to Carstens, Jan. 29, 1965, geheim: both PA/AA, B 150, Bd. 45.

5. Joachim Steffen, "Nassers Erpressungsversuch," *Lübecker Morgen* (SPD-affiliated), Jan. 28, 1965; Joachim Besser, "Die Hall-Steinzeit," *Kölner Stadt-Anzeiger*, Jan. 30; Hans Reiser, "Probe auf die Hallstein-Doktrin," *Süddeutsche Zeitung*, Feb. 3.

6. "Michaelis," "Selbstgefesselt—Druck auf Bonn ermöglicht," *Nürnberger Nachrichten*, Feb. 3, 1965; "Fass ohne Boden," *NRZ: Rhein-Ruhr-Zeitung*, Feb. 17, 1965. This interpretation received a full treatment in *Der Spiegel*, which elaborated this thesis with the examples of Algeria and Indonesia. "Bratpfanne vor der Sonne," *Der Spiegel*, Mar. 17, 1965, 32.

7. Deutscher Bundestag, *Sten. Ber.*, 4. WP, 160. Sitzung (Jan. 29, 1965), 7878A. Jürgen Tern of the *Frankfurter Allgemeine* endorsed this standpoint wholeheartedly, remarking that "nothing good comes of treading lightly with development aid" ("Keinen Pfennig," *FAZ*, Jan. 30, 1965, 1).

8. CDU-Fraktion, Feb. 9, 1965: ACDP, VIII-001-1010/1, pp. 191–92.

9. Ibid., p. 189. Schröder's fears of a chain reaction are also evident in his comments of January 28 to the Bundestag's Foreign Affairs Committee, cited in n. 1 above

10. Willy Weyer, "Kein Fall für die Hallstein-Doktrin," *fdk* 16, no. 9 (Feb. 2, 1965): 2–3. The article was ghostwritten by the FDP's press secretary, Wolfgang Schollwer, a longtime critic of the isolation policy. Schollwer, *FDP im Wandel*, 243.

11. For Scheel's comments in the cabinet meeting of February 3, 1965, see Osterheld, *Außenpolitik*, 154–55.

12. In private conversations, Schröder routinely commented that he had been opposed to the weapons deal in the first place. As the U.S. embassy observed, this pass-the-buck attitude won him few friends in Bonn during the crisis. US Bonn (McGhee) 3104, Feb. 18, 1965, confidential: NARA, RG 59, ANF 64–66, Box 2226 (Pol Ger W—Near E).

13. On the cabinet meeting, see Osterheld, *Außenpolitik*, 152–53. Throughout the crisis, reliable information about the exact state of the arms shipments was hard to come by, even for top-level decision makers. The figure of DM 150 million derives from a memo by Jansen, Dec. 22, 1964, vertraulich: *AAPD* 1964, 1557–58.

14. Klaus Mehnert, a political scientist with close government ties, wrote to the chancellor that the agreements with Israel were unconstitutional and that they threatened to demolish "a structure of German foreign policy erected carefully in the course of a decade and a half, one that concerns a central question for us—the relationship to Pankow." Mehnert argued (much as in Chapter 6 above) that Erhard had brought the crisis on himself by refusing to act sooner to throttle the military aid to Israel. Mehnert to Erhard, Jan. 31, 1965: BAK, B 136, Bd. 6228.

15. Carstens, Vermerk (StS 9/65), Feb. 3, 1965, streng geheim: PA/AA, B 150, Bd. 46.

16. DG Cairo (Müller) 135, Feb. 8, 1965, geheim, citissime: *AAPD* 1965, 275–76.

17. For an excerpt from Erhard's letter to Eshkol, see Timm, *Hammer, Zirkel, Davidstern*, 192. On the approval of the CDU/CSU's foreign policy circle, see the memo by Ref. L 1 (Balken), Feb. 9, 1965: PA/AA, B 1, Bd. 219. See also Westrick's comments to Felix Shinnar on Feb. 11: *AAPD* 1965, 298–99.

18. DG Cairo (Müller) 152, Feb. 11, 1965: PA/AA, B 36, Bd. 480; DG Cairo 156, Feb. 12, 1965: PA/AA, B 1, Bd. 219. On the mediation by the Marquis de Nerva, secretary-general of Spain's Foreign Ministry, see the conversation Carstens/Nerva, Feb. 12, 1965: *AAPD* 1965, 307–12.

19. For a sense of the uproar, see the press conference of Feb. 12, 1965, 15:30: BPA, Pressemagazin, Jan.–June 1965; also the questions posed to Carstens in the Bundestag session of Feb. 17 (see the following note). Finally, Jürgen Tern, "Waffenlieferugen und Erpressung," *FAZ*, Feb. 12, 1965, 1.

20. Deutscher Bundestag, 4. WP, 164. Sitzung (Feb. 17, 1965): *Sten. Ber.*, 8076. In the telegram "Plurex 360" of Jan. 29, 1965, Carstens had instructed Bonn's ambassadors in the Arab world to undertake démarches, commenting, among other things, that the Federal Republic would certainly not establish diplomatic relations with Israel *before the fall Bundestag elections*. On Feb. 17 and on several subsequent occasions, Carstens denied ever having issued orders in which Bonn promised *in general* not to establish relations with Israel

21. For a good example of the pro-Israel lobby, see the telegram sent by Heinz Gollwitzer to Erhard on February 12: "In the name of over 400 German university teachers whose signatures follow, I ask you, honored Herr Chancellor, to prevent a capitulation to Arab extortion—lest all the moral reconstruction [since 1945] be demolished. Keep us from having to be ashamed once again of being German and of belonging to this state." The text of this telegram was repeated in a note from Gollwitzer to all the members of the Bundestag's Foreign Affairs committee, Feb. 18, 1965: ACDP, NL Birrenbach, I-483-16/2.

22. "A Message to the Conscience of the World," *New York Times*, Feb. 18, 1965, p. 23. See also, on p. 5 of the same issue, "Jews to Discuss Boycott of Bonn." Here the chairman of the Conference of Presidents of Major American Jewish Organizations, Dr. Joachim Prinz, is quoted as saying that the Federal Republic had a moral obligation to ensure the safety and security of the surviving victims of Nazism.

23. The "world Jewry" observation originated with Karl-Günther von Hase, chief of the Federal Press Office; see Carstens's notes on a meeting between Erhard and his top ministers on Feb. 20, 1965, streng geheim: *AAPD* 1965, 365. For requests for American assistance in dealing with Israel, see Rusk/Knappstein conversation, Feb. 18, 1965, confidential; McGhee/Schröder conversation, reported in US Bonn 3148, Feb. 22, 1965, secret; and McGhee's conversation with CDU whip Will Rasner, reported in US Bonn 3149, Feb. 22, 1965, confidential, priority: all NARA, Box 2226, cited in n. 12 above. German records of the first two conversations appear in *AAPD* 1965, 351–55, 367–72.

24. See Hase's comments in the press conference of January 29, 1965, emphasizing that the government must retain maneuvering room in deciding how to respond to Nasser's affront. BPA, Pressemagazin, Jan.–June 1965. On February 9, Erhard reiterated this standpoint in a backgrounder with Cyrus Sulzberger. LES, NL Erhard, Bd. NE 335.

25. Erhard to the CDU-Fraktion: ACDP, VIII-001-1010/1, p. 197; Erhard to the Bundestag: *DzD*, 205–9, esp. 207. For an indication of Carstens's differentiated plans for responding to the course of the Ulbricht visit, see his handwritten note "VAR-Israel: Linie," penned on the night of Feb. 18/19, 1965: BAK, NL Carstens, Bd. 583.

26. DG Cairo (Müller) 174, Feb. 17, 1965: PA/AA, B 1, Bd. 220.

27. DG Amman 21, Feb. 15, geheim: *AAPD* 1965, 329–31. On the purpose of Böker's trip, see Sachs, Vermerk, Feb. 5, 1965: PA/AA, B 150, Bd. 46.

28. On the Arab League's resolution, see DG Cairo (Müller) 211, Feb. 23, NfD, cito: PA/AA, B 36, Bd. 481. Jordan's King Hussein, who had initially sought to mediate between Cairo and Bonn, was furious after learning about all the hardware under way to Tel Aviv—particularly because Böker had failed to underscore this during their conversation a few days earlier. See DG Amman 23, Feb. 19, geheim, citissime mit Vorrang: PA/AA, B 150, Bd. 47; this includes the text of a sharply worded letter from Hussein to President Lübke.

29. Blasius, "'Völkerfreundschaft' am Nil," 766.

30. "Bleibt die 'Hallstein-Doktrin' weiter bestehen?," *General-Anzeiger*, Feb. 8, 1965; "Am Ende einer Doktrin," *Nürnberger Nachrichten*, Feb. 10, 1965; "Läßt Bonn die Hallstein-Doktrin fallen?," *Weser-Kurier* (Bremen), Feb. 24, 1965; Fritz René Allemann, "Tod einer Doktrin," *Die Weltwoche*, Mar. 5, 1965; "Zerbricht die Hallstein-Doktrin?," *Der Spiegel*, Mar. 17, 1965. (This was a cover story for *Der Spiegel*.)

31. Deutscher Bundestag, 4. WP, 164. Sitzung (Feb. 17, 1965): *Sten. Ber.*, 8111–15. Despite sharp criticisms of the government's handling of the crisis thus far, Erler deliberately refrained from prescribing any solutions. He most certainly did not advocate abandoning the Hallstein Doctrine; see his comments to the SPD caucus on Feb. 15, 1965, in Weber, Hölscher, and Potthoff, *SPD-Fraktion im Deutschen Bundestag*, 3:582.

32. "Beweglich geworden," *FAZ*, Feb. 16, 1965, p. 1. The Bonn *General-Anzeiger* took a similar line; see US Bonn (McGhee) 3080, Feb. 17, 1965, confidential: NARA, Box 2226.

33. US Bonn (McGhee) 3080, Feb. 17, 1965, confidential: NARA, Box 2226.

34. Carstens to DG Washington, Paris, and London Plurex 766, Feb. 17, 1965, geheim: *AAPD* 1965, 344–51, esp. 350.

35. The situation in Tanzania is described in greater detail in Chapter 6. On "downgrading" vs. "upgrading," see DG The Hague (Berger) 46, Feb. 9, 1965: PA/AA, B 34, Bd. 606.

36. Carstens, Plurex 766, cited in n. 34 above.

37. For the British response, see *AAPD* 1965, 350 n. 61. It is worth noting that the working level of London's Foreign Office perceived "a very considerable interest of our own in helping the Germans as far as we can." Western Department (Ledwidge), "The Hallstein Doctrine in Danger," Feb. 3, 1965, confidential: PRO, FO 371/183009. On the French offer for regular conversations on the Hallstein Doctrine, see DG Paris (Knoke) 276, Feb. 18, 1965, geheim, citissime: PA/AA, B 150, Bd. 47. French advice on Tanzania came on Feb. 17 and 26; see *AAPD* 1965, 342–43, esp. n. 8.

38. DG Washington (Knappstein) 561, Feb. 18, 1965, geheim: *AAPD* 1965, 351–55, quote on 354. On the outcome of the U.S. soundings in Israel, see below.

39. DG Dar-es-Salaam 99, Feb. 28, 1965, vertraulich, citissime: *AAPD* 1965, 408–11.

40. On Nyerere's announcement, see ibid., note 13. In late January, West German officials placed the sum total of Bonn's aid to Tanzania, including commitments for 1965, at DM 183.85 million; of this, DM 129.45 million had not yet been disbursed. Abt. III (Pauls), Aufz., "Entwicklungshilfe für Tansania; hier: Auswirkungen, die eine Einstellung der deutschen Entwicklungshilfe für Tansania haben würde," Jan. 27, 1965, vertraulich: PA/AA, B 150, Bd. 45. In practice, Nyerere's highly publicized refusal of West German aid appears to have been a face-saving gesture; see DG Dar 100, Mar. 1, 1965, geheim, citissime mit Vorrang: ibid., Bd. 48.

41. Comments by the deputy chief of mission at the German embassy in Dar-es-Salaam, reported in US Dar-es-Salaam 1733, Feb. 13, 1965, confidential: NARA, RG 59, ANF 64–66, Box 2204 (Pol 16 Ger E). For the reaction in Bonn, see "Tansania bereitet Bonn Kopfzerbrechen," *Süddeutsche Zeitung*, Mar. 2, 1965. For samples of angry press commentary, see Werner Holzer, "Bonner Undank," Mar. 2, 1965; and Albrecht von Kessel, "Schlechter Stil," *Die Welt*, Mar. 3, 1965.

42. Staatliche Plankommission/Abteilung Außenhandel, "Zur Erhöhung des Regierungskredites," Feb. 19, 1965: BA-SAPMO, DY 30, Bd. 3665.

43. See the joint communiqué of Mar. 1, 1965: *DADDR* 1965, 852–58, esp. 857, which mentions all points except the consulate in East Berlin. For an excellent analysis of the Nasser-Ulbricht conversations (and the protocols themselves), see Blasius, "'Völkerfreundschaft' am Nil," 766–71, 775–805.

44. See Erhard's detailed comments on this point to the three ambassadors of the Western Allies, Mar. 5, 1965, 11:30 A.M.: *AAPD* 1965, 457–59. Speaking independently with the French ambassador on March 6, Erhard confirmed that he was in favor of a break in diplomatic relations. Osterheld, *Außenpolitik*, 167.

45. See Osterheld's description of excerpts from a memorandum for Erhard in *Außenpolitik*, 161. On Adenauer's position, see his letter to Erhard of Mar. 3: LES, I. 1), Bd. 10–11. On Hallstein's trip from Brussels (where he had served since 1958 as president of the European Commission), see US Brussels Ecbus 928, Feb. 26, 1965, secret: NARA, RG 59, ANF 64–66, Box 2227 (Pol Ger W—UAR).

46. On reservations presented by Schröder, Scheel, Carstens, and Economics Minister Kurt Schmücker in a ministerial meeting on March 2, 1965, see Carstens's memorandum of that date: *AAPD* 1965, 422–25; also Wolffsohn, "Von der verordneten zur freiwilligen 'Vergangenheitsbewältigung'?," 118–22.

47. The "ruthless" demeanor of the American ambassador, George McGhee, greatly embittered Horst Osterheld, while the French ambassador, who was also present at the McGhee-Erhard conversation of March 5, later remarked that "no Russian could command Ulbricht more openly than McGhee just did [Erhard]." Osterheld, *Außenpolitik*, 166. For the official German protocol (drafted by Osterheld) of McGhee's exchange with Erhard, see *AAPD* 1965, 459.

48. For earlier suggestions that Bonn should recognize Israel in retaliation, see the observations by Jean Soutou about a "coup de frein," noted in DG Paris (Knoke) 248, Feb. 15, 1965, geheim, citissime: *AAPD* 1965, 332; and—even earlier—Fritz Erler in the Bundestag's Foreign Affairs Committee on January 28 (cited in n. 1 above). On Barzel's meetings with American Jewish leaders, see Shafir, *Ambiguous Relations*, 245–46.

49. On the decision-making process, compare Osterheld, *Außenpolitik*, 168–69; US Bonn 3467, Mar. 12, 1965, secret: NARA, Box 2226; and "Aus familiären Gründen,"

Der Spiegel, Mar. 17, 1965, 27–29. All emphasize Barzel's role, stressing his concern with the CDU's precipitous decline in opinion polls.

50. On the surprise at the Foreign Office, see US Bonn 3364, Mar. 7, 9:00 P.M., confidential, immediate: NARA, Box 2226 (as cited in n. 12 above). This report treats as credible information circulated by the CDU party headquarters, which placed both Barzel and Schröder at the center of the decision. Nevertheless, the foreign minister's anger in subsequent conversations suggests that he gave his assent only reluctantly. Osterheld, *Außenpolitik*, 171–72. Hentschel, *Erhard*, 557, suggests that Schröder was not consulted at all.

51. Birrenbach, *Meine Sondermissionen*, 98–105.

52. On the embassy burnings, see *Keesing's Contemporary Archives* 15 (1965): 20741; on the meeting of the Arab League, see Ref. I B 4 (Redies), Aufz., "Reaktion der arabischen Staaten auf die Aufnahme diplomatischer Beziehungen zu Israel": *AAPD* 1965, 521–22.

53. On Bonn's damage control strategy in the Middle East, see Böker, Aufz., Mar. 19, geheim: *AAPD* 1965, 540–48.

54. For example, a representative of the German firm Hochtief told the Syrian government that if it did not break relations, Bonn would make an additional DM 150 million in Hermes credits available toward the construction of the Euphrates Dam. DG Damascus (Mangoldt) 122, Mar. 30, 1965, citissime: PA/AA, B 38, Bd. 117. The State Department registered concern over "certain inconsistencies in Ger[man] aid policies in Near East"; see Circular 1831, Mar. 30, 1965, secret: NARA, Box 2226.

55. Technically, though, only nine were able to break diplomatic relations with the Federal Republic, since Bonn had established only consular relations with Kuwait so as not to antagonize Iraq. Krapf to DG Baghdad, Nov. 24, 1961: PA/AA, B 12, Bd. 124.

56. Carstens to DG Paris/NATO 160, Feb. 9, 1965, citissime mit Vorrang: PA/AA, B 136, Bd. 142. Later, Bonn did have at least two specific requests: that representatives from NATO states in Cairo not attend any receptions in honor of Ulbricht and that they discourage other countries from attending. US Paris (Finletter) Polto 1217, Feb. 23, 1965, confidential: NARA, Box 2227.

57. In December 1964, the State Department saw disaster coming and opted to duck: "FRG now appears to be playing very active game in Middle East. We believe it desirable for US to avoid involvement in FRG activities. Our experience with Adenauer last year reflects FRG tendency to cast blame on US for difficult decisions." DepSta Circular 1139 (to Bonn and the Arab capitals), Dec. 17, 1964, secret: NARA, Box 2226. On March 10, the Johnson administration informed the Israelis of its willingness to deliver the remaining tanks directly. *AAPD* 1965, 503, note 15.

58. France agreed to represent West German interests in Iraq, Syria, Lebanon, Jordan, and Sudan; Italy played this role in Yemen and Egypt; and Switzerland assumed it in Algeria. In each case, a West German section was created within the host embassy. The German diplomats posted to these sections were not allowed direct access to foreign ministries; formal communications had to be conveyed via the host embassies.

59. For examples of the "self-isolation" critique, see Conrad Ahlers, "Die Hallstein-Neurose," *Frankfurter Rundschau*, Mar. 8, 1960; and Marcel Schulte, "Eine zweifelhafte Doktrin," *Frankfurter Neue Presse*, May 18, 1961.

60. Schröder in the CDU-Fraktion, Feb. 9, 1965: ACDP, VIII-001-1010/1, p. 191.

61. Pauls to Oncken, Feb. 16, 1965: PA/AA, B 38, Bd. 4. Similar arguments could be heard in some portions of the CDU/CSU; see the conversation between Hamburg deputy Erik Blumenfeld and W. W. Rostow sent in US Bonn Airgram A-1580, Mar. 17, 1965, secret: NARA, RG 59, ANF 64–66, Box 2207 (Pol 1 Ger W).

62. Carstens, Aufz., "Vorschläge zur Deutschlandpolitik," Mar. 10, 1965, geheim, p. 10: PA/AA, B 150, Bd. 48.

63. Ibid., p. 4. By contrast, the Foreign Office's chief of planning, Herbert Müller-Roschach, remained bullish about the deterrent value of Bonn's action against Ceylon; see his memorandum "Kontinuierliche Deutschlandpolitik mit und ohne die sog. 'Hallstein-Doktrin,'" Feb. 5, 1965: *AAPD* 1965, 251–59, esp. 252–53.

64. Deutscher Bundestag, 4. WP, 170. Sitzung (Mar. 10, 1965): *Sten. Ber.*, 8507–9. The timing of this question-and-answer session was hardly coincidental; the Arab League had not yet met to formulate a response to the Federal Republic's recognition of Israel, and the West Germans wished to warn the Arab leaders against a recognition of the GDR.

65. As an additional bone to this camp, Schröder remarked during this session, "I prefer to avoid speaking too often of doctrines." Countess Marion Dönhoff wrote enthusiastically of a "new Hallstein Doctrine," which offered Bonn the possibility of a scaled reaction rather than just the "massive retaliation" of breaking diplomatic relations. "Deutsches Dilemma," *Die Zeit*, Mar. 12, 1965: *DzD* IV/11, 273–74.

66. See the talking points dated February 25, prepared by Guttenberg for use by President Lübke in a conversation with Erhard. BAK, NL Guttenberg, Bd. 48, Bl. 5–8.

67. Guttenberg disguised his comments about an "Anwesenheitsdoktrin" as an attack on Erich Mende; but clearly Schröder was his intended target. Deutscher Bundestag, 4. WP, 183. Sitzung (May 14, 1965): *Sten. Ber.*, 9162–63. Here again, the public conversation had an external purpose as well: Bonn had just exchanged ambassadors with Israel and was hoping that the effects in the Arab world might yet be contained.

68. On January 4, 1966, several Referate, including the Latin America and reunification desks, agreed that Colombia's dependence on coffee exports made it particularly vulnerable to trade-related pressure, particularly since the Federal Republic was Colombia's second-biggest coffee market. Ref. I B 2 (Meyer-Lohse), Aufz., "Deutsche Handelspolitische Gegenmaßnahmen gegen ein weiteres Vordringen der SBZ in Kolumbien" (Entwurf), Jan. 11, 1966: PA/AA, B 38, Bd. 110. For the project's cancellation by the head of the Countries Department, see notes in ibid. by Ref. I B 2 and Ref. II A 1, both dated January 26.

69. In West Africa, Chad and Nigeria refused landing rights to Interflug, while Mali and Guinea granted them. Hardenberg to DG Paris, Sept. 2, 1966: PA/AA, B 38, Bd. 108. In November 1966, Interflug service to Conakry opened with a laughable degree of pomp; see Troche, *Ulbricht und die Dritte Welt*, 59.

70. Schröder to Westrick, Kabinettsvorlage, "Verdrängung der 'Interflug' von Zypern; hier: Ersatz durch Aufnahme eines Lufthansa-Dienstes," Mar. 4, 1965, vertraulich: PA/AA, B 150, Bd. 48. By pushing Interflug out of Cyprus, the Foreign Office was hoping to create difficulties for the airline's service to Cairo.

71. At the FDP party congress in Frankfurt on March 22, 1965, Erich Mende intoned

that "this doctrine is, at least today, no longer a suitable instrument of foreign policy when it comes to upholding the Federal Republic's claim to sole representation [of Germany]." *DzD* IV/11, 312.

72. Schröder to Erhard, July 17, 1965, vertraulich: *AAPD* 1965, 1184–87.

73. Mende's stance reflected in part the convictions of officials in the FDP central headquarters like Wolfgang Schollwer and Hans-Dietrich Genscher, who considered "the FDP chairman as executor of the Hallstein Doctrine" to be a "macabre vision." Schollwer, *FDP im Wandel*, 271. On the cabinet's discussions, see Carstens, Aufz., Aug. 25, 1965, vertraulich: *AAPD* 1965, 1378–79. Both the Chancellor's Office and the Foreign Office tried to revive the project in November; see Ministerbüro (Simon), Vermerk, Nov. 4, 1965: PA/AA, B 36, Bd. 141.

74. Schröder, "Germany Looks at Eastern Europe," 24.

75. Abt. II (Krapf), Aufz., "Herstellung der Bewegungsfreiheit in der Deutschland-Politik," Jan. 28, 1965, streng geheim: *AAPD* 1965, 203–5.

76. [CSU], "Arbeitspapier zum Regierungsprogramm," October 1965, pp. 4–5: BAK, NL Carstens, Bd. 638. On October 5, 1965, Guttenberg supplied Lübke with another round of material intended to compromise Schröder; see BAK, NL Guttenberg, Bd. 48, Bl. 78–79, 118–19. On Lübke's efforts to stop Schröder—a questionable use of his office—see Morsey, *Heinrich Lübke*, 462–65.

77. Carstens, notes of conversation with Erhard on Oct. 8, 1965: BAK, NL Carstens, Bd. 638.

78. Carstens to Erhard, Oct. 11, 1965, pp. 7–8: ibid.

79. Lenkungsausschuß, 96. Sitzung, Jan. 14, 1965, p. 17: BAK, B 213, Bd. 1529. One day earlier, the Bundestag's Budget Committee had cut the budgetary allotment by DM 100 million, from DM 700 million.

80. The Development Aid Ministry made this calculation in early 1965, after Minister Scheel expressed his concern that the Hallstein Doctrine might be distorting Bonn's aid distribution. Officials found that 40 percent of Bonn's capital aid and 33 percent of its technical aid went to countries where the Hallstein Doctrine played at least some role; but when India was excluded, these proportions sank to 12 and 24 percent, respectively. The report did note that some twenty minor countries would probably never have received West German aid were it not for the Hallstein Doctrine, but the sums involved were not great. Dr. Walter Rau (Unterabteilungsleiter II A), Aufz., "Hallstein-Doktrin und Entwicklungshilfe," Jan. 26, 1965, esp. pp. 3–4 and Anlage: ACDP, NL Vialon, I-475-016/3.

81. Draft of a joint cabinet resolution by the Development Aid Ministry, the Economics Ministry, and the Foreign Office, undated [prob. Dec. 1965], p. 2: BAK, B 213, Bd. 1533. See also the memo prepared for Scheel's speech to the Bundestag Foreign Affairs Committee on Jan. 19, 1966, p. 2, which makes reference to the GDR's activities in 23 developing countries: ACDP, NL Vialon, I-475-016/4.

82. Lenkungsausschuß, 112. Sitzung, Jan. 12, 1966: BAK, B 213, Bd. 1534.

83. Böker, Aufz., "Zusätzliche Hilfe für die Palästina-Flüchtlinge," Aug. 19, 1966, vertraulich: *AAPD* 1966, 1092–94.

84. On these general conditions, which dated back to a cabinet decision of May 20, 1965, see the conversation in the Lenkungsausschuß, 105. Sitzung, July 29, 1965, pp. 7–10: BAK, B 213, Bd. 1532.

85. On the continuation of projects in these countries (including military assistance in the case of Sudan), see Lenkungsausschuß, ibid. See also Carstens to Erhard, Mar. 7, 1966, geheim: *AAPD* 1966, 270–71, which reported that Sudan was planning to bring up a motion in the Arab League meeting of March 14 allowing the Arab states to regulate their relations with West Germany as each country saw fit.

86. On the Arab reaction, see Böker's comments to a joint meeting of the Bundestag Foreign Affairs and Development Aid Committees on June 16, 1966, as noted in a memo of the Ministry of All-German Affairs of June 22, pp. 2–3: BAK, B 137, Bd. 5851. On the terms of the West German-Israeli treaty, see p. 1 of the same document.

87. This decision was later criticized as a half-measure, since an unofficial West German trade fair agency immediately stepped in to run the German pavilion on the government's behalf. Ref. I B 4 (Gehlhoff), Aufz., Dec. 19, 1966: B 38, Bd. 106.

88. On the Italians in Yemen, who protested routinely on behalf of the West Germans, see various telegrams from September through November 1966 in PA/AA, B 38, Bd. 116. The word invoked repeatedly by the reunification desk in such cases was "Gewöhnung"—"getting used to" the presence of two German flags, two German delegations, or two German states. See, for example, Ref. II A 1 (Wentker), Vermerk, July 25, 1966: PA/AA, B 38, Bd. 106.

89. US Baghdad Airgram A-29, July 13, 1966, confidential (enclosure 2): NARA, RG 59, ANF 64–66, Box 2204 (Pol 16 Ger E). On the long list of top East German leaders making the pilgrimage to Cairo, see the glib remark by an American diplomat in Cairo: "Like Avis, they have to try harder." US Cairo (Battle) Airgram A-1031, June 7, 1966, p. 3: NARA, RG 59, ANF 64–66, Box 2205 (Ger E—UAR). The report is entitled "The Pankow Recognition Offensive in Egypt or They Care Enough to Send Their Very Best."

90. These figures come from a lengthy planning document on the GDR's credit relations with the socialist and nonsocialist worlds; Politbüro, Protokoll Nr. 33/66, Aug. 18, 1966, Anl. 3, p. 25: BA-SAPMO, DY 30/J IV 2/2, Bd. 1072.

91. Politbüro, Protokoll Nr. 8/67, Feb. 21, 1967, Anl. 2, pp. 1–3: BA-SAPMO, DY 30/J IV 2/2, Bd. 1100.

92. Ibid., pp. 4–5.

93. Böker, Aufz., "Deutsch-ceylonesische Beziehungen nach Bildung der neuen Regierung," Apr. 1, 1965: PA/AA, B 38, Bd. 112.

94. On the negotiations between State Secretary Lahr and Senanayake, see DG Colombo 179, Sept. 30, 1965, citissime mit Vorrang: *AAPD* 1965, 1550–55; also Lahr, *Zeuge von Fall und Aufstieg*, 432–33. Bonn's aid offers were quite generous: DM 32 million in instant credit, a further DM 18 million in project aid, and DM 6 million in technical aid. Lenkungsausschuß, Oct. 8, 1965, pp. 18–19: BAK, B 213, Bd. 1532.

95. DG Dar (Schroeder) 156, July 2, 1966, citissime: PA/AA, B 34, Bd. 671.

96. DG Accra (Steltzer), Ber. 231/66, "Politische Tragweite des Umsturzes in Ghana," Mar. 7, 1966: PA/AA, B 38, Bd. 105. Some 170 East Germans had to leave Ghana right away; one of Steltzer's Western diplomatic colleagues remarked that "the Federal Republic is one of the biggest winners from the new political constellation" (pp. 6–7). On the spy school, see Troche, *Ulbricht und die Dritte Welt*, 64.

97. Meyer-Lindenberg, Aufz., "Staatsstreich in Indonesien," Oct. 4, 1965: PA/AA, B 38, Bd. 114.

98. Abeilung Internationale Verbindungen, "Gedanken für die erste Beratung zur Verwirklichung des PB-Beschlusses vom 22. 3. 1966," June 21, 1966: BA-SAPMO, DY 30/IV A 2/20, Bd. 7.

99. Politbüro, Protokoll Nr. 33/66, Aug. 16, 1966, Anl. 3, p. 26: BA-SAPMO, DY 30/J IV 2/20, Bd. 1072.

100. For a clue to Ulbricht's motives, see marginalia on a memo describing a conversation between Georg Stibi and the Czech foreign minister on Dec. 25, 1965: BA-SAPMO, DY 30, Bd. 3669.

101. Conversation Winzer/U Thant, July 26, 1966: BA-SAPMO, DY 30, Bd. 3669.

102. Report by Kurt Olivier, the ADN correspondent in New York, Apr. 8, 1966, 1–2: BA-SAPMO, DY 30/IV A 2/20, Bd. 53. On Winzer's trip to Mali, see his conversation with Soviet foreign minister Gromyko, Apr. 15, 1966: BA-SAPMO, DY 30, Bd. 3669. In April, Mali had assumed the chairmanship of the UN Security Council for one year; Winzer was hoping that Mali might push to have the East German application transferred to a subcommittee for further discussions.

103. DG UN (von Braun) 316, Apr. 15, 1966, geheim: *AAPD* 1966, 468–71.

104. In March 1965, Carstens observed that within the WHO, the GDR was extremely close to achieving a breakthrough; see his "Vorschläge zur Deutschlandpolitik," Mar. 10, 1965, geheim, p. 5: PA/AA, B 150, Bd. 48.

105. Meeting of the "SBZ-Referate," Oct. 26, 1966: PA/AA, B 38, Bd. 104. NGO questions came up in almost every one of the bimonthly "SBZ-Referate" meetings; of special importance is the discussion of Oct. 7, 1964: PA/AA, B 80, Bd. 372.

106. For a sample of Bonn's efforts to sway the vote of the International Olympic Committee, see Lahr, Runderlaß, July 21, 1965: PA/AA, B 80, Bd. 471. British observers later commented that West German pressure "caused considerable resentment and was rather a boomerang." Exeter to Holmer, Nov. 8, 1965: PRO, FO 371/183165. On the general problem, see Geyer, "Der Kampf um nationale Repräsentation" and Kilian, *Hallstein-Doktrin*, chap. 11.

107. Carstens, Aufz., "Deutschland-Politik," Jan. 27, 1966, vertraulich: *AAPD* 1966, 81–82, 85.

108. Carstens, Aufz., "Die Problematik unserer Deutschland-Politik," Oct. 17, 1966: *AAPD* 1966, 1378–79.

109. Comments by Gerhard Kegel to a meeting of the "Arbeitsgruppe Strategie und Taktik der Partei auf dem Gebiet der Außenpolitik," a working group within the SED's Abteilung Internationale Verbindungen, o. D. [December 1966]: BA-SAPMO, DY 30/IV A 2/20, Bd. 7.

110. Carstens, Aufz., "Die Problematik unserer Deutschland-Politik," (cited in n. 107 above), 1378.

111. Krapf, Runderlaß, June 14, 1965: PA/AA, B 80, Bd. 471. It should be noted, however, that these results are skewed by the fact that Germans had been asked the *same* basket of questions since 1951. Understandably, then, items which had once ranked very high on the list, such as housing and unemployment, had diminished in importance, leaving reunification as the topic that 47 percent of those polled deemed the most important task at hand.

112. Gradl to Kissinger, Apr. 20, 1965: ACDP, NL Gradl, I-294-77/1.

113. UK Bonn (Roberts), Oct. 13, 1965, confidential: PRO, FO 371/153054. Schütz's

Reform der Deutschlandpolitik appeared in late September 1965; the title given here is that of the English translation published two years later.

114. For reliable statistics on East German growth, see Steiner, "Von 'Hauptaufgabe' zu 'Hauptaufgabe,'" 236–37. On the many journalists reporting about the GDR in glowing terms in the second half of the 1960s, see Hacker, *Deutsche Irrtümer*, 384–88; Bender, *Die "Neue Ostpolitik" und ihre Folgen*, 121–24.

115. Memo by one of Mende's associates at the Ministerium für gesamtdeutsche Fragen, July 28, 1965: BAK, B 137, Bd. 3334.

116. This idea had been mooted by the philosopher Karl Jaspers as early as 1960—much to the horror of West German television audiences. See *DzD* IV/5, 145–46, and Ref. 700 (Bock), Aufz., Aug. 17, 1960: PA/AA, B 80, Bd. 295.

117. Brandt speech to the SPD party congress in Dortmund, June 1, 1966: *DzD* IV/12, 812–13. Dichgans in *Die Zeit* of May 27, 1966: *DzD* IV/12, 793–96.

118. See Mende's comments in an interview with the *Kölner Stadtanzeiger*, Feb. 4, 1966: *DZD* IV/12, 165–69; also his comments to the FDP caucus on Apr. 26, 1966, p. 4: ADL, A040-777.

119. See the report by the nonpartisan group Kuratorium Unteilbares Deutschland, "8 Grundsätze für eine offensive Deutschlandpolitik," Mar. 29, 1966: *DzD* IV/12, 406–7.

120. On the legal issues, see comments by CDU deputy Benda, May 2, 1966: *DzD* IV/12, 627–29.

121. Speech by Albert Norden, June 29, 1966: *DzD* IV/12, 1007.

122. Comments by Ernst Majonica at a conference of the "Außenpolitische Gemeinschaft" of the Evangelische Akademie in Loccum, Mar. 12, 1966, p. 12: ACDP, NL Birrenbach, Bd. 17/1.

123. Selvage, "Poland, the German Democratic Republic, and the German Question," 202–22.

124. On the origins of (and limitations of) the peace note, see Blasius, "Erwin Wickert und die Friedensnote der Bundesregierung."

125. For criticism along these lines, see Dichgans to Westrick (head of the Chancellor's Office), May 13, 1966: BAK, B 136, Bd. 6502. Many in the Chancellor's Office had doubts about the "white book's" potential impact; see BAK, B 136, Bd. 6779.

126. Erhard to the CDU caucus on Apr. 26, 1966, pp. 277–78: ACDP, VIII-001-035.

127. FDP-Fraktion, Apr. 26, 1966: ADL, A040-777.

128. The phrase "Sommer des Mißvergnügens" was used in private letters by Erik Blumenfeld, a CDU Bundestag deputy from Hamburg, to express the feeling of malaise in West Germany. Blumenfeld to Barzel, July 26, 1966, and to Gerrard Eichenberg, July 29, 1966: both BAK, NL Blumenfeld, Bd. 6.

129. In a meeting with Erhard on July 12, Mende demanded diplomatic relations with Eastern Europe by the fall of 1966. FDP-Fraktion, July 27, 1966, p. 2: ADL, A040-774. On the SPD, see the resolution adopted by the Dortmund Party Congress on June 4, 1966: *DzD* IV/12, 851.

130. Even in October 1966, Erhard "was still held back by a determined minority in the CDU/CSU headed by Baron Guttenberg," according to Carstens. US Bonn (McGhee) 4330, Oct. 11, 1966, secret: NARA, RG 59, ANF 64–66, Box 2227 (Pol Ger W—Rom).

131. For this judgment, and also a useful clarification of the nature of the Federal Republic's recession and budgetary difficulties, see Hentschel, *Ludwig Erhard*, 614.

132. McGhee, *At the Creation of a New Germany*, 188–93. Also of interest is a conversation between Erhard's successor, Kiesinger, and President Johnson on Apr. 26, 1967: *FRUS 1964–68/XV*, 530.

133. Johnson speech to the National Conference of Editorial Writers, New York, Oct. 7, 1966, analyzed by Hans Hellmuth Ruete, Oct. 11, 1966, p. 4: BAK, NL Carstens, Bd. 629.

134. Carstens, Aufz., "Heutige Kabinettsitzung," Oct. 14, 1966, geheim: BAK, NL Carstens, Bd. 640; Carstens, Aufz., "Die Problematik unserer Deutschlandpolitik," Oct. 17, 1966: *AAPD*, 1380.

135. "Wiedervereinigung—Schweigen Ehrensache," *Der Spiegel*, Oct. 24, 1966, 27–28; Hentschel, *Ludwig Erhard*, 644–48; Hildebrand, *Von Erhard zur Großen Koalition*, 226–28.

CHAPTER EIGHT

1. Hildebrand, *Von Erhard zur Großen Koalition*, 272; Bahr, *Zu meiner Zeit*, 212.

2. *DzD* V/1, 56.

3. Ibid., 57–99.

4. This point is implicit in Kiesinger's declaration that the government's highest goal was peace. Brandt made the point explicit on many occasions; see, for example, his comments to British foreign minister George Brown on Apr. 12, 1967: *AAPD* 1967, 571.

5. In an interview with *Die Welt* on Dec. 15, 1966, Herbert Wehner dismissed the designation "SBZ" as "bureaucrats' German." Hard-liners like Wilhelm Grewe wrote in to the Foreign Office, protesting that they had worked for years to encourage their Western colleagues to speak of the "SBZ." In the cabinet meeting of Dec. 20, Kiesinger backed Wehner on this point, suggesting the phrase "das andere Teil Deutschlands" (the other part of Germany). PA/AA, B 38, Bd. 144; see also ibid. for Grewe's protest (DG NATO, Dec. 21, 1966.)

6. Diehl, Aufz., "Besprechungen in Washington vom 21. bis 27. Januar," Feb. 1, 1967, vertraulich: *AAPD* 1967, 212–19, esp. 216.

7. Conversation Kiesinger/Seydoux, Mar. 3, 1967, vertraulich: *AAPD* 1967, 380–81.

8. Conversation Rusk/Brandt/Couve/Brown, Dec. 14, 1966, secret: *FRUS 1964–68/XV*, 468.

9. In the Foreign Office's vocabulary, this meant distinguishing between "sole representation" (*Alleinvertretung*) and "sole presence" (*Alleinpräsenz*), with the latter being considered less critical. Diehl, Aufz., "Ergebnis der Deutschlanddiskussion," Mar. 17, 1967, geheim: *AAPD* 1967, 483–88; see also Diehl, *Zwischen Politik und Presse*, 384–87.

10. In a brainstorming session on February 27, 1967, Bahr called for a strategy of "Wiedervereinigung durch Umarmung" (reunification through embracing) to replace the unsuccessful efforts at "Wiedervereinigung durch Anschluß" (reunification through annexation). Ref. II A 1 (Jung), Aufz., Mar. 2, vertraulich: *AAPD* 1967, 394–95. On Bahr's outlook during the Grand Coalition years, see Vogtmeier, *Egon Bahr und die deutsche Frage*, 98–117.

11. Kroegel, *Einen Anfang finden!*, 141–68.

12. Ref. II A 1 (Jung), Aufz., Apr. 12, 1967, geheim: *AAPD* 1967, 575–79.

13. Ibid. See also the conversation of February 27, 1967, cited in n. 10 above.

14. DG Bamako (von Rom) 43, May 11, 1967, vertraulich: *AAPD* 1967, 732–34.

15. Abt. I (Meyer-Lindenberg), Aufz., "Beziehungen Singapore/DDR," June 23, 1967: PA/AA, B 38, Bd. 113; Böker, Aufz., Jan. 8, 1968: PA/AA, B 38, Bd. 117.

16. On Böker's continuing use of the designation "SBZ," see his memo cited in n. 15 above; it was drafted by Heinrich Bassler of the Southeast Asia desk, another fervent proponent of the isolation campaign. On bureaucratic inertia, see End, *Zweimal deutsche Außenpolitik*, 80.

17. This involved not only Strauss at the Finance Ministry, but also the installment of Baron Guttenberg (actually Strauss's greatest rival within the CSU) as state secretary in the Chancellor's Office. In his new post, Guttenberg had to *defend* the coalition's policy of détente; see his letters to Heinrich Krone of Mar. 17 and Apr. 24, 1967: ACDP, NL Krone, Bd. I-028-11/7.

18. Interesting in this regard are Kiesinger's comments during (unsuccessful) coalition negotiations with the FDP on November 24, 1966. The chancellor-to-be expressed concern about an "avalanche" or "chain reaction" of recognitions in the wake of relations with Romania, and wondered, "Are we really in such a hurry?" See the handwritten notes in ACDP, VIII-001-290/4.

19. Schütz, Runderlaß (Dipex Nr. 2), Jan. 13, 1967, geheim, citissime: *AAPD* 1967, 103–5. This telegram sounded out Third World governments about their likely reactions to the planned step. For a note circulated to all foreign missions in Bonn on January 31, 1967, see *DzD* V/1, 431–32. For the Quai's instructions, which betrayed a certain weariness with the Hallstein Doctrine, see Quai (de Beaumarchais) to AF Damascus, Baghdad, Beirut, Cairo, and Algiers, Jan. 30, 1967, réservé: MAE, EU 61–70, RFA, Z169.

20. See, for example, Guttenberg's comments in a TV interview of Jan. 30, 1967: *DzD* V/1, 420–22.

21. Abt. I (Meyer-Lindenberg), Aufz., "Wiederaufnahme der diplomatischen Beziehungen mit Jordanien," Feb. 21, 1967, geheim: *AAPD* 1967, 310–12. On the success of the "covering operation," see the reference to Ruete's memo of February 11, 1967, in *AAPD* 1967, 569 n. 13.

22. On Hungary's attitude, see the report by the East German ambassador in Budapest, Meissner, on his conversation with Kadar: MfAA, G-A 411, Bl. 43–45. In the summer of 1967, the Czech government allowed the opening of a West German trade mission in Prague analogous to the ones already up and running in Warsaw, Budapest, and Sofia. Bahr, *Zu meiner Zeit*, 220–22.

23. Sodaro, *Moscow, Germany, and the West*, 92–100. From a close reading of published speeches, Sodaro deduces that Brezhnev had not entirely given up hope on the Grand Coalition; but the thrust of Brezhnev's remarks nevertheless indicated that Bonn must change course at once.

24. Selvage, "Poland, the German Democratic Republic, and the German Question," 229–42.

25. For such hopes at the Foreign Ministry (which Axen considered unrealistic), see Axen to Winzer, Apr. 13, 1967: MfAA, G-A 411, Bl. 129–33.

26. Detailed summaries of both the Soviet memorandum and the instructions to Soviet ambassadors can be found in the Winzer/Abrassimov conversation, Apr. 4,

1967: MfAA, G-A 411, Bl. 85–91; quote from p. 7 of the transcript. For further evidence on Soviet thinking, see remarks by the Soviet ambassador to Cairo, reported in Winzer's note to Ulbricht of Apr. 17, 1967: BA-SAPMO, NY 4182, Bd. 1337.

27. See Winzer's report of May 22, 1967, p. 6: BA-SAPMO, NY 4182, Bd. 1337.

28. See the report by the East German consul in Damascus, Horst Grunert, summarized in Winzer to Ulbricht et al., June 5, 1967: BA-SAPMO, NY 4182, Bd. 1334.

29. Timm, *Hammer, Zirkel, Davidstern*, 212–13. The contents of Stoph's letter are apparent from conversations between East German diplomats and Arab counterparts; see especially the cables from Damascus (Grunert) Nr. 215/67, June 11, 1967, and Cairo (Scholz) Nr. 159/67, June 12, 1967: MfAA, G-A 412, Bl. 128 and 146–48.

30. Remarks by the Yemeni ambassador to Iraq, reported in Baghdad (Jaeschke) Nr. 97/67, June 11, 1967; see also the report from Algiers (Lösch) Nr. 255/67, June 13, 1967: MfAA, G-A 412, Bl. 130 and 149–51.

31. Conversation Weiss/Nasser, July 9, 1967: BA-SAPMO, DY 30, Bd. 3666, Bl. 49–51.

32. Conversation Weiss/Atassi, July 19, 1967, esp. 4–8, of the protocol drafted by Grunert: BA-SAPMO, NY 4182, Bd. 1334.

33. Ulbricht to Brezhnev, Aug. 1, 1967, p. 10: BA-SAPMO, DY 30, Bd. 3666.

34. Conversation Ulbricht/Ali Sabri (held in Moscow), Nov. 8, 1967, pp. 8–9: BA-SAPMO, NY 4182, Bd. 1337. The GDR did not, in fact, offer to pay for the *transport* of the jets, which proved to be a serious hurdle for the Syrians; see Winzer to Ulbricht et al., Nov. 15, 1967: MfAA, G-A 414, Bl. 85–88. The value of the GDR's military aid to Egypt after the Six Day War has been estimated at $45 million; Troche, *Ulbricht und die Dritte Welt*, 66.

35. See the extensive plan for East German relations with Egypt, Syria, and Iraq, approved by the Politburo on Oct. 10, 1967: BA-SAPMO, DY 30/J IV 2/2, Bd. 1138, Anl. 3.

36. Weiss, Aufz., Jan. 20, 1968: BA-SAPMO, NY 4182, Bd. 1334.

37. Politbüro, Protokoll Nr. 4/68, Feb. 6, 1968: BA-SAPMO, DY 30/J IV 2/2, Bd. 1153, Anl. 3.

38. Brandt to Kiesinger, Mar. 6, 1967, geheim: *AAPD* 1967, 412–15.

39. At the Quai, the Direction d'Europe observed that although most Third World countries appeared to have accepted Bonn's modification of the Hallstein Doctrine with respect to Romania, certain countries (the Congo, Egypt, Iraq, Algeria, Cambodia) did not really follow Bonn's reasoning; they would be very unlikely to take the doctrine at all seriously if Bonn were to renew ties with Belgrade. Note, Feb. 16, 1967, pp. 7–8: MAE, EU 61–70, RFA Z169. Resistance to the Yugoslavia initiative remained strong in the CDU Bundestag caucus through December 1967; see Kroegel, *Einen Anfang finden!*, 196–97.

40. Winzer to Ulbricht et al., Jan. 3, 1968, esp. pp. 4–6: BA-SAPMO, NY 4182, Bd. 1238.

41. On Kiesinger's conversation with Indira Gandhi, see DG New Delhi (Mirbach) 924, Nov. 24, 1967, vertraulich, citissime: *AAPD* 1967, 1540–42.

42. For Gandhi's response, see ibid.; for the comments of Ne Win of Burma, see *AAPD* 1967, 1536. See also Kiesinger's report to the Bundestag's Foreign Affairs Committee on December 14, 1967, recorded in a memorandum of the Ministry for All-German Affairs of Dec. 15: BAK, B 137, Bd. 5851.

43. See the telegram by Eric Harder, a German diplomat attached to the Italian embassy in Cairo, Jan. 29, 1968, geheim: *AAPD* 1968, 109–12. Several months earlier, another German diplomat had observed that the Egyptians did not take the Hallstein Doctrine very seriously; he concluded that if Egypt were to reestablish relations with Bonn, it would likely reserve the right to establish them with East Berlin shortly thereafter. Lothar Lahn to the Foreign Office, Sept. 27, 1967, vertraulich: *AAPD* 1967, 1315–16.

44. Mortimer, *The Third World Coalition in International Politics*, 20–22.

45. Wischnewski to the Bundestag, Oct. 11, 1967, in *DzD* V/1, 1798. For similar views expressed by Chancellor Kiesinger, see his comments to Japanese journalists on May 8, 1969: ACDP, NL Kiesinger, I-226-A008-1, esp. p. 6.

46. On Mali, see Lahr to DG Bamako, Mar. 8, 1967, vertraulich, citissime: PA/AA, B 150, Bd. 98, Bl. 2331. In the case of Algeria, West German officials were careful not to hint too strongly; see, for example, Wischnewski's conversation with the Algerian foreign minister in New York on Nov. 29, 1967, in *AAPD* 1967.

47. One anomaly here was Senegal. On the implications of the WHO vote, see Frank, Aufz., May 16, 1968, geheim: *AAPD* 1968, 614–22. For a roughly comparable assessment by the international organizations desk at the East German foreign ministry, see Information Nr. 152/VII, July 31, 1968: SAPMO, DY 30/IV A 2/20, Bd. 53.

48. Shortly before the WHO episode, the Soviet ambassador in Bonn told State Secretary Duckwitz that Moscow would be watching West German behavior during the vote very closely. *AAPD* 1968, 617, note 15.

49. Sodaro, *Moscow, Germany, and the West*, 116–18. Here again, Sodaro devotes most of his attention to arguing that Moscow's line was less firm that East Berlin's—a valid point, but one that should not distract from the intensity of the pressure the Soviets were bringing to bear on the Federal Republic.

50. Morsey, *Heinrich Lübke*, chap. 21.

51. On Kiesinger's Nazi past, see Kroegel, *Einen Anfang finden!*; on the election of the NPD to various state parliaments, see Hildebrand, *Von Erhard zur Großen Koalition*, 475–77.

52. A demonstration of May 11, 1968, in Bonn explicitly linked the "emergency laws" to Nazi practices; see the photograph in Hildebrand, *Von Erhard zur Großen Koalition*, 357.

53. Rusinek, "Von der Entdeckung der NS-Vergangenheit zum generellen Faschismusverdacht," 124. On the student protests more generally, see Thränhardt, *Geschichte der Bundesrepublik Deutschland*, 175–81.

54. On the GDR's April pronouncements, see a memorandum prepared at the Department of State, May 5, 1968, confidential: *FRUS* 1964–68/XV, 663–64. On the June demands, see Kroegel, *Einen Anfang finden!*, 229–32.

55. Soviet memoranda of Nov. 21, 1967, and July 5, 1968: *DzD* V/1, 2050, and *DzD* V/2, 972.

56. Schwarz, "Die Regierung Kiesinger und die Krise in der CSSR 1968," 182–85.

57. Siekmeier, *Restauration oder Reform?*, pt. 4.

58. Brauers, *Liberale Deutschlandpolitik 1949–1969*, 169–70; Brandt speech: *DzD* V/2, 464.

59. CDU-Fraktion, Mar. 26, 1968, pp. 8–10: ACDP, VIII-001-1016/1. See also the conversation in the coalition's "Dienstagskreis" of that day, pp. 3–4: ACDP, I-226-

A010. For Bahr's views, see Stoessel/Bahr conversation, Apr. 9, 1968, confidential: NARA, RG 59, ANF 67–69, Box 2081 (Pol 1 Eur E-Ger W).

60. Brandt assured the CDU Bundestag caucus of this on January 23, 1968: ACDP, VIII-001-1015/2 (pp. 21–22).

61. Two of many examples encountered during research for this project include the Ring Katholischer Deutscher Burschenschaften, ordinarily marked by its conservatism, and the Bremer Jungsozialisten. US Munich (Creel) A-238, Dec. 13, 1968; US Bremen (Goodman) A-58, Apr. 3, 1969: NARA, RG 59, ANF 67–69, Boxes 2214–15 (Pol 16 Ger E).

62. Resolution of the Extraordinary Party Congress in Bad Godesberg, reprinted in *SPD-Jahrbuch* 1968/69, 427–28.

63. On Heinemann's election, see Baring, *Machtwechsel*, 120–23.

64. Hildebrand, *Von Erhard zur Großen Koalition,* 372 (where the process is described rather neutrally as the Union's effort to reintegrate dissatisfied voters).

65. Krone to Kiesinger, Feb. 8, 1968: ACDP, NL Krone, I-028-12/15.

66. Kiesinger, interview with *Stuttgarter Nachrichten*, Oct. 11, 1967, printed in *DzD* V/1, 1795–97.

67. On the CDU's suspicions of Egon Bahr, triggered especially by Bahr's secret contacts with the SED via the Italian Communist Party, see Kroegel, *Einen Anfang finden!*, 212–24, and Schmoeckel and Kaiser, *Die vergessene Regierung*, 185–200. On Schröder's turn against the new Eastern policy, see US Bonn (Lodge) 14386, July 12, 1968, confidential: NARA, RG 59, ANF 67–69, Box 2129 (Pol 15-1).

68. On Kiesinger's growing isolation within the CDU/CSU, demonstrated by the choice of Schröder as the party's (unsuccessful) candidate for Federal President, see Kroegel, *Einen Anfang finden!*, 275–82.

69. See especially Rusk's comments to Brandt during the quadripartite foreign ministers' dinner on Dec. 12, 1967: *FRUS* 1964–68/XV, 613–15; *AAPD* 1967, 1642–43.

70. In the summer of 1968, British officials debated the problem of East German recognition quite intensively; see the minute "Recognition of the GDR: Possibilities and Implications," July 19, 1968, secret: PRO, FCO 33/225. Paragraph 11 summarizes British concerns; paragraph 9 refers to a little-known initiative by Rusk to avert direct German-German talks by having representatives from each side meet under the aegis of the Four Powers. In the same archival volume, see also the notes of the conversation on July 25, 1968.

71. This interpretation is, admittedly, informed primarily by a reading of British documents; diplomats at London's Foreign and Commonwealth Office showed a particular sensitivity to every nuance of France's policy on German unification. Desk officers in London complained with some justification that a double standard was at work: German public opinion looked the other way when de Gaulle flirted with Ulbricht, but many Germans still had not forgiven Britain for Macmillan's softness during the Berlin Crisis of 1958–59. See, for example, FO (Gibbs) to UK Bonn, Dec. 14, 1968, confidential, and UK Bonn (Gladstone), Jan. 2, 1968, confidential: both PRO, FCO 33/244.

72. Baring, *Machtwechsel*, 139–47.

73. US Bonn (Fessenden) 5817, May 2, 1969, secret: NARA, RG 59, ANF, Box 2115 (Pol 16 Ger E); Ref. I B 4 (Gehlhoff), May 7, 1969, geheim: *AAPD* 1969, 564–65.

74. US Bonn (Hillenbrand) 885, July 22, 1967, confidential: NARA, RG 59, ANF 67–

69, Box 1930 (Pol Camb-Ger W). For a thorough West German account, see PA/AA, B 38, Bd. 199.

75. *AAPD* 1967, 1315 n. 9.

76. CDU-Fraktion, May 13, 1969, pp. 34–37: ACDP, VIII-001-1019/1. Interestingly, Rainer Barzel, the caucus chairman, seemed inclined to regard Cambodia as a special case analogous to Finland.

77. Kroegel, *Einen Anfang finden!*, 311; US Bonn 6432 (Fessenden), May 15, 1969, confidential: NARA, RG 59, ANF 67–69, Box 1930 (Pol Camb-Ger W).

78. The U.S. report cited in n. 77 above notes that Brandt stormed out of the cabinet meeting of May 14, "saying he would not be responsible for the consequences if relations were severed." For the views of Brandt's circle and the Foreign Office leadership, see Ahlers, Aufz., May 16, 1969, and Ruete, Aufz., May 29, 1969: *AAPD* 1969, 596–98 and 648–53. State Secretary Duckwitz remarked to Allied diplomats that he had been opposed to the Hallstein Doctrine for years; see US Bonn (Fessenden) 7196, May 29, 1969, confidential: NARA, RG 59, ANF 67–69, Box 2115 (Pol 16 Ger E).

79. See the resolution of the SPD-Parteivorstand of May 16, 1969: AdsD, PV, May–Aug. 1969.

80. Brandt speech to the Gesellschaft für Auslandskunde in Munich, May 20, 1969, pp. 16–20: PA/AA, B 37, Bd. 467. A useful summary appears in D. C., "Brandt will der 'DDR' nicht das Feld überlassen," *FAZ*, May 21, 1969, 3.

81. US Bonn (Fessenden) 6946, May 24, 1969, confidential, priority: NARA, RG 59, ANF 67–69, Box 1930 (Pol Camb-Ger W).

82. Kroegel, *Einen Anfang finden!*, 313. See also Kiesinger's background talk with journalists on May 29, 1969, pp. 1–4: ACDP, NL Kiesinger, I-226-A008-1.

83. Duckwitz to Ankara 302, May 23, 1969, geheim, citissime mit Vorrang: *AAPD* 1969, 622–23; Frank, *Entschlüsselte Botschaft*, 330–31.

84. Bahr to Brandt, May 29, 1969: *AAPD* 1969, 654–55.

85. "Zwischen null und eins," *Der Spiegel*, June 2, 1969, 27–28.

86. On the June 2 meeting and the later confusion, see Bahr, *Zu meiner Zeit*, 217–19. The record of the "Kressbonn Circle" meeting largely confirms Bahr's account; it also provides some insight into what the CDU/CSU planned. Karl Carstens pointed out that the Vienna Convention on Diplomatic Relations allowed for the possibility that a mission could be permanently or temporarily closed *without* this constituting a break in diplomatic relations. Dienstagskreis, 32. Protokoll, June 2, 1969, pp. 17–18: ACDP, I-226-A010.

87. Auswärtiges Amt, *Außenpolitik der Bundesrepublik Deutschland*, 325.

88. Troche, *Ulbricht und die Dritte Welt*, 81.

89. Bahr, *Zu meiner Zeit*, 219. Brandt and Schmidt later defended the Cambodia decision to the SPD Parteirat in quite thoughtful terms, however: see the Parteirat meeting of June 27, 1969, AdsD.

90. "Grundsatzerklärung der Bundesregierung zur Deutschland- und Friedens-politik," May 30, 1969: *Texte zur Deutschlandpolitik* 3, 254–55. The statement also proclaimed that "friendship and cooperation resting upon mutual trust is . . . only possible with those countries that take the side of the German people in the funda-mental question of national unity." On Wehner's responsibility for having formulated this, see Booz, "*Hallsteinzeit*," 125–26.

91. See the memorandum by the Foreign Ministry, "Die Hauptaufgaben der Aussenpolitik der Deutschen Demokratischen Republik im Jahre 1969," Mar. 27, 1969, p. 17: SAPMO, DY 30/J IV 2/2A, Bd. 1365. Tellingly, the Politburo rejected the memo during its April 8 meeting, insisting that the entire paper be organized upon the theme "Die Hauptaufgaben der Aussenpolitik in Vorbereitung des 20. Jahrestages der DDR."

92. Politbüro, Protokoll Nr. 7/69, Feb. 18, 1969, Anl. 2: BA-SAPMO, DY 30/J IV 2/2, Bd. 1215.

93. Cables 264 and 267 from the East German consul in Damascus (Marter), Apr. 29 and 30, 1969: both BA-SAPMO, NY 4182, Bd. 1334.

94. Winzer to Ulbricht et al., Apr. 25 and 29, 1969: BA-SAPMO, NY 4182, Bd. 1333 and MfAA, G-A 418, Bl. 147.

95. See the compilation of telegrams from Baghdad (particularly 249 and 251) passed along from the Foreign Ministry to Ulbricht et al. on May 2, 1969: BA-SAPMO, NY 4182, Bd. 1333.

96. On the Winzer/Sihanouk conversation, see Winzer's cable from Phnom Penh of Mar. 9, 1968: BA-SAPMO, NY 4182, Bd. 1325.

97. Skepticism can be read between the lines of an arcane dispute between the East Germans and the Cambodians as to the wording of the communiqué announcing diplomatic relations. Abteilung Information, Information Nr. 44/V, May 9, 1969: BA-SAPMO, DY 30/IV A 2/20, Bd. 676. See also telegrams 159 and 165 from Phnom Penh, in ibid.

98. Regarding the embassy, see Axen to Stoph, May 12, 1969: ibid. On the other items, see the negotiating instructions approved in the Politbüro, Protokoll Nr. 20/69, May 20, 1969, Anl. 2: BA-SAPMO, DY 30/J IV 2/2, Bd. 1228.

99. Abteilung Information, Information Nr. 81/VI, June 16, 1969: BA-SAPMO, DY 30/IV A 2/20, Bd. 676.

100. Politbüro, Arbeitsprotokoll Nr. 19/69, May 13, 1969, Anl. 6: BA-SAPMO, DY 30/J IV 2/2A, Bd. 1371.

101. Telegram Nr. 88/69 (Bierbach) from Cairo, May 24, 1969: MfAA, G-A 419, Bl. 53–54.

102. Before the military coup in late May, the Sudanese cabinet had been sharply divided over the question of whether to recognize East Germany or reestablish relations with West Germany. The coup brought to the fore pro-Egyptian forces sharply critical of Bonn's support for Israel. Establishing diplomatic relations with the GDR was, in fact, the first major decision of any sort taken by the new government. US Khartoum 610, May 29, 1969, confidential: NARA, RG 59, ANF 67–69, Box 2115 (Pol 16 Ger E).

103. For varying rumors of this sort pertaining to Syria, see telegram 268 from Damascus, Apr. 30, 1969, and Winzer's conversation with the Soviet ambassador in Damascus, June 4, 1969: both BA-SAPMO, NY 4182, Bd. 1334.

104. Ref. I B 4, Aufz., June 11, 1969, geheim: AAPD 1969, 700–701.

105. This was rather transparent in the case of Iraq, which boasted of turning down an offer of £80 million ($192 million) from West Germany since Baghdad did not want to turn the question of recognition into a "business" arrangement. Telegram 251 from Baghdad, cited in n. 95 above. Nasser himself claimed that West Germany had offered Egypt $125 million; see Weiss/Nasser conversation, July 12, 1969, an

account of which was sent by Kohrt to Ulbricht et al. on July 14: BA-SAPMO, NY 4182, Bd. 1338.

106. For the Iraq figure, see Troche, *Ulbricht und die Dritte Welt*, 75; the amount for Sudan (VM 50 million) was approved by the Politburo in circulation, May 30, 1969 (see the Protokoll Nr. 21/69, Anl. 3): BA-SAPMO, DY 30/J IV 2/2, Bd. 1129.

107. In Syria's case, this merely involved signing a document that had been initialed back on May 1. The Politburo actually considered backdating the Syrian decision so that it would appear to have come before Iraq's. Arbeitsprotokoll Nr. 19/69, May 13, 1969, p. 5 of Anl. 6: BA-SAPMO, DY 30/J IV 2/2A, Bd. 1371. On the VM 30 million to South Yemen, see the Foreign Ministry's proposal of June 30 (approved by the Politburo on July 1): BA-SAPMO, DY 30/J IV 2/2A, Bd. 1378, Bl. 63–66.

108. US Berlin (Klein) 1006, June 9, 1969: NARA, RG 59, ANF 67–69, Box 2114 (Pol 7 Ger E).

109. See the remarks by Conrad Ahlers reported in US Bonn 9031, July 9, 1969: NARA, RG 59, ANF 67–69, Box 2117 (Pol Ger E-UAR).

110. For these figures (VM 300 and 150 million, respectively), see the Foreign Ministry's proposal of Sept. 19, 1969: BA-SAPMO, DY 30/J IV 2/2A, Bd. 1396, Bl. 103–9. The $75 million in government credits would have included $25 million left unused from the GDR-Egyptian aid agreement of 1965.

111. Guinea's decision came as a disappointment; SED ideologist Albert Norden had led a delegation to Conakry seeking diplomatic relations. Politbüro, Arbeitsprotokoll Nr. 31/69, Aug. 5, 1969: BA-SAPMO, DY 30/J IV 2/2A, Bd. 1384. On India's standpoint, see US Delhi 13480, Sept. 18, 1969, confidential: NARA, RG 59, ANF 67–69, Box 2115 (Pol 16 Ger E).

112. South Yemen had only recently been constituted as an independent state centered around the former British colony of Aden. The Federal Republic established diplomatic relations in December 1967. Even before South Yemen's recognition of the GDR, the status of Bonn's promised aid of £1 million ($2.4 million) was in jeopardy, since Aden refused to accept a "Berlin clause" in the treaty. Later in 1969, Bonn proceeded to restore diplomatic relations with the North Yemeni regime based in Sana'a—relations that Sana'a had broken in 1965 in retaliation for Bonn's exchange of ambassadors with Israel. US Aden 609, June 30, 1969, and US Aden A-119, Aug. 6, 1969: NARA, RG 59, ANF 67–69, Box 2115 (Pol 16 Ger E) and Box 2135 (Pol Ger W-Yemen).

113. Sihanouk made these points to Winzer during the latter's visit to Phnom Penh in early 1968; see Winzer's telegram of Mar. 9, 1968: SAPMO, NY 4182, Bd. 1325.

114. Wolle, *Die heile Welt der Diktatur*, 45–51.

115. Politbüro, Arbeitsprotokoll Nr. 38/69, Oct. 14, 1969: BA-SAPMO, DY 30/J IV 2/2A, Bd. 1395. See especially the accompanying documents by Axen and Böhm on Bl. 110–13 of Bd. 1396.

116. Putensen, *Im Konfliktfeld zwischen Ost und West*, 251–92. As Putensen shows, delays in the realization of the Helsinki Conference led the Finnish government to propose a new tack in September 1971: the simultaneous establishment of diplomatic relations with both German states. Bonn resisted this option until January 1973.

117. US Bonn (Rush) 14518, Nov. 5, 1969, secret: NARA, RG 59, ANF 67–69, Box 2128 (Pol 15).

118. For the views of Scheel and other members of the Brandt cabinet, see Frank,

Aufzeichnung, "Außenbeziehungen der DDR (Mitgliedschaft der DDR in internationalen staatlichen Organisationen)," Dec. 5, 1969, streng geheim: *AAPD* 1969, 1365–67. See also Brandt's comments to U.S. secretary of state William P. Rogers on Dec. 8, 1969: *AAPD* 1969, 1985.

119. Scheel, Runderlaß 4271 Plurex, Oct. 30, 1969: *AAPD* 1969, 1195–96; Booz, "*Hallsteinzeit,*" 139–45.

120. See the complaints of United Nations representatives conveyed in DG UN (Böker) 1241, Nov. 5, 1969, vertraulich, Citissime: *AAPD* 1969, 1221–24. One should, of course, bear in mind that Alexander Böker, at this time serving as the West German observer at the United Nations, had earlier expended a tremendous amount of energy resisting East German encroachments around the developing world; he was thus predisposed to worry about the policy of the Brandt-Scheel coalition.

121. *AAPD* 1970, 2262, note 12; also Kilian, *Hallstein-Doktrin,* 169–70.

122. Horstmeier, "Die DDR und Belgien"; Pekelder, "Zwischen 'Sowjet-Deutschland' und 'sozialistischem Modellstaat'"; Becker, *DDR und Großbritannien.*

123. Muth, *DDR-Außenpolitik,* 284; on Algeria, see Troche, *Ulbricht und die Dritte Welt,* 84.

124. For a complex international history of the negotiations surrounding the Basic Treaty, see Sarotte, *Dealing with the Devil.*

125. For a list, in painstaking chronological order, of the countries that established diplomatic relations with the GDR, see Muth, *DDR-Außenpolitik,* 234–37. On U.S. reservations, see Grunert, *Für Honecker auf glattem Parkett.*

CONCLUSION

1. See, for example, several of the essays in Schwanitz, *Jenseits der Legende.* On the bitterness of the former diplomats, see Lahann, *Geliebte Zone,* 316–26.

2. On the term "affiliation," see Winrow, *The Foreign Policy of the GDR in Africa,* 9–15. Of more general interest here: Siebs, *Außenpolitik der DDR 1976–1989*; Ostermann, "East Germany and the Horn Crisis."

3. Frank, *Entschlüsselte Botschaft,* 185–86.

4. Analogies to Cold War nuclear doctrines first surfaced during the Near Eastern crisis of March 1965. See Marion Gräfin Dönhoff, "Deutsches Dilemma," *Die Zeit,* Mar. 12, 1965; and the comments by Bundestag President Eugen Gerstenmaier and his interviewer in *Der Spiegel,* Mar. 17, 1965.

BIBLIOGRAPHY

PRIMARY SOURCES

Archival Sources
Archiv der sozialen Demokratie (AdsD), Bonn
    SPD: Bundesvorstand 1955–69
    Nachlässe
        Fritz Erler
        Erich Ollenhauer
Archiv des Deutschen Liberalismus (ADL), Gummersbach
    FDP: Bestand Bundespartei
        Bundeshauptausschuß (A 12)
    FDP: Bestand Bundestagsfraktion (A 40)
        Fraktionsprotokolle
        Fraktionsvorstandsprotokolle
Archiv für christlich-demokratische Politik (ACDP), St. Augustin
    CDU/CSU-Fraktion im Bundestag (VIII-001)
        Sitzungen des CDU/CSU-Fraktionsvorstands (1955–65)
        Sitzungen der CDU/CSU-Fraktion (1955–65)
        Arbeitskreissitzungen
            Kurzprotokolle 1962–66
    Arbeitskreis V der CDU/CSU-Fraktion im Bundestag (VIII-006)
        Protokolle des Arbeitskreises, 1954–61
    Nachlässe
        I-433: Kurt Birrenbach
        I-010: Felix von Eckardt
        I-210: Eugen Gerstenmaier
        I-294: Johann Baptist Gradl
        I-149: Josef Jansen
        I-028: Heinrich Krone
        I-148: Hans-Joachim von Merkatz
        I-475: Friedrich Karl Vialon
Bundesarchiv Berlin-Lichterfelde (BAL)
    Stiftung Archiv der Parteien und Massenorganisation der DDR (SAPMO)
        Politbüro des ZK—Reinschriftenprotokolle, Arbeitsprotokolle
        Abteilung Internationale Beziehungen des ZK
        Außenpolitische Kommission beim Politbüro des ZK
        Büro Ulbricht

Nachlässe
NY 4090: Otto Grotewohl
NY 4182: Walter Ulbricht
DL 2: Ministerium für Außenhandel und innerdeutschen Handel
Bundesarchiv Koblenz (BAK)
B 136: Bundeskanzleramt
B 137: Bundesministerium für gesamtdeutsche Fragen (BMG)
B 145: Presse- und Informationsamt der Bundesregierung (BPA)
B 213: Bundesministerium für wirtschaftliche Zusammenarbeit (BMZ)
Nachlässe
N 1371: Rainer Barzel
N 1388: Erik Blumenfeld
N 1351: Herbert Blankenhorn
N 1239: Heinrich von Brentano
N 1337: Karl Carstens
N 1397: Karl Theodor Freiherr von und zu Guttenberg
N 1236: Walter Hallstein
N 1018: Jakob Kaiser
Ludwig-Erhard-Stiftung (LES), Bonn
Nachlaß Ludwig Erhard
Korrespondenz
Pressekonferenzen (NE 335)
Ministère des Affaires Étrangères/Archives Étrangères (MAE), Paris
Série Europe 1944–60
Allemagne 1949–55
Allemagne 1956–60
République Démocratique Allemande 1956–60
Yougoslavie 1956–60
Série Europe 1961–70
République Fédérale d'Allemagne
République Démocratique Allemande
National Archives and Record Administration (NARA), College Park, Md.
RG 59, Records of the Department of State
Central Decimal Files, 1950–63
462A series (West German trade)
462B series (East German trade)
601.62A&B (diplomatic representation)
602.62A&B (consular representation)
611.62A&B (U.S. relations with West, East Germany)
648.62A&B (Polish relations with West, East Germany)
662A series (West German diplomatic relations)
662B series (East German diplomatic relations)
762A&B (politics and government in each German state)
762A.02, 762B.02 (recognition of, respectively, West and East Germany)
Alpha-Numeric Files, 1963–69
Aid W Ger
Pol E Ger

Pol W Ger

UN Ger E, W

Pol Tanzania

Pol Zanzibar

Lot Files, Europe

Entry 3088: EUR/GER—Numerical Files Relating to the GDR

Entry 3090: EUR/GER—Alpha-Numeric Files Relating to the FRG

Parlamentsarchiv des Deutschen Bundestages, Bonn

Ausschuß für Auswärtige Angelegenheiten

Sitzungsprotokolle (1954–65)

Ausschuß für Entwicklungshilfe

Sitzungsprotokolle (1961–69)

Politisches Archiv des Auswärtigen Amtes (PA/AA), Bonn

B 1: Ministerbüro

B 2: Büro Staatssekretär

B 10: Abteilung 2

B 11: Abteilung 3

B 12: Abteilung 7

B 30: United Nations (Referat 300/I B 1)

B 33: Latin America (Referat 306/I B 2)

B 34: Sub-Saharan Africa (Referat 307/I B 3)

B 36: Near and Middle East (Referat I B 4)

B 37: South, Southeast, and East Asia (Referat I B 5)

B 38: Unifaction (Referat II A 1)

B 80: International Law (Referat 500/V 1)

Nachlaß Wilhelm Grewe

Nachlaß Albrecht von Kessel

B 150: Aktenkopien zur Edition *Akten zur Auswärtigen Politik*

Bestand MfAA

Leitungssitzungen (1955–64)

Correspondence of Staatssekretär/Minister Winzer

Unterredungen mit den Leitern der Auslandsvertretungen

Presse- und Informationsamt der Bundesregierung (BPA), Bonn

Abteilung Pressedokumentation

Pressemagazin

Public Records Office (PRO), London

FO 371: Foreign Office: Political Relations, 1906–present

FCO 33: Foreign & Commonwealth Office: Western Department, Registered

PREM 11: Prime Minister's Office

Stiftung Bundeskanzler-Adenauer-Haus (StBKAH), Rhöndorf

Nachlaß Konrad Adenauer

Microfilm Collections

Confidential U.S. State Department Central Files. Bethesda, Md.: University
Publications of America.

Federal Republic of Germany: Internal Affairs, 1950–54 [FRG-IA 50–54]

Federal Republic of Germany: Internal Affairs, 1955–59 [FRG-IA 55–59]

Federal Republic of Germany: Foreign Affairs, 1950–54 [FRG-FA 50–54]
Federal Republic of Germany: Foreign Affairs, 1955–59 [FRG-FA 55–59]
Germany: Internal Affairs and Foreign Affairs 1955–59 [G-FA 55–59]
Soviet Union: Foreign Affairs 1955–59 [USSR-FA 55–59]
Records of the U.S. Department of State Relating to Internal Affairs of East Germany,
1955–59 [GDR-IA 55-59]. Wilmington, Del.: Scholarly Resources, 1988.
Records of the U.S. Department of State Relating to Internal Affairs of the Russian Zone,
1950–54 [GDR-IA 50–54]. Wilmington, Del.: Scholarly Resources, 1987.

Official Document Collections

Akten zur Auswärtigen Politik der Bundesrepublik Deutschland. 1949–52, 1963–70.
Munich: Oldenbourg, 1994– .
Auswärtiges Amt, ed. *Aussenpolitik der Bundesrepublik Deutschland. Dokumente von*
1949 bis 1994. Cologne: Verlag Wissenschaft und Politik, 1995.
——. *Die Bemühungen der deutschen Regierung und ihrer Verbündeten um die Einheit*
Deutschlands 1955–1966. Bonn: Bundesdruckerei, 1966.
——. *40 Jahre Außenpolitik der Bundesrepublik Deutschland.* Stuttgart: Bonn Aktuell,
1989.
Conference of Heads of State or Government of Non-Aligned Countries. Belgrade:
Yugoslavia, 1961.
Conference of Heads of State or Government of Non-Aligned Countries. Cairo: National
Publication House, 1964.
Deutscher Bundestag. *Verhandlungen des Deutschen Bundestages. Stenographische*
Berichte.
Documents diplomatiques français. 1954–61. Paris: Imprimerie Nationale.
Dokumente zur Außenpolitik der Regierung der Deutschen Demokratischen Republik.
Berlin: Staatsverlag der DDR, 1954– .
Dokumente zur Deutschlandpolitik.
II. Reihe, 1945–50. 3 vols. Munich: Oldenbourg, 1996–97.
III. Reihe, May 5, 1955–November 9, 1958. 4 vols. Frankfurt: Metzner, 1961–69.
IV. Reihe, November 10, 1958–November 30, 1966. 12 vols. Frankfurt: Metzner,
1971–81.
V. Reihe, December 1, 1966–December 31, 1968. 2 vols. Frankfurt: Metzner, 1984–
87.
Foreign Relations of the United States. Washington, D.C.: Government Printing Office.
1949/III. *Council of Foreign Ministers; Germany and Austria.*
1950/IV. *Central and Eastern Europe; The Soviet Union.*
1951/III. *European Security and the German Question.*
1952–54/VII. *Germany and Austria.*
1955–57/V. *Austrian State Treaty; Summit and Foreign Ministers Meetings, 1955.*
1955–57/XXV. *Eastern Europe.*
1955–57/XXVI. *Central and Southeastern Europe.*
1958–60/VIII. *Berlin Crisis 1958–59.*
1958–60/IX. *Berlin Crisis 1959–60; Germany; Austria.*
1958–60/XIV. *Africa.*
1961–63/IX. *Foreign Economic Policy.*
1961–63/XIV. *Berlin Crisis 1961–62.*

1961–63/XV. *Berlin Crisis 1962–63.*
1961–63/XVI. *Eastern Europe.*
1961–63/XXI. *Africa.*
1964–68/XV. *Germany and Berlin.*
Die Kabinettsprotokolle der Bundesregierung. Vols. 1–10. Boppard am Rhein: Harald
Boldt Verlag, 1982–2000.
Texte zur Deutschlandpolitik. Edited by the Bundesministerium für gesamtdeutsche
Fragen. Bonn: Deutscher Bundes-Verlag, 1968–1982.

Thematic Document Collections and Party Publications

Beziehungen DDR-UdSSR 1949 bis 1955. 2 vols. Berlin: Staatsverlag der Deutschen
Demokratischen Republik, 1975.
Buchstab, Günter, ed. *Adenauer: "Wir haben wirklich etwas geschaffen." Die Protokolle
des CDU-Bundesvorstandes 1953–57.* Düsseldorf: Droste, 1990.
———. *Adenauer: ". . . Um den Frieden zu gewinnen." Die Protokolle des CDU-
Bundesvorstandes 1957–1961.* Düsseldorf: Droste, 1994.
———. *Adenauer: "Stetigkeit in der Politik." Die Protokolle des CDU-Bundesvorstandes
1961–1965.* Düsseldorf: Droste, 1998.
Frankland, Noble, and Vera King, eds. *Documents on International Affairs 1956.*
Oxford: Oxford University Press, 1959.
Jacobsen, Hans-Adolf, and Mieczyslaw Tomala, eds. *Bonn-Warschau 1945–1991. Die
deutsch-polnischen Beziehungen. Analyse und Dokumentation.* Cologne: Verlag
Wissenschaft und Politik, 1992.
Jelinek, Yeshayahu, ed. *Zwischen Moral und Realpolitik. Deutsch-Israelische
Beziehungen 1945–1965. Eine Dokumentensammlung.* Gerlingen: Bleicher, 1997.
Lappenküper, Ulrich, ed. *Die Bundesrepublik Deutschland und Frankreich: Dokumente
1949–1963.* Vol. 1, *Außenpolitik und Diplomatie.* Munich: Saur, 1997.
Merritt, Anna J., and Richard L. Merritt, eds. *Public Opinion in Semisovereign
Germany: The HICOG Surveys, 1949–1955.* Urbana: University of Illinois Press,
1980.
Ruhm von Oppen, Beate, ed. *Documents on Germany Under Occupation 1945–1954.*
London: Oxford University Press, 1955.
Todt, Manfred, ed. *Anfangsjahre der Bundesrepublik Deutschland. Berichte der
Schweizer Gesandtschaft in Bonn 1949–1955.* Munich: Oldenbourg, 1987.
Weber, Petra, Wolfgang Hölscher, and Heinrich Potthoff, eds. *Die SPD-Fraktion im
Deutschen Bundestag. Sitzungsprotokolle 1949–66.* 3 vols. Düsseldorf: Droste,
1993.
Wengst, Udo, ed. *FDP-Bundesvorstand: Sitzungsprotokolle 1949–1968.* Düsseldorf:
Droste, 1990–93.

Reference Works

Baumgartner, Gabriele, and Dieter Hebig, eds. *Biographisches Handbuch der
SBZ/DDR 1945–1990.* Munich: Saur, 1997.
Müller-Enbergs, Helmut, Jan Wielgohs, and Dieter Hoffmann, eds. *Wer war wer in
der DDR? Ein biographisches Lexikon.* Berlin: Links, 2000.
Ritter, Gerhard A., and Merith Niehuss. *Wahlen in Deutschland 1946–1991. Ein
Handbuch.* Munich: Beck, 1991.

Zimmermann, Hartmut, Horst Ulrich, and Michael Fehlauer, eds. *DDR Handbuch*, 3rd ed. Cologne: Verlag Wissenschaft und Politik, 1985.

Memoirs, Correspondence, and Conversations

Adenauer, Konrad. *Briefe 1955–57*. Edited by Hans Peter Mensing. Berlin: Siedler, 1998.

——. *Briefe 1957–59*. Edited by Hans Peter Mensing. Paderborn: Schöningh, 2000.

——. *Erinnerungen*. 4 vols. Stuttgart: Deutsche Verlags-Anstalt, 1965–67.

——. *Teegespräche 1955–58*. Edited by Hanns Jürgen Küsters. Berlin: Siedler, 1986.

——. *Teegespräche 1959–61*. Edited by Hanns Jürgen Küsters. Berlin: Siedler, 1988.

——. *Teegespräche 1961–63*. Edited by Hans Peter Mensing. Berlin: Siedler, 1992.

Adenauer-Heuss: Unter vier Augen. Gespräche aus den Gründerjahren 1949–1959. Edited by Hans Peter Mensing. Berlin: Siedler, 1997.

Allardt, Helmut. *Politik vor und hinter den Kulissen. Erfahrungen eines Botschafters zwischen Ost und West*. Düsseldorf: Econ, 1979.

Bahr, Egon. *Zu meiner Zeit*. Munich: Karl Blessing, 1996.

Baring, Arnulf, ed. *Sehr verehrter Herr Bundeskanzler! Heinrich von Brentano im Briefwechsel mit Konrad Adenauer*. Hamburg: Hoffmann und Campe, 1974.

Birrenbach, Kurt. *Meine Sondermissionen. Rückblick auf zwei Jahrzehnte bundesdeutscher Außenpolitik*. Düsseldorf: Econ, 1984.

Brandt, Willy. *Begegnungen und Einsichten. Die Jahre 1960–1975*. Hamburg: Hoffmann und Campe, 1976.

Carstens, Karl. *Erinnerungen und Erfahrungen*. Boppard am Rhein: Harald Boldt, 1993.

Diehl, Günter. *Zwischen Politik und Presse. Bonner Erinnerungen 1949–1969*. Frankfurt: Societäts-Verlag, 1994.

Eckardt, Felix von. *Ein unordentliches Leben*. Düsseldorf: Econ, 1967.

Frank, Paul. *Entschlüsselte Botschaft. Ein Diplomat macht Inventur*. Stuttgart: Deutsche Verlags-Anstalt, 1981.

Grewe, Wilhelm. *Rückblenden 1976–1951*. Frankfurt: Propyläen, 1979.

Grunert, Horst. *Für Honecker auf glattem Parkett. Erinnerungen eines DDR-Diplomaten*. Berlin: Edition Ost, 1995.

Kroll, Hans. *Lebenserinnerungen eines Botschafters*. Cologne: Kiepenheuer & Witsch, 1967.

Krone, Heinrich. "Aufzeichnungen zur Deutschland- und Ostpolitik 1954–1969." In *Adenauer-Studien III*, edited by Rudolf Morsey and Konrad Repgen, 134–301. Mainz: Matthias-Grünewald-Verlag, 1974.

——. *Tagebücher 1945–1961*. Edited by Hans-Otto Kleinmann. Düsseldorf: Droste, 1995.

Lahr, Rolf. *Zeuge von Fall und Aufstieg. Private Briefe 1934–1974*. Hamburg: Albrecht Knaus, 1981.

McGhee, George. *At the Creation of a New Germany: From Adenauer to Brandt*. New Haven, Conn.: Yale University Press, 1989.

Mende, Erich. *Von Wende zu Wende, 1962–1982*. Munich: Herbig, 1986.

Micunovic, Veljko. *Moscow Diary*. Translated by David Floyd. New York: Doubleday, 1980.

Morrow, John H. *First American Ambassador to Guinea*. New Brunswick, N.J.:
 Rutgers University Press, 1968.
Osterheld, Horst. *Außenpolitik unter Bundeskanzler Ludwig Erhard 1963–1966. Ein
 dokumentarischer Bericht aus dem Bundeskanzleramt*. Düsseldorf: Droste, 1992.
———. *"Ich gehe nicht leichten Herzens . . . ": Adenauers letzte Kanzlerjahre—ein
 dokumentarischer Bericht*. Mainz: Matthias-Grünewald-Verlag, 1986.
Peckert, Joachim. *Zeitwende zum Frieden. Ostpolitik miterlebt und mitgestaltet*.
 Herford: Busse Seewald, 1990.
Sahm, Ulrich. *"Diplomaten taugen nichts." Aus dem Leben eines Staatsdieners*.
 Düsseldorf: Droste, 1994.
Schmid, Carlo. *Erinnerungen*. Bern: Scherz, 1979.
Schollwer, Wolfgang. *FDP im Wandel. Aufzeichnungen 1960–1966*. Munich:
 Oldenbourg, 1994.
Schütz, Klaus. *Logenplatz und Schleudersitz. Erinnerungen*. Berlin: Ullstein, 1992.
Seydoux, François. *Dans l'intimité franco-allemande. Une mission diplomatique*. Paris:
 Editions Albatros, 1977.
Wischnewski, Hans-Jürgen. *Mit Leidenschaft und Augenmaß. In Mogadischu und
 anderswo*. Munich: Bertelsmann, 1989.

SECONDARY SOURCES

Books and Articles

Abelshauser, Werner, and Walter Schwengler. *Anfänge westdeutscher
 Sicherheitspolitik 1945–1956*. Vol. 4, *Wirtschaft und Rüstung, Souveränität und
 Sicherheit*. Munich: Oldenbourg, 1997.
Ahonen, Pertti. "Domestic Constraints on West German *Ostpolitik*: The Role of the
 Expellee Organizations in the Adenauer Era." *Central European History* 31, nos. 1
 & 2 (1998): 31–64.
Altmann, Normen. *Konrad Adenauer im Kalten Krieg. Wahrnehmungen und Politik
 1945–1956*. Mannheim: Palatium, 1993.
Andereggen, Anton. *France's Relationship with Subsaharan Africa*. Westport, Conn.:
 Praeger, 1994.
Anderson, Sheldon. *A Cold War in the Soviet Bloc: Polish–East German Relations,
 1945–1962*. Boulder, Colo.: Westview, 2001.
Anic de Osona, Marija. *Die erste Anerkennung der DDR. Der Bruch der deutsch-
 jugoslawischen Beziehungen 1957*. Baden-Baden: Nomos, 1990.
Außenpolitik der DDR: Drei Jahrzehnte sozialistische deutsche Friedenspolitik. Berlin:
 Staatsverlag der DDR, 1979.
Badstübner, Rolf. "Die sowjetische Deutschlandpolitik im Lichte neuer Quellen." In
 Loth, *Die deutsche Frage in der Nachkriegszeit*, 102–35.
Bark, Dennis, and David Gress. *A History of West Germany*. Vol. 2, *Democracy and Its
 Discontents, 1963–1991*. 2nd ed. Cambridge, Mass.: Blackwell, 1993.
Baring, Arnulf. *Außenpolitik in Adenauers Kanzlerdemokratie*. Munich: Oldenbourg,
 1969.
———. *Machtwechsel. Die Ära Brandt-Scheel*. Stuttgart: Deutsche Verlags-Anstalt, 1982.
Becker, Bert. *Die DDR und Großbritannien 1945/49 bis 1973. Politische, wirtschaftliche*

und kulturelle Kontakte im Zeichen der Nichtanerkennungspolitik. Bochum: Universitätsverlag Brockmeyer, 1991.

Bellers, Jürgen. *Außenwirtschaftspolitik der Bundesrepublik Deutschland 1949–1989.* Münster: Lit, 1990.

Bender, Peter. "Berlinkrise—Geburtsstunde der neuen Ostpolitik?" *Deutschland Archiv* 30, no. 6 (1997): 934–39.

———. *Episode oder Epoche? Zur Geschichte des geteilten Deutschland.* Munich: dtv, 1996.

———. *Die "Neue Ostpolitik" und ihre Folgen. Vom Mauerbau bis zur Vereinigung.* Munich: dtv, 1995.

———. *Zehn Gründe für die Anerkennung der DDR.* Frankfurt am Main: Fischer, 1968.

Benz, Wolfgang. *Die Gründung der Bundesrepublik. Von der Bizone zum souveränen Staat.* 5th ed. Munich: dtv, 1999.

Berggötz, Sven Olaf. *Nahostpolitik in der Ära Adenauer. Möglichkeiten und Grenzen 1949–1963.* Düsseldorf: Droste, 1998.

Beschloss, Michael. *The Crisis Years: Kennedy and Khrushchev, 1960–1963.* New York: Harper Collins, 1991.

Besson, Waldemar. *Die Außenpolitik der Bundesrepublik. Erfahrungen und Maßstäbe.* Munich: Piper, 1970.

Bingen, Dieter. *Die Polenpolitik der Bonner Republik von Adenauer bis Kohl.* Baden-Baden: Nomos, 1998.

Bingen, Dieter, and Jansz Jozef Wec. *Die Deutschlandpolitik Polens 1945–1991. Von der Status-quo-Orientierung bis zum Paradigmawechsel.* Cracow: Jagellonian University, 1993.

Birke, Adolf M. *Nation ohne Haus. Deutschland 1945–1961.* Special edition. Berlin: Siedler, 1994.

Bischof, Günter. "The Making of the Austrian Treaty and the Road to Geneva." In Bischof and Dockrill, *Cold War Respite: The Geneva Summit of 1955,* 117–54.

Bischof, Günter, and Saki Dockrill, eds. *Cold War Respite: The Geneva Summit of 1955.* Baton Rouge: Louisiana State University Press, 2000.

Blasius, Rainer A. "Erwin Wickert und die Friedensnote der Bundesregierung vom 25. März 1966." *Vierteljahrshefte für Zeitgeschichte* 43, no. 3 (1995): 539–53.

———. "Geschäftsfreundschaft statt diplomatischer Beziehungen. Zur Israel-Politik 1962/63." In Blasius, *Von Adenauer zu Erhard,* 154–210.

———. *Hasso von Etzdorf. Ein deutscher Diplomat im 20. Jahrhundert.* Zurich: Haumesser Verlag, 1994.

———. " 'Völkerfreundschaft' am Nil: Ägypten und die DDR im Februar 1965." *Vierteljahrshefte für Zeitgeschichte* 46, no. 4 (1998): 747–805.

———, ed. *Von Adenauer zu Erhard. Studien zur Auswärtigen Politik der Bundesrepublik Deutschland 1963.* Munich: Oldenbourg, 1994.

Bodemer, Klaus. *Entwicklungshilfe—Politik für wen? Ideologie und Vergabepraxis der deutschen Entwicklungshilfe in der ersten Dekade.* Munich: Weltforum, 1974.

Booz, Rüdiger Marco. *"Hallsteinzeit." Deutsche Außenpolitik 1955–1972.* Bonn: Bouvier, 1995.

Bouvier, Beatrix W. *Zwischen Godesberg und Großer Koalition. Der Weg der SPD in die Regierungsverantwortung.* Bonn: Dietz, 1990.

Brands, H. W. *The Specter of Neutralism: The United States and the Emergence of the Third World, 1947–1960*. New York: Columbia University Press, 1989.

Brauers, Christoph. *Liberale Deutschlandpolitik 1949–1969. Positionen der F.D.P. zwischen nationaler und europäischer Orientierung*. Münster: Lit, 1993.

Braunthal, Gerard. *Parties and Politics in Modern Germany*. Boulder, Colo.: Westview, 1996.

Broszat, Martin, ed. *Zäsuren nach 1945. Essays zur Periodisierung deutscher Nachkriegsgeschichte*. Munich: Oldenbourg, 1990.

Buchheim, Hans. *Deutschlandpolitik 1949–1972. Der diplomatisch-politische Prozeß*. Stuttgart: Deutsche Verlags-Anstalt, 1984.

Bührer, Werner. "Der BDI und die Aussenpolitik der Bundesrepublik in den fünfziger Jahren." *Vierteljahrshefte für Zeitgeschichte* 40, no. 2 (1992): 241–61.

Buffet, Cyril. "De Gaulle et Berlin: Une certaine idée d'Allemagne." *Revue d'Allemagne* 22, no. 4 (October–December 1990): 525–38.

Burns, William J. *Economic Aid and American Policy toward Egypt, 1955–1981*. Albany: State University of New York Press, 1985.

Burr, William. "Avoiding the Slippery Slope: The Eisenhower Administration and the Berlin Crisis, November 1958–January 1959." *Diplomatic History* 16, no. 2 (1994): 177–205.

Cary, Noel. "Reassessing Germany's *Ostpolitik*." *Central European History* 33, no. 2 (2000): 235–62.

Castigliola, Frank. "The Pursuit of Atlantic Community: Nuclear Arms, Dollars, and Berlin." In *Kennedy's Quest for Victory: American Foreign Policy, 1961–63*, edited by Thomas G. Paterson, 24–56. New York: Oxford University Press, 1989.

Clayton, Anthony. *The Zanzibar Revolution and Its Aftermath*. Hamden, Conn.: Archon, 1981.

Conze, Eckart. *Die gaullistische Herausforderung. Die deutsch-französischen Beziehungen in der amerikanischen Europapolitik 1958–1963*. Munich: Oldenbourg, 1995.

——. "No Way Back to Potsdam: The Adenauer Government and the Geneva Summit." In Bischof and Dockrill, *Cold War Respite*, 190–214.

Czempiel, Ernst-Otto. *Macht und Kompromiß. Die Beziehungen der Bundesrepublik Deutschland zu den Vereinten Nationen 1956–1970*. Düsseldorf: Bertelsmann Universitätsverlag, 1971.

Danckwortt, Dieter. *Zur Psychologie der deutschen Entwicklungshilfe*. Baden-Baden: Verlag August Lutzeyer, 1962.

Dann, Uriel. *Iraq under Qassem: A Political History, 1958–1963*. New York: Praeger, 1969.

Dennert, Jürgen. *Entwicklungshilfe geplant oder verwaltet? Entstehung und Konzeption des Bundesministeriums für wirtschaftliche Zusammenarbeit*. Bielefeld: Bertelsmann Universitätsverlag, 1968.

Deutschkron, Inge. *Israel und die Deutschen. Das besondere Verhältnis*. Cologne: Verlag Wissenschaft und Politik, 1983.

Di Nolfo, Ennio, ed. *Power in Europe? II: Great Britain, France, Germany, and Italy, and the Origins of the EEC, 1952–1957*. Berlin: Walter de Gruyter, 1992.

Doering-Manteuffel, Anselm, ed. *Adenauerzeit. Stand, Perspektiven, und methodische Aufgaben der Zeitgeschichtsforschung (1955–1967)*. Bonn: Bouvier, 1993.

Döscher, Hans-Jürgen. *Verschworene Gesellschaft. Das Auswärtige Amt unter Adenauer zwischen Neubeginn und Kontinuität.* Berlin: Akademie Verlag, 1995.

Dröge, Heinz, Fritz Münch, and Ellinor von Puttkamer. *The Federal Republic of Germany and the United Nations.* New York: Carnegie Endowment, 1967.

Eibl, Franz. *Politik der Bewegung. Gerhard Schröder als Außenminister 1961–1966.* Munich: Oldenbourg, 2001.

Emerson, Rupert. *From Empire to Nation: The Rise to Self-Assertion of Asian and African Peoples.* Cambridge, Mass.: Harvard University Press, 1960.

End, Heinrich. *Zweimal deutsche Außenpolitik. Internationale Dimensionen des innerdeutschen Konflikts 1949–1972.* Cologne: Verlag Wissenschaft und Politik, 1973.

Engel, Ulf, and Hans-Georg Schleicher. *Die beiden deutschen Staaten in Afrika: Zwischen Konkurrenz und Koexistenz 1949–1990.* Hamburg: Institut für Afrika-Kunde, 1998.

Engelmann, Roger, and Paul Erker. *Annäherung und Abgrenzung. Aspekte deutsch-deutscher Beziehungen 1956–1969.* Munich: Oldenbourg, 1993.

Faulenbach, Bernd, and Heinrich Potthoff, eds. *Sozialdemokraten und Kommunisten nach Nationalsozialismus und Krieg. Zur historischen Einordnung der Zwangsvereinigung.* Essen: Klartext, 1998.

Felken, Detlef. *Dulles und Deutschland. Die amerikanische Deutschlandpolitik 1953–1959.* Bonn: Bouvier, 1993.

Foot, Rosemary. *The Practice of Power: US Relations with China since 1949.* Oxford: Clarendon, 1995.

Foschepoth, Josef. "Adenauers Moskaureise 1955." *Aus Politik und Zeitgeschichte* 22 (1986): 30–46.

——, ed. *Adenauer und die deutsche Frage.* 2nd ed. Göttingen: Vandenhoeck & Ruprecht, 1990.

Frei, Norbert. *Vergangenheitspolitik. Die Anfänge der Bundesrepublik und die NS-Vergangenheit.* Munich: Beck, 1996.

Frei, Otto. "Die Bemühungen der DDR um internationale Anerkennung." In *Die internationale Politik 1963*, edited by Wilhelm Cornides, Dietrich Mende, and Wolfgang Wagner, 235–56. Munich: Oldenbourg, 1969.

Frohn, Axel. "Adenauer und die deutschen Ostgebiete in den fünfziger Jahren." *Vierteljahrshefte für Zeitgeschichte* 44, no. 4 (1996): 484–525.

Gaddis, John Lewis. "History, Theory, and Common Ground." *International Security* 22, no. 1 (Summer 1997): 75–85.

——. *The Long Peace: Inquiries into the History of the Cold War.* New York: Oxford University Press, 1987.

——. *We Now Know: Rethinking Cold War History.* New York: Oxford University Press, 1997.

Gallus, Alexander. *Die Neutralisten. Verfechter eines vereinten Deutschland zwischen Ost und West 1945–1990.* Düsseldorf: Droste, 2001.

Garton Ash, Timothy. *In Europe's Name: Germany and the Divided Continent.* New York: Random House, 1993.

Gearson, John P. S. *Harold Macmillan and the Berlin Wall Crisis, 1958–1962: The Limits of Interests and Force.* New York: St. Martin's, 1998.

Gehler, Michael. "Österreichs außenpolitische Emanzipation und die deutsche Frage 1945–1955." In *Österreich unter alliierter Besatzung 1945–1955*, edited by Alfred Ableitinger, Siegfried Beer, and Eduard G. Staudinger, 205–68. Vienna: Böhlau, 1998.

Gerber, Therese Steffen. "Zwischen Neutralitätspolitik und Anlehnung and den Westen. Die Beziehungen zwischen der Schweiz und der DDR (1949–1972)." In Pfeil, *Die DDR und der Westen*, 329–49.

Geyer, Martin H. "Der Kampf um nationale Repräsentation. Deutsch-deutsche Sportbeziehungen und die 'Hallstein-Doktrin.'" *Vierteljahrshefte für Zeitgeschichte* 44, no. 1 (1996): 55–86.

Görgey, Laszlo. *Bonn's Eastern Policy 1964–1971: Evolution and Limitations*. Hamden, Conn.: Archon, 1972.

Grieder, Peter. *The East German Leadership, 1946–1973: Conflict and Crisis*. Manchester: Manchester University Press, 1999.

Gürbey, Gülüzar. *Die Türkei-Politik der Bundesrepublik Deutschland unter Konrad Adenauer (1949–1963)*. Pfaffenweiler: Centaurus-Verlagsgesellschaft, 1990.

Hacke, Christian. *Weltmacht wider Willen. Die Außenpolitik der Bundesrepublik Deutschland*. Updated, expanded edition. Frankfurt: Ullstein, 1993.

Hacker, Jens. *Deutsche Irrtümer. Schönfärber und Helfershelfer der SED-Diktatur im Westen*. Berlin: Ullstein, 1992.

Hafez, Kai. "Von der nationalen Frage zur Systempolitik. Perioden der DDR-Nahostpolitik, 1949–1989." *Orient* 36, no. 1 (1995): 77–95.

Hahn, Karl-Eckhard. *Wiedervereinigung im Widerstreit. Einwirkungen und Einwirkungsversuche westdeutscher Entscheidungsträger auf die Deutschlandpolitik Adenauers von 1949 bis zur Genfer Viermächtekonferenz 1959*. Hamburg: Kovac, 1993.

Hanrieder, Wolfram. *Germany, America, Europe: Forty Years of German Foreign Policy*. New Haven, Conn.: Yale University Press, 1989.

Harrison, Hope. "Ulbricht and the Concrete 'Rose': New Archival Evidence on the Dynamics of Soviet–East German Relations and the Berlin Crisis." Cold War International History Project, Working Paper No. 5. Washington, D.C.: Woodrow Wilson International Center, 1993.

Heidemeyer, Helge. *Flucht und Zuwanderung aus der SBZ/DDR 1945/1949–1961*. Düsseldorf: Droste, 1994.

Hentschel, Volker. *Ludwig Erhard. Ein Politikerleben*. Munich: Olzog, 1996.

Herf, Jeffrey. *Divided Memory: The Two Germanys and the Nazi Past*. Cambridge, Mass.: Harvard University Press, 1997.

Herzfeld, Hans. "Das geteilte Deutschland." In *Die internationale Politik 1958–1960*, edited by Wilhlem Cornides, Dietrich Mende, and Wolfgang Wagner, 564–618. Munich: Oldenbourg, 1971.

Hildebrand, Klaus. "'Atlantiker' versus 'Gaullisten.' Zur Außenpolitik der Bundesrepublik Deutschland während der sechziger Jahre." *Revue d'Allemagne* 22, no. 4 (1990): 583–92.

——. *Von Erhard zur großen Koalition*. Stuttgart: Deutsche Verlags-Anstalt, 1984.

Hölscher, Wolfgang. "Krisenmanagement in Sachen EWG. Das Scheitern des Beitritts Großbritanniens und die deutsch-französischen Beziehungen." In Blasius, *Von Adenauer zu Erhard*, 9–44.

Hoff, Henning. "'Largely the Prisoners of Dr. Adenauer's Policy.' Großbritannien und die DDR (1949–1973)." In Pfeil, *Die DDR und der Westen*, 185–206.

Holbik, Karel, and Henry Allen Myers. *West German Foreign Aid, 1956–1966: Its Economic and Political Aspects*. Boston: Boston University Press, 1968.

Hoppe, Christoph. *Zwischen Teilhabe und Mitsprache: Die Nuklearfrage in der Allianzpolitik Deutschlands 1959–1966*. Baden-Baden: Nomos, 1993.

Horstmeier, Carel. "Die DDR und Belgien (1949–1972)." In Pfeil, *Die DDR und der Westen*, 309–27.

Hünseler, Peter. *Die außenpolitische Beziehungen der Bundesrepublik Deutschland zu den arabischen Staaten von 1949–1980*. Frankfurt am Main: Peter Lang, 1990.

Ihme-Tuchel, Beate. "Das Bemühen der SED um die staatliche Anerkennung durch Jugoslawien 1956/57." *Zeitschrift für Geschichtswissenschaft* 42 (1994): 695–702.

Ingimundarson, Valur. "The Eisenhower Administration, the Adenauer Government, and the Political Uses of the East German Uprising of 1953." *Diplomatic History* 20, no. 3 (Summer 1996): 381–409.

Jacobsen, Hans-Adolf, Gert Leptin, Ulrich Scheuner, and Eberhard Schulz, eds. *Drei Jahrzehnte Außenpolitik der DDR. Bestimmungsfaktoren, Instrumente, Aktionsfelder*. Munich: Oldenbourg, 1979.

Jansen, G. H. *Nonalignment and the Afro-Asian States*. New York: Praeger, 1966.

Jarausch, Konrad. "Care and Coercion: The GDR as Welfare Dictatorship." In *Dictatorship as Experience: Towards a Socio-Cultural History of the GDR*, edited by Konrad Jarausch, translated by Eve Duffy. New York: Berghahn, 1999.

Jelinek, Yeshayahu, and Rainer A. Blasius. "Ben Gurion und Adenauer im Waldorf Astoria. Gesprächsaufzeichnungen vom israelisch-deutschen Gipfeltreffen in New York am 14. März 1960." *Vierteljahrshefte für Zeitgeschichte* 45, no. 2 (1997): 309–43.

Jodl, Marcus. *Amboß oder Hammer? Otto Grotewohl—Eine politische Biographie*. Berlin: Aufbau Taschenbuch, 1996.

Karabell, Zachary. *Architects of Intervention: The United States, the Third World, and the Cold War, 1946–1962*. Baton Rouge: Louisiana State University Press, 1999.

Katzer, Nikolaus. *"Eine Übung im Kalten Krieg." Die Berliner Außenministerkonferenz von 1954*. Cologne: Verlag Wissenschaft und Politik, 1994.

Kilian, Werner. *Die Hallstein-Doktrin. Der diplomatische Krieg zwischen der BRD und der DDR 1955–1973*. Berlin: Duncker & Humblot, 2001.

Kitzinger, Uwe. *German Electoral Politics: A Study of the 1957 Campaign*. Oxford: Clarendon, 1960.

Kleinmann, Hans-Otto. *Geschichte der CDU*. Stuttgart: Deutsche Verlags-Anstalt, 1993.

Kleßmann, Christoph. *Zwei Staaten, eine Nation. Deutsche Geschichte 1955–1970*. 2nd ed. Bonn: Bundeszentrale für politische Bildung, 1997.

Klingl, Friedrich. *Das ganze Deutschland soll es sein! Thomas Dehler und die politischen Weichenstellungen der fünfziger Jahre*. Munich: Olzog, 1987.

Klotzbach, Kurt. *Der Weg zur Staatspartei. Programmatik, praktische Politik und Organisation der deutschen Sozialdemokratie 1945–1965*. Bonn: Dietz, 1982.

Knipping, Franz, and Klaus-Jürgen Müller, eds. *Aus der Ohnmacht zur Bündnismacht. Das Machtproblem in der Bundesrepublik Deutschland 1945–1960*. Paderborn: Schöningh, 1995.

Köhler, Henning. *Adenauer. Eine politische Biographie*. Frankfurt am Main: Propyläen, 1994.

Koerfer, Daniel. *Kampf ums Kanzleramt. Erhard und Adenauer*. Stuttgart: Deutsche Verlags-Anstalt, 1987.

Kopstein, Jeffrey. *The Politics of Economic Decline in East Germany, 1945–1989*. Chapel Hill: University of North Carolina Press, 1987.

Kosthorst, Daniel. *Brentano und die deutsche Einheit. Die Deutschland- und Ostpolitik des Außenministers im Kabinett Adenauer 1955–1961*. Düsseldorf: Droste, 1993.

———. "Sowjetische Geheimpolitik in Deutschland? Chruschtschow und die Adschubej-Mission 1964." *Vierteljahrshefte für Zeitgeschichte* 44, no. 2 (April 1996): 257–93.

Kroegel, Dirk. *Einen Anfang finden! Kurt Georg Kiesinger in der Außen- und Deutschlandpolitik der Großen Koalition*. Munich: Oldenbourg, 1997.

Kunz, Diane B., ed. *The Diplomacy of the Crucial Decade: American Foreign Relations during the 1960s*. New York: Columbia University Press, 1994.

Küsters, Hanns Jürgen. *Die Gründung der Europäischen Wirtschaftsgemeinschaft*. Baden-Baden: Nomos, 1982.

———. "Kanzler in der Krise. Journalistenberichte über Adenauers Hintergrundgespräche zwischen Berlin-Ultimatum und Bundespräsidentenwahl 1959." *Vierteljahrshefte für Zeitgeschichte* 36, no. 4 (1988): 733–68.

———. "Konrad Adenauer und Willy Brandt in der Berlin-Krise 1958–1963." *Vierteljahrshefte für Zeitgeschichte* 40, no. 4 (1992): 483–542.

Lahann, Birgit. *Geliebte Zone. Geschichte aus dem neuen Deutschland*. Stuttgart: Deutsche Verlags-Anstalt, 1997.

Lamm, Hans Siegfried, and Siegfried Kupper. *DDR und Dritte Welt*. Munich: Oldenbourg, 1976.

Lappenküper, Ulrich. "'Ich bin wirklich ein guter Europäer.' Ludwig Erhards Europapolitik 1949–1966." *Francia* 18, no. 3 (1991): 85–120.

Lavy, George. *Germany and Israel: Moral Debt and National Interest*. London: Frank Cass, 1996.

Lee, Sabine. "Perception and Reality: Anglo-German Relations during the Berlin Crisis, 1958–1959." *German History* 15, no. 1 (1995): 47–69.

———. *An Uneasy Partnership: British-German Relations between 1955 and 1961*. Bochum: Brockmeyer, 1996.

Lees, Lorraine M. *Keeping Tito Afloat: The United States, Yugoslavia, and the Cold War*. University Park: Pennsylvania State University Press, 1997.

Lemke, Michael. *Die Berlinkrise 1958 bis 1963. Interessen und Handlungsspielräume der SED im Ost-West-Konflikt*. Berlin: Akademie Verlag, 1995.

———. "'Doppelte Alleinvertretung.' Die nationalen Wiedervereinigungs-konzepte der beiden deutschen Regierungen und die Grundzüge ihrer politischen Realisierung in der DDR (1949–1952/53)." *Zeitschrift für Geschichtswissenschaft* 40, no. 6 (1992): 531–43.

———. *Einheit oder Sozialismus? Die Westpolitik der SED 1949–1961*. Cologne: Böhlau, 2001.

———. "Kampagne gegen Bonn. Die Systemkrise der DDR und die West-Propaganda der SED 1960–1963." *Vierteljahrshefte für Zeitgeschichte* 41, no. 2 (1993): 153–74.

———. "Der nahe Osten, Indien und die Grotewohlreise von 1959. Zur

Anerkennungspolitik der DDR in der zweiten Hälfte der fünziger Jahre." *asien afrika lateinamerika* 20 (1993): 1027–42.

Lesch, David W. *Syria and the United States: Eisenhower's Cold War in the Middle East*. Boulder, Colo.: Westview, 1992.

Lindemann, Mechthild. "Anfänge einer neuen Ostpolitik? Handelsvertragsverhandlungen und die Errichtung von Handelsvertretungen in den Ostblock-Staaten." In Blasius, *Von Adenauer zu Erhard*, 45–96.

Lohse, Eckart. *Östliche Lockungen und westliche Zwänge. Paris und die deutsche Teilung 1949 bis 1955*. Munich: Oldenbourg, 1995.

Lorenzen, Jan T. "Die Jugoslawien-Politik der DDR 1953–1957 und die Haltung der Bundesrepublik." *Deutschland Archiv* 29, no. 1 (1996): 58–66.

Loth, Wilfried. *Stalin's Unwanted Child: The Soviet Union, the German Question, and the Founding of the GDR*. Translated by Robert F. Hogg. New York: St. Martin's, 1998.

——, ed. *Die deutsche Frage in der Nachkriegszeit*. Berlin: Akademie, 1994.

——. *Walter Hallstein: The Forgotten European?* Translated by Bryan Ruppert. New York: St. Martin's, 1998.

Maier, Charles S. *Dissolution: The Crisis of Communism and the End of East Germany.* Princeton, N.J.: Princeton University Press, 1997.

Major, Patrick. *The Death of the KPD: Communism and Anti-Communism in West Germany, 1945–1956*. Oxford: Clarendon, 1997.

Marcowitz, Reiner. *Option für Paris? Unionsparteien, SPD und Charles de Gaulle 1958 bis 1969*. Munich: Oldenbourg, 1996.

——. "Wendejahre 1963/64. Die deutsch-französischen Beziehungen in der Endphase der 'Ära Adenauer' und zu Beginn der Kanzlerschaft Erhards." *Francia* 22, no. 3 (1995): 83–102.

Martin, Edwin W. *Divided Counsel: The Anglo-American Response to Communist Victory in China*. Lexington: University Press of Kentucky, 1986.

Mastny, Vojtech. *The Cold War and Soviet Insecurity: The Stalin Years*. New York: Oxford University Press, 1996.

Mauer, Victor. "Macmillan und die Berlin-Krise 1958/59." *Vierteljahrshefte für Zeitgeschichte* 44, no. 2 (1996): 229–56.

Mayer, Frank A. "Adenauer and Kennedy: An Era of Distrust in German-American Relations?" *German Studies Review* 17, no. 1 (1994): 83–104.

McAdams, A. James. *Germany Divided: From the Wall to Reunification*. Princeton, N.J.: Princeton University Press, 1993.

——. "Revisiting the *Ostpolitik* in the 1990s." *German Politics and Society* 30 (Fall 1993): 49–60.

McMahon, Robert J. *The Cold War on the Periphery: The United States, India, and Pakistan*. New York: Columbia University Press, 1994.

Merseburger, Peter. *Der schwierige Deutsche. Kurt Schumacher—Eine Biographie*. Stuttgart: Deutsche Verlags-Anstalt, 1995.

Millikan, Max F., and W. W. Rostow. *A Proposal: Key to an Effective Foreign Policy*. New York: Harper & Brothers, 1957.

Morsey, Rudolf. *Heinrich Lübke. Eine politische Biographie*. Paderborn: Schöningh, 1996.

BIBLIOGRAPHY

Morsey, Rudolf, and Konrad Repgen, eds. *Adenauer-Studien III*. Mainz: Matthias-Grünewald-Verlag, 1974.

Mortimer, Robert A. *The Third World Coalition in International Politics*. 2nd ed. Boulder, Colo.: Westview, 1984.

Müller, Claus. *Relaunching German Diplomacy: The Auswärtiges Amt in the 1950s*. Münster: Lit, 1996.

Müller, Klaus-Jürgen. "Die Bundesrepublik Deutschland und der Algerienkrieg." *Vierteljahrshefte für Zeitgeschichte* 38, no. 4 (1990): 609–41.

Muth, Ingrid. *Die DDR-Außenpolitik 1949–1972. Inhalte, Strukturen, Mechanismen*. 2nd ed. Berlin: Links, 2001.

Ndumbe, Kum'a, III. *Was will Bonn in Afrika? Zur Afrikapolitik der Bundesrepublik Deutschland*. Pfaffenweiler: Centaurus, 1992.

Nicholls, Anthony J. *Freedom with Responsibility: The Social Market Economy in Germany, 1918–1963*. Oxford: Clarendon, 1994.

Noack, Paul. "Hallstein-Doktrin." In *Handwörterbuch der deutschen Einheit*, edited by Werner Weidenfeld and Karl-Rudolf Korte, 369–76. Frankfurt: Campus, 1992.

Ostermann, Christian. "East Germany and the Horn Crisis. Documents on SED Afrikapolitik." *Cold War International History Project Bulletin* 8/9 (Winter 1996/97): 47–49.

——. " 'Die Ostdeutschen an einen langwierigen Kampf gewöhnen.' Die Vereinigten Staaten und der Aufstand vom 17. Juni 1953." *Deutschland Archiv* 30, no. 3 (1997): 350–68.

——, ed., *Uprising in East Germany, 1953: The Cold War, the German Question, and the First Major Upheaval behind the Iron Curtain*. Budapest: Central European University Press, 2001.

Padgett, Stephen, ed. *Adenauer to Kohl: The Development of the German Chancellorship*. London: Hurst, 1994.

Pape, Matthias. "Die deutsch-österreichischen Beziehungen zwischen 1945 und 1955. Ein Aufriß." *Historisch-politische Mitteilungen* 2 (1995): 149–72.

——. "Mozart und der Kalte Krieg. Die Entsendung einer DDR- 'Delegation' zum internationalen musikwissenschaftlichen Kongreß in Wien 1956." *Deutschland Archiv* 31, no. 5 (1998): 760–72.

Pautsch, Ilse Dorothee. "Im Sog der Entspannungspolitik. Die USA, das Teststopp-Abkommen und die Deutschland-Frage." In Blasius, *Von Adenauer zu Erhard*, 118–53.

Pawelka, Peter. *Die UNO und das Deutschlandproblem*. Tübingen: Mohr, 1971.

Pekelder, Jacco. "Zwischen 'Sowjet-Deutschland' und 'sozialistischem Modellstaat.' Niederländische Wahrnehmungen der DDR und die Anerkennungsdebatte 1961 bis 1973." *Deutschland Archiv* 31, no. 4 (1998): 599–604.

Peterson, M. J. *Recognition of Governments: Legal Doctrine and State Practice, 1815–1995*. New York: St. Martin's, 1997.

Pfeil, Ulrich, ed. *Die DDR und der Westen. Transnationale Beziehungen 1949–1989*. Berlin: Links, 2001.

Poppinga, Anneliese. *"Das Wichtigste ist der Mut." Konrad Adenauer—die letzten fünf Kanzlerjahre*. Bergisch Gladbach: Gustav Lübbe, 1994.

Pridham, Geoffrey. *Christian Democracy in Western Germany: The CDU/CSU in Government and Opposition, 1945–1976*. London: Croom Helm, 1977.

Putensen, Dörte. *Im Konfliktfeld zwischen Ost und West. Finnland, der Kalte Krieg und die deutsche Frage (1947–73)*. Berlin: Arno Spitz, 2000.

Ramet, Pedro. *The Soviet-Syrian Relationship since 1955: A Troubled Alliance*. Boulder, Colo.: Westview, 1990.

Rivière, Claude. *Guinea: The Mobilization of a People*. Translated by Virginia Thompson and Richard Adloff. Ithaca, N.Y.: Cornell University Press, 1977.

Rubinstein, Alvin Z. *Yugoslavia and the Nonaligned World*. Princeton, N.J.: Princeton University Press, 1970.

Rupieper, Hermann-Josef. *Der besetzte Verbündete. Die amerikanische Deutschlandpolitik 1949–1955*. Opladen: Westdeutscher Verlag, 1991.

Rusinek, Bernd-A. "Von der Entdeckung der NS-Vergangenheit zum generellen Faschismusverdacht—akademische Diskurse in der Bundesrepublik der 60er Jahre." In Schildt, Siegfried, and Lammers, *Dynamische Zeiten*, 114–47.

Sarotte, Mary Elise. *Dealing with the Devil: East Germany, Détente, and Ostpolitik, 1969–1973*. Chapel Hill: University of North Carolina Press, 2001.

Scheffler, Thomas. "Deutsche Sozialdemokraten und israelische Sozialisten im Kalten Krieg (1945–1965)." In Schwanitz, *Jenseits der Legende*, 152–60.

———. *Die SPD und der Algerienkrieg (1954–1962)*. Berlin: Das Arabische Buch, 1995.

Schertz, Adrian. *Die Deutschlandpolitik Kennedys und Johnsons. Unterschiedliche Ansätze innerhalb der amerikanischen Regierung*. Cologne: Böhlau, 1992.

Schildt, Axel, Detlef Siegfried, and Karl Christian Lammers, eds. *Dynamische Zeiten. Die 60er Jahre in den beiden deutschen Gesellschaften*. Hamburg: Christians, 2000.

Schlarp, Karl-Heinz. "Alternativen zur deutschen Außenpolitik 1952–1955: Karl Georg Pfleiderer und die 'Deutsche Frage.'" In *Aspekte deutscher Außenpolitik im 20. Jahrhundert. Aufsätze Hans Rothfels zum Gedächtnis*, edited by Wolfgang Benz and Hermann Graml, 211–48. Stuttgart: Deutsche Verlags-Anstalt, 1976.

Schleicher, Harry. "Wandlungen der jugoslawischen Deutschland-Politik." *Europa-Archiv* 18, no. 3 (February 10, 1963): 99–106.

Schleicher, Ilona, and Hans-Georg Schleicher. *Die DDR im südlichen Afrika. Solidarität und Kalter Krieg*. Hamburg: Institut für Afrika-Kunde, 1997.

Schmoeckel, Reinhard, and Bruno Kaiser. *Die vergessene Regierung. Die große Koalition 1966 bis 1969 und ihre langfristigen Wirkungen*. Bonn: Bouvier, 1991.

Schneppen, Heinz. "Eine Insel und zwei deutsche Staaten. Sansibar und die Hallstein-Doktrin 1964–66." *Deutschland Archiv* 32, no. 3 (May/June 1999): 409–19.

Scholz, Michael F. "Östen Undén und die DDR. Schwedische Deutschlandpolitik in den fünfziger Jahren." *Vierteljahrshefte für Zeitgeschichte* 41, no. 3 (1993): 391–417.

Schröder, Gerhard. "Germany Looks at Eastern Europe." *Foreign Affairs* 44, no. 1 (October 1965): 15–25.

Schuster, Rudolf. "Die 'Hallstein-Doktrin.' Ihre rechtliche und politische Bedeutung und die Grenzen ihrer Wirksamkeit." *Europa-Archiv* 18, no. 18 (September 15, 1963): 675–90.

Schwanitz, Wolfgang. "Wasser, Uran und Paktfreiheit? Zur Geschichte der Beziehungen zwischen der DDR und Sudan (1955–1970)." In Schwanitz, *Jenseits der Legende*, 137–51.

———, ed. *Jenseits der Legende: Araber, Juden, Deutsche*. Berlin: Dietz, 1994.

BIBLIOGRAPHY

Schwarz, Hans-Peter. *Adenauer. Der Staatsmann 1952–1967*. Munich: dtv, 1994.

———. *Die Ära Adenauer. Epochenwechsel, 1957–1963*. Stuttgart: Deutsche Verlags-Anstalt, 1983.

———. *Die Ära Adenauer. Gründerjahre der Republik, 1949–1957*. Stuttgart: Deutsche Verlags-Anstalt, 1981.

———. "Die Regierung Kiesinger und die Krise in der CSSR 1968." *Vierteljahrshefte für Zeitgeschichte* 47, no. 2 (April 1999): 159–86.

———. "Vortasten nach Warschau." *Die politische Meinung* 43, no. 346 (1997): 87–95.

Shafir, Shlomo. *Ambiguous Relations: The American Jewish Community and Germany Since 1945*. Detroit: Wayne State University Press, 1999.

Siebenmorgen, Peter. *Gezeitenwechsel. Aufbruch zur Entspannungspolitik*. Bonn: Bouvier, 1990.

Siebs, Benno-Eide. *Die Außenpolitik der DDR 1976–1989. Strategien und Grenzen*. Paderborn: Schöningh, 1999.

Siekmeier, Mathias. *Restauration oder Reform? Die FDP in den sechziger Jahren— Deutschland- und Ostpolitik zwischen Wiedervereinigung und Entspannung*. Cologne: Janus, 1998.

Smith, Gordon W. "'Ostpolitik' since Reunification." *German Life and Letters*, n.s., 49, no. 1 (January 1996): 88–100.

Smyser, W. R. *From Yalta to Berlin: The Cold War Struggle over Germany*. New York: St. Martin's, 1999.

Sodaro, Michael J. *Moscow, Germany, and the West from Khrushchev to Gorbachev*. Ithaca, N.Y.: Cornell University Press, 1990.

Soell, Hartmut. *Fritz Erler. Eine politische Biographie*. 2 vols. Berlin: Dietz, 1976.

Spanger, Hans-Joachim. *Die beiden deutschen Staaten in der Dritten Welt. Die Entwicklungspolitik der DDR—Eine Herausforderung für die Bundesrepublik?* Opladen: Westdeutscher Verlag, 1987.

Spaulding, Robert Mark. *Osthandel and Ostpolitik: German Trade Policies in Eastern Europe from Bismarck to Adenauer*. Providence, R.I.: Berghahn, 1997.

Speier, Hans. "The Hallstein Doctrine." In *Force and Folly: Essays on Foreign Affairs and the History of Ideas*, 135–53. Cambridge, Mass.: MIT Press, 1969.

Staritz, Dietrich. *Geschichte der DDR*, expanded edition. Frankfurt am Main: Suhrkamp, 1996.

———. *Die Gründung der DDR. Von der sowjetischen Besatzungsherrschaft zum sozialistischen Staat*, 3rd ed. Munich: dtv, 1995.

Stehle, Hansjakob. "Adenauer, Polen, und die deutsche Frage." In Foschepoth, *Adenauer und die deutsche Frage*, 80–98.

Steiner, André. "Von 'Hauptaufgabe' zu 'Hauptaufgabe.' Zur Wirtschaftsentwicklung der langen 60er Jahre in der DDR." In Schildt, Siegfried, and Lammers, *Dynamische Zeiten*, 218–47.

Steininger, Rolf. *Der Mauerbau. Die Westmächte und Adenauer in der Berlinkrise 1958–1963*. Munich: Olzog, 2001.

Stevens, Christopher A. *The Soviet Union and Black Africa*. London: Macmillan, 1976.

Thränhardt, Dietrich. *Geschichte der Bundesrepublik Deutschland*, expanded edition. Frankfurt: Suhrkamp, 1996.

———. "Wahlen und Wiedervereinigung: Die Absicherung des Weststaats." In Foschepoth, *Adenauer und die deutsche Frage*, 250–70.

Timm, Angelika. *Hammer, Zirkel, Davidstern. Das gestörte Verhältnis der DDR zu Zionismus und Staat Israel*. Bonn: Bouvier, 1997.

Trachtenberg, Marc. *A Constructed Peace: The Making of the European Settlement, 1945–1963*. Princeton, N.J.: Princeton University Press, 1999.

———. *History and Strategy*. Princeton, N.J.: Princeton University Press, 1991.

Trimbur, Dominique. *De la Shoah à la réconciliation? La question des relations RFA-Israël (1949–1956)*. Paris: CNRS-Éditions, 2000.

Troche, Alexander. *Ulbricht und die Dritte Welt. Ost-Berlins "Kampf" gegen die Bonner "Alleinvertretungsanmaßung."* Erlangen: Palm & Enke, 1996.

Turner, Henry Ashby. *Germany from Partition to Unification*. New Haven, Conn.: Yale University Press, 1992.

Tusa, Ann. *The Last Division: Berlin and the Wall*. London: Hodder & Stoughton, 1996.

Verheyen, Dirk. *The German Question: A Cultural, Historical, and Geopolitical Exploration*. 2nd ed. Boulder, Colo.: Westview, 1999.

Vogel, Rolf, ed. *Der deutsch-israelische Dialog*. Vol 1. Munich: Saur, 1987.

Vogtmeier, Andreas. *Egon Bahr und die deutsche Frage. Zur Entwicklung der sozialdemokratischen Ost- und Deutschlandpolitik vom Kriegsende bis zur Vereinigung*. Bonn: Dietz, 1996.

Weber, Petra. *Carlo Schmid 1896–1979—Eine Biographie*. Munich: Beck, 1996.

Wei, Liang-Tsai. *Peking versus Taipei in Africa, 1960–1978*. Taipei: Asia and World Institute, 1982.

Wenger, Andreas. "Der lange Weg zur Stabilität. Kennedy, Chruschtschow und das gemeinsame Interesse der Supermächte am Status quo in Europa." *Vierteljahrshefte für Zeitgeschichte* 46, no. 1 (1998): 69–100.

Wengst, Udo. *Thomas Dehler 1897–1967. Ein politische Biographie*. Munich: Oldenbourg, 1997.

Wettig, Gerhart. *Bereitschaft zu Einheit in Freiheit? Die sowjetische Deutschland-Politik 1945–1955*. Munich: Olzog, 1999.

———. "Die sowjetische Politik während der Berlin-Krise von 1958 bis 1962. Der Stand der Forschungen." *Deutschland Archiv* 30, no. 3 (1997): 383–98.

Wiggershaus, Norbert. "Die Entscheidung für einen westdeutschen Verteidigungsbeitrag 1950." In *Anfänge westdeutscher Sicherheitspolitik*, Vol. 1, *Von der Kapitulation bis zum Pleven-Plan*, edited by Roland G. Foerster et al., 325–402. Munich: Oldenbourg, 1982.

Wilson, Henry S. *African Decolonization*. London: Edwin Arnold, 1994.

Winrow, Gareth M. *The Foreign Policy of the GDR in Africa*. Cambridge: Cambridge University Press, 1990.

Wippel, Andreas. *Die Außenwirtschaftsbeziehungen der DDR zum Nahen Osten. Einfluß und Abhängigkeit der DDR und das Verhältnis von Außenwirtschaft zu Außenpolitik*. Berlin: Das Arabische Buch, 1995.

Wolle, Stefan. *Die heile Welt der Diktatur*. Munich: Econ & List, 1999.

Wolffsohn, Michael. "Von der verordneten zur freiwilligen 'Vergangenheitsbewältigung'? Eine Skizze der bundesdeutschen Entwicklung 1955/65." *German Studies Review* 12, no. 1 (February 1989): 111–37.

Wyden, Peter. *Wall: The Inside Story of Divided Berlin*. New York: Simon and Schuster, 1989.

Yahya, Ali M. *Egypt and the Soviet Union, 1955–1972: A Study in the Power of the Small State*. Washington, D.C.: Harbinger, 1989.

Zimmermann, Hubert. " '. . . they have got to put something in the family pot!': The Burden-Sharing Problem in German-American Relations, 1960–1967." *German History* 14, no. 3 (1996): 325–46.

Zubok, Vladislav M. "Soviet Policy Aims at the Geneva Conference." In Bischof and Dockrill, *Cold War Respite*, 55–74.

Dissertations

Ahonen, Pertti. "The Expellee Organizations and West German Ostpolitik, 1949–1969." Ph.D. diss., Yale University, 1999.

Granieri, Ronald J. "America's Germany, Germany's Europe: Konrad Adenauer, the CDU/CSU, and the Politics of German *Westbindung*, 1949–1963." Ph.D. diss., University of Chicago, 1996.

Gray, William Glenn. "The Hallstein Doctrine: West Germany's Global Campaign to Isolate East Germany, 1949–1969." Ph.D. diss., Yale University, 1999.

Ingimundarson, Valur. "East Germany, West Germany, and U.S. Cold War Strategy, 1950–1954." Ph.D. diss., Columbia University, 1993.

Kirby, Stephen. "The Two Germanys in Subsaharan Africa, 1957–1972: Ideological Universalism versus Traditional Statecraft." Ph.D. diss., University of Virginia, 1993.

Maulucci, Thomas Wayne. "The Creation and Early History of the West German Foreign Office, 1945–55." Ph.D. diss., Yale University, 1997.

Selvage, Douglas E. "Poland, the German Democratic Republic and the German Question, 1955–1967." Ph.D. diss., Yale University, 1998.

Trimbur, Dominique. "La question des rélations germano-israéliènnes (1949–1956)." Ph.D. diss., Metz, 1995

INDEX

Abs, Hermann-Josef, 170

Adenauer, Konrad, 10, 117, 123, 124, 131–32, 140, 251 (n. 82), 255 (n. 123), 287 (n. 111); on GDR and problems of German unity, 6, 8, 11–12, 24–25, 43, 97, 101, 195, 224, 229–30; on isolation campaign, 23–24, 39–40, 126, 136, 143, 145, 184, 231; on relations with Soviet Union, 30, 31–32, 34–37, 95, 133; on relations with Eastern Europe, 38, 58–59, 70–72, 74, 76, 78, 79, 81–82, 86; on relations with Arab states and Israel, 58, 64, 68, 69, 89, 90, 99, 172, 180, 259 (n. 30), 268 (n. 9), 293 (n. 36); on relations with France, 96, 141; on relations with Africa, 108, 110, 120

Algeria, 114, 122, 124, 125, 147, 152, 153, 166, 168, 169, 181, 188, 204, 218

All-African Peoples' Congress, 122

Allgemeiner deutscher Nachrichtendienst (ADN), 110, 111, 112

Allied High Commission. *See* Western Allies

Angola, 152

Arab League, 19, 171, 177, 181, 309 (n. 64)

Argentina, 300 (n. 137)

"Atlanticists." *See* Christian Democratic Union/Christian Social Union

Atlee, Clement, 13

Auer, Theodor, 155

Austria, 31, 32, 46, 192, 245 (n. 12), 252 (n. 87)

Axen, Hermann, 152, 153, 315 (n. 25)

Baghdad Pact, 69

Bahr, Egon, 199, 207, 208, 211, 217, 232

Bandaranaike, Sirimavo, 153, 154, 155, 156, 188, 189, 218

Bandung Conference, 28, 42, 48, 60, 61, 125, 169

Bargen, Werner von, 237 (n. 5), 289 (n. 128)

Barzel, Rainer, 180, 181, 301 (n. 151), 319 (n. 76)

Bassler, Heinrich, 135–36, 315 (n. 16)

Becker, Walter, 53

Belgium, 14, 103, 122, 218

Belgrade Conference, 116, 125–29, 130, 131, 134, 135, 139, 162, 227

Ben Bella, Ahmed, 166

Bender, Peter, 7, 207

Berger, Hans, 253 (n. 106)

Berlin, 201, 208; military missions in, 22; access to, 49–50, 87, 206, 254 (n. 109); wall through, 116, 125, 126, 158; holiday passes to, 145–46

Berlin Crisis, 87, 92, 95–99, 100–102, 110, 115, 124, 133, 140, 163, 168, 227

Birrenbach, Kurt, 181, 280 (n. 13)

Blankenhorn, Herbert, 77, 78, 80, 82, 254 (n. 113), 261 (n. 68)

Blücher, Franz, 52, 59–60, 69

Blumenfeld, Erik, 309 (n. 61), 313 (n. 128)

Böhm, Franz, 293 (n. 38)

Böker, Alexander, 155, 168, 169, 170, 177, 199, 223, 322 (n. 120)

Bolz, Lothar, 60, 102

Bonn Group, 49, 255 (n. 116)

Brandt, Willy: as chancellor, 7, 8, 217, 218; as mayor of West Berlin, 102, 131, 145–46, 192, 285 (n. 79); as foreign minister, 196, 197, 198, 199, 203, 207, 208, 210–11, 212, 226, 231, 232

Bräutigam, Otto, 245 (n. 7), 248 (n. 47)

Brazil, 152

Brentano, Heinrich von, 121, 133, 142, 143, 281 (n. 17); and relations with Eastern Europe, 32, 36, 71–74, 77, 78–79, 81, 82–83, 84, 262 (n. 81); and isolation campaign, 37, 39–40, 44, 45–46, 50, 62, 75, 82, 86, 98–99, 128–29, 132, 184, 245 (n. 12); and relations with Arab states and Israel, 54, 65, 66, 67, 69, 105, 260 (n. 58), 285–86 (n. 82); and relations with Africa, 100, 108, 110–14, 120; and relations with GDR, 101

Brezhnev, Leonid, 202

Britain, 64, 69, 76, 90, 103, 122, 142, 155, 157, 163, 208–9, 218, 219, 239 (n. 20), 249–50 (n. 66); Foreign Office, 11, 21–23, 36, 42, 50, 80, 82, 265 (n. 131), 270 (n. 50), 296 (n. 80), 306 (n. 37), 318 (n. 70); embassy of in Bonn, 105, 108, 192, 259 (n. 37). See also Western Allies

Bucerius, Gerd, 248 (n. 50)

Bulganin, Nikolai, 31, 36, 37, 38

Bulgaria, 142, 149

Bundestag, 10, 36, 62, 99, 114, 119, 120, 123, 141, 144, 147, 175, 177, 193, 204, 286 (n. 89); elections to, 10, 72, 74, 76, 131, 181, 191; addresses by Adenauer to, 11–12, 23–25, 39–40, 44, 184; Foreign Affairs Committee of, 32, 37–38, 39–40, 51, 67, 84, 231, 243 (n. 77), 251 (n. 84), 257 (n. 137), 258 (n. 17), 266 (n. 147), 273 (n. 93), 277 (n. 142); addresses by Brentano to, 62, 67, 72, 184

Burma, 28, 33–34, 86, 88, 92, 94, 102, 106, 121, 149, 152, 153, 154, 203, 205, 222, 248 (n. 53), 252 (n. 85), 274 (n. 99), 284 (n. 64)

Cairo Conference, 162–70 passim

Cambodia, 6, 135–36, 137, 149, 154, 205, 226, 228; recognition of GDR, 196–97, 209–10, 211–12, 213–14, 232. See also Sihanouk, Norodom

Cameroon, 121

Carstens, Karl, 3, 44, 131, 134, 136, 138, 155, 159–60, 161, 169, 172, 177, 179, 183, 186, 191, 195, 199, 259 (n. 31), 264 (n. 122), 286 (n. 89), 288 (n. 119), 292 (n. 30), 295 (n. 75), 296 (n. 85), 302 (n. 160), 319 (n. 86)

Ceylon, 4, 98, 103, 118, 121, 122, 124, 136, 152, 153, 159, 160, 162, 170, 203, 218, 225, 228; East German consulate in, 154, 155, 156, 158, 184, 188–89

China, People's Republic of, 13, 60, 65, 92, 100, 140, 143, 155, 160, 168, 169, 291 (n. 12)

Christian Democratic Union/Christian Social Union (CDU/CSU), 10; parliamentary caucus, 37, 39, 78, 133, 141, 146, 176, 177, 243 (n. 75); early reservations about Hallstein Doctrine, 66, 77, 82; performance in elections, 71–72, 74, 76, 131, 191; endorsement of Hallstein Doctrine, 83–84, 132, 139, 180, 185–86, 209, 210, 231–32; split between Gaullists and Atlanticists, 140, 144, 145, 172, 178, 197, 200; resistance to détente, 142, 143–44, 193, 196, 197, 203–4, 208

Claudius, Eduard, 69–70

Colombia, 185

Conant, James B., 254 (n. 109)

Congo (Brazzaville), 218

Congo (Leopoldville), 122, 124, 275 (n. 107)

Conté, Seydou, 110, 111, 112, 113

Cuba, 115, 124, 138–39, 140, 148, 162, 168, 296 (n. 92)

Cyprus, 130, 159, 169

Czechoslovakia, 41, 64, 71, 104, 107, 149, 196, 200, 206, 208

Dahomey, 169, 275 (n. 107), 282 (n. 29), 289 (n. 129)

De Gaulle, Charles, 91, 96, 140, 141, 195, 209, 227

Dehler, Thomas, 43, 230, 287 (n. 103)

Denmark, 253 (n. 106)

Dertinger, Georg, 15

Détente, 7, 140–41, 142–44, 149, 196,

197, 200, 217, 229; and peaceful coexistence, 127, 128

Development aid, 114, 116–23, 186; technical assistance, 105, 118; capital aid, 119; Steering Committee and, 121–22, 123, 134–35, 136, 137. *See also* Foreign Office; Hermes credits

Dichgans, Hans, 192

Diehl, Günter, 35, 48, 211

Dittmann, Herbert, 267 (n. 148), 272 (n. 69)

Dönhoff, Marion Countess, 266 (n. 145), 309 (n. 65), 322 (n. 4)

Duckwitz, Georg Ferdinand, 98, 268 (n. 7), 271 (n. 62), 295 (n. 76), 298 (n. 114), 319 (n. 78)

Dulles, John Foster, 34, 71, 77, 80, 82, 84, 89, 96, 250 (n. 72), 266–67 (n. 148)

Dumke, Horst, 275 (n. 109), 280 (n. 7), 288 (n. 116)

Eckardt, Felix von, 77, 111, 252 (n. 89), 273 (n. 93), 274 (n. 96)

Economic and Social Council of the UN (ECOSOC), 22

Economic Council of Europe (ECE), 17, 46, 50–51, 242 (n. 64), 250 (nn. 67, 75), 252 (n. 89)

Egypt, 26, 43, 51, 52, 55, 63, 67, 73, 85, 87, 152, 204, 225, 226, 227, 228, 229; relations with FRG, 19, 20, 51, 52–54, 68, 69, 105–6, 146, 181, 185, 242 (n. 66), 243 (n. 78), 291 (n. 12); early relations with GDR, 19–20, 28, 41–42, 47–48, 52–54, 67, 88, 90; Aswan Dam, 20, 59, 89, 99, 117, 121; Suez Canal, 64–65, 68; East German consulate in, 87, 92–93, 94, 99–100, 105–6, 134, 160, 168–69; Office of the Plenipotentiary of the GDR to the Arab States, 88–89; East German aid to, 88–90, 124, 172, 179–80, 188, 202, 213, 214, 217; West German aid to, 89, 117–18, 119, 121, 166–67, 170, 177, 214, 285–86 (n. 82); recognition of GDR, 215. *See also* Nonaligned movement

Eisenhower, Dwight D., 109, 113, 227, 270 (n. 54)

Eisenhower Doctrine, 85

Erhard, Ludwig: as minister of economics, 69, 119, 121, 132, 287 (n. 112); as chancellor, 140, 141, 144–45, 146, 163, 167, 171, 172, 174, 176, 177, 180, 182, 186, 191, 192, 193, 194–95, 198, 231; and "peace note," 193–94

Erler, Fritz, 145, 178, 231, 289 (n. 138), 299 (n. 123), 301 (n. 151), 307 (n. 48)

Eshkol, Levi, 167, 176

Ethiopia, 104, 126, 220

Etzdorf, Hasso von, 1, 105, 113, 114, 272 (n. 80)

Euphrates Dam. *See* Syria: Euphrates Dam

European Economic Community (EEC), 85, 103, 117, 138, 141, 166, 204

Exequatur, 53, 67, 105, 106, 136, 137, 252 (n. 92), 275 (n. 112), 289 (n. 128)

Expellees, 71–72, 76

Federal Republic of Germany (FRG), 2; constitution of, 10; sovereignty of, 12, 30; cabinets of, 23, 24, 52, 81, 82, 83, 111, 157, 159, 170, 174, 175, 179, 180, 185, 186, 193, 197, 204, 211, 212, 251 (n. 77)

—institutions of: Ministry of Economics, 54, 134–35, 170, 186; Press and Information Office, 102; Ministry for Economic Cooperation, 132–33, 170, 186; Ministry for All-German Affairs, 243 (n. 80), 274 (n. 95). *See also* Bundestag; Foreign Office

Finland, 8, 27, 40, 42, 94, 109, 152; trade agreement with GDR, 14, 221; equal treatment of FRG and GDR, 18, 32, 33; promotion of European Security Conference, 217

Florin, Peter, 283 (n. 49)

Foreign Office (*Auswärtiges Amt*), 5, 40, 41, 98, 126, 162, 190; employment of former Nazis, 1, 19; law professors in, 8, 23, 45, 145; expansion of diplomatic network, 15, 16, 18; ambassadors' conferences, 31, 44–48, 51, 53, 54, 55, 66, 104–5, 114–15, 257 (n. 142), 275 (n. 114), 279 (n. 172), 281 (nn. 17, 27); organization of, 44–45, 97–98, 155, 271 (n. 60); and public relations, 94–95, 102–3

—prosecution of isolation campaign: 2–3, 5–6, 26–27, 37–39, 44–49, 114–15, 143, 144–45, 163, 164, 168–70, 174, 182–85, 198–99, 224; subordination of trade to political interests, 34, 45; development of "managed relationships," 55, 137, 224–25; efforts to replace Hallstein Doctrine, 97–98, 182–84, 198–99, 210–11, 231; suppression of East German symbols, 106–7, 187; linkage of aid to, 117, 130, 131, 134–39, 140–41, 157–59, 169–70, 204, 225

—views of: on relations with Eastern Europe, 5, 38–39, 45–46, 72–74, 77–78, 79, 97–98, 142, 148–49, 185; on relations with Arab states and Israel, 18–20, 52–54, 65–70, 86, 166–67, 171–72, 186–87, 246 (n. 24); on relations with Soviet Union, 34, 36–38; on relations with Africa, 87, 91, 100, 103–4, 108–9, 110–13, 122, 159

Four Powers, 111; responsibility for German affairs, 7, 42, 78, 95–96, 140, 195; conferences of, 21, 30, 31, 34, 35, 42–43, 51, 94, 96–97, 100–101

France, 63–64, 103, 108, 109, 120, 122, 143, 164, 178, 180, 182, 219; Quai d'Orsay, 22, 42, 50, 76, 80, 82, 84, 163, 179, 249 (nn. 61, 66), 254 (n. 114), 255 (n. 116), 265 (n. 132), 315 (n. 19), 316 (n. 39); embassy in Bonn, 35, 92, 198, 249 (n. 64), 254 (n. 110), 256 (n. 128), 262 (n. 96), 268 (n. 17), 275 (nn. 111, 115), 281 (n. 26), 286 (n. 92), 297 (n. 93). See also Western Allies

François-Poncet, André, 242 (n. 66), 246 (n. 24)

Frank, Paul, 223

Frankfurter Allgemeine Zeitung, 48, 53, 84, 178, 253 (nn. 98, 103), 256

(n. 131), 266 (nn. 144, 145), 267 (n. 154), 269 (n. 42), 271 (n. 64), 277 (n. 145), 285 (n. 76), 286 (n. 94), 298 (n. 110), 304 (n. 7)

Frankfurter Rundschau, 253 (n. 101), 289 (n. 137), 293 (n. 33), 296 (n. 89), 308 (n. 59)

Free Democratic Party (FDP), 10, 43, 66, 98, 117, 130, 131–32, 138, 139, 145, 146, 176, 180, 185, 191, 195, 197; calls for diplomatic relations with Eastern Europe, 45, 72, 77, 83–84, 194, 207, 230, 264 (n. 116); parliamentary caucus, 82, 119, 133, 287 (n. 106)

Friedrich Ebert Foundation, 119

Gandhi, Indira, 204

"Gaullists." See Christian Democratic Union/Christian Social Union: split between Gaullists and Atlanticists

Genscher, Hans-Dietrich, 310 (n. 73)

German Democratic Republic (GDR), 2, 143; attitudes of population, 6, 21, 123–25; founding of, 10–11; sovereignty of, 12, 21–22, 40, 42; economic situation in, 124, 192; Twentieth anniversary of, 212–13, 217

—diplomatic efforts of: strategy for achieving recognition, 3, 5, 7, 14–15, 19–20, 58, 94, 147–52, 221–23; propaganda by, 11, 101, 124, 149, 152; use of targeted trade deals, 27–28; choice of main points of concentration, 152–53, 154; use of development aid, 153–54, 161, 187–88, 217

—institutions of: Ministry for Foreign Affairs, 11, 14–15, 41, 60, 65, 189, 221, 283 (n. 48); Ministry for Intra-German and Foreign Trade, 19–20, 28; Chamber for Foreign Trade, 33; Ministry for State Security (Stasi), 189, 220

—symbols of: flag, 2, 106, 187; license plates, consular and diplomatic, 4, 70, 106, 187

—views of: on relations with FRG, 6, 218–19, 229; on relations with Arab states and Israel, 59, 63–64, 65, 69–70, 196–97, 201–3

German Information Center (New York), 102

Germany, Federal Republic of. *See* Federal Republic of Germany

Gerstenmaier, Eugen, 77, 108, 121, 171, 293 (n. 36), 322 (n. 4)

Ghana, 8, 69, 103, 117, 120, 122, 124, 129, 130, 135, 149, 152, 168, 170, 189, 228, 237 (n. 4)

Gomulka, Wladislaw, 70, 75–76, 77, 80

Gradl, Johann Baptist, 192

Grand Coalition: new Eastern policy of, 196, 197–98, 200–201, 203, 231–32; Kressbonn Circle, 211, 212

Greece, 117, 118, 159

Grewe, Wilhelm, 36, 38–39, 44–45, 46–47, 48–49, 65, 70, 73, 75, 81, 84–85, 97, 98, 137, 224, 243 (n. 84), 246 (nn. 28, 31), 247–48 (nn. 34, 46), 257 (n. 141)

Grotewohl, Otto, 11, 76, 87, 91, 92–94, 99, 100, 126, 276 (n. 128), 283 (n. 51)

Guevara, Ernesto "Che," 115, 206

Guinea, 1–2, 87, 104, 122, 215, 223; East German aid to, 91, 107–8; West German aid to, 100, 108–9, 115, 120, 137; aborted recognition of GDR, 109–14. *See also* Sékou Touré, Ahmed

Guttenberg, Baron Karl Theodor von und zu, 184, 274 (n. 102), 292 (nn. 22, 23), 310 (n. 76), 313 (n. 130), 315 (n. 17)

Guyana, British, 4, 294 (n. 58)

Gyptner, Richard, 89, 258 (n. 8), 268 (n. 13)

Hager, Kurt, 126

Hallstein, Walter, 23, 25, 33, 34, 36, 44, 47–48, 49, 55, 62, 65, 66–67, 68, 75, 76, 79, 80, 82–83, 84–86, 97, 98, 137, 180, 245 (n. 7), 248 (n. 47), 249 (n. 62), 257 (n. 137), 263 (n. 108); circular instructions of, to ambassadors, 25–26, 32, 38; on use of threats, 51–52

Hallstein Doctrine, 2, 7, 31, 51, 55, 72, 97, 98, 99, 100, 102, 105, 110, 114, 115, 117, 122, 129–42 passim, 145, 146, 148, 153, 154, 156, 157, 158–59, 162, 165, 170–86 passim, 194–204 passim, 207, 209, 210, 212, 215, 218, 221–32 passim; coining of, 5–6, 49, 84–85; Soviet Union as sole exception to, 38, 72–73, 109; and question of automatically breaking relations, 49, 111; "birth defect" argument regarding, 73, 200

Hase, Karl-Günther von, 272 (n. 76), 304 (n. 23)

Hassel, Kai-Uwe von, 281 (n. 22)

Heinemann, Gustav, 208

Hermes credits, 118–19, 121, 159, 225

Herter, Christian, 120

Heuss, Theodor, 69

Hitler, Adolf, 10, 64, 201, 211

Holocaust, legacy of, 19, 171

Honecker, Erich, 220, 233

Hoyer Millar, Frederick, 243 (n. 74), 250 (n. 69)

Hungary, 70, 71, 75, 140, 142, 149, 200

India, 43, 51, 55, 73, 85, 143; relations with GDR, 26–27, 59–60, 87, 88, 92, 93–94, 126–27, 154, 156, 215; relations with FRG, 27, 52, 59–60, 68, 117, 118, 119, 121, 203–4, 224–25.*See also* Nehru, Jawarlahal; Nonaligned movement

Indonesia, 26, 27, 28, 94, 103, 149, 152–53, 154, 169, 170, 178, 189, 223, 228, 265 (n. 138), 286 (n. 92); East German consulate in, 106, 136–37; West German aid to, 117, 121

Interflug, 185

International Monetary Fund, 117

Iran, 68, 69, 118, 120, 221, 242 (n. 66)

Iraq, 4, 69, 87, 89–90, 92, 93, 94, 103, 117, 119, 137, 181, 187, 224; East German consulate in, 136; recognition of GDR, 209, 213, 214

Israel, 63, 129, 219; political and military relations with FRG, 5, 19, 20, 53–

54, 64, 69, 146, 167, 171, 172, 176, 177, 180–81, 181–82, 187
Italy, 122, 178, 182, 187, 208, 249 (n. 60)

Jansen, Josef, 155, 156, 157, 170, 244 (n. 97), 272 (n. 68), 299 (n. 122), 303 (n. 183)
Japan, 210, 257 (n. 137), 265 (n. 138)
Johnson, Lyndon B., 194–95
Jordan, 90, 119, 181, 187, 200, 306 (n. 28)

Kaiser, Jakob, 245 (n. 8)
Kalbitzer, Helmut, 120, 281 (n. 17)
Karume, Abeid, 160, 161
Kaufmann, Erich, 23, 252 (n. 91)
Kaunda, Kenneth, 168
Keita, Modibo, 128, 149
Kennan, George F., 125, 300 (n. 138)
Kennedy, John F., 144
Kenya, 152, 169
Kessel, Albrecht von, 80, 98, 103, 246–47 (n. 32), 262 (n. 86), 264 (n. 121), 267 (n. 151), 307 (n. 41)
Khrushchev, Nikita, 31, 36, 40, 61, 63, 70, 71, 75, 86, 87, 93, 95–97, 101, 147, 227
Kidd, Coburn, 246–47 (n. 32)
Kiesewetter, Wolfgang, 112, 268 (nn. 8, 12)
Kiesinger, Kurt Georg, 196, 198, 199, 200, 203, 206, 207, 208, 210, 211, 226, 231, 232, 266 (n. 145)
Kirkpatrick, Ivone, 36
Kissinger, Henry, 103, 192
Knappstein, Karl Heinrich, 274 (n. 101)
Kopf, Wilhelm, 33–34, 252 (n. 85), 283 (n. 44)
Korth, Erich, 272 (n. 79)
Krapf, Franz, 174–75, 300 (n. 141)
Kroll, Hans, 265 (n. 138)
Krone, Heinrich, 39, 143, 208
Kurella, Alfred, 1, 112, 113
Kuwait, 181

Lahr, Rolf, 156, 166, 170, 223, 290 (n. 140)

Laos, 4
Lebanon, 20, 28, 41, 52, 85, 90, 181
Leuschner, Bruno, 153–54
Liberia, 69
Libya, 181
Lloyd, Selwyn, 82, 96
Lübke, Heinrich, 108, 121, 186–87, 199, 206, 231, 287 (n. 110)
Lufthansa, 138, 185
Lumumba, Patrice, 124, 282 (n. 39)
Luxembourg, 14

McCloy, John J., 240 (n. 37)
McGhee, George, 178, 284 (n. 59), 307 (n. 47)
Macmillan, Harold, 50, 96, 227, 270 (n. 54), 273 (n. 92)
Majonica, Ernst, 137, 313 (n. 122)
Mali, 120, 122, 124, 128, 129, 137, 168, 190, 199, 204, 205
Media. See Press, West German
Mehnert, Klaus, 304 (n. 14)
Meissner, Boris, 34, 270 (n. 44)
Melchers, Wilhelm, 241 (n. 46)
Mende, Erich, 130, 138, 145, 185, 192
Merchant, Livingston, 35
Merkatz, Hans-Joachim von, 69, 121, 129
Meyer, Ernst Wilhelm, 27, 33, 52
Mikoyan, Anastas, 95, 270 (n. 54)
Mirbach, Baron Dietrich von, 256 (n. 130), 302 (n. 164)
Molotov, Vyacheslav, 42–43
Mommer, Karl, 175, 255 (n. 119), 293 (n. 36), 303 (n. 186)
Morocco, 126, 134–35, 148, 181
Mozambique, 152
Müller-Roschach, Herbert, 272 (n. 68), 309 (n. 63)
Multilateral nuclear force. See Nuclear weapons: multilateral force
Murphy, Robert, 80
Myrdal, Gunnar, 17

Nasser, Gamal Abdul, 4, 6, 20, 41, 52–54, 58, 61–62, 64, 65, 69, 88, 89, 90, 91, 92–93, 94, 100, 105, 121–22, 125,

INDEX

129, 141, 158, 166, 167, 171–73, 180,
201, 202, 215, 222, 267 (n. 156); invitation to Ulbricht, 173, 174, 175, 176,
177, 178
National Democratic Party (NPD), 206,
208
Nehru, Jawarlahal, 27, 28–29, 41, 52,
58, 59–60, 61–62, 69, 93, 128, 129–
30, 227, 267 (n. 156)
Netherlands, 14, 218, 239 (n. 20), 245
(n. 14)
Nigeria, 103, 161
Nkrumah, Kwame, 4, 112, 122, 126, 128,
135, 149, 168, 189, 222
Nohr, Karl, 110, 112, 113
Nöhring, Herbert, 241 (n. 46), 249
(n. 59)
Nonaligned movement, 3, 28–29, 61–
62, 125, 204, 222. *See also* Bandung
Conference; Belgrade Conference;
Cairo Conference
Nongovernmental organizations
(NGOs), 190–91
Norden, Albert, 193, 321 (n. 111)
North Atlantic Treaty Organization
(NATO), 3, 23, 25, 50, 64, 77, 82, 83,
97, 182, 217, 222, 260 (n. 54); West
German contribution to, 16, 30, 142
Nuclear weapons, 127; German access
to, 109, 149, 152, 164; multilateral
force, 141–42, 145, 172. *See also* Test
Ban Treaty, Limited
Nyerere, Julius, 160, 161, 178, 179, 189

Oberländer, Theodor, 69
Ollenhauer, Erich, 24, 36, 40, 110, 230,
250 (n. 76)
Olympics, 8, 190–91
Osterheld, Horst, 47

Pakistan, 69, 121, 203, 248–49 (n. 58),
251 (n. 78)
Pauls, Rolf, 169, 181, 309 (n. 61)
Pfleiderer, Karl-Georg, 52, 62–63, 77–
78, 79, 81, 83, 230, 251 (n. 84)
Pieck, Wilhelm, 11
Poland, 58, 70, 76–77, 78; Oder-Neisse

boundary, 73, 75–76, 79, 84, 97, 194,
200–201, 207; relations with FRG,
71–74, 77–78, 84, 140, 142, 149
Politburo. *See* Socialist Unity Party:
Politburo of
Portugal, 122, 152, 164
Press, West German, 12, 110, 114, 192;
and isolation campaign, 48–49, 85,
98, 137–38, 158, 161, 178, 184; and
Eastern Europe, 70–71, 78, 79, 83–84
Public opinion, West German, 68, 175;
on GDR, 11, 13, 128; and student
movements, 206, 207

Qassem, Abdul Karim, 90–91, 93, 94,
112, 136
Quwatli, Shukri al-, 64, 67

Rapacki, Adam, 78
Rau, Heinrich, 41, 59–60, 64, 88, 90,
244 (n. 90), 255 (n. 118), 268 (n. 14)
Rauschning, Hermann, 24
Recognition under international law,
14, 46–47. *See also* Exequatur
Reich, German, 10, 192
Rheinischer Merkur, 137
Roberts, Frank, 265 (n. 133)
Romania, 73, 142, 149, 194, 196, 200,
225
Rusk, Dean, 143, 163, 165, 179, 291
(n. 7), 318 (n. 69)

Saudi Arabia, 181
Scheel, Walter, 132, 134, 170, 176, 217,
218, 281 (n. 17)
Scherpenberg, Albert Hilger van, 97–
98, 99, 105, 109, 111, 134, 266
(n. 139), 276 (n. 129)
Schlesinger, Arthur, Jr., 284 (n. 59)
Schlitter, Kurt, 282 (n. 29)
Schmid, Carlo, 146–47, 239 (n. 12), 266
(n. 147)
Schollwer, Wolfgang, 286 (n. 94), 304
(n. 10), 310 (n. 73)
Scholz, Ernst, 259 (n. 42)
Scholz, Paul, 126
Schröder, Gerhard: as foreign minister,

133–34, 141–42, 144, 155, 163, 172, 174, 175–76, 180, 181, 183, 184, 185, 186, 193, 226, 297 (n. 100); and isolation campaign, 137, 161–62; and policy of movement, 142, 146; as minister of defense, 197, 208

Schroeder, Herbert, 111, 113, 157, 161, 275 (n. 109), 277 (n. 138), 283 (n. 44), 296 (n. 79)

Schumacher, Kurt, 10, 11, 230, 238 (n. 3)

Schütz, Klaus, 199

Schütz, Wilhelm Wolfgang, 192

Schwelien, Joachim, 84–85, 262 (n. 95)

Sékou Touré, Ahmed, 1, 2, 6, 91, 100, 108–13, 114, 157, 223

Self-determination, 4, 24, 87, 103, 109, 122, 126, 127, 131, 164, 168, 198

Senegal, 100

Sihanouk, Norodom, 128, 135, 209, 210, 211, 212, 213

Singapore, 199

Six Day War, 196, 202, 228

Social Democratic Party (SPD), 120; criticism of CDU/CSU foreign policy, 10, 40, 43, 82, 83–84, 98, 119, 178, 196, 197, 209, 211–12; calls for better relations with GDR, 24, 145–46, 193, 194, 207, 231–32; support of isolation campaign, 25, 36, 110–11, 114, 139, 146–47, 230–31; performance in elections, 76, 131

Socialist Unity Party (SED), 9, 10–11, 30–31, 86, 111, 191, 193, 221, 222; Politburo of, 41, 60, 90, 94, 107, 112, 148, 154, 188, 213, 214, 217, 279 (n. 163), 283 (n. 47), 320 (n. 91); foreign policy commission of, 152, 164; International Relations Department, 189

Somalia, 130, 218, 283 (n. 44)

South Africa, 152, 164

Soviet Union, 127, 142; support for recognition of GDR, 7, 16, 21–22, 40, 58, 63, 65, 75, 108, 153, 189–90, 201, 215; relations with FRG, 31–33, 34–37, 38, 39, 142, 195, 221; stance on German unification, 40, 226–27; relations

with Arab states and Israel, 50, 63–64, 68, 70, 89, 117–18, 202–3, 228–29, 257–58 (n. 3); relations with Africa, 107–10, 283 (n. 41); on separate peace with GDR, 124, 147, 163; and Bonn's new Eastern policy, 196, 200–201, 205–6. *See also* Berlin Crisis

Spain, 99–100, 176, 182

Spiegel, Der, 112, 134, 195, 266 (n. 145), 288 (n. 113), 298 (n. 112), 302 (n. 173), 304 (n. 6), 306 (n. 30)

Sri Lanka. *See* Ceylon

Steering Committee. *See* Development aid: Steering Committee and

Steltzer, Hans, 281 (n. 27)

Stoph, Willi, 199, 202

Strauss, Franz-Josef, 69, 143, 172, 175, 180, 197, 208

Strobel, Robert, 137

Sudan, 52, 148, 181, 187, 211, 214, 250 (n. 67), 255 (n. 116), 259 (n. 24)

Süddeutsche Zeitung, 237 (n. 1), 263 (n. 110), 266 (n. 145), 269 (n. 42), 271 (n. 64), 277 (n. 145), 304 (n. 5)

Sukarno, Ahmed, 4, 69, 121–22, 127–28, 129, 136–37, 178, 189

Sweden, 14, 15, 22, 26, 27, 46, 109, 221, 239 (n. 21)

Switzerland, 15, 19, 22, 26, 32, 109, 192, 221, 240 (n. 24), 248–49 (n. 58)

Syria, 20, 26, 52, 63–64, 85, 86, 87, 149, 181, 228, 308 (n. 54); East German consulate in, 65–68, 69–70, 99; East German aid to, 88, 188, 201, 202–3, 213; Euphrates Dam, 121, 137; recognition of GDR, 214–15

Taiwan, 13, 168

Tanganyika, 152, 157, 160. *See also* Tanzania

Tanzania, 4, 160–61, 178, 179, 184, 189, 228

Terminology, West German, 3, 12, 106, 198, 199, 237 (n. 3), 297 (n. 100)

Test Ban Treaty, Limited, 142–43, 144

Thailand, 120, 121

Thant, U, 190

Tito, Josip Broz, 40, 52, 58–59, 61–63, 74–76, 79–81, 86, 99, 125, 127, 128, 130, 147, 165, 203
Togo, 126, 283 (n. 44)
Tunisia, 69, 103, 104, 120, 181
Turkey, 54, 68, 117, 118, 159, 211, 242 (n. 66)

Uganda, 152
Ulbricht, Walter, 3, 7, 8, 11, 22, 61, 63, 74, 126, 140, 143, 147, 149, 152, 153, 173, 174, 175, 189–90, 193, 201, 202, 203, 212, 220, 223, 224, 232, 233, 238 (n. 6), 255 (n. 118); visit to Cairo, 173–83 passim; and "Ulbricht Doctrine," 201
Unfriendly act, 23, 33, 39, 44, 62, 73, 79, 111, 134, 203, 212
Unification, German, 191–92, 193–94, 195, 198
United Arab Republic: formation and dissolution of, 87, 88. See also Egypt; Syria
United Kingdom. See Britain
United Nations, 2, 7, 17, 18, 28, 50, 109, 117, 131, 189–90, 206, 221, 242 (n. 56), 252 (n. 92), 291 (n. 12), 301 (n. 159). See also Economic Council of Europe; Economic and Social Council of the UN; World Health Organization
United Nations Educational, Scientific, and Cultural Organization (UNESCO), 189, 250 (n. 75)
United States, 17, 22, 77, 90, 117, 141, 178, 208–9, 219; Department of State, 22–23, 36, 71, 76–77, 79, 80, 84, 119, 157, 165, 180, 181–82; embassy in Bonn, 38, 39, 114, 253 (n. 99), 264 (n. 118), 272 (n. 73), 277 (n. 144), 278 (n. 159), 298 (n. 117); and nonaligned movement, 125, 281 (n. 28); and détente, 142, 194; and Africa, 155, 157; and Israel, 167, 177, 179, 182. See also Western Allies
Uruguay, 41, 244 (n. 96)

Vietnam, 92, 228
Voigt, Hermann, 256 (n. 129), 257 (nn. 137, 139)
Von der Esch, Hansjoachim, 66–68

Warsaw Pact, 30, 64, 200–201
Wehner, Herbert, 197, 212, 232
Welck, Baron Wolfgang von, 33–34, 77, 244 (n. 5), 261 (n. 80), 265 (n. 138)
Welt, Die, 253 (n. 102), 257 (n. 140), 263–64 (nn. 110, 115), 266 (nn. 144, 145), 269 (n. 42), 271 (n. 63), 273 (n. 94), 277 (n. 145), 284 (n. 64), 298 (n. 110), 314 (n. 5)
Western Allies, 10, 30, 36, 115; policy of blocking recognition of GDR, 7, 13–14, 27, 95–96, 101–2, 189–90, 222, 226; support of isolation campaign, 9, 15–17, 22–23, 25, 42, 49–50, 98, 104, 138, 162–64, 168, 178–79, 200, 208–9, 223, 227–28
Westrick, Ludger, 20, 66, 172, 176
Winzer, Otto, 148, 162, 187, 190, 201, 203, 213, 214
Wischnewski, Hans-Jürgen, 114, 166, 204, 214, 231, 283 (n. 42), 290 (n. 139), 317 (n. 46)
World Bank, 117, 272 (n. 77)
World Health Organization (WHO), 16, 204–5

Yemen (later North Yemen), 147, 181, 187, 188, 301 (n. 148)
Yemen, South, 215
Yugoslavia, 8, 43, 51, 78, 109, 230; aid and restitution treaty with FRG, 52, 62–63, 76, 82–83; recognition of GDR, 58–59, 74–75, 76–77, 79–82, 224; relations with GDR, 60–61, 63, 75, 86; and nonaligned movement, 61–62, 63, 125, 127, 130, 162, 222; further relations with FRG, 82–84, 85, 99, 118, 165–66, 168; reestablishment of diplomatic relations with FRG, 196, 203–4, 205, 226. See also Tito, Josip Broz

Zambia, 168, 169
Zanzibar, 8, 155, 156–57, 160–61, 162, 178, 224. See also Tanzania
Zeit, Die, 248 (n. 50), 260–61 (nn. 64, 65, 78), 266 (n. 145), 277 (n. 145), 279 (n. 169), 285 (n. 76)

THE NEW COLD WAR HISTORY

William Glenn Gray, *Germany's Cold War:*
   The Global Campaign to Isolate East Germany, 1949–1969 (2003).

Matthew J. Ouimet, *The Rise and Fall of the Brezhnev Doctrine in Soviet Foreign Policy*
   (2003).

Pierre Asselin, *A Bitter Peace:*
   Washington, Hanoi, and the Making of the Paris Agreement (2002).

Jeffrey Glen Giauque, *Grand Designs and Visions of Unity:*
   The Atlantic Powers and the Reorganization of Western Europe, 1955–1963 (2002).

Chen Jian, *Mao's China and the Cold War* (2001).

M. E. Sarotte, *Dealing with the Devil:*
   East Germany, Détente, and Ostpolitik, 1969–1973 (2001).

Mark Philip Bradley, *Imagining Vietnam and America:*
   The Making of Postcolonial Vietnam, 1919–1950 (2000).

Michael E. Latham, *Modernization as Ideology:*
   American Social Science and "Nation Building" in the Kennedy Era (2000).

Qiang Zhai, *China and the Vietnam Wars, 1950–1975* (2000).

William I. Hitchcock, *France Restored: Cold War Diplomacy and the*
   Quest for Leadership in Europe, 1944–1954 (1998).